Fodor's 04

PARIS

Where to Stay and Eat for All Budgets

Must-See Sights and Local Secrets

Ratings You Can Trust

Fodor's Travel Publications New York, Toronto, London, Sydney, Auckland
www.fodors.com

FODOR'S PARIS 2004
Editor: Melissa Klurman

Editorial Production: Tom Holton
Editorial Contributors: Nancy Coons, Ethan Gilsdorf, Simon Hewitt, Satu Hummasti, Rosa Jackson, Nicola Keegan, Christopher Mooney
Maps: David Lindroth *cartographer;* Bob Blake and Rebecca Baer, *map editors*
Design: Fabrizio La Rocca, *creative director;* Guido Caroti, *art director;* Melanie Marin, *senior photo editor*
Production/Manufacturing: Angela L. McLean
Cover Photo: (Paris bookstall): Robert Holmes/Corbis

COPYRIGHT

ISBN 1-4000-1252-X

ISSN 0149-1288

SPECIAL SALES

Fodor's Travel Publications are available at special discounts for bulk purchases for sales promotions or premiums. Special editions, including personalized covers, excerpts of existing guides, and corporate imprints, can be created in large quantities for special needs. For more information, contact your local bookseller or write to Special Markets, Fodor's Travel Publications, 1745 Broadway, New York, NY 10019. Inquiries from Canada should be directed to your local Canadian bookseller or sent to Random House of Canada, Ltd., Marketing Department, 2775 Matheson Boulevard East, Mississauga, Ontario L4W 4P7. Inquiries from the United Kingdom should be sent to Fodor's Travel Publications, 20 Vauxhall Bridge Road, London SW1V 2SA, England.

AN IMPORTANT TIP & AN INVITATION

Although all prices, opening times, and other details in this book are based on information supplied to us at press time, changes occur all the time in the travel world, and Fodor's cannot accept responsibility for facts that become outdated or for inadvertent errors or omissions. So **always confirm information when it matters,** especially if you're making a detour to visit a specific place. Your experiences—positive and negative—matter to us. If we have missed or misstated something, **please write to us.** We follow up on all suggestions. Contact the Paris editor at editors@fodors.com or c/o Fodor's at 1745 Broadway, New York, New York 10019.

PRINTED IN THE UNITED STATES OF AMERICA

10 9 8 7 6 5 4 3 2 1

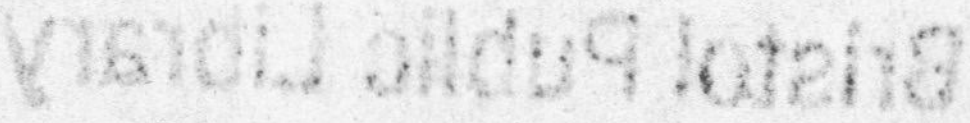

DESTINATION PARIS

A quai-side vista that takes in the Seine, a passing boat, the Ile de la Cité, Notre-Dame, the mansard roofs, and a few wispy clouds all in one generous sweep is enough to convince you that Paris is indeed the most beautiful city on earth. Stroll along formal footpaths in the Jardin du Luxembourg and lose yourself in the halls of the Louvre. Meander through Montmartre and promenade down broad boulevards off the Arc de Triomphe. Master métro lines and river curves. Immerse yourself in the city's patchwork of villages. Linger in a Left Bank café and indulge in gastronomic delights. Admire the architectural filigree—the woven metal of the Eiffel Tower and the plastic tubing encasing the Centre Pompidou. Listen to vendors hawking the season's produce in the markets of Montorgueil and Mouffetard. Paris is all about people and the pleasure of enjoying its beauty, art, culture, and cuisine. This is, after all, a city where café-sitting is a culture, a simple walk can be an extraordinary experience filled with visual delights, and a meal is an almost sacred ritual. Bon voyage!

Karen Cure

Karen Cure, Editorial Director

CONTENTS

Maps

CloseUps

ABOUT THIS BOOK

	There's no doubt that the best source for travel advice is a like-minded friend who's just been where you're headed. But with or without that friend, you'll have a better trip with a Fodor's guide in hand. Once you've learned to find your way around its pages, you'll be in great shape to find your way around your destination.
SELECTION	Our goal is to cover the best properties, sights, and activities in their category, as well as the most interesting communities to visit. We make a point of including local food-lovers' hot spots as well as neighborhood options, and we avoid all that's touristy unless it's really worth your time. You can go on the assumption that everything you read about in this book is recommended wholeheartedly by our writers and editors. Flip to **On the Road with Fodor's** to learn more about who they are. It goes without saying that no property mentioned in the book has paid to be included.
RATINGS	Orange stars ★ denote sights and properties that our editors and writers consider the very best in the area covered by the entire book. These, the best of the best, are listed in the **Fodor's Choice** section in the front of the book. Black stars ★ highlight the sights and properties we deem **Highly Recommended,** the don't-miss sights within any region. Fodor's Choice and Highly Recommended options in each region are usually listed on the title page of the chapter covering that region. Use the index to find complete descriptions. Sights pinpointed with numbered map bullets ❶ in the margins tend to be more important than those without bullets.
SPECIAL SPOTS	**Pleasures & Pastimes** focuses on types of experiences that reveal the spirit of the destination. Watch for **Off the Beaten Path** sights. Some are out of the way, some are quirky, and all are worth your while. If the munchies hit while you're exploring, look for **Need a Break?** suggestions.
TIME IT RIGHT	Wondering when to go? Check **On the Calendar** up front and chapters' **Timing** sections for weather and crowd overviews and best days and times to visit.
SEE IT ALL	Use Fodor's exclusive **Great Itineraries** as a model for your trip. (For a good overview of the entire destination, follow those that begin the book, or mix regional itineraries from several chapters.) **Good Walks** guide you to important sights in each neighborhood; ⚑ indicates the starting points of walks and itineraries in the text and on the map.
BUDGET WELL	Hotel and restaurant price categories from **¢ to $$$$** are defined in the opening pages of each chapter—expect to find a balanced selection for every budget. For attractions, we always give standard adult admission fees; reductions are usually available for children, students, and senior citizens. Look in **Discounts & Deals** in Smart Travel Tips for information on destination-wide ticket schemes.
BASIC INFO	**Smart Travel Tips** lists travel essentials for the entire area covered by the book. To find the best way to get around, see the transportation section; see individual modes of travel ("By Car," "By Train") for details. We assume you'll check Web sites or call for particulars.

ON THE MAPS	Maps throughout the book show you what's where and help you find your way around. Black and orange numbered bullets ❶ ❶ in the text correlate to bullets on maps.
BACKGROUND	In general, we give background information within the chapters in the course of explaining sights as well as in CloseUp boxes and in Understanding France at the end of the book. To get in the mood, review the suggestions in Books & Movies. The glossary can be invaluable.
DON'T FORGET	Restaurants are open for lunch and dinner daily unless we state otherwise; we mention dress only when there's a specific requirement and reservations only when they're essential or not accepted—it's always best to book ahead. Hotels have private baths, phone, TVs, and air-conditioning and operate on the European Plan (EP, meaning without meals). We always list facilities but not whether you'll be charged extra to use them, so when pricing accommodations, find out what's included.

SYMBOLS

Many Listings

- ★ Fodor's Choice
- ★ Highly recommended
- Physical address
- Directions
- Mailing address
- Telephone
- Fax
- On the Web
- E-mail
- Admission fee
- Open/closed times
- Start of walk/itinerary
- Metro stations
- Credit cards

Hotels & Restaurants

- Hotel
- Number of rooms
- Facilities
- Meal plans
- Restaurant
- Reservations
- Dress code
- Smoking
- BYOB
- Hotel with restaurant that warrants a visit

Other

- Family-friendly
- Contact information
- See also
- Branch address
- Take note

ON THE ROAD WITH FODOR'S

A trip takes you out of yourself. Concerns of life at home completely disappear, driven away by more immediate thoughts—about, say, what marvels will beguile the next day, or where you'll have dinner. That's where Fodor's comes in. We make sure that you know all your options, so that you don't miss something that's around the next bend just because you didn't know it was there. Because the best memories of your trip might well have nothing to do with what you came to Paris to see, we guide you to sights large and small all over the region. You might set out to explore the Louvre or see the Eiffel Tower, but back at home you find yourself unable to forget strolling along the Seine or enjoying a crêpe from a corner stand. With Fodor's at your side, serendipitous discoveries are never far away.

Our success in showing you every corner of the City of Light is a credit to our extraordinary writers. Although there's no substitute for travel advice from a good friend who knows your style, our contributors are the next best thing—the kind of people you would poll for travel advice if you knew them.

Nancy Coons has lived in France for many years and has written many books for Fodor's, including *Provence and the Côte d'Azur, Escape to Provence,* and *Escape to the Riviera.*

Ethan Gilsdorf first paused in Paris in high school, then college, and finally bought his one-way ticket in 1999. When he's not roving little-known quartiers in an endless quest for the ultimate hotel—a hobby now bordering on obsession—he writes on culture, food, cinema, and travel for the *Washington Post, Boston Globe, Time Out, the New York Post,* and other publications.

Simon Hewitt headed to Paris straight from studying French and art history at Oxford. It was a return to base: his grandmother was French, as are his wife and daughter. He moved to Versailles a few years ago to gain a different perspective on life in and around the French capital. When not contemplating the Sun King's bicep-flexing Baroque, his thoughts often turn to cricket—he is captain of the French national team.

Rosa Jackson's love affair with French pastries began at age four, when she spent her first year in Paris before returning to the Canadian north. Early experiments with eclairs and croissants led her to enroll in the Paris Cordon Bleu, where she learned that even great chefs make mistakes. A food writer for the past ten years and a Parisian since 1995, Rosa has eaten in hundreds of Paris restaurants—and always has room for dessert.

Nicola Keegan was born in Ireland and raised in Iowa. But after spending one year at the Sorbonne she knew Paris was going to be her home forever. Now famous for crossing the city on foot even in the worst storms, and her uncanny knowledge of where to purchase absolute necessities from truffle oil to that perfect pair of gold-hued boots, she brings all her hard-earned "savoir faire" to the Shopping and Sports chapters, as well as the Smart Travel Tips section.

Christopher Mooney originally came to Paris to study French philosophy, smoke Gîtanes cigarettes, and hang out in cafés. More than a dozen years later he's still there, but his taste for Gallic thought and tobacco has given way to an unslakeable thirst for fine Burgundy vintages. For this edition, this passionate writer (his pet computer often doubles as an additional pillow when he's traveling on the road to update *Fodor's France*) devoted his efforts to finding the best of Paris for the Exploring chapter and the hottest spots for Nightlife and the Arts.

WHAT'S WHERE

The first thing you need to do is learn the difference between the Rive Droite (Right Bank) and the Rive Gauche (Left Bank). In the most stereotypical terms, the Rive Droite is traditionally more elegant and commercial, though its less central areas (the Marais, the Bastille, and Belleville, for example) are the hip places of the moment. The Rive Gauche, on the other hand, is the artistic area; the Sorbonne and the Quartier Latin are here, along with the haunts of literary greats, budding artists, and fashion designers. Between the two banks you have the Ile de la Cité, where you'll find Notre-Dame, and the smaller Ile St-Louis. When you move beyond the classic, core arrondissements Paris becomes less a theme park and more a vital urban center in constant evolution. To experience the true Paris, explore the winding side streets of its lesser-known communities—Belleville, Bercy, Parmentier-Charonne, Tolbiac, Gobelins–Butte aux Cailles.

The Islands

1er & 4e Arrondissements

The Ile de la Cité is where our story starts, some 2,300 years ago, when the island was the strategic stronghold of a Gallic tribe called the Parisii, who held off all comers until 52 BC, the year Julius Caesar's soldiers finally rebuffed the Gauls and established a colony. Today, three buildings here—Notre-Dame, the Conciergerie, and the Sainte-Chapelle—still overawe through their sheer scale and unadulterated historical and architectural grandeur. This is as it should be, for you are now in the very heart of the city. Although large tracts of the island were bulldozed by Baron Haussmann in the mid-19th century, there are still enchanting nooks, notably the Ancient Cloître Quarter, tucked beneath the shadows of the cathedral, and the pretty garden below Pont Neuf in the square du Vert-Galant. Just over the little footbridge behind the cathedral is the Ile St-Louis, the smaller of the two islands, still home to some of the most charming streets in Paris, and, at Berthillon, its best ice cream.

Louvre, Faubourg-St-Honoré & Opéra

1er, 2e & 9e Arrondissements

In the 1er arrondissement, you can see one of the largest collections of art in the world, a theater which has been staging productions for the past 200 years, and a few of the places Louis XIV used to live: not a bad harvest for a single 15-minute walk. For most people, the Louvre remains the greatest museum, period. If the Louvre doesn't satisfy your taste for grandiosity, with its Leonardos, Raphaels, Rubenses, and Davids, collect yourself with a stroll to place de la Concorde through the majestic Jardin des Tuileries. Head over to the Pont Alexandre-III, a bridge that has all the elements that characterized the Belle Epoque: style, class, power, exuberance. Double back along the rue de Rivoli to the serene courtyard gardens of the Palais Royal, where the Comédie Française is the permanent playground for the ghosts of Great French Theater. After being seduced by the luxe boutiques of the Palais-Royal arcades (Thomas Jefferson was a frequent customer here back when), spend some time window-shopping along rue St-Honoré and Faubourg St-Honoré, still the world's most exclusive shopping strip. Next, promenade through the place Vendôme, the bejeweled mecca of *haute joaillerie* (fancy jewelry), followed by a quick restorative at the Ritz, and then it's on to the sumptuous, entirely renovated Palais Garnier, immortalized by Degas's paintings, Pavlova's dancing, and the Phantom's crashing chandelier. Surrounding the Opéra are some of the great boulevards of Paris, where 19th-century Parisians first perfected the art of promenading.

The Marais, Beaubourg & Les Halles

3e & 4e Arrondissements

Le Marais translates as "the swamp." Although this appellation refers to the formerly overwhelming presence of the Seine in this area, this lively neighborhood is anything but stuck in the mud. Three decades ago, some of the chicest people in Paris made the Marais the home of the hip by renovating the multitude of 17th- and 18th-century mansions in the quarter, opening gorgeous shops, and transforming several *hôtels particuliers* (mansions) into museums, including the Musée Carnavalet and Musée Picasso. At the end of the boutique-busy rue des Francs-Bourgeois is the Marais's showplace, the eternally elegant place des Vosges. Today the lively atmosphere of the Marais makes it one of the city's best areas for eating, drinking, walking, and exploring—its narrow, labyrinthine streets still hold all manner of surprises, including the venerable Jewish Quarter, centered around rue des Rosiers, and the rue Ste-Croix-de-la-Bretonnerie and rue Vieille-du-Temple, the lifelines of gay life in Paris. To the west of the Marais lies the Beaubourg quartier, known for eight centuries as the "belly" of Paris, not just for its location but because this was where you went to get grub at any hour of the day or night. Then, in 1969, the iron-and-glass-roofed pavilions of Les Halles were torn down, leaving a large hole in the city's stomach that was filled 10 years later with a hideous but extremely successful shopping mall. While food still fuels the hip pedestrian area around rue Montorgueil, elsewhere fashion boutiques have taken over where butchers and bakers used to hold sway. The area was given much-needed cultural sustenance when the Centre Georges Pompidou opened its doors at Beaubourg in 1977; its sloping plaza, rooftop restaurant, chaos of a lobby, and adjacent place Igor Stravinsky (landmarked by the wild fountain of Jean Tinguely and Niki de St-Phalle) are among Paris's best people-watching spots.

Quartier Latin

5e Arrondissement

The backbone of French intellectual life for more than 700 years, the Quartier Latin has always attracted the intellectually restless, the politically discontent, the artistically inspired, and those who like to hang out with them to its universities, cafés, garrets, and alleys. Home to most of the country's major centers of learning (the Sorbonne, the Ecole Normale Supérieure, the Ecole Polytechnique, the College de France), the Latin Quarter has also been the site of the city's fiercest street battles: in 1871 against the State; in 1945 against the Germans; and in 1968 against everyone over 30. The medieval labyrinth of streets surrounding rue de la Huchette gives a sense of what the city was like before Haussmann and the automobile transformed everything. At the bouquiniste stalls along the Seine you can rummage through rare books, posters, and postcards. A quick hop down the leafy steps to the river's edge brings you to the Bateaux Mouches (river barges) and the *café-peniches* (restaurant barges) that line the quai. Artistic treasures can be found in the Musée National du Moyen-Age (National Museum of the Middle Ages), housed in the famous Cluny mansion, and the Panthéon church.

St-Germain-des-Prés

6e Arrondissement

One of the chicest (yet most tourist-friendly) neighborhoods in Paris, this quarter is centered around the venerable tower of the church of St-Germain-des-Prés, the oldest house of worship in Paris. Aswarm with bookstores and cafés—most notably Café Flore and Les Deux Magots, where Picasso, Camus, Sartre, and de Beauvoir spent their days working and their nights drinking—St-Germain has almost been gentrified into unconsciousness: on some streets, expensive boutiques sit next to expensive galleries which are, more often than not, next to expensive restaurants. But wander off traffic-clogged boulevard St-Germain (a street that fairly cries out for you to shop till you drop), and you'll find winding streets, ancient facades, and hidden courtyards. Particularly pleasing is rue St-André-des-Arts, a pedestrian street lined with sidewalk cafés; near here you'll find what many people consider the most beautiful spot in all Paris—the Cour de Rohan, a cul-de-sac off the Cour de Commerce St-André, an alley where time seems frozen in the 18th century. If you love decorative arts, head straight to the Carré Rive Gauche district off the quai Voltaire (rue de Bac, rue de l'Université, rue de Lille, rue des St-Pères), packed with 120 antiques stores. A stroll a little farther south brings you to the sylvan glades of the Luxembourg Gardens.

Invalides & Eiffel Tower

7e Arrondissement

Hidden behind high walls and heavy doors is the staid, serious 7th arrondissement, home of government ministries (including Hôtel Matignon, the Prime Minister's HQ), foreign embassies, and magnificent hôtels particuliers, still occupied by ducs, vicomtes, and princes of France's first families. Blueblood Central, the area attracts tourists for three good reasons: the impressive collections of late 19th-century art at the Musée d'Orsay, the Eiffel Tower, and Napoléon's final resting spot—or spots; his remains are divided into six coffins—at the vast Esplanade des Invalides. Yet the district offers much more, including the Musée Rodin (in an 18th-century mansion within a rose garden), the tea salons and shops along the Rue du Bac, and the fabulous food floor of Au Bon Marché, the city's oldest and poshest department store. Next to the Eiffel Tower, the single most photographed monument in the neighborhood is the superb Art Nouveau building by Jules Lavirotte on avenue Rapp. And don't forget the odoriferous offerings underfoot in the Paris sewer system; guided tours are offered daily.

Champs-Élysées, Trocadéro & Monceau-Batignolles

8e, 16e & 17e Arrondissements

Majestic with a capital "M," Napoléon's Arc de Triomphe crowns the Étoile, a star of the first magnitude with 12 streams of light; by day, you'll see these are avenues, the leading ray of which is the Champs-Élysées. From the Arc de Triomphe, follow the avenue Hoche and head northeast to Parc Monceau, with its mock ruins and grottoes and surrounding ring of neoclassical mansions, among the most expensive and ostentatious in the city. The Champs was once an aristocratic pleasure park, then deteriorated into a garish sprawl of pricey cafés, car showrooms, and bland shopping malls. Today a restorative face-lift has replaced some of its lost grandeur. Adjoining streets like avenue Montaigne, with their palatial hotels, haute-couture shops, and power-lunch bistros, are already posher than ever. Crossing avenue Marceau into the 16e arrondissement ups the ante even further: this is another stylish area, rich in Art Nouveau and Art Deco houses and laden with museums (the free Musée de l'Art Moderne and the avant-garde Palais de Tokyo lead the pack).

Bastille, Nation & Bercy

11e & 12e Arrondissements

The only folks storming the Bastille these days are Opéra-goers lining up for seats at the Opéra Bastille and young Parisians bent on painting the town rouge. The area around the former (now-vanished) prison has been gentrified: galleries, shops, theaters, cafés, restaurants, and bars replaced the formerly decrepit buildings and alleys, bringing an artsy crowd to mingle with blue-collar locals—and jacking up the prices. To get away from the crowds, avoid rue de Lappe and stick to the parallel streets. Rue Keller and rue des Taillandiers hide cool art galleries and nifty clothing and music stores. Stroll down the redbrick Viaduc des Arts, a stylish walkway with flowers and benches above and haute design shops below. Leave the Bastille column and head east along the Faubourg St-Antoine, once an area of small tradesmen, now a trendy but still unpretentious extension of the Bastille. Farther on and you are smack in the middle of the bustling Aligre street market, where the best produce and cheapest vintage clothing in the city can be found. Then on to the oft-forgotten neighborhood of Nation, where the Revolution took its heaviest toll. You can view the graves of some 1,300 guillotined nobles at the nearby and little-known St-Picpus cemetery. A jog south towards the Seine brings you to the Bercy district. Once the Paris center of the wine trade, it is now a thriving business and shopping area.

Chinatown, Tolbiac, Buttes-aux-Cailles & Gobelins

13e Arrondissement

Not nearly as concentrated or ornate as its counterpart in San Francisco or New York, Paris's Chinatown is more eclectic than either, offering a wide choice of Asian cuisine—Cambodian, Thai, Laotian, Chinese, Japanese—often in the same restaurant. A 20-minute walk from here is the revamped Tolbiac district. Once an ugly tangle of rusting factories, the area is now the site of Paris's controversial national library, the Bibliothèque François-Mitterand. The nearby rue Louise Weiss has become Paris's epicenter of contemporary art. Still in the 13e arrondissement is the Butte-aux-Cailles (Quail Hill), which offers more of a village atmosphere, especially at the cheap bar, bistro, and apple-tree-lined junction of the rue des Cinq-Diamants and the rue de la Butte-aux-Cailles.

Montparnasse

14e Arrondissement

Hemingway, Henry Miller, Picasso, and Sartre all showed up in the cafés, boulevards, and villas of Montparnasse to create or philosophize. Something of them remains in the cemetery, on plaques in front of houses, and chiseled into the tables of bars they frequented, but little elsewhere. The quartet of cafés on the corner of boulevard du Montparnasse and boulevard Raspail—La Coupole, Le Dôme, Le Sélect, and La Rotonde—were the center for a "lost generation" of American writers in the years surrounding World War I. Papa Hemingway, Gertrude Stein, and Zelda and F. Scott Fitzgerald held court here, rubbing shoulders with the likes of Albert Camus, Anaïs Nin, and Marcel Duchamp. The four cafés are still here (though only Le Sélect still draws a stylish crowd, while La Coupole remains the American favorite). The rest of the neighborhood looks much as it did in the 1920s, were it not for the oppressive shadow of the Tour Montparnasse, continental Europe's tallest office tower and Paris's biggest eyesore. For cutting-edge contemporary art-lovers, Jean Nouvel's glass-cubed Fondation Cartier is hard to top. The Parc Montsouris and Cité Universitaire area is a great place to meet other foreigners in Paris.

Passy, Auteuil & the Bois de Boulogne

16e Arrondissement

Proust's Paris, the Passy and Auteuil neighborhoods on the far west side, form the city's largest and one of its most elegant wards. On one side

Passy and Auteuil are bordered by the Seine, on the other by the Bois de Boulogne, an extensive wooded park with lakes, flower gardens, the Bagatelle mansion (built in just 60 days on a bet with Marie-Antoinette), and the fabled Pré-Catalan restaurant. Benjamin Franklin and Honoré de Balzac once resided in the nearby abodes, and the streets of both Passy and Auteuil are still adorned with Paris's choicest selection of Art Nouveau buildings. Along with the mansions designed by Hector Guimard, the paintings of Claude Monet will draw you to the 16e arrondissement, to the Musée Marmottan–Claude Monet.

Montmartre, Pigalle & Abbesses

18e Arrondissement

Rising above the city on the highest hill in Paris is Montmartre (the name means "hill of martyrs"), site of the Basilique du Sacré-Coeur and once the favorite haunt of the bohemian artist community. Despite the tourist hordes that daily pack the narrow backstreets and steep stairways of the "Butte," Montmartre and neighboring Abbesses have retained more of an authentic village flavor than most Paris areas. Strolling here offers glimpses of gardens, small cafés, and wine bars filled with locals, while an essential part of the Montmartre experience is to make your way up the steep stairways that have great views of Paris. Third-rate artists sell their sidewalk masterpieces on the place du Tertre, but real artists live northwest of the place in million-dollar homes on avenue Junot (the little alley at No. 25 is probably one of the most picturesque in Paris). Locals will tell you that rue Lépic remains the best street market in the city. At the bottom of the hill Lépic spills into the netherworld of Pigalle, which still cashes in on its reputation as the sin center of Paris. Steer clear of the portholed "bars américaines" but the Musée de l'Erotisme and the Moulin Rouge remain safe sexy bets. On the other side of the hill, a different Paris waits, especially at La Goutte d'Or, a principally West and North African neighborhood, with pockets of Serb, Pakistani, Portuguese, and Parisian bohemian thrown in to enliven the mix.

Northeast Paris

10e, 11e & 20e Arrondissements

Princes of the Paris night will tell you that the Bastille's bubble has burst, Pigalle is passé, and the Latin Quarter is for the quaint of heart. The real happening scene has retreated northeast, to the edges of the 11th arrondissement and beyond. Oberkampf has been the nocturnal center of things for a few years now, but the areas around are catching up quickly. Particularly thriving is the area around République and the Canal St-Martin, whose locks, bridges, and waterside cafés conjure up an unexpected flavor of Amsterdam. Farther north along the canal brings you to Parc de la Villette, once Paris's largest complex of slaughterhouses and stockyards, now a giant park with loads of high-tech buildings. Belleville, too, long a center of immigrant, working-class Paris, has become a focal point for artists, musicians, and other like-minded folk. Piaf would barely recognize her childhood home, the neighborhood of Ménilmontant-Belleville, thanks to construction, but the stretch between the original Belleville, centered around rue de Ménilmontant and up to Père-Lachaise cemetery, offers some of the most rewarding rambling anywhere. Not to be missed is the Parc des Buttes-Chaumont; as for the fabled Père-Lachaise cemetery, head here if you wish to tell Oscar Wilde, Jim Morrison, Marcel Proust, or Piaf all your problems and have them listen for eternity.

Paris with Arrondissements

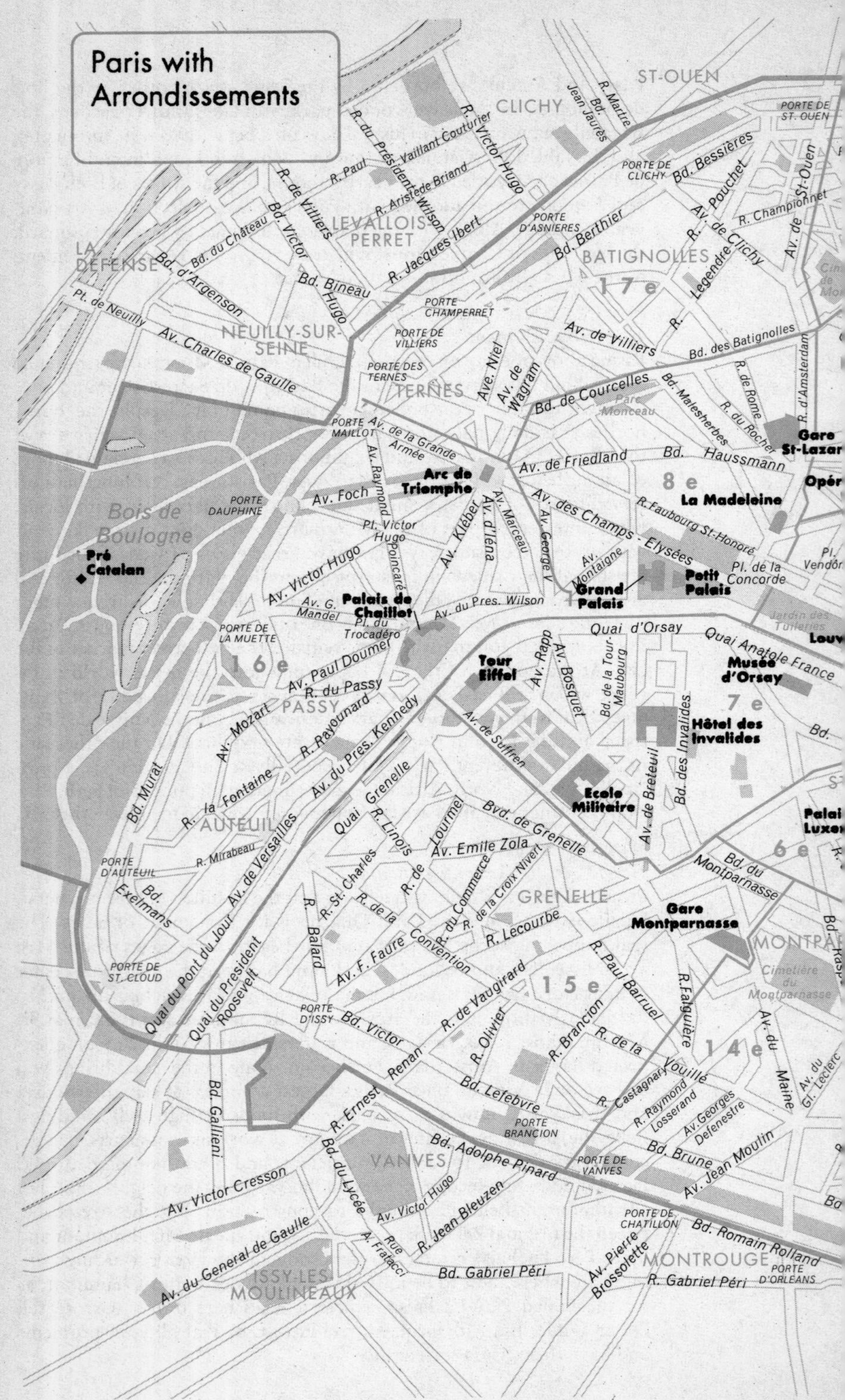

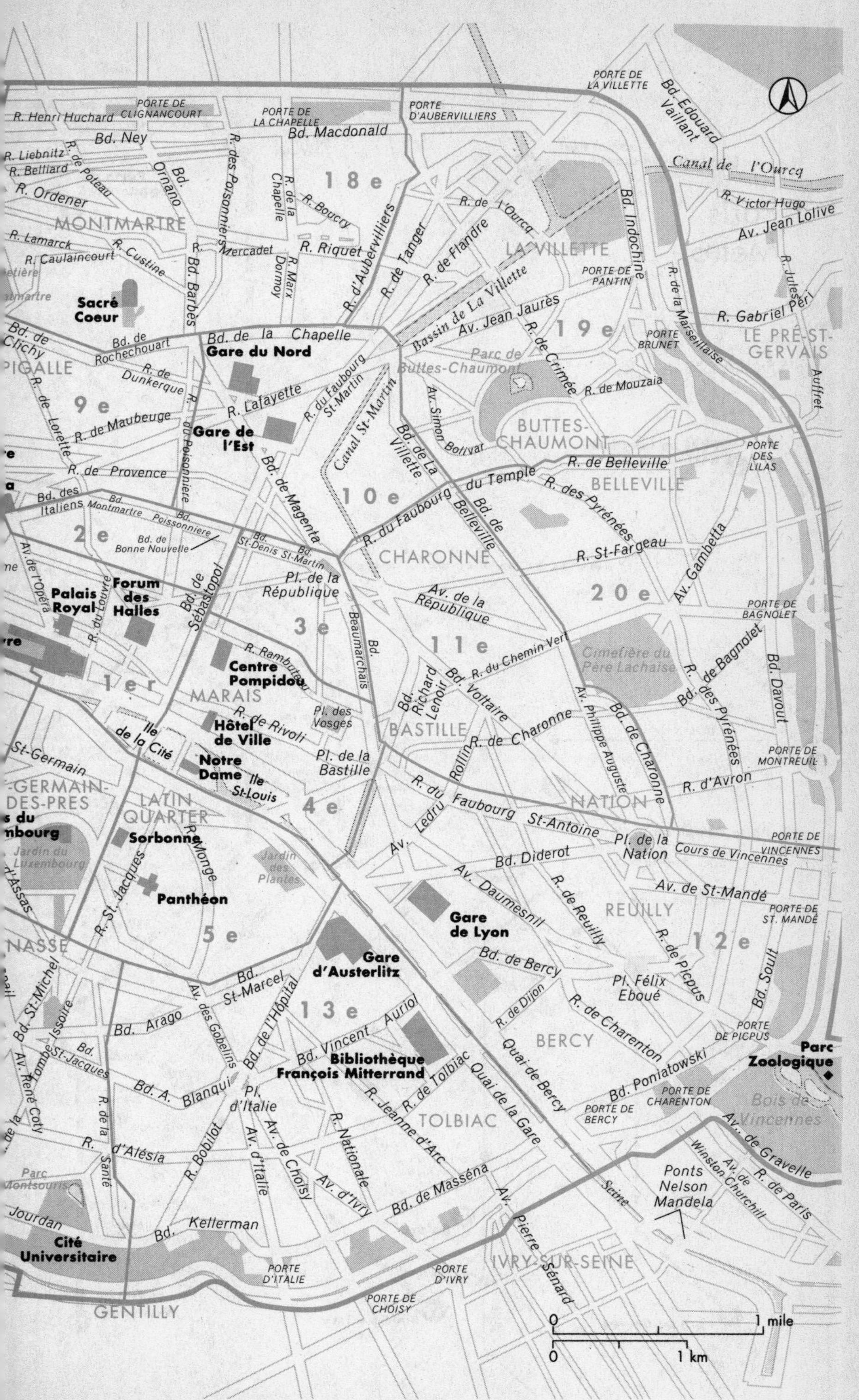
PORTE DE LA VILLETTE
Bd. Edouard Vaillant
R. Henri Huchard
PORTE DE CLIGNANCOURT
PORTE DE LA CHAPELLE
PORTE D'AUBERVILLIERS
Bd. Ney
Bd. Macdonald
Canal de l'Ourcq
R. Liebnitz
R. Belliard
R. de Poteau
Bd. Ornano
R. des Poissonniers
R. de la Chapelle
18e
R. Ordener
R. Boucry
R. de l'Ourcq
Bd. Indochine
R. Victor Hugo
MONTMARTRE
Av. Jean Lolive
R. Lamarck
R. Custine
R. Mercadet
R. Riquet
R. de Tanger
R. de Flandre
LA VILLETTE
R. Caulaincourt
R. Marx Dormoy
R. d'Aubervilliers
Bassin de La Villette
PORTE DE PANTIN
R. de la Marseillaise
R. Jules
Sacré Coeur
Bd. Barbès
Av. Jean Jaurès
R. Gabriel Péri
Bd. de Clichy
Bd. de Rochechouart
Bd. de la Chapelle
R. de Crimée
19e
PORTE BRUNET
LE PRÉ-ST-GERVAIS
PIGALLE
Gare du Nord
Parc de Buttes-Chaumont
R. de Dunkerque
R. du Faubourg St-Martin
R. de Mouzaia
Auffret
9e
R. de Lorette
R. Lafayette
Canal St-Martin
Av. Simon Bolivar
BUTTES-CHAUMONT
R. de Maubeuge
R. du Poissonnière
Gare de l'Est
Bd. de La Villette
PORTE DES LILAS
R. de Provence
Bd. de Magenta
R. de Belleville
Bd. des Italiens
Bd. Montmartre
Bd. Poissonnière
R. du Faubourg du Temple
R. des Pyrénées
BELLEVILLE
10e
Bd. de Belleville
2e
Bd. de Bonne Nouvelle
Bd. St-Denis
Bd. St-Martin
CHARONNE
R. St-Fargeau
Av. Gambetta
Av. de l'Opéra
Forum des Halles
Palais Royal
R. du Louvre
Bd. de Sébastopol
Pl. de la République
Av. de la République
20e
PORTE DE BAGNOLET
3e
Bd. Beaumarchais
11e
R. Rambuteau
Centre Pompidou
R. du Chemin Vert
Cimetière du Père Lachaise
R. de Bagnolet
Bd. Davout
1er
MARAIS
Bd. Richard Lenoir
Bd. Voltaire
R. des Pyrénées
Pl. des Vosges
BASTILLE
Av. Philippe Auguste
Bd. de Charonne
Ile de la Cité
Hôtel de Ville
R. de Rivoli
R. de Charonne
R. Rollin
PORTE DE MONTREUIL
St-Germain
Notre Dame
Pl. de la Bastille
R. d'Avron
ST-GERMAIN-DES-PRES
Ile St-Louis
R. du Faubourg St-Antoine
NATION
LATIN QUARTER
4e
Av. Ledru
Pl. de la Nation
Cours de Vincennes
PORTE DE VINCENNES
Sorbonne
R. Monge
Jardin du Luxembourg
Jardin des Plantes
Bd. Diderot
Av. Daumesnil
R. de Reuilly
Av. de St-Mandé
R. d'Assas
R. St. Jacques
Panthéon
REUILLY
PORTE DE ST. MANDÉ
Gare de Lyon
12e
5e
R. de Picpus
Gare d'Austerlitz
Bd. de Bercy
Bd. St-Marcel
Pl. Félix Eboué
Bd. Soult
Bd. St-Michel
Av. des Gobelins
13e
R. de Dijon
R. de Charenton
Bd. Arago
Bd. de l'Hôpital
Bd. Vincent Auriol
BERCY
PORTE DE PICPUS
Parc Zoologique
Bd. St-Jacques
Bibliothèque François Mitterrand
Quai de Bercy
Bd. Poniatowski
Av. René Coty
R. de la Tombe Issoire
Bd. A. Blanqui
Pl. d'Italie
R. de Tolbiac
Quai de la Gare
PORTE DE CHARENTON
R. de la Santé
R. Jeanne d'Arc
TOLBIAC
PORTE DE BERCY
Bois de Vincennes
R. d'Alésia
R. Bobillot
Av. d'Italie
Av. de Choisy
R. Nationale
Av. de Gravelle
Av. Winston Churchill
R. de Paris
Parc Montsouris
Av. d'Ivry
Bd. de Masséna
Seine
Ponts Nelson Mandela
Jourdan
Bd. Kellerman
Av. Pierre Sénard
Cité Universitaire
PORTE D'ITALIE
PORTE D'IVRY
IVRY-SUR-SEINE
PORTE DE CHOISY
GENTILLY
0
1 mile
0
1 km

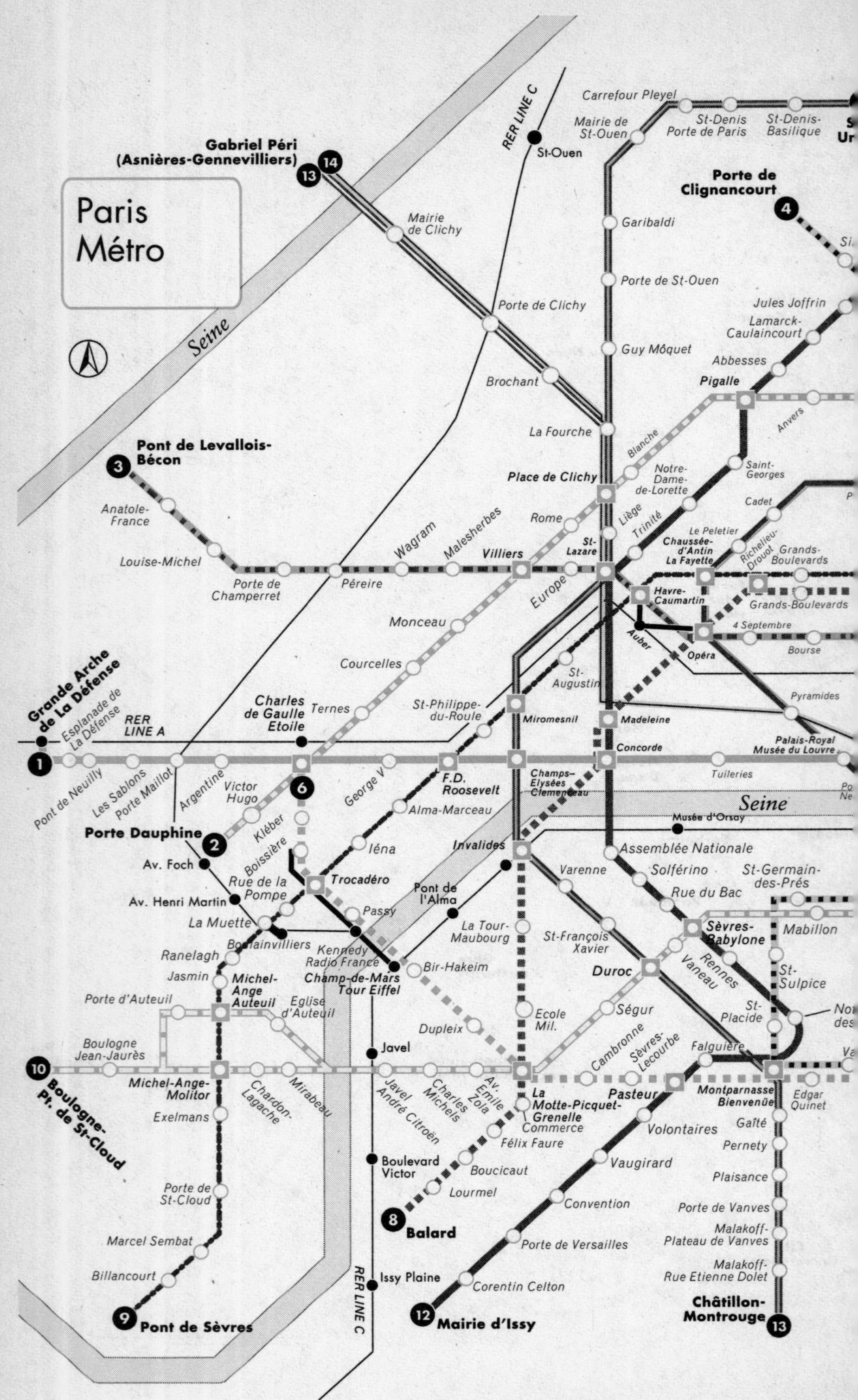
Paris Métro
Seine
RER LINE C
RER LINE A
Gabriel Péri (Asnières-Gennevilliers)
Mairie de Clichy
Porte de Clichy
Brochant
La Fourche
Place de Clichy
St-Ouen
Carrefour Pleyel
Mairie de St-Ouen
St-Denis Porte de Paris
St-Denis-Basilique
Porte de Clignancourt
Garibaldi
Porte de St-Ouen
Guy Môquet
Jules Joffrin
Lamarck-Caulaincourt
Abbesses
Pigalle
Anvers
Blanche
Notre-Dame-de-Lorette
Saint-Georges
Cadet
Le Peletier
Chaussée-d'Antin La Fayette
Richelieu-Drouot
Grands-Boulevards
Havre-Caumartin
Auber
Opéra
4 Septembre
Bourse
Pyramides
Palais-Royal Musée du Louvre
Tuileries
Pont de Levallois-Bécon
Anatole-France
Louise-Michel
Porte de Champerret
Péreire
Wagram
Malesherbes
Villiers
Rome
Liège
Trinité
St-Lazare
Europe
Monceau
Courcelles
Ternes
Charles de Gaulle Etoile
St-Augustin
St-Philippe-du-Roule
Miromesnil
Madeleine
Concorde
Grande Arche de La Défense
Esplanade de La Défense
Pont de Neuilly
Les Sablons
Porte Maillot
Argentine
Victor Hugo
George V
F.D. Roosevelt
Champs-Elysées-Clemenceau
Musée d'Orsay
Assemblée Nationale
Porte Dauphine
Av. Foch
Av. Henri Martin
Kléber
Boissière
Iéna
Alma-Marceau
Invalides
Varenne
Solférino
Rue du Bac
St-Germain-des-Prés
Rue de la Pompe
Trocadéro
Passy
Pont de l'Alma
La Tour-Maubourg
St-François Xavier
Sèvres-Babylone
Mabillon
La Muette
Boulainvilliers
Kennedy Radio France
Champ-de-Mars Tour Eiffel
Bir-Hakeim
Duroc
Vaneau
Rennes
St-Sulpice
Ranelagh
Jasmin
Michel-Ange Auteuil
Eglise d'Auteuil
Porte d'Auteuil
Ecole Mil.
Ségur
St-Placide
Boulogne Jean-Jaurès
Dupleix
Cambronne
Sèvres-Lecourbe
Falguière
Boulogne-Pt. de St-Cloud
Michel-Ange-Molitor
Chardon-Lagache
Mirabeau
Javel
Javel André Citroën
Charles Michels
Av. Emile Zola
La Motte-Picquet-Grenelle
Commerce
Pasteur
Montparnasse Bienvenüe
Edgar Quinet
Exelmans
Félix Faure
Volontaires
Gaîté
Pernety
Boulevard Victor
Boucicaut
Vaugirard
Plaisance
Porte de St-Cloud
Lourmel
Convention
Porte de Vanves
Marcel Sembat
Balard
Porte de Versailles
Malakoff-Plateau de Vanves
Billancourt
Issy Plaine
Corentin Celton
Malakoff-Rue Etienne Dolet
Pont de Sèvres
Mairie d'Issy
Châtillon-Montrouge
1
2
3
4
6
8
9
10
12
13
14

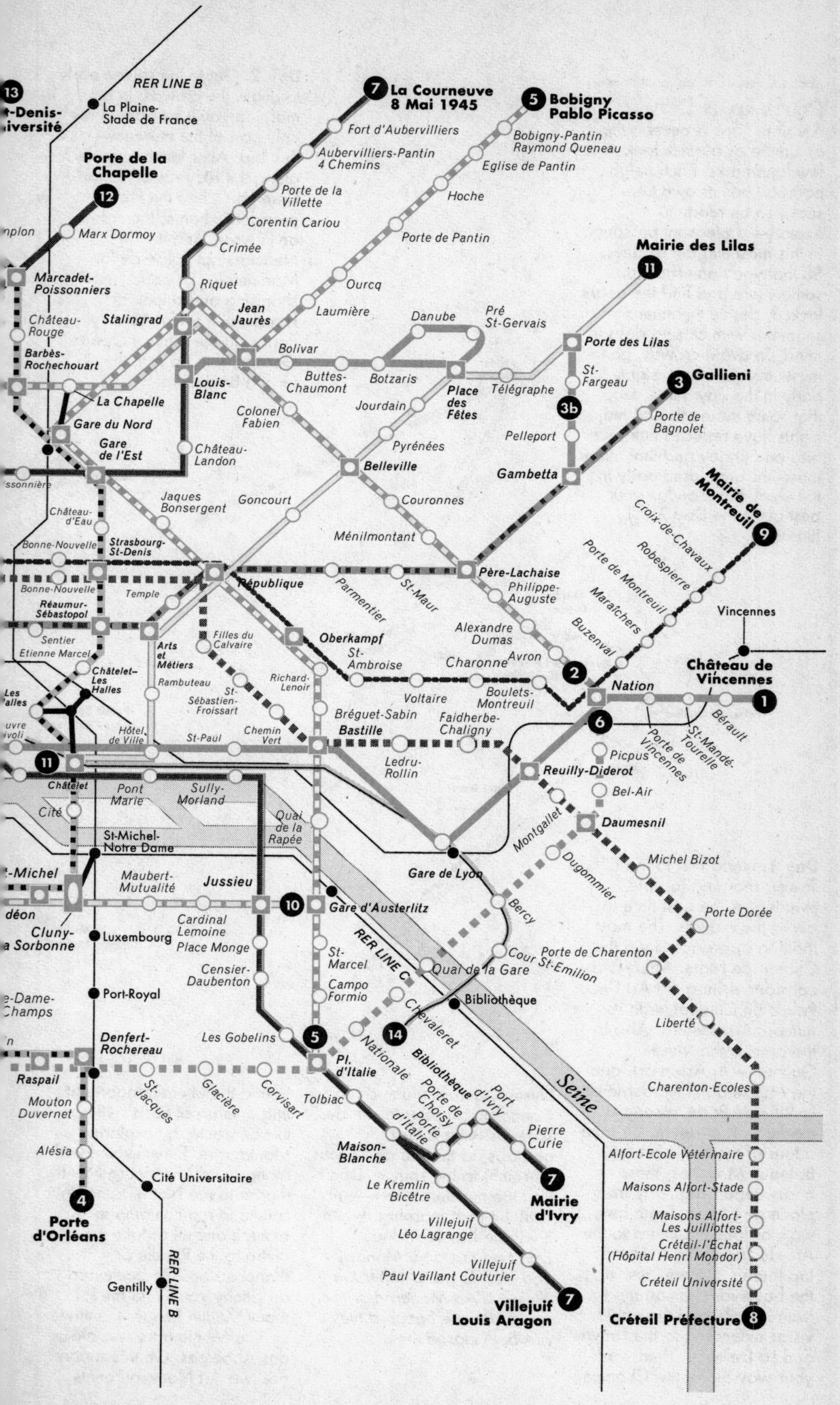
RER LINE B
La Plaine-Stade de France
7 La Courneuve 8 Mai 1945
5 Bobigny Pablo Picasso
Fort d'Aubervilliers
Aubervilliers-Pantin 4 Chemins
Bobigny-Pantin Raymond Queneau
Eglise de Pantin
Porte de la Chapelle
12
Porte de la Villette
Hoche
Marx Dormoy
Corentin Cariou
Porte de Pantin
Crimée
Mairie des Lilas
11
Marcadet-Poissonniers
Riquet
Ourcq
Château-Rouge
Stalingrad
Jean Jaurès
Laumière
Danube
Pré St-Gervais
Porte des Lilas
Barbès-Rochechouart
Bolivar
Louis-Blanc
Buttes-Chaumont
Botzaris
Place des Fêtes
Télégraphe
St-Fargeau
3 Gallieni
La Chapelle
Colonel Fabien
Jourdain
3b
Porte de Bagnolet
Gare du Nord
Gare de l'Est
Pyrénées
Pelleport
Château-Landon
Belleville
Gambetta
Mairie de Montreuil
Château-d'Eau
Jaques Bonsergent
Goncourt
Couronnes
Croix-de-Chavaux
Bonne-Nouvelle
Strasbourg-St-Denis
Ménilmontant
9
Robespierre
Porte de Montreuil
Bonne-Nouvelle
Temple
République
Parmentier
St-Maur
Père-Lachaise
Philippe-Auguste
Maraîchers
Réaumur-Sébastopol
Vincennes
Sentier
Filles du Calvaire
Oberkampf
Alexandre Dumas
Buzenval
Etienne Marcel
Arts et Métiers
St-Ambroise
Avron
Châtelet-Les Halles
Charonne
Château de Vincennes
Richard-Lenoir
2
Nation
Rambuteau
St-Sébastien-Froissart
Voltaire
Boulets-Montreuil
1
Bréguet-Sabin
Faidherbe-Chaligny
Bérault
6
Hôtel de Ville
St-Paul
Chemin Vert
Bastille
Porte de Vincennes
St-Mandé-Tourelle
Picpus
11
Ledru-Rollin
Reuilly-Diderot
Châtelet
Pont Marie
Sully-Morland
Bel-Air
Cité
Quai de la Rapée
Montgallet
Daumesnil
St-Michel-Notre Dame
Michel Bizot
Dugommier
Gare de Lyon
Maubert-Mutualité
Jussieu
Bercy
10
Gare d'Austerlitz
Porte Dorée
Cluny-La Sorbonne
Cardinal Lemoine
Luxembourg
Place Monge
RER LINE C
St-Marcel
Cour St-Emilion
Porte de Charenton
Censier-Daubenton
Quai de la Gare
Campo Formio
Chevaleret
Bibliothèque
Port-Royal
Liberté
Denfert-Rochereau
Les Gobelins
5
14
Nationale
Bibliothèque
Raspail
Pl. d'Italie
Porte de Choisy
Port d'Ivry
St-Jacques
Glacière
Corvisart
Seine
Charenton-Ecoles
Mouton Duvernet
Tolbiac
Porte d'Italie
Pierre Curie
Alésia
Maison-Blanche
Alfort-Ecole Vétérinaire
Cité Universitaire
7
Le Kremlin Bicêtre
Mairie d'Ivry
Maisons Alfort-Stade
4
Porte d'Orléans
Villejuif Léo Lagrange
Maisons Alfort-Les Juilliottes
Créteil-l'Echat (Hôpital Henri Mondor)
RER LINE B
Villejuif Paul Vaillant Couturier
Gentilly
Créteil Université
7
Villejuif Louis Aragon
Créteil Préfecture
8

GREAT ITINERARIES

Paris in 5 Days

A visit to Paris is never quite as simple as a quick look at a few landmarks. Each neighborhood has its own treasures, so be ready to explore—a pleasant prospect in this most elegant of cities. So that you don't show up somewhere and find the doors locked, shuffle the itinerary segments with closing days in mind. To avoid crowds, go to museums and major sights early in the day. Note, too, that some museums and major sights have reduced entrance fees on Sunday and that many museums are closed early in the week (on Monday your best bet is the Day 2 itinerary).

Day 1. Head first to the Eiffel Tower: morning (or late evening) is the best time to avoid the crowds. The most thrilling approach is via the Champ de Mars. Afterwards consider visiting the Art Deco Palais de Chaillot, with its numerous museums. Also in the area is the Musée Guimet, with Asian art, and the Musée d'Art Moderne de la Ville de Paris, a superb modern art museum. Or take a tour of the Seine on the Bateaux Mouches; these boats depart regularly from place de l'Alma. From here, walk or take the métro to the Arc de Triomphe; from the top there's a great view of the boulevards emanating from L'Étoile and the noble vistas extending to the Louvre and La Défense. Then work your way along the Champs-Élysées, across place de la Concorde and the Jardin des Tuileries (with a visit, perhaps, to the Jeu de Paume museum) to the Louvre. Don't visit the museum now—wait until the next morning, when it will be less crowded. *Don't do this on a Monday if you plan to go to either the Musée d'Art Moderne or the Jeu de Paume because they are both closed then.*

Day 2. Get to the Louvre early to avoid the crowds; in a morning you'll be able to see only part of the museum—it's that big. After lunch, wander along the ritzy rue St-Honoré. Here you'll find the French president's home, the Palais de l'Élysée, and the Neoclassical Église de la Madeleine. For good shopping and a look at Haussmann's 19th-century Paris and the famous Opéra Garnier, join up with the Grand Boulevards.

Spend the late afternoon getting a sense of Paris's village-like character by exploring Montmartre. Either walk (north along rue du Faubourg Montmartre to rue Notre-Dame de Lorette to rue Fontaine to place Blanche) or take the métro to the Pigalle or Blanche stop. On boulevard de Clichy you'll find the famous Moulin Rouge. Continue up into Montmartre, via place des Abbesses. On this square are two Art Nouveau gems:

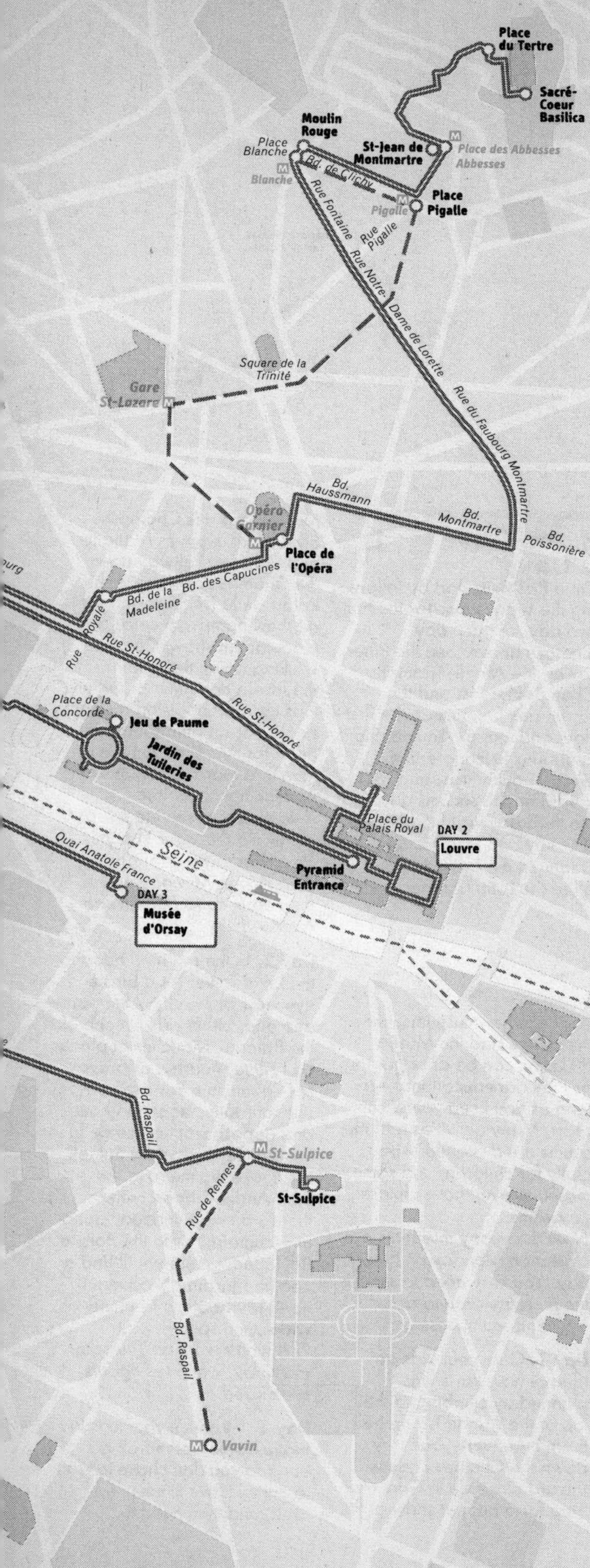

the church of St-Jean de Montmartre, and the Art Nouveau Guimard entrance to the Abbesses métro station. From here walk through the winding, hilly streets to place du Tertre, and then on to Sacré-Coeur, where there's a tremendous view of the city below.
This is fine any day but Tuesday, when the Louvre is closed.

Day 3. Start the morning admiring the Impressionists in the Musée d'Orsay; arrive early to avoid the crowds. Then head west to the Palais Bourbon, home of the Assemblée Nationale (the French parliament), and the Hôtel des Invalides, with its impressive Église du Dôme. If you're up for another museum, visit the Musée Rodin; if not, see its rose garden, filled with Rodin's sculptures. Continue east toward the enormous church of St-Sulpice. From here it's just three stops to the Vavin métro station in Montparnasse.
This won't work on Monday, when the Musée d'Orsay and the Musée Rodin are closed.

Day 4. Begin by visiting Notre-Dame Cathedral and Sainte-Chapelle on Ile de la Cité. Then head over to the neighboring Ile St-Louis and wander the narrow streets. Cross over the Seine to explore the Latin Quarter, using the Panthéon dome as a landmark. Set aside more time if you plan to see the Musée National du Moyen-Age or the Institut du Monde Arabe, relax in the Jardin du Luxembourg, or sip coffee in a neighborhood café. In the afternoon visit the Centre Pompidou and explore the winding streets of the Marais. The Musée Picasso is in one of this old neighborhood's hôtels particuliers (mansions). The elegant place des Vosges is pleasant for a break.
Closings make this a problem on Monday (Institut du

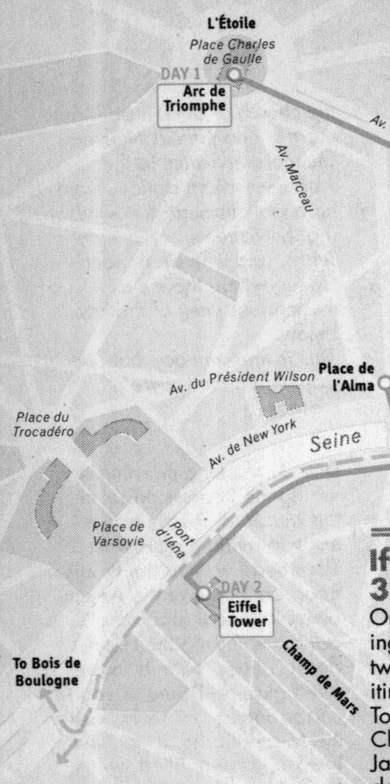

Monde Arabe), Tuesday (Musée du Moyen-Age, Centre Pompidou, Musée Picasso), and Wednesday (Musée Picasso).

Day 5. To get a sense of the splendor in which French royalty lived, spend most of the day visiting Versailles.
This is fine any day but Monday when the château and other sights are closed.

If You Have More Time

You can attack the smaller museums like the Maillol and the Marmottan and explore the funky Bastille, elegant Passy, and up-and-coming Bercy neighborhoods. Or take the métro to see attractions on the edge of the city: Père-Lachaise Cemetery, the Parc de La Villette, or the Bois de Boulogne or Bois de Vincennes, Paris's two largest parks. Or take a day trip to Fontainebleau, Chartres, or other points of interest around Paris.

If You Have 3 Days

On a first visit, start by following the suggestions for the first two days of the 5-day itinerary above: See the Eiffel Tower, the Arc de Triomphe, Champs-Élysées, and the Jardin des Tuileries on the first day; and tour the Louvre, the Faubourg St-Honoré, the Grand Boulevards, and Montmartre on the second day. On the third day visit the Musée d'Orsay and then Notre-Dame; in the afternoon explore the Latin Quarter.

Paris with Kids

Paris's major museums, like the Louvre and the Musée d'Orsay, can be as engaging as they are educational—as long as you keep your visits short. Many activities and museums are designed especially for children, and some museums even have children's programs.
Note that many museums are closed on Monday or Tuesday. You may need to shuffle the itinerary around according to museum closings.

Day 1. Give your kids an idea of how Paris was planned by climbing to the top of the Arc de Triomphe. From here work your way down the Champs-Élysées toward place de la Concorde. Stop for a puppet show at the Marionettes des Champs-Élysées, at avenues Matignon and Gabriel, halfway down the Champs. Or head to the Palais de la Découverte, just off the Champs, to catch a planetarium show. Continue walking down the Champs, to the Jardin des Tuileries, where kids can sail boats on a small pond. For an afternoon treat, head for Angélina (on rue de Rivoli), a tearoom famous for its thick hot chocolate.
If you want to see the puppet show, do this on a Wednesday, Saturday, or Sunday. Skip this on Monday when the Palais de la Découverte is closed.

Day 2. In the morning head to the Eiffel Tower for a bird's-eye view of the city. After you descend, either ride on one of the Bateaux Mouches at place de l'Alma, nearby; or brave Les Égouts, the Paris sewers (the tour takes about an hour and departs from place de la Résistance, across the Seine). Next take the métro to the Parc André-Citroën, where there's a computerized "dancing fountain," or to the Boisde Boulogne, where you'll find a zoo (the Jardin d'Acclimatation), rowboats, and plenty of wide-open space.
This won't work on Thursday or Friday, when Les Égouts are closed.

Day 3. Introduce your kids to Notre-Dame Cathedral; go early so you don't have to wait to get in. Have lunch in the area, and then head to

Berthillon on the Ile St-Louis for some of the city's best ice cream. Afterward cross the Seine and walk or take the métro to the Odéon stop. From here walk around the colonnaded Théâtre de l'Odéon to the Jardin du Luxembourg, where there's a playground, a pond where kids can rent miniature boats, a café, a marionette theater, and plenty of places to sit. Ready for more? Walk to the Centre de la Mer et des Eaux, an aquarium nearby, then continue on foot or by bus to the Arènes de Lutèce, one of the few vestiges of the former Roman city. Not far on foot or by métro is the Jardin des Plantes, a botanical garden with the state-of-the-art Grande Galerie de l'Évolution, a museum exhibiting a collection of taxidermy of all kinds of animals. Also just a métro ride away in Montparnasse are the Catacombs, Roman quarries that served as headquarters for the French Resistance during World War II.

Don't try to see the Catacombs on Monday or the Grande Galerie de l'Évolution on Tuesday, when they're closed.

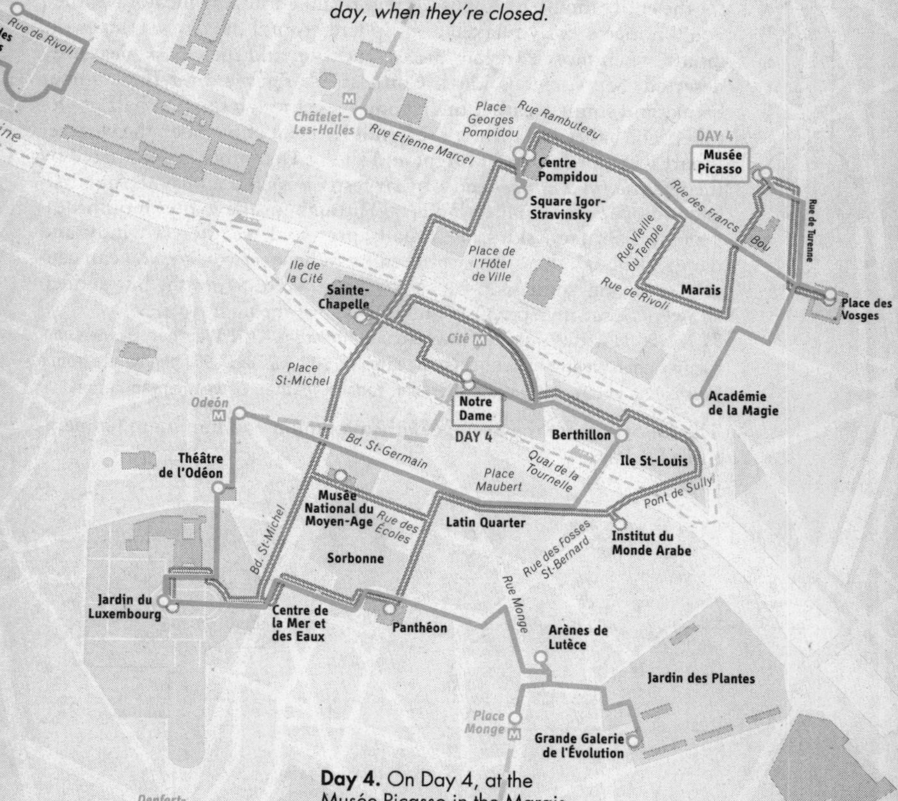

Day 4. On Day 4, at the Musée Picasso in the Marais, show your kids the paintings and sculptures of one of France's finest artists. Nearby, pick up a sandwich to eat on a bench in the place des Vosges. If your children are up for another museum, one that's more child-oriented, head for the Académie de la Magie and catch a magic show. Or take in the Centre Pompidou; either see an exhibit (often there are special kids' programs related to the shows) or simply ride the escalator to the top for a great view of Paris. Around the corner, on the Square Igor-Stravinsky, watch the imaginative, moving sculptures in the fountain. Another option is to take the métro from Châtelet–Les-Halles to the Porte de La Villette; in the whimsical park of the same name are an interactive science museum, a museum of musical instruments, an IMAX theater, and various innovative structures to play on and in.

Because of closings, do this between Thursday and Sunday: The Parc de La Villette is closed Monday, the Centre Pompidou Tuesday, the Musée Picasso Tuesday and Wednesday, and the Académie de la Magie every day except Wednesday and weekends.

WHEN TO GO

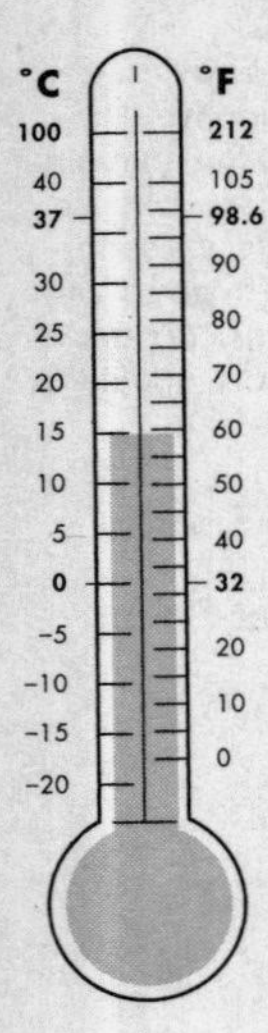

The major tourist season in France stretches from Easter to mid-September, but Paris has much to offer in every season. If you're dreaming of Paris in the springtime, May is your best bet, not rainy March and April—regardless of what songs say about the latter. Paris in the early spring can be disappointingly damp, though it's relatively tourist-free; May and June are delightful, with good weather and plenty of cultural and other attractions. July and August can be sultry, stuffy, and uncomfortable, intensified by pollution which has been getting worse each year. Moreover, many theaters and some of the smaller restaurants and shops close for the entire month of August. If you're undeterred by the hot weather, you'll notice a fairly relaxed atmosphere around the city, as this is the month when most Parisians are on vacation and the city is pleasantly deserted. September is ideal. Cultural life revives after the summer break, and sunny weather often continues through the first half of October. The ballet and theater are in full swing in November, the weather is part wet and cold, part bright and sunny. December is dominated by the *fêtes de fin d'année* (end-of-year festivities) and a busy theater, ballet, and opera season into January. Throughout the winter months, especially February, skies are usually grey and weather is windy and damp, although there's very little snow. Whenever you go, you can usually count on some rain—August is the wettest month, but sudden showers occur in September and in January through April.

Forecasts **AccuWeather** www.accuweather.com. **CNN Weather** www.cnn.com/weather. **Weather Channel Connection** 900/932–8437, 95¢ per minute from a Touch-Tone phone www.weather.com. **Yahoo Weather** weather.yahoo.com.

The following are the average daily maximum and minimum temperatures for Paris.

Jan.	43F	6C	May	68F	20C	Sept.	70F	21C
	34	1		49	10		53	12
Feb.	45F	7C	June	73F	23C	Oct.	60F	16C
	34	1		55	13		46	8
Mar.	54F	12C	July	76F	25C	Nov.	50F	10C
	39	4		58	14		40	5
Apr.	60F	16C	Aug.	75F	24C	Dec.	44F	7C
	43	6		58	14		36	2

ON THE CALENDAR

ONGOING

May–Late Sept.	**Grandes Eaux Musicales** is a fountain display at the Château de Versailles (Sunday only).
Late May–Early June	The **Festival de Jazz de Boulogne-Billancourt** attracts big names and varied styles of jazz in Boulogne-Billancourt, a suburb of Paris.
Late May–Early June	The **French Open Tennis Championships** (🌐 www.french-open.com) takes place at Roland Garros Stadium. The **Grand Steeple Chase** takes place at the Porte D'Auteuil racetrack.

WINTER

Late Nov.–Late Dec.	The festive **Christmas Market** (✉ Pl. du 11-Novembre-1918, 10e Ⓜ Métro: Gare de l'Est) has crafts, gifts, and toys from every region of France.
Late Dec.	**Christmas** is highlighted by illuminations throughout the city, particularly on the Champs-Élysées, avenue Montaigne, and boulevard Haussmann. Many churches open their doors with free Sunday-afternoon concerts, the mayor's office sponsors free rides for children on all merry-go-rounds in the city for a period of two weeks, and major department stores and luxury meccas vie for your attention with amazing window displays. Outside the Hôtel de Ville are a giant crèche plus an ice-skating rink free to the public.
Dec. 31–Jan. 1	On **New Year's Eve** check out the spectacular fireworks illuminating the Eiffel Tower.
Jan. 6	**Epiphany** is when *galettes des rois* ("kings' pastries")—deliciously light almond cakes available in all bakeries—are traditionally served; whoever gets the porcelain charm embedded in each is king or queen for the day.
Feb.	**Foire à la Feraille de Paris** is an antiques and bric-a-brac fair held in the Bois de Vincennes. **Salon d'Agriculture** (🌐 www.salon-agriculture.com), an agricultural smorgasbord and a favorite with some Parisians, is held mid-month at the Porte de Versailles.

SPRING

Mar.	**Salon du Livre,** an international book exposition, is held annually at the end of the month.
Mar.–Apr.	**Foire du Trône,** an amusement park, is set up in the Bois de Vincennes. The **Prix du Président de la République** takes place at the Auteuil Racecourse. The **Paris Film Festival** (🌐 www.festival.wannadoo.fr) is held at the Cinema Gaumont Matignan on the Champs Élysées.
Late Apr.	The **International Marathon of Paris** (🌐 www.parismarathon.com) runs through the city and large parks on the outskirts.
Early May	At the **Foire de Paris** (🌐 www.comexpo-paris.com), hundreds of booths display everything from crafts to wines. The **Novotel-Perrier French Open** takes place at the national golf course in les Yvelines just outside of Paris.

SUMMER	
June	The Paris Air Show, is a display of old and new planes at Le Bourget Airport. The colorful Gay Pride Parade takes place mid-month.
Mid-June–Mid-July	Festival du Marais features everything from music to dance to theater in the churches and historic mansions of the Marais (tickets ✉ 44 rue François-Miron, 4e ☎ 01–48–87–60–08 Ⓜ Métro: St-Paul). A similar celebration takes place at the Butte Montmartre Festival (☎ 01–42–62–46–22). Just outside Paris, the Festival de St-Denis takes place this year with live music, theater, and dance.
Late June	The Grand Prix de Paris, is held on the flat at Longchamp Racecourse. The 45th International Air Show takes place in Le Bourget.
July 13	Bals des Sapeurs-Pompiers (Firemen's Balls), held to celebrate the eve of Bastille Day, spill into the streets of every arrondissement. Head to any *caserne* (fire station) in Paris and dance the night away to live music; spectacular party locations also include historic landmarks in the Marais and a barge on the Seine.
July 14	Bastille Day celebrates the storming of the Bastille prison in 1789. There's a military parade along the Champs-Élysées in the morning and fireworks at night at Trocadéro.
Late July	The Tour de France (🌐 www.letour.com), the world's leading bicycle race, speeds to a Sunday finish on the Champs-Élysées.
Late July–End Aug.	The Fête Musique en l'Ile (☎ 01–45–23–18–25 for details) is a series of concerts held in the picturesque 17th-century Église St-Louis on Ile St-Louis.
FALL	
Mid–Late Sept.	Biennale des Antiquaires (even-numbered years only), an antiques fair, takes place at the Carrousel du Louvre.
Late Sept.	On the Journée du Patrimonie, the third Sunday in September, normally closed historic buildings—such as the state residences of the President and Prime Minister—are open to the public. The world-class (second only to Tokyo"s) Salon Mondial de l'Automobile auto show takes place this month. The (very) loud Techno Parade winds its way through the streets of Paris to finish at Trocadéro.
Early Oct.	The Montmartre Grape Harvest (🌐 www.montmartrenet.com), held the first Saturday of October, celebrates the grape harvest in the Montmartre vineyard, at the corner of rue des Saules and rue St-Vincent. FIAC (International Fair of Contemporary Art) takes place at Porte de Versailles. The Prix de l'Arc de Triomphe, Europe's top flat race, is the first Sunday of the month at Longchamp Racecourse.
Mid-Oct.–Early Nov.	The Fête de Jazz de Paris (☎ 01–47–83–33–58 for information) is a two-week celebration that includes lots of big-name musicians.
Oct.–Nov.	The Fête d'Art Sacré (☎ 01–42–77–92–26 for information) is a series concerts and exhibitions held in churches throughout the city.
Nov. 11	Armistice Day ceremonies at the Arc de Triomphe include a military parade down the Champs-Élysées.

Third Thurs. in Nov.	**Beaujolais Nouveau,** that light, fruity wine from the Beaujolais region of France, is officially released at midnight on Wednesday; its arrival is celebrated in true Dionysian form in cafés and restaurants around the city.
Late Nov.	**Salon des Caves Particulières** brings French producers to the exhibition center at Porte de Versailles for a wine-tasting jamboree. Galleries and museums also will open their doors for "Le Mois de la Photo" (Photo Month).

PLEASURES & PASTIMES

Where Art Comes First

Paris's museums range from the ostentatiously grand to the delightfully obscure—the French seem bent on documenting everything any of its citizens have ever done. Not just repositories of masterworks, the city's museums also reveal the endlessly fascinating nuances of French culture. It is fitting that the Musée d'Orsay, a Belle Epoque former train station, houses the city's legacy of art from 1848 to 1914: railroads and other everyday phenomena were—shockingly so at the time—favorite subjects of the period's artists, especially the Impressionists, who enjoy pride of place under the glass-vaulted roof. And it was the French Revolution that opened the Louvre to the masses, so that all can now view the extraordinary collection amassed in good part by seven centuries of monarchs, while imagining the history-shaping intrigues that once fermented in these same salons. A proletarian spirit also dominates the Centre Pompidou, where the world's largest collection of modern art is displayed; though opened in 1977, it has been so popular that a recent renovation means it is looking better than ever.

In addition to these big three, other favorites include museums which began life not as museums, but as sumptuous houses. Many of these gilded time-machines are filled with salons aglitter with gilt *boiserie* (carved wood panels), chandeliers, and flocked red velvet walls literally oozing Parisian elegance. For these unique peeps into yesteryear, top bets include the decorative arts treasures found at the Musée Nissim de Camondo, the Musée Jacquemart-André, and the Musée Carnavalet. Skip through the centuries at some modern art museums, as both the Musée Rodin and the Musée Picasso are housed in historic hôtels particuliers—mansions built as private homes for the rich and famous. For a true trip back to the 17th, 18th or 19th centuries, discover overlooked jewels like the Hôtel Lauzun on the Ile St-Louis, the Atelier Delacroix on the Place Furstenberg, and the Musée de la Vie Romantique (where the likes of Chopin and Georges Sand once rendezvoused) at the foot of Montmartre.

Bon Appétit!: The Pleasures of Eating

"Animals feed, men eat, but only wise men know the art of dining," wrote the French gastronome Anthelme Brillat-Savarin. Join them in the pursuit of this art and don't feel guilty if you spend as much time of your stay in Paris in its restaurants as in its museums. Eating is the heart and soul of French culture. Give yourself over to the leisurely meal; two hours for a three-course menu is par, and you may, after relaxing into the routine, begin to feel pressed at less than three. Whether your dream meal is savoring truffle-studded fois gras served on Limoges china or sharing a baguette with *jambon* (ham) and Brie *sur l'herbe* (on the grass), eating in Paris can be a memorable experience. Needless to say, it's well worth splurging on a dinner of outstanding haute cuisine in formal splendor (and many of those restaurants feature historically dazzling interiors, worthy of any museum). But also keep in mind that many famous chefs have opened bistro annexes where you can sample their cooking for less. In addition, younger chefs are setting up shop in more affordable, outlying parts of Paris, where they are serving their own innovative versions of bistro classics. Some of these locations can mean a long métro or cab ride, but it will give you the opportunity to discover restaurants in neighborhoods that you might not otherwise see. End any proper meal with a sublime cheese course, then dessert (the more decadent and creamy the better), then an *express* (coffee taken black, with sugar).

The best introductions to French food are the open-air street markets. The biggest is on boulevard de Reuilly between rue de Charenton and place Félix-Eboué (12e, métro: Dugommier), open Tuesday and Friday; while others are the south end of rue Mouffetard (5e, métro: Monge); rue de Buci (6e, métro: Odéon, in the heart of St-Germain-des-Prés); rue Daguerre (14e, métro: Denfert-Rochereau) in Montparnasse; and rue Lepic (18e, métro: Blanche or Abbesses) in Montmartre. Or head instead to the delightful grocery stores of Paris. Whether you buy the baguettes lined up soldier-style at the *boulangerie* (bakery), where you can also get fine sandwiches, or seductively displayed pastries at the pâtisserie, or *charcuteries,* where butchers sells cold cuts, or *épiceries*—the French equivalent of a deli—or at the *fromagerie* (cheese shop), you'll find it easy to create the fixings for a pique-nique in one of the city's parks. As you'll discover, who needs to pay a fortune to dine amid the Art Nouveau splendors of Maxim's when you can enjoy a peach and Brie on a bench in that even more gorgeous showplace, the 17th-century place des Vosges?

Café Society

Along with air, water, and wine, the café remains one of the basic necessities of life in Paris. You may prefer a posh perch at a renowned spot such as the Deux Magots on boulevard St-Germain or opt for a tiny *café du coin* (corner café) where you can have a quick cup of coffee at the counter. Those on the grands boulevards (such as boulevard St-Michel, boulevard St-Germain, and the Champs-Élysées) and in the big tourist spots (near the Louvre, the Opéra, and the Eiffel Tower, for example) will almost always be the most expensive and the least interesting. The more modest establishments (look for nonchalant locals) are the places to really get a feeling for French café culture. And we do mean culture—Les Deux Magots is still milking its reputation as one of the Left Bank's prime meeting places for intelligentsia as the former hangout of Verlaine, Rimbaud, Gide, Picasso, and Breton. In spite of its heart-stopping prices, the Flore still packs them in—you can't help imagining that something profound is being uttered at the next table, any more than you can resist the ultrarich onion soup. At La Closerie des Lilas an expensive drink allows you to rest your derrière on the spots once favored by Baudelaire, Apollinaire, and Hemingway. Delightfully, all these cafés are still crammed with locals, so grab a seat, order a Lillet, and settle in for a round of serious people-watching.

Rues with a View: Scenic Strolls & Bus Routes

The French have a word for it: *flâner,* which means to saunter, and this is the way to best appraise Paris. Ignore any urges to speed—just relax and let the *esprit de Paris* take over. It's hard to get lost, thanks to very visible monuments that serve as landmarks. Some favorite walks are from place St-Michel through the Latin Quarter to the Panthéon, and down rue Mouffetard; along the banks of the Canal St-Martin and Canal de l'Ourcq up to the Parc de la Villette; through the small, winding streets of the Marais from place de la Bastille to the Pompidou Center; along busy rue Faubourg St-Honoré; from the Élysée Palace to the Madeleine; place Vendôme, and the gardens of the Palais-Royal; and along the streets and riverbanks of

Ile St-Louis from east to west, ending at Pont St-Louis for a classic view of the Seine and Notre-Dame.

There are also several bus lines that you can take for a good, cheap tour of Paris, sans irritating commentary. Some of these lines are traveled by buses with small balconies in the rear, though the proximity to gusts of carbon monoxide is less than pleasant. No. 29: the interesting section of the 29 stretches from Gare St-Lazaare, past Opéra Garnier and the Pompidou, and through the heart of the Marais, crossing the place des Vosges before ending up at the Bastille. This is one of the few lines that run primarily through the small streets of a neighborhood. No. 69: get on at the Champ de Mars (the park right by the Eiffel Tower) and ride through parts of the Quartier Latin, across the bridge to the Right Bank near the Louvre, by the Hôtel de Ville (City Hall), and on to the Bastille area. No. 72: river-lovers will appreciate this line. It follows the Seine from the Hôtel de Ville west past the Louvre, Trocadéro, and most of the big-name Right Bank sights. You also get good views of the Left Bank, including the Eiffel Tower.

Shopping: Bon Chic, Bon Genre

Quotidian activities are elevated to high art in Paris, and shopping is no exception. Sophisticated city dwellers that they are—many natives live by the motto *bon chic, bon genre* ("well dressed, well bred")—Parisians approach this exercise as a ritual, and an elaborate ritual at that. Picking produce at the open-air markets on rue Mouffetard or rue Montorgueil or at the Marché d'Aligre, or searching for haute couture at Jean-Paul Gaultier, Sonia Rykiel, or Christian Dior, they cast a discerning eye on the smallest detail and demand the highest quality—which may explain why the city's shopkeepers are so famously grouchy. Browsing through old books and maps in the stalls of *bouquinistes* (secondhand booksellers) on quai de l'Hôtel de Ville along the Seine, or prowling through castoffs at the Marché aux Puces St-Ouen, Parisians show their practicality, their sense of economy, and their ability to turn even a piece of junk into an inventively chic treasure. The city's lairs of consumerism are celebrated—the fashion salons, venerable antiques shops around the rue de Beaune and rue Jacob, august fashion showrooms, and *grands magasins* (department stores) such as Au Bon Marché, Au Printemps, and the Galeries Lafayette, which flaunt Belle Epoque extravagance and trendy designers.

Splendid Stones: Churches to Palaces

It may be due to a heightened sense of aesthetics or just typical Gallic disdain, but Parisians always seem to view with skepticism the architectural innovations continually rising in their midst—all the while assembling the most beautiful city on earth. "C'est magnifique," say some Parisians of the grandiose glass pyramid by architect I. M. Pei that sprouted in 1989 from the Cour Napoléon at their beloved Louvre. "C'est horrible," say others. The Grand Palais was tolerated only as a frothy oddity when it went up as a temporary pavilion for the World's Fair of 1900, but it's still there, a reassuring glass and iron presence on the bank of the Seine. And some Parisians sniffingly refer to the high-rise complex of La Défense as "Houston on the Seine," though this futuristic area and such other glassy creations as the Institut du Monde Arabe, completed in 1988, continue to provide the visual theatrics with which Paris astonishes. Even the Eiffel Tower wasn't spared Parisian scorn: when the city's graceful icon first appeared above the rooftops in 1889, naysayers quipped that they enjoyed ascending to the top because it was the only place they didn't have to look at the darn thing. Still, the memories you cherish most may be of burnished jewels like the Palais de Chaillot, St-Sulpice, Notre-Dame, or the Sainte-Chapelle. More glass than stone, the latter is one of the supreme achievements of the Middle Ages and its heavenly light has not dimmed over the ages.

FODOR'S CHOICE

Fodor'sChoice ★

The sights, restaurants, hotels, and other travel experiences on these pages are our editors' top picks—our Fodor's Choices. They're the best of their type in the area covered by the book—not to be missed and always worth your time. In the chapters that follow, you will find all the details.

RESTAURANTS

$$$$ **Alain Ducasse.** Whether Croesus-rich or sublimely light, Ducasse's culinary triumphs will guarantee you an advanced degree in nouvelle finesse.

$$$$ **Les Élysées du Vernet.** A glass ceiling designed by Gustave Eiffel, intoxicating creations by Alain Solivères (try his *Parmentier de sanglier au panais,* or shepherd's pie of roasted boar with garlic parsnips), and alluring touches—women are presented with a rose on their adieu—put this place in the running for your grand Parisian blow-out.

$$$$ **Taillevent.** Perhaps the most traditional of all Paris luxury restaurants, this grande dame is still the city's finest representative of French *haute cuisine.*

$$$–$$$$ **L'Astrance.** Paris has gone wild over this cool and contemporary spot, thanks to the kitchen's fusion fireworks—anyone for coconut-curry mousseline of scallops studded with tiny green apple ice cubes?

$$$ **La Régalade.** Is Yves Camdeborde the chef of the moment? Only time will tell, but as the leading priest who marries bistro and nouvelle cookery—who can resist his soup of lentils and puréed chestnuts poured over a mound of fois gras?—his remains one of the hardest reservations to snag.

$–$$ **Chez Savy.** The Art Deco cream-and-burgundy interior cossets; the rib-sticking specialties from the Auvergne in central France—lentil salad with bacon, beautifully charred lamb with feather-light shoestring *frites,* poached peach with sorbet—delight.

$–$$ **Ze Kitchen Galerie.** Unbridled creativity and lots of pure fun (check out the windowed kitchen) are the draws here.

BUDGET RESTAURANTS

$ **L'Ardoise.** Just because this contemporary bistro is making waves in Paris doesn't mean you'll have to get a second mortgage to sample dishes such as crab flan in a creamy parsley emulsion.

¢–$ **Les Pipos.** With conversation that flows as freely as the wine, this is everything you can ask for in a Latin Quarter bistro.

LODGING

$$$$ **Hôtel Montalembert.** This cutting-edge designer pad keeps pace with modern times with wireless high-speed Internet, sleek lines and colors, and concept-shattering cuisine.

$$$$ **L'Hôtel.** Empire style opulence abounds at this erstwhile literary haunt and palace of love, now the city's most distinctive boutique

hotel. The Jacques Garcia–designed rooms are crammed with over-the-top antiques and gilt 19th-century details.

$$$ **Hôtel Relais Saint-Sulpice.** On a dead-quiet street near place St-Sulpice is this tiny find, a thoughtfully decorated hideaway whose decor combines Jazz Age Shanghai with treasures from your grandfather's African safari.

$$$ **Hôtel des Grands Hommes.** The serene face-lift at this place du Panthéon hotel will make you feel worthy of being enshrined in the adjacent temple to France's big men (and women). Top-floor balconies have views stretching to Sacre Coeur.

$$ **Hôtel du Lys.** One of Paris's oldest former residences, this 350-year-old hotel has a modest but historical character, with all the beams and twisty narrow corridors preserved from the period. Plus, it's family run, with friendly faces behind the front desk.

$–$$ **Hôtel de Nesle.** Despite having few expected services, the attention to decoration wins you over at the Nesle. Rooms have cartoon frescoes and furnishings evoking historical events and themes. The interior jardin is a welcome respite from around-the-corner Odéon.

$–$$ **Hôtel Langlois.** Its starring role in a recent Hollywood film hasn't gone to its head—the Langlois still offers impeccably well-kept rooms with Art Nouveau and Belle Epoque settings, easily competing with hotels double the price.

BUDGET LODGING

$ **Ermitage Hôtel.** This tranquil spot is as filled with history—it dates from Napoléon III's time and has mirrored armoires, chandeliers, and antiques—as it is lacking in high-tech gadgetry.

$ **Hôtel du Champ de Mars.** A B&B feel, modern amenities, and a location near the Eiffel Tower make this a great spot to base your Paris trip—-and don't forget there's a leafy private garden, too.

$ **Port-Royal Hôtel.** With an antiques-filled lobby, bleached stone-strewn breakfast court, wrought-iron beds, and tile bathrooms, it would be easy to think that this off-the-beaten-path Latin Quarter hotel was a much more expensive place to stay.

MUSEUMS & MASTERPIECES

Centre Georges Pompidou. After a lengthy restoration, the oddest-looking building in Paris and its giant collection are back, better and brassier than ever. Drawing from more than 40,000 works, exhibits are rotated constantly, reinforced by a dynamic program of temporary exhibitions.

Musée Carnavalet. The Hôtel Carnavalet, once the home of Madame de Sévigne, contains just about everything important to the city of Paris, from Proust's bedroom to Louis XVI's shaving kit.

Musée d'Art Moderne. Though often overshadowed by the Pompidou, the collection of modern and contemporary works is very strong, and the temporary exhibits (from Francis Picabia to Matthew Barney to Mark Rothko) are world-class.

Musée d'Orsay. Once a Beaux Arts train station, now a trove of late-19th-century art. The impressive Impressionist and Post-Impressionist section, though inexplicably cramped into a corner upstairs, includes the most important works of Van Gogh, Monet, Manet, and Gauguin.

Musée du Louvre. Incomparable. With more than 800,000 artworks and antiquities in 650,000 square feet of exhibition space, this is, no question, the biggest and best museum in the world.

Musée Nissim de Camondo. Although constructed only in the 19th century by an art-loving millionaire, this mansion showcases the crème de la crème of Rococo and Neoclassical decorative arts and remains the connoisseur's connoisseur's favorite.

Musée Rodin. Rodin's hôtel particulier and its gardens house the sculptor's greatest works, including *The Kiss, Burghers of Calais,* and *The Thinker,* as well as paintings by Van Gogh, Monet, and Renoir. Devote extra time to the marble sculptures of Rodin's mistress-pupil Camille Claudel.

QUINTESSENTIAL PARIS

Arènes de Lutèce. Once the site of Roman gladiator fights and theater performances. Destroyed in AD 3, and not rediscovered until 1869, it is now a favorite of picnickers and boule players.

Café de Flore. The St-Germain neighborhood's gone to the fashion dogs, but this is still the city's essential intellectual gathering place. Neophytes like the cafés wraparound terrace, but insiders prefer the first floor.

Canal St Martin. One of the city's most picturesque spots, slightly off-the-beaten track but oh so Parisian. A barge ride takes you through the canal's nine locks, a perfect way to enjoy the pretty bridges and leafy plane trees that border the water.

Jardin du Luxembourg. Children riding ponies or vying for brass rings on the merry-go-round, students reading under the shady plane trees or napping in the green metal chairs around the fountain: this is as picture-perfect Parisian as it gets.

Au Lapin Agile. The avant-garde cabaret of 19th-century Montmartre bohemia still draws a night crowd. The decor has hardly changed since the composer Erik Satie jammed on the house piano back in the 1880s.

Clignancourt Flea Market. For the hard-core bargain hunter, vintage clothing enthusiast, and astute antiques hunter, the sprawling Marché aux puces at Porte de Clignancourt is the center of the world.

SPECTACULAR SIGHTS

Église du Dôme. Under the dome of this commanding Baroque church, part of Les Invalides, Napoléon rests in imperial splendor.

Tour Eiffel. There is perhaps no other sight more closely associated with Paris than the magnificent steel structure of the Eiffel Tower. Come at night for a particularly illuminating view of the City of Light.

Notre-Dame Cathedral. After seeing the spectacular interior, head up to the twin towers to visit the gargoyles and see the 13-ton bell, which still rings on special occasions.

Sainte-Chapelle. Ascending into this chapel, built by Louis IX to house what he believed to be the Crown of Thorns from Christ's crucifixion and still shimmering with walls of stained glass, is like climbing into a jewel box.

SMART TRAVEL TIPS

Finding out about your destination before you leave home means you won't squander time organizing everyday minutiae once you've arrived. You'll be more streetwise when you hit the ground as well, better prepared to explore the aspects of Paris that drew you here in the first place. The organizations in this section can provide information to supplement this guide; contact them for up-to-the-minute details, and consult the A to Z sections that end the Side Trips chapter for facts on the various topics as they relate to the areas around Paris. Happy landings!

ADDRESSES

Addresses in Paris are fairly straightforward: there is the number, the street name and, often, the location in one of Paris's 20 arrondissements (districts); for instance, Paris 75010 or, simply, the last two digits, 10^{e}, each of which indicates that the address is in the 10th. Due to its large size, the 16^{e} arrondissement has two numbers assigned to it: 75016 and 75116. For the layout of Paris's arrondissements, consult the map at the end of this section. They are laid out in a spiral, beginning from the area around the Louvre (1er arrondissement), then moving clockwise through the Marais, the Quartier Latin, St-Germain, and then out from the city center to the outskirts until it reaches Menilmontant/Père-Lachaise (20e arrondissement). Occasionally you may see an address with a number plus *bis*—for instance, 20 bis rue Vavin. This indicates the next entrance or door down from 20 rue Vavin. Please note that in France you enter a building on the ground floor, or *rez-de-chaussée* (RC or 0), and go up one floor to the first floor, or *premier étage*. General address terms used in this book to keep in mind are: *av.* (abbreviation for avenue); *bd.* (abbreviation for boulevard); *carrefour* (crossway); *cours* (promenade); *passage* (passageway); *quai* (quay/wharf/pier); *rue* (street); *sq.* (abbreviation for square).

AIR TRAVEL TO & FROM PARIS

As one of the premier destinations in the world, Paris is serviced by a great many international carriers and a surprisingly large number of U.S.-based airlines. Air France is the French flag carrier and offers numerous flights (often several per day) between Paris's Charles de Gaulle airport and New York City's JFK airport; Newark, New Jersey; Washington, D.C.'s Reagan airport; as well as the cities of Miami, Chicago, Houston, San Francisco, Los Angeles, Toronto, Montréal, and Mexico City. American-based carriers are usually less expensive but offer, on the whole, fewer nonstop direct flights. Delta Airlines is a popular U.S.–France carrier; its departures to Paris leave from Atlanta, Cincinnati, and New York City's JFK. Travelers in the northeast and southwest of the United States often use Continental Airlines, whose nonstop Paris flights generally depart from Newark and Houston; in peak season, they often offer daily departures. United Airlines, has nonstop flights to Paris from Chicago; Washington, D.C.; and San Francisco. American Airlines offers daily nonstop flights to Paris's Orly airport from numerous cities, including New York City's JFK, Boston, Miami, Chicago, and Dallas/Fort Worth. Northwest has a daily departure to Paris from its hub in Detroit. In Canada, Air France and Air Canada are the leading choices for departures from Toronto and Montréal; in peak season, departures are often on a daily basis. From London, Air France, British Airways, and British Midland are the leading carriers, with up to 15 flights daily in peak season. In addition, direct routes link Manchester, Edinburgh, and Southampton with Paris. A number of discount carriers are cornering the market to numerous European destinations. Ryanair, Easyjet, and Buzz offer direct service from Paris to Dublin, London, Glasgow, Amsterdam, and Brussels, to name just a few. To save money, these companies use the smaller airports outside the major cities (Beauvais in Paris, Luton in London), which necessitate a 20-minute to one-hour shuttle service at minimal cost (€10–€15). Don't worry: although prices may be slashed, safety standards, security, and pilots are top-notch, following the same strict European standards as the major carriers. Tickets are available on the Web only and need to be booked well in advance to get the best prices—a one-way ticket from Paris to Dublin costs a mere €30, for example.

BOOKING

When you book, **look for nonstop flights** and **remember that "direct" flights stop at least once.** Try to avoid connecting flights, which require a change of plane. Two airlines may operate a connecting flight jointly, so ask whether your airline operates every segment of the trip; you may find that the carrier you prefer flies you only part of the way. To find more booking tips and to check prices and make online flight reservations, log on to www.fodors.com.

Major Airlines **Air Canada** ☎ 800/776-3000 in the U.S. and Canada; 08-25-88-08-81 in France. **Air France** ☎ 800/237-2747 in the U.S.; 08-20-82-08-20 in France ⊕ www.airfrance.com. **American Airlines** ☎ 800/433-7300 in the U.S.; 08-10-87-28-72 in France ⊕ www.aa.com. **British Airways** ☎ 800/247-9297 in the U.S.; 0345/222-111 in the U.K.; 08-25-82-54-00 in France ⊕ www.britishairways.com. **Continental** ☎ 800/231-0856 in the U.S.; 01-42-99-09-09 in France ⊕ www.continental.com. **Delta** ☎ 800/241-4141 in the U.S.; 08-00-35-40-80 in France ⊕ www.delta.com. **Northwest** ☎ 800/225-2525 in the U.S.; 08-10-55-65-56 in France ⊕ www.nwa.com. **Qantas** ☎ 800/227-4500 in the U.S.; 08-20-82-05-00 in France ⊕ www.qantas.com. **United** ☎ 800/538-2929 in the U.S.; 08-10-72-72-72 in France ⊕ www.unitedairlines.com. **US Airways** ☎ 800/428-4322 in the U.S.; 08-10-63-22-22 in France ⊕ www.usairways.com.

Travel between the U.K. & France **Air France** ☎ 020/8742-6600 in the U.K.; 08-02-80-28-02 in France ⊕ www.airfrance.com. **British Airways** ☎ 0345/222-111 in the U.K.; 08-02-80-29-02 in France ⊕ www.britishairways.com. **British Midland** ☎ 020/8754-7321, 0345/554-554 in the U.K.; 01-53-43-25-27 in France ⊕ www.britishmidland.com.

Discount Airlines **Buzz** ☎ 01-55-17-42-42 in France ⊕ www.buzzaway.com. **Easyjet** ☎ 08-25-08-25-08 in France ⊕ www.easyjet.com. **Ryan Air** ☎ 08-92-55-56-66 in France ⊕ www.ryanair.com

Within France **Air France** ☎ 800/237-2747 in the U.S.; 08-02-80-28-02 in France ⊕ www.airfrance.com. **AirLib Express** ☎ 08-25-09-09-09 ⊕ www.airlibexpress.com.

CHECK-IN & BOARDING

Security measures in France have always been stringent, especially on international flights; check-in lines are long, slow, and frustrating if you're running late, so plan to arrive at the airport about 2 hours before your scheduled departure time for domestic flights and 2½ to 3 hours before international flights. You may need to arrive earlier if you're flying from one of the busier airports during peak air-traffic times such as the Christmas holidays. To avoid delays at airport security checkpoints both home and abroad, try not to wear any metal. Jewelry, belt and other buckles, steel-toe shoes, barrettes, and under-wire bras are among the objects that can set off detectors.

Always **ask your carrier about its check-in policy.** Assuming that not everyone with a ticket will show up, airlines routinely overbook planes. When everyone does, airlines ask for volunteers to give up their seats. In return, these volunteers usually get a several-hundred-dollar flight voucher, which can be used toward the purchase of another ticket, and are rebooked on the next flight out. If there are not enough volunteers, the airline must choose who will be denied boarding. The first to get bumped are passengers who checked in late and those flying on discounted tickets, so **get to the gate and check in as early as possible,** especially during peak periods.

Always **bring a government-issued photo ID to the airport;** even when it's not required, a passport is best.

CUTTING COSTS

You can save on air travel within Europe if you plan on traveling to and from Paris aboard Air France. If you sign up for Air France's Euro Flyer program, you can buy coupons that enable you to travel to any Air France destination. Rates are calculated per miles covered and are divided into zones: a Zone One coupon costs $60 and covers an area of 0–150 mi; Zone 2 costs $90 and covers 151–500 mi; up to Zone 6 ($200) which covers an area of over 2,000 mi. You can only purchase these coupons in the United States, and you must ask for them specifically. These coupons are a great investment for those who are planning on traveling from city to city and don't want to worry about the cost of one-way travel.

The least expensive airfares to Paris are priced for round-trip travel and must usually be purchased in advance. Airlines generally allow you to change your return date for a fee; most low-fare tickets, however, are nonrefundable. It's smart to **call a number of airlines and check the Internet;** when you are quoted a good price, **book it on the spot**—the same fare may not be available the next day, or even the next hour. Always **check different routings** and look into using alternate airports. Also, price off-peak flights, which may be significantly less expensive than others. Travel agents, especially low-fare specialists (⇨ Discounts & Deals), are helpful.

Consolidators are another good source. They buy tickets for scheduled flights at reduced rates from the airlines, then sell them at prices that beat the best fare available directly from the airlines. Sometimes you can even get your money back if you need to return the ticket. Carefully read the fine print detailing penalties for changes and cancellations, purchase the ticket with a credit card, and **confirm your consolidator reservation with the airline.**

When you fly as a courier, you trade your checked-luggage space for a ticket deeply subsidized by a courier service. There are restrictions on when you can book and how long you can stay. Some courier companies list with membership organizations, such as the Air Courier Association and the International Association of Air Travel Couriers; these require you to become a member before you can book a flight.

Consolidators **AirlineConsolidator.com** ☎ 888/468-5385 🌐 www.airlineconsolidator.com; for international tickets. **Best Fares** ☎ 800/576-8255 or 800/576-1600 🌐 www.bestfares.com; $59.90 annual membership. **Cheap Tickets** ☎ 800/377-1000 or 888/922-8849 🌐 www.cheaptickets.com. **Expedia** ☎ 404/728-8787 or 800/397-3342 🌐 www.expedia.com. **Hotwire** ☎ 866/468-9473 or 920/330-9418 🌐 www.hotwire.com. **Now Voyager Travel** ✉ 45 W. 21st St., 5th floor, New York, NY 10010 ☎ 212/459-1616 🖷 212/243-2711 🌐 www.nowvoyagertravel.com. **Onetravel.com** 🌐 www.onetravel.com. **Orbitz** ☎ 888/656-4546 🌐 www.orbitz.com. **Priceline.com** 🌐 www.priceline.com. **Travelocity** ☎ 888/709-5983; 877/282-2925 in Canada; 0870/111-7060 in the U.K. 🌐 www.travelocity.com.

Courier Resources **Air Courier Association/Cheaptrips.com** ☎ 800/282-1202 🌐 www.aircourier.org or www.cheaptrips.com. **International Association of Air Travel Couriers** ☎ 308/632-3273 🌐 www.courier.org.

ENJOYING THE FLIGHT

State your seat preference when purchasing your ticket, and then repeat it when you confirm and when you check in. For more legroom, you can request one of the few emergency-aisle seats at check-in, if you are capable of lifting at least 50 pounds—a Federal Aviation Administration requirement of passengers in these seats. Seats behind a bulkhead also offer more legroom, but they don't have underseat storage. Don't sit in the row in front of the emergency aisle or in front of a bulkhead, where seats may not recline.

Ask the airline whether a snack or meal is served on the flight. If you have dietary concerns, **request special meals when booking.** These can be vegetarian, low-cholesterol, or kosher, for example. It's a good idea to pack some healthful snacks and a small (plastic) bottle of water in your carry-on bag. On long flights, try to maintain a normal routine to help fight jet lag. At night, **get some sleep.** By day, **eat light meals, drink water** (not alcohol), and **move around the cabin** to stretch your legs. For additional jet-lag tips consult *Fodor's FYI: Travel Fit & Healthy* (available at bookstores everywhere).

Smoking policies vary from carrier to carrier. Many airlines prohibit smoking on all of their flights; others allow smoking only on certain routes or certain departures. Ask your carrier about its policy.

FLYING TIMES

Flying time to Paris is 7 hours from New York, 9½ hours from Chicago, and 11 hours from Los Angeles. Flying time from the United Kingdom to Paris is 1½ hours.

HOW TO COMPLAIN

If your baggage goes astray or your flight goes awry, complain right away. Most carriers require that you **file a claim immediately.** The Aviation Consumer Protection Division of the Department of Transportation publishes *Fly-Rights,* which discusses airlines and consumer issues and is available on-line. You can also find articles and information at mytravelrights.com, the Web site of the nonprofit Consumer Travel Rights Center.

Airline Complaints **Aviation Consumer Protection Division** ✉ U.S. Department of Transportation, C-75, Room 4107, 400 7th St. SW, Washington, DC 20590 ☎ 202/366-2220 ⊕ airconsumer.ost.dot.gov/ **Federal Aviation Administration Consumer Hotline** ✉ for inquiries: FAA, 800 Independence Ave. SW, Washington, DC 20591 ☎ 800/322-7873 ⊕ www.faa.gov.

RECONFIRMING

Check the status of your flight before you leave for the airport. You can do this on your carrier's Web site, by linking to a flight-status checker (many Web booking services offer these), or by calling your carrier or travel agent. Always confirm international flights at least 72 hours ahead of the scheduled departure time.

AIRPORTS & TRANSFERS

The major airports are Charles de Gaulle (also known as Roissy), 26 km (16 mi) northeast of Paris, and Orly, 16 km (10 mi) south of Paris. It doesn't really matter which one you fly into; both are easily accessible from Paris, though Roissy is the only one with a TGV (high-speed train) station. Whether you take a car or bus to travel from Paris to the airport on your departure, always allot an extra half hour (at least) due to the often horrendous traffic tie-ups within the airports proper (especially in peak seasons and at peak hours): once you arrive at the airports, you'll often need to take the inter-airport buses to shuttle you from one terminal to another, and if this bus is held up due to traffic congestion (often the case), a serious case of nail-biting will result.

Airport Information **Charles de Gaulle/Roissy** ☎ 01-48-62-22-80 in English ⊕ www.paris-airports.com. **Orly** ☎ 01-49-75-15-15 ⊕ www.paris-airports.com.

AIRPORT TRANSFERS

Charles de Gaulle/Roissy: From the Charles de Gaulle airport, **the least expensive way to get into Paris is on the RER-B line,** the suburban express train. Each terminal has an exit where the free RER shuttle bus (a white and yellow bus with the letters ADP in gray) will pass every 7–15 minutes to take you on the short ride to the nearby RER station: Terminal 2A (exit A8), Terminal 2C (exit C8), Terminal 2B (exit B6), Terminal 2D (exit D6), Terminal 2F (exit 2.08). Trains to central Paris (Les Halles, St-Michel, Luxembourg) depart every 15 minutes. The fare (including métro connection) is €8, and journey time is about 30 minutes. Note that you will have to carry your luggage down to the train tracks, and trains will be crowded if you are traveling during rush hour.

You don't need to have flown Air France to take their comfortable shuttle service to the city. Line One goes from the airport to Charles-de-Gaulle Étoile and Porte Maillot from 5:45 AM to 11 PM. It leaves every

12 minutes and costs €10, which you can pay on board. Passengers arriving in Terminal 1 need to take exit 34; Terminal 2A and 2C, exit 5; Terminal 2B and 2D, exit 6, Terminal 2F, exit 0.07. Line Four goes to Montparnasse and the Gare de Lyon from 7 AM to 9 PM. Buses run every 30 minutes and cost €12. Passengers arriving in Terminal 1 need to look for exit 34; Terminal 2A and 2C need to take either exit 2 or 2C; Terminal 2B and 2D, exit 2 or 2B; and Terminal 2F, exit 0.07.

Another option is to take Roissybus, operated by the Paris Transit Authority, which runs between Charles de Gaulle and the Opéra every 20 minutes from 5:45 AM to 11 PM; the cost is €8. Note that you have to hail the bus that you want—it will not stop automatically—and that rush-hour traffic can make for a slow ride.

You can arrange a ride with Paris Airports Service or Airport Shuttle, and a bilingual driver will be waiting with a minivan to drive you, and often a few other travelers, to your destination. Rates are set so there are no unpleasant surprises due to poor traffic conditions—approximately €19 for one person and €13 per person for two or more people traveling together, and can be prepaid by credit card. It is best to call, fax, or e-mail your request at least 24 hours in advance, noting your flight number, expected time of arrival, and your destination address in Paris.

Journey times for taxis, and as a consequence, prices, are unpredictable. At best, the journey takes 30 minutes, but it can take as long as an hour. The average fare falls between €30 and €45. You can ask for a quote before getting into the taxi, but it is almost certain that your driver will respond with a shrug. There is also a €.90 supplement per piece of luggage. Please note that drivers can no longer refuse to take a fourth person; it's the law.

Orly: From the Orly airport **the most economical way to get into Paris is to take the RER-C or Orlyrail line;** catch the free shuttle bus from the terminal to the train station. Trains to Paris leave every 15 minutes. Passengers arriving in either the South or West Terminal need to use exit G. The fare is €6, and journey time is about 35 minutes. Another option is to take the monorail service, Orlyval, which runs between the Antony RER-B station and Orly airport every four to eight minutes. The fare to downtown Paris is €9.

You can also take an Air France bus from Orly to Les Invalides on the Left Bank and Montparnasse; these run every 12 minutes from 6 AM to 11:30 PM (you need not have flown on Air France to use this service). The fare is €8, and journey time is between 30 and 45 minutes, depending on traffic. The Paris Transit Authority's Orlybus is yet another option; buses leave every 15 minutes for the Denfert-Rochereau métro station; the cost is €6.

With advance reservations Paris Airports Services or Airport Shuttle can pick you up at Orly and drive you directly to your destination. If possible make your reservations at least 24 hours in advance; MasterCard and Visa are accepted and the operators speak English. The fare for one person traveling alone is €17 or €13 per person with two or more people traveling together. At best, taxis take around 25 minutes from Orly to downtown Paris; the fare falls between €15 and €30.

Taxis & Shuttles **Air France Bus** ☎ 01-41-56-89-00 recorded information in English 🌐 www.cars-airfrance.com. **Airport Shuttle** ☎ 01-30-11-11-90; 888/426-2705 toll free from the U.S. 📠 01-30-11-11-99 🌐 www.airportshuttle.fr. **Paris Airports Services** ☎ 08-21-80-08-01 📠 01-49-62-78-79 🌐 www.parisairportservice.com.

DUTY-FREE SHOPPING

Duty-free shopping is no longer possible when you are traveling within the European Union; you will benefit from duty-free prices only when you are leaving European territory.

BOAT & FERRY TRAVEL

Linking France and the United Kingdom, a boat or ferry trip across the Channel can range from a mere 35 minutes (via hovercraft) to 95 minutes (via ferryboat). Trip length also depends on your departure point: popular routes link Boulogne and Folkestone, Le Havre and Portsmouth, and, the most booked passage, Calais and Dover.

Hoverspeed travels the route from Dover, England, to Calais, France, up to 15 times a day by hovercraft and catamaran. The crossings take 35 minutes (Hovercraft) or 95 minutes (catamaran). They also link Folkestone, England, with Boulogne, France, with 10 35-minute crossings per day. P&O European Ferries links Portsmouth and Le Havre. They have up to 25 sailings a day; the crossing takes about 75 minutes. Seafrance operates up to 15 sailings a day from Dover to Calais; the crossing takes either 70 or 90 minutes depending on the ship.

Driving distances from the French ports to Paris are as follows: from Calais, 290 km (180 mi); from Boulogne, 243 km (151 mi); from Le Havre 230 km (120 mi). The fastest routes to Paris from each port are via N43, A26, and A1 from Calais and the Channel Tunnel; via N1 from Boulogne; and via N15 from Le Havre.

Boat & Ferry Travel **Hoverspeed** ✉ International Hoverport, Marine Parade, Dover, Kent CT17 9TG England ☎ 0870/240-8070 🌐 www.hoverspeed.fr. **P&O European Ferries** ✉ Channel House, Channel View Rd., Dover, Kent CT17 9TJ England ☎ 0870/242-4999 🌐 www.poportsmouth.com. **Seafrance** ✉ 23 rue Louis-le-Grand, 75002 Paris ☎ 08-25-04-40-45 🌐 www.seafrance.net.

FARES & SCHEDULES

Schedules and tickets are available at any travel agency throughout France or via the Internet. Travel agencies accept traveler's checks, major credit cards, and cash. Fares vary, but a round-trip from Dover to Calais completed within five days costs €40 for one person, €220 for two adults plus a car. The price doubles if the visit exceeds five days.

BUSINESS HOURS

BANKS & OFFICES

On weekdays, banks are open generally 9:30 AM–4:30 or 5 PM (note that the Banque de France closes at 3:30), and some banks are also open Saturday 9–5 as well. In general, government offices and businesses are open 9–5.

GAS STATIONS

Gas stations in the city are generally open 7:30 AM–8 PM, though those near the city's *portes* (or principal entranceways) near the *périphérique* (beltway) are open 24 hours a day.

MUSEUMS & SIGHTS

Most museums are closed one day a week—usually either Monday or Tuesday—and on national holidays. Generally, museums and national monuments are open from 10 AM to 5 or 6 PM. A few close for lunch (noon–2) and are open Sunday only in the afternoon. Many of the large museums have one *nocturne* (nighttime) opening per week, when they are open until 9:30 or 10 PM. The Louvre is closed Tuesday and stays open late Wednesday until 9:45 PM. The Centre Pompidou is closed Tuesday and has late opening hours daily until 10 PM. The Musée d'Orsay is closed Monday and stays open until 9:30 PM Thursday. All national museums are free to the public the first Sunday of every month.

PHARMACIES

Pharmacies are generally open Monday–Saturday 8:30 AM–8 PM. Nearby pharmacies that stay open late, or for 24 hours, or Sunday, are listed on the door.

SHOPS

Generally, large shops are open from 9:30 or 10 AM to 7 or 8 PM Monday to Saturday and remain open through lunchtime. Many of the large department stores stay open until 10 PM Wednesday or Thursday. Smaller shops and many supermarkets often open earlier (8 AM) but take a lengthy lunch break (1 PM–3 PM) and generally close around 8 PM; small food shops are often open Sunday mornings 9 AM–1 PM. There is always a small corner grocery store that stays open late, usually until 11 PM, if you're in a bind for basic necessities like diapers, bread, cheese, and fruit (and perhaps the unnecessary bottle of chilled champagne or the disposable plastic rain hat, circa 1950). Note that prices are substantially higher in such outlets than in the larger supermarkets. Most shops close all day Sunday, except in the Marais (where shops that stand side by side on rue des Francs Bourgeois, from antiques dealers to chic little designers, jewelry to home decoration, open their doors to welcome hordes of Sunday browsers); the Bastille, the Latin Quarter, and the Ile de la Cité also have shops that open Sunday.

BUS TRAVEL TO & FROM PARIS

The excellent national train service in France means that long-distance bus service in the country is practically nonexistent; regional buses are found where train service is spotty. Local bus information to the rare rural areas where trains do not have access can be obtained from the SNCF.

The largest international operator is Eurolines France, whose main terminal is in the Parisian suburb of Bagnolet (a half-hour métro ride from central Paris, at the end of métro line 3). Eurolines runs international routes to over 1,500 cities in Europe.

FARES & SCHEDULES

It is possible to take a bus (via ferry) to Paris from the United Kingdom; just be aware that what you save in money will almost certainly cost you in time—the bus trip takes about seven hours as opposed to the three it takes on the Eurostar train line (Victoria Station–Gare du Nord). In general, the price of a round-trip bus ticket is 50% less than that of a plane and 25% less than a train ticket, so if you have the time and the energy, this is a good way to cut the cost of travel. Eurolines also offers a 15-day (€285), 30-day (€425), or 60-day (€490) pass if you're planning on doing the grand European tour. Ask about one of the "circle tours" that depart from Paris, for example, via London, Amsterdam, then back to Paris again). Eurolines operates a service from London's Victoria Coach Station, via the Dover–Calais ferry, to Paris's Porte de Bagnolet. There is a 9 AM departure that arrives in Paris at 4 PM, a 2 PM departure that arrives at 9 PM, and the overnight trip from 9:30 PM, which arrives in Paris at 7 AM. Fares are £60 round-trip (under-25 youth pass £56), £35 one-way. Other Eurolines routes include the following: Amsterdam (7 hours, €70); Barcelona (15 hours, €150); and Berlin (10 hours, €132). There are also international-only arrival-departures from Avignon, Bordeaux, Lille, Lyon, Toulouse, and Tours. Hoverspeed offers up to four daily departures from London's Victoria Coach Station. Fares are £60 round-trip, £38 one-way.

Bus Information **Eurolines** ✉ 28 av. Général-de-Gaulle, Bagnolet 93541 ☎ 08-92-89-90-91 in France; 020/7730-3499 in the U.K. 🌐 www.eurolines.fr. **Hoverspeed** ✉ International Hoverport, Marine Parade, Dover CT17 9TG England ☎ 0870/240-8070 🌐 www.hoverspeed.fr. **Paris Vision** ✉ 1 rue d'Auber, 75009 Paris ☎ 01-47-42-27-40. **SNCF** ✉ 88 rue St-Lazare, 75009 Paris ☎ 08-36-35-35-39 in English.

BUS TRAVEL WITHIN PARIS

Bus travel in Paris has always had the reputation of catering to that very small population of people who actually have the time to sit in the bus and read a good book as it snails its way through impossible Parisian traffic. All that changed in 2002 when special protected bus lanes were created throughout Paris—more than 41 km (25 mi) of them in every arrondissement except the 13e. Travel time has been cut, on the average, by a whopping 50%; for example, a trip from Saint-Michel to the place de la Concorde now takes 9 minutes instead of the usual 25. This, of course is to discourage the stubborn Parisian population from taking their cars to work and creating impossible congestion in the city, but it can benefit you, too: Buses are a scenic, convenient, and efficient way to see the city, and the new ones are equipped with air-conditioning—something to think about on those sweltering August days.

Paris buses are green and white; route number and destination are marked in front, and major stopping places along the sides. The brown bus shelters, topped by red-and-yellow circular signs, contain timetables and route maps; note that buses must be hailed at these larger bus shelters, as they service multiple lines and routes. Smaller stops are designated simply by a pole bearing bus numbers.

Of Paris's 250 bus routes, three main lines circle the *grands boulevards* and are known as the *petite ceinture* (small belt). These constitute bus numbers PC 1, PC 2, and PC 3, which run in a continuous circle covering the major *portes*, or entryways, into the city center. More than 200 other bus routes run throughout Paris, reaching virtually every nook and cranny of the city. During weekdays and Saturday, buses run every five minutes (as opposed to the 15- to 20-minute wait on Sunday and national holidays). One ticket will take you anywhere within the city; once you get off at any point, that ticket is no longer valid.

Bus transport is ideal for the elderly, women with children (easy access with strollers), and anyone who likes to take the scenic route. Needless to say, seats are more difficult to find during rush hours.

A map of the bus system is on the flip side of every métro map, in all métro stations, and at all bus stops. Maps are also found in each bus. A recorded message announces the name of the next stop. To get off, press one of the red buttons mounted on all the silver poles that run the length of the bus and the *arrêt demandé* (stop requested) light directly behind the driver will light up. Use the rear door to exit.

The Balabus, a public orange-and-white bus that runs between May and September, gives an interesting 50-minute tour around the major sights. You can use your Paris-Visite, Carte Orange, or Mobilis pass, or one to three bus tickets depending on how far you ride. The route runs from La Défense to the Gare de Lyon.

FARES & SCHEDULES

Regular buses accept métro tickets, your best bet is to buy a *carnet* of 10 tickets for €9.60 at any métro station, or you can buy a single ticket on board (exact change appreciated) for €1.30. If you have individual tickets, you should be prepared to **punch your ticket in the red-and-gray machines located at the entrance of the bus.** You need to show (but not punch) weekly, monthly, and Paris-Visite/Mobilis tickets to the driver. Tickets can be bought on buses, in the métro, or in any bar/tabac store displaying the lime-green métro symbol above its street sign.

Most routes operate from 7 AM to 8:30 PM (or 20h30 to the French); some continue to midnight. After 8:30 PM you must either take the métro or one of the 18 "Noctambus" lines (indicated by a brown owl symbol at bus stops). These bus lines operate hourly (1:30 AM–5:30 AM) between Châtelet and various nearby suburbs; they can be stopped by hailing them at any point on their route. Paris-Visite/Mobilis passes are accepted on the Noctambus. A regular ticket costs €2.30 and allows for one transfer.

Bus Information RATP ✉ Pl. de la Madeleine, 75008 Paris ✉ 53 bis quai des Grands Augustins, 75006 Paris ☎ 08-36-68-41-14 🌐 www.ratp.com.

CAMERAS & PHOTOGRAPHY

If you need to get your camera repaired, your best bet is to go to one of the FNAC stores in Paris. Note that it might take some time for the camera to be fixed. The *Kodak Guide to Shooting Great Travel Pictures* (available at bookstores everywhere) is loaded with tips.

Camera Repair & Photo Developing FNAC ✉ 26–30 av. des Ternes, 17e ✉ in the Forum des Halles ✉ 1–7 rue Pierre-Lescot, 1er ✉ 136 rue St-Lazare, 9e ✉ 157 rue du Faubourg St-Antoine, 11e.

Photo Help Kodak Information Center ☎ 800/242–2424 🌐 www.kodak.com.

EQUIPMENT PRECAUTIONS

Don't pack film and equipment in checked luggage, where it is much more susceptible to damage. X-ray machines used to view checked luggage are extremely powerful and therefore are likely to ruin your film. Try to **ask for hand inspection of film,** which becomes clouded after repeated exposure to airport X-ray machines, and **keep videotapes and computer disks away from metal detectors.** Always **keep film, tape, and computer disks out of the sun.** Carry an extra supply of batteries, and **be prepared to turn on your camera, camcorder, or laptop** to prove to airport security personnel that the device is real.

FILM & DEVELOPING

The easiest place to get film developed and printed is at one of the various FNAC stores around the city. Keep in mind that it is expensive to have film developed and printed in Paris—around US$20 per 36-exposure roll.

VIDEOS

Video systems are not the same all over the world. The United States, for instance, uses NTSC and France uses SECAM. Other European countries, including the United Kingdom, use PAL. This means that you probably won't be able to play videotapes from the United States in France. You should also **bring extra blank videotapes with you from home** for your camcorder as you may not be able to find compatible tapes in France.

CAR RENTAL

Rates in Paris begin at approximately $70 a day and $200 a week for an economy car with air-conditioning, manual transmission, and unlimited mileage. This does not include tax on car rentals, which is 19.6% or, if you are picking one up at the airport, the airport tax. To save money, make reservations before you go; you can generally get a much better deal. Note that driving in Paris is best avoided, and parking is very difficult to find. You're better off renting a car only when you want to take excursions out of the city.

Renting a car through a local French agency has a number of disadvantages, the biggest being price, as they simply cannot compete with the larger international companies. These giants combine bilingual service, the security of name recognition, extensive services (such as 24-hour hot lines), and fully automatic vehicles. Easycar, an Internet-only rental service, offers the wonderful Smartcar, a tiny two-seater Mercedes perfect for zipping around the city. SNAC, a France-based agency, can be useful if you are interested in luxury cars (convertible BMWs) or large family vans (Renault Espace, for example).

Major Agencies **Alamo** ☎ 800/522-9696 🌐 www.alamo.com. **Avis** ☎ 800/331-1084; 800/879-2847 in Canada; 0870/606-0100 in the U.K.; 02/9353-9000 in Australia; 09/526-2847 in New Zealand 🌐 www.avis.com. **Budget** ☎ 800/527-0700; 0870/156-5656 in the U.K. 🌐 www.budget.com. **Dollar** ☎ 800/800-6000; 0124/622-0111 in the U.K., where it's affiliated with Sixt; 02/9223-1444 in Australia 🌐 www.dollar.com. **Hertz** ☎ 800/654-3001; 800/263-0600 in Canada; 0870/844-8844 in the U.K.; 02/9669-2444 in Australia; 09/256-8690 in New Zealand 🌐 www.hertz.com. **National Car Rental** ☎ 800/227-7368; 0870/600-6666 in the U.K. 🌐 www.nationalcar.com.

CUTTING COSTS

For a good deal, **book through a travel agent who will shop around.** Do **look into wholesalers,** companies that do not own fleets but rent in bulk from those that do and often offer better rates than traditional car-rental operations. Prices are best during off-peak periods. Rentals booked through wholesalers often must be paid for before you leave home.

Local Agencies **Easycar** 🌐 www.easycar.com. **SNAC** ✉ 82 rue Lauriston ☎ 01-44-05-33-99 🌐 www.automobiles-snac.fr

Wholesalers **Auto Europe** ☎ 207/842-2000 or 800/223-5555 🖷 207/842-2222 🌐 www.autoeurope.com. **Destination Europe Resources (DER)** ✉ 9501 W. Devon Ave., Rosemont, IL 60018 ☎ 800/782-2424 🌐 www.der.com. **Europe by Car** ☎ 212/581-3040 or 800/223-1516 🖷 212/246-1458 🌐 www.europebycar.com. **Kemwel** ☎ 800/678-0678 🖷 207/842-2124 🌐 www.kemwel.com.

INSURANCE

When driving a rented car you are generally responsible for any damage to or loss of the vehicle. Collision policies that car-rental companies sell for European rentals typically do not cover stolen vehicles. Before you rent—and purchase collision or theft coverage—see what coverage you already have under the terms of your personal auto-insurance policy and credit cards.

REQUIREMENTS & RESTRICTIONS

In France, you drive on the right and **yield to drivers coming from streets to the right.** However, this rule does not necessarily apply at roundabouts, where you should watch out for just about everyone. You must **wear your seat belt,** and children under 12 may not travel in the front seat. Speed limits are 130 kph (80 mph) on expressways (*autoroutes*), 110 kph (70 mph) on divided highways (*routes nationales*), 90 kph (55 mph) on other roads (*routes*), 50 kph (30 mph) in cities and towns (*villes et villages*).

In France your own driver's license is acceptable. An International Driver's Permit is not necessary unless you are planning on a long-term stay; you can get one from the American or Canadian Automobile Association, and, in the United Kingdom, from the Automobile Association or Royal Automobile Club. You must be 18 years old to drive, but there is no top age limit for those whose faculties are intact. To rent a car you must be 21 or older and have a major credit card, although you will be permitted to rent a car for a €17 per day supplement if you're under 25.

SURCHARGES

Before you pick up a car in one city and leave it in another, **ask about drop-off charges or one-way service fees,** which can be substantial. Note, too, that some rental agencies charge extra if you return the car before the time specified in your contract. To avoid a hefty refueling fee, **fill the tank just before you turn in the car,** but be aware that gas stations near the rental outlet may overcharge. It's almost never a deal to buy the tank of gas that's in the car when you rent it; the understanding is that you'll return it empty, but some fuel usually remains.

CAR TRAVEL

France's roads are classified into five types, numbered and prefixed *A* (*autoroute*), *N* (*route nationale*), *D* (*route départmentale*), and the smaller *C*, or *V*. Roads marked *A* (*autoroutes*) are expressways. There are excellent links between Paris and most French cities. When trying to get around Ile-de-France, it is often difficult to avoid Paris—just try to **steer clear of rush hours** (7–9:30 AM and 4:30–7:30 PM). A *péage* (toll) must be paid on most expressways: the rate varies but can be steep. Certain booths allow you to pay with your credit card.

There are two major rings that run parallel to each other and encircle Paris: the *périférique intérieur,* the inside ring also known as the *grands boulevards* (not to be confused with the major avenue layout in the center of Paris's Right Bank) and the *périférique extérieur,* the outside ring, which is a major highway and from which *portes* (gates) connect Paris to the major highways of France. The names of these highways function on the same principal as the métro, with the final destination as the determining point in the direction you must take.

Heading north, look for Porte de la Chapelle (direction Lille and Charles de Gaulle airport); east, for Porte de Bagnolet (direction Metz and Nancy); south, for Porte d'Orléans (direction Lyon and Bordeaux); and west, for Porte d'Auteuil (direction Rouen and Chartres) or Porte de St-Cloud.

EMERGENCY SERVICES

If your car breaks down on an expressway, pull your car as far off the road as possible, set your emergency indicators, and, if possible, put the emergency triangle located in the trunk of your car at least 30 yards behind your car to warn oncoming traffic; then **go to a roadside emergency telephone.** These phones put you in direct contact with the police, automatically indicating your exact location, and are available every 3 km (2 mi). If you have a breakdown anywhere else, find the nearest garage or contact the police. There are also 24-hour assistance hot lines valid throughout France (available through rental agencies and supplied to you when you rent the car), but do not hesitate to call the police in case of any roadside emergency, for they are quick and reliable and the phone call is free. There are special phones just for this purpose on all highways—just pick up the phone and dial 17.

Police ☎ 17. **Club Automobile de l'Ile de France** ☎ 01-40-55-43-00 is for members only.

GASOLINE

Gas is expensive and prices vary enormously; anything from €.85 to €1.40 per liter. Credit cards are accepted in every gas station. There are very few self-service gas stations in Paris.

PARKING

Finding parking in Paris is very difficult. Meters and ticket machines (pay and display) are common: make sure you have a supply of €.50 coins. If you're planning on spending a lot of time in Paris with a car, **buy a parking card** (*carte de stationnement*) for €15 or €30 at any café displaying the red TABAC sign. This card works like a credit card in the parking meters, allowing you to avoid the inconvenience of finding exact change. After depositing enough money (or using your parking card) in the ticket machine, you will receive a receipt; be sure to display the receipt on the inside window of the vehicle, the dashboard on the passenger side being best. Note that in August, parking is free in certain residential areas. However, only parking meters with a dense yellow circle on them indicate free parking in August; if you do not see the circle, pay up. Parking tickets are expensive, and there is no shortage of the blue-uniformed parking police. Parking lots, indicated by a blue sign with a white *P,* are usually underground and are generally expensive (due to the 24-hour surveillance systems).

ROAD MAPS

For the best, most detailed directional information, do what the French do and invest in a Michelin road map—available at almost any gas station or bookstore. You can buy either regional or national maps for approximately €6.

RULES OF THE ROAD

A native quirk that takes some getting used to is the famous *priorité à droite* law that states that all drivers must yield to any vehicle coming from the right—to be safe, slow down at *all* crosswalks and make sure no one is coming from the right.

Some important traffic terms and signs to note: *Sortie* (Exit); *Sens Unique* (One Way); *Stationnement Interdite* (No Parking); *Impasse* (Dead End). Blue rectangular signs indicate a highway; triangles carry illustrations of a particular traffic hazard; speed limits are indicated in a circle with the maximum speed circled in red.

THE CHANNEL TUNNEL

Short of flying, taking the "Chunnel" is the fastest way to cross the English Channel: 35 minutes from Folkestone to Calais, 60 minutes from motorway to motorway, or three hours from London's Waterloo Station to Paris's Gare du Nord. Reservations are essential at peak times and a good idea at any time. Cars don't drive in the Chunnel but are loaded onto trains. The comfortable Eurostar train is a particularly civilized way to make the crossing, especially if you choose one of the upper classes of service where meals and drinks are served throughout your trip. There are often upgrade offers for a nominal price; check when making your reservation.

Car Transport **Eurotunnel** ☎ 0870/535–3535 in the U.K.; 070/223210 in Belgium; 03–21–00–61–00 in France 🌐 www.eurotunnel.com. **French Motorail/Rail Europe** ☎ 0870/241-5415 🌐 www.frenchmotorail.com.

Passenger Service **Eurostar** ☎ 1233/617–575 or 0870/518–6186, in the U.K. 🌐 www.eurostar.co.uk. **Rail Europe** ☎ 800/942–4866 or 800/274–8724; 0870/584–8848 U.K. inquiries and credit-card bookings 🌐 www.raileurope.com.

CHILDREN IN PARIS

Fodor's Around Paris with Kids (available in bookstores everywhere) can help you plan your days together.

If you are renting a car, don't forget to **arrange for a car seat** when you reserve. For general advice about traveling with children, consult *Fodor's FYI: Travel with Your Baby* (available in bookstores everywhere).

BABY-SITTING

Agencies can provide English-speaking baby-sitters with just a few hours' notice. The hourly rate is approximately €6 (three-hour minimum) plus an agency fee of €10. Many hotels offer baby-sitting services as well.

Agencies **A. G. Prestige** ✉ 69 rue Louis Michel, 92300 Levallois ☎ 01–41–40–07–45. **Allo Maman Poule** ✉ 7 Villa Murat, 16ᵉ ☎ 01–45–20–96–96. **Baby-Sitting Service** ✉ 18 rue Tronchet, 8ᵉ ☎ 01–46–37–51–24.

FLYING

When booking, **confirm carry-on allowances** if you're traveling with infants. In general, for babies charged 10% to 50% of the adult fare you are allowed one carry-on bag and a collapsible stroller; if the flight is full, the stroller may have to be checked or you may be limited to less.

Experts agree that it's a good idea to use safety seats aloft for children weighing less than 40 pounds. Airlines set their own policies: if you use a safety seat, U.S. carriers usually require that the child be ticketed, even if he or she is young enough to ride free, because the seats must be strapped into regular seats. And even if you pay the full adult fare for the seat, it may be worth it, especially on longer trips. Do **check your airline's policy about using safety seats during takeoff and landing.** Safety seats are not allowed everywhere in the plane, so get your seat assignments as early as possible.

When reserving, **request children's meals or a freestanding bassinet** (not available at all airlines) if you need them. But note that bulkhead seats, where you must sit to use the bassinet, may lack an overhead bin or storage space on the floor.

SIGHTS & ATTRACTIONS

Paris has plenty of diversions for the young (noted by a duck icon in the margin throughout this book), and almost all museums and movie theaters offer discounted rates to children. *Le Pariscope* and *L'Officiel des Spectacles* are two weekly publications that have sections in English about entertainment for children. The **CIDJ,** the Centre d'Information et de Documentation pour la Jeunesse (Center for Information and Documentation for Young People), also has information about activities and events for youngsters in Paris.

SUPPLIES & EQUIPMENT

Supermarkets carry several major brands of diapers (*couches*), universally referred to as Pampers (pronounced "pawm-paires"). Junior sizes are hard to come by, as the French toilet-train early. Baby formula is available in grocery stores or pharmacies. There are two types of formula: *lait premier age,* for infants 0–4 months, and *lait deuxième age,* for 4 months or older. French formulas come in powder form and need to be mixed with a pure, low-mineral-content bottled water like Evian or Volvic (the French *never* mix baby formula with tap water). American formulas do not exist in France. If you're looking for treats for your little ones, some items to keep in mind are *coloriage* (coloring books); *crayons de couleur* (crayons); *pâte à modeler* (modeling clay); and *feutres* (markers).

COMPUTERS ON THE ROAD

If you use a major Internet provider, getting on-line in Paris shouldn't be difficult. Call your Internet provider to get the local access number in Paris. Many hotels have business services with Internet access and even in-room modem lines. You will, however, need an adapter for your computer for the European-style plugs. If you're traveling with a laptop, carry a spare battery and adapter. **Never plug your computer into any socket before asking about surge protection.** IBM sells a pen-size modem tester that plugs into a telephone jack to check if the line is safe to use.

Access Numbers in Paris **AOL** ☎ 01-41-45-81-00. **Compuserve** ☎ 08-03-00-60-00, 08-03-00-80-00, or 08-03-00-90-00.

Internet Cafés **Café Orbital** ✉ 13 rue de Médicis, 6ᵉ, Latin Quarter ☎ 01-43-25-76-77. **Cybercafé** ✉ 72-74 passage de Choiseul, 2ᵉ, Opéra/Grands Boulevards ☎ 01-47-03-36-12 🌐 www.cari.com. **Cybercafé de Paris** ✉ 15 rue des Halles, 1ᵉʳ, Beaubourg/Les Halles ☎ 01-42-21-11-11. **EasyEverything** ✉ 37 bd. Sébastopol, 1ᵉʳ, Beaubourg/Les Halles ☎ 01-40-41-09-10. **Les Jardins de l'Internet Cybercafé** ✉ 79 bd. St-Michel, 4ᵉ, Latin Quarter ☎ 01-44-07-22-20 🌐 www.jardin-internet.net Ⓜ Métro: Cluny La Sorbonne. **Web Bar** ✉ 32 rue de Picardie, 3ᵉ, République ☎ 01-42-72-66-55 🌐 www.webbar.fr Ⓜ Métro: République.

CONCIERGES

Concierges, found in many hotels, can help you with theater tickets and dinner reservations: a good one with connections may be able to get you seats for a hot show or prime-time dinner reservations at the restaurant of the moment. You can also turn to your hotel's concierge for help with travel arrangements, sightseeing plans, services ranging from aromatherapy to zipper repair, and emergencies. Always, **always tip** a concierge who has been of assistance (⇨ Tipping).

CONSUMER PROTECTION

Whether you're shopping for gifts or purchasing travel services, **pay with a major credit card** whenever possible, so you can cancel payment or get reimbursed if there's a problem (and you can provide documentation). If you're doing business with a particular company for the first time, **contact your local Better Business Bureau and the attorney general's offices** in your state and (for U.S. businesses) the company's home state as well. Have any complaints been filed? Finally, if you're buying a package or tour, always **consider travel insurance** that includes default coverage (⇨ Insurance).

BBBs **Council of Better Business Bureaus** ✉ 4200 Wilson Blvd., Suite 800, Arlington, VA 22203 ☎ 703/276-0100 📠 703/525-8277 🌐 www.bbb.org.

CUSTOMS & DUTIES

When shopping abroad, **keep receipts** for all purchases. Upon reentering the country, **be ready to show customs officials what you've bought.** Pack purchases together in an easily accessible place. If you think a duty is incorrect, appeal the assessment. If you object to the way your clearance was handled, note the inspector's badge number. In either case, first ask to see a supervisor. If the problem isn't resolved, write to the appropriate authorities, beginning with the port director at your point of entry.

IN AUSTRALIA

Australian residents who are 18 or older may bring home A$400 worth of souvenirs and gifts (including jewelry), 250 cigarettes or 250 grams of cigars or other tobacco products, and 1,125 ml of alcohol

(including wine, beer, and spirits). Residents under 18 may bring back A$200 worth of goods. Members of the same family traveling together may pool their allowances. Prohibited items include meat products. Seeds, plants, and fruits need to be declared upon arrival.
Australian Customs Service Regional Director, Box 8, Sydney, NSW 2001 02/9213-2000 or 1300/363263; 02/9364-7222 or 1800/803-006 quarantine-inquiry line 02/9213-4043 www.customs.gov.au.

IN CANADA

Canadian residents who have been out of Canada for at least seven days may bring in C$750 worth of goods duty-free. If you've been away fewer than seven days but more than 48 hours, the duty-free allowance drops to C$200. If your trip lasts 24 to 48 hours, the allowance is C$50. You may not pool allowances with family members. Goods claimed under the C$750 exemption may follow you by mail; those claimed under the lesser exemptions must accompany you. Alcohol and tobacco products may be included in the seven-day and 48-hour exemptions but not in the 24-hour exemption. If you meet the age requirements of the province or territory through which you reenter Canada, you may bring in, duty-free, 1.5 liters of wine *or* 1.14 liters (40 imperial ounces) of liquor *or* 24 12-ounce cans or bottles of beer or ale. Also, if you meet the local age requirement for tobacco products, you may bring in, duty-free, 200 cigarettes and 50 cigars. Check ahead of time with the Canada Customs and Revenue Agency or the Department of Agriculture for policies regarding meat products, seeds, plants, and fruits.

You may send an unlimited number of gifts (only one gift per recipient, however) worth up to C$60 each duty-free to Canada. Label the package UNSOLICITED GIFT—VALUE UNDER $60. Alcohol and tobacco are excluded.
Canada Customs and Revenue Agency 2265 St. Laurent Blvd., Ottawa, Ontario K1G 4K3 800/461-9999, 204/983-3500, or 506/636-5064 www.ccra.gc.ca.

IN FRANCE

If you're coming from outside the European Union (EU), you may import duty free: (1) 200 cigarettes or 100 cigarillos or 50 cigars or 250 grams of tobacco (twice that if you live outside Europe); (2) 2 liters of wine and, in addition, (a) 1 liter of alcohol over 22% volume (most spirits) or (b) 2 liters of alcohol under 22% volume (fortified or sparkling wine) or (c) 2 more liters of table wine; (3) 50 ml of perfume and 250 ml of toilet water; (4) 200 grams of coffee, 100 grams of tea; and (5) other goods to the value of €46 (€15.3 for those under 15).

If you're arriving from an EU country, you may be required to declare all goods and prove that anything over the standard limit is for personal consumption. But there is no limit or customs tariff imposed on goods carried within the EU.

Any amount of euros or foreign currency may be brought into France, but foreign currencies converted into euros may be reconverted into a foreign currency only up to the equivalent of €769.
Direction des Douanes 16 rue Yves Toudic, 10e 01-40-40-39-00.

IN NEW ZEALAND

All homeward-bound residents may bring back NZ$700 worth of souvenirs and gifts; passengers may not pool their allowances, and children can claim only the concession on goods intended for their own use. For those 17 or older, the duty-free allowance also includes 4.5 liters of wine or beer; one 1,125-ml bottle of spirits; and either 200 cigarettes, 250 grams of tobacco, 50 cigars, *or* a combination of the three up to 250 grams. Meat products, seeds, plants, and fruits must be declared upon arrival to the Agricultural Services Department.
New Zealand Customs Head office: The Customhouse, 17-21 Whitmore St., Box 2218, Wellington 09/300-5399 or 0800/428-786 www.customs.govt.nz.

IN THE U.K.

If you are a U.K. resident and your journey was wholly within the European Union, you probably won't have to pass through customs when you return to the United Kingdom. If you plan to bring back large quantities of alcohol or tobacco, check EU limits beforehand. In most cases, if you bring back more than 200 cigars, 3,200 cigarettes, 10 liters of spirits, 110

liters of beer, and/or 90 liters of wine, you have to declare the goods upon return.
HM Customs and Excise ✉ Portcullis House, 21 Cowbridge Rd. E, Cardiff CF11 9SS ☎ 0845/010-9000 or 0208/929-0152; 0208/929-6731 or 0208/910-3602 complaints 🌐 www.hmce.gov.uk.

IN THE U.S.

U.S. residents who have been out of the country for at least 48 hours may bring home, for personal use, $800 worth of foreign goods duty-free, as long as they haven't used the $800 allowance or any part of it in the past 30 days. This exemption may include 1 liter of alcohol (for travelers 21 and older), 200 cigarettes, and 100 non-Cuban cigars. Family members from the same household who are traveling together may pool their $800 personal exemptions. For fewer than 48 hours, the duty-free allowance drops to $200, which may include 50 cigarettes, 10 non-Cuban cigars, and 150 ml of alcohol (or 150 ml of perfume containing alcohol). The $200 allowance cannot be combined with other individuals' exemptions, and if you exceed it, the full value of all the goods will be taxed. Antiques, which the U.S. Bureau of Customs and Border Protection defines as objects more than 100 years old, enter duty-free, as do original works of art done entirely by hand, including paintings, drawings, and sculptures. This doesn't apply to folk art or handicrafts, which are in general dutiable.

You may also send packages home duty-free, with a limit of one parcel per addressee per day (except alcohol or tobacco products or perfume worth more than $5). You can mail up to $200 worth of goods for personal use; label the package PERSONAL USE and attach a list of its contents and their retail value. If the package contains your used personal belongings, mark it AMERICAN GOODS RETURNED to avoid paying duties. You may send up to $100 worth of goods as a gift; mark the package UNSOLICITED GIFT. Mailed items do not affect your duty-free allowance on your return.

To avoid paying duty on foreign-made high-ticket items you already own and will take on your trip, register them with Customs before you leave the country. Consider filing a Certificate of Registration for laptops, cameras, watches, and other digital devices identified with serial numbers or other permanent markings; you can keep the certificate for other trips. Otherwise, bring a sales receipt or insurance form to show that you owned the item before you left the United States.
U.S. Bureau of Customs and Border Protection ✉ for inquiries and equipment registration, 1300 Pennsylvania Ave. NW, Washington, DC 20229 ☎ 877/287-8667, 202/354-1000 🌐 www.customs.gov ✉ for complaints, Customer Satisfaction Unit, 1300 Pennsylvania Ave. NW, Room 5.5D, Washington, DC 20229.

DISABILITIES & ACCESSIBILITY

Although the city of Paris is doing much to ensure that public facilities accommodate people with mobility difficulties, it still has a long way to go. Some sidewalks now have low curbs, and many arrondissements have public rest rooms and telephone boxes that are accessible to travelers using wheelchairs.
Local Resources **Association des Paralysés de France** ✉ 22 rue de Pére Guerin, 75013 Paris ☎ 01-44-16-83-83 is a very helpful organization.

RESERVATIONS

When discussing accessibility with an operator or reservations agent, **ask hard questions.** Are there any stairs, inside *or* out? Are there grab bars next to the toilet *and* in the shower/tub? How wide is the doorway to the room? To the bathroom? For the most extensive facilities meeting the latest legal specifications, **opt for newer accommodations.** If you reserve through a toll-free number, consider also calling the hotel's local number to confirm the information from the central reservations office. Get confirmation in writing when you can.

TRANSPORTATION

The Paris métro is a labyrinth of winding stairs, malfunctioning doors, and hordes of scurrying Parisians, all of which make it a less than ideal mode of transport for travelers with disabilities. In addition, very few métro and RER stations are wheelchair-accessible with the exception of the new, fully automated line Météor. For those with walking difficulties, all stairs have handrails, and nearly two-thirds of the stations have at least one escalator. Avoid peak hours between 8 and 9 AM and 6 and 7 PM. Bus lines Nos. 38, 62, 68, and 91 are wheelchair-accessible, but note that you will be more comfortable traveling with someone who can help you. For information about accessibility, **get the RER and métro access guide,** available at most stations and from the Paris Transit Authority. The SNCF has special accommodations in the first-class departments of trains that are reserved exclusively for people using wheelchairs (and are available for the second-class price). It is essential to **reserve special train tickets in advance**—this not only assures a comfortable seat but guarantees assistance at the station. Taxi drivers are required by law to assist travelers with disabilities in and out of their vehicles.

The Airhop shuttle company runs adapted vehicles to and from the airports; Orly–Paris costs €27.50 and Charles de Gaulle–Paris costs €38.15; this service is available weekdays only. Reservations (in French) must be made in advance. Note that you must pay €2.40 for every 15 minutes there is a delay.

Local Resources **Airhop** ☎ 01-41-29-01-29. **G.I.H.P.** ✉ 2-24 rue Henri Barbusse, 93000 Bobigny ☎ 01-41-83-15-15. **Paris Transit Authority** RATP; (✉ 54 quai de la Rapée, 75599, Cedex 12 ☎ 08-36-68-77-14 🌐 www.ratp.com.

Complaints **Aviation Consumer Protection Division** (⇨ Air Travel) for airline-related problems. **Departmental Office of Civil Rights** ✉ for general inquiries, U.S. Department of Transportation, S-30, 400 7th St. SW, Room 10215, Washington, DC 20590 ☎ 202/366-4648 🖷 202/366-9371 🌐 www.dot.gov/ost/docr/index.htm. **Disability Rights Section** ✉ NYAV, U.S. Department of Justice, Civil Rights Division, 950 Pennsylvania Ave. NW, Washington, DC 20530 ☎ ADA information line 202/514-0301, 800/514-0301, 202/514-0383 TTY, 800/514-0383 TTY 🌐 www.ada.gov. **U.S. Department of Transportation Hotline** ☎ for disability-related air-travel problems, 800/778-4838 or 800/455-9880 TTY.

TRAVEL AGENCIES

In the United States, the Americans with Disabilities Act requires that travel firms serve the needs of all travelers. Some agencies specialize in working with people with disabilities.

Travelers with Mobility Problems **Access Adventures** ✉ 206 Chestnut Ridge Rd., Scottsville, NY 14624 ☎ 585/889-9096 ✉ dltravel@prodigy.net, run by a former physical-rehabilitation counselor. **CareVacations** ✉ No. 5, 5110-50 Ave., Leduc, Alberta T9E 6V4 Canada ☎ 780/986-6404 or 877/478-7827 🖷 780/986-8332 🌐 www.carevacations.com, for group tours and cruise vacations. **Flying Wheels Travel** ✉ 143 W. Bridge St., Box 382, Owatonna, MN 55060 ☎ 507/451-5005 🖷 507/451-1685 🌐 www.flyingwheelstravel.com.

DISCOUNTS & DEALS

Be a smart shopper and **compare all your options** before making decisions. A plane ticket bought with a promotional coupon from travel clubs, coupon books, and direct-mail offers or purchased on the Internet may not be cheaper than the least expensive fare from a discount ticket agency. And always keep in mind that what you get is just as important as what you save.

Paris Tourist Offices, railroad stations, major métro stations, and participating museums sell the *Carte Musées et Monuments* (Museums and Monuments Pass), which offers unlimited access to 74 museums and monuments in Paris—including the Louvre, Musée d'Orsay, Sainte-Chapelle, and Versailles, but not the Eiffel Tower, temporary exhibits, or guided tours—over a one-, three-, or five-consecutive-day period; the cost, respectively, is €15, €30, and €40. From the looks of it, only the most rabid museum goer will benefit from this pass: you'd have to do three museums in one day, or six in three days, to make any real saving—and it's even less of an attractive proposition now that the museums owned by the City of Paris are free. However, the pass also allows access to museums and monuments without having to wait in line (something to consider if you're going to make the Louvre your home away from home). If you don't plan on seeing that many museums or monuments, you may be better off paying at each site.

Museum Passes **Association InterMusées** ✉ 4 rue Brantôme, 75003 Paris ☎ 01-44-61-96-60 🌐 www.intermusees.com.

DISCOUNT RESERVATIONS

To save money, **look into discount reservations services** with Web sites and toll-free numbers, which use their buying power to get a better price on hotels, airline tickets (⇨ Air Travel), even car rentals. When booking a room, always **call the hotel's local toll-free number** (if one is available) rather than the central reservations number—you'll often get a better price. Always ask about special packages or corporate rates.

When shopping for the best deal on hotels and car rentals, **look for guaranteed exchange rates,** which protect you against a falling dollar. With your rate locked in, you won't pay more, even if the price goes up in the local currency.

Airline Tickets **Air 4 Less** ☎ 800/AIR4LESS; low-fare specialist.

Hotel Rooms **Accommodations Express** ☎ 800/444-7666 or 800/277-1064 🌐 www.accommodationsexpress.com. **Hotels.com** ☎ 800/246-8357 🌐 www.hotels.com. **International Marketing & Travel Concepts** ☎ 800/790-4682 🌐 www.imtc-travel.com. **Steigenberger Reservation Service** ☎ 800/223-5652 🌐 www.srs-worldhotels.com. **Turbotrip.com** ☎ 800/473-7829 🌐 www.turbotrip.com.

PACKAGE DEALS

Don't confuse packages and guided tours. When you buy a package, you travel on your own, just as though you had planned the trip yourself. Fly/drive packages, which combine airfare and car rental, are often a good deal. In cities, ask the local visitor's bureau about hotel packages that include tickets to major museum exhibits or other special events.

ELECTRICITY

To use your U.S.-purchased electric-powered equipment, **bring a converter and adapter.** The electrical current in Paris is 220 volts, 50 cycles alternating current (AC); wall outlets take continental-type plugs, with two round prongs.

If your appliances are dual-voltage, you'll need only an adapter. Don't use 110-volt outlets marked FOR SHAVERS ONLY for high-wattage appliances such as blow-dryers. Most laptops operate equally well on 110 and 220 volts and so require only an adapter.

EMBASSIES

Australia ✉ *4 rue Jean-Rey, 75724, Paris, 15e* ☎ *01-40-59-33-00* Ⓜ *Métro: Bir-Hakeim* ⏲ *Weekdays 9:15-12:15.*

Canada ✉ *35 av. Montaigne, Paris, 8e* ☎ *01-44-43-29-00* Ⓜ *Métro: Franklin-D.-Roosevelt* ⏲ *Weekdays 8:30-11.*

New Zealand ✉ *7 ter rue Léonardo da Vinci, Paris, 16e* ☎ *01-45-00-24-11* Ⓜ *Métro: Victor-Hugo* ⏲ *Weekdays 9-1.*

United Kingdom ✉ *35 rue du Faubourg-St-Honoré, Paris, 8e* ☎ *01-44-51-31-00* Ⓜ *Métro: Madeleine* ⏲ *Weekdays 9:30-12:30 and 2:30-5.*

United States ✉ *2 rue St-Florentin, Paris, 1er* ☎ *01-43-12-22-22 in English; 01-43-12-23-47 emergencies* Ⓜ *Métro: Concorde* ⏲ *Weekdays 9-3.*

EMERGENCIES

The French National Health Care system has been organized to provide fully equipped, fully staffed hospitals within 30 minutes of every resident in Paris. For signage, hospitals are indicated by a rectangular blue box with a white cross. This guidebook does not list the major Paris hospitals, as the French government prefers an emergency operator to make the judgment call and assign you the best and most convenient option for your emergency. Note that if you are able to walk into a hospital emergency room by yourself, you are often considered "low priority" and the wait can be interminable. So if time is of the essence, the best thing to do is to call the fire department (☎ 18); a fully trained team of paramedics will usually arrive within five minutes. You may also dial for a Samu ambulance (☎ 15); there is usually an English-speaking physician available who will help you assess the situation and either dispatch an ambulance immediately or advise you as to your best course of action. It's important to check with your insurance company before you leave for your trip to make sure that you are covered internationally.

In a less urgent situation, do what the French do and call SOS Doctor or SOS Dental services; like magic, a certified, experienced doctor or dentist arrives at the door well within an hour, armed with an old leather doctor case filled with the essentials to diagnose and treat the patient (at an average cost of €55). He or she may or may not be bilingual, but will, at worst, have a rudimentary understanding of English. This is a very helpful 24-hour service to use for common benign illnesses that need to be treated quickly for comfort, such as high fevers, toothaches, or stomach flus (which seem to have the unfortunate habit of announcing themselves late at night).

The American Hospital and the Hertford British Hospital both have 24-hour emergency hot lines with bilingual doctors and nurses who can provide advice. For small problems, go to a pharmacy, marked by a green neon cross. Pharmacists are authorized to administer first aid and recommend over-the-counter drugs, and they can be very helpful in advising you in English or sending you to the nearest English-speaking pharmacist.

Call the police (☎ 17) if there has been a crime or an act of violence. On the street, some French phrases that may be needed in an emergency are: *Au secours!* (Help!), *urgence* (emergency), *samu* (ambulance), *pompiers* (firemen), *poste de station* (police station), *médicin* (doctor), and *hôpital* (hospital).

CONTACTS

Doctors & Dentists **SOS Dentists** ☎ 01-43-37-51-00. **SOS Doctors** ☎ 01-47-07-77-77.
Emergency Services **Ambulance** ☎ 15. **Fire Department** ☎ 18. **Police** ☎ 17. These numbers are toll-free and can be dialed from any phone.
Hospitals **The American Hospital** ✉ 63 bd. Victor-Hugo, Neuilly ☎ 01-46-41-25-25. **The Hertford British Hospital** ✉ 3 rue Barbès, Levallois-Perret ☎ 01-46-39-22-22.
Hot Lines **FACTS-Line I** ☎ 01-47-23-80-8, open Monday, Wednesday, and Friday 6–10 PM, offers HIV/AIDS support in English. **SOS Help** ☎ 01-47-23-80-80, open daily 3–11 PM, is an English-language crisis and information hot line.
Late-Night & 24-Hour Pharmacies **Dhéry** ✉ Galerie des Champs, 84 bd. des Champs-Élysées, 8e ☎ 01-45-62-02-41 is open 24 hours. **Pharmacie des Arts** ✉ 106 bd. Montparnasse, 14e is open daily until midnight. **Pharmacie Internationale** ✉ 5 pl. Pigalle, 9e ☎ 01-48-78-38-12. **Pharmacie Matignon** ✉ rue Jean-Mermoz, at the Rond-Point de Champs-Élysées, 8e is open daily until 2 AM.

ENGLISH-LANGUAGE MEDIA

BOOKS

For information about bookstores in Paris, *see* Specialty Shops *in* Chapter 6. The American Library in Paris is another resource for English-language books; it's open Tuesday–Saturday 10–7.
Bookstores *See* Chapter 6, Shopping.

NEWSPAPERS & MAGAZINES

A number of free magazines in English, with all kinds of listings, including events, bars, restaurants, shops, films, and museums, are available in Paris. Look for *Time Out Paris, FUSAC, The Paris Free Voice,* and *Irish Eyes,* which are available at both tourist offices and all Anglo-American restaurants, bars, and bookshops. Besides a large selection of French newspapers and magazines, all kinds of English-language newspapers and magazines can be found at newsstands, especially in major tourist areas, including the *International Herald Tribune, USA Today,* the *New York Times,* the *European Financial Times,* the *Times* of London, *Newsweek, The Economist, Vogue,* and *Elle.*

RADIO & TELEVISION

Radio in France is an eclectic mix, with a greater variety of music than you'd expect. Most stations broadcast in French. A number of them play Top 40 music, including Cherie FM (91.3), Skyrock (96), NRJ (100.3), Radio Nova (101.5), and Fun Radio (101.9). A wide range of music can be found on FIP (105.1); classical on Radio Classique (101.1); '60s–'90s on Nostalgie (90.4); techno on Radio FG (98.2); and the news (in French) on France Info (105.5).

Turn on the television and you'll notice many American shows dubbed into French (Canal Jimmy, Channel 8, shows American shows in their original, undubbed format). France has both national stations (TF1, France 2, France 3, La Cinq/Arte, and M6) and cable stations (most notably CanalPlus, France's version of HBO). Every morning at 7:05 AM, ABC News (from the night before) is aired. You can also find CNN, BBC World, and BBC Prime on cable.

ETIQUETTE & BEHAVIOR

When meeting someone for the first time, whether in a social or a professional setting, it is appropriate to shake hands. Other than that, the French like to kiss—they kiss close friends, men kiss men, women kiss women, French children kiss other French children. For the Parisians, it's two quick smacks, one on each cheek.

The French like to look at people, that's why they created cafés and fashion—they'll look at your shoes, your watch, they'll check out what you're wearing, what you're reading—what they will not do is maintain steady eye contact or smile. If a stranger of the opposite sex smiles at you, it is best to do as the French do and give a blank, haughty, cutting look before turning away. If you smile back, you might find yourself in a Pepé Le Pew–type situation.

Some basic pleasantries in French include: "bonne journée," have a nice day; "bonne soirée," have a nice evening; "enchanté," nice to meet you; "s'il vous plaît," please; and "je vous en prie," you're welcome.

When visiting a French home, don't expect to be invited into the kitchen or to take a house tour. The French have a very definite sense of personal space, and you'll be escorted to what are considered the guest areas. If you're invited to dinner, be sure to bring a gift, such as wine, champagne, flowers, or chocolates.

When dining out, note that the French only fill their wine glasses until they are half full—it's considered bad manners to fill it to the brim. They never serve themselves before serving the rest of the table. They never order coffee or tea with dessert, always after. They always keep their hands above the table, and most usually keep their elbows off the table. They often divide the check evenly between couples or individuals, even if someone only ordered a salad and others had a full meal. Bread is broken, never cut, and placed next to the plate, never on the plate.

BUSINESS ETIQUETTE

In a business situation, greetings are typically made with a friendly handshake. A suit is appropriate for business meetings for both men and women. Professional presentation is extremely important: casual Fridays are unheard of, sneakers are saved for weekends. The French don't like overfamiliarity in any form; use formal surname greetings unless a mutual decision has been made to use first names.

GAY & LESBIAN TRAVEL

In Paris, several gay and lesbian organizations provide information on events, medical care, and counseling to one of the largest homosexual communities in the world. A number of informative newspapers and magazines that cover the Parisian gay-lesbian scene are available at stores and kiosks in the city, including *TETU,* and *Lesbia* magazines.

Organizations **Association des Médecins Gais** ☎ 01-48-05-81-71 and **Écoute Gaie** ☎ 01-44-93-01-02 after 6 PM give advice and information over the phone. **Centre Gai et Lesbien** ✉ 3 rue Keller, 11e ☎ 01-43-57-21-47 regroups a multitude of associations ready to respond to any questions you may have; a great source of information. **Les Mots à la Bouche** ✉ 6 rue Ste-Croix-de-la-Bretonnerie, 4e ☎ 01-42-78-88-30 is Paris's largest gay bookstore and is always a rich resource for current happenings and literature.

Gay- & Lesbian-Friendly Travel Agencies **Different Roads Travel** ✉ 8383 Wilshire Blvd., Suite 520, Beverly Hills, CA 90211 ☎ 323/651-5557 or 800/429-8747 (Ext. 14 for both) 🖷 323/651-3678 ✉ lgernert@tzell.com. **Kennedy Travel** ✉ 130 W. 42nd St., Suite 401, New York, NY 10036 ☎ 212/840-8659 or 800/237-7433 🖷 212/730-2269 🌐 www.kennedytravel.com. **Now, Voyager** ✉ 4406 18th St., San Francisco, CA 94114 ☎ 415/626-1169 or 800/255-6951 🖷 415/626-8626 🌐 www.nowvoyager.com. **Skylink Travel and Tour** ✉ 1455 N. Dutton Ave., Suite A, Santa Rosa, CA 95401 ☎ 707/546-9888 or 800/225-5759 🖷 707/636-0951; serving lesbian travelers.

GUIDEBOOKS

Plan well and you won't be sorry. Guidebooks are excellent tools—and you can take them with you. You may want to check out color-photo-illustrated *Fodor's Exploring Paris,* thorough on culture and history, and pocket-size *Citypack Paris,* with a supersize city map. Both are available at on-line retailers and bookstores everywhere.

HOLIDAYS

With 11 national holidays (*jours feriés*) and five weeks of paid vacation, the French have their share of repose. In May there is a holiday nearly every week, so be prepared for stores, banks, and museums to shut their doors for days at a time. If a holiday falls on a Tuesday or Thursday, many businesses *font le pont* (make the bridge) and close on that Monday or Friday as well. But some exchange booths in tourist areas, small grocery stores, restaurants, cafés, and bakeries usually remain open. Bastille Day (July 14) is observed in true French form. Celebrations begin on the evening of the 13th, when city firemen open the doors to their stations, often classed as historical monuments, to host their much-acclaimed all-night balls and finish the next day with the annual military parade and air show.

Note that these dates are for the calendar year 2004: January 1 (New Year's Day); April 11–12 (Easter Sunday/Monday);

May 1 (Labor Day); May 8 (VE Day); May 20 (Ascension); May 30–31 (Pentecost Sunday/Monday); July 14 (Bastille Day); August 15 (Assumption); November 1 (All Saints); November 11 (Armistice); December 25 (Christmas).

INSURANCE

The most useful travel-insurance plan is a comprehensive policy that includes coverage for trip cancellation and interruption, default, trip delay, and medical expenses (with a waiver for preexisting conditions).

Without insurance you'll lose all or most of your money if you cancel your trip, regardless of the reason. Default insurance covers you if your tour operator, airline, or cruise line goes out of business. Trip-delay covers expenses that arise because of bad weather or mechanical delays. Study the fine print when comparing policies.

If you're traveling internationally, a key component of travel insurance is coverage for medical bills incurred if you get sick on the road. Such expenses aren't generally covered by Medicare or private policies. U.K. residents can buy a travel-insurance policy valid for most vacations taken during the year in which it's purchased (but check preexisting-condition coverage). British and Australian citizens need extra medical coverage when traveling overseas.

Always **buy travel policies directly from the insurance company**; if you buy them from a cruise line, airline, or tour operator that goes out of business you probably won't be covered for the agency or operator's default, a major risk. Before making any purchase, **review your existing health and home-owner's policies** to find what they cover away from home.

Travel Insurers In the United States: **Access America** ✉ 6600 W. Broad St., Richmond, VA 23230 ☎ 800/284-8300 📠 804/673-1491 or 800/346-9265 🌐 www.accessamerica.com. **Travel Guard International** ✉ 1145 Clark St., Stevens Point, WI 54481 ☎ 715/345-0505 or 800/826-1300 📠 800/955-8785 🌐 www.travelguard.com.

In the United Kingdom: **Association of British Insurers** ✉ 51 Gresham St., London EC2V 7HQ ☎ 020/7600-3333 📠 020/7696-8999 🌐 www.abi.org.uk. In Canada: **RBC Insurance** ✉ 6880 Financial Dr., Mississauga, Ontario L5N 7Y5 ☎ 800/565-3129 📠 905/813-4704 🌐 www.rbcinsurance.com. In Australia: **Insurance Council of Australia** ✉ Insurance Enquiries and Complaints, Level 3, 56 Pitt St., Sydney, NSW 2000 ☎ 1300/363683 or 02/9251-4456 📠 02/9251-4453 🌐 www.iecltd.com.au. In New Zealand: **Insurance Council of New Zealand** ✉ Level 7, 111-115 Customhouse Quay, Box 474, Wellington ☎ 04/472-5230 📠 04/473-3011 🌐 www.icnz.org.nz.

LANGUAGE

The French may appear prickly at first to English-speaking visitors. But it usually helps if you **make an effort to speak a little French.** A simple, friendly *bonjour* (hello) will do, as will asking if the person you are greeting speaks English (*Parlez-vous anglais?*). Be patient, and speak English slowly. *See* the French Vocabulary and Menu Guide at the back of the book for more suggestions.

LANGUAGES FOR TRAVELERS

A phrase book and language-tape set can help get you started. *Fodor's French for Travelers* (available at bookstores everywhere) is excellent.

MAIL & SHIPPING

Post offices, or PTT, are scattered throughout every arrondissement and are recognizable by a yellow LA POSTE sign. They are usually open weekdays 8 AM–7 PM, Saturday 8 AM–noon.

Post Offices **Main office** ✉ 52 rue du Louvre, 1er, open 24 hours seven days a week. **Champs-Élysées office** ✉ 10 rue Balzar, 8e, Monday to Saturday, open until 7 PM.

OVERNIGHT SERVICES

Sending overnight mail from Paris is relatively easy. Besides DHL, Federal Express, and UPS, the French post office has an overnight mail service called Chronopost that has special prepaid boxes for international use (and also boxes specifically made to mail wine). All agencies listed can be used as drop-off points and all have information in English.

Major Services **DHL** ✉ 6 rue des Colonnes, 7e ☎ 01-55-35-30-30 🌐 www.dhl.com ✉ 59 rue Iéna, 16e ☎ 01-45-01-91-00. **Federal Express** ✉ 63 bd. Haussmann, 8e ☎ 01-40-06-90-16 🌐 www.fedex.com/fr ✉ 2 rue 29 Juillet, 1er ☎ 01-49-26-04-66; 08-00-12-38-00 information in English about pickups 🌐 www.ups.com. **UPS** ✉ 34 bd. Malesherbes, 8e ✉ 107 rue Réaumur, 2e ☎ 08-00-87-78-77.

POSTAL RATES

Airmail letters to the United States and Canada cost €.67 for 20 grams, €1.25 for 40 grams, and €1.98 for 60 grams. Letters to the United Kingdom cost €.46 for up to 20 grams, as they do within France. Postcards cost €.46 within France and EU countries and €.67 to the United States and Canada. Stamps can be bought in post offices and cafés displaying a red TABAC sign.

RECEIVING MAIL

If you're uncertain where you'll be staying, have mail sent to American Express (if you're a card member) or to "poste restante" at any post office.

MÉTRO

Métro stations are recognizable either by a large yellow *M* within a circle or by the distinctive curly green Art Nouveau railings and archway bearing the full title (Métropolitain). Taking **the métro is the most efficient way to get around Paris.** *See* the Métro map, *below.*

Fourteen métro and two RER (Réseau Express Régional, or the Regional Express Network) lines crisscross Paris and the suburbs, and you are seldom more than 500 yards from the nearest station. The métro network connects at several points in Paris with the RER, the commuter trains that go from the city center to the suburbs. RER trains crossing Paris on their way from suburb to suburb can be great time-savers because they make only a few stops in the city (you can use the same tickets for the métro and the RER within Paris).

It's essential to **know the name of the last station on the line you take,** as this name appears on all signs. A connection (you can make as many as you like on one ticket) is called a *correspondance.* At junction stations, illuminated orange signs bearing the name of the line terminus appear over the correct corridors for each correspondance. Illuminated blue signs marked *sortie* indicate the station exit. Note that tickets are valid only inside the gates, or *limites.*

Métro service starts at 5:30 AM and continues until 1 AM, when the last train on each line reaches its terminus. Some lines and stations in Paris are a bit risky at night, in particular Lines 2 and 13. But in general, the métro is relatively safe throughout, providing you **don't walk around with your wallet hanging out of your back pocket or travel alone late at night.**

FARES & SCHEDULES

All **métro tickets and passes are valid not only for the métro but also for all RER and bus travel within Paris.** Métro tickets cost €1.30 each; a *carnet* (10 tickets for €9.30) is a better value. The best deal is the unlimited usage *carte orange* ticket, sold according to zone. Zones 1 and 2 cover the entire métro network; tickets cost €13.25 a week or €44.35 a month. If you plan to take suburban trains to visit places in Ile-de-France, consider a four-zone (Versailles, St-Germain-en-Laye; €21.65 a week) or six-zone (Rambouillet, Fontainebleau; €28.10 a week) ticket. For these weekly/monthly tickets, you need a pass (available from rail and major métro stations) and a passport-size photograph (many stations have photo booths).

A one-day (Mobilis) and the two- to five-day (Paris-Visite) tickets assure unlimited travel on the entire RATP network: métro, RER, bus, tram, funicular (Montmartre), and noctambus (night bus). Unlike the coupon jaune, which is good from Monday morning to Sunday evening, Mobilis and Paris-Visite passes are valid starting any day of the week and give you discounts on a limited number of museums and tourist attractions. The price is €8.38 (one-day), €13.70 (two-day), €18.30 (three-day), and €26.70 (five-day) for Paris only. Rates for children ages 4–11 are approximately half of these prices. Suburbs such as Versailles and St-Germain-en-Laye cost €23.60 (one-day). EuroDisney costs €23.60, €34.30, €42.70, and €53.35 respectively for a one- to four-day pass.

Access to métro and RER platforms is through an automatic ticket barrier. Slide your ticket in and pick it up as it pops out. Be certain to **keep your ticket during your journey;** you'll need it to leave the RER system and in case you run into any green-clad ticket inspectors, who will impose a hefty fine if you can't produce your ticket.

Métro Information RATP ✉ Pl. de la Madeleine, 8e ✉ 53 bis quai des Grands-Augustins, 6e ☎ 08-36-68-41-14 🌐 www.ratp.fr, open daily 9-5.

MONEY MATTERS

Like many capital cities, Paris is expensive; the good news is that if you avoid the obvious tourist traps, you can find plenty of affordable places to eat and shop. Prices tend to reflect the standing of an area in the eyes of Parisians; much-sought-after residential arrondissements such as the 7ᵉ, 16ᵉ, and 17ᵉ—of limited visitor interest—are far more expensive than the student-oriented, much-visited Latin Quarter. The tourist area where value for money is most difficult to find is the 8ᵉ arrondissement, on and around the Champs-Élysées. Places where you can generally be certain to shop, eat, and stay without overpaying include the streets surrounding Montmartre (not the Butte, or hilltop, itself); the St-Michel/Sorbonne area on the Left Bank; the mazelike streets around Les Halles and the Marais in central Paris; in Montparnasse, south of the boulevard; and the Bastille, République, and Belleville areas of eastern Paris.

Note that in cafés, bars, and some restaurants **it's less expensive to eat or drink standing at the counter than it is to sit at a table.** Two prices are listed—*au comptoir* (at the counter) and *à salle* (at a table)—and sometimes a third for the terrace. A cup of coffee, standing at a bar, costs from €1.05; if you sit, it will cost €1.50–€6.10. A glass of beer costs from €1.50 standing and from €2.30 to €6.10 sitting; a soft drink costs between €1.50 and €3.05. A ham sandwich will cost between €2.60 and €4.60.

Expect to pay €6.10–€10.70 for a short taxi ride. Museum entry is €3.05–€6.90, though there are hours or days of the week when admission is reduced or free.

Prices throughout this guide are for adults. Substantially reduced fees are almost always available for children, students, and senior citizens. For information on taxes, *see* Taxes.

ATMS

ATMs are one of the easiest ways to get euros. Although transaction fees may be higher abroad than at home, banks usually offer excellent wholesale exchange rates through ATMs. You may, however, have to look around for Cirrus and Plus locations; it's a good idea to get a list of locations from your bank before you go. Note, too, that you may have better luck with ATMs if you're using a credit card or debit card that is also a Visa or MasterCard rather than just your bank card.

To get cash at ATMs in Paris, **your PIN must be four digits long,** If you are having trouble remembering your pin, do not try more than twice, because at the third attempt, the machine will eat your card and you will have to go back the next morning to retrieve it. Note, too, that you may be charged by your bank for using ATMs overseas; inquire at your bank about charges.

CREDIT CARDS

Throughout this guide, the following abbreviations are used: AE, American Express; DC, Diners Club; MC, MasterCard; and V, Visa.

Reporting Lost Cards **American Express** ☎ 336/939–1111 or 336/668–5309; call collect. **Diners Club** ☎ 303/799–1504; call collect. **MasterCard** ☎ 0800/90–1387. **Visa** ☎ 0800/90–1179; 410/581–9994 collect.

CURRENCY

On January 1, 2002, the new single European Union (EU) currency, the euro, became the official currency of the 12 countries participating in the European Monetary Union (with the notable exceptions of Great Britain, Denmark, and Sweden). In France, the long-awaited physical debut of the euro was rather anticlimactic; banks closed their doors for an extra day to prepare for a bustle and confusion that never came. In fact, the transition went quite smoothly (some French equipped themselves with special pocket calculators that automatically calculated euro-franc conversions, out of an unfounded fear that with the change of currency, prices would rise). Actually, the toughest task for Europeans was to familiarize themselves with the newly issued coins and bills so shiny and fresh they had the odd perfection of play money in a new set of Monopoly. But, money is, after all, just money, and with that philosophical nod to reality, the European Monetary Union, over 300 million strong, was born. The first thing you will notice is that the euro system has quite a lot of coins, eight to be exact: 1 and 2 euros, plus 1, 2, 5, 10, 20, and 50 cents. All coins have one side that has the value of the euro on it, while the opposite side is adorned with each country's own unique national symbol. There are seven colorful notes: 5, 10, 20, 50, 100, 200, and 500 euros. Notes have the principal architectural styles from antiquity onwards on one side and the map and the flag of Europe on the other and are the same for all countries. The first thing you must do when you change your money is to memorize the coins as soon as you can (notes are much easier to grasp, as they start off at €5) and you'll undoubtedly find yourself quickly weighted down with all those coins. This was the first complaint most Europeans made with this new system, and this, in turn, led to the second complaint: due to their high nickel content, euro coins pose a problem for people with an allergic sensitivity to the metal (if you're sensitive to nickel, try to handle the coins as little as possible, and if you do come in contact with them rinse your hands as soon as you can).

All that aside, you'll soon realize just how easy the advent of the euro makes any whirlwind grand European tour. From France you'll glide through the borders of Austria, Germany, Italy, Spain, Holland, Ireland, Greece, Belgium, Finland, Luxembourg, and Portugal with no pressing need to run to the local exchange booth to change yet another currency before you even had the time to become familiar with the last. You're also able to assess the value of a purchase (for example, to realize that eating a three-course meal in a small restaurant in Lisbon is cheaper than the ham sandwich you bought on the Champs Élysées). Along with the facility of movement from country to country, the euro has another benefit in that it was created as a direct competitor with the U.S. dollar and, therefore, their rates of conversion are quite similar. At press time (summer 2003), one euro equaled approximately U.S.$1.2.

Don't be alarmed if you've forgotten some rumpled francs at home this trip—you have until midnight, February 17, 2005, to change coins and until midnight February 17, 2012, to change notes at the Banque of France (a fixed rate of exchange was established: 1 euro equaling 6.55957 French francs). After these dates, however, you may as well frame those remaining francs and hang them on the wall for posterity, not to say prosperity.

Such are the ground rules when it comes to the euro and the old EU currencies. But when it comes to the dollar (and all other currencies that are not part of the EU community), you still have to pay close attention to where you change your money—shop around for the best exchange rates (and also check the rates before leaving home) when it comes to non-EU currencies, such as the U.S. dollar, the Japanese yen, and the British pound. The rates of conversion between the euro and other local currencies have been irrevocably fixed: 1 euro = 1.95 German marks; 0.78 Irish punts; 13.76 Austrian schillings; 1,936.26 Italian lira; 40.33 Belgian francs; 166.38 Spanish pesetas; 2.20 Dutch guilders; 200.48 Portuguese escudos; 40.33 Luxembourg francs; and 5.94 Finnish markkas. Outside the EU, at time of writing, 1 euro = 1.39 Canadian dollars; 1.79 Australian dollars; 2.14 New Zealand dollars; and 0.62 pound sterling.

CURRENCY EXCHANGE

The easiest way to get euros is through ATMs; you can find them in airports, train stations, and throughout the city. ATM rates are excellent because they are based on wholesale rates offered only by major banks. It's a good idea, however, to bring some euros with you from home and always to have some cash and traveler's checks as backup. For the best deal when exchanging currencies not within the Monetary Union purview (the U.S. dollar, the yen, and the English pound are examples), compare rates at banks (which usually have the most favorable rates) and booths, and look for exchange booths that clearly state "no commission." At exchange booths always confirm the rate with the teller before exchanging money. You won't do as well at exchange booths in airports or rail and bus stations, in hotels, in restaurants, or in stores. Of all the banks in Paris, the Banque de France has the best rates. To avoid lines at airport exchange booths, **get enough euros before you leave home to cover any immediate necessity.**

Exchange Services **International Currency Express** ✉ 427 N. Camden Dr., Suite F, Beverly Hills, CA 90210 ☎ 888/278-6628 orders 📠 310/278-6410 🌐 www.foreignmoney.com. **Thomas Cook Currency Services** ☎ 800/287-7362 orders and retail locations 🌐 www.us.thomascook.com.

TRAVELER'S CHECKS

Do you need traveler's checks? It depends on where you're headed. If you're going to rural areas and small towns, go with cash; traveler's checks are best used in cities. Lost or stolen checks can usually be replaced within 24 hours. To ensure a speedy refund, buy your own traveler's checks—don't let someone else pay for them: irregularities like this can cause delays. The person who bought the checks should make the call to request a refund.

PACKING

You'll notice it right away: the women dress well to go shopping, to go to the cinema, to have a drink near the canal; the men look good when they are fixing their cars. The Parisians are a people who still wear hats to the races, well-cut clothes for fine meals; you will not see them in sweats unless they are doing something *sportif* and you will not see them in casual clothes unless it's a Sunday afternoon and they are melting cheese for fondue. When you are in Paris there are certain essential clothing points to remember: don't wear combinations of shorts, sweats, or sneakers if you want to blend in, these are considered only appropriate for children. Good food in good settings deserve good clothing, not necessarily a suit and tie, but long-sleeved shirt and pants for him, something nice for her. For some unknown reason trendy discos and clubs won't let men who are wearing sandals in, it's shoes or nothing. The most essential items to pack are rain gear, a shawl or sweater for cool churches and museums, and a comfortable pair of walking shoes. A small package of tissues is always a good idea for the rustic bathrooms in cafés, airports, and train stations. You can find almost every toiletry in a Parisian pharmacy; if you have the Latin name of your prescription drug it, too, can be found.

In your carry-on luggage, **pack an extra pair of eyeglasses or contact lenses and enough of any medication** you take to last a few days longer than the entire trip. You may also ask your doctor to write a spare prescription using the drug's generic name, as brand names may vary from country to country. In luggage to be checked, **never pack prescription drugs, valuables, or undeveloped film.** And don't forget to carry with you the addresses of offices that handle refunds of lost traveler's checks. Check *Fodor's How to Pack* (available at on-line retailers and bookstores everywhere) for more tips.

To avoid customs and security delays, carry medications in their original packaging. Don't pack any sharp objects in your carry-on luggage, including knives of any size or material, scissors, and corkscrews, or anything else that might arouse suspicion.

To avoid having your checked luggage chosen for hand inspection, don't cram bags full. The U.S. Transportation Security Administration suggests packing shoes on top and placing personal items you don't want touched in clear plastic bags.

CHECKING LUGGAGE

You're allowed to carry aboard one bag and one personal article, such as a purse or a laptop computer. Make sure what you carry on fits under your seat or in the overhead bin. Get to the gate early, so you can board as soon as possible, before the overhead bins fill up.

Baggage allowances vary by carrier, destination, and ticket class. On international flights, you're usually allowed to check two bags weighing up to 70 pounds (32 kilograms) each, although a few airlines allow checked bags of up to 88 pounds (40 kilograms) in first class. Some international carriers don't allow more than 66 pounds (30 kilograms) per bag in business class and 44 pounds (20 kilograms) in economy. On domestic flights, the limit may be 50 pounds (23 kilograms) per bag. Most airlines won't accept bags that weigh more than 100 pounds (45 kilograms) on domestic or international flights. Check baggage restrictions with your carrier before you pack.

Airline liability for baggage is limited to $2,500 per person on flights within the United States. On international flights it amounts to $9.07 per pound or $20 per kilogram for checked baggage (roughly $640 per 70-pound bag) and $400 per passenger for unchecked baggage. You can buy additional coverage at check-in for about $10 per $1,000 of coverage, but it often excludes a rather extensive list of items, shown on your airline ticket.

Before departure, **itemize your bags' contents** and their worth, and label the bags with your name, address, and phone number. (If you use your home address, cover it so potential thieves can't see it readily.) Include a label inside each bag and **pack a copy of your itinerary.** At check-in, **make sure each bag is correctly tagged** with the destination airport's three-letter code. Because some checked bags will be opened for hand inspection, the U.S. Transportation Security Administration recommends that you leave luggage unlocked or use the plastic locks offered at check-in. TSA screeners place an inspection notice inside searched bags, which are resealed with a special lock.

If your bag has been searched and contents are missing or damaged, file a claim with the TSA Consumer Response Center as soon as possible. If your bags arrive damaged or fail to arrive at all, file a written report with the airline before leaving the airport.

Complaints U.S. Transportation Security Administration Consumer Response Center ☎ 866/289-9673 🌐 www.tsa.gov.

PASSPORTS & VISAS

When traveling internationally, **carry your passport** even if you don't need one (it's always the best form of ID) and **make two photocopies of the data page** (one for someone at home and another for you, carried separately from your passport). If you lose your passport, promptly call the nearest embassy or consulate and the local police.

U.S. passport applications for children under age 14 require consent from both parents or legal guardians; both parents must appear together to sign the application. If only one parent appears, he or she must submit a written statement from the other parent authorizing passport issuance for the child. A parent with sole authority must present evidence of it when applying; acceptable documentation includes the child's certified birth certificate listing only the applying parent, a court order specifically permitting this parent's travel with the child, or a death certificate for the nonapplying parent. Application forms and instructions are available on the Web site of the U.S. State Department's Bureau of Consular Affairs (🌐 www.travel.state.gov).

ENTERING FRANCE

All citizens of Australia, Canada, New Zealand, the United States, and the United Kingdom, even infants, need only a valid passport to enter France for stays of up to 90 days. If you lose your passport, promptly call the nearest embassy or consulate and the local police.

Australian Citizens Australian Passport Office ☎ 131-232 🌐 www.passports.gov.au.

PASSPORT OFFICES

The best time to apply for a passport or to renew is in fall and winter. Before any trip, check your passport's expiration date, and, if necessary, renew it as soon as possible.

Australian Citizens Passports Australia ☎ 131-232 🌐 www.passports.gov.au.

Canadian Citizens Passport Office ✉ to mail in applications: 200 Promenade du Portage, Hull, Québec J8X 4B7 ☎ 819/994-3500 or 800/567-6868 🌐 www.ppt.gc.ca.

New Zealand Citizens New Zealand Passports Office ☎ 0800/22-5050 or 04/474-8100 🌐 www.passports.govt.nz.

U.K. Citizens U.K. Passport Service ☎ 0870/521-0410 🌐 www.passport.gov.uk.

U.S. Citizens National Passport Information Center ☎ 900/225-5674 or 900/225-7778 TTY (calls are 55¢ per minute for automated service or $1.50 per minute for operator service); 888/362-8668 or 888/498-3648 TTY (calls are $5.50 each) 🌐 www.travel.state.gov.

REST ROOMS

Use of public toilet facilities in cafés and bars is usually reserved for customers. Bathrooms are often downstairs and are usually unisex, which may mean walking by a men's urinal to reach the cubicle. Turkish-style toilets—holes in the ground surrounded by porcelain pads for your feet—are still found. Stand as far away as possible when you press the flushing mechanism in order to avoid water damage to your shoes. In certain cafés the lights will not come on in the bathroom until the cubicle door is locked. These lights work on a three-minute timer to save electricity. Simply press the button again if the lights go out. Clean public toilets are available in fast-food chains, department stores, and public parks. You can also find pay-per-use toilet units on the street, which require €.30 (small children, however, should not use these alone, as the self-sanitizing system works with weight-related sensors that might not detect a child's presence). There are bathrooms in the larger métro stations and in all train stations for a cost of €.15–€.30.

SAFETY

Don't wear a money belt or a waist pack, both of which peg you as a tourist. Distribute your cash and any valuables (including your credit cards and passport) between a deep front pocket, an inside jacket or vest pocket, and a hidden money pouch. Do not reach for the money pouch once you're in public.

Paris is one of the safest big cities in the world, good news for the traveling lone female. Although times are changing, it is still felt that women traveling alone are fair game for troublesome comments and the like; however, *dragueurs* (men who persistently profess their undying love to hapless female passersby) are a dying breed in this increasingly politically correct world. Certain neighborhoods can still pose problems, thanks to the night trade that goes on around Les Halles and St-Denis and on boulevard Clichy in Pigalle. Some off-the-beaten-path neighborhoods—particularly the outlying suburban communities around Paris, heavily populated by working-class and immigrant populations—may warrant extra precaution. Note that smiling automatically out of politeness is not part of French culture and can be quickly misinterpreted. If you encounter a problem, don't be afraid to show your irritation. When in doubt, stick to the boulevards, memorize the time of the last métro train to your station, ride in the first car by the conductor, and just use your common sense. Paris is a giant metropolis, so it is always best to be street-wise and alert.

SENIOR-CITIZEN TRAVEL

Travelers to Paris 60 years or older can take advantage of many discounts, such as reduced admissions of 20%–50% to museums and movie theaters. For rail travel outside of Paris, the Carte Senior entitles travelers 60 years and older to discounts.

To qualify for age-related discounts, **mention your senior-citizen status up front** when booking hotel reservations (not when checking out) and before you're seated in restaurants (not when paying the bill). Be sure to have identification on hand. When renting a car, ask about promotional car-rental discounts, which can be cheaper than senior-citizen rates.

Educational Programs **Elderhostel** ✉ 11 Ave. de Lafayette, Boston, MA 02111-1746 ☎ 877/426-8056; 978/323-4141 international callers; 877/426-2167 TTY 📠 877/426-2166 🌐 www.elderhostel.org. **Interhostel** ✉ University of New Hampshire, 6 Garrison Ave., Durham, NH 03824 ☎ 603/862-1147 or 800/733-9753 📠 603/862-1113 🌐 www.learn.unh.edu.

SIGHTSEEING TOURS

There are many ways to see Paris on a guided tour.

BIKE TOURS

A number of companies organize bike tours around Paris and its environs (Versailles, Chantilly, and Fontainebleau) for about €12–€30 per person.

Butterfield & Robinson ✉ 70 Bond St., Toronto M5B 1X3 Canada ☎ 416/864-1354 or 800/678-1147. **Bikenroller** ✉ 38 rue Fabert, 7e ☎ 01-45-50-38-27 🌐 www.bikenroller.fr. **Maison Roue Libre** ✉ 1 passage Mondétour, 1er ☎ 01-48-15-28-88 🌐 www;citefutee.com. **Paris Velo** ✉ 2 rue Fer-á-Moulin, 5e ☎ 01-43-37-59-22 🌐 www.paris- velo-rent-a-bike.fr. **Paris à Vélo, C'est Sympa** ✉ 37 bd. Bourdon, 4e ☎ 01-48-87-60-01.

BOAT TOURS

Boat trips along the Seine run throughout the day and evening for a cost of €6–€15. Many of the tours include lunch or dinner for an average cost of €46–€90. Reservations for meals are usually essential, and some require jacket and tie.

Bateaux Mouches boats depart from the Pont de l'Alma (Right Bank) 10–noon, 2–7, and 8:30–10:30. Lunch is served at 1 PM and dinner at 8:30 PM. Bateaux Parisiens–Tour Eiffel boats depart from the Pont d'Iéna (Left Bank) every half hour in summer and every hour in winter, starting at 10 AM. The last boat leaves at 9 PM (11 PM in summer). There are lunch and dinner cruises. Bat-O-Bus's trip along the Seine, without commentary, give you the advantage of being able to get on and off at any one of seven stops along the river, including the Eiffel Tower, Musée d'Orsay, St. Germain-des-Prés, the Louvre, Notre-Dame, Hôtel de Ville, and the Champs-Élysées. Get a one-day pass for €10, or buy a two-consecutive-day pass for €12.

Note that it operates from May 1 to October 31, departs every half hour between 10 and 6. Canauxrama organizes leisurely canal tours in flat-bottom barges along the St-Martin and Ourcq canals in East Paris. Departures from the quai de la Loire are at 9:15 and 2:45, and departures from the Bassin de l'Arsenal (opposite 50 boulevard de la Bastille) are at 9:30 and 2:30. The trip lasts about 2½ hrs. Reservations should be made. Paris Canal runs 3-hr trips with bilingual commentary between the Musée d'Orsay and the Parc de La Villette, between April and mid-November only. Reservations are essential. Vedettes du Pont Neuf boats depart every half hour from square du Vert Galant, 10–noon, 1:30–6:30, and 9–10:30 from March to October. Yachts de Paris organizes 2½-hr "gourmand cruises" (for about €135) year-round.

Bateaux Mouches ✉ Pont de l'Alma, 8e ☎ 01-42-25-96-10 🌐 www.bateauxmouches.com. **Bateaux Parisiens-Tour Eiffel** ✉ Pont d'Iéna, 7e ☎ 01-44-11-33-44 🌐 www.bateauxparisiens.com. **Bat-O-Bus** ✉ Pont d'Iéna, 7e ☎ 01-44-11-33-44 or 01-44-11-33-99 🌐 www.ratp.com. **Canauxrama** ✉ 5 bis quai de la Loire, 19e ✉ Bassin de l'Arsenal, 12e ☎ 01-42-39-15-00 🌐 www.canauxrama.com. **Paris Canal** ✉ 19 quai de la Loire, 19e ☎ 01-42-40-96-97. **Vedettes du Pont Neuf** ✉ Ile de la Cité, 1er ☎ 01-46-33-98-38. **Yachts de Paris** ✉ Port de Javel ☎ 01-44-54-14-70 🌐 www.yachtsdeparis.com.

BUS TOURS

For a 2-hr orientation tour by bus, the standard price is about €23. The two largest bus-tour operators are Cityrama and Paris Vision; for a more intimate—albeit expensive—tour of the city, Cityrama also runs several minibus excursions per day. Paris Bus gives tours in a London-style double-decker bus. You can catch the bus at any of nine pickup points; tickets cost €21 and allow you unlimited use for two days. For €23 the "Paris Open Tour" gives you two (consecutive) days of freedom to visit Paris in a double-decker bus with an open top. The bilingual tour lasts about 2 hrs, but you can get on and off as you please, since the bus stops at more than 20 spots along a circular route. These tours are slow and lose their charm after approximately the first 20 minutes, especially with the long and rather exasperating multilingual commentary. For a more interesting, authentic, and economical trip, why not take a regular Parisian bus for a mere €1.30 per ticket? A copy of the timetables for these tours is available from the main Paris Tourist Office. RATP (Paris Transit Authority) also gives guide-accompanied excursions in and around Paris by bus.

Cityrama ✉ 4 pl. des Pyramides, 1er ☎ 01-44-55-61-00. **Paris Bus** ☎ 01-42-30-55-50. **Paris Vision** ✉ 214 rue de Rivoli, 1er ☎ 01-42-60-31-25. **RATP** ✉ Pl. de la Madeleine, 8e ✉ 53 bis quai des Grands-Augustins, 6e ☎ 08-36-68-41-14.

HELICOPTER TOURS

For a spectacular aerial view of Paris, Delta Lima offers a helicopter tour; it takes off from Toussus le Noble (15 minutes from Paris). Tours last 35 minutes and cost €147 per person.

Delta Lima ☎ 01-40-68-01-23.

MINIBUS TOURS

Paris Bus and Paris Major Limousine organize tours of Paris and environs by luxury minibuses (for 4 to 15 passengers) for a minimum of 4 hrs. The price varies from €260 to €397. Reservations are essential.

Paris Bus ✉ 22 rue de la Prévoyance, Vincennes ☎ 01-43-65-55-55 🌐 www.touring-france.com. **Paris Major Limousine** ✉ 6 pl. de la Madeleine, 8e ☎ 01-44-52-50-00 🌐 www.parislimousine.fr.

WALKING TOURS

The team at Paris Walking Tours offer a wide selection of tours, from neighborhood visits to museum tours and theme tours such as "Hemingway's Paris," "The Marais," "Montmartre," and "The Latin Quarter." A 2-hr tour costs about €10.

Black Paris Tours offers tours exploring the places made famous by African-American musicians, writers, artists, and political exiles. Tours include a 4- to 5-hr walking-bus-métro tour (€80) that offers first-time visitors a city orientation and a primer in the history of African-Americans in Paris. Other options include "Montmartre/Pigalle: The 1920s Harlem of Paris" and tours of top African and soul-food restaurants.

A list of walking tours is also available from the Caisse Nationale des Monuments Historiques, in the weekly magazine *Pariscope,* and in *L'Officiel des Spectacles,* which lists walking tours under the heading

"*Conférences*" (most are in French, unless otherwise noted).

Black Paris Tours ☎ 01-46-37-03-96. **Paris Walking Tours** ☎ 01-48-09-21-40 🌐 www.paris-walks.com. **Butterfield & Robinson** ✉ 70 Bond St., Toronto M5B 1X3 Canada ☎ 416/864-1354 or 800/678-1147. **Caisse Nationale des Monuments Historiques** ✉ Bureau des Visites/Conférences, Hôtel de Sully, 62 rue St-Antoine, 4e ☎ 01-44-61-21-70.

STUDENTS IN PARIS

For a detailed listing of deals for students in Paris, ask for the brochure *Jeunes à Paris* from the main tourist office. *France-USA Contacts* (*FUSAC*), a twice-monthly publication available free in restaurants and bookstores, also has useful information.

IDs & Services **STA Travel** ✉ 10 Downing St., New York, NY 10014 ☎ 212/627-3111 or 800/777-0112 📠 212/627-3387 🌐 www.sta.com. **Travel Cuts** ✉ 187 College St., Toronto, Ontario M5T 1P7 Canada ☎ 416/979-2406, 800/592-2887, 866/246-9762 in Canada 📠 416/979-8167 🌐 www.travelcuts.com.

TAXES

All taxes must be included in affixed prices in France. Prices in **restaurants and hotel prices must by law include taxes and service charges:** If these appear as additional items on your bill, you should complain.

VALUE-ADDED TAX

VAT (value-added tax, known in France as TVA), at a standard rate of 19.6% (33% for luxury goods), is included in the price of many goods, but foreigners are often entitled to a refund. To be eligible for the VAT, an item (or items) must be purchased in one day in one place and must equal or exceed €182. You cannot combine purchases from different shops to total the required amount, or combine purchases from various days to total the required amount. The VAT for services (restaurants/theater, etc.) is not refundable. When making a purchase, **ask for a VAT refund form** and find out whether the merchant gives refunds—not all stores do, nor are they required to. Have the form stamped like any customs form by customs officials when you leave the country or, if you're visiting several European Union countries, when you leave the EU. Be ready to show customs officials what you've bought (pack purchases together, in your carry-on luggage); budget extra time for this. In France, you then put the letter into any one of the mailboxes at the airport—postage is already paid and there's usually a mailbox near the TVA counter. Your refund will arrive either as a credit to your credit card or as a check in U.S. dollars. You can also go to the French consulate with your plane tickets, your VAT forms, and the items you purchased to receive the stamp, but it will cost you $21; there is a three-month (after date of purchase) time limit.

A refund service can save you some hassle, for a fee. Global Refund is a Europe-wide service with 190,000 affiliated stores and more than 700 refund counters—located at every major airport and border crossing. Its refund form is called a Tax Free Check. The service issues refunds in the form of cash, check, or credit-card adjustment, minus a processing fee. If you don't have time to wait at the refund counter, you can mail in the form instead.

VAT Refunds **Global Refund** ✉ 99 Main St., Suite 307, Nyack, NY 10960 ☎ 800/566-9828 📠 845/348-1549 🌐 www.globalrefund.com.

TAXIS

Taxi rates are based on location and time. Daytime rates, A (7 AM–7 PM), within Paris are €.55 per kilometer (½ mi), and nighttime rates, B, are around €.90 per kilometer. Suburban zones and airports, C, are €1.10 per kilometer. There is a basic hire charge of €2 for all rides, a €.90 supplement per piece of luggage, and a €.75 supplement if you're picked up at an SNCF station. Waiting time is charged at €19.85 per hour. The easiest way to get a taxi is to **ask your hotel or a restaurant to call a taxi for you, or go to the nearest taxi stand** (you can find one every couple of blocks); cabs with their signs lit can be hailed but are annoyingly difficult to spot (and they are not all a single, uniform color). In July 2001, a new law was (finally) implemented requiring chauffeurs to take a fourth passenger for an average supplement of €2.30. It is customary to tip the driver about 10%.

Taxi Companies **Airport Taxi** ☎ 08-25-16-66-66. **Airtaxi** ☎ 08-91-70-25-50. **Taxi Bleu** ☎ 08-25-16-10-10. **Taxi G7** ☎ 01-47-39-47-39.

TELEPHONES

AREA & COUNTRY CODES

The country code for France is 33. The first two digits of French numbers are a prefix determined by zone: Paris and Ile-de-France, 01; the northwest, 02; the northeast, 03; the southeast, 04; and the southwest, 05. Pay close attention to numbers beginning with 08. Calls that begin with 08 followed by 00 are toll-free, but calls that begin with 08 followed by 36—like the information lines for the SNCF for example—cost €.35 per minute, so be careful. Numbers that begin with 06 are reserved for cell phones.

Note that **when dialing France from abroad, drop the initial 0 from the telephone number** (all numbers listed in this book include the initial 0, which is used for calling numbers *from within* France). To call a telephone number in Paris from the United States, dial 011–33 plus the phone number, but minus the initial 0 listed for the specific number in Paris. In other words, the local number for the Louvre is 01–40–20–51–51. To call this number from New York City, dial 011–33–1–40–20–51–51. To call this number from within Paris, dial 01–40–20–51–51. To call France from the United Kingdom, dial 00–33, then dial the number in France minus the initial 0 of the specific number.

DIRECTORY & OPERATOR ASSISTANCE

To find a number in France, **dial 12 for information.** For international inquiries, dial 00–33 plus the country code. These calls have a fixed rate of €.60.

Another source of information is the Minitel, an on-line network similar to the Internet. You can use one—they look like small computer terminals—free in most post offices. To access the on-line phone book, hit the *appel* (call) key, then type the name you are looking for, and hit *envoi* (return). It is also useful for tracking down services: tap in *piscine* (swimming pool) under *activité* (activity), for example, and it will give you a list of all the pools in Paris. Go to other lines or pages by hitting the *suite* (next) key. Newer models will connect automatically when you hit the book-icon key. To disconnect, hit *fin* (end).

INTERNATIONAL CALLS

To make a direct international call out of France, dial 00 and wait for the tone; then dial the country code (1 for the United States and Canada, 44 for the United Kingdom, 61 for Australia, and 64 for New Zealand) and the area code (minus any initial 0) and number.

Good news—telephone rates are actually decreasing in France due to the fact that the France Telecom monopoly now has some stringent competition. As in most countries, the highest rates fall between 8 AM and 7 PM and average out to a hefty €.25 per minute to the United States, Canada, and the closer European countries including Germany and Great Britain. Rates are greatly reduced from 7 PM to 8 AM with an average €.12 per minute.

To call home with the help of an operator, dial 00–33 plus the country code. There is an automatic €6.80 service charge.

Telephone cards are sold that enable you to make long-distance and international calls from any phone. Don't hesitate to invest in one if you plan on making calls from your hotel, as hotels often accumulate service charges and also have the most expensive rates.

LOCAL CALLS

Since all local numbers in Paris and the Ile-de-France begin with a 01, you must dial the full 10-digit number, including the initial 0. A local call costs €.11 for every three minutes.

LONG-DISTANCE CALLS

To call from region to region within France, dial the full 10-digit number, including the initial 0.

LONG-DISTANCE SERVICES

AT&T, MCI, and Sprint access codes make calling long-distance relatively convenient, but you may find the local access number blocked in many hotel rooms. First ask the hotel operator to connect you. If the hotel operator balks, ask for an international operator, or dial the international operator yourself. One way to improve your odds of getting connected to your long-distance carrier is to travel with more than one company's calling card (a hotel may block Sprint, for example, but not MCI). If all else fails, call from a pay phone.

Access Codes **AT&T Direct** ☎ 08-00-99-00-11 or 08-00-99-01-11; 800/222-0300 information. **MCI WorldPhone** ☎ 08-00-99-00-19; 800/444-4444 information. **Sprint International Access** ☎ 08-00-99-00-87; 800/793-1153 information.

PHONE CARDS

Practically all French pay phones are operated by *télécartes* (phone cards), which you can buy from post offices, tabacs, magazine kiosks, and any métro station. These phone cards will save you money and hassle, since it is almost impossible to find phones that take change these days. There are as many phone cards these days as bakeries, so to be safe, request the *télécarte international,* which, despite its name, allows you to make either local or international calls and offers greatly reduced rates. Instructions are in English and the cost is €8 for 60 units and €16 for 120 units. You may also request the simple *télécarte,* which allows you to make calls in France (the cost is €8 for 50 units; €15 for 120 units). You can also use your credit card in much the same way as a télécarte.

PUBLIC PHONES

Public telephone booths can almost always be found in post offices, métro stations, bus stops, and in most cafés, as well as on the street.

TIME

The time difference between New York and Paris is 6 hours (so when it's 1 PM in New York, it's 7 PM in Paris). The time difference between London and Paris is 1 hour; between Sydney and Paris, 8–9 hours; and between Auckland and Paris, 12 hours. All schedules, be it train, plane, or theater, work on a 24-hour or "continual" clock in France, which means that 8 AM is 8h00 but 8 PM is 20h00. Midnight is 24h00.

TIPPING

Bills in bars and restaurants must, by law, include service, but it is customary to round out your bill with some small change unless you're dissatisfied. The amount varies—from €.15 for a beer to €1.50–€2.30 after a meal. In expensive restaurants, it's common to leave an additional 5% of the bill on the table.

Tip taxi drivers and hairdressers about 10% of the bill. Give theater and cinema ushers €.25–€.50. In some theaters and hotels, cloakroom attendants may expect nothing (watch for signs that say *pourboire interdit*—tipping forbidden); otherwise, give them €.75. Washroom attendants usually get €.30, though the sum is often posted.

If you stay more than two or three days in a hotel, it is customary to leave something for the chambermaid—about €1.50 per day. Expect to pay about €1.50 (€.75 in a moderately priced hotel) to the person who carries your bags or who hails you a taxi. In hotels providing room service, give €.75 to the waiter (this does not apply if breakfast is routinely served in your room). If the chambermaid does some pressing or laundering for you, give her €.75–€1.50 on top of the bill. If the concierge has been very helpful, it is customary to leave a tip of €8–€16, depending on the type of hotel and the level of service.

Service-station attendants get nothing for pumping gas or checking oil but €.75 or €1.50 for checking tires. Train and airport porters get a fixed sum (€.90–€1.50) per bag. Museum guides should get €1.50–€3 after a guided tour. It is standard practice to tip bus drivers about €1.50 after an excursion.

TOURS & PACKAGES

Because everything is prearranged on a prepackaged tour or independent vacation, you spend less time planning—and often get it all at a good price.

BOOKING WITH AN AGENT

Travel agents are excellent resources. But it's a good idea to collect brochures from several agencies, as some agents' suggestions may be influenced by relationships with tour and package firms that reward them for volume sales. If you have a special interest, find an agent with expertise in that area; the American Society of Travel Agents (ASTA; ⇨ Travel Agencies) has a database of specialists worldwide.

Make sure your travel agent knows the accommodations and other services of the place being recommended. Ask about the hotel's location, room size, beds, and whether it has a pool, room service, or programs for children, if you care about these. Has your agent been there in person or sent others whom you can contact?

Do some homework on your own, too: local tourism boards can provide information about lesser-known and small-niche operators, some of which may sell only direct.

BUYER BEWARE

Each year consumers are stranded or lose their money when tour operators—even large ones with excellent reputations—go out of business. So check out the operator. Ask several travel agents about its reputation, and try to **book with a company that has a consumer-protection program.** (Look for information in the company's brochure.) In the United States, members of the National Tour Association and the United States Tour Operators Association are required to set aside funds to cover payments and travel arrangements in the event that the company defaults. It's also a good idea to choose a company that participates in the American Society of Travel Agents' Tour Operator Program; ASTA will act as mediator in any disputes between you and your tour operator.

Remember that the more your package or tour includes, the better you can predict the ultimate cost of your vacation. Make sure you know exactly what is covered, and **beware of hidden costs.** Are taxes, tips, and transfers included? Entertainment and excursions? These can add up.

Tour-Operator Recommendations **American Society of Travel Agents** (⇨ Travel Agencies). **National Tour Association** (NTA) ✉ 546 E. Main St., Lexington, KY 40508 ☎ 859/226-4444 or 800/682-8886 🖷 859/226-4404 🌐 www.ntaonline.com. **United States Tour Operators Association** (USTOA) ✉ 275 Madison Ave., Suite 2014, New York, NY 10016 ☎ 212/599-6599 or 800/468-7862 🖷 212/599-6744 🌐 www.ustoa.com.

TRAIN TRAVEL

The SNCF, France's rail system, is fast, punctual, comfortable, and comprehensive. There are various options: local trains, overnight trains with sleeping accommodations, and the high-speed TGV, or Trains à Grande Vitesse (averaging 255 kph [160 mph] on the Lyon/southeast line and 300 kph [190 mph] on the Lille and Bordeaux/southwest lines).

The TGVs, the fastest way to get around the country, operate between Paris and Lille/Calais, Paris and Lyon/Switzerland/the Riviera, Paris and Angers/Nantes, Paris and Tours/Poitiers/Bordeaux, Paris and Brussels, and Paris and Amsterdam. As with other main-line trains, a small supplement may be assessed at peak hours.

Paris has six international rail stations: Gare du Nord (northern France, northern Europe, and England via Calais or Boulogne); Gare St-Lazare (Normandy, England via Dieppe); Gare de l'Est (Strasbourg, Luxembourg, Basel, and central Europe); Gare de Lyon (Lyon, Marseille, the Riviera, Geneva, Italy); and Gare d'Austerlitz (Loire Valley, southwest France, Spain). Note that Gare Montparnasse has taken over as the main terminus for trains bound for southwest France since the introduction of the new TGV-Atlantique service.

CUTTING COSTS

To save money, look into rail passes. But be aware that if you don't plan to cover many miles, you may come out ahead by buying individual tickets.

RAIL PASSES

If you plan to travel outside of Paris by train, consider purchasing a France Rail Pass, which allows 3 days of unlimited train travel in a one-month period. If you travel solo, first class will run you $240, while second class is $210: you can add up to 6 days on this pass for $30 a day. For two people traveling together on a Saver Pass, the cost is $196, while in second class, it is $171; additional days (up to 6) cost $25 each. Other options include the France Rail 'n Drive Pass (combining rail and rental car), France Rail 'n Fly Pass (rail travel and one air-travel journey within France), and the France Fly Rail 'n Drive Pass (a rail, air, and rental-car program all in one).

France is one of 17 countries in which you can use EurailPasses, which provide unlimited first-class rail travel in all the participating countries for the duration of the pass. If you plan to rack up the miles, get a standard pass. These are available for 15 days ($572), 21 days ($740), one month ($918), two months ($1,298), and three months ($1,606). If your plans call for only limited train travel, look into a

Europass, which costs less money than a EurailPass. Unlike with the EurailPasses, however, you get a limited number of travel days in a limited number of countries during a specified time period. For example, a two-month Europass ($360–$710) allows between 5 and 15 days of rail travel but costs around $200 less than the least expensive EurailPass. Keep in mind, however, that the Europass is good only in France, Germany, Italy, Spain, and Switzerland, and the number of countries you can visit is further limited by the type of pass you buy

In addition to standard EurailPasses, ask about special rail-pass plans. Among these are the Eurail Youthpass (for those under age 26), the Eurail Saver Pass (which gives a discount for two or more people traveling together), a Eurail Flexipass (which allows a certain number of travel days within a set period), the Euraildrive Pass, and the Europass Drive (train and rental car).

Whichever of the above passes you choose, remember that **you must purchase your Eurail and Euro passes at home before leaving for France.**

Another option is to purchase one of the discount rail passes available only for sale in France from SNCF.

When traveling together, **two people (who don't have to be a couple) can save money with the Prix Découverte à Deux.** You'll get a 25% discount during *périodes bleus* (blue periods: weekdays and not on or near any holidays). Note that you have to be with the person you said you would be traveling with.

You can get a reduced fare if you're a senior citizen (over 60). There are two options: for the Prix Découverte Senior, all you have to do is show a valid ID with your age and you're entitled to up to a 25% reduction in fares in first and second class. The second, the Carte Senior, is better if you're planning on spending a lot of time traveling; it costs €44.20, is valid for one year, and entitles you to up to a 50% reduction on most trains with a guaranteed minimum reduction of 25%. It also entitles you to a 30% discount on trips outside of France.

With the Carte Enfant Plus, for €53.35 children under 12 and up to four accompanying adults can get up to 50% off on most trains for an unlimited number of trips. This card is perfect if you're planning on spending a lot of time traveling in France with your children, as it's valid for one year. You can also opt for the Prix Découverte Enfant Plus: when you buy your ticket, simply show a valid ID with your child's age and you can get a significant discount for your child and a 25% reduction for up to four accompanying adults.

If you purchase an individual ticket from SNCF in France and you're under 26, you automatically get a 25% reduction (a valid ID, such as an ISIC card or your passport, is necessary). If you're going to be using the train quite a bit during your stay in France and if you're under 26, consider buying the Carte 12–25 (€41.15), which offers unlimited 50% reductions for one year (provided that there's space available at that price; otherwise you'll just get the standard 25% discount).

If you don't benefit from any of these reductions and if you plan on traveling at least 200 km (132 mi) round-trip and don't mind staying over a Saturday night, look into the Prix Découverte Séjour. This ticket gives you a 25% reduction.

Don't assume that your rail pass guarantees you a seat on the train you wish to ride. You need to **book seats ahead even if you're using a rail pass.**

FARES & SCHEDULES

You can call for train information or reserve tickets in any Paris station, irrespective of destination. If you know what station you'll depart from you can get a free schedule there (while supplies last), or you can access the new, multilingual computerized schedule information network at any Paris station. You can also make reservations and buy your ticket while at the computer. Go to the Grandes Lignes counter for travel within France and to the Billets Internationaux desk if you're heading out of the country. Note that calling the SNCF's 08 number costs €.35 per minute, which quickly adds up; to save this cost, either go to the nearest station and make the reservations in person or visit the SNCF Web site 🌐 www.sncf.fr.

Seat reservations are required on TGVs and are a good idea on trains that may be crowded—particularly in summer and holidays on popular routes. You also need a reservation for sleeping accommodations.

Train Information **BritRail Travel** ☎ 800/677-8585 in the U.S.; 020/7834-2345 in the U.K. **Eurostar** ☎ 08-36-35-35-39 in France; 0345/881-881 in the U.K. 🌐 www.eurostar.com. **InterCity Europe** ✉ Victoria Station, London ☎ 020/7834-2345 or 020/7828-0892; 0990/848-848 credit-card bookings. **Rail Europe** ☎ 800/942-4866 in the U.S. 🌐 www.raileurope.com. **SNCF** ✉ 88 rue St-Lazare, 75009 Paris ☎ 08-36-35-35-35 🌐 www.sncf.fr.

BETWEEN THE U.K. & FRANCE

Short of flying, taking the "Chunnel" is the fastest way to cross the English Channel: three hours from London's central Waterloo Station to Paris's central Gare du Nord, 35 minutes from Folkestone to Calais, and 60 minutes from motorway to motorway. There is a vast range of prices for Eurostar—round-trip tickets range from €520 for first class to €105.35 for second class depending on when you travel. It's a good idea to **make a reservation if you're traveling with your car on a Chunnel train**; cars without reservations, if they can get on at all, are charged 20% extra.

British Rail also has four daily departures from London's Victoria Station, all linking with the Dover–Calais/Boulogne ferry services through to Paris. There is also an overnight service on the Newhaven–Dieppe ferry. Journey time is about eight hours. Credit-card bookings are accepted by phone or in person at a British Rail Travel Centre.

Car Transport **Eurotunnel** ☎ 0870/535-3535 in the U.K.; 070/223210 in Belgium; 03-21-00-61-00 in France 🌐 ww2.eurotunnel.com.

Passenger Service **Eurostar** ☎ 1233/617-575 or 0870/518-6186 in the U.K. 🌐 www.eurostar.co.uk; **Rail Europe** ☎ 800/942-4866 or 800/274-8724; 0870/584-8848 U.K. credit-card bookings 🌐 www.raileurope.com.

TRAVEL AGENCIES

A good travel agent puts your needs first. Look for an agency that has been in business at least five years, emphasizes customer service, and has someone on staff who specializes in your destination. In addition, **make sure the agency belongs to a professional trade organization.** The American Society of Travel Agents (ASTA)—the largest and most influential in the field with more than 20,000 members in some 140 countries—maintains and enforces a strict code of ethics and will step in to help mediate any agent-client disputes involving ASTA members if necessary. ASTA (whose motto is "Without a travel agent, you're on your own") also maintains a Web site that includes a directory of agents. (If a travel agency is also acting as your tour operator, *see* Buyer Beware *in* Tours & Packages.)

Local Agent Referrals **American Society of Travel Agents** (ASTA) ✉ 1101 King St., Suite 200, Alexandria, VA 22314 ☎ 703/739-2782; 800/965-2782 24-hr hot line 📠 703/739-3268 🌐 www.astanet.com. **Association of British Travel Agents** ✉ 68-71 Newman St., London W1T 3AH ☎ 020/7637-2444 📠 020/7637-0713 🌐 www.abtanet.com. **Association of Canadian Travel Agents** ✉ 130 Albert St., Suite 1705, Ottawa, Ontario K1P 5G4 ☎ 613/237-3657 📠 613/237-7052 🌐 www.acta.ca. **Australian Federation of Travel Agents** ✉ Level 3, 309 Pitt St., Sydney, NSW 2000 ☎ 02/9264-3299 📠 02/9264-1085 🌐 www.afta.com.au. **Travel Agents' Association of New Zealand** ✉ Level 5, Tourism and Travel House, 79 Boulcott St., Box 1888, Wellington 6001 ☎ 04/499-0104 📠 04/499-0786 🌐 www.taanz.org.nz.

Paris Agencies **American Express** ✉ 11 rue Scribe, 8e ☎ 01-47-77-77-07 ✉ 38 av. de Wagram, 8e ☎ 01-42-27-58-80. **Nouvelles Frontières** ✉ 5 av. de l'Opéra, 1er ☎ 08-03-33-33-33. **Soltours** ✉ 48 rue de Rivoli, 4e Ⓜ Métro: Hôtel de Ville ☎ 01-42-71-24-34.

VISITOR INFORMATION

Learn more about foreign destinations by checking government-issued travel advisories and country information. For a broader picture, consider information from more than one country.

France Tourist Information **France On-Call** ☎ 410/286-8310 weekdays 9-7 🌐 www.francetourism.com. **Chicago** ✉ 676 N. Michigan Ave., Chicago, IL 60611 ✉ fgto@mcs.net. **Los Angeles** ✉ 9454 Wilshire Blvd., Suite 715, Beverly Hills, CA 90212 ☎ 310/271-6665 📠 310/276-2835 ✉ fgto@gte.net. **New York City** ✉ 444 Madison Ave., 16th fl., New York, NY 10022 ☎ 212/838-7800 📠 212/838-7855 ✉ info@francetourism.com. **Canada** ✉ 1981 av. McGill College, Suite 490, Montréal, Québec H3A 2W9 ☎ 514/288-4264 📠 514/845-4868 ✉ mfrance@mtl.net. **U.K.** ✉ 178 Piccadilly, London W1V OAL ☎ 020/76399-3500 📠 020/76493-6594. **Australia** ✉ 25 Bligh St., Sydney NSW 2000 ☎ 02/9231-5244 📠 02/9221-8682.

Local Tourism Information **Espace du Tourisme d'Ile-de-France** ✉ Carrousel du Louvre, 99 rue de Rivoli, 75001 Paris ☎ 08-03-81-80-00 or

01-44-50-19-98. **Office du Tourisme de la Ville de Paris** Paris Tourist Office ✉ 127 bd. des Champs-Élysées ☎ 01-49-52-53-54; 01-49-52-53-56 recorded information in English. **Office du Tourisme et de Congrès Paris** Paris Convention and Visitors Bureau ✉ 127 bd. des Champs-Élysées, 75008 ☎ 08-92-68-31-12, €.30 per minute.

Government Advisories **U.S. Department of State** ✉ Overseas Citizens Services Office, Room 4811, 2201 C St. NW, Washington, DC 20520 ☎ 202/647-5225 interactive hot line; 888/407-4747 🌐 www.travel.state.gov; enclose a cover letter with your request and a business-size SASE. **Consular Affairs Bureau of Canada** ☎ 800/267-6788 or 613/944-6788 🌐 www.voyage.gc.ca. **U.K. Foreign and Commonwealth Office** ✉ Travel Advice Unit, Consular Division, Old Admiralty Bldg., London SW1A 2PA ☎ 020/7008-0232 or 020/7008-0233 🌐 www.fco.gov.uk/travel. **Australian Department of Foreign Affairs and Trade** ☎ 02/6261-1299 Consular Travel Advice Faxback Service 🌐 www.dfat.gov.au. **New Zealand Ministry of Foreign Affairs and Trade** ☎ 04/439-8000 🌐 www.mft.govt.nz.

WEB SITES

Do check out the World Wide Web when planning your trip. You'll find everything from weather forecasts to virtual tours of famous cities. Be sure to **visit Fodors.com** (🌐 www.fodors.com), a complete travel-planning site. You can research prices and book plane tickets, hotel rooms, rental cars, vacation packages, and more. In addition, you can post your pressing questions in the Travel Talk section. Other planning tools include a currency converter and weather reports, and there are loads of links to travel resources.

Paris/France Web Sites For more specific information on Paris, visit one of the following: **French Embassy** 🌐 www.france.diplomatie.fr. **French Government Tourist Office** 🌐 www.francetourism.com. **French Ministry of Culture** 🌐 www.culture.fr. **Paris Convention and Visitors Bureau** 🌐 www.paris-touristoffice.com. **Paris Tourist Office** 🌐 www.paris.org.

EXPLORING PARIS

1

FODOR'S CHOICE

Ancien Cloître Quartier, Ile de la Cité
Arènes de Lutèce, Latin Quarter
Café de Flore, St-Germain-des-Prés
Canal St-Martin, Paris
Centre Georges Pompidou, Beaubourg/Les Halles
Cour de Rohan, St-Germain-des-Prés
Hôtel des Invalides, Invalides
Jardin du Luxembourg, St-Germain-des-Prés
Louvre, Louvre/Tuileries
Musée d'Art Moderne de la Ville de Paris, Trocadéro/Eiffel Tower
Musée Carnavalet, Le Marais
Musée Nissim de Camondo, Parc Monceau
Musée d'Orsay, St-Germain-des-Prés
Musée Rodin, Invalides
Notre-Dame, Ile de la Cité
Sainte-Chapelle, Ile de la Cité
Tour Eiffel (Eiffel Tower), Trocadéro/Eiffel Tower

Many other sights and attractions enliven Paris. For other favorites, look for the black stars as you read the chapter.

Revised and updated by Christopher Mooney

Introduction by Nancy Coons

YOU'LL ALWAYS HAVE PARIS. Like the champagne-frosted idyll Bogie and Bergman reminisced about in *Casablanca,* the time you spend in this endlessly resonant city will remain a lifelong reference point. Over and over, as in a reverie, you'll conjure up its sensory assault—the sting in the nostril of a fresh-lit Gitane cigarette, the rippling of lights on the misty Seine, the confetti flutter of antique prints over the stand of a *bouquiniste* (booksellers), the aromatic bedlam of a street food market, the waves battering the prow of the *Medusa* in Géricault's epic canvas at the Louvre. And you'll go all moony again.

Whether weaned on Hemingway or Henry James, Doisneau or Cartier-Bresson, Brassaï or Cecil Beaton, Westerners share an image of Paris as the city of lovers, from Rodin's brawny duo to smoldering apache dancers, from *La Bohème*'s Mimi and Rodolfo weeping in a chilly garret to Anaïs Nin's flappers naked under fur. The Hollywood propaganda machine melted the hearts of any stubborn holdouts: who could stand firm in the face of Leslie Caron's blushes as she danced in Gene Kelly's arms along the Seine in *An American in Paris,* Audrey Hepburn's fine-boned take on the *Winged Victory* in *Funny Face,* or the punched-in-the-gut look on Bogie's face when he remembered the German tanks rolling in?

The real love affair is with the city of Paris itself, and it can play you like a violin. Around every corner, down every *ruelle,* or little street, lies a resonance-in-waiting. You can stand on rue du Faubourg St-Honoré at the very spot where Edmond Rostand set Ragueneau's pastry shop in *Cyrano de Bergerac.* You can peruse the letters of Madame de Sévigné in her erstwhile hôtel particulier, now the Musée Carnavalet. You can hear the words of Racine resound in the hair-raising diction of the Comédie Française. You can breathe in the fumes of hubris before the extravagant porphyry tomb of Napoléon at Les Invalides. You can climb into César Franck's organ loft at the church of Ste-Clotilde. You can gaze through the gate at the Ile St-Louis mansion where Voltaire honed his wit, and then lay a garland on Oscar Wilde's grave.

No matter which way you head, any trip through Paris will be a voyage of discovery. But choosing the Paris of your dreams is a bit like choosing a perfume or cologne. Do you prefer young and dashing, or elegant and worldly? Something sporty, or divinely glamorous? No matter—beneath touristy Paris, historic Paris, fashion-conscious Paris, pretentious-bourgeois Paris, practical working-class Paris, or the legendary bohemian Paris of undying attraction, you will find your own Paris, and it will be vivid, exciting, unforgettable. Veterans know that Paris is a city of regal perspectives and ramshackle streets, of formal *espaces vertes,* or green open spaces, and quiet squares, and this combination of the pompous and the private is one of the secrets of its perennial lure.

Another draw is its scale: Paris is relatively small as capitals go, with distances between many of its major sights and museums eminently walkable. The city's principal tourist axis is less than 6½ km (4 mi) long, running parallel to the north bank of the Seine from the Arc de Triomphe to the Bastille. In fact, the best way to get to know Paris is on foot, although public transportation—particularly the métro subway system—is excellent. Serious explorers should buy a *Plan de Paris* booklet: a city map-guide with a street-name index that also shows métro stations (note that all métro stations have a detailed neighborhood map just inside the entrance).

For the first-timer, there will always be several "musts" at the top of the list—the Louvre, Notre-Dame, and the Eiffel Tower, among them—

but a visit to Paris will never be quite as simple as a quick look at a few landmarks. Every *quartier,* or neighborhood, has its own treasures, and you should be ready to explore—a very pleasant prospect in this most elegant of cities. It is no exaggeration to say that the most assiduous explorers of Paris are the Parisians themselves. Each quartier has its own personality and unsuspected charms, which are discovered best on foot. Ultimately, your route will depend on your own preferences and your curiosity—as well as your degree of fatigue. You can wander for hours without getting bored—though not, perhaps, without getting lost. By the time you have seen only a few neighborhoods, drinking in the rich variety they have to offer, you should not only be culturally replete but downright exhausted, and hungry, too. Again, take your cue from the Parisians and plan your next stop at a sidewalk café. So you've heard stories of a friend of a friend who paid $6 for a coffee at a famous café? So what? What you're paying for is time, and the opportunity to watch the intricate drama of Parisian street life unfold. Hemingway knew the rules: he'd be just another sports writer if the café waiters of Paris had hovered around him impatiently.

After enjoying your ringside seat at the street theater, you're ready to explore the city as a living art gallery. Paris provides, at nearly every turn, a familiar work of art, framed in reality: *promeneurs* in the Bois de Boulogne in perfect pointillist silhouette, broad street perspectives flashing from gold to pink to silver under scudding Impressionist clouds, a woman's abstracted stare over a glass of green liqueur at a Montmartre café, and fine-boned ladies in stylish black and white delicately sniffing at Guerlain's perfume counter.

You'll learn it's all so familiar and all so terribly . . . Parisian. *Rillettes* (preserved goose spread) and *poilâne* (the ubiquitous chewy sourdough bread from Poilâne bakery) and Beaujolais. Ranks of posters, eight at a time, plastered over scaffolding. The discreet hiss of the métro's rubber wheels. The street sweeper guiding rags along the rain gutters with a twig broom. The coins in the saucer by the *pissoir.* The tantalizing hidden carriage courtyards lined with boxwood, gravel, and Peugeots. The shriek of the espresso machine as it steams the milk for your café crème, the flip-lid sugar bowl on the zinc bar. The illuminated monuments looming like Mayan idols. The lovers buried in each others' necks along the banks of the Seine.

Yes, you'll always have Paris. So what are you waiting for?

FROM NOTRE-DAME TO PLACE DE LA CONCORDE

No matter how you approach Paris—historically, geographically, emotionally—it is the Seine River that beckons you. The city owes both its development and much of its visual appeal to the Seine, which weaves through its very heart. Each bank of the river has its own personality; the Rive Droite (Right Bank), with its spacious boulevards and formal buildings, generally has a more sober and genteel feel than the more carefree Rive Gauche (Left Bank) to the south. In between, the river harbors two tiny islands that stand at the center of the city—the Ile de la Cité and the Ile St-Louis. Both seem to be gliding downriver, as if the latter were being towed by the former. It is the Ile de la Cité that forms the city's historic ground zero.

It was here, for obvious reasons of defense and in the hope of controlling the trade that passed along the Seine, that the earliest inhabitants

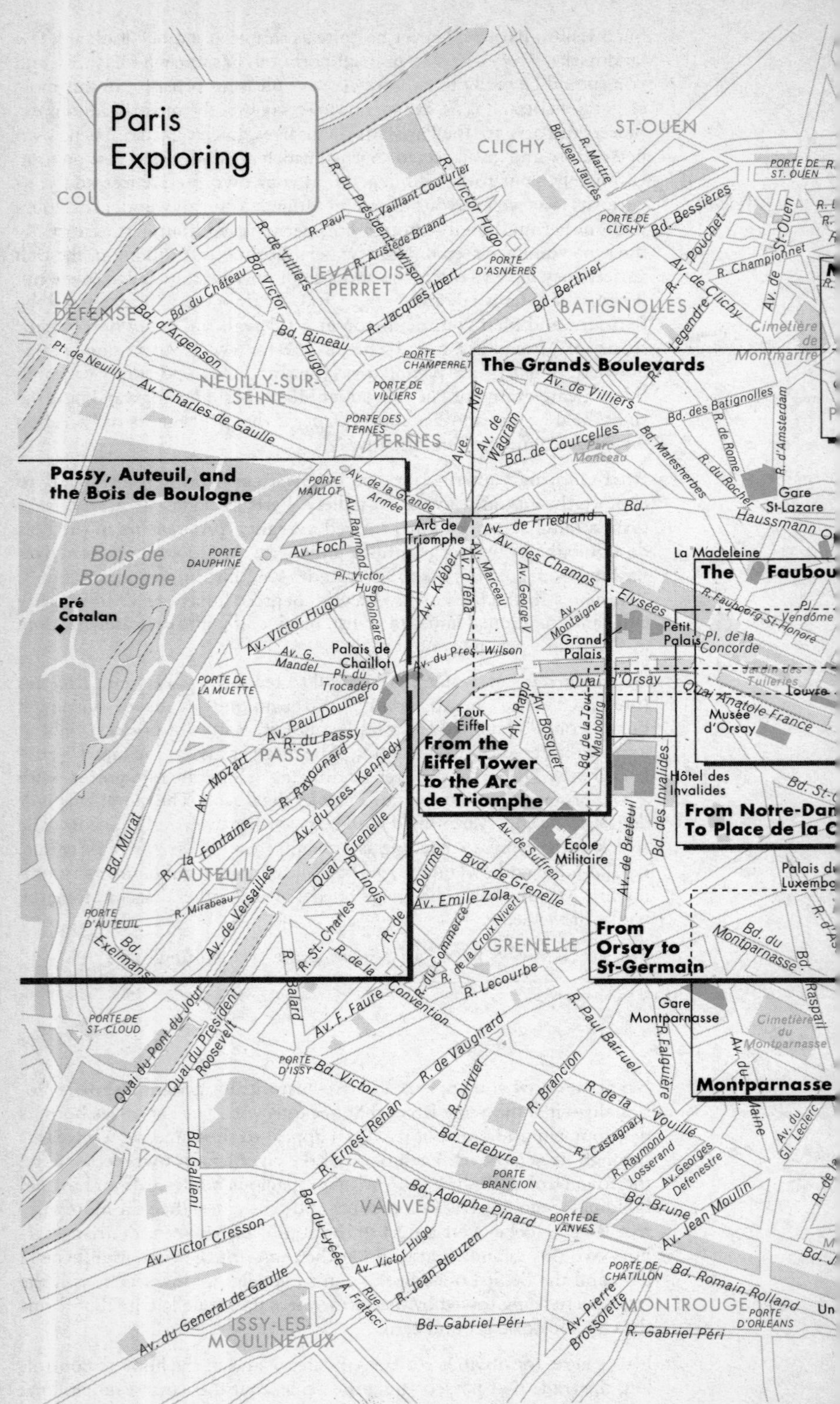
Paris Exploring
The Grands Boulevards
Passy, Auteuil, and the Bois de Boulogne
From the Eiffel Tower to the Arc de Triomphe
The Faubou
From Notre-Dam To Place de la C
From Orsay to St-Germain
Montparnasse
CLICHY
ST-OUEN
LEVALLOIS-PERRET
LA DÉFENSE
NEUILLY-SUR-SEINE
TERNES
BATIGNOLLES
PASSY
AUTEUIL
GRENELLE
VANVES
MONTROUGE
ISSY-LES-MOULINEAUX
Bois de Boulogne
Pré Catalan
Arc de Triomphe
Palais de Chaillot
Pl. du Trocadéro
Tour Eiffel
Grand Palais
Petit Palais
La Madeleine
Gare St-Lazare
Musée d'Orsay
Hôtel des Invalides
Ecole Militaire
Gare Montparnasse
Palais du Luxembourg
Cimetière de Montmartre
Cimetière du Montparnasse
Parc Monceau
Jardin des Tuileries
Louvre
Pl. de la Concorde
Pl. Vendôme
PORTE DE ST. OUEN
PORTE DE CLICHY
PORTE D'ASNIERES
PORTE CHAMPERRET
PORTE DE VILLIERS
PORTE DES TERNES
PORTE MAILLOT
PORTE DAUPHINE
PORTE DE LA MUETTE
PORTE D'AUTEUIL
PORTE DE ST. CLOUD
PORTE D'ISSY
PORTE BRANCION
PORTE DE VANVES
PORTE DE CHATILLON
PORTE D'ORLEANS
Av. Charles de Gaulle
Pt. de Neuilly
Bd. d'Argenson
Bd. du Château
Bd. Victor Hugo
Bd. Bineau
R. de Villiers
R. Paul Vaillant Couturier
R. du Président Wilson
R. Aristide Briand
R. Victor Hugo
R. Jacques Ibert
Bd. Jean Jaurès
R. Martre
Bd. Bessières
R. Pouchet
Av. de Clichy
R. Championnet
Av. de St-Ouen
Bd. Berthier
R. Legendre
Av. de Villiers
Bd. des Batignolles
R. de Rome
R. d'Amsterdam
Bd. de Courcelles
Bd. Malesherbes
R. du Rocher
Bd. Haussmann
Ave. Niel
Av. de Wagram
Av. de la Grande Armée
Av. Foch
Av. Raymond Poincaré
Pl. Victor Hugo
Av. Victor Hugo
Av. G. Mandel
Av. de Friedland
Av. des Champs Elysées
Av. Kléber
Av. d'Iéna
Av. Marceau
Av. George V
Av. Montaigne
Av. du Pres. Wilson
R. Faubourg St-Honoré
Quai d'Orsay
Quai Anatole France
Av. Rapp
Av. Bosquet
Bd. de la Tour Maubourg
Bd. des Invalides
Av. de Breteuil
Av. de Suffren
Bd. St-G
Av. Paul Doumer
R. du Passy
R. Raynouard
Av. du Pres. Kennedy
Av. Mozart
R. la Fontaine
Quai Grenelle
R. Linois
R. Mirabeau
Av. de Versailles
R. St. Charles
R. de la Convention
R. de Lourmel
Bvd. de Grenelle
Av. Emile Zola
R. du Commerce
R. de la Croix Nivert
R. Lecourbe
Bd. Murat
Bd. Exelmans
R. Balard
Av. F. Faure
Quai du Pont du Jour
Quai du Président Roosevelt
Bd. Victor
R. de Vaugirard
R. Olivier
R. Brancion
R. Paul Barruel
R. Falguière
R. de la Vouillé
R. Castagnary
R. Raymond Losserand
Av. Georges Defenestre
Bd. du Montparnasse
Bd. Raspail
Av. du Maine
Av. du Gl. Leclerc
R. Ernest Renan
Bd. Lefebvre
Bd. Adolphe Pinard
Bd. Brune
Av. Jean Moulin
Bd. Gallieni
Bd. du Lycée
Av. Victor Cresson
Av. Victor Hugo
R. Jean Bleuzen
Av. du General de Gaulle
Rue A. Fratacci
Bd. Gabriel Péri
Av. Pierre Brossolette
Bd. Romain Rolland
R. Gabriel Péri

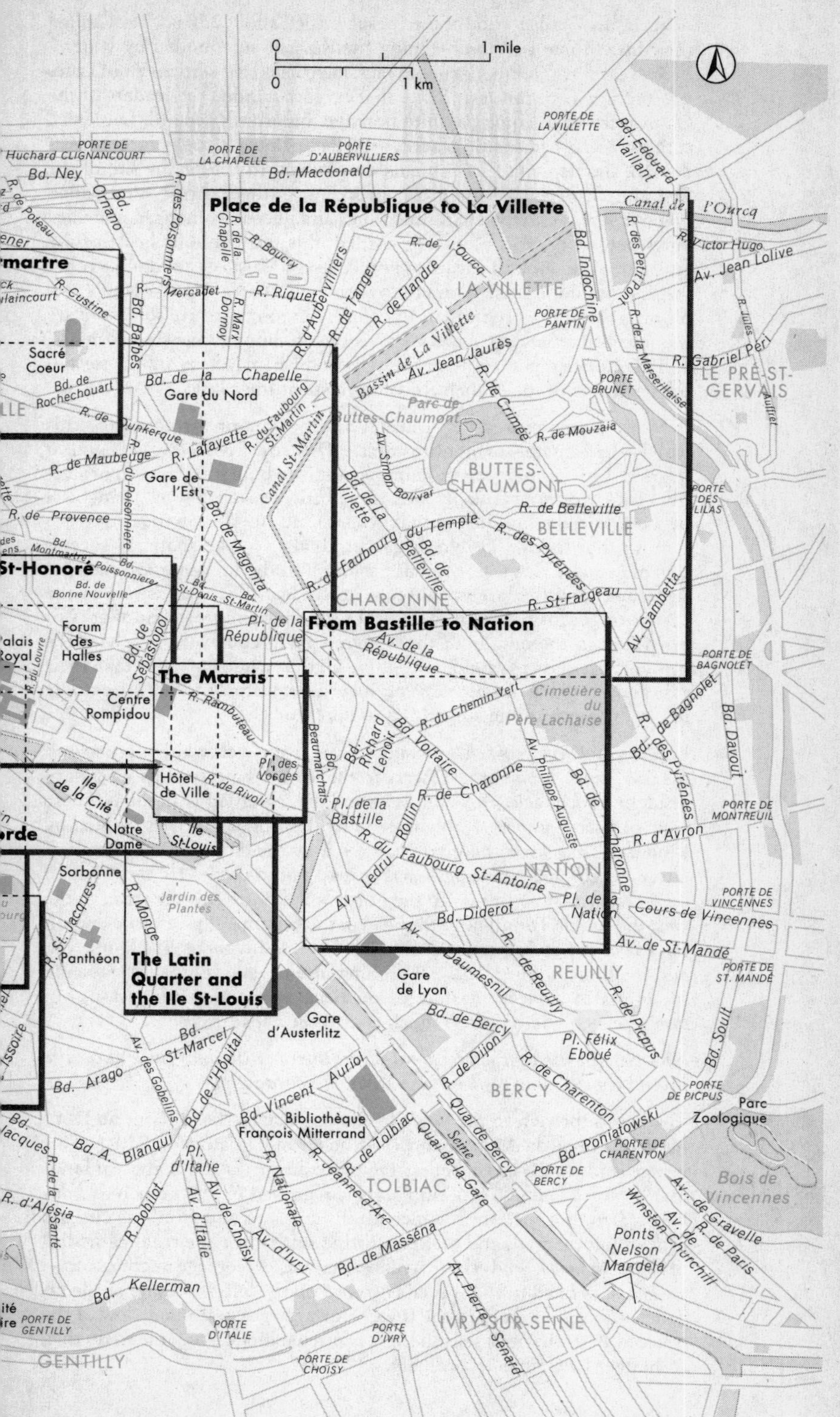

0
1 mile
0
1 km
Place de la République to La Villette
From Bastille to Nation
The Marais
The Latin Quarter and the Ile St-Louis
St-Honoré
LA VILLETTE
BUTTES-CHAUMONT
BELLEVILLE
CHARONNE
NATION
REUILLY
BERCY
TOLBIAC
LE PRÉ-ST-GERVAIS
IVRY-SUR-SEINE
GENTILLY
PORTE DE CLIGNANCOURT
PORTE DE LA CHAPELLE
PORTE D'AUBERVILLIERS
PORTE DE LA VILLETTE
PORTE DE PANTIN
PORTE BRUNET
PORTE DES LILAS
PORTE DE BAGNOLET
PORTE DE MONTREUIL
PORTE DE VINCENNES
PORTE DE ST. MANDÉ
PORTE DE PICPUS
PORTE DE CHARENTON
PORTE DE BERCY
PORTE D'IVRY
PORTE D'ITALIE
PORTE DE CHOISY
PORTE DE GENTILLY
Sacré Coeur
Gare du Nord
Gare de l'Est
Forum des Halles
Centre Pompidou
Palais Royal
Hôtel de Ville
Notre Dame
Ile de la Cité
Ile St-Louis
Sorbonne
Panthéon
Jardin des Plantes
Gare de Lyon
Gare d'Austerlitz
Bibliothèque François Mitterrand
Parc de Buttes-Chaumont
Cimetière du Père Lachaise
Pl. de la République
Pl. de la Bastille
Pl. des Vosges
Pl. de la Nation
Pl. Félix Eboué
Pl. d'Italie
Parc Zoologique
Bois de Vincennes
Ponts Nelson Mandela
Canal de l'Ourcq
Bassin de La Villette
Canal St-Martin
Seine
Bd. Ney
Bd. Macdonald
Bd. Ornano
Bd. Barbès
Bd. de Rochechouart
Bd. de la Chapelle
Bd. de Magenta
Bd. de Sébastopol
Bd. Richard Lenoir
Bd. Voltaire
Bd. Beaumarchais
Bd. de Charonne
Bd. de Belleville
Bd. de La Villette
Bd. Indochine
Bd. Edouard Vaillant
Bd. Davout
Bd. Soult
Bd. Diderot
Bd. de Bercy
Bd. Poniatowski
Bd. de Masséna
Bd. Kellerman
Bd. Vincent Auriol
Bd. Arago
Bd. St-Marcel
Bd. de l'Hôpital
Bd. A. Blanqui
Bd. de Bagnolet
Av. Jean Jaurès
Av. Jean Lolive
Av. Simon Bolivar
Av. de la République
Av. Gambetta
Av. Philippe Auguste
Av. Ledru Rollin
Av. Daumesnil
Av. de St-Mandé
Av. des Gobelins
Av. d'Italie
Av. de Choisy
Av. d'Ivry
Av. Pierre Sénard
Av. de Gravelle
Av. de Winston Churchill
Cours de Vincennes
R. de Crimée
R. de Flandre
R. de Tanger
R. d'Aubervilliers
R. Riquet
R. de Belleville
R. des Pyrénées
R. St-Fargeau
R. du Faubourg du Temple
R. du Faubourg St-Antoine
R. de Charonne
R. du Chemin Vert
R. de Rivoli
R. Rambuteau
R. Lafayette
R. de Maubeuge
R. de Provence
R. du Faubourg St-Martin
R. de Dunkerque
R. du Poisonnière
R. des Poissonniers
R. Custine
R. de Mouzaia
R. Gabriel Péri
R. d'Avron
R. de Reuilly
R. de Picpus
R. de Charenton
R. de Dijon
R. de Tolbiac
R. Jeanne d'Arc
R. Nationale
R. Bobillot
R. Monge
R. St. Jacques
R. d'Alésia
R. de la Santé
R. de Paris
Quai de Bercy
Quai de la Gare

of Paris, the Gaulish tribe of the Parisii, settled about 250 BC. They called their little home Lutetia, meaning "settlement surrounded by water." In the year 53 BC Julius Caesar, in fact, mentioned the settlement of Lutetia, and it was to this island city that he commanded the leaders of the Gaulish tribes to come pay him homage, before his general, Labienus, ruthlessly crushed them. Whereas the Ile St-Louis is today largely residential, the Ile de la Cité remains deeply historic and is the site of the first church of Paris—the great, brooding Cathedral of Notre-Dame. Napoléon was crowned here, and kings and queens exchanged marriage vows before its great altar. The cathedral is the symbolic heart of the city, if not the symbolic heart of France itself. Most of the island's other medieval buildings fell victim to town planner Baron Haussmann's ambitious rebuilding program of the 1860s. Among the rare survivors are the jewel-like Sainte-Chapelle, a vision of shimmering stained glass, and the Conciergerie, the former city prison where Marie-Antoinette and other victims of the French Revolution spent their last days.

If Notre-Dame represents Church, another major attraction of this walk—the Louvre—symbolizes State. This royal palace was begun in the mid-13th century, when Philippe-Auguste built a fortress to protect the city's western flank. It was not until pleasure-loving François I began a partial rebuilding of that original rude fortress in the early 16th century that today's Louvre began gradually to take shape. A succession of French rulers were responsible for filling this immense, symmetrical structure, now the largest museum in the world as well as one of the easiest to get lost in, with the world's greatest paintings and works of art. Right in the middle of the Louvre's main courtyard is I. M. Pei's shimmering glass pyramid, reminding all that while Parisians take their role as custodians of a glorious heritage most seriously, they are equally intent on bequeathing something to the future.

Before you leave Notre-Dame, take a cue from Victor Hugo and climb the 387 steps of one of its towers to the former haunts of its legendary resident hunchback, Quasimodo. You'll be rewarded with the ultimate view of Paris—unforgettably framed by the stone gargoyles created by Viollet-le-Duc. From here you can see how the city—like the trunk of a tree developing new rings—has spread out in circles from the island on which you now stand. To the north is the Butte Montmartre; to the west the Arc de Triomphe at the head of the Champs-Élysées; to the south the towers of St-Sulpice and the domes of the Invalides, the Panthéon, and the Luxembourg Palace. Drinking in the view, you could stay here for hours in a pleasant state of medieval suspended animation, but don't delay—you have too much else to see ahead.

Numbers in the text correspond to numbers in the margin and on the From Notre-Dame to the Place de la Concorde map.

a good walk

The best approach to the Ile de la Cité is to cross the Pont au Double from quai de Montebello (St-Michel métro stop or RER). This bridge leads to the large, pedestrian place du Parvis and that great landmark, Notre-Dame. Place du Parvis is regarded by the French as *kilomètre zéro,* the spot from which all distances to and from the city are officially measured, and makes a fitting setting for the regal cathedral of **Notre-Dame** 1. Study the magnificent facade, explore the interior, then—you have to head to the special entrance on the left-hand side of the facade—toil up the steps to the towers for a gargoyle-framed view of the heart of Paris. In peak season there is often a block-long line to do this, so budget your time accordingly.

To escape the crowds, however, relief is just a short—and magical—stroll away. Few people venture to the **Ancient Cloître** ②, a nook of medieval Paris that is tucked behind the northern (or left-hand side as you face the cathedral) buttresses of Notre-Dame. First, history and art buffs will want to visit the **Musée de Notre-Dame** ③ on rue du Cloître-Notre-Dame. Then enter the quarter—originally the area where seminary students boarded with the church canons—by taking one of the adjoining side streets and head north toward the Seine to reach rue Chanoinesse, once the seminary's cloister walk. Here, at No. 10, is the house that was once paradise to those fabled lovers of the Middle Ages, Héloïse and Abelard. Past some pretty houses (notably No. 24), you'll find rue de Columbe, but make a right at No. 5—a private house which still contains the ruins of the medieval chapel of St-Aignan—to turn onto rue des Ursins. This will take you to a lovely flower garden set by steps leading up to the riverside quai aux Fleurs. While taking a time-out on the steps, feast your eyes (if not your stomach—this is a good spot for a picnic) on one of the island's most beautiful medieval mansions. Just a step away is rue des Chantres, which seems to exist only so as to strikingly frame Notre-Dame's spire in the distance. Once your Nikon has immortalized this view, head back to the cathedral and take a walk around Notre-Dame's walls, which nicely sets the whole place in proportion, with the gardens between the cathedral and the Seine offering splendid views of the sophisticated medieval masonry. Head through the gardens to **Square Jean-XXIII** ④ and turn right to cross Pont de l'Archevêché for the best view of all, with Notre-Dame's flying buttresses (archlike structural supports enabling the walls to soar heavenward) lending the heavy apse a magical lightness.

Walk (or dance—this is where Leslie Caron and Gene Kelly so memorably pas-de-deuxed in *An American in Paris*)—along quai de la Tournelle until you reach the Petit Pont, then cross back over the Seine and head straight on to rue de Lutèce. Turn left here, pass the flower market, and continue on to boulevard du Palais and the imposing **Palais de Justice** ⑤, the 19th-century law courts; you can wander around the buildings among the black-robed lawyers or attend a court hearing. But the real interest here is the late-Gothic **Sainte-Chapelle** ⑥, which many consider the most beautiful church in the world, tucked away to the left of the main courtyard. Turn left as you leave the Palais de Justice, then left again onto quai de l'Horloge, named for the oldest *horloge* (clock) in Paris, marking time since 1370 from high up on the **Conciergerie** ⑦, the prison where Marie-Antoinette and other blue bloods awaited their slice of history at the guillotine. Quai de l'Horloge leads to rue de Harlay and historic **place Dauphine** ⑧. Cross this old-fashioned square to **square du Vert-Galant** ⑨, with its equestrian statue of Henri IV. Steps on the right lead down to the waterside where Vedette motorboats set off for their tours along the Seine.

Cross **Pont Neuf** ⑩—actually the oldest bridge in Paris—to the Rive Droite and turn left along quai du Louvre, past the Art Deco Samaritaine department store, to reach the great **Louvre** ⑪ museum, entering through the elegant Baroque East Front designed by Claude Perrault in the 1660s. This entry portal leads into Cour Carrée, a grandiose courtyard that has something of the assured feel of an Oxford or Cambridge quadrangle, though on a much grander scale. Through the massive archway of the domed Pavillon de l'Horloge, straight ahead you can make out the palace's controversial main entrance: I. M. Pei's famous glass pyramid. Settle in for a visit to the home of the *Venus de Milo,* the *Winged Victory of Samothrace,* and the mystifying countenance of the *Mona Lisa.*

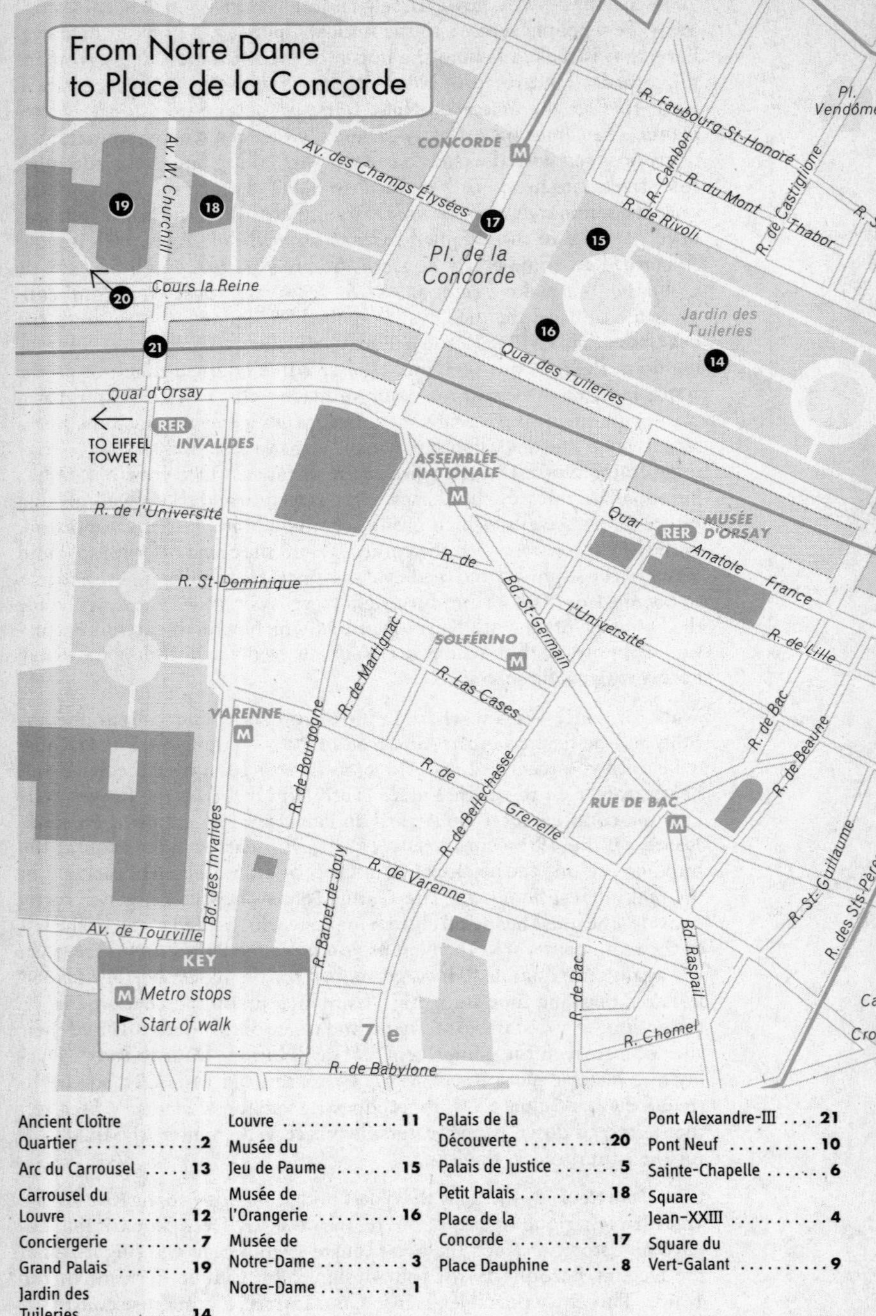

Ancient Cloître Quartier 2
Arc du Carrousel 13
Carrousel du Louvre 12
Conciergerie 7
Grand Palais 19
Jardin des Tuileries 14
Louvre 11
Musée du Jeu de Paume 15
Musée de l'Orangerie 16
Musée de Notre-Dame 3
Notre-Dame 1
Palais de la Découverte 20
Palais de Justice 5
Petit Palais 18
Place de la Concorde 17
Place Dauphine 8
Pont Alexandre-III 21
Pont Neuf 10
Sainte-Chapelle 6
Square Jean-XXIII 4
Square du Vert-Galant 9

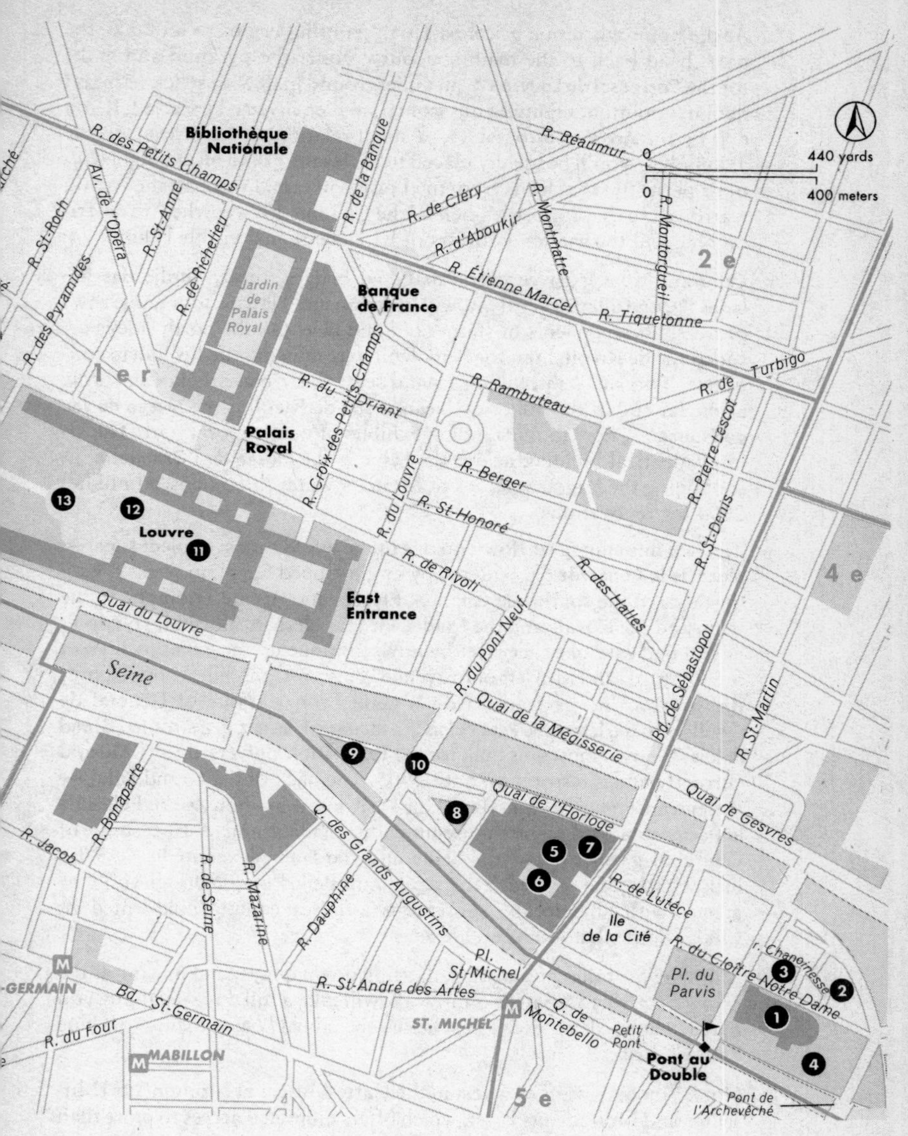
Bibliothèque Nationale
Banque de France
Palais Royal
Jardin de Palais Royal
Louvre
East Entrance
Seine
Ile de la Cité
Pl. du Parvis
Pont au Double
Petit Pont
Pont de l'Archevêché
Pl. St-Michel
ST. MICHEL
MABILLON
-GERMAIN
1er
2e
4e
5e
440 yards
400 meters
R. des Petits Champs
R. Réaumur
R. de la Banque
R. de Cléry
R. d'Aboukir
R. Étienne Marcel
R. Montmartre
R. Montorgueil
R. Tiquetonne
R. de Turbigo
R. Rambuteau
R. Pierre Lescot
R. St-Denis
R. Berger
R. St-Honoré
R. de Rivoli
R. des Halles
R. du Louvre
R. Croix des Petits Champs
R. du Oriant
R. de Richelieu
R. St-Anne
Av. de l'Opéra
R. St-Roch
R. des Pyramides
Quai du Louvre
R. du Pont Neuf
Quai de la Mégisserie
Bd. de Sébastopol
R. St-Martin
Quai de Gesvres
Quai de l'Horloge
R. de Lutèce
R. du Cloître Notre Dame
r. Chanoinesse
Q. des Grands Augustins
R. Dauphine
R. Mazarine
R. de Seine
R. Bonaparte
R. Jacob
Bd. St-Germain
R. du Four
R. St-André des Artes
Q. de Montebello

At the point when one priceless Titian painting begins to look like the next, head back to the main concourse under the pyramid and make for the **Carrousel du Louvre** ⑫, an underground mall with snack bars and designer boutiques fanning out from a smaller, inverted pyramid. If you exit by the **Arc du Carrousel** ⑬—a small relation to the distant Arc de Triomphe—you'll be ideally placed to assess the grand vista (aligned *almost* perfectly) that leads from the Louvre pyramid through the Arc du Carrousel to the Concorde obelisk, the Champs-Élysées, the Arc de Triomphe, and the shadowy towers of La Défense just visible behind.

Continue west, past eccentric diagonal hedges, to the **Jardin des Tuileries** ⑭, or Tuileries Gardens, with its manicured lawns, fountains, rows of trees, and regiments of statues old and new. On the north side is arcaded rue de Rivoli, built for Napoléon to commemorate his Italian conquests. Two smallish buildings stand sentinel by place de la Concorde, at the far end of the Tuileries. Nearest rue de Rivoli is the **Musée du Jeu de Paume** ⑮, host to outstanding exhibits of contemporary art. The almost identical building nearer the Seine is the **Musée de l'Orangerie** ⑯, containing the largest versions of Monet's *Water Lilies* (closed until fall 2004 for renovations).

The two museums gaze down on one of the world's most opulent squares, **place de la Concorde** ⑰, centered by its gilt-tipped Egyptian obelisk, with the Seine to the south, the Champs-Élysées and Arc de Triomphe to the west, and rue Royale and the Madeleine church to the north. If you don't have a bad case of gallery feet by now, continue up the Champs-Élysées for 500 yards and turn left onto avenue Winston-Churchill. Looming over the street corner is Jean Cardot's giant bronze statue of General de Gaulle. On the left is the **Petit Palais** ⑱, facing the larger, glass-roofed **Grand Palais** ⑲—two museums built for the Exposition Universelle of 1900 and currently under restoration until 2005. The back of the Grand Palais—the entrance is on avenue Franklin-D.-Roosevelt—houses the **Palais de la Découverte** ⑳, a science museum with a planetarium. A 10-ft statue of Churchill gazes toward the Seine and the **Pont Alexandre-III** ㉑. With luck, by the time you reach this exuberant Belle Epoque bridge you'll be greeted with a memorable sunset to set off the gleaming, gold-leafed Invalides dome that looms up ahead.

TIMING Allowing for toiling up towers, dancing down quays, and musing at the *Mona Lisa,* this 5½-km (3½-mi) walk will take a full day—enabling you to reach Pont Alexandre-III just before the fabled *l'heure bleue*—the blue hour of dusk.

Note: You may want to invest in the **Carte Musées et Monuments** (Museums and Monuments Pass), which offers unlimited access to more than 65 museums and monuments over a one-, three-, or five-consecutive-day period; the cost, respectively, is €15, €30, and €40. Considering that most Paris museums other than the Louvre (which charges €10) cost between €4 and €7, you have to be serious about museum going to make this pay off, but there is one incredible plus: you get to jump to the head of the line by displaying it—quite a feat when there are 600 people lined up to get into the Musée d'Orsay. Since most museums don't charge for kids under 18, a family of four need buy only two passes. The Pass is available at Paris's tourist offices and métro stations and at all participating museums. Note that many museums are closed on Monday and Tuesday. Information: 🌐 www.intermusees.com.

What to See

2 **Ancien Cloître Quartier.** Hidden in the shadows of Notre-Dame and just a few steps away from its seething crowds is this magical and often overlooked nook of Paris. Thankfully, when Baron Haussmann knocked down much of the Ile de la Cité in the 19th century, he spared this sector, still set with medieval mansions—lucky folk from the 15th-century including composer Pierre du Bellay; Ludwig Bemelmans, creator of the beloved *Madeleine*; and the Aga Khan once called these home—and winding alleys. Back in the Middle Ages this was the quarter where canons boarded students of the cathedral seminary, and one of these was the celebrated Peter Abelard (1079–1142)—questioner of the faith, philosopher, founder of the University of Paris, and scandalizer of the civilized world for his penchant for *les femmes*. Abelard came to this quarter to reside with Canon Fulbert to teach his niece, Héloïse, resulting in a love affair whose denouement—she became pregnant, he was castrated by the law (but survived to become a famous teacher)—is the stuff of legend. Their house, completely redone in the 19th century, stands at No. 10 rue Chanoinesse—a plaque commemorates the lovers on the quayside facade. In the Ancien Cloître there are no famous sights per se, so just follow your nose and explore its storybook streets. Although defaced by a modern police station and garage, the tiny warren of six streets still casts a spell, particularly at the intersection of rue des Ursins and rue des Chantres, where a lovely medieval palace, tiny flower garden, and quayside steps form a cul-de-sac where time seems to be holding its breath. ✉ *Rue du Cloître-Notre-Dame north to quai des Fleurs, Ile de la Cité* Ⓜ *Cité.*

Fodor'sChoice ★

13 **Arc du Carrousel.** Often the setting for fashion-magazine photo spreads, this small triumphal arch between the Louvre and the Tuileries was erected by Napoléon between 1806 and 1808. The four bronze horses on top were originally the famous gilded horses that Napoléon looted from Venice; when these were returned in 1815, Bosio designed four new ones harnessed to a chariot driven by a goddess symbolizing the Restoration (of the monarchy). Ⓜ *Palais-Royal.*

12 **Carrousel du Louvre.** Part of the early 1990s' Louvre renovation program, this subterranean shopping complex is centered on an inverted glass pyramid (overlooked by the regional Ile-de-France tourist office) and contains a wide array of stores, spaces for fashion shows (this is Paris, after all), an auditorium, and a huge parking garage. At lunchtime, museum goers rush to the mall-style food court where fast food goes international. Note that you can get into the museum, and avoid some lines, by entering through the mall. ✉ *Entrance on rue de Rivoli or by the Arc du Carrousel, Louvre/Tuileries* Ⓜ *Palais-Royal.*

need a break?

Avoid the throngs and the trashy fast food at the Carrousel du Louvre's food court and opt instead for the quiet comfort of **Le Fumoir** (☎ 01–42–92–00–24), a cozy, book-lined bar just across the street from the eastern exit of the Louvre. The crowd here is chic and cosmopolitan, drawn by the beautiful waitresses, racks of international newspapers, and some of the best hot chocolate in the city. For deeper appetites, hot dishes are served from noon until past midnight, and Sunday brunch is excellent.

7 **Conciergerie.** This is the famous prison in which dukes and duchesses, lords and ladies, and, most famously, Queen Marie-Antoinette were all imprisoned during the French Revolution before being carted off to the guillotine. By the end of the Reign of Terror (1793–95), countless others fell foul of the revolutionaries, including their own leaders Danton and

Robespierre. Originally part of the royal palace on the Ile de la Cité, the turreted medieval building still holds Marie-Antoinette's cell (with some objects connected with the ill-fated queen); a chapel, embellished with the initials M. A., occupies the true site of her confinement. Out of one of these windows, Toni (the queen's nickname) notoriously saw her best friend, the Comtesse de Lamballe—lover of the arts and daughter of the richest duke in France—torn to pieces by a wild mob, her dismembered limbs then displayed on pikes. Elsewhere are the courtyard and fountain where victims of the Terror spent their final days playing piquet, writing letters to their loved ones, and waiting for the dreaded climb up the staircase to the Chamber of the Revolutionary Council to hear its final verdict. You can also visit the guardroom, complete with hefty Gothic vaulting and intricately carved columns, and the monumental Salle des Gens d'Armes, whence a short corridor leads to the kitchen, with its four vast fireplaces. The building takes its name from the palace's *concierge,* or governor, whose considerable income was swollen by the privilege he enjoyed of renting out shops and workshops. ✉ *1 quai de l'Horloge, Louvre/Tuileries* ☎ *01–53–73–78–50* 🌐 *www.monum.fr* 🎫 *€5.50, joint ticket with Sainte-Chapelle €8* ⏲ *Apr.–Sept., daily 9:30–6:30; Oct.–Mar., daily 10–5* Ⓜ *Cité.*

19 **Grand Palais.** With its curved glass roof and florid Belle Epoque ornament, the Grand Palais is unmistakable when approached from either the Seine or the Champs-Élysées, and forms an attractive duo with the Petit Palais on the other side of avenue Winston-Churchill. Both these stone buildings, adorned with mosaics and sculpted friezes, were built for the world's fair of 1900, and, as with the Eiffel Tower, were not intended to remain as permanent additions to the city. But once they were up no one seemed inclined to take them down. Today the adjoining galleries play host to major exhibitions, but the giant iron-and-glass interior of the Grand Palais itself is closed for renovation until 2007, when it will reopen as a exhibition space for contemporary art. ✉ *Av. Winston-Churchill, Champs-Élysées* ☎ *01–44–13–17–17* 🌐 *www.rmn.fr/galeriesnationalesdugrandpalais* 🎫 *€11.10 10–1 (reservation only), €10 after 1* ⏲ *Daily 10–1 by reservation; Thurs.–Mon. 1–8, Wed. 1–10* Ⓜ *Champs-Élysées–Clemenceau.*

14 **Jardin des Tuileries** (Tuileries Gardens). Monet and Renoir captured this impressive garden—really more of a long park—with paint and brush, Left Bank songstresses warble about its beauty, and all Parisians know it as a charming place to stroll and survey the surrounding cityscape. The planting of the Tuileries—the name comes from an ancient clay pit formerly on this spot that supplied material for many of the tile roofs of Paris—is typically French: formal and neatly patterned, with statues, rows of trees, and gravel paths, often adorned with a string quartet or jugglers entertaining large crowds on weekends. No wonder the Impressionists liked this city park—note how the gray, austere light of Paris makes green trees look even greener. ✉ *Bordered by quai des Tuileries, pl. de la Concorde, rue de Rivoli, and the Louvre, Louvre/Tuileries* Ⓜ *Tuileries.*

need a break?

Stop off for a snack or lunch at **Dame Tartine** (☎ 01–47–03–94–84), one of the two designer brasseries erected in the Tuileries in the late 1990s (it's on the left as you arrive from place de la Concorde). With its glass-paneled walls and roof and light wood and aluminum accents, the restaurant is sober and airy. The cuisine is inventive and offers good value—try the lamb flan with tomato purée and a carafe of red Ventoux from the Rhône. You can also eat outdoors in the leafy shade.

Louvre

Egyptian Antiquities: **11, 21**
French Paintings:
14th–17th cent. **31**
18th–19th cent. **33**
19th cent. (large) **25, 34**
French Sculptures:
17th–18th cent. **1**
17th–19th cent. **7**
Middle Ages, Renaissance **6**
Greek, Etruscan and Roman Antiquities:
Bronzes and Precious Objects **23**
Ceramics and Terracotta **22**
Greek Antiquities **4, 12**
Etruscan and Roman Antiquities **13**
Venus de Milo **12**
Islamic and Asia Minor Antiquities:
Arab Antiquities **10**
Iranian Antiquities **9**
Islamic Art **2**
Mesopotamia **8**
Italian Paintings: **26**
Mona Lisa **27**
Italian Sculptures:
11th–15th cent. **5**
16th–19th cent. **14**
Michelangelo's The Dying Slave **14**
Medieval Louvre: **3**
Northern School Paintings:
Holland, Flanders, Germany **29**
Northern Sculptures:
17th–19th cent. **14**
Objets d'Art:
17th–18th cent. **18, 20**
Galerie d'Apollon (Crown Jewels) **24**
Middle Ages, Renaissance **17**
Napoléon III Apartments **15**
19th cent. **16, 19**
Prints and Drawings:
French 17th cent. **32**
Italian School **28**
Northern Schools **30**

11 Fodor's Choice ★ **Louvre.** Leonardo da Vinci's *Mona Lisa* and *Virgin and Saint Anne,* van Eyck's *Madonna of Chancellor Rolin,* Giorgione's *Concert Champêtre,* and Delacroix's *Liberty Guiding the People* . . . you get the picture. This is the world's greatest art museum—and the largest. In days of yore visitors would arrive at its front door, race along its miles of corridors—passing the *Venus de Milo,* the *Winged Victory,* and the *Mona Lisa*—and 40 minutes later collapse while exclaiming, "At last, we have seen the Louvre!" Today, of course, nearly everyone respects the fact that you don't go to the Louvre to speed past major milestones in civilization. Many thousands of treasures are newly cleaned and lighted, so plan on seeing it all—from the red brocaded Napoléon III salons to the fabled Egyptian collection, from the 186-carat Regent Diamond to the rooms crowded with Botticellis, Caravaggios, Poussins, and Géricaults. The Louvre is now a coherent, unified structure, and search parties no longer need to be sent in to find you and guide you out.

To get into the Louvre you may have to wait in two long lines: one outside the Pyramide entrance portal and another downstairs at the ticket booths. You can avoid the first by entering through the Carrousel du Louvre, but you often can't avoid the second. Your ticket will get you into any and all of the wings as many times as you like during one day. If you find the crowds too overwhelming, try coming around 4 PM on Monday or Wednesday when the Louvre has evening hours. This is when many day visitors are heading back to their hotels and evening visitors have yet to arrive. As enormous as the Louvre is, we've outlined a simple guide in the following pages that is broken up by location (wing, floor, collection, and room number). If you want a more exhaustively comprehensive guide, the museum bookstore sells—in addition to the general maps at the information desk—a plethora of books and leaflets in English.

The Louvre is much more than a museum—it is a saga that began centuries ago. Begun as a fortress by Philippe-Auguste in the 13th century, it was not until 300 years later, under François I, that today's Louvre began to take shape. Through the years, Henri IV (1589–1610), Louis XIII (1610–43), Louis XIV (1643–1715), Napoléon I (1804–14), and Napoléon III (1852–70) all contributed to its construction. Before rampaging revolutionaries burned part of it down during the bloody Paris Commune of 1871, the building was even larger. The open section facing the Tuileries Gardens was originally the Palais des Tuileries, the royal family's main Paris residence.

The uses to which the building has been put have been almost equally varied. Though Charles V (1364–80) made the Louvre his residence—parts of the original medieval fortress have been excavated and can be seen during your visit—later French kings preferred to live elsewhere, mainly in the Loire Valley. Even after François I decided to make the Louvre his permanent home, and accordingly embarked on an ambitious rebuilding program (most of which came to nothing), the Louvre never became more than a secondary palace.

The construction of the stately Cour Carrée (Square Court), mainly during the reign of Louis XIII, marked the beginning of the Louvre as you see it today. When a competition for architects to design a suitably imposing east facade was held in 1668, a young draftsman named Claude Perrault teamed up with the seasoned illustrator and painter Charles Le Brun to produce the winning proposal. You'd have thought its muscular rhythms would have wowed the Sun King, but he left the city for Versailles in 1682. Then, during the remainder of Louis's reign, the palace underwent a rapid decline. After the Revolution, however, a national assembly voted to turn part of the Louvre into a public museum. The galleries were stocked with nationalized art taken from the churches, the king, and other members of the French nobility, but the greatest boon to the collection came when a Corsican corporal measured his power by how much great art he could ransack from the rest of the world. Napoléon Bonaparte moved into the Louvre in 1800 as his armies were marching across Europe. They bravely captured the world's most famous treasures and brought them all back to the Louvre. With Napoléon's fall from grace, the new museum was forced in 1815 to return many of its works to the original owners. Napoléon's stay, however, did not prevent the three remaining French kings—Louis XVIII (1814–24), Charles X (1824–30), and Louis-Philippe (1830–48)—from making the Louvre their home. Fast-forward to the 20th century. During World War II the invading Germans looted the Louvre and used it as office space; a classical art buff, Hitler had the *Winged Victory of Samothrace* installed near his desk. Most of the stolen pieces were recovered after the Liberation, but no large-scale changes or innovations were made until François Mitterrand was elected President in 1981.

Reflecting Mitterrand's desire to make his mark on the city, he commissioned the design and construction of I. M. Pei's **Pyramide** (or glass pyramid) surrounded by three smaller pyramids in the Cour Napoléon. Unveiled in March 1989, it's more than just a grandiloquent gesture. The pyramid provided a new, and much needed, museum entrance; it also tops a large museum shop, café, and restaurant. Moreover, it acts as the originating point for the most celebrated city view in Europe, a majestic vista stretching through the Arc du Carrousel, the Tuileries Gardens, across place de la Concorde, up the Champs-Élysées to the towering Arc de Triomphe, and ending at the giant modern arch at La Défense, 4 km (2½ mi) farther west.

Among many other improvements is the entrance at the Porte des Lions, from quai des Tuileries overlooking the Seine. And thanks to the addition of the underground Carrousel du Louvre—a mall with upscale shops selling clothing, records, and other decidedly non-Louvre-related merchandise—there is even a massive fast-food court. Now you can get a Universal Burger before checking out David's *Coronation of Napoléon I* without ever having to go above ground. For more soigné dining, be sure to check out the museum's stylish Café Marly.

The quality and sheer variety of the Louvre's extraordinary collections are overwhelming. The number one attraction is Leonardo da Vinci's enigmatic *Mona Lisa.* While Leonardo's portrait may need some tracking down, this is not a bad thing: along the way you'll find the Louvre packed with legendary collections, divided into seven areas: Asian antiquities, Egyptian antiquities, Greek and Roman antiquities, sculpture, objets d'art, paintings, and prints and drawings. What follows is no more than a selection of favorites, chosen to act as key points for your exploration.

RICHELIEU WING

Below Ground and Ground Floor: As you enter the Richelieu Wing from the Pyramide, on the left and up a flight of stairs is a gallery that displays temporary exhibits comprised of the Louvre's most recent acquisitions in French sculpture. Straight ahead is **Salle 20** ("salle" is French for room) filled with more French sculpture, including frilly busts of members of the court of Louis XIV, but most people pass through this room to get to the dramatic Cour Marly to the west or Cour Puget to the east. The **Cour Marly** is filled with sculptures, many from the park at Marly commissioned by Louis XIV at the end of the 17th century to provide a lighthearted contrast to the pompous statuary at neighboring Versailles. The Cour Puget is named for the artist who created the sculpture at place des Victoires, now mostly reassembled in the lower court. Back to the southeast corner of Cour Marly, you will find **Salle 1** of French sculpture. In **Salle 2** are fragments of Romanesque chapels from Cluny, the powerful abbey in Burgundy that dominated French Catholicism in the 11th century. In **Salles 4–6** you can see the refinement of sculpture encouraged by the wealthy communities in the Ile-de-France. The funerary art of **Salles 7–10** ranges from spooky to risible. The late-15th-century tomb of Philippe Pot in **Salle 10** is especially eerie: you see Philippe stretched out in eternal prayer, held aloft by eight black-robed pallbearers. Walking through **Salles 11–19,** you can see how the piety and stiffness of medieval French sculpture began to give way to the more natural style of the Italian Renaissance.

To the north of the Cour Puget are **Salles 25–33,** filled with the products of the Académie Royale, the art school of 18th-century France. The smaller works in **Salle 25** are all qualification pieces for the Académie—once admitted into the school based on previous works, the student was asked to produce a sculpture as proof of continuing worth. To the east of the Cour Puget is the start of the Louvre's **Oriental Antiquities** collection. Within the glass case of **Salle 1** are many ancient Mesopotamian carvings, including a 2-inch Neolithic figure dating from the 6th millennium BC. Facing the case are the pieced-together fragments of the 3rd-millennium BC Stela of the Vultures, containing the oldest known written history, including images of King Eannatum catching his enemies in a net. Farther along, **Salle 1b** has countless examples of the wide-eyed alabaster statues produced by the Sumerians during the 3rd millennium BC. The centerpiece of **Salle 3** is the "Codex of Hammurabi," an 18th-century BC diorite stela containing the world's oldest written code of laws. Near the top of the text you can see Hammurabi, king of the first Babylonian dynasty, meeting a seated Shamash, the god of justice. On the east side of Salle 3 is a bas-relief lion in glazed terra-cotta tiles, one of numerous such beasts from the 6th-century BC Gates of Babylon.

Salle 4 is the Cour Khorsabad, a re-creation of the temple erected by the Assyrian king Sargon II in the 8th century BC at the palace of Dur-Sharrukin. Walking among the temple's five massive, winged bulls known as *lamassu,* or benign demigods, is one of the most spectacular experiences in the Louvre, even though only three of the bulls and almost none of the reerected reliefs are authentic. The originals were lost on a frigate that sank.

First Floor: Restored rooms from the royal apartments of Napoléon III fill the southwest of the first floor of the Richelieu Wing. Salle 79 is the most spectacular; the corner reception room, decorated for Napoléon III's secretary of state, gives you a good idea of the eye-popping luxury of the Second Empire.

Second Floor: Just to the east of the escalators is **Salle 1,** which begins the section devoted to French and Northern School paintings. At the entrance to this room is a single 14th-century gold-backed painting of John the Good—the oldest known individual portrait from north of Italy. In **Salle 4** is *The Madonna of Chancellor Rolin,* by the 15th-century Early Netherlandish master Jan van Eyck. The first artist to use oil paints extensively, van Eyck defined what became known as the "northern style," characterized by a light source illuminating one area on an otherwise dark background. You almost need a microscope to drink in all the detail in this painting, which ranks as one of the top 10 paintings in the Louvre collection. One of the first self-portraits ever painted—a disheveled offering by Albrecht Dürer (1471–1528)—hangs in **Salle 8.** Walking through **Salles 9–17,** you can see how the Dutch developed a fluid and comfortable representation of the body while playing with the shiny, dark palette of oil paints.

The most dramatic gallery in this section is **Salle 18,** where a cycle of giant matching canvases by Peter Paul Rubens (1577–1640) recounts Maria de' Medici's journey from Florence to Paris—an overbearing immortalization of a relatively cushy trip. The swirling Baroque paintings were commissioned by Maria herself and originally hung in the nearby Palais du Luxembourg). The riveting *Disembarkation of Maria de' Medici at the Port of Marseille* memorably portrays an artificially slimmed-down Maria about to skip over the roly-poly daughters of Poseidon as a personified France beckons her to shore. In **Salle 31** are several paintings by Rembrandt van Rijn (1606–69). In his 1648 *Supper at Emmaus,* he challenges many painting conventions, such as centering the subject and delineating objects with bold brush strokes. The masterpiece of the Dutch collection is *The Lacemaker,* by Jan Vermeer (1632–75), in **Salle 38.** Obsessed with optical accuracy, Vermeer painted the red thread in the foreground as a slightly blurred jumble, just as one would actually see it if focusing on the girl.

SULLY WING

The entrance into the Sully Wing is more impressive than the entrances to the others—you get to walk around and through the foundations and moat of the castle built by Philippe-Auguste in the 13th century and expanded by Charles V in the 14th with a series of Cinderella-like towers and moats.

Ground Floor: The northern galleries of the Sully are a continuation of the ancient **Iranian collection** started on the ground floor of the Richelieu Wing. **Salle 12,** housing the Greek, Etruscan, and Roman collections, is also home to the famous 2nd-century BC *Venus de Milo.* The armless statue, one of the most reproduced and recognizable works of art in the world, is actually as beautiful as they say—it is worth your trouble to push past the lecturing curators and tourist groups to get a closer look at the incredible skill with which the Greeks turned cold marble into something vibrant and graceful. Oddly enough, her face is strikingly like the *Mona Lisa*'s, with an additional mystery being the original form of her missing arms—were they holding a mirror or a net? In the 19th century the Venus was dug up on the Greek island of Milos, then sold for 6,000 francs to the French ambassador in Constantinople, who presented her to King Louis XVIII. **Salles 13–17** are filled with all kinds of statuary: funerary stelae, body fragments, architectural details.

First Floor: The northern galleries of the first floor continue with the **objets d'art collection** started in the Richelieu Wing, picking up at the 17th century and continuing through the Revolution to the Restoration.

Second Floor: Sully picks up French painting where the Richelieu Wing leaves off, somewhere around the 17th century. At this point, a conscious battle was under way in French art between the northern style (epitomized by magical, candlelit canvases of Georges de La Tour and the more impassive Le Nain brothers and centered on the work of the Dutch) and the southern one (headed by Poussin, and coming from Florence, Venice, and Rome). The result was a blending of northern style and method (darkly painted interiors and oil paints) with southern subjects and technique (ruined landscapes and single-point perspective). Charles Le Brun (1619–90), Louis XIV's principal adviser on the arts and the man who designed many of the greatest salons at Versailles, painted massive "history paintings" jam-packed with excruciating details from biblical, historical, or mythological stories. Displayed in **Salle 32** are the four colossal canvases of his late-17th-century *Story of Alexander,* with a powerful view of the trials of the emperor (and no small reference to Louis XIV).

An academic painter of a different genre was Antoine Watteau (1684–1721), long considered the greatest French painter of the 18th century. In scenes such as his 1717 *Pilgrimage to the Island of Cythera* in **Salle 36,** he depicted in wispy pastel brush strokes the bucolic and often frivolous lifestyle of the Baroque-age court set, here depicted arriving on (or departing from) Cythera, the mythological isle of love. Here he concentrates on creating an equally poetic mood, but there is an extra layer of emotion: the gallant gentlemen and courtly women seem drugged by the pleasures about to be enjoyed but disturbingly aware of their transitory nature, too. Maurice Quentin de La Tour (1704–88) was another favorite court painter; his 1755 *Marquise de Pompadour* in **Salle 45** captures the leading fashion plate of Louis XV's court. Madame de Pompadour, mistress to the king, is shown with everything a good courtesan should have: books, music manuscripts, engravings, fine clothing, and, of course, pale skin.

One revolution and two republics after the court painters of the 17th and 18th centuries, the Académie continued to define Good Taste. In **Salle 60** you can see the paintings of Jean-Auguste Ingres (1780–1867), which depict the exotic themes popular in the Age of Empires. His 1862 *Turkish Bath* portrays an orgy of steamy women who look anything but Turkish. One of these ladies was the subject of his *La Grande Odalisque*; here, exoticism and the French classical tradition gel to produce a strikingly elegant image.

DENON WING

Below Ground: To the south and east of the Pyramide entrance are galleries displaying Italian sculpture from the early Renaissance, including a 15th-century *Madonna and Child* by the Florentine Donatello (1386–1466).

Ground Level: In the former imperial stables (**Salle 4**) you can see the 1513–15 *Slaves* of Michelangelo. After carefully selecting his slab of marble, Michelangelo (1475–1564) would spend days envisioning the form of the sculpture within the uncut stone. The sculptures that finally emerged openly eroticized the male body. The fact that many were left "unfinished" (i.e., parts of the marble were left rough, making it look as if the sculptures were trying to free themselves from the stone blocks) was controversial at first, but the style was to inspire Rodin and other modern artists.

To the east of the Italian sculpture collection are the galleries containing the sculptures of the **Greek, Etruscan,** and **Roman periods.** In **Salle 18** is the 6th-century BC *Etruscan Sarcophagus* from Cerveteri, showing a married couple pieced together from thousands of clay fragments.

First Floor: Stretching out from a tiny entry next to the Sully Wing is the **Galerie d'Apollon,** a 17th-century hall decorated by the painter Charles Le Brun (who immortalized himself in one of the portraits on the wall) that now holds what remains of France's **Crown Jewels.** Around the corner from the jewels, the sublime *Winged Victory of Samothrace* stands regally, if headless, at the top landing of the grand **Escalier Daru.** The spectacular 3rd-century BC statue was found on a tiny Greek island in the northern Aegean. Depicted in the act of descending from Olympus, the *Winged Victory,* or *Nike,* to use the ancient Greek name, originally came from the isle of Samothrace and was carved by an unknown master in 305 BC to commemorate the naval victory of Demetrius Poliorcetes over the Turks.

The **Italian painting** collection begins at the western end of the Denon Wing. The paintings in **Salle 6** (also known as the Salle des États) are large-scale canvases from the 16th-century Venetian School. Dominating the room is the massive 1562 *Feast at Cana* by Veronese (1528–88), a sumptuous scene (restored in the 1980s) centered on Jesus's turning water into wine. When painted, it was considered scandalous to adorn the holy story with so much contemporary dress and fashionable 16th-century detail, so the painter was obliged to rename the painting *Feast in the House of Levi.*

And now for the Most Famous Painting in the World: the *Mona Lisa* (also known as *La Gioconda,* or *La Joconde* to the French), painted by Leonardo da Vinci (1452–1519) in 1503–06. As the portrait of the wife of one Francesco del Giocondo, a 15th-century Florentine millionaire, Leonardo's masterpiece is now believed by some historians to have been painted as a memorial after the lady's death. To those who recall Théophile Gautier's words "a sphinx of beauty," the portrait is a bit of a disappointment. The picture is smaller than you might expect and kept behind protective glass; it is invariably surrounded by a crowd of worshipers intent on studying her enigmatic expression (or is it she who is studying them?). Once you get in front of the videotaping tourists, you, too, may find yourself asking "Is this it?" when faced with this 2½- by 1¾-ft painting of an eyebrow-less woman with yellowing skin and an annoyingly smug smile. In fact, most art historians award the beauty prize instead to Leonardo's *Virgin and St. Anne,* hanging nearby. Here in this room, you'll find other legendary works of the High Renaissance, including Raphael's *La Belle Jardiniére.*

The 1458 *Calvary* in **Salle 8,** painted by Andrea Mantegna (1431–1506), a follower of the Florentine architect Brunelleschi's treatises on perspective, is one of the first paintings ever with a vanishing point. Although equally renowned during his lifetime as an anatomist and inventor, Leonardo da Vinci was originally trained as a painter. His breathtaking 1483 *Virgin of the Rocks* has an interesting sense of spatial relationships—the four figures create the four corners of a pyramid, while their glances and gestures keep all activity contained within this form.

Behind the *Feast at Cana* are two passages leading to **Salles 75–77,** home to great epic-scale canvases produced in Paris during the 19th century. When official court painter Louis David (1748–1825) produced the *Coronation of Napoléon* on December 2, 1804, now hanging in Salle 75, he wisely decided not to capture the moment when Napoléon snatched the crown from the hands of Pope Pius VII to place it upon his own head—choosing instead to paint the new emperor turning to crown Josephine.

Also in Salle 75 hang two of the most famous works in the history of French painting: the 1819 *Raft of the Medusa* by Théodore Géricault (1791–1824) and the 1830 *Liberty Leading the People* by Eugène Delacroix (1798–1863). Géricault's epic work conveys a gloomily Romantic view of the human state, nightmarish despite its heroism and grand scale. Painted when Géricault was only 27 years old, it was inspired by the real-life story of the wreck of a French merchant ship: the captain lost control, the ship was without lifeboats or supplies, and ultimately the survivors resorted to cannibalism. The painting caused a stir with the government, which took offense at the stab made at the inefficiency of authority. The Académie was aghast for formal reasons: the painting had no central subject, no hero, no resolution. The survivors are a mess of living and dead bodies jumbled in and out of ominous, sickly green shadows.

Even though Delacroix wasn't directly involved in the "Trois Glorieuses"—a three-day revolution in 1830 that ousted Charles X's autocracy and brought in a parliamentary monarchy with Louis-Philippe as king—he was compelled to paint *Liberty* to commemorate the Parisians who attempted to restore the Republic. Once again, it is an unorthodox subject for a painting: poorly armed bourgeoisie and pugnacious street urchins step over the dead bodies of comrades and slay other French folk in the name of an ultimately short-lived government. The allegorical figure of Liberty is quite a character: she is shown walking barefoot over barricades, her peasant dress falling away from her breasts, the tricolore (French flag) held aloft with one well-muscled limb while the other grips a rifle.

The above highlights of the Louvre collection are simply the merest tip of the iceberg. You'll also find walls virtually wallpapered with masterpieces by Fra Angelico, Botticelli, Holbein, Hals, Brueghel, El Greco, Murillo, Boucher, Goya, and Caravaggio—whose *Death of the Virgin* towers over La Grande Galerie—just to mention a few of the famous names, along with one-hit wonders like Enguerrand Quarton's magnificent 15th-century *Pietà*. Other collections here will delight connoisseurs, such as the examples of French furniture—the grandiose 17th- and 18th-century productions of Boulle and Riesener, marvels of intricate craftsmanship and elegant luxury, are prized by those with a fondness for opulent decoration.

Admission is often charged for a full calendar of other art-related events at the museum. Lectures take place in the Louvre Auditorium; the films there showcase everything from silent works to the history of art in Paris. A smattering of films, lectures, concerts, and exhibits is included in what's called Les Midis du Louvre. For recorded information in five languages (French, English, Spanish, German, and Italian), call 01–40–21–51–51 (press 2 for English). Be sure to pick up the free three-month schedule of events called *Louvre* at the information desk under the Pyramide, or look at the TV monitors behind the desk.

If you have time for only one visit, these selections give you an idea of the riches of the museum. But try to make repeat visits—the Louvre is one-third cheaper on Sunday (free the first Sunday of each month) and after 3 PM on other days. (Unless you plan to go to a number of museums every day, the one-, three-, and five-day tourist museum passes probably aren't worth your money, since you could easily spend a whole day at the Louvre alone.) Study the plans at the entrance to get your bearings and pick up a map to take with you. ✉ *Palais du Louvre, Louvre/Tuileries (it's faster to enter through the Carrousel du Louvre mall on rue de Rivoli than through the pyramid)* ☎ *01–40–20–51–51 information* 🌐 *www.louvre.fr* 🎫 *€10, €8 after 3 PM and all day Sun., free 1st Sun. of month, €5 for Napoléon Hall exhibitions* ⏲ *Thurs.–Sun. 9–6, Mon. and Wed. 9 AM–9:45 PM. Some sections open limited days* Ⓜ *Palais-Royal.*

⓯ **Musée du Jeu de Paume.** Renovations transformed this museum, at the entrance to the Tuileries Gardens, into an ultramodern, white-walled showcase for excellent temporary exhibits of bold contemporary art. The building was once used for *jeu de paume* (literally, "palm game"—a forerunner of tennis). Starting in late 2004, the museum is scheduled to incorporate the collections of the Centre National de la Photographie and show only photography, video, and multimedia exhibitions. ✉ *1 pl. de* *la Concorde, Louvre/Tuileries* ☎ *01–42–60–69–69* € *5.80* ⏲ *Tues. noon–9:30, Wed.–Fri. noon–7, weekends 10–7* Ⓜ *Concorde.*

16 **Musée de l'Orangerie.** Set to open in fall 2004 after years of renovation, this museum is most famous as the home of several of Claude Monet's largest *Water Lilies* canvases. Set in the Tuileries Gardens, the museum also has a noted selection of early 20th-century paintings, with works by Renoir, Cézanne, Matisse, and Marie Laurencin, among other masters. ✉ *Pl. de la Concorde, Louvre/Tuileries* ☎ *01–42–97–48–16* €6 Ⓜ *Concorde.*

1 **Notre-Dame.** Looming above place du Parvis on the Ile de la Cité is the Cathédrale de Notre-Dame, the most enduring symbol of Paris. Begun in 1163, completed in 1345, badly damaged during the Revolution, and restored by Viollet-le-Duc in the 19th century, Notre-Dame may not be France's oldest or largest cathedral, but in terms of beauty and architectural harmony it has few peers—as you can see by studying the facade from the open square. The doorways seem like hands joined in prayer, the sculpted kings form a noble procession, and the rose windows gleam with what seems like divine light. Above, the gallery breaks the lines of the stone vaults and, between the two high towers, the spire soars above the transept crossing. Seen from the front, the cathedral gives an impression of strength, dignity, and majestic serenity; seen from the Pont de l'Archevêché, it has all the proud grace of a seagoing vessel, the cross on its steeple borne like the flag on a tall mast.

Fodor's Choice ★

An army of stonemasons, carpenters, and sculptors arrived in 1163, working on a site that had previously seen a Roman temple, an early Christian basilica, and a Romanesque church. The chancel and altar were consecrated in 1182, but the magnificent sculptures surrounding the main doors were not put into position until 1240. The north tower was finished 10 years later. If both towers seem to some a bit top-heavy, that's because two needlelike spires were originally conceived to top them but were never built. If you look carefully, you will see that the tower on the left is wider than the one on the right.

Despite various changes in the 17th century, the cathedral remained substantially unaltered until the French Revolution, when it was transformed into a Temple of Reason—busts of Voltaire and Rousseau replaced those of saints. The statues of the kings of Israel were hacked down by the mob, chiefly because they were thought to represent the despised royal line of France, and everything inside and out that was deemed "anti-Republican" was stripped away. An interesting postscript to this destruction occurred in 1977, when some of the heads of these statues were discovered salted away in a bank vault on boulevard Haussmann. They'd apparently been hidden there by an ardent royalist who owned the small mansion that now forms part of the bank. (The restored heads are now on display in the Musée National du Moyen-Age.)

By the early 19th century the excesses of the Revolution were over, and the cathedral went back to fulfilling its religious functions. Napoléon crowned himself emperor here in May 1804 (David's heroic painting of the lavish ceremony can be seen in the Louvre)—you can stand on the step where he stood when he crowned Josephine. Full-scale restoration started in the middle of the century, the most conspicuous result of which was the reconstruction of the spire. It was then, too, that Haussmann demolished the warren of little buildings in front of the cathedral, creating place du Parvis.

The facade divides neatly into three levels. At the first-floor level are the three main entrances, or portals: the Portal of the Virgin on the left, the Portal of the Last Judgment in the center, and the Portal of St. Anne on the right. All three are surmounted by magnificent carvings—most of them 19th-century copies of the originals—of figures, foliage, and biblical scenes. Above these are the restored statues of the kings of Israel, the Galerie des Rois. Above the gallery is the great rose window and, above that, the Grand Galerie, at the base of the twin towers. The south tower houses the great bell of Notre-Dame, as tolled by Quasimodo, Victor Hugo's fictional hunchback. The 387-step climb to the top of the towers (use the separate entrance to the left of the facade as you face it) is worth the effort for a close-up of the famous gargoyles—most of them added in the 19th century—and the expansive view of the city. Unfortunately, some of those views are now ruined by safety railings.

As you enter by the Portal of the Virgin, the faith of the early builders permeates all, and the miracle of the quiet, persuasive interior provides an apt contrast to the triumphant glory of the exterior, with the soft glow of the stained-glass windows replacing the statues of saints, virgins, prophets, and apostles. The best time to visit is early in the morning, when the cathedral is at its brightest and least crowded. At the entrance are the massive 12th-century columns supporting the twin towers. Look down the nave to the transepts—the arms of the church—where, at the south (right) entrance to the chancel, you'll glimpse the haunting 12th-century statue of Notre-Dame de Paris, *Our Lady of Paris*. The chancel itself owes parts of its decoration to a vow taken by Louis XIII in 1638. Still without an heir after 23 years of marriage, he promised to dedicate the entire country to the Virgin Mary if his queen produced a son. When this miraculous event came to pass, Louis set about redecorating the chancel and choir. On the south side of the chancel is the **Trésor** (treasury), with a collection of garments, reliquaries, and silver and gold plate.

Under the square in front of the cathedral is the **Crypte Archéologique,** Notre-Dame's archaeological museum. It contains remains of previous churches on the site, scale models charting the district's development, and relics and artifacts dating from the Parisii, who lived here 2,000 years ago, unearthed during excavations in the 1960s. Slides and models detail the history of the Ile de la Cité. The foundations of the 3rd-century Gallo-Roman rampart and of the 6th-century Merovingian church can also be seen.

3 If your interest in the cathedral is not yet sated, duck into the **Musée de Notre-Dame** (✉ 10 rue du Cloître-Notre-Dame, Ile de la Cité), across the street opposite the North Door. The museum's paintings, engravings, medallions, and other objects and documents chart the history of the Cathedral of Notre-Dame. ✉ *Pl. du Parvis, Ile de la Cité* ☎ *01–44–32–16–72* 🌐 *www.monum.fr* 🎫 *Cathedral free, towers €5.50, crypt €3.50, treasury €2.50, museum €2.50* ⏲ *Cathedral daily 8–7. Towers Apr.–Sept., daily 9:30–7:30; Oct.–Mar., daily 10–5. Treasury Mon.–Sat. 9:30–11:30 and 1–5:30. Crypt Tues.–Sun. 10–6. Museum Wed. and weekends 2:30–6* Ⓜ *Cité.*

20 **Palais de la Découverte** (Palace of Discovery). A planetarium, working models, and scientific and technological exhibits on such topics as optics, biology, nuclear physics, and electricity make up this science museum behind the Grand Palais. ✉ *Av. Franklin-D.-Roosevelt, Champs-Élysées* ☎ *01–56–43–20–21* 🌐 *www.palais-decouverte.fr* 🎫 *€5.60, €3.10 extra for planetarium* ⏲ *Tues.–Sat. 9:30–6, Sun. 10–7* Ⓜ *Champs-Élysées–Clemenceau.*

5 **Palais de Justice** (Law Courts). The city's courts were built by Baron Haussmann in his characteristically weighty neoclassical style in about 1860. You can wander around the buildings, watch the bustle of the lawyers, or attend a court hearing. The solidity of Haussmann's buildings seems to emphasize the finesse of two important sights enclosed within the complex spared by Haussmann: La Conciergerie and Sainte-Chapelle. ✉ *Bd. du Palais, Ile de la Cité* ⏲ *Mon.–Sat. 8–6* Ⓜ *Cité.*

18 **Petit Palais.** The smaller counterpart to the Grand Palais, just off the Champs-Élysées, usually presents a permanent collection of French painting and furniture, with splendid canvases by Courbet and Bouguereau, but is closed for restoration until January 2005. You can, however, still admire the two fine statues that flank the building: French World War I hero Georges Clemenceau, facing the Champs-Élysées; and Jean Cardot's resolute image of Winston Churchill, facing the Seine. ✉ *Av. Winston-Churchill, Champs-Élysées* ☎ *01–42–65–12–73* 🌐 *paris-france.org/musees* Ⓜ *Champs-Élysées–Clemenceau.*

17 **Place de la Concorde.** This majestic square at the foot of the Champs-Élysées is undoubtedly one of the most balanced and harmoniously beautiful spaces in the world. Originally consecrated to the glory of Louis XV, it was laid out in the 1770s, but there was nothing in the way of peace or concord about its early years, for it was here that his successor, Louis XVI, and Marie-Antoinette were guillotined, along with more than 2,000 other people between 1793 and 1795. And it was here that Madame Roland cried, "Liberty, what crimes are committed in thy name." When the blood of the victims had been washed away and the yells of the *sans culottes* political extremists had died down, the square was renamed Concorde and, in place of a statue of Louis XV, another monument, freer of political significance, was erected in 1833: a 107-ft obelisk, originally quarried in the 8th century BC, and a present from the viceroy of Egypt (its gilded cap was restored in 1998). Among the handsome, symmetrical 18th-century buildings facing the square is the deluxe Hôtel Crillon, originally built by Gabriel—architect of the Petit Trianon—as an 18th-century home for three of France's wealthiest families. At the near end of high-walled rue Royale is the legendary Maxim's restaurant, but unless you choose to eat here, you won't be able to see the riot of crimson velvets and florid Art Nouveau furniture inside. Ⓜ *Concorde.*

8 **Place Dauphine.** The Surrealists loved place Dauphine, which they called "le sexe de Paris" because of its location—at the western tail end of the Ile de la Cité—and suggestive V shape. Its origins were much more proper: built by Henri IV, the king named the place in homage to his successor, the Dauphin, who grew up to become Louis XIII. The triangular place is lined with some 17th-century houses which the writer André Maurois felt represented the very quintessence of Paris and France. Take a seat on the park bench, enjoy a picnic, and see if you agree. Ⓜ *Cité.*

21 **Pont Alexandre-III.** No other bridge over the Seine epitomizes the fin-de-siècle frivolity of the Belle Epoque (or Paris itself) like the exuberant, bronze lamp–lined Pont Alexandre-III. An urban masterstroke that seems as much created of cake frosting and sugar sculptures as of stone and iron, it makes an alluring backdrop for fashion shoots and the surrounding Parisian landmarks. The bridge was built, like the Grand and Petit Palais nearby, for the 1900 world's fair; it was inaugurated by the visiting Russian czar, the ill-fated Nicholas II, and ingratiatingly named in honor of his father. Ⓜ *Invalides.*

10 **Pont Neuf** (New Bridge). Crossing the Ile de la Cité, just behind square du Vert-Galant, is the oldest bridge in Paris, confusingly called the New

Bridge. It was completed in 1607 and was the first bridge in the city to be built without houses lining either side because, so some historians believe, Henri IV wanted a clear view of Notre-Dame from his windows at the Louvre. It's a romantic spot to take in a view of Seine. *Pont Neuf*

6 **Sainte-Chapelle** (Holy Chapel). One of the supremely dazzling achievements of the Middle Ages, a Gothic jewel, and home to the most ancient stained-glass windows in Paris, this chapel was built by the pious Louis IX (1226–70), whose good works ensured his subsequent canonization. Constructed in less than three years, it was conceived as an enormous reliquary—a receptacle for what Louis believed to be the crown of thorns from Christ's crucifixion and fragments of the true cross, acquired from the impoverished Emperor Baldwin of Constantinople at phenomenal expense.

Fodor's Choice ★

The building is actually two chapels in one. The plainer first-floor chapel, made gloomy by insensitive mid-19th-century restorations (which could do with restoration themselves), was for servants and lowly members of the court. The infinitely more spectacular upper chapel, up a dark spiral staircase, was reserved for the king and important members of the court. The chapel walls (if you can call them that) consist mainly of stained glass and constitute a technical tour de force. Here, again, some clumsy 19th-century work has added a deadening touch, but the glory of the chapel—the stained glass—is magically intact. The chapel is airy and diaphanous, the walls glowing and sparkling as light plays on the windows. Notice how the walls, in fact, consist of at least twice as much glass as masonry: the entire aim of the architects was to provide the maximum amount of window space.

Architecturally, for all its delicate and ornate exterior decoration—notice the open latticework of the pencil-like *flèche,* or spire, on the roof—the design of the building is simplicity itself. In essence it's no more than a thin, rectangular box, much taller than it is wide. But think of it first and foremost as an enormous magic lantern, illuminating 1,130 figures from the Bible, to create—as one writer poetically put it—"the most marvelous colored and moving air ever held within four walls." Come early in the day to avoid the crowds—better still, try to attend one of the regular, candlelit concerts. ✉ *4 bd. du Palais, Ile de la Cité* ☎ *01–43–54–30–09 concert information* 🌐 *www.monum.fr* 🎫 *€5.50, joint ticket with Conciergerie €8* ⏲ *Apr.–Sept., daily 9:30–6:30; Oct.–Mar., daily 10–5* Ⓜ *Cité.*

4 **Square Jean-XXIII.** When it comes to views of Notre-Dame, no visit to the great cathedral is complete without a riverside walk past the cathedral through Square Jean-XXIII. It offers a breathtaking sight of the east end of the cathedral, ringed by flying buttresses and surmounted by the spire. From here the building seems to float above the Seine like some vast stone ship. Ⓜ *Cité.*

9 **Square du Vert-Galant.** The equestrian statue of the Vert Galant himself—amorous adventurer Henri IV—surveys this leafy square at the western end of the Ile de la Cité. Henri, king of France from 1589 until his assassination in 1610, was something of a dashing figure, by turns ruthless and charming, a stern upholder of the absolute rights of monarchy, and a notorious womanizer. He is probably best remembered for his cynical remark that "*Paris vaut bien une messe*" ("Paris is worth a mass"), a reference to his readiness to renounce Protestantism to gain the throne of predominantly Catholic France and, indeed, be allowed to enter the city. To ease his conscience he issued the Edict of Nantes in 1598, according French Protestants (almost) equal rights with their Catholic counterparts. It was Louis XIV's revocation of the edict nearly 100 years later that led

to the massive Huguenot exodus from France—an economic catastrophe for the country. The square itself is a fine spot to linger on a sunny afternoon and is the departure point for the glass-topped Vedette tour boats on the Seine (at the bottom of the steps to the right). *Pont Neuf*

FROM THE EIFFEL TOWER TO THE ARC DE TRIOMPHE

The Eiffel Tower lords over southwest Paris, and from nearly wherever you are on this walk you can see it looming. For years many Parisians felt the Tour Eiffel was an iron eyesore and compared it to a giraffe, a giraffe that weighed 15 million pounds and whose head rose 1,000 ft high. Then gradually the tower became part of the Parisian landscape and entered the hearts and souls of Parisians and visitors alike. Thanks to its stunning nighttime illumination, topped by four 6,000-watt projectors creating a lighthouse beacon visible for 80 km (50 mi) around, it continues to make Paris live up to its moniker *La Ville Lumière*—the City of Light.

Water is the second theme of this walk: fountains playing beneath place du Trocadéro; tours along the Seine on the Bateaux Mouches; and an underground prowl through the city's sewers, if you can stand it. Museums are the third; the area around Trocadéro is full of them. Military grandeur is the fourth; the Arc de Triomphe is Napoléon's most eye-popping legacy to Paris (the young general often surveyed his troops on the Champ de Mars, near the start of this walk). The arch stands foursquare at the top of the city's most famous avenue: the Champs-Élysées. This grand boulevard is the last leg of the Tour de France bicycle race on the third or fourth Sunday in July, and the site of vast ceremonies on Bastille Day (July 14) and Armistice Day (November 11). Its trees are often decked with the French tricolore and foreign flags to mark visits from heads of state.

Explore its commercial upper half (its verdant lower section, sloping down gracefully to place de la Concorde, the Tuileries Gardens, and the Louvre is covered in the first walking tour). Local charm is not a plus of this grand sector of western Paris. The French moan that it is losing its character and, as you notice the number of fast-food joints, you'll know what they mean—though renovation has gone some way to restoring the avenue's legendary elegance. For a real dose of high style, head to nearby avenue Montaigne, the address of some of the top names in world fashion.

Numbers in the text correspond to numbers in the margin and on the Eiffel Tower to Arc de Triomphe map.

a good walk

Graced by the stately facade of the **École Militaire** 1 ⚑, the verdant expanse of the **Champ de Mars** 2—once used as a parade ground and then as site of the world exhibitions—provides a thrilling approach to the iron symbol of Paris: the **Tour Eiffel** 3. As you get nearer, the Eiffel Tower's colossal bulk (it's far bigger and sturdier than pictures suggest) becomes spectacularly evident. (If you want to skip this walk through the parade grounds, just take the RER directly to Champ de Mars for the Eiffel Tower.)

Across the Seine from the Eiffel Tower, above stylish gardens and fountains on the heights of the Trocadéro, is the Art Deco **Palais de Chaillot** 4, a cultural center containing three museums. Pause on the piazza, lined by gold statues, to admire the view of the Eiffel Tower. The south wing of the Palais, to your left as you arrive from the Seine, houses the

Musée de l'Homme 5, an anthropology museum, and the **Musée de la Marine** 6, a maritime museum. The right wing was badly damaged by fire in 1997, and its **Musée des Monuments Français** 7, with copies of statues, columns, and archways from throughout France, is undergoing renovation and will reopen in 2005, when it will share space with the Institut Français d'Architecture.

From the Palais head right down avenue du Président-Wilson, with its street lamps designed by Frank Lloyd Wright. On the next block down on your right, surrounded most days by no fewer than nine French tricolore flags, is another Art Deco building fronted by a rotunda lined with mosaics and alternating pinkish beige and pebble-dash concrete: the Conseil Economique et Social (Economic and Social Council). Echoing it across place d'Iéna is another, slightly older rotunda, topped by a pineapple—the **Musée Guimet** 8, with its extensive collection of Indo-Chinese and Far Eastern art. Farther down avenue du Président-Wilson, the equally pompous architecture of the **Palais Galliéra** 9, an exhibition hall for displays of clothing design and fashion, squares up to the cool gray outlines of the 1930s **Musée d'Art Moderne de la Ville de Paris** 10, a venue for temporary exhibits as well as the city's high-powered collection of modern art. Directly next door is the **Palais de Tokyo** 11, a vestige of the 1930 Universal Exposition which, after being derelict for more than a decade, reopened in 2002 as an ultrahip contemporary art center.

Continue down to place de l'Alma, where a giant golden torch appears to be saluting the memory of Diana, Princess of Wales, who died in a car crash in the tunnel below in 1997. Across the **Pont de l'Alma** 12 (to the left) is the entrance to **Les Égouts** 13, Paris's sewers. If you prefer a less malodorous tour of the city, stay on the Right Bank and head down the sloping side road to the left of the bridge to the embarkation point of the **Bateaux Mouches** 14 (motorboats) and their tours of Paris by water.

From place de l'Alma head up the grand thoroughfare of avenue Montaigne, one of the leading showcases for the great haute-couture houses such as Dior, Chanel, Nina Ricci, Valentino, Prada, and Dolce & Gabbana. After some world-class window-shopping, continue on to the Rond-Point des Champs-Élysées, the main traffic nexus of Paris's most famous avenue, and turn left up the **Champs-Élysées** 15. At No. 116 is the famous **Lido** 16 nightclub, opposite the venerable Le Fouquet's restaurant-café, once frequented by Orson Welles and James Joyce. Stop in at the **Office de Tourisme de la Ville de Paris** 17 (the main city Tourist Office) at No. 127, on the left-hand side of the avenue. Continue up to the top of the avenue and place Charles-de-Gaulle, known to Parisians as L'Étoile, or the Star—a reference to the streets that fan out from it—and site of the colossal, 164-ft **Arc de Triomphe** 18. L'Étoile is Europe's most chaotic traffic circle: short of attempting a death-defying dash, your only way of getting to the Arc de Triomphe in the middle is to take an underground passage from the top right of avenue des Champs-Élysées. The view from the top of the Arc de Triomphe reveals the star effect of the 12 radiating avenues and enables you to admire the vista down the Champs-Élysées toward place de la Concorde and the distant Louvre. West of the Champs-Élysées, and visible from the Arc de Triomphe, are the verdant Bois de Boulogne; the posh suburb of Neuilly; and the towering office buildings and ultramodern arch of La Défense. (The Charles-de-Gaulle–Étoile métro and RER station, which sprawls underground beneath L'Étoile, provides quick access to the western suburbs if you want to make the excursion now.)

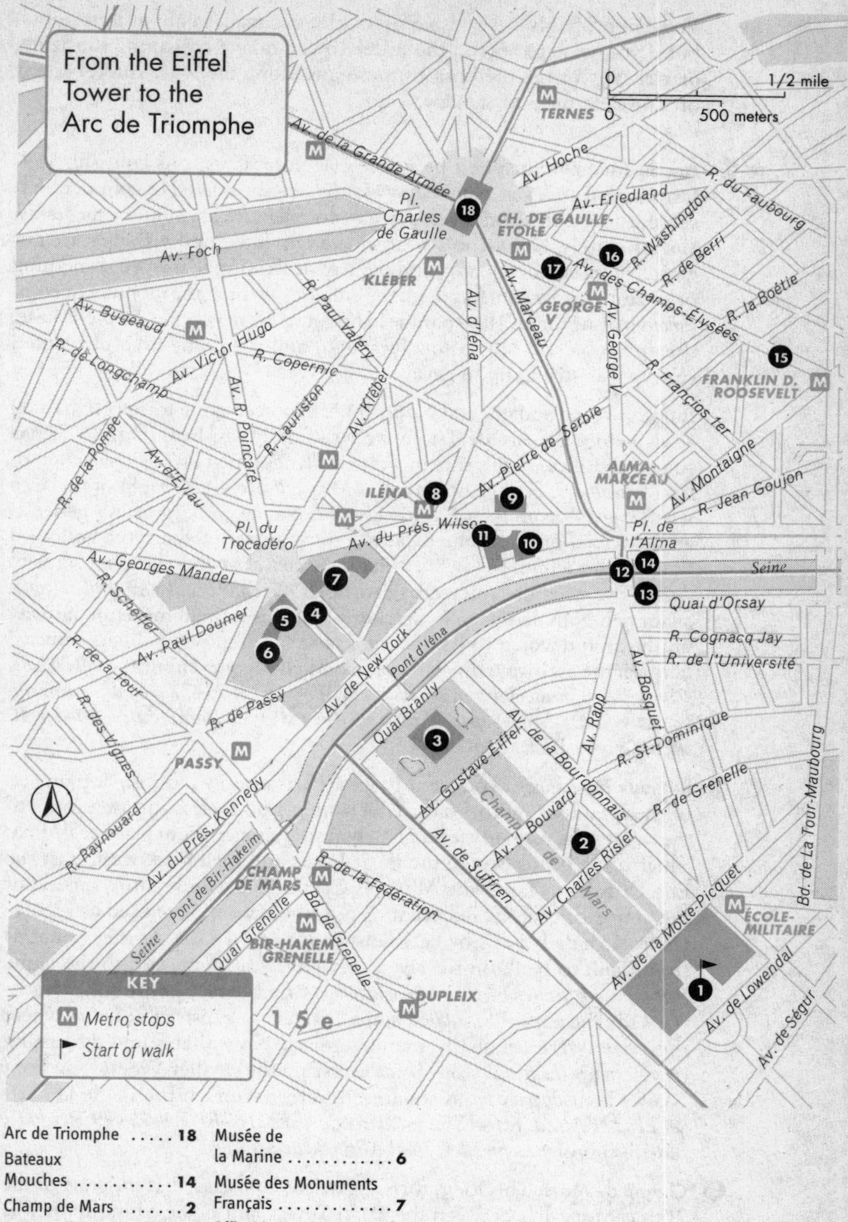

Arc de Triomphe 18
Bateaux Mouches 14
Champ de Mars 2
Champs-Élysées 15
École Militaire 1
Les Égouts 13
Lido 16
Musée d'Art Moderne de la Ville de Paris 10
Musée Guimet 8
Musée de l'Homme 5
Musée de la Marine 6
Musée des Monuments Français 7
Office de Tourisme de la Ville de Paris 17
Palais de Chaillot 4
Palais Galliéra 9
Palais de Tokyo 11
Pont de l'Alma 12
Tour Eiffel (Eiffel Tower) 3

TIMING You can probably cover this 5½-km (3½-mi) walk in about four hours, but if you wish to ascend the Eiffel Tower, take a trip along the Seine, or visit any of the plethora of museums along the way, you'd be best off allowing most of the day.

What to See

★ 18 **Arc de Triomphe.** Inspired by Rome's Arch of Titus, this colossal, 164-ft triumphal arch was planned by Napoléon—who liked to consider himself the heir to the Roman emperors—to celebrate his military successes. Unfortunately, Napoléon's strategic and architectural visions were not entirely on the same plane, and the Arc de Triomphe proved something of an embarrassment. Although the emperor wanted the monument completed in time for an 1810 parade in honor of his new bride, Marie-Louise, the arch was still only a few feet high, and a dummy arch of painted canvas was strung up to save face.

Empires come and go, and Napoléon's had been gone for more than 20 years before the Arc de Triomphe was finally finished, in 1836. It has some magnificent sculpture by François Rude, such as *The Departure of the Volunteers,* better known as *La Marseillaise,* to the right of the arch when viewed from the Champs-Élysées. Names of Napoléon's generals are inscribed on the stone facades—those underlined are the hallowed figures who fell on the fields of battle. After showing alarming signs of decay, the structure received a thorough overhaul in 1989 and is once again neo-Napoleonic in its splendor. There is a small museum halfway up the arch devoted to its history. France's Unknown Soldier is buried beneath the archway; the flame is rekindled every evening at 6:30. ✉ *Pl. Charles-de-Gaulle, Champs-Élysées* ☎ *01–55–37–73–77* 🌐 *www.monum.fr* 🎟 *€7* ⏲ *Apr.–Sept., daily 9:30–11; Oct.–Mar., daily 10–10:30* Ⓜ *Métro or RER: Étoile.*

14 **Bateaux Mouches.** If you want to view Paris in slow motion, hop on one of these famous motorboats, which set off on their hour-long tours of the city waters regularly (every half hour in summer) from place de l'Alma. Their route heads east to the Ile St-Louis and then back west, past the Eiffel Tower, as far as the Allée des Cygnes and its miniature version of the Statue of Liberty. Believe it or not, these were once used as regular ferries on a daily basis by Parisians up until the 1930s. As they bounced from bank to bank on the river, they gave rise, some say, to the name *Bateaux Mouches* (which translates as "fly boats"); more sober historians say the name "mouche" actually refers to a district of Lyon, where the boats were originally manufactured. Note that some discerning travelers prefer to take this Seine cruise on the smaller Vedettes du Pont Neuf which depart from square du Vert-Galant on the Ile de la Cité. ✉ *Pl. de l'Alma, Eiffel Tower/Trocadéro* ☎ *01–40–76–99–99* 🌐 *www.bateaux-mouches.fr* 🎟 *€7* Ⓜ *Alma-Marceau.*

2 **Champ de Mars.** This long, formal garden, landscaped at the start of the 20th century, lies between the Eiffel Tower and École Militaire. It was previously used as a parade ground and was the site of the world exhibitions of 1867, 1889 (date of the construction of the Eiffel Tower), and 1900. Ⓜ *École Militaire; RER: Champ de Mars.*

15 **Champs-Élysées.** Marcel Proust lovingly described the *recherché* elegance of the world's most famous avenue, the Champs-Élysées, during its Belle Epoque heyday, when its cobblestones resounded to the clatter of horses and carriages rather than the screech of tires. Although there's still a certain thrill to strutting along Les Champs, the abundance of bland shops and chain restaurants (and the absence of actual Parisians) makes the experience feel suspiciously like a trip to the mall. Originally an ex-

panse of green frequented by cattle, the 2-km (1¼-mi) Champs-Élysées was laid out in the 1660s by the landscape gardener André Le Nôtre as a park sweeping away from the Tuileries. Today, in a losing battle against all those airline offices, car showrooms, and movie theaters, the city has planted extra trees, broadened sidewalks, installed coordinated designer street furnishings (everything from benches and lighting to traffic lights, telephone booths, and trash cans), refurbished (i.e., Disneyfied) Art Nouveau newsstands, built underground parking to alleviate congestion, and clamped down on garish storefronts. To find the beauteous avenue of yore, look for the elegant 19th-century park pavilions along the lower half of the avenue, which continue to house the historic restaurants Ledoyen, Laurent, and Le Pavillon Élysées. Ⓜ *Champs-Élysées–Clemenceau, Franklin-D.-Roosevelt, George V, Étoile.*

1 **École Militaire** (Military Academy). Napoléon was one of the more famous graduates of this military academy, whose harmonious 18th-century building facing the Eiffel Tower across the Champ de Mars is still in use for army training, and, consequently, not open to the public. ☒ *Pl. du Maréchal-Joffre, Trocadéro/Eiffel Tower* Ⓜ *École Militaire.*

13 **Les Égouts** (The Sewers). Everyone visits the Louvre, so surprise your friends back home by telling them you toured the infamous sewers of Paris. Brave their unpleasant—though tolerable—smell to follow an underground city of banks, passages, and footbridges famously immortalized as the escape routes of Jean Valjean in *Les Misérables* and the Phantom of the Opera. Signs indicate the streets above you, and detailed panels and displays illuminate the history of waste disposal in Paris, whose sewer system is the largest in the world after Chicago's. The tour takes about an hour. ☒ *Opposite 93 quai d'Orsay, Trocadéro/Eiffel Tower* ☎ *01–53–68–27–81* *€3.80* ⊙ *Feb.–Dec., Sat.–Wed. 11–5* Ⓜ *Alma-Marceau; RER: Pont de l'Alma.*

off the beaten path

American Church. The staff of this Left Bank neo-Gothic church, built in 1927–31, offers help and advice to English-speaking foreigners. The church hosts free classical music concerts on Sunday from September to June at 6 PM. ☒ *65 quai d'Orsay, Trocadéro/Eiffel Tower* ☎ *01–40–62–05–00* Ⓜ *Alma-Marceau; RER: Pont de l'Alma.*

16 **Lido.** Free-flowing champagne, foot-stomping melodies in French and English, and topless razzmatazz pack in the crowds (mostly tourists) every night for the show at this famous nightclub, which has been around since 1946. ☒ *116 av. des Champs-Élysées, Champs-Élysées* ☎ *01–40–76–56–0* 🌐 *www.lido.fr* Ⓜ *George V.*

10 **Musée d'Art Moderne de la Ville de Paris** (Paris Museum of Modern Art).

Fodor's Choice ★

Both temporary exhibits and a permanent collection of top-quality 20th-century art can be found at this museum. It takes over, chronologically speaking, where the Musée d'Orsay leaves off: among the earliest works are Fauvist paintings by Vlaminck and Derain, followed by Picasso's early experiments in Cubism. Its vast, unobtrusive, white-walled galleries provide an ideal backdrop for the bold statements of 20th-century art. Loudest and largest are the canvases of Robert Delaunay. Other highlights include works by Braque, Rouault, Gleizes, Da Silva, Gromaire, and Modigliani. There is also a large room devoted to Art Deco furniture and screens, where Jean Dunand's gilt and lacquered panels consume oceans of wall space. There is a pleasant, if expensive, museum café and an excellent bookshop specializing in 19th- and 20th-century art and architecture, with many books in English. ☒ *11 av. du Président-Wilson, Trocadéro/Eiffel Tower* ☎ *01–53–67–40–00* 🌐 *www.*

paris.org *Permanent collection free, temporary exhibitions €7* *Tues.–Fri. 10–5:30, weekends 10–6:45* *Iéna.*

★ 8 **Musée Guimet.** One of the most refined and cherished of Paris museums, this Belle Epoque treasure was founded by Lyonnais industrialist Émile Guimet, who traveled around the world in the late 19th century amassing priceless Indo-Chinese and Far Eastern objets d'art. A highlight is the largest collection of Cambodian art this side of Cambodia, with celebrated works from the Angkor culture. *6 pl. d'Iéna, Trocadéro/Eiffel Tower* *01–56–52–53–00* *www.museeguimet.fr* *€5.50* *Iéna or Boissiére.*

5 **Musée de l'Homme** (Museum of Mankind). Picasso, it is said, discovered the bold lines of African masks and sculpture here and promptly went off to paint his *Desmoiselles d'Avignon* and create Cubism. You, too, may be inspired by the impressive artifacts, costumes, and domestic tools from around the world mounted here, the earliest dating from prehistoric times. This earnest anthropological museum is in the south wing of the Palais de Chaillot. To find the entrance, just look for the giant totem pole from British Colombia. *17 pl. du Trocadéro, Trocadéro/Eiffel Tower* *01–44–05–72–72* *www.mnhn.fr* *€5* *Wed.–Mon. 9:45–5:15* *Trocadéro.*

6 **Musée de la Marine** (Maritime Museum). In the west wing of the Palais de Chaillot, this museum contains ship models and seafaring paraphernalia illustrating French naval history up to the age of the nuclear submarine. *17 pl. du Trocadéro, Trocadéro/Eiffel Tower* *01–53–65–69–69* *€7* *Wed.–Mon. 10–6* *Trocadéro.*

7 **Musée des Monuments Français** (French Monuments Museum). One of the most fascinating museums in Paris closed after a fire in 1997 and is scheduled to reopen in 2005, when it will share space with the Institut Français d'Architecture and the Chaillot school, which trains architects in restoration. Founded in 1879 by architect-restorer Viollet-le-Duc (the man mainly responsible for the extensive renovation of Notre-Dame and countless other Gothic cathedrals), it is a vast repository of copies of statues, columns, archways, and frescoes from the Romanesque and Gothic periods (roughly 1000–1500) and forms an excellent (if somewhat bogus) introduction to French medieval architecture. *1 pl. du Trocadéro, Trocadéro/Eiffel Tower* *01–44–05–39–10* *Trocadéro.*

17 **Office de Tourisme de la Ville de Paris** (Paris Tourist Office). This modern, spacious office near the Arc de Triomphe is worth a visit at the start of your stay to pick up free maps, leaflets, and information on upcoming events. Most of the staff speak English and can also help book accommodations or tickets for shows. You can also exchange money here and buy métro tickets and souvenirs. *127 av. des Champs-Élysées, Champs-Élysées* *08–92–68–31–12* *www.paris-touristoffice.com* *Daily 9–8* *Charles-de-Gaulle–Étoile.*

4 **Palais de Chaillot** (Chaillot Palace). This honey-color Art Deco cultural center was built in the 1930s to replace a Moorish-style building constructed for the World Exhibition of 1878. It contains the new Institut Français d'Architecture, the Chaillot school, which trains architects as restorers and three large museums: the **Musée de l'Homme,** the **Musée de la Marine,** and the **Musée des Monuments Français.** The tumbling gardens leading to the Seine contain sculptures, dramatic fountains, and a large aquarium currently undergoing renovation until 2005. The palace terrace, flanked by gilded statuettes (and often invaded by roller skaters and skateboarders), offers a wonderful picture-postcard view of

the Eiffel Tower and is a favorite spot for fashion photographers. ✉ *Pl. du Trocadéro, Trocadéro/Eiffel Tower* Ⓜ *Trocadéro.*

need a break?

You'll get a tremendous view of the Eiffel Tower and the Invalides dome with your ice cream, cocktail, or lunch at **Le Totem** (✉ Pl. du Trocadéro, Trocadéro/Eiffel Tower ☎ 01–47–27–28–29), an elegant bar and restaurant in the south wing of the Palais de Chaillot.

9 **Palais Galliera.** This luxurious mansion, built in 1888 for the Duchesse de Galliera, houses rotating exhibits on costumery and clothing design. ✉ *10 av. Pierre-1er-de-Serbie, Trocadéro/Eiffel Tower* ☎ *01–56–52–86–00* 🌐 *www.paris-france.org/musees* 🎫 *€7* 🕒 *Tues.–Sun. 10–6* Ⓜ *Iéna.*

★ 11 **Palais de Tokyo.** Derelict for more than a decade, the Art Nouveau monstrosity next door to the Musée d'Art Moderne has reemerged as a contemporary art center with unorthodox and ambitious programming. This is arguably the most dynamic cultural institution in town, with two gargantuan floors of ever-changing exhibits, plus debates, DJ-driven music concerts, readings, fashion shows, and a good, inexpensive restaurant. ✉ *13 av. du Président-Wilson, Trocadéro/Eiffel Tower* ☎ *01–47–23–54–01* 🌐 *www.palaisdetokyo.com* 🎫 *€5* 🕒 *Tues.–Sun. noon–midnight* Ⓜ *Iéna.*

12 **Pont de l'Alma** (Alma Bridge). This bridge is best known for the chunky stone Zouave statue carved into one of the pillars. Zouaves were Algerian infantrymen recruited into the French army and famous for their bravura and colorful uniforms. There is nothing quite so glamorous, or colorful, about the Alma Zouave, however, whose hour of glory comes in times of watery distress: Parisians use him to judge the level of the Seine during heavy rains. Ⓜ *Alma-Marceau.*

3 Fodor's Choice ★ **Tour Eiffel** (Eiffel Tower). If the Statue of Liberty is New York, if Big Ben is London, if the Kremlin is Moscow, then the Eiffel Tower is Paris. For two years French engineer Gustave Eiffel—already famous for building viaducts and bridges—worked to erect this monument, which was designed to exalt the technical era that had begun to shine in the lamp of Edison and to stammer in the first telephone of Bell. It was created for the World Exhibition of 1889, inaugurated by Edward VII, then Prince of Wales, and was still in good shape to celebrate its 100th birthday in 1989. Such was Eiffel's engineering wizardry that even in the strongest winds his tower never sways more than 4½ inches.

Since its colossal bulk exudes a feeling of mighty permanence, you may have trouble believing that it nearly became 7,000 tons of scrap iron when its concession expired in 1909. Many Parisians first hated the structure and agreed with designer William Morris, who arrived at its site one day to exclaim, "Why on earth have I come here? Because it's the only place I can't see it from." Only its potential use as a radio antenna saved the day (it still bristles with a forest of radio and television transmitters). By the days of the German occupation, however, Paris trembled when it was suggested that the 12,000 pieces of metal and its 2,500,000 rivets should be "requisitioned." The nocturnal illumination is breathtaking—every girder highlighted in glorious detail. If you're full of energy, stride up the stairs as far as the third deck. If you want to go to the top, you'll have to take the elevator. The view at 1,000 ft may not beat that from the Tour Montparnasse skyscraper, but the setting makes it considerably more romantic, especially if you come in the late evening, after the crowds have dispersed. ✉ *Quai Branly, Trocadéro/Eiffel Tower* ☎ *01–44–11–23–23* 🌐 *www.tour-eiffel.fr* 🎫 *By elevator: 2nd fl. €3.70, 3rd fl. €6.90, 4th fl. €9.90. Climbing: 2nd and 3rd fl.*

only, €3 ⏲ July–Aug., daily 9 AM–midnight; Sept.–June, daily 9 AM–11 PM Ⓜ *Bir-Hakeim; RER: Champ de Mars.*

need a break?

Shlepping up and down the tower can bring on an appetite. If you don't want to break the bank at the excellent Jules Verne restaurant on the second level of the tower, or if you're stuck in the dead zone between lunchtime and dinner, head to the **Café du Marché** (✉ 38 rue Cler, Trocadéro/Eiffel Tower ☎ 01–47–05–51–27), a relaxed, all-day restaurant where the drinks are cheap, the salads gigantic, and the daily specials truly special.

THE FAUBOURG ST-HONORÉ

Fashions change, but the Faubourg St-Honoré—the area just north of the Champs-Élysées and the Tuileries—firmly maintains its tradition of high style. As you progress from the President's Palace past a wealth of art galleries and the neoclassic Madeleine Church to the stately place Vendôme, you will see that all is luxury and refinement here. On the ritzy square, famous boutiques sit side by side with famous banks—after all, elegance and finance has never been an unusual combination. It is not surprising to learn that one of the main arteries of the area, rue de Castiglione, was named after one of its former residents—the glamorous fashion-plate Countess de Castiglione, sent to plead the cause of Italian unity with Napoléon III. The emperor was persuaded (he was easily susceptible to feminine charms), and the area became a Kingdom of Woman: famous dressmakers, renowned jewelers, exclusive perfume shops, and the most chic hotel in Paris, the Ritz, made this *faubourg* (district) a symbol of luxury throughout the world.

Today the tradition continues, with leading names in fashion found farther east on place des Victoires, close to what was, for centuries, the gastronomic heart of Paris: Les Halles (pronounced "lay-*al*"), once the city's main market. These giant glass-and-iron market halls were demolished in 1969 and replaced by a park and a modern shopping mall, the Forum des Halles. The surrounding streets underwent a transformation and are now filled with shops, cafés, restaurants, and chic apartment buildings. The brash modernity of the mall stands in contrast to the august church of St-Eustache nearby. Similarly, the incongruous black-and-white columns in the classical courtyard of Richelieu's neighboring Palais-Royal present a further case of daring modernity—or architectural vandalism, depending on your point of view.

Numbers in the text correspond to numbers in the margin and on the Faubourg St-Honoré map.

a good walk

Start your walk in front of the most important home in France: the **Palais de l'Élysée** 1 ⚑, the Presidential Palace; barriers and gold-braided guards keep the public at bay. There's more to see in the plethora of art galleries and luxury fashion boutiques lining rue du Faubourg St-Honoré, where you will also see Sotheby's auction house and the British embassy. From rue du Faubourg St-Honoré, turn left onto rue Boissy-d'Anglas and cut right through an archway into Cité Berryer, a smart courtyard with several trendy shops. It leads to rue Royale, a classy street lined with jewelry stores. Looming to the left is the sturdy **Église de la Madeleine** 2.

Cross boulevard de la Madeleine and take rue Duphot down to rue St-Honoré, where you'll find **Notre-Dame de l'Assomption** 3, noted for its huge dome and solemn interior. Continue to rue de Castiglione; then head left to one of the world's most opulent squares, the **place Vendôme** 4, ringed with jewelers. That's Napoléon standing at the top of the square's bronze central column—and that's the Ritz, fronted by those Rolls-Royces, halfway down on the left. Return to rue St-Honoré and continue to the mighty church of **St-Roch** 5. It's worth having a look inside to see the bombastically Baroque altarpiece in the circular Lady Chapel at the far end.

Take the next right onto rue des Pyramides and cross place des Pyramides, with its gilded statue of Joan of Arc on horseback, to the northwest wing of the Louvre, home to the **Union Centrale des Arts Décoratifs** 6, with three separate museums dedicated to fashion, publicity, and the decorative arts. Stay on arcaded rue de Rivoli to place du Palais-Royal. On the far side of the square is the **Louvre des Antiquaires** 7, a chic shopping mall housing upscale antiques stores. Opposite, beyond the exuberant fountains of place André-Malraux, Garnier's 19th-century Opéra beckons at the far end of the avenue of the same name.

Just beyond Jean-Michel Othaniel's aluminum and psychedelic glass entrance canopy to the Palais-Royal métro station is the **Comédie Française** 8, the time-honored setting for performances of classical French drama. To the right of the theater is the unobtrusive entrance to the **Palais-Royal** 9; its courtyard is a surprising oasis in the heart of the city and a study in both classical and contemporary French landscape architecture. Walk down to the far end of the garden and peek into the glossy 19th-century interior of Le Grand Véfour, one of the swankiest restaurants in the city.

One block north of here, on rue de Richelieu, stands what used to be France's main national library, the **Bibliothèque Nationale Richelieu** 10. Rue des Petits-Champs heads east to the circular **place des Victoires** 11: that's Louis XIV astride the plunging steed in the center of the square. You'll find some of the city's most upscale fashion shops here and on the surrounding streets, along with the 17th-century church of **Notre-Dame des Victoires** 12. Head south down rue Croix-des-Petits-Champs, past the nondescript Banque de France on your right, and take the second street on the left to the circular **Bourse du Commerce** 13, the Commercial Exchange. Alongside it is a 100-ft-high fluted column, the **Colonne de Ruggieri.**

Today most of the market area that once sat alongside is occupied by the **Jardin des Halles** 14, dominated on the left by the bulky outline of the church of **St-Eustache** 15, a curious architectural hybrid of Gothic and classical styles. Take bustling rue de Montorgueil beyond the church, and then turn right on rue Étienne-Marcel to admire the **Tour Jean Sans Peur** 16, a tower built into the old city walls in 1409. Backtrack a few yards and turn right onto rue Française, right again along quaint rue Tiquetonne, and then take your first left into rue Dussoubs. Just to your right is the entrance to one of the city's most elegant covered galleries, the **Passage du Grand-Cerf** 17. Turn right at the end of the gallery and go down rue St-Denis to the cozy medieval church of **St-Leu–St-Gilles** 18.

Stay on rue St-Denis and take a third right, along rue des Prêcheurs, to reach the **Forum des Halles** 19, a modern, multilevel shopping mall. Turn left on rue Pierre-Lescot to reach square des Innocents, with its handsome 16th-century Renaissance fountain. Farther east you can see the futuristic funnels of the Centre Pompidou jutting above the surrounding buildings.

From the far end of square des Innocents, rue St-Denis leads to place du Châtelet, with its theaters, fountain, and the **Tour St-Jacques** 20 looming up to your left—all that remains of a church that once stood here.

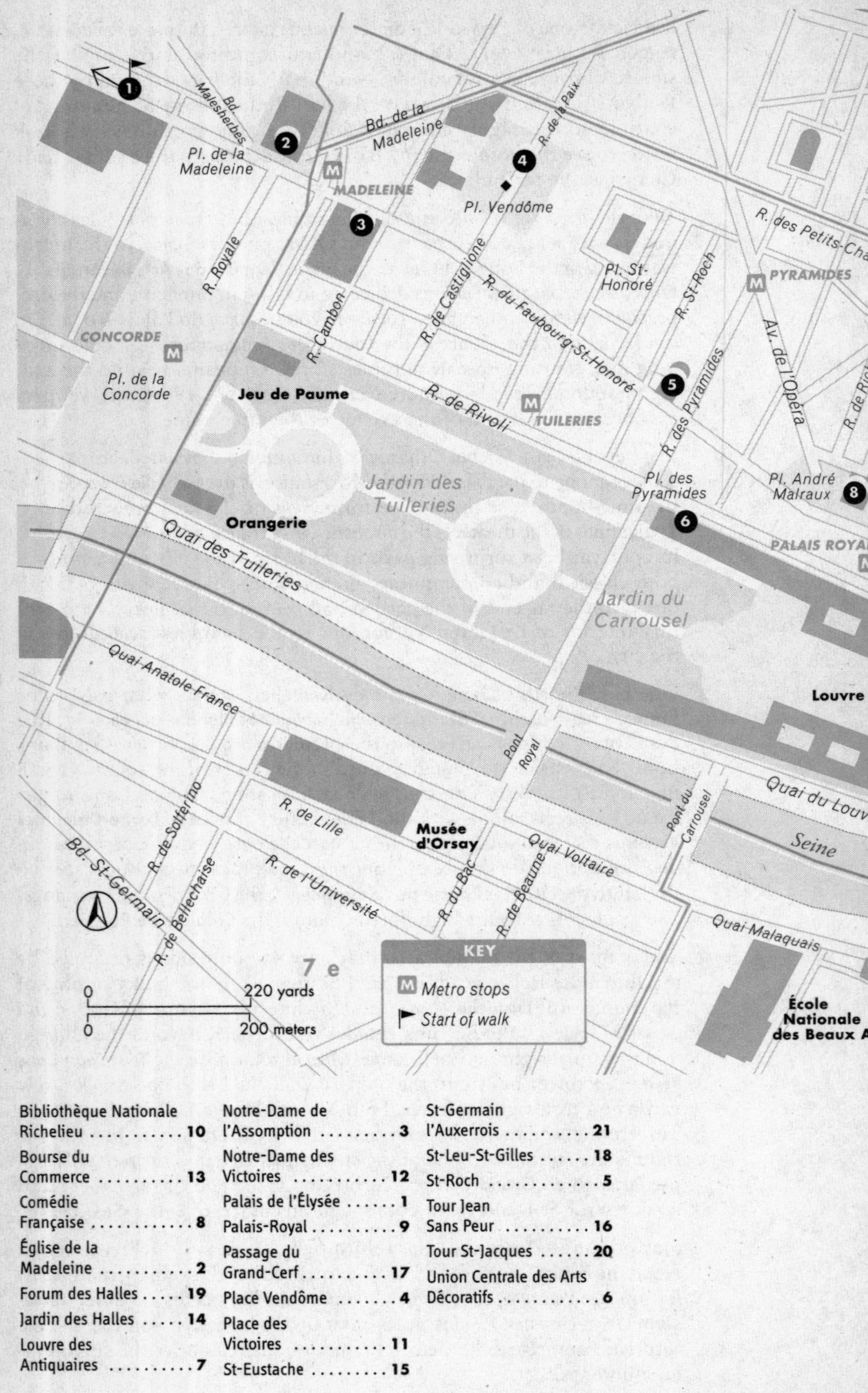
Bd. Malesherbes
Pl. de la Madeleine
Bd. de la Madeleine
R. de la Paix
MADELEINE
Pl. Vendôme
R. des Petits-Cha
R. Royale
R. Cambon
R. de Castiglione
R. du Faubourg-St.-Honoré
Pl. St-Honoré
R. St-Roch
PYRAMIDES
Av. de l'Opéra
CONCORDE
Pl. de la Concorde
Jeu de Paume
R. de Rivoli
TUILERIES
R. des Pyramides
R. de Ri
Jardin des Tuileries
Pl. des Pyramides
Pl. André Malraux
Orangerie
PALAIS ROYA
Quai des Tuileries
Jardin du Carrousel
Quai Anatole France
Louvre
Pont Royal
R. de Lille
Musée d'Orsay
Quai du Louv
R. de Solferino
Pont du Carrousel
Seine
Bd. St-Germain
R. de Bellechaise
R. de l'Université
R. du Bac
R. de Beaune
Quai Voltaire
Quai Malaquais
KEY
Metro stops
Start of walk
7e
0
220 yards
0
200 meters
École Nationale des Beaux A

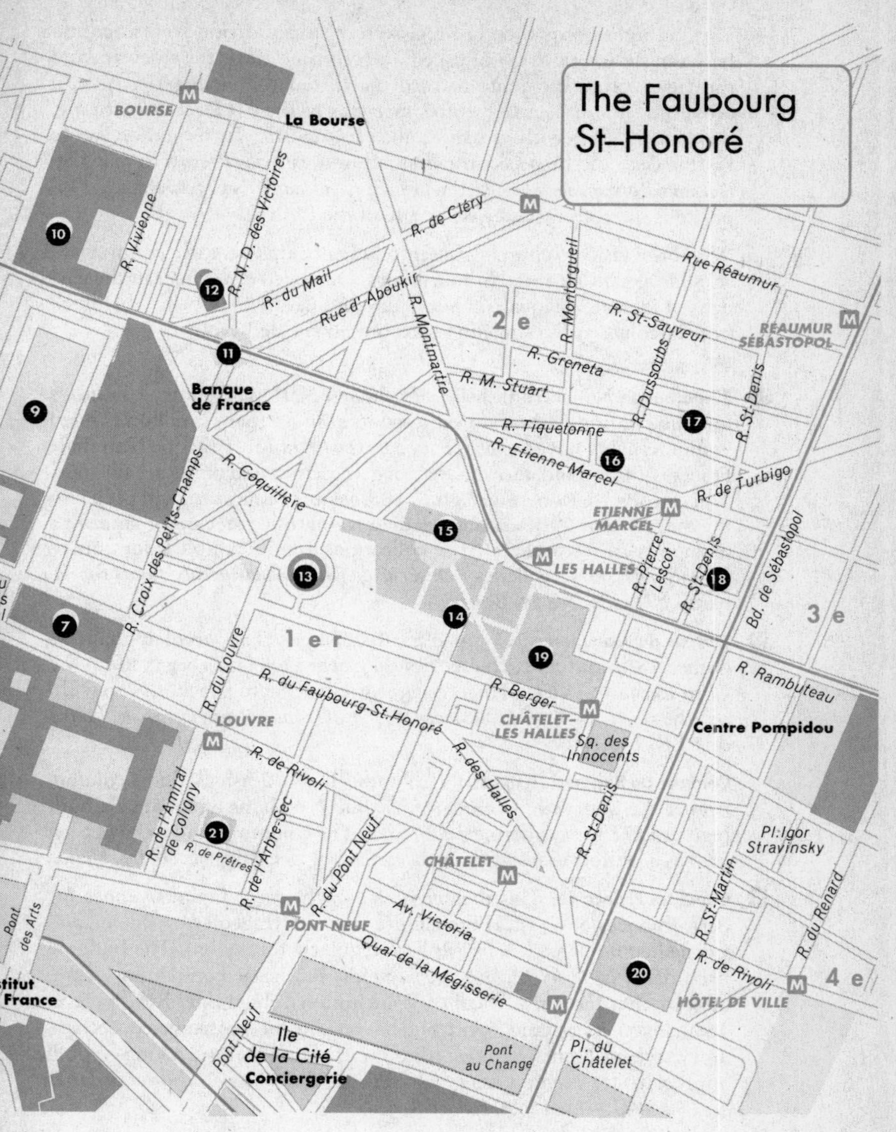
The Faubourg St–Honoré
BOURSE
La Bourse
R. Vivienne
R. N. D. des Victoires
R. de Cléry
R. du Mail
Rue d' Aboukir
R. Montmartre
R. Montorgueil
Rue Réaumur
R. St-Sauveur
RÉAUMUR SÉBASTOPOL
2 e
R. Greneta
R. M. Stuart
R. Dussoubs
R. St-Denis
Banque de France
R. Tiquetonne
R. Etienne Marcel
R. de Turbigo
R. Coquillère
R. Croix des Petits-Champs
ETIENNE MARCEL
LES HALLES
R. Pierre Lescot
Bd. de Sébastopol
3 e
1 e r
R. du Louvre
R. du Faubourg-St.Honoré
R. Berger
R. Rambuteau
LOUVRE
CHÂTELET-LES HALLES
Sq. des Innocents
Centre Pompidou
R. de Rivoli
R. des Halles
R. de l'Amiral de Coligny
R. de Prêtres
R. de l'Arbre-Sec
R. du Pont Neuf
CHÂTELET
Pl. Igor Stravinsky
R. St-Martin
R. du Renard
Pont des Arts
PONT NEUF
Av. Victoria
Quai de la Mégisserie
R. de Rivoli
4 e
HÔTEL DE VILLE
France
Pont Neuf
Ile de la Cité
Conciergerie
Pont au Change
Pl. du Châtelet
10
12
11
9
7
13
15
14
19
16
17
18
21
20

Turning right on quai de la Mégisserie, you can divide your attention between the exotic array of caged birds for sale along the sidewalk and the view across the Seine toward the turreted Conciergerie. As you cross rue du Pont Neuf, the birds give way to the Art Deco Samaritaine department store with its panoramic rooftop café. Turn right on rue de l'Arbre-Sec, and then take the first left onto rue des Prêtres to reach **St-Germain l'Auxerrois** (21), once the French royal family's parish church. Opposite is the colonnaded east facade of the Louvre.

TIMING With brief visits to churches and monuments, this 5½-km (3½-mi) walk should take about three to four hours. On a nice day, linger in the gardens of the Palais-Royal; on a cold day, indulge in an unbelievably thick hot chocolate at the Angélina tearoom on rue de Rivoli.

What to See

10 **Bibliothèque Nationale Richelieu** (Richelieu National Library). France's longtime national library used to contain more than 7 million printed volumes; many have been removed to the giant Bibliothèque Nationale François-Mitterrand, though original manuscripts and prints are still here. You can admire Robert de Cotte's 18th-century courtyard and peep into the magnificent 19th-century reading room, but you cannot enter (it's open only to researchers). The collections are on exhibit from time to time in the library's galleries. ⊠ *58 rue de Richelieu, Opéra/Grands Boulevards* ⏲ *Daily 9–8* Ⓜ *Bourse.*

13 **Bourse du Commerce** (Commercial Exchange). The circular, shallow-domed 18th-century exchange building near Les Halles began life as the Corn Exchange; Victor Hugo waggishly likened it to a jockey's cap without the peak. ⊠ *Rue de Viarmes, Opéra/Grands Boulevards* Ⓜ *Métro or RER: Les Halles.*

Colonne de Ruggieri (Ruggieri's Column). The 100-ft-high fluted column, behind the Bourse du Commerce, is all that remains of a mansion built here in 1572 for Catherine de' Medici. The column is said to have been used as a platform for stargazing by her astrologer, Ruggieri. Ⓜ *Les Halles.*

8 **Comédie Française.** This theater is one of the most famous venues for performances of classical French drama, with tragedies by Racine and Corneille and comedies by Molière regularly on the bill. The building itself dates from 1790, but the Comédie Française company was created by that most theatrical of French monarchs, Louis XIV, back in 1680. If you understand French and have a taste for the mannered, declamatory style of French acting—it's a far cry from method acting—you'll appreciate an evening here. ⊠ *2 rue de Richelieu, Louvre/Tuileries* ☎ *01–44–58–15–15* Ⓜ *Palais-Royal.*

2 **Église de la Madeleine.** With its rows of uncompromising columns, this sturdy neoclassical edifice—designed in 1814 but not consecrated until 1842—looks more like a proudly inflated, though unfaithful, version of a Greek temple than a Christian church. The loose interpretation was intentional: the overproportioned porticoes, the interior barrel vaults-cum-domes, and the opulent versions of the Ionic and Corinthian orders were meant to be Parisian one-uppings of anything Athens had to offer. Changing political moods continued to alter the building's purpose—a Greek basilica one day, a temple to Napoléon's glory another, a National Assembly hall the next. At one point, in fact, La Madeleine, as it is known, was nearly selected as Paris's first train station. Inside, the only natural light comes from three shallow domes. The walls are richly and harmoniously decorated; gold glints through the murk. Nowadays the opulent interior is the site of lots of expensive concerts as well as daily masses. And if sitting in the cool interior of a Catholic

church is not enough to make you reflect upon your faults, try viewing the huge fresco of the Last Judgment above you. A simpler crypt offers intimate weekday masses. Free classical music concerts and organ recitals are held throughout the week. ✉ *Pl. de la Madeleine, Opéra/Grands Boulevards* ⏲ *Mon.–Sat. 7:30–7, Sun. 8–7* Ⓜ *Madeleine.*

need a break?

Fauchon (✉ 26 pl. de la Madeleine, Opéra/Grands Boulevards ☎ 01–47–42–60–11), the city's poshest food emporium, has an equally posh tearoom. It's best to visit on a sunny day, otherwise the interior can be somewhat dreary. The terrace, however, is very romantic, with a spectacular view of the church across the street. Teas are served with glass sand timers to ensure perfect steeping; cakes and pastries are special treats.

1

19 **Forum des Halles.** Les Halles, the iron-and-glass halls of the central Paris food market, were closed in 1969 and replaced in the late '70s by the Forum des Halles, a characterless, modern shopping mall. Nothing remains of either the market or the rambunctious mise-en-scène that led 19th-century novelist Émile Zola to dub Les Halles *le ventre de Paris* ("the belly of Paris"), although rue de Montorgueil, behind St-Eustache, retains something of its original bustle. Unfortunately, much of the plastic, concrete, glass, and mock-marble facade of the multilevel shopping mall is already showing signs of wear and tear. This state of affairs is not much helped by the hordes of teenagers and down-and-outs who invade it toward dusk. Nonetheless, if you are a serious shopper, you might want to check out the French chain stores, the few small boutiques, and the weekly fashion shows by up-and-coming young designers held here. ✉ *Main entrance: rue Pierre-Lescot, Beaubourg/Les Halles* Ⓜ *Les Halles; RER: Châtelet Les Halles.*

14 **Jardin des Halles** (Les Halles Garden). This garden, crisscrossed with paths and alleyways flanked by bushes, flower beds, and trim little lawns, takes up much of the site once occupied by Les Halles, the city's central market. Children love the bush shaped like a rhinoceros. Ⓜ *Les Halles; RER: Châtelet Les Halles.*

7 **Louvre des Antiquaires.** This "shopping mall" of super-elegant antiques dealers, off place du Palais-Royal opposite the Louvre, is a minimuseum in itself. Its stylish, glass-walled corridors—lined with Louis XVI *boiseries* (wainscoting), Charles Dix bureaus, and the pretty sort of bibelots that would have gladdened the heart of Marie-Antoinette—deserve a browse whether you intend to buy or not. For more Antiques Heaven, head over to the area around rue Jacob on the Left Bank. ✉ *Main entrance: Pl. du Palais-Royal, Louvre/Tuileries* ⏲ *Tues.–Sun. 11–7* Ⓜ *Palais-Royal.*

need a break?

Once patronized by Proust, founded in 1903, **Angélina** (✉ 226 rue de Rivoli, Louvre/Tuileries ☎ 01–42–60–82–00) is a famous *salon de thé* (tearoom), lined with seaside frescoes and huge mirrors, noted for its irresistible €6 *chocolat africain*, a cup of hot, thick chocolate served with whipped cream. The famous writer would probably sniff at the shopworn air of the place today and reserve his affections for the still-elegant teas served at historic Ladurée, 12 blocks to the east at 16 rue Royale.

3 **Notre-Dame de l'Assomption.** This 1670 church, with its huge dome and solemn interior, was the scene of Lafayette's funeral in 1834. It is now a chapel for Paris's Polish community. ✉ *Rue Cambon, Louvre/Tuileries* Ⓜ *Concorde.*

⓬ **Notre-Dame des Victoires.** Visit this central Paris church, built from 1666 to 1740, to see the 30,000 ex-voto tablets that adorn its walls. ✉ *Pl. des Petits-Pères, Beaubourg/Les Halles* Ⓜ *Sentier.*

⚑ ❶ **Palais de l'Élysée.** Madame de Pompadour, Napoléon, Joséphine, the Duke of Wellington, and Queen Victoria all stayed at this "palace," today the official home of the French president. Originally constructed as a private mansion in 1718, the Élysée—incidentally, when Parisians talk about "L'Élysée," they mean the president's palace, whereas the Champs-Élysées is known simply as "Les Champs"—has housed presidents only since 1873. President Félix Faure died here in 1899 in the arms, so it is said, of his mistress. Although you can catch a glimpse of the palace forecourt and facade through rue du Faubourg St-Honoré gateway, it is difficult to get much idea of the building's size, or of the extensive gardens that stretch back to the Champs-Élysées, because it is closed to the public. ✉ *55 rue du Faubourg St-Honoré, Champs-Élysées* Ⓜ *Miromesnil.*

★ ❾ **Palais-Royal** (Royal Palace). One of the most Parisian sights in all of Paris, the Palais-Royal is especially loved for its gardens, where children play, lovers whisper, and senior citizens crumble bread for the sparrows. The *palais* dates from the 1630s, and is *royal* only in that all-powerful Cardinal Richelieu (1585–1642) magnanimously bequeathed it to Louis XIII. In his early days as king, Louis XIV preferred the relative intimacy of this place to the intimidating splendor of the nearby Louvre (of course, he soon decided that his own intimidating splendor warranted a more majestic home; hence, Versailles). During the French Revolution, it became Le Palais Egalité (the Palace of Equality) because its owner, Louis-Philippe d'Orléans, the king's cousin, professed revolutionary ideas, one of which was to convert the arcades of the palace into boutiques and cafés (Louis XVI reputedly quipped, "My cousin, now that you are going to keep shop I suppose we shall see you only on Sundays"). Before one of these shops Camille Desmoulins gave the first speech calling for the French Revolution in 1789.

Today the Palais-Royal contains a block of apartments (former residents include André Malraux, Jean Cocteau, and Colette) and the French Ministry of Culture, whose buildings—not open to the public—overlook a colonnaded courtyard with black-and-white-striped half columns and revolving silver spheres that slither around in two fountains, the controversial work of architect Daniel Buren. The splendid gardens beyond are bordered by arcades harboring discreet boutiques and are divided by rows of perfectly trimmed little trees. Back in the early 19th century this was the haunt of prostitutes and gamblers: a veritable sink of vice. These days it's hard to imagine anyplace more hoity-toity. ✉ *Pl. du Palais-Royal, Louvre/Tuileries* Ⓜ *Palais-Royal.*

⓱ **Passage du Grand-Cerf.** This pretty, glass-roofed *passage* (gallery) is filled with crafts shops offering an innovative selection of jewelry, paintings, and ceramics. ✉ *Entrances on rue Dussoubs, rue St-Denis, Beaubourg/Les Halles* Ⓜ *Étienne Marcel.*

❹ **Place Vendôme.** Snobbish and self-important, this famous square is also gorgeous; property laws have kept away cafés and other such banal establishments, leaving the plaza stately and refined, the perfect home for the rich and famous (Chopin lived and died at No. 12; today's celebs camp out at the Hotel Ritz at No. 15, while a lucky few, including the family of the Sultan of Brunei, actually own houses here). With its granite pavement and Second Empire street lamps, Jules-Hardouin Mansart's rhythmic, perfectly proportioned example of 17th-century urban architecture shines in all its golden-stone splendor. The square is a fitting showcase for the cluster of jewelry display windows found here. Interestingly, when the square was first built, only the facades of the hôtels particuliers were constructed, to maintain a uniform appearance—the lots behind the facades were then sold to buyers who custom-tailored their palaces to individual tastes. Napoléon had the square's central column made from the melted bronze of 1,200 cannons captured at the Battle of Austerlitz in 1805, and stands vigilantly on the top. Painter Gustave Courbet headed the revolutionary hooligans who, in 1871, toppled the column (into a pile of manure, no less) and shattered it into thousands of metallic pieces. The Third Republic stuck them together again and sent him the bill. To raise a glass of champagne in honor of the place's famous ghosts, repair to Hemingway's Bar at the Ritz (⇨ Close-Up Box, Hemingway's Paris, *below*). Ⓜ *Opéra.*

11 **Place des Victoires.** This circular square, now home to many of the city's top fashion boutiques, was laid out in 1685 by Jules Hardouin-Mansart in honor of the military victories of Louis XIV, that indefatigable warrior whose nearly continuous battles may have brought much prestige to his country but came perilously close to bringing it to bankruptcy, too. Louis is shown galloping along on a bronze horse in the middle; his statue dates from 1822 and replaced one destroyed during the Revolution. Louis was so taken with this plaza that he commissioned the architect, who also designed much of Versailles, to build another, place Vendôme, on the other side of avenue de l'Opéra. Ⓜ *Sentier.*

15 **St-Eustache.** Since the demolition of the 19th-century iron-and-glass market halls at the beginning of the '70s, St-Eustache has reemerged as a dominant element on the central Paris skyline. It is a huge church, the "cathedral" of Les Halles, built as the market people's Right Bank reply to Notre-Dame on the Ile de la Cité. St-Eustache dates from a couple of hundred years later than Notre-Dame. With the exception of the feeble west front, added between 1754 and 1788, construction lasted from 1532 to 1637, spanning the decline of the Gothic style and the emergence of the Renaissance. As a consequence, the church is a curious architectural hybrid. Its exterior flying buttresses are Gothic, but its column orders, rounded arches, and thick, comparatively simple window tracery are unmistakably classical. Few buildings bear such eloquent witness to stylistic change. St-Eustache also hosts occasional organ concerts and contemporary art exhibitions. ⊠ *2 rue du Jour, Beaubourg/Les Halles* ☎ *01–46–27–89–21 concert information* ⊙ *Daily 8–7* Ⓜ *Les Halles; RER: Châtelet Les Halles.*

21 **St-Germain l'Auxerrois.** Until 1789, this church was used by the French royal family as its Paris parish church, in the days when the adjacent Louvre was a palace rather than a museum. The fluid stonework of the facade reveals the influence of 15th-century Flamboyant Gothic style, enjoying its final shrieks before the classical takeover of the Renaissance. Notice the unusually wide windows in the nave and the equally unusual double aisles. The triumph of classicism is evident, however, in the fluted columns around the choir, the area surrounding the altar. These were added in the 18th century and are characteristic of the desire of 18th-century clerics to dress up medieval buildings in the architectural raiment of their own day. ⊠ *Pl. du Louvre, Louvre/Tuileries* Ⓜ *Louvre-Rivoli.*

18 **St-Leu–St-Gilles.** Near the Centre Pompidou, this intimate church presents a stylistic contrast between its large-windowed, 14th-century nave and the raised, 17th-century Renaissance choir. ⊠ *Rue St-Denis, Beaubourg/Les Halles* Ⓜ *Étienne Marcel.*

HEMINGWAY'S PARIS

THERE IS AN OLD FAMILIAR SAYING: *"Everyone has two countries, his or her own—and France." For the "Lost Generation" after World War I, these words rang particularly true. Disillusioned by America's Depression and Prohibition, lured by favorable exchange rates and a booming artistic scene, many American writers, composers, and painters moved to Paris in the 1920s and 1930s. F. Scott Fitzgerald, Gertrude Stein, Ezra Pound, E. E. Cummings, Janet Flanner, and John dos Passos are just a few of the famous figures, with Ernest Hemingway heading the list. "Papa" found Paris a veritable Land of Cockaigne, where every man does what he pleases, where all could allow their personal idiosyncracies full play and apologize for them with the simple remark,* Je suis comme ça. *"I am like that." It is this freedom that, back then, made Paris the cultural—and hoopla—capital of the world. And the best witnesses to that amazing era were the many expatriates who came to admire, and remained to praise.*

Hemingway arrived in Paris with his first wife, Hadley, in December 1921, and made for the Left Bank—the Hôtel Jacob et d'Angleterre, to be exact (still operating at 44 rue Jacob). To celebrate their arrival, the couple went to the Café de la Paix for a meal they nearly couldn't afford. In 1922 they moved to 74 rue du Cardinal Lemoine (his writing studio was around the corner on the top floor of 39 rue Descartes), then in early 1924 the couple and their baby son settled at 113 rue Notre-Dame des Champs. Nearby, he settled in at La Closerie des Lilas café to write much of The Sun Also Rises. *It was a time "when we were very young and very happy" as he wrote in* A Moveable Feast.

Not happy for long. In 1926 Hemingway left Hadley and next year wedded his mistress Pauline Pfeiffer across town at St Honoré-d'Eylau, then moved to 6 rue Férou, near the Musée du Luxembourg, whose collection of Cézanne landscapes (now in the Musée d'Orsay) he revered. Hemingway once declared that "unless you have geography, background, you have nothing." You can follow the steps of Jake and Bill in The Sun Also Rises *as they "circle" the Ile St-Louis before the "steep walking . . . all the way up to the place de la Contrescarpe," then right along rue du Pot-de-Fer to the "rigid north and south" of rue St-Jacques and on to boulevard du Montparnasse.*

For gossip and books, Papa would visit Shakespeare & Company at 12 rue de l'Odéon, owned by Sylvia Beach, an early buddy (the bookstore can now be found at 37 rue de la Bûcherie). For cash and cocktails, Hemingway usually headed to the upscale Right Bank. The first was found at the Guaranty Trust Company, at 1 rue des Italiens. The second, when he was flush, at the bar of the Hôtel Crillon, or, when poor, at the Caves Mura, at 19 rue d'Antin, or Harry's Bar, still in brisk business at 5 rue Daunou, with photos of Papa gazing down from the walls. Hemingway's legendary association with the Hotel Ritz, where he now has his own bar named for him, dates from the Liberation in 1944, when he strode in at the head of his platoon and "liberated" the joint by ordering 73 dry martinis. Here Hemingway asked Mary Welsh to become his fourth wife, and also righted the world with Jean-Paul Sartre, George Orwell, and Marlene Dietrich. Paris loves naming streets after adopted sons and it is only fitting that Hemingway has a plaque of his own, heralding short rue Ernest-Hemingway in the 15^{e} arrondissement. This, after all, was the man who wrote: "There is never any ending to Paris."

5 **St-Roch.** Designed by Lemercier in 1653 but completed only in the 1730s, this huge church is almost as long (138 yards) as Notre-Dame, thanks to Hardouin-Mansart's domed Lady Chapel at the far end, with its elaborate Baroque altarpiece. Classical playwright Pierre Corneille (1606–84) is buried here; a commemorative plaque honors him at the left of the entrance. ✉ *Rue St-Honoré, Louvre/Tuileries* Ⓜ *Tuileries.*

16 **Tour Jean Sans Peur.** This sturdy medieval tower was built by Jean Sans Peur (John the Fearless), Duke of Burgundy, in 1409 to defend his long-since-vanished Paris mansion. You can explore the spiral staircase and admire the magnificent vaulting with its intertwined array of sculpted vines, hops, and hawthorn flowers. Ask for an English translation for all the banners detailing Paris's medieval architecture. ✉ *20 rue Étienne-Marcel, Beaubourg/Les Halles* ☎ *01–40–26–20–28* 🎫 *€4.60* ⏲ *Sept.–June, Wed. and weekends 1:30–6; July–Aug., Tues.–Sun. 1:30–6* Ⓜ *Étienne Marcel.*

20 **Tour St-Jacques.** An ornate 170-ft stump tower that belonged to a 16th-century church destroyed in 1797, it sits forlornly, swallowed up by traffic. Currently under renovation, it is scheduled to open to the public in late 2004. ✉ *Pl. du Châtelet, Beaubourg/Les Halles* Ⓜ *Châtelet.*

need a break?

Twenty different international beers are available on draft, and more than 180 in bottles, at **Le Trappiste** (✉ 4 rue St-Denis, Beaubourg/Les Halles ☎ 01–42–33–08–50), just north of place du Châtelet. Mussels and french fries are the traditional accompaniment, although various other snacks such as hot dogs and sandwiches are also available.

★ 6 **Union Centrale des Arts Décoratifs** (Decorative Arts Center). A must for lovers of fashion and the decorative arts, this northwestern wing of the Louvre building houses three famously chic museums: the **Musée de la Mode,** devoted to costumes and accessories dating back to the 18th century, usually displayed in temporary exhibitions devoted to a single theme or designer—needless to say, the place is a second home to Paris's enormous fashion community; the **Musée des Arts Décoratifs,** with furniture, tapestries, glassware, paintings, and other necessities of life from the Middle Ages through Napoléon's time and beyond—a highlight here are the sumptuous period-style rooms (note the ostentatious number of chairs in the salon); and the **Musée de la Publicité,** perhaps less of interest for its temporary exhibits of advertisements and posters than for Jean Nouvel's brash decor—described by one Paris critic as "hi-tech miserabalism"—combining metal-plaqued walls with exposed brickwork and faded gilding, black-lacquered parquet floors, leopard-skin pillars, and a battery of TV monitors over the bar. ✉ *107 rue de Rivoli, Louvre/Tuileries* ☎ *01–44–55–57–50* 🌐 *www.ucad.fr* 🎫 *€7* ⏲ *Tues.–Sun. 11–6* Ⓜ *Palais-Royal.*

THE GRANDS BOULEVARDS

Famously immortalized in the canvases of Monet, Renoir, and Pissarro, the Grands Boulevards are the long chain of avenues that join the Madeleine to the Opéra, continue via the ancient gates of St-Denis and St-Martin to place de la République, and on to the Bastille. Together they constitute the longest, most commercial, most representative artery of Paris, and the most diverse. Parisians have always loved to promenade down their great avenues to feel the pulse of the city throbbing at its strongest. The focal point of this walk is the avenue that runs west to east from St-Augustin, the city's grandest Second Empire church, to place de la République, whose very name symbolizes the ultimate downfall of the imperial regime. The avenue's name changes six times along the way, which is why Parisians refer to it, in the plural, as "Les Grands Boulevards."

This walk starts at the Parc Monceau, heart of one of the most fashionable residential neighborhoods, but the makeup of the neighborhoods along the Grands Boulevards changes steadily as you head from the posh 8^e *arrondissement* (district) toward working-class east Paris. The *Grands Magasins* (department stores) at the start of the walk epitomize upscale Paris shopping. They stand on boulevard Haussmann, named in honor of the regional prefect who oversaw the reconstruction of the city in the 1850s and 1860s. The opulent Opéra Garnier, just past the Grands Magasins, is the architectural showpiece of the period (often termed Second Empire and corresponding to the rule of Napoléon III).

Haussmann's concept of urban planning proved grand enough to ward off the postwar skyscrapers and property sharks that bedevil so many other European cities (Paris's urban planners have relegated them to the outskirts). Though lined with the seven-story blocks typical of Haussmann's time, the boulevards date from the 1670s, when they were created on the site of the city's medieval fortifications. These were razed when Louis XIV's military triumphs appeared to render their raison d'être obsolete, and were replaced by leafy promenades known from the outset as "boulevards" (the word has the same origin as bulwark).

This walk takes in some of the older sights on both sides of the boulevard, including the city's traditional auction house, the colonnaded stock exchange, and the Sentier district with its busy fabric traders. It ends on the tranquil banks of the little-known Canal St-Martin.

Numbers in the text correspond to numbers in the margin and on The Grand Boulevards map.

a good walk

Take the métro to Monceau in the tony 8e arrondissement and step through gold-topped iron gates to enter the **Parc Monceau** (1) —the heart of an elegant residential neighborhood once called home by the likes of Paderewski, Rostand, and Sarah Bernhardt. Once past the sculpted busts of Gounod, Chopin, and Bizet, near the middle of the park, head left to avenue Velasquez, which is ornamented with spectacular gates and mansions. One such mansion is the **Musée Cernuschi** (2), which has a refined collection of Chinese art from Neolithic pottery to contemporary paintings, but is closed until June 2004. Continue on to boulevard Malesherbes and turn right, then right again onto rue de Monceau, to reach the **Musée Nissim de Camondo** (3), whose aristocratic interiors sumptuously bring to life the days of the ancien régime.

More splendor awaits at the **Musée Jacquemart-André** (4). Continue down rue de Monceau and turn left onto rue de Courcelles, then left again onto boulevard Haussmann to find this imposing 19th-century marble palace filled with lacquered antiques and great old-master paintings amassed by a Parisian millionaire. Continue eastward along the boulevard and cross the square in front of the church of St-Augustin. Stay on boulevard Haussmann then turn right down rue d'Anjou to enter the leafy, intimate square Louis XVI with its **Chapelle Expiatoire** (5), dedicated to Louis XVI and Marie-Antoinette. Be sure to take a look at the amusing stone carvings on the gleaming 1930s-style facade of the bank at the corner of rue Pasquier and rue Mathurins. Some 300 yards farther down boulevard Haussmann are the Grands Magasins, Paris's most renowned department stores. First comes **Au Printemps** (6), then **Galeries Lafayette** (7). Marks & Spencer, across the street, provides an out-

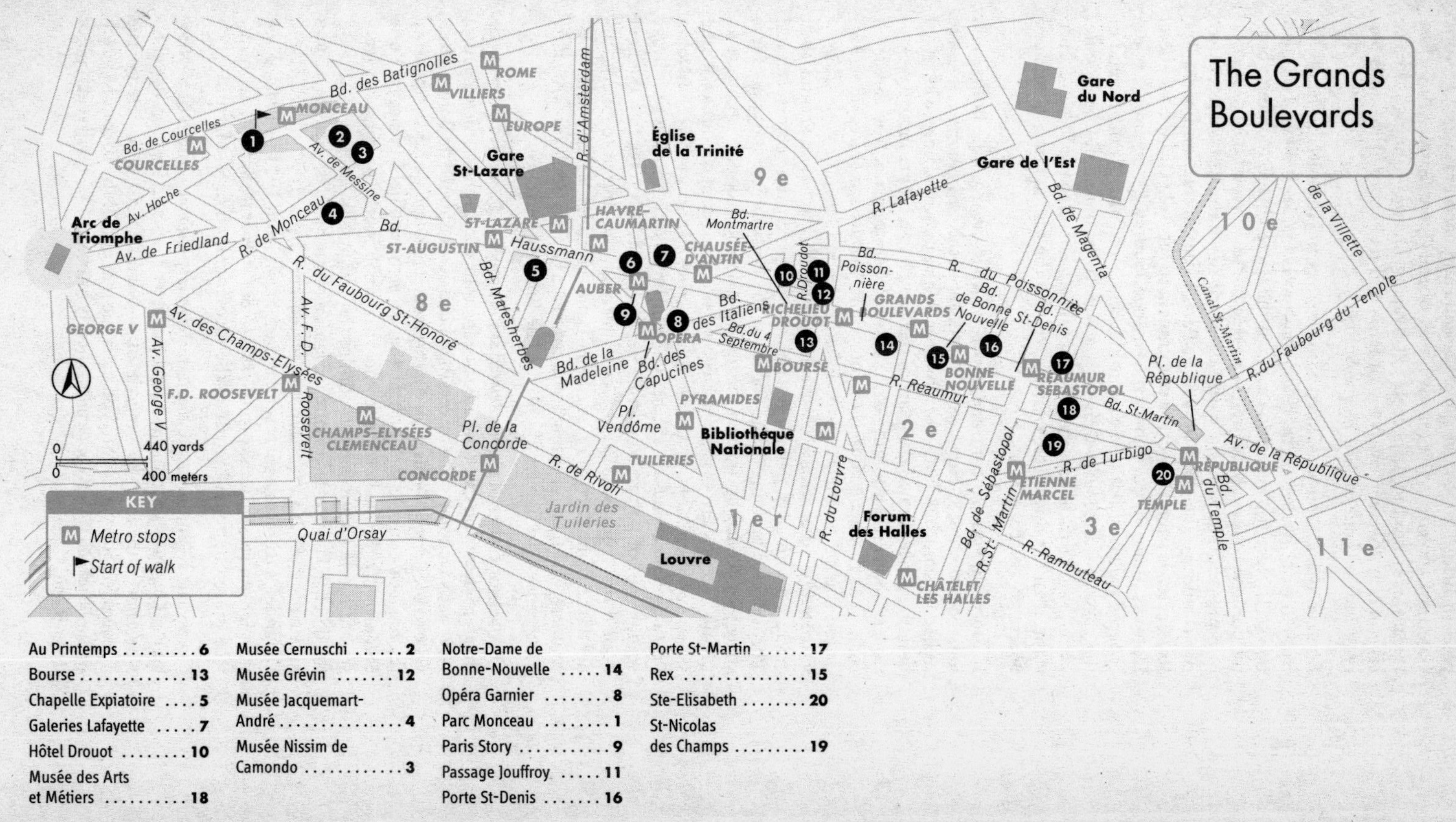

Au Printemps 6
Bourse 13
Chapelle Expiatoire 5
Galeries Lafayette 7
Hôtel Drouot 10
Musée des Arts et Métiers 18
Musée Cernuschi 2
Musée Grévin 12
Musée Jacquemart-André 4
Musée Nissim de Camondo 3
Notre-Dame de Bonne-Nouvelle 14
Opéra Garnier 8
Parc Monceau 1
Paris Story 9
Passage Jouffroy 11
Porte St-Denis 16
Porte St-Martin 17
Rex 15
Ste-Elisabeth 20
St-Nicolas des Champs 19

post for British goods like ginger biscuits and bacon rashers. Opposite Galeries Lafayette is the massive bulk of the **Opéra Garnier** 8. Before venturing around to inspect its extravagant facade, you might like to take in a multiscreen overview of Paris and its history at the **Paris Story** 9 movie venue at No. 11 rue Scribe.

Boulevard des Capucines, lined with cinemas and restaurants, heads left from in front of the Opéra, becoming boulevard des Italiens. Look left up rue Laffitte for a startling view of the Sacré-Coeur, looming above the porticoed church of Notre-Dame-de-Lorette. Just after the intersection of boulevard Haussmann with boulevard des Italiens, turn left down rue Drouot to the **Hôtel Drouot** 10, Paris's central auction house. Rue Rossini leads from Drouot, as it is known, to rue de la Grange-Batelière. Halfway along on the right is the **Passage Jouffroy** 11, one of the many covered galleries that honeycomb the center of Paris. At the far end of the passage is the **Musée Grévin** 12, a waxworks museum. Cross boulevard Montmartre to passage des Panoramas, leading to rue St-Marc. Turn right, then left down rue Vivienne, to find the foursquare, colonnaded **Bourse** 13, the Paris Stock Exchange.

If you wish, you can continue down rue Vivienne from the Bourse and join the Faubourg St-Honoré walk at the Bibliothèque Nationale. If you're feeling adventurous, head east along rue Réaumur, whose huge-windowed buildings once formed the heart of the French newspaper industry—stationery shops still abound—and cross rue Montmartre. You can catch sight of St-Eustache church to your right; the distant spires of St-Ambroise emerge on the horizon. Take the second left up rue de Cléry, a narrow street that is the exclusive domain of fabric wholesalers and often crammed with vans, pallets, and delivery people creating colorful chaos. The lopsided building at the corner of rue Poissonnière looks as if it is struggling to stay upright on the district's drunken slopes. Continue up rue de Cléry as far as rue des Degrés—not a street at all but a 14-step stairway—then look for the clock and crooked turnip tower of **Notre-Dame de Bonne-Nouvelle** 14, hemmed in by rickety housing that looks straight out of Balzac. You can enter via No. 19 bis (meaning the next door down from No. 19) and cross through the church to emerge beneath the front portico on rue de la Lune. Head left as far as rue Poissonnière, and then turn right to return to the Grands Boulevards, by now going under the name of boulevard de Bonne-Nouvelle.

On the near corner of the boulevard stands the **Rex** 15, an Art Deco movie theater where you can take a backstage tour. Cross the boulevard for a view of its wedding-cake tower; then head up boulevard de Bonne-Nouvelle to the **Porte St-Denis** 16, a newly cleaned triumphal arch dating from the reign of Louis XIV. A little farther on is the smaller but similar **Porte St-Martin** 17. From here take rue St-Martin south, pausing on leafy square Émile-Chautemps to admire the red marble–pillared facade of the derelict Théâtre de la Gaîté Lyrique, a music hall designed by Jacques Hittorff in 1862; Offenbach conducted here from 1873 to 1875, and Diaghilev's Russian ballets set the stage alight from 1911 to 1913. Then turn left on rue Réaumur to the **Musée des Arts et Métiers** 18, an industrial museum, housed partly in the former church of St-Martin.

Across rue Réaumur is the high, narrow, late-Gothic church of **St-Nicolas des Champs** 19. Continue past the cloister ruins and Renaissance gateway that embellish the far side of St-Nicolas, and head left on rue Turbigo for 500 yards until you meet the rear end of the Baroque church of **Ste-Elisabeth** 20 on your right. Shortly afterward you will reach place de la République.

TIMING The distance between Parc Monceau and place de la République is about 7 km (4½ mi), which will probably require at least four hours to walk, including coffee breaks and window-shopping.

What to See

6 **Au Printemps.** Founded in 1865 by Jules Jaluzot—former employee of Au Bon Marché, which opened 13 years earlier on the Left Bank—Au Printemps swiftly became the mecca of Right Bank shoppers, enabling the current opulent Belle Epoque buildings, with their domes and gold-and-green mosaic signs, to be erected by the turn of the 20th century. The glass cupola in Café Flo dates from 1923; and the rooftop cafeteria has a splendid view of the Paris skyline. ✉ *64 bd. Haussmann, Opéra/Grands Boulevards* Ⓜ *Havre Caumartin.*

13 **Bourse** (Stock Exchange). The Paris Stock Exchange, a serene, colonnaded 19th-century building, is a far cry from Wall Street. Bring your passport if you want to tour it. ✉ *Rue Vivienne, Opéra/Grands Boulevards* *€4.50* ⏲ *Guided tours only (in French), weekdays every ½ hr 1:15–4* Ⓜ *Bourse.*

need a break? A family-run *épicerie* (grocery store) and wine shop in the elegant Galerie Vivienne, **Legrand Filles et Fils** (✉ 1 rue Banque, Bourse ☎ 01-42-60-07-12) has been the place to go for eatables and drinkables since 1880. Now the Legrand family has added a wine bar in the back, serving simple, delicious fare and a superb selection of wines. For a €15 corking fee, they'll open any bottle in the cellar. Château Pétrus 1961 anyone?

5 **Chapelle Expiatoire.** This unkempt mausoleum emerges defiantly from the lush undergrowth of verdant square Louis-XVI off boulevard Haussmann, marking the initial burial site of Louis XVI and Marie-Antoinette after their turns at the guillotine on place de la Concorde. Two stone tablets are inscribed with the last missives of the doomed royals: touching pleas for forgiveness for their revolutionary enemies. When compared to the pomp and glory of Napoléon's memorial at the Invalides, this tribute to royalty seems halfhearted and trite. ✉ *29 rue Pasquier, Opéra/Grands Boulevards* ☎ *01-44-32-18-00* 🌐 *www.monum.fr* *€2.50* ⏲ *Thurs.–Sat. 1–5* Ⓜ *St-Augustin.*

7 **Galeries Lafayette.** This turn-of-the-20th-century department store has a vast, shimmering Belle Epoque glass dome that can be seen only if you venture inside. ✉ *40 bd. Haussmann, Opéra/Grands Boulevards* Ⓜ *Chaussée d'Antin; RER: Auber.*

10 **Hôtel Drouot.** Hidden away in a grid of narrow streets not far from the Opéra is Paris's central auction house, where everything from stamps and toy soldiers to Renoirs and 18th-century commodes is sold. The 16 salesrooms make for fascinating browsing, and there's no obligation to bid. The mix of ladies in fur coats with money to burn, penniless art lovers desperate to unearth an unidentified masterpiece, and scruffy dealers trying to look anonymous makes up Drouot's unusually rich social fabric. Sales are held most weekdays, with viewings in the morning; anyone can attend. For centuries, the French government refused to allow foreign firms to stage auctions, but that changed in 2001, and Drouot now faces very stiff competition from Sotheby's and Christie's, who have set up shop in Paris. ✉ *9 rue Drouot, Opéra/Grands Boulevards* ☎ *01-48-00-20-00* ⏲ *Viewings mid-Sept.–mid-July, Mon.–Sat. 11–noon and 2–6, with auctions starting at 2* Ⓜ *Richelieu Drouot.*

off the beaten path

Musée Gustave Moreau. A visit to this town house and studio of painter Gustave Moreau (1826–98), doyen of the Symbolist movement, is one of the most distinctive artistic experiences in Paris. The Symbolists strove to convey ideas through images, but many of the ideas Moreau was trying to express were so obscure that the artist had to provide explanatory texts, which rather confuses the point. But it's easy to admire his extravagant colors and flights of fantasy, influenced by Persian and Indian miniatures. From the Trinité church, take rue Blanche to the right, and then turn right on rue de la Tour-des-Dames; the museum is at the far end of rue de la Rochefoucauld. ✉ *14 rue de la Rochefoucauld, Opéra/Grands Boulevards* ☎ *01–48–74–38–50* 🎫 *€3.40* ⏲ *Thurs.–Sun. 10–12:45 and 2–5:15, Mon. and Wed. 11–5:15* Ⓜ *Trinité.*

18 **Musée des Arts et Métiers** (National Technical Museum). The former church and priory of St-Martin des Champs was built between the 11th and 13th centuries. Confiscated during the Revolution, it was used first as an educational institution, then as an arms factory, before becoming, in 1799, the Conservatoire des Arts et Métiers. Today the church and the splendid 13th-century refectory, a large hall supported by central columns, form part of the National Technical Museum, a crafts and industrial museum with a varied collection of models (locomotives, vehicles, and agricultural machinery), astronomical instruments, looms, and glass, together with displays on printing, photography, and the history of television. ✉ *60 rue Réaumur, Beaubourg/Les Halles* ☎ *01–53–01–82–00* 🌐 *www.cnam.fr/museum* 🎫 *€5.50* ⏲ *Tues.–Sun. 10–6, Thurs. 10–9:30* Ⓜ *Arts et Métiers.*

need a break?

A tiny Chinatown has popped up near the Arts et Métiers, especially on and around rue au Maire. Chinese and Vietnamese restaurants are dotted everywhere; most are unremarkable, but if you're in a hurry and couldn't possibly stomach another mediocre croque monsieur or crepe, try the delicious *phô* (beef noodle soup) at tiny **Shun Da** (✉ 16 rue Volta ☎ 01–42–72–71–11), a five-table Vietnamese restaurant in a 14th-century timbered building on rue Volta. If it's packed, as is often the case, the larger **Song Heng** (✉ 6 rue Volta ☎ 01–42–36–71–66) across the street is just as good—though the building is a spring chicken by comparison: mid-1600s.

2 **Musée Cernuschi.** Closed for renovation until June 2004, this museum is set within an aristocratic town house. A connoisseur's favorite, the collection includes Chinese art from Neolithic pottery (3rd century BC) to funeral statuary, painted 8th-century silks, and contemporary paintings, as well as ancient Persian bronze objects. ✉ *7 av. Velasquez, Parc Monceau* ☎ *01–55–74–61–30* 🌐 *www.paris-france.org/musees* 🎫 *Free* ⏲ *Tues.–Sun. 10–5:40* Ⓜ *Monceau.*

12 **Musée Grévin.** Founded in 1882, this waxworks museum, around the corner from the Hôtel Drouot, ranks in scope and ingenuity with Madame Tussaud's in London. Wax renderings of 250 historical and contemporary celebrities are on display; your ticket also allows entry to a 1900 Palace of Illusion. ✉ *10 bd. Montmartre, Opéra/Grands Boulevards* ☎ *01–47–70–85–05* 🌐 *www.grevin.com* 🎫 *€15* ⏲ *Daily 10–7* Ⓜ *Grands Boulevards.*

★ 4 **Musée Jacquemart-André.** Often compared to New York City's Frick Collection, this was one of the grandest private residences of 19th-century Paris. Built between 1869 and 1875, it found Hollywood fame when used as Gaston Lachaille's mansion in the 1958 musical *Gigi.* Edouard

André and his painter wife Nélie Jacquemart, the house's actual owners, were rich and cultured, so art from the Italian Renaissance and 18th-century France compete for attention here. Note the freshly restored Tiepolo frescoes in the staircase and on the dining-room ceiling, while salons done in the fashionable "Louis XVI–Empress" style (favored by Empress Eugénie) are hung with great paintings, including Uccello's *Saint George Slaying the Dragon,* Rembrandt's *Pilgrims of Emmaus,* Jean-Marc Nattier's *Mathilde de Canisy,* and Jacques-Louis David's *Comte Antoine-Français de Nantes.* You can tour the house with the free English audio guide. The Tiepolo salon now contains a café, where you can lunch on salads named after the great painters Fragonard, Mantegna, and Chardin. ✉ *158 bd. Haussmann, Parc Monceau* ☎ *01–45–62–11–59* 🌐 *musee-jacquemart-andre.com* 🎫 *€8* ⏲ *Daily 10–6* Ⓜ *St-Philippe-du-Roule or Miromesnil.*

need a break?

An abbreviation of *boulangerie-épicerie,* **Be** (✉ 73 bd. de Courcelles, Parc Monceau ☎ 01–46–22–20–20) is a hybrid bakery and corner store run by superchef Alain Ducasse and renowned baker Eric Kayser. Stocked with gastronomic grocery items like candied tomatoes and walnut oil from the Dordogne, it is also the perfect drop-in spot for delicious soups and gourmet sandwiches.

3 **Musée Nissim de Camondo.** Molière made fun of the *bourgeois gentilhomme,* the middle-class man who aspired to the class of his royal betters, but the playwright would have been in awe of Comte Moïse de Camondo, whose sense of style, grace, and refinement could have taught the courtiers at Versailles a thing or two. After making a fortune in the late 19th century, the businessman built this grand hôtel particulier in the style of the Petit Trianon and proceeded to furnish it with some of the most exquisite furniture, boiseries, and bibelots of the mid- to late 18th century. His wife and children (the museum is named after his son, who died in combat during World War I) then moved in and lent the house enormous warmth and charm. From ancien régime splendor, however, the family descended to the worst horrors of World War II: after the death of Count Moïse in 1935, the estate left the family's house and treasures to the government, while shortly thereafter, family descendants were packed off to Auschwitz by the Nazis, where several of them were murdered. Today the wealthy matrons of Paris have made this museum their own, and it shines anew with the beauty of the 18th century. If you want to see these enchanting salons in all their candlelit glory, view a video of *Valmont,* Milos Forman's 1989 filmed version of *Les Liaisons Dangereuses.* ✉ *63 rue de Monceau, Parc Monceau* ☎ *01–53–89–06–50* 🌐 *www.ucad.fr* 🎫 *€4.60* ⏲ *Wed.–Sun. 10–5* Ⓜ *Villiers.*

Fodor's Choice ★

14 **Notre-Dame de Bonne-Nouvelle.** This wide, soberly neoclassical church is tucked away off the Grands Boulevards. The previous church (the second) on the spot was ransacked during the Revolution, and the current one, built in 1823–29 after the restoration of the French monarchy, was ransacked by Communard hooligans in May 1871. The highlight is the semicircular apse behind the altar, featuring some fine 17th-century paintings beneath a three-dimensional 19th-century grisaille composition by Abel de Pujol. Note the many pictures, statues, and works of religious art in the side chapels. ✉ *Rue de la Lune, Opéra/Grands Boulevards* Ⓜ *Bonne Nouvelle.*

8 **Opéra Garnier.** Haunt of the Phantom of the Opera, the real-life setting for some of Degas's famous ballet paintings, and still the most opulent theater in the world, the Paris Opéra was begun in 1862 by Charles Gar-

nier at the behest of Napoléon III. Due to its lavishness, it was not completed until 1875, five years after the emperor's abdication. Awash with Algerian colored marbles and gilded putti, it is said to typify Second Empire architecture: a pompous hodgepodge of styles with about as much subtlety as a Wagnerian cymbal crash. The composer Debussy famously compared it to a Turkish bathhouse, but lovers of pomp and splendor will adore it. Hitler is said to have called it the most beautiful building in the world.

To see the theater and lobby, you don't actually have to attend a performance: after paying an entry fee you can stroll around at leisure and view the foyer and have a peek into the auditorium. The monumental Grand Foyer is nearly as big as the auditorium (together they fill 3 acres). After all, this was a theater for Parisians who came to the opera primarily to be seen; on opening nights, you can still see Rothschilds and rock stars preen and prance on the grand staircase. If the lavishly upholstered auditorium seems small, it is only because the stage is the largest in the world—more than 11,000 square yards, with room for up to 450 performers. Marc Chagall painted the ceiling in 1964. The **Opera Museum,** containing a few paintings and theatrical mementos, is unremarkable. If you want a full burst of Parisian grandeur, make sure you catch a performance here—while technically the official home of the Paris Ballet, this auditorium usually mounts one or two full-scale operas a season (most operas are presented at the drearily modern Opéra de la Bastille). ✉ *Pl. de l'Opéra, Opéra/Grands Boulevards* ☎ *01–40–01–22–63* 🌐 *www.opera-de-paris.fr* 🎫 *€6* ⏲ *Daily 10–4:30. Guided tours in English at 3* PM Ⓜ *Opéra.*

need a break?

Few cafés are as grand as the Belle Epoque **Café de la Paix** (✉ 5 pl. de l'Opéra, Opéra/Grands Boulevards ☎ 01–40–07–30–10). Once described as "the center of the civilized world," it was a regular meeting place for the glitterati of 19th- and 20th-century Paris; the prices are as grand as the setting. Today probably only the waiters speak French.

❶ **Parc Monceau.** The most picturesque gardens on the Right Bank were laid out as a private park in 1778 and retain some of the fanciful elements then in vogue, including mock ruins and a faux pyramid. In 1797 André Garnerin, the world's first-recorded parachutist, staged a landing in the park. The rotunda—known as the Chartres Pavilion—is surely the city's grandest public rest room; it started life as a tollhouse. All in all, this remains one of the snobbiest parks in Paris and certainly one of the prettiest—no wonder director Vincente Minnelli used it as a backdrop in his film *Gigi.* ✉ *Entrances on bd. de Courcelles, av. Velasquez, av. Ruysdaël, av. van Dyck, Parc Monceau* Ⓜ *Monceau.*

❾ **Paris Story.** Victor Hugo is your "guide" on this 45-minute split-screen presentation of Paris and its history, with spectacular photography and tasteful musical accompaniment, with St-Saëns's Organ Symphony employed to majestic effect. It's a fun introduction to the city. Be sure to get headphones to hear the English translation. ✉ *11 bis rue Scribe, Opéra/Grands Boulevards* ☎ *01–42–66–62–06* 🌐 *www.paris-story.com* 🎫 *€8* ⏲ *Apr.–Oct., daily 9–8; Nov.–Mar., daily 9–7; screenings on the hr* Ⓜ *Opéra.*

⓫ **Passage Jouffroy.** Built in 1846, as its giant clock will tell you, this shops-filled *passage* (gallery) was one of the first precursors to the modern-day shopping mall. ✉ *Entrances on bd. Montmartre, rue de la Grange-Batelière, Opéra/Grands Boulevards* Ⓜ *Richelieu Drouot.*

16 **Porte St-Denis.** Not as grandiose as the Arc de Triomphe, but triumphant nonetheless, Paris's second-largest arch (76-ft) was erected by François Blondel in 1672 to celebrate the victories of Ludovico Magno (as Louis XIV is here styled) on the Rhine. The bas-reliefs by François Girardon include campaign scenes and trophies stacked on shallow, slender pyramids. The arch faces rue St-Denis—formerly the royal processional route into Paris from the north (last so used by Queen Victoria in 1855) but now better known for activity along the sidewalk. ✉ *Bd. St-Denis, Opéra/Grands Boulevards* Ⓜ *Strasbourg St-Denis.*

17 **Porte St-Martin.** This 56-ft triumphal arch, slightly smaller and younger than the neighboring Porte St-Denis, was designed by Blondel's pupil Pierre Bullet in 1674. Louis XIV's victories at Limburg (in Flanders) and Besançon in Franche-Comté get bas-relief coverage from Martin Desjardins. ✉ *Bd. St-Denis, Opéra/Grands Boulevards* Ⓜ *Strasbourg St-Denis.*

15 **Rex.** If you're a movie buff, you may want to inspect Europe's self-styled "Grandest Cinema," built in 1932—although the 50-minute back-screen tour, full of special effects and loudspeaker commentary (available in English), gives only a tantalizing glimpse of the 2,700-seat auditorium, with its star-spangled roof and onstage fountains. You're surreptitiously filmed as you go around, with an individualized souvenir video (€6) available as you leave. If you still want more, see a movie here. ✉ *1 bd. Poissonnière, Opéra/Grands Boulevards* ☎ *08–36–68–70–23* *€7* ⏲ *Wed.–Sun. 10–7* Ⓜ *Bonne Nouvelle.*

20 **Ste-Elisabeth.** This studied essay in Baroque (built 1628–46) is pleasantly unpretentious; there's no soaring bombast here. The church has brightly restored wall paintings and a wide, semicircular apse around the choir, where biblical scenes are carved into stupendous 17th-century wood paneling transferred from an abbey in Arras in northern France. ✉ *Rue du Temple, République* Ⓜ *Temple.*

19 **St-Nicolas des Champs.** The rounded arches and Doric capitals in the chancel of this church date from 1560 to 1587, a full century later than the pointed-arch nave (1420–80). There is a majestic mid-17th-century organ and a fine *Assumption of the Virgin* (1629) by Simon Vouet above the high altar. The south door (1576) on rue au Maire is gloriously carved and surrounded by a small but unexpectedly well-tended lawn complete with rosebushes. ✉ *Rue St-Martin, Opéra/Grands Boulevards* Ⓜ *Arts et Métiers.*

FROM RÉPUBLIQUE TO LA VILLETTE

Place de la République is the gateway to northeast Paris, a largely residential area that is often underestimated by tourists, but not by the natives: princes of the Paris night will now tell you that the Bastille bubble has burst, and the eventide pulse has beaten a retreat northeast into the heartland of the 11e arrondissement. For stylemeisters, rue Oberkampf, rue St-Maur, and rue Jean-Pierre-Timbaud are where it's all happening. Another flash point for trendies is the newly cool area around the Canal St-Martin, which forms the focal point of this walk. Today its barges transport mainly visitors and pleasure boats, but it was once a busy thoroughfare linking the Seine to the city's central slaughterhouse at La Villette. The Mitterrand era saw La Villette landscaped beyond recognition, with science and music museums and a concert hall built amid a wittily designed postmodern park. Nearby, 19th-century city planner Baron Haussmann let his hair down at the tumbling Buttes-Chaumont Park, going to town with a lake, a waterfall, a grotto, and phony cliffs.

Numbers in the text correspond to numbers in the margin and on place de la République to La Villette map.

a good walk

Begin your walk at **place de la République** 1 . Cross the square and head up rue du Faubourg-du-Temple to the **Canal St-Martin** 2, whose locks and pale-green footbridges conjure up an unexpected flavor of Amsterdam. At this point, the canal emerges from a 2½-km (1½-mi) tunnel that starts beyond the Bastille. To explore the trendy Oberkampf district, continue along rue du Faubourg-du-Temple until you hit rue St-Maur, then take it south a few blocks to rue Jean-Pierre-Timbaud and rue Oberkampf. Backtrack north to the **Hôpital St-Louis** 3, Paris's oldest hospital, with its serene courtyard and chapel still intact. Leave the hospital on rue de la Grange-aux-Belles and turn left, then right down rue Bichat, to find the Canal St-Martin bending beneath the unassuming white facade of the **Hôtel du Nord** 4, made famous by the film of the same name. The canal continues north to the circular **Rotonde de La Villette** 5. It surveys both the elevated métro line and the unruffled sheen of the Bassin de La Villette, where boats leave on a mile-long trip to the **Parc de La Villette** 6, with its postmodern science and music museums. If you prefer to take the 30-minute walk along the canal to the park, keep to the left bank of quai de la Seine and go past the tiny, 18th-century Portuguese Jewish cemetery at No. 44. Cross over the canal on the Pont de Crimée, near the church of St-Jacques–St-Christophe, before continuing up quai de la Marne. Yet another option is to follow avenue Secrétan southeast from the Rotonde to the picturesque **Parc des Buttes-Chaumont** 7. Wend your way left around this tumbling park—once a quarry—and skirt the lake before climbing to the top of the manmade cliff for a panoramic view of the city.

Leave the park from the eastern corner. Turn left on rue Botzaris, and then right up rue de Crimée. Take the first left up a flight of stairs to the dowdy little street called villa Albert-Robida. You're now on the fringe of the **Quartier d'Amérique** 8, so called because stone quarried in the Buttes-Chaumont is said to have been used to build the White House. The two- and three-story houses around here—originally quarriers' cottages—are a far cry from the seven-story buildings dominating the rest of Paris. Turn left down rue Arthur-Rozier and continue to rue de Mouzaïa. These days these small houses are very desirable: some of the prettiest are found in the *villas* or mews, leading off of rue de Mouzaïa. Venture up quaint, cobbled villa Émile-Lobet on the right—the five gray skyscrapers looming at the far end are a chilling architectural contrast to the colorful paint and ivy-covered railings of the houses. Turn left and left again down flagstone-paved villa de Bellevue and cross to villa du Progrès. Take a left at the bottom of the street and then a right down rue de la Fraternité to reach **place du Rhin-et-Danube** 9.

More mewsy alleyways can be found on either side of rue Miguel-Hidalgo, with a cute view of the foursquare brick tower of the church of St-Francis d'Assisi at the far end of villa des Boërs. From here, take a right on rue Compans and head up to the **Cimetière de La Villette** 10. The entrance is flanked by a grim stone cube that once served as the local morgue. Admire the windows and roofline of the school opposite; then take allée Darius-Milhaud along the side of the cemetery. This promenade curves through the heart of the district, becoming allée Arthur-Honegger and ending in a flight of steps topped by the bulky silhouette of the Cité de la Musique, a modern music academy. The entry to the Parc de La Villette is down to the left.

TIMING If you want to enjoy lunch, dinner, or the sizzling night scene at one of Oberkampf's trendy outposts, begin your exploration at midday. The

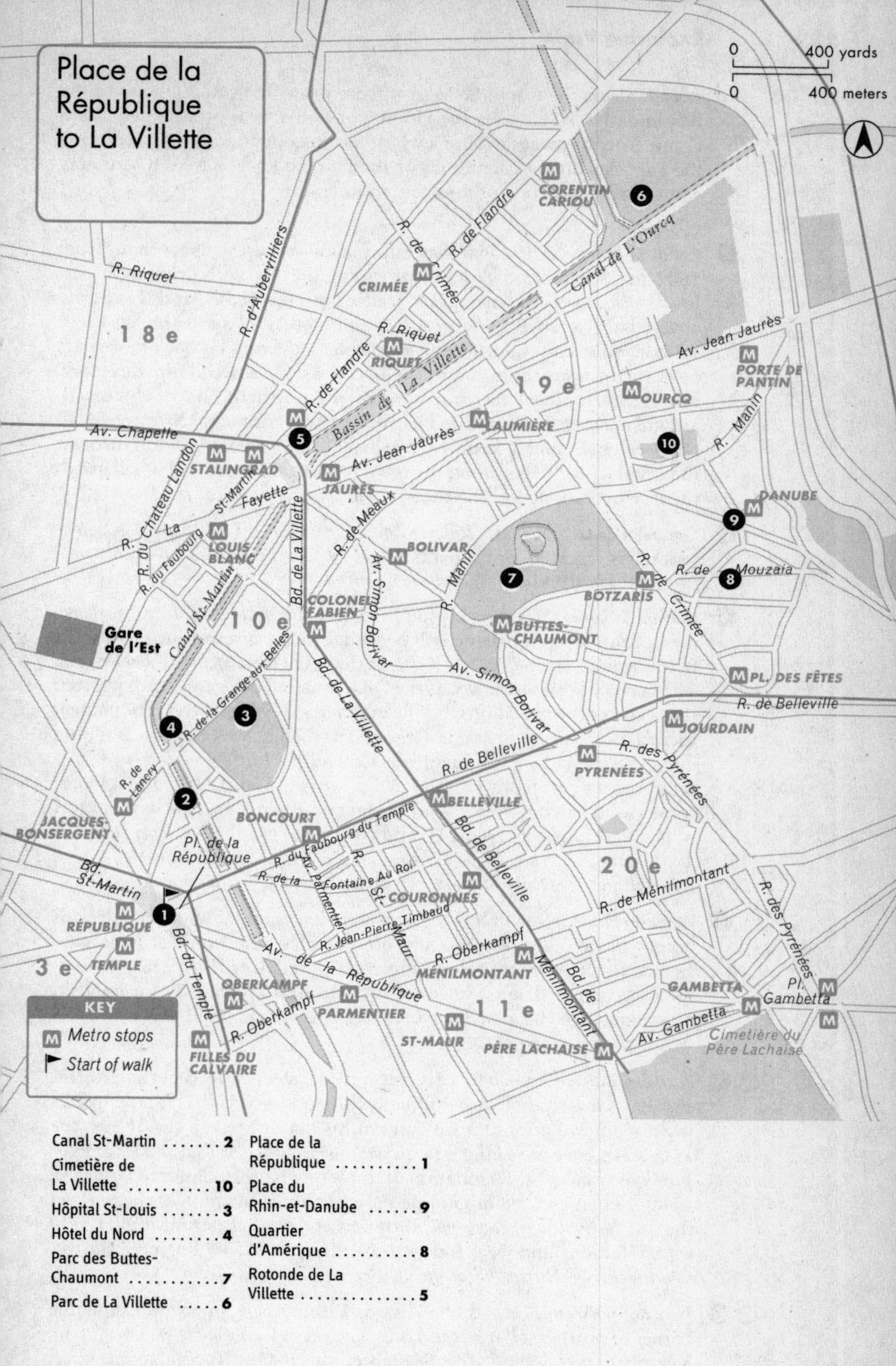

Canal St-Martin 2
Cimetière de La Villette 10
Hôpital St-Louis 3
Hôtel du Nord 4
Parc des Buttes-Chaumont 7
Parc de La Villette 6
Place de la République 1
Place du Rhin-et-Danube 9
Quartier d'Amérique 8
Rotonde de La Villette 5

stretch along the Canal St-Martin from place de la République to the Bassin de La Villette, via the Hôpital St-Louis, is approximately 2 km (1 mi). You may want to allot a whole morning or afternoon to exploring the Parc des Buttes-Chaumont or the Parc de La Villette. Or you may want to return to one of these on another day.

What to See

2 **Canal St-Martin.** The canal was built, at the behest of Napoléon, from 1802 to 1825, with the aim of providing the city with drinking water. It was not assigned to navigable traffic until the 1850s, and was partly covered (between Bastille and République) by Haussmann in 1862. With its quiet banks, locks, and footbridges, the canal is one of the city's most picturesque spots and much loved by novelists and film directors. Major development has transformed the northern end of the canal, around place de Stalingrad and its 18th-century rotunda. There are €1.50 **barge rides** (✉ Embarkation at 13 quai de la Loire, La Villette) through the canal's nine locks along the once-industrial Bassin de La Villette to the nearby Parc de La Villette. *Jacques-Bonsergent, Jaurès.*

Fodor's Choice ★

10 **Cimetière de La Villette** (La Villette Cemetery). One of Paris's smallest cemeteries, it is reserved for residents of the 19e arrondissement. ✉ *Entrance on rue d'Hautpoul, La Villette* Ⓜ *Ourcq.*

3 **Hôpital St-Louis** (St. Louis Hospital). Though it's not, technically speaking, a tourist sight, no one will begrudge you a discreet visit to Paris's first hospital, erected in 1607–10, at the same time as place des Vosges. The main courtyard, known as the Quadrilatère Historique, with its steep roofs and corner pavilions, has been remarkably preserved. The chapel, tucked away along rue de la Grange-aux-Belles, was the first building in Paris to be lit by gaslight and shelters *Suffer Little Children to Come unto Me,* a painting by Charles de La Fosse (1636–1716), and a handsome wood balcony carved with trumpeting angels and the monograms of hospital founders Henri IV and Maria de' Medici. ✉ *Entrances on av. Richerand, rue de la Grange-aux-Belles, av. Claude-Vellefaux, République* ⏲ *Daily 5 AM–9 PM; chapel weekday afternoons.*

4 **Hôtel du Nord** (North Hotel). Despite its unassuming white facade, this hotel—thoroughly restored and now a café-restaurant—is famous in France for its starring role in director Marcel Carné's 1938 movie of the same name. There are concerts and stand-up comedy (in English) most nights. ✉ *102 quai de Jemmappes, République* ☎ *01–40–40–78–78* Ⓜ *Jacques-Bonsergent.*

7 **Parc des Buttes-Chaumont.** This picturesque, steep-sloped park in northeast Paris has a lake, waterfall, and cliff-top folly. Until Napoléon III's town planner Baron Haussmann got his hands on it in the 1860s, the area was a garbage dump and quarry—legend has it that the local gypsum was used in the foundation of the White House. Children large and small will enjoy the **Guignol de Paris** (an open-air puppet theater) on the northern side of the park; shows start (weather permitting) at 3:30 PM Wednesday and weekends (€2.50 charge). ✉ *Rue Botzaris, Buttes-Chaumont* Ⓜ *Buttes-Chaumont, Botzaris.*

6 **Parc de La Villette.** Until the 1970s this 130-acre site, in an unfashionable corner of northeast Paris commonly known as La Villette, was originally a cattle market and *abattoir* (slaughterhouse). Only the slaughterhouse, known as **La Grande Halle** (Great Hall), remains: a magnificent iron-and-glass structure ingeniously transformed into an exhibition-cum-concert center. But everything else here—from the science museum and spherical cinema to the music academy, all connected by designer gardens with canopied walkways and red cubical follies—is futuristic.

Although La Villette breathes the architectural panache of the Mitterrand era, the late president only oversaw one project himself: the **Cité de la Musique,** a giant postmodern music academy designed by architect Christian de Portzamparc, complete with a state-of-the-art concert hall and the spectacular **Musée de la Musique** (Music Museum; ✉ 221 av. Jean-Jaurès, La Villette ☎ 01–44–84–44–84 🎫 €6.10 ⏲ Tues.–Sat. noon–6). The museum contains a mind-tingling array of 900 instruments; their sounds and story are evoked with wireless headphones (ask for English commentary).

The **park** itself, laid out in the 1980s to the design of Bernard Tschumi—now dean of Columbia University's architecture department and a heavyweight of the cerebral postmodern movement—links the academy to the science museum half a mile away. Water and the Grande Halle are the park's focal elements. Two bridges cross the Canal de l'Ourcq, which bisects the park; one becomes a covered walkway, running parallel to the Canal St-Denis, and continues up to the science museum—itself surrounded by the unruffled sheen of a broad moat, reflecting the spherical outline of **La Géode.** This looks like a huge silver golf ball but is actually a cinema made of polished steel, with an enormous hemispherical screen.

The pompously styled **Cité des Sciences et de l'Industrie** (Industry and Science Museum) tries to do for science and industry what the Centre Pompidou does for modern art. Adrien Fainsilber's rectangular building, also conceived in the 1970s, even looks like the Centre Pompidou, minus the gaudy piping. Inside, displays are bright and thought-provoking, though many are in French only. The brave attempt to render technology fun and easy involves 60 do-it-yourself contraptions that make you feel more participant than onlooker. Lines (especially during school holidays) can be intimidating. ✉ *30 av. Corentin-Cariou, La Villette* ☎ *01–40–05–80–00* 🌐 *www.cite-sciences.fr* 🎫 *€7.50, planetarium €2.50* ⏲ *Tues.–Sun. 10–6* Ⓜ *Porte de La Villette, Porte de Pantin.*

1 **Place de la République.** This large oblong square, laid out by Haussmann in 1856–65, is dominated by a matronly, Stalin-size statue symbolizing *The Republic* (1883). The square is often used as a rallying point for demonstrations. République has more métro lines than any other station in Paris. Ⓜ *République.*

9 **Place du Rhin-et-Danube.** Although seven streets intersect at this square in the Quartier d'Amérique, it retains a rural, unhurried feel. The small white statue of a young girl clutching a sheaf of wheat recalls the area's pastoral origins, before it was absorbed into Paris in the 19th century. The métro station underneath was built in a former quarry. Ⓜ *Danube.*

8 **Quartier d'Amérique** (America Quarter). This neighborhood is so named because the gypsum that was once quarried here (mostly on the site that was transformed into the Parc des Buttes-Chaumont in the 1860s) was shipped to America and used, so the story goes, in building the White House. The quartier is made up of a grid of streets and narrow mews (known as "villas") lined with modest two- and three-story houses once inhabited by quarriers—now some of the most sought-after homes in the city. Ⓜ *Botzaris.*

5 **Rotonde de La Villette.** This strange circular building was one of the tollhouses built around the edge of Paris by Nicolas Ledoux in the 1780s. Most of these austere, daunting buildings, symbols, to the populace, of taxes and oppression, were promptly dismantled during the Revolution. Luckily, the Rotunda survived as a relic of Ledoux's thrilling architecture. Like Mitterrand, Ledoux was fascinated by masonic symbols such as spheres and pyramids. Although the Rotunda is partly obscured by the aboveground métro as you approach from the south, its clean-cut outlines and honey-color stonework can be admired from the north, where a paved courtyard overlooks the Bassin de La Villette and the barges lining up at the lock to reach the Canal St-Martin. ✉ *Pl. de Stalingrad, La Villette* Ⓜ *Stalingrad.*

FROM BASTILLE TO NATION

At the center of the Bastille neighborhood is place de la Bastille, site of the infamous prison attacked by the Parisian people on July 14, 1789—an event that came to symbolize the beginning of the French Revolution. The only folks likely to storm the Bastille these days are theatergoers lining up for seats at the modern Opéra Bastille. They are joined by hipsters, who now flock here as the neighborhood—along with the adjacent sectors of Belleville and Menilmontant (the latter immortalized in the Oscar-winning 1957 film of Albert Lamorrise, *The Red Balloon*)—was gentrified, largely in commemoration of the bicentennial of the Revolution in 1989. Soon this area became one of the liveliest in Paris, and galleries, shops, theaters, cafés, restaurants, and bars still fill formerly decrepit buildings and alleys. After a decade of the artsy crowd's mingling with the blue-collar natives, many of the former have moved on, but the hip spots are holding on and still making fashion waves. Southeast of the Bastille are the imposing place de la Nation and the up-and-coming Bercy neighborhood. Other highlights of this tour include the verdant Bois de Vincennes, the spectacular Bibliothèque Nationale François-Mitterrand, and the evocative Père-Lachaise cemetery, final resting place of Balzac, Proust, Wilde, and many other famous figures.

Numbers in the text correspond to numbers in the margin and on the From Bastille to Nation map.

a good walk

Start your walk at **place de la Bastille** ❶ ⚑, which is easily accessible by métro. Today the square is dominated by the Colonne de Juillet and the curving glass facade of the modern **Opéra de la Bastille** ❷. Leading away from the square is rue de la Roquette, a street alive with shops and cafés, which in turn leads first to vibrant rue de Lappe, lined with bars, clubs, and restaurants, then to rue des Taillandiers and rue Keller, with their bookshops and music stores. All these streets are worth exploring—and rue de Lappe is especially hopping at night. Turn right at the end of rue de Lappe onto rue de Charonne to reach rue du Faubourg-St-Antoine, famous for its cabinetmakers. You'll see why if you take the unevenly cobbled passage du Chantier, just opposite. Its boutiques sell furniture and nothing else. (Peek into other *passages* as well for more glimpses of the behind-the-scenes life of the Bastille.)

Continue along rue du Faubourg-St-Antoine, and then take a right down avenue Ledru-Rollin, crossing rue Charenton and passing the modern church of St-Antoine, to reach avenue Daumesnil. The disused railroad viaduct has been tastefully transformed into a series of designer boutiques with a walkway on top—restyled the **Viaduc des Arts** ❸.

Saunter down as far as rue Hector-Malot; then turn right across avenue Daumesnil and head down boulevard Diderot to Gare de Lyon métro station. If you'd like to visit the giant national library, the **Bibliothèque Nationale François-Mitterrand** ❹, take Line 14 from Gare de Lyon for three stops to the Bibliothèque station. Or get off one stop earlier at Cour St-Emilion and explore the revamped **Bercy** ❺ neighborhood, with its restored wine warehouses and innovative park. The four L-shape towers of the national library loom across the Seine as you head west toward

Bercy 5
Bibliothèque Nationale François-Mitterrand 4
Bois de Vincennes. 9
Cimetière du Père-Lachaise 8
Cimetière de Picpus 6
Opéra de la Bastille. 2
Place de la Bastille. 1
Place de la Nation 7
Viaduc des Arts 3

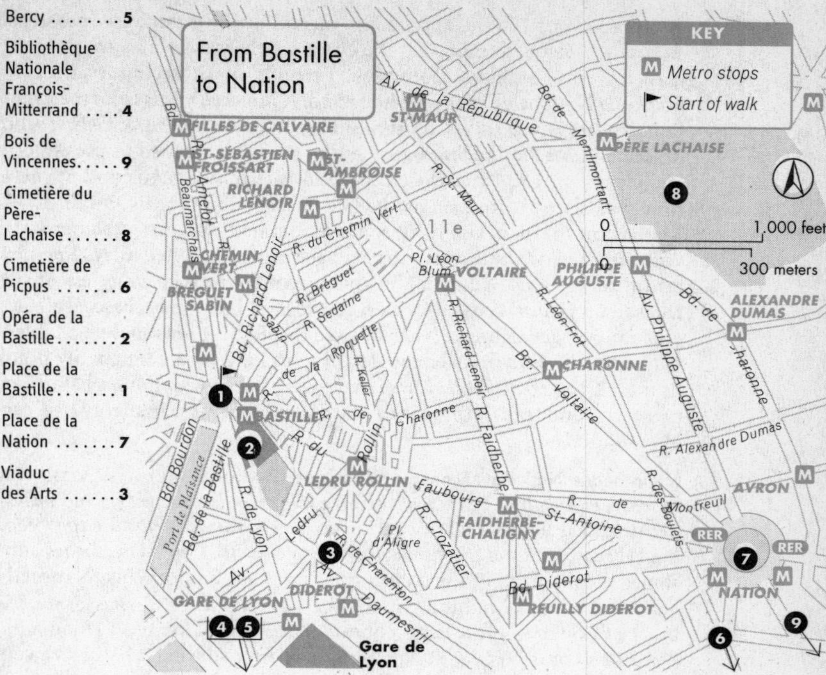

the grass-covered walls of the Palais Omnisports stadium. Follow rue de Bercy, under the elephantine Ministère des Finances, and then turn right through the tunnel, up to rue de Rambouillet. Here rejoin avenue de Daumesnil and the Viaduc des Arts. Head up the steps to see what's on top of the viaduct: gone are the tracks, ousted by the Promenade Plantée, a walkway lined with trees and flowers. The walkway continues for another 2½ km (1½ mi). But you might just want to stay on it for about 1 km (½ mi) before turning left on rue de Picpus. Some 350 yards up on the right is the entry to the **Cimetière de Picpus** 6, where General Lafayette is buried.

Continue on rue de Picpus for about 250 yards, and then cross rue Fabre-d'Eglantine to reach the majestic **place de la Nation** 7, flanked to the right by two towering columns that once marked the eastern entry to Paris. From here it's a short métro ride to the city's most famous cemetery, the **Cimetière du Père-Lachaise** 8, or to the **Bois de Vincennes** 9, a large wooded park with lakes, a castle, and a zoo.

TIMING The walk from place de la Bastille to place de la Nation, including an excursion to the Bercy neighborhood, is about 7 km (4½ mi) long and takes about four hours to complete. Count on more time if you also plan to visit the national library.

What to See

5 **Bercy.** Bercy is a testament to the French genius for urban renewal. Tucked away on the Right Bank of the Seine, south of the Gare de Lyon in the 12e arrondissement, this colorful district was for decades filled with warehouses storing wine from the provinces. Now sport and finance set the tone. The first thing you'll see as you emerge from the Bercy métro station is the mighty glass wall of the **Ministère des Finances** (Finance Ministry). To the left is the ingeniously sloping, grass-walled **Palais Omnisports,** a weird-looking stadium that hosts sports and music

events and seats 17,000, approached on all sides by gleaming white steps. Across the Seine, dominating the city's southeast skyline, are the four glass towers of architect Dominique Perrault's national library, the Bibliothèque Nationale François-Mitterrand. A hundred yards from the Palais Omnisports is a quirky, Cubist building designed by Frank Gehry, who described it as "a dancing figure in the park." It opened as the American Center in 1994 but closed in 1996 for lack of funds and at press time was slated to reopen as the **Cinémathèque Français** in fall 2004. The *jardin* (garden) opposite is a witty, state-of-the-art designer park with trim lawns, vines, rose-strewn arbors, and cobbled alleys lined by centurion trees providing a ghostly map of the former wineries. At the **Maison du Jardin** (Garden Center; ✉ rue Paul-Belmondo, Bercy/Tolbiac) you can get gardening advice and see displays of seasonal vegetables. Curved walkways fly over rue de Dijon to land by a Chinese lily pond near the Cour St-Emilion, where two rows of wine warehouses have been preserved and transformed into boutiques and cafés. Ⓜ *Bercy or Cour St-Emilion.*

❹ **Bibliothèque Nationale François-Mitterrand** (National Library). As the last of former president François Mitterrand's *grands travaux* (grand building projects) before he left office, the *Très Grande Bibliothèque* (Very Big Library, as some facetiously call it) opened in 1997. The library subsumes the majority of the collections in the old Bibliothèque Nationale and, with some 11 million volumes between its walls, surpasses the Library of Congress as the largest library in the world. Architect Dominique Perrault's controversial design comprises four soaring 24-story towers that house most of the books. The design is thought-provoking—the four towers imitate four open volumes—but criticism was heaped on the project since books are housed in the towers (whose windows need to be covered to protect the stacks), while library goers are relegated to underground reading rooms. A stunning interior courtyard—sunk beneath ground level and invisible as you approach, despite its thicket of full-size evergreens—provides breathing space. You can visit part of the library for free or pay to inspect one of the temporary exhibits or to consult some of the more than 300,000 books (millions more are available to qualified researchers). The library is fronted by a giant flight of wooden steps overlooking the Seine (note the red *Batofar* lightship, now used for techno concerts), but be warned—the library's two entrances are tucked away almost secretively at either end. ✉ *11 quai François-Mauriac, Bercy/Tolbiac* ☎ *01–53–79–59–59* 🌐 *www.bnf.fr* 🎫 *Library €3, exhibitions €5* ⏲ *Mid-Sept.–Aug., Tues.–Sat. 10–7, Sun. noon–6* Ⓜ *Métro or RER: Bibliothèque.*

❾ **Bois de Vincennes** (Vincennes Woods). Sandwiched between the unexciting suburb of Charenton and the working-class district of Fontenay-sous-Bois, to the southeast of Paris, Bois de Vincennes is often considered a poor man's Bois de Boulogne. But the comparison is unfair: the Bois de Vincennes is no more difficult to get to and has equally illustrious origins. It, too, was landscaped under Napoléon III, although a park had already been created here by Louis XV in 1731. The park has several lakes, notably **Lac Daumesnil,** with two islands, and **Lac des Minimes,** with three; rowboats can be hired at both. In addition, the park contains a zoo, a tribal-art museum, the **Hippodrome de Vincennes** (a cinder-track racecourse), a castle, a flower garden, and several cafés. In spring there's an amusement park, the **Foire du Trône.** Bikes can be rented from the Château de Vincennes métro station for €4 an hour or €15 a day. Note that the Bois suffered severe damage in the hurricane that lashed Paris in 1999, and although new trees have been planted, it will take the woods a few decades to return to their full sylvan glory. To reach the park, take the métro to Porte Dorée and then transfer to Bus 46.

Some 1,200 mammals and birds can be seen at the Bois de Vincennes's 33-acre **Parc Zoologique,** the largest zoo in France. The most striking element is the 210-ft steel and concrete Grand Rocher, an artificial rock built in 1934, inhabited by wild mountain sheep and penguins. You can take an elevator (€3) to the top. ✉ *53 av. de St-Maurice, Bois de Vincennes* ☎ *01–44–75–20–10* 🎫 *€8* ⏲ *Apr.–Oct., daily 9–6; Nov.–Mar., daily 9–5* Ⓜ *Porte Dorée.*

The **Musée des Arts d'Afrique et d'Océanie** (Museum of the Arts of Africa and Oceania) is at the Porte Dorée entrance to the Bois de Vincennes. It's housed in an Art Deco building—opened for the Colonial Exhibition in 1931—whose awesome facade is covered with a sculpted frieze depicting sites and attractions of France's erstwhile overseas empire. Inside, headdresses, bronzes, jewelry, masks, statues, and pottery from former French colonies are spaciously displayed under subtle spotlighting. There is also a tropical aquarium in the basement, with rows of tanks filled with colorful tropical fish. Note: most of the museum's collections have been moved to the new Musée du Quai-Branly, which will open its doors in 2005, but the aquarium and many of the displays are still open to the public. ✉ *293 av. Daumesnil, Bois de Vincennes* ☎ *01–44–74–84–80* 🎫 *€5.60, €4.20 Sun.* ⏲ *Wed.–Mon. 10–5:30* Ⓜ *Porte Dorée.*

The historic **Château de Vincennes** is on the northern edge of the Bois de Vincennes. Built in the 15th century by various French kings, the castle is France's medieval Versailles, an imposing, high-walled castle surrounded by a dry moat and dominated by a 170-ft keep. The sprawling castle grounds also contain a modest replica (built 1379–1552) of the Sainte-Chapelle on the Ile de la Cité and two elegant, classical wings designed by Louis Le Vau in the mid-17th century, that house the archives of the French armed forces and are closed to the public. ✉ *Av. de Paris, Bois de Vincennes* ☎ *01–48–08–31–20* 🌐 *www.monum.fr* 🎫 *€5.50* ⏲ *Apr.–Sept., daily 10–noon and 1:15–6:30; Oct.–Mar., daily 10–noon and 1:15–5* Ⓜ *Château de Vincennes.*

The **Parc Floral de Paris** (Paris Floral Park) is the Bois de Vincennes's 70-acre flower garden. It includes a lake and water garden and is renowned for its seasonal displays of blooms. It also contains a miniature train, a game area, and an "exotarium" with tropical fish and reptiles. ✉ *Rte. de la Pyramide, Bois de Vincennes* ☎ *01–55–94–20–20* 🎫 *€1.50* ⏲ *Apr.–Sept., daily 9:30–8; Oct.–Mar., daily 9:30–5* Ⓜ *Château de Vincennes.*

★ 8 **Cimetière du Père-Lachaise** (Father Lachaise Cemetery). The world's most illustrious necropolis, the 118-acre Père-Lachaise cemetery is the final stop for more illustrious people than you could ever meet in a lifetime. Plots are prime real estate and now only the outrageously wealthy can afford to be laid to rest with the famous. Jim Morrison's fans rage on at the eternal party in Division 6, but otherwise a serene Gothic aura persists, as tombs compete in grandiosity, originality, and often, alas, dilapidation. Cobbled avenues, steep slopes, and lush vegetation create a powerful atmosphere. Named after the Jesuit father—Louis XIV's confessor—who led the reconstruction of the Jesuit Rest House completed here in 1682, the cemetery houses the tombs of the famed medieval lovers Héloïse and Abelard; composer Chopin; the playwright Molière; the writers Honoré Balzac, Marcel Proust, Paul Eluard, Oscar Wilde, and Gertrude Stein and Alice B. Toklas (buried in the same grave); the popular French actress Simone Signoret and her husband, singer-actor Yves

Montand; and Edith Piaf. Perhaps the most popular shrine is to rock star Morrison, where dozens of Doors fans, following the trail of spray-painted graffiti, come to pay homage to the songwriter. (Now, along with the fans, there's a guard who makes sure you don't stay too long.) Of less dubious taste is the sculpted tomb of Romantic artist Théodore Géricault, shown brush in hand above a bronze relief plaque replicating his *Raft of the Medusa*. The cemetery was the site of the Paris Commune's final battle, on May 28, 1871, when the rebel troops were rounded up, lined against the Mur des Fédérés (Federalists' Wall) in the southeast corner, and shot. Get hold of a map at the entrance—Père-Lachaise is an easy place in which to get lost. ✉ *Entrances on rue des Rondeaux, bd. de Ménilmontant, and rue de la Réunion, Père Lachaise* ⏲ *Easter–Sept., daily 8–6; Oct.–Easter, daily 8 AM–dusk* Ⓜ *Gambetta, Philippe-Auguste, Père-Lachaise.*

need a break?

Just next door to the cemetery is the mother of all neighborhood restaurants, **La Mère Lachaise** (✉ 78 bd. Ménilmontant, Père Lachaise ☎ 01–47–97–61–60), a bustling restaurant/brasserie where the service is exceedingly friendly and the fare—traditional gratins, soups, savory tarts, and sausages—is copious and delicious. On a warm day, grab a table on the pretty terrace. It's open for *grignotage* (snacks) all day, but for lunch, dinner, or the very popular Sunday brunch, reserve in advance. There's live music most evenings.

6 **Cimetière de Picpus.** Most of the 1,300 people executed at the guillotine on place de la Nation in 1794 were buried in a mass grave at the nearby Picpus Cemetery. Also buried here is General Lafayette, whose grave site can be identified by its U.S. flag. ✉ *Entrance at 35 rue Picpus (once inside, ring bell of caretaker's home for access to cemetery), Bastille/Nation* ☎ *01–43–44–18–54* 🎫 *€2.30* ⏲ *Oct.–Easter, Tues.–Sat. 2–4; Easter–Sept., Tues.–Sat. 2–6. Guided visits Tues.–Sun. at 2:30 and 4* Ⓜ *Métro or RER: Nation.*

2 **Opéra de la Bastille** (Bastille Opera). Designed by Argentine-born architect Carlos Ott, the state-of-the-art Bastille Opera, on the south side of place de la Bastille, opened on July 14, 1989, in commemoration of the bicentennial of the French Revolution and in hope of making Paris once more the center of European opera. The steeply sloping auditorium seats more than 3,000 and has earned more plaudits than the curving glass facade, which strikes Parisians as depressingly like that of yet another modern office building. ✉ *Pl. de la Bastille, Bastille/Nation* ☎ *01–40–01–19–70* 🎫 *Guided tours €10, €5 under 26 years of age (call ahead to book)* Ⓜ *Bastille.*

1 **Place de la Bastille.** Nothing remains of the infamous Bastille prison destroyed at the beginning of the French Revolution. Until 1988 there was little more to see here than a huge traffic circle and the **Colonne de Juillet** (July Column). As part of the countrywide celebrations for July 1989, the bicentennial of the French Revolution, the Opéra de la Bastille was erected, inspiring substantial redevelopment on the surrounding streets, especially along rue de Lappe—once a haunt of Edith Piaf—and rue de la Roquette. What was formerly a humdrum neighborhood rapidly became one of the most sparkling and attractive in the city. Streamlined art galleries, funky jazz clubs, and Spanish-style tapas bars set the tone.

The Bastille, or, more properly, the Bastille St-Antoine, was a massive building protected by eight immense towers and a wide moat (its ground plan is marked by paving stones set into the modern square). It was built by Charles V in the late 14th century. He intended it not as a prison but as a fortress to guard the eastern entrance to the city. By the reign of Louis XIII (1610–43), however, the Bastille was used almost exclusively to house political prisoners. Voltaire, the Marquis de Sade, and the mysterious Man in the Iron Mask were all incarcerated here, along with many other unfortunates. It was this obviously political role—specifically, the fact that the prisoners were nearly always held by order of the king—that led the "furious mob" (in all probability no more than a largely unarmed rabble) to break into the prison on July 14, 1789, kill the governor, steal what firearms they could find, and free the seven remaining prisoners.

Later in 1789, the prison was knocked down. A number of the original stones were carved into facsimiles of the Bastille and sent to each of the provinces as a memento of royal oppression. The key to the prison was given to George Washington by Lafayette, and it has remained at Mount Vernon ever since. The power of legend being what it is, what soon became known as the Storming of the Bastille was elevated to the status of a pivotal event in the course of the French Revolution, demonstrating the newfound power of a long-suffering population. Thus it was that July 14 became the French national day, an event now celebrated with patriotic fervor throughout the country. Ⓜ *Bastille.*

7 **Place de la Nation.** The towering early 19th-century, statue-topped columns on majestic place de la Nation stand sentinel at the Gates of Paris—the eastern sector's equivalent of the Arc de Triomphe, with the bustling but unpretentious Cours de Vincennes providing a down-to-earth echo of the Champs-Élysées. Place de la Nation (known as place du Trône—Throne Square—until the Revolution) was the scene of 1,300 executions at the guillotine in 1794. Most were buried in a mass grave at the nearby Cimetière de Picpus. Ⓜ *Métro or RER: Nation.*

3 **Viaduc des Arts** (Arts Viaduct). With typical panache, Paris planners have converted this redbrick viaduct—originally the last mile of the suburban railroad that led to place de la Bastille (the site of the Bastille Opéra was once a station)—into a stylish promenade. Upscale art, crafts, and furniture shops occupy the archways below, and a walkway, with shrubs, flowers, and benches, has replaced the tracks up above. ✉ *Av. Daumesnil, Bastille/Nation* Ⓜ *Gare de Lyon, Daumesnil, Bel-Air.*

THE MARAIS

The Marais is one of Paris's oldest, most picturesque, and most sought-after residential districts. Renovation is the keynote; well into the '70s this was one of the poorest areas, filled with dilapidated tenements and squalid courtyards. The area's regeneration was sparked by the building of the Centre Pompidou (known to Parisians as Beaubourg), which ranks alongside Frank Gehry's Guggenheim Museum in Bilbao, Spain, as one of Europe's most architecturally whimsical museums. The gracious architecture of the 17th and early 18th centuries, however, sets the tone for the rest of the Marais. Today most of the Marais's *hôtels particuliers*—loosely, "mansions," onetime residences of aristocratic families—have been restored by rich, with-it couples, and many of the buildings are now museums, the grandest of them being the Musée Carnavalet and the most visited of them the Musée Picasso. There are trendy boutiques and cafés among the kosher shops of the traditionally Jewish neighborhood around rue des Rosiers.

The history of the Marais—the word, incidentally, means marsh or swamp—goes back to when Charles V, king of France in the 14th century, moved his court here from the Ile de la Cité. However, it wasn't until Henri IV laid out place Royale, today place des Vosges, in the early 17th century, that the Marais became *the* place to live. Aristocratic dwellings began to dot the neighborhood, and their salons filled with the beau monde. But following the French Revolution the Marais rapidly became one of the most deprived, dissolute areas in Paris.

It was spared the attentions of Baron Haussmann, the man who rebuilt so much of Paris in the mid-19th century—so, though crumbling, the Marais's ancient, golden-hue buildings and squares remained intact. You won't be able to get into many of the historic homes that spangle the neighborhood but this shouldn't stop you from admiring their handsome facades or trying to glimpse through the formal portals (*portes cochères*) to study the discreet courtyards that lurk behind them.

Jewish heritage is also an important part of the Marais's history. Jewish immigrants began settling in this area in the 13th century, though the main wave of immigrants (from Russia and Central Europe) came in the 19th century. Another wave—of Sephardic Jews from North Africa—arrived here in the 1960s following Algerian independence. Today there are still many kosher shops and restaurants among the trendy, newer arrivals.

Numbers in the text correspond to numbers in the margin and on the Marais map.

a good walk

Begin this walk in front of the **Hôtel de Ville** 1 ⚑. You can't inspect the lavish interior, but head left to the traffic-free square, with its fountains and forest of street lamps, to admire the exuberant facade. Turn left along quai de l'Hôtel de Ville; bouquinistes line the Seine, and you may catch a glimpse of the towers of Notre-Dame through the trees. Take the next left up picturesque rue des Barres to the church of **St-Gervais–St-Protais** 2, one of the last Gothic constructions in the country and a newly cleaned riot of Flamboyant decoration. From the church, head up to rue de Rivoli and take a left to get to rue du Temple. On your way, you'll pass one of the city's most popular department stores, the Bazar de l'Hôtel de Ville, or BHV, as it's known. Take rue de la Verrerie, the first street on your left, and pause as you cross rue du Renard to take in an impressive clash of architectural styles: to your left, the medieval silhouette of Notre-Dame; to the right, the gaudy colored pipes of the Centre Pompidou.

Cross rue du Renard and take the second right to the ornate 16th-century church of **St-Merri** 3. Rue St-Martin, full of stores, restaurants, and galleries, leads past the designer Café Beaubourg. Turn right to reach **Square Igor-Stravinsky** 4 with its unusual fountain; on one side of the square is IRCAM, where you can hear performances of contemporary classical music. Up ahead looms the **Centre Georges Pompidou** 5, overlooking a sloping piazza that is often aswarm with musicians, mimes, dancers, and fire-eaters. On the far side you can visit the **Atelier Brancusi** 6 before crossing rue Rambuteau to the Quartier de l'Horloge; take pedestrian rue de Brantôme and turn left onto rue Bernard-de-Clairvaux to admire Le Défenseur du Temps, a modern mechanical clock that whirs into action on the hour as St. George defends Time against a dragon, an eagle, or a crab (symbols of fire, air, and water). At noon, 6 PM, and 10 PM he takes on all three at once.

Return to rue Rambuteau, turn left, and cross rue Beaubourg. If you're with children, duck into impasse Berthaud to visit the **Musée de la Poupée** 7, or doll museum. Otherwise, stay on rue Rambuteau and turn left onto rue du Temple, where the **Musée d'Art et d'Histoire du Judaïsme** 8 is in the stately Hôtel de St-Aignan at No. 71. The **Hôtel de Mont-**

mor ⑨ at No. 79 is another splendid 17th-century mansion. Take a right onto rue des Haudriettes; just off to the left at the next corner is the **Musée de la Chasse et de la Nature** ⑩, the Museum of Hunting and Nature, housed in one of the Marais's grandest mansions. Head right on rue des Archives, crossing rue des Haudriettes, and admire the medieval gateway with two fairy-tale towers, now part of the **Archives Nationales** ⑪, the archives museum entered from rue des Francs-Bourgeois around to the left.

Continue past the Crédit Municipal (the city's grandiose pawnbroking concern), the Dôme du Marais restaurant (housed in a circular 18th-century chamber originally used for auctions), and the church of **Notre-Dame des Blancs-Manteaux** ⑫, with its superb inlaid pulpit. A corner turret signals rue Vieille-du-Temple; turn left past the palatial Hôtel de Rohan (now part of the Archives Nationales), then right onto rue de la Perle to the **Musée Bricard** ⑬, occupying a mansion as impressive as the assembly of locks and keys within. From here it is a step down rue de Thorigny (opposite) to the palatial 17th-century Hôtel Salé, now the **Musée Picasso** ⑭. Church lovers may wish to detour up rue de Thorigny and along rue du Roi-Doré to admire the severe neoclassical portico of **St-Denis-du-St-Sacrement** ⑮ and the Delacroix *Deposition* inside.

Backtrack along rue de Thorigny and turn left onto rue du Parc-Royal. Halfway down rue Elzévir is the **Musée Cognacq-Jay** ⑯, a must if you are interested in 18th-century furniture, porcelain, and paintings. If you can't face another museum, take the next right, rue Payenne, instead, and tarry in the sunken garden at square Georges-Cain, opposite the 16th-century Hôtel de Marle, now used as a Swedish culture center. Next door you can enjoy a rear view of the steep-roofed Cognacq-Jay building. Rue Payenne becomes rue Pavée as you pass beneath a lookout turret. Peek into the next courtyard on the left at the cheerfully askew facade of the Bibliothèque Historique de la Ville de Paris. Continuing on rue Pavée takes you to rue des Rosiers, with its excellent Jewish bakeries and falafel shops. Back on rue des Francs-Bourgeois is the **Musée Carnavalet** ⑰, the Paris History Museum, in perhaps the swankiest edifice in the Marais, and famous for its period rooms and collection of the decorative arts. A short walk along rue des Francs-Bourgeois takes you to large, pink-brick **place des Vosges** ⑱, lined with covered arcades, and the most beautiful legacy of the French Renaissance still intact in Paris. At No. 6 you can visit the **Maison de Victor Hugo** ⑲, where the workaholic French author once lived.

Exit the square by rue de Birague to reach rue St-Antoine: to the left is the church of **Ste-Marie** ⑳; to the right is the **Hôtel de Sully** ㉑, which houses the Caisse Nationale des Monuments Historiques (Historic Monuments Trust) at No. 62 and a textbook example of 17th-century architecture. Across rue St-Antoine, pause to admire the mighty Baroque church of **St-Paul–St-Louis** ㉒. Take the left-hand side door out of the church into narrow passage St-Paul, and then turn right onto rue St-Paul, past the grid of courtyards that make up the Village St-Paul antiques-shops complex. Children enjoy the **Académie de la Magie** ㉓ farther down at No. 11. At rue de l'Ave-Maria, turn right to reach the painstakingly restored **Hôtel de Sens** ㉔, a strange mixture of defensive stronghold and fairy-tale château. If you are a photography fan, head up rue Figuier, then down rue de Fourcy to the **Maison Européenne de la Photographie** ㉕. Head left on rue François-Miron past the 17th-century **Hôtel de Beauvais** ㉖. Note the two half-timber houses, among the oldest in Paris, across the street at Nos. 11 and 13, and the Belle Epoque bakery Au Petit Versailles, at the corner of Rue Tiron. The next left, rue Geoffroy-l'Asnier, leads

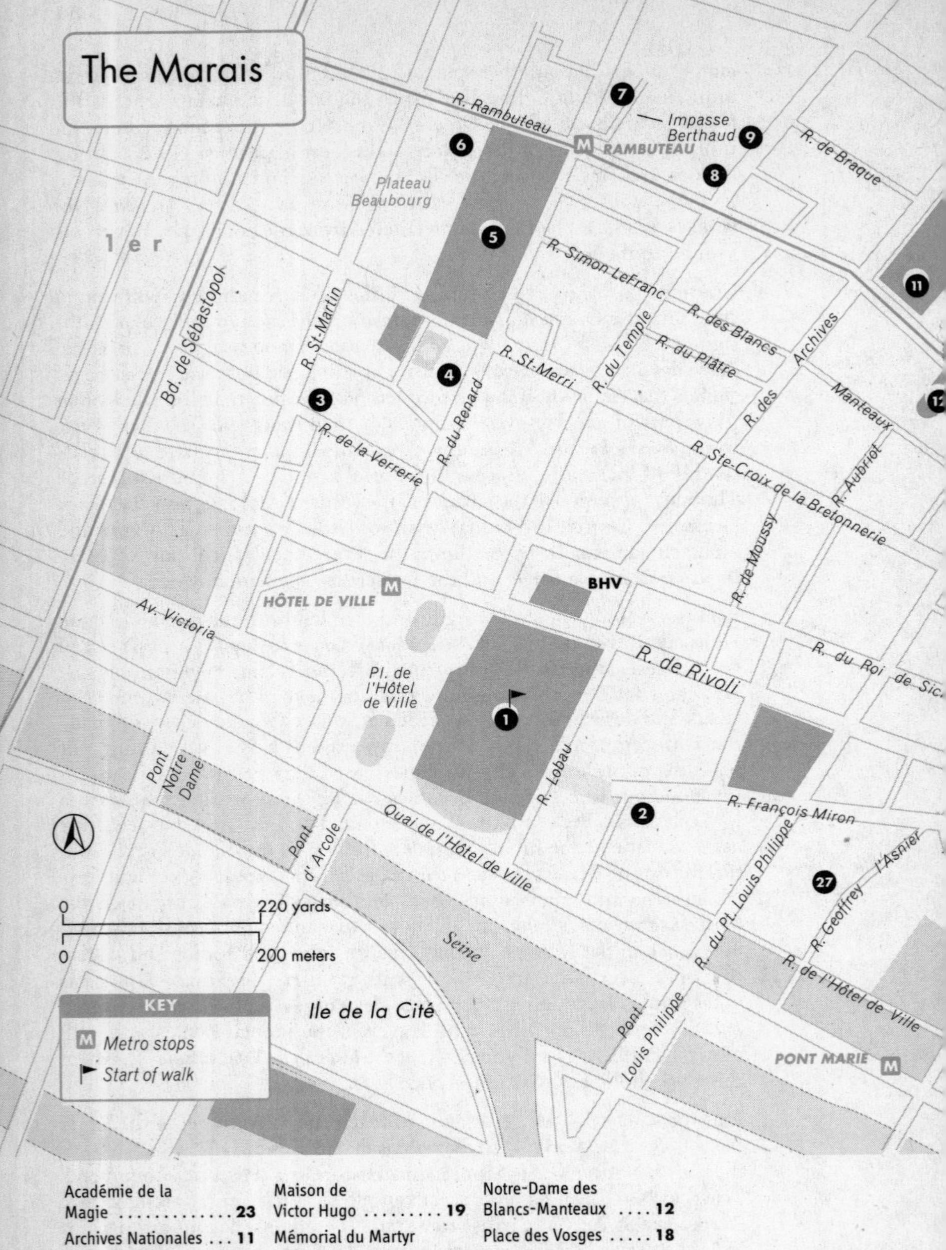

Académie de la Magie **23**
Archives Nationales . . . **11**
Atelier Brancusi **6**
Centre Pompidou **5**
Hôtel de Beauvais **26**
Hôtel de Montmor **9**
Hôtel de Sens **24**
Hôtel de Sully **21**
Hôtel de Ville **1**
Maison Européenne de la Photographie **25**
Maison de Victor Hugo **19**
Mémorial du Martyr Juif Inconnu **27**
Musée d'Art et d'Histoire du Judaïsme . . **8**
Musée Bricard **13**
Musée Carnavalet **17**
Musée de la Chasse et de la Nature **10**
Musée Cognacq-Jay . . . **16**
Musée Picasso **14**
Musée de la Poupée . . . **7**
Notre-Dame des Blancs-Manteaux **12**
Place des Vosges **18**
St-Denis-du-St-Sacrement **15**
St-Gervais-St-Protais . . . **2**
St-Merri **3**
St-Paul-St-Louis **22**
Ste-Marie **20**
Square Igor-Stravinsky **4**

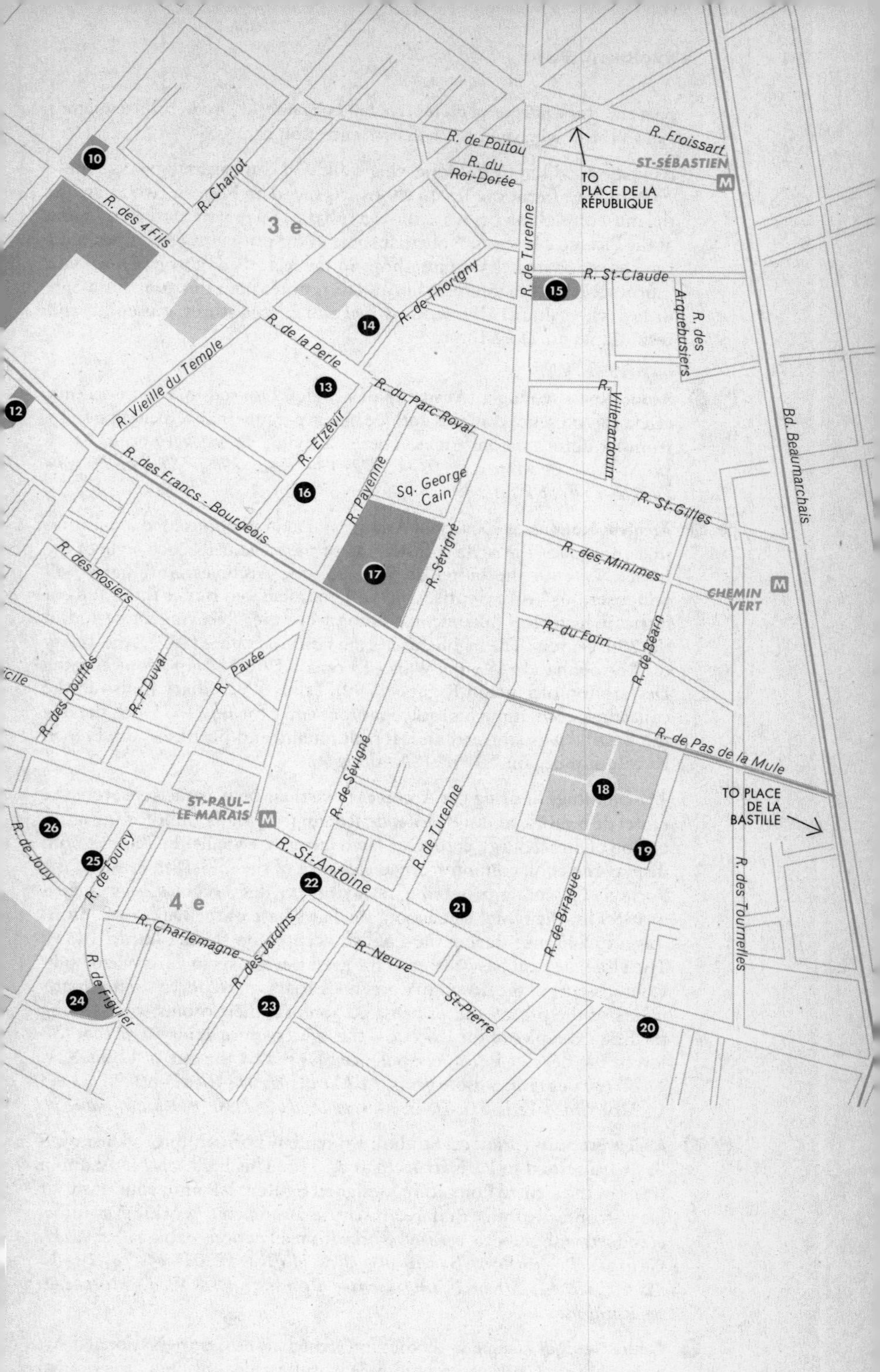

R. de Poitou
R. Froissart
R. du Roi-Dorée
ST-SÉBASTIEN
TO PLACE DE LA RÉPUBLIQUE
10
R. Charlot
R. des 4 Fils
3 e
R. de Turenne
R. St-Claude
15
R. de Thorigny
14
R. des Arquebusiers
R. de la Perle
R. Vieille du Temple
13
R. du Parc Royal
R. Villehardouin
12
R. Elzévir
Bd. Beaumarchais
R. des Francs - Bourgeois
16
R. Payenne
Sq. George Cain
R. St-Gilles
R. Sévigné
17
R. des Minimes
R. des Rosiers
CHEMIN VERT
R. du Foin
R. de Béarn
R. des Douffes
R. F. Duval
R. Pavée
R. de Pas de la Mule
R. de Sévigné
18
TO PLACE DE LA BASTILLE
ST-PAUL-LE MARAIS
R. de Turenne
26
R. de Jouy
R. St-Antoine
19
25
R. de Fourcy
22
R. des Tournelles
4 e
21
R. de Birague
R. Charlemagne
R. des Jardins
R. Neuve St-Pierre
R. de Figuier
24
23
20

past the stark **Mémorial du Martyr Juif Inconnu** 27, a huge bronze memorial to those who died in Nazi concentration camps.

TIMING At just over 5 km (3 mi) long, this walk will comfortably take a whole morning or afternoon. If you choose to spend an hour or two in any of the museums along the way, allow a full day. Be prepared to wait in line at the Picasso Museum. Note that some of the museums don't open until the afternoon and that many shops in the Marais don't open until late morning. If you're interested in Judaica, don't plan this tour for a Saturday, when almost all Jewish-owned and related stores, museums, and restaurants are closed.

What to See

23 **Académie de la Magie** (Academy of Magic). Housed in a 16th-century cellar, this museum contains antique magic paraphernalia, including some from Houdini's bag of tricks. There's a magic show every hour. ✉ *11 rue St-Paul, Le Marais* ☎ *01–42–72–13–26* *€7* *Wed. and weekends 2–7* Ⓜ *St-Paul.*

★ 11 **Archives Nationales** (National Archives). Palatially housed in a mansion that showcases the earliest flowering of the elegant Rococo style of the Louis XV era—the Hôtel de Soubise—the Archives Nationales will tempt serious history buffs, who will be fascinated by the thousands of intricate historical documents, dating from the Merovingian period to the 20th century. The highlights are the Edict of Nantes (1598), the Treaty of Westphalia (1648), the wills of Louis XIV and Napoléon, and the Declaration of Human Rights (1789). Louis XVI's diary is also in the collection, containing his sadly ignorant entry for July 14, 1789, the day the Bastille was stormed and, for all intents and purposes, the French Revolution began: "*Rien*" ("Nothing").

The buildings housing the Archives have their own attractions, too: the **Hôtel de Soubise** and the **Hôtel de Rohan** (originally built for the archbishop of Strasbourg), across the lawn facing rue Vieille-du-Temple, both display the cool, column-fronted elegance of the mid-18th century; the Porte de Clisson, a turreted gateway on rue des Archives, was erected in 1380 for the Hôtel de Clisson, the Paris base of the Duke of Bedford (regent of France during the English occupation from 1420 to 1435). The Hôtel de Soubise was one of the grandest houses in Paris when built. Connoisseurs of the decorative arts flock to this museum to see the apartments of the prince and princess de Soubise; their rooms were among the first examples of the Rococo—the lighter, more dainty style that followed the heavier Baroque opulence favored by the age of Louis XIV. ✉ *60 rue des Francs-Bourgeois, Le Marais* ☎ *01–40–27–60–96* *€3* *Mon. and Wed.–Fri. 10–5:30, weekends 2–5:30* Ⓜ *Rambuteau.*

6 **Atelier Brancusi** (Brancusi Studio). Romanian-born sculptor Constantin Brancusi settled in Paris in 1898 at age 22. This light, airy museum in front of the Centre Pompidou, designed by Renzo Piano, contains four glass-fronted rooms that reconstitute Brancusi's working studios, crammed with smooth, stylized works from all periods of his career. ✉ *Pl. Georges-Pompidou, Beaubourg/Les Halles* ☎ *01–44–78–12–33* *€5.50, €8.50 including Centre Pompidou* *Wed.–Mon. 2–6* Ⓜ *Rambuteau.*

5 **Centre Georges Pompidou** (Pompidou Center). The Centre National d'Art et de Culture Georges-Pompidou is its full name, although it is known to Parisians simply as Beaubourg (for the neighborhood). Georges Pompidou (1911–74) was the president of France who launched the project. Unveiled in 1977, three years after his death, the Centre Pompidou was soon attracting more than 8 million visitors a year—five times

Fodor's Choice ★

more than intended. Hardly surprising, then, that it was soon showing signs of fatigue: the much-vaunted, gaudily painted service pipes snaking up the exterior (painted the same colors that were used to identify them on the architects' plans) needed continual repainting, while the plastic tubing enclosing the exterior escalators was cracked and grimy. The center was closed for two years of top-to-bottom renovation before reopening on the first day of the new millennium.

Place Georges-Pompidou, a gently sloping piazza with a giant gold flowerpot in one corner and the Atelier Brancusi in the other, leads to the center's sprawling, stationlike, concrete-floored entrance hall, with huge, psychedelically colorful signs, ticket counters on the back left, and an extensive art shop to your right, topped by a café. Head left for the escalator that climbs the length of the building, offering spectacular views of Paris, ranging from the Tour Montparnasse to the left, around to the Sacré-Coeur on its hill to the right. Since the renovations, the **Musée National d'Art Moderne** (Modern Art Museum, entrance on Level 4) has doubled in size to occupy most of the center's top two stories: one devoted to modern art—including major works by Matisse, the Surrealists, Modigliani, Duchamp, and Picasso—the other to contemporary art since the '60s, including video installations. Also look for rotating exhibits of contemporary art. In addition, there's a public reference library, a language laboratory, an industrial design center, two cinemas, and a rooftop restaurant, Georges, which is noted for its great view of the skyline and Eiffel Tower. ✉ *Pl. Georges-Pompidou, Beaubourg/Les Halles* ☎ *01–44–78–12–33* 🌐 *www.centrepompidou.fr* 🎫 *€8.50, including Atelier Brancusi; €5.50 for permanent collection only; free 1st Sun. of month* ⏲ *Wed.–Mon. 11–9* Ⓜ *Rambuteau.*

need a break?

The view at night of the Eiffel Tower from **Georges** (✉ Pl. Georges-Pompidou, Beaubourg/Les Halles ☎ 01–44–78–47–99), the restaurant on the roof of the Centre Pompidou, is a marvel. The food is not up to the decor, but the buzz about this place draws a fun crowd.

26 **Hôtel de Beauvais.** Dating from 1655, this newly renovated mansion is one of the finest in the Marais. It was built for Pierre de Beauvais with surprisingly generous funding from the normally parsimonious Louis XIV. The reason for the Sun King's unwonted largesse: a reward for de Beauvais's willingness to turn a blind eye to the activities of his wife, Catherine-Henriette Bellier, in educating the young monarch in matters sexual. Louis, who came to the throne in 1643 at the age of 4, was 14 when de Beauvais's wife first gave him the benefit of her expertise; she was 40. ✉ *68 rue François-Miron, Le Marais* Ⓜ *St-Paul.*

9 **Hôtel de Montmor.** This 17th-century mansion was built by M. Montmor, Louis XIII's financial adviser. His son ran a salon here frequented by such luminaries as philosopher and mathematician Pierre Gassend, physicist Gilles de Roberval, writer and professor of medicine Gui Patin, and Dutch astronomer Christian Huygens. This informal gathering of the "Boffins" prompted the creation of the Académie des Sciences in 1666. Note the huge windows and intricate ironwork on the second-floor balcony. ✉ *79 rue de Temple, Le Marais* Ⓜ *Rambuteau.*

24 **Hôtel de Sens.** One of a handful of civil buildings in Paris to have survived from the Middle Ages—witness the pointed corner towers, Gothic porch, and richly carved decorative details—this sumptuous Marais mansion was built in 1474 for the archbishop of Sens. Its best-known occupants were Henri IV and his queen, Marguérite, philanderers both.

While Henri dallied with his mistresses—he is said to have had 56—at a series of royal palaces, Marguérite entertained her almost equally large number of lovers here. Today the building houses occasional exhibits and a fine-arts library, the **Bibliothèque Forney.** ✉ *1 rue du Figuier, Le Marais* ☎ *01–42–78–14–60* 🎫 *Exhibitions €3* ⏲ *Tues.–Sat. 1:30–8* Ⓜ *Pont Marie.*

21 **Hôtel de Sully.** A major monument of the French Renaissance style, this mansion, begun in 1624, has a stately garden and a majestic courtyard with statues, richly carved pediments, and dormer windows. It is the headquarters of the **Caisse Nationale des Monuments Historiques,** responsible for administering France's historic monuments. Guided visits to Paris sites and buildings begin here, though all are conducted in French. The excellent bookshop, just inside the gate, has a plethora of publications on Paris, many of them in English. The bookshop is open daily 10–12:45 and 1:45–6. ✉ *62 rue St-Antoine, Le Marais* ☎ *01–44–61–20–00* Ⓜ *St-Paul.*

1 **Hôtel de Ville** (City Hall). Overlooking the Seine, City Hall is the residence of the mayor of Paris. Until 1977, Paris was the only city in France without a mayor; with the creation of the post and the election of Jacques Chirac (elected president of France in 1995), leader of the right-of-center Gaullist party, the position became pivotal in both Parisian and French politics. It comes as no surprise, therefore, that Chirac oversaw a thorough restoration of the Hôtel de Ville, both inside and out.

The square in front of the Hôtel de Ville was relaid in the 1980s and adorned with fancy lamps and fountains; an open-air ice rink is installed from December through February. Back in the Middle Ages this was the site of public executions. Most victims were hanged, drawn, and quartered; the lucky ones were burned at the stake. Following the short-lived restoration of the Bourbon monarchy in 1830, the building became the seat of the French government, a role that came to a sudden end with the uprisings in 1848. During the Commune of 1871 the Hôtel de Ville was burned to the ground. Today's exuberant building, based closely on the 16th-century Renaissance original, went up between 1874 and 1884. In 1944, following the liberation of Paris from Nazi rule, General de Gaulle took over the leadership of France from here. ✉ *Pl. de l'Hôtel-de-Ville, Le Marais* ⏲ *For special exhibitions only* Ⓜ *Hôtel de Ville.*

25 **Maison Européenne de la Photographie** (European Photography Center). This museum combines spacious modern galleries with the original stonework of a venerable hôtel particulier. Despite its name, the museum has an impressive collection of both European and American photography and stages up to four different exhibitions every three months. ✉ *5 rue de Fourcy, Le Marais* ☎ *01–44–78–75–00* 🌐 *www.mep-fr.org* 🎫 *€5, free Wed. after 5 PM* ⏲ *Wed.–Sun. 11–8* Ⓜ *St-Paul.*

19 **Maison de Victor Hugo** (Victor Hugo's Home). The workaholic French author famed for *Les Misérables* and the *Hunchback of Notre-Dame* lived in a corner of beautiful place des Vosges between 1832 and 1848. The memorabilia here include several of his atmospheric, Gothic-horror-movie-like ink sketches, tribute to Hugo's unsuspected talent as an artist, along with illustrations for his writings by other artists, including Bayard's rendition of Cosette (from "Les Miz," which has graced countless T-shirts). The rooms upstairs represent Hugo's living style in several of his many homes; the central room of the floor, for instance, is decorated with Chinese-theme panels and woodwork he created for his mistress's home outside Paris. ✉ *6 pl. des Vosges, Le Marais* ☎ *01–42–72–10–16* 🎫 *€5.50* ⏲ *Tues.–Sun. 10–5:45* Ⓜ *St-Paul.*

27 **Mémorial du Martyr Juif Inconnu** (Memorial of the Unknown Jewish Martyr). This memorial was erected at the **Centre de Documentation Juive Contemporaine** (Center for Contemporary Jewish Documentation) to honor the memory of the 6 million Jews who died "without graves" at the hands of the Nazis. The basement crypt has a dramatic black-marble Star of David containing the ashes of victims from Nazi death camps in Poland and Austria. The center has archives, a library, and a gallery that hosts temporary exhibitions. ✉ *17 rue Geoffroy-l'Asnier, Le Marais* ☎ *01–42–77–44–72* *€2.30* ⏲ *Sun.–Fri. 10–1 and 2–5:30* Ⓜ *Pont Marie.*

8 **Musée d'Art et d'Histoire du Judaïsme** (Museum of Jewish Art and History). With its clifflike courtyard ringed by giant pilasters, the Hôtel St-Aignan, completed in 1650 to the design of Pierre le Muet, is one of the most awesome sights in the Marais. It opened as the city's Jewish museum in 1998, after a 20-year restoration. The interior has been renovated to the point of blandness, but the exhibits have good explanatory English texts on Jewish history and practice, and you can ask for a free audio guide in English. Highlights include 13th-century tombstones excavated in Paris; wooden models of destroyed East European synagogues; a roomful of early Chagalls; and Christian Boltanski's stark, two-part tribute to Shoah (Holocaust) victims, in the form of plaques on an outer wall naming the (mainly Jewish) inhabitants of the Hôtel St-Aignan in 1939, and canvas hangings with the personal data of the 13 residents who were deported and died in concentration camps. Jewish people settled in France in the Rhône Valley as early as the 1st century BC; there was a synagogue in Paris by 582; an expulsion order was issued by Charles VI in 1394 but fitfully enforced; and 40,000 French Jews were granted full citizenship by the Revolution in 1791. France's Jewish population sank from 300,000 to 180,000 through deportation and flight during World War II but has since grown to around 700,000. ✉ *71 rue du Temple, Le Marais* ☎ *01–53–01–86–60* *€6* ⏲ *Sun.–Fri. 11–6* Ⓜ *Rambuteau or Hôtel de Ville.*

13 **Musée Bricard.** Also called the Musée de la Serrure (Lock Museum), this museum is housed in a exquisitely elegant Baroque mansion designed for himself in 1685 by the architect of Les Invalides, Libéral Bruant. Anyone with a taste for fine craftsmanship will appreciate the intricacy and ingenuity of many of the older locks displayed here. One represents an early security system—it would shoot anyone who tried to open it with the wrong key. Another was made in the 17th century by a master locksmith who was himself held under lock and key while he labored over it—the task took him four years. ✉ *1 rue de la Perle, Le Marais* ☎ *01–42–77–79–62* *€4.60* ⏲ *Weekdays 2–5* Ⓜ *St-Paul.*

17 **Musée Carnavalet.** To get a picture of the eternal yet ever-changing face of Paris through the ages, head to these two adjacent mansions in the heart of the Marais. Devoted to Parisian history, they include many salons filled with antiques and historical artifacts. Material dating from the city's origins until 1789 is in the Hôtel Carnavalet, and material from 1789 to the present is in the Hôtel Peletier St-Fargeau. In the late 17th century the Hôtel Carnavalet was the setting for the most brilliant salon in Paris, presided over by Madame de Sévigné, best known for the hundreds of letters she wrote to her daughter; they've become one of the most enduring chronicles of French high society in the 17th century. The Hôtel Carnavalet, transformed into a museum in 1880, is full of maps and plans, furniture, and busts and portraits of Parisian worthies down the ages. The section on the Revolution includes riveting models of guillotines and objects associated with the royal family's final days, including

Fodor's Choice ★

the king's razor and the chess set used by the royal prisoners at the approach of their own endgame. Lovers of the decorative arts will enjoy the period rooms here, especially those devoted to that most French of French styles, the 18th-century Rococo. Most entertaining, however, are the re-creations of Marcel Proust's cork-lined bedroom, the late-19th-century Fouquet jewelry shop, and a room from the Art Nouveau monument the Café de Paris. ✉ *23 rue de Sévigné, Le Marais* ☎ *01–44–59–58–58* 🌐 *www.paris-france.org/musees* 🎟 *Free for permanent collection, €6 for exhibits* ⏲ *Tues.–Sun. 10–5:40* Ⓜ *St-Paul.*

need a break?

Marais Plus (✉ 20 rue des Francs-Bourgeois, Le Marais ☎ 01–48–87–01–40), on the corner of rue Elzévir and rue des Francs-Bourgeois, is a delightful, artsy gift shop with a cozy salon de thé in the back.

10 **Musée de la Chasse et de la Nature** (Museum of Hunting and Nature). This museum is housed in the Hôtel de Guénégaud, designed around 1650 by François Mansart and one of the Marais's most stately mansions. There's an extensive collection of hunting paraphernalia, including a series of immense 17th- and 18th-century still lifes (notably by Desportes and Oudry) of dead animals and a wide variety of swords, guns, muskets, and taxidermy. ✉ *60 rue des Archives, Le Marais* ☎ *01–42–72–86–42* 🎟 *€4.60* ⏲ *Wed.–Mon. 11–6* Ⓜ *Rambuteau.*

16 **Musée Cognacq-Jay.** Another rare opportunity to see how cultured and rich Parisians once lived, this mansion is devoted to the arts of the 18th century and contains an outstanding collection in boiseried rooms of furniture, porcelain, and paintings—notably by Watteau, Boucher, and Tiepolo—amassed by Ernest Cognacq, founder of La Samaritaine, the city's largest department store, and his wife, Louise Jay. ✉ *8 rue Elzévir, Le Marais* ☎ *01–40–27–07–21* 🌐 *www.paris-france.org/musees* 🎟 *Free for permanent collection, €4.60 for exhibits* ⏲ *Tues.–Sun. 10–5:40* Ⓜ *St-Paul.*

★ 14 **Musée Picasso.** The Picasso Museum opened in fall 1985 and shows no signs of losing its immense popularity. The building itself, put up between 1656 and 1660 for financier Aubert de Fontenay, quickly became known as the Hôtel Salé—*salé* meaning, literally, "salted"—referring to the enormous profits made by de Fontenay as the sole appointed collector of the salt tax. The mansion was luxuriously restored by the French government as a permanent home for the pictures, sculptures, drawings, prints, ceramics, and assorted works of art given to the government by Picasso's heirs after the painter's death in 1973 in lieu of death duties. Unfortunately, these days the hôtel particulier is showing the wear and tear of being one of the city's most popular museums; on peak summer afternoons this place is more congested than the Gare du Lyon. It's the largest collection of works by Picasso in the world—no masterpieces, but "Picasso's Picassos," all works kept and sentimentally valued by Picasso himself. There are pictures from every period of his life: a grand total of 230 paintings, 1,500 drawings, and nearly 1,700 prints, as well as works by Cézanne, Miró, Renoir, Braque, Degas, and Matisse. The scuffed yet palatial surroundings of the Hôtel Salé add to the pleasures of a visit. ✉ *5 rue de Thorigny, Le Marais* ☎ *01–42–71–25–21* 🎟 *€5.50, Sun. €4, free 1st Sun. of month* ⏲ *Wed.–Mon. 9:30–5:30* Ⓜ *St-Sébastien.*

7 **Musée de la Poupée** (Doll Museum). If you love dolls, make a detour to this quaint, low-ceiling house in a cul-de-sac behind the Centre Pompidou to admire the rarefied collection of 300 French dolls dating back to the 1850s—many wearing their original costumes. Bisque-head dolls with enamel eyes were the Paris specialty, with Steiner, Bru, and Jumeau

among the leading makers represented here. Two of the museum's six rooms are devoted to temporary exhibits, and there's a well-stocked gift shop. ✉ *Impasse Berthaud, Beaubourg/Les Halles* ☎ *01–42–72–73–11* 🎫 *€6* ⏲ *Tues.–Sun. 10–6* Ⓜ *Arts et Métiers or Hôtel de Ville.*

need a break?

Harry Potter fans, take note: the real Nicolas Flanel, the alchemist whose sorcerer's stone is the source of immortality in the popular book series, used to live at 51 rue Montmorency, in what is not only the oldest building in Paris, dating from 1407, but also a pretty good restaurant. The copious lunch at the **Auberge Nicolas Flanel** (✉ 51 rue de Montmorency, Le Marais ☎ 01–42–71–77-78) won't make you live forever, but it will definitely keep you going till dinner.

1

⓬ **Notre-Dame des Blancs-Manteaux.** The Blancs Manteaux were white-robed 13th-century mendicant monks whose monastery once stood on this spot. For the last 100 years this late-17th-century church has had an imposing 18th-century facade that belonged to a now-destroyed church on the Ile de la Cité. Unfortunately, the narrow streets of the Marais leave little room to step back and admire it. The inside has fine woodwork and a Flemish-style Rococo pulpit whose marquetry panels are inlaid with pewter and ivory. ✉ *Rue des Blancs-Manteaux, Le Marais* Ⓜ *Rambuteau.*

★ ⓲ **Place des Vosges.** The oldest monumental square in Paris—and probably still its most nobly proportioned—place des Vosges was laid out by Henri IV at the start of the 17th century. Originally known as place Royale, it has kept its Renaissance beauty nearly intact, although its buildings have been softened by time, their pale pink brick crumbling slightly in the harsh Parisian air and the darker stone facings pitted with age. It stands on the site of a former royal palace, the Palais des Tournelles, which was abandoned by the Italian-born queen of France Catherine de' Medici when her husband, Henri II, was killed in a tournament here in 1559. It was always a highly desirable address, reaching a peak of glamour in the early years of Louis XIV's reign, when the nobility were falling over themselves for the privilege of living here. The two larger buildings on either side of the square were originally the king and queen's pavilions. The statue in the center is of Louis XIII. It's not the original; that was melted down in the Revolution, the same period when the square's name was changed in honor of the French département of the Vosges, the first in the country to pay the new revolutionary taxes. With its arcades, symmetrical pink-brick town houses, and trim green garden bisected by gravel paths and edged with plane trees, the square achieves harmony and balance: it's a pleasant place to tarry on a sultry summer afternoon. Better yet, grab an arcade table at one of the many cafés lining the square—even a simple cheese crepe becomes a feast in this setting. To actually enter one of the square's imposing town houses, visit the **Maison de Victor Hugo** at No. 6. Ⓜ *Chemin Vert.*

⓯ **St-Denis-du-St-Sacrement.** This severely neoclassical edifice dates from the 1830s. It is a formidable example of architectural discipline, oozing restraint and monumental dignity (or banality, according to taste). The grisaille frieze and gilt fresco above the semicircular apse have clout if not subtlety; the Delacroix *Deposition* (1844), in the front right-hand chapel as you enter, has both. ✉ *Rue de Turenne, Le Marais* Ⓜ *St-Sébastien.*

❷ **St-Gervais–St-Protais.** This imposing church near the Hôtel de Ville is named after two Roman soldiers martyred by the emperor Nero in the 1st century AD. The original church—no trace remains of it now—was built in the 7th century. The present church, a riot of Flamboyant-style decoration, went up between 1494 and 1598, making it one of the last Gothic constructions in the country. Pause to look at the facade, constructed between 1616 and 1621. It's an early example of French architects' use of the classical orders of decoration on the capitals (topmost sections) of the columns. Those on the first floor are plain and sturdy Doric; the more elaborate Ionic is used on the second floor; and the most ornate of all—Corinthian—is used on the third floor. The church hosts occasional organ and choral concerts. ✉ *Pl. St-Gervais, Le Marais* ☎ *01–47–26–78–38 concert information* ⏲ *Tues.–Sun. 6:30 AM–8 PM* Ⓜ *Hôtel de Ville.*

3 **St-Merri.** This church near the Centre Pompidou, completed in 1552, has a turret containing the oldest bell in Paris (cast in 1331) and an 18th-century pulpit supported on carved palm trees. ✉ *Rue de la Verrerie, Beaubourg/Les Halles* Ⓜ *Hôtel de Ville.*

22 **St-Paul–St-Louis.** The leading Baroque church in the Marais, its elegant dome rising 180 ft above the crossing, was begun in 1627 by the Jesuits and partly modeled on their Gesù church in Rome. Look for Delacroix's dramatic *Christ on the Mount of Olives* high up in the transept, and the two huge shells, used as fonts, presented by Victor Hugo when he lived on nearby place des Vosges. ✉ *Rue St-Antoine, Le Marais* Ⓜ *St-Paul.*

20 **Ste-Marie.** Constructed in 1632–34 by François Mansart as the chapel of the Convent of the Visitation, this is now a Protestant "reformed" church. The large dome above the distinctive nave rotunda is one of the earliest in Paris. ✉ *Rue St-Antoine, Le Marais* Ⓜ *Bastille.*

4 **Square Igor-Stravinsky.** The café-lined square, next to the Centre Pompidou and backed by the church of St-Merri, has a fountain animated by the colorful and imaginative sculptures of French artist Niki de St-Phalle, together with the aquatic mechanisms of her Swiss partner, Jean Tinguely. The fountain (sculptures and all) was erected in 1980. It is not part of the Centre Pompidou, but it fits right in. Ⓜ *Rambuteau.*

THE LATIN QUARTER & THE ILE ST-LOUIS

South of Ile de la Cité on the Left Bank of the Seine is the bohemian Quartier Latin, with its warren of steep sloping streets populated largely by Sorbonne students and academics who fill the air of the cafés with their ideas—and tobacco smoke. The name Latin Quarter comes from the university tradition of studying and speaking in Latin, a tradition that disappeared during the Revolution. The university began as a theological school in the Middle Ages; in 1968 the student revolution here had an explosive effect on French politics, resulting in major reforms in the education system.

In fact, since ancient times, this quartier has detested the staid *bourgeoisie,* for here walks the ghost of Villon, that great poet and rapscallion who died sordidly in a tavern brawl. And here Verlaine, among the students and the shopkeepers of rue Mouffetard, drank his absinthe and wrote his poems. Today, however, the area is becoming increasingly upscale, with dozens of boutiques and antiques stores offering Right Bank luxury rubbing elbows with the bookstores. A grim modern skyscraper at the Jussieu campus, the science division of the University of Paris, reiterates the area's yen for learning yet fails to outgun the mighty dome of the Panthéon in its challenge for skyline supremacy. Most of the district's appeal is less emphatic: Roman ruins, tumbling street markets, the two oldest trees in Paris, and chance glimpses of Notre-Dame all await your discovery.

As does the Ile St-Louis. Of the two islands in the Seine—the Ile de la Cité is located just to the west—it is the Ile St-Louis that best retains the romance and loveliness of *le Paris traditionnel.* It has remained in the heart of Parisians as it has remained in the heart of every tourist who came upon it by accident, and without warning—a tiny universe unto itself, shaded by trees, bordered by Seine-side quais, and overhung with ancient stone houses. These have long comprised some of the most prized addresses in Paris—Voltaire, Daumier, Cézanne, Baudelaire, Chagall, Helena Rubenstein, and the Rothschilds are just some of the lucky people who have called the Ile St-Louis home. Up until the 1800s it was reputed that some island residents never crossed the bridges to get to Paris proper—and once you discover the island's quiet charm, you may understand why.

Numbers in the text correspond to numbers in the margin and on the Latin Quarter and the Ile St.-Louis map.

a good walk

Start at the Seine along the Pont au Double and head to square René-Viviani, where you'll find a battered acacia—which vies with a specimen in the Jardin des Plantes for the title of oldest tree in Paris—and a spectacular view of Notre-Dame. Behind the square lie the church of **St-Julien-le-Pauvre** 1, built at the same time as Notre-Dame, and the tiny, elegant streets of the Maubert district. Turn left out of the church and cross rue St-Jacques to the elegantly proportioned church of **St-Séverin** 2. The surrounding streets are for pedestrians only and crammed with cheap restaurants fronted by suave waiters touting customers at most hours of the day and night. Take rue St-Séverin, a right on rue Xavier-Privas, and a left on rue de la Huchette—where you'll find Paris's smallest theater and oldest jazz club—to reach **place St-Michel** 3. The grandiose fountain, depicting St. Michael slaying the dragon, is a popular meeting spot at the nerve center of the Left Bank.

Turn left up boulevard St-Michel and cross boulevard St-Germain. To your left, behind some forbidding railings, lurks a garden with ruins that date from Roman times. These belong to the Hôtel de Cluny, fabled repository of the **Musée National du Moyen-Age** 4, the National Museum of the Middle Ages. The entrance is down rue Sommerard, the next street on the left. Cross place Paul-Painlevé, in front of the museum, up toward the **Sorbonne** 5 university, fronted by a small plaza where the Left Bank's student population congregates after classes. Continue uphill until you are confronted, up rue Soufflot on your left, by the menacing domed bulk of the **Panthéon** 6, originally built as a church but now a monument to France's most glorious historical figures. On the far left corner of place du Panthéon stands **St-Étienne-du-Mont** 7, a church whose facade is a mishmash of architectural styles. Explore the top of quaint rue de la Montagne-Ste-Geneviève alongside; then turn right onto rue Descartes to reach **place de la Contrescarpe** 8. This square looks almost provincial during the day as Parisians flock to the daily market on rue Mouffetard.

Duck into the old church of **St-Médard** 9 at the foot of rue Mouffetard; then head left for 250 yards along rue Censier and turn left again into rue du Gril to discover the beautiful white **Mosquée** 10, complete with minaret. Blink twice and you'll be convinced you've left Paris behind. On the far side of the mosque extends the **Jardin des Plantes** 11, spacious botanical gardens; the first building you'll come to is the **Grande Galerie de l'Evolution** 12, a museum with a startling collection of taxidermy,

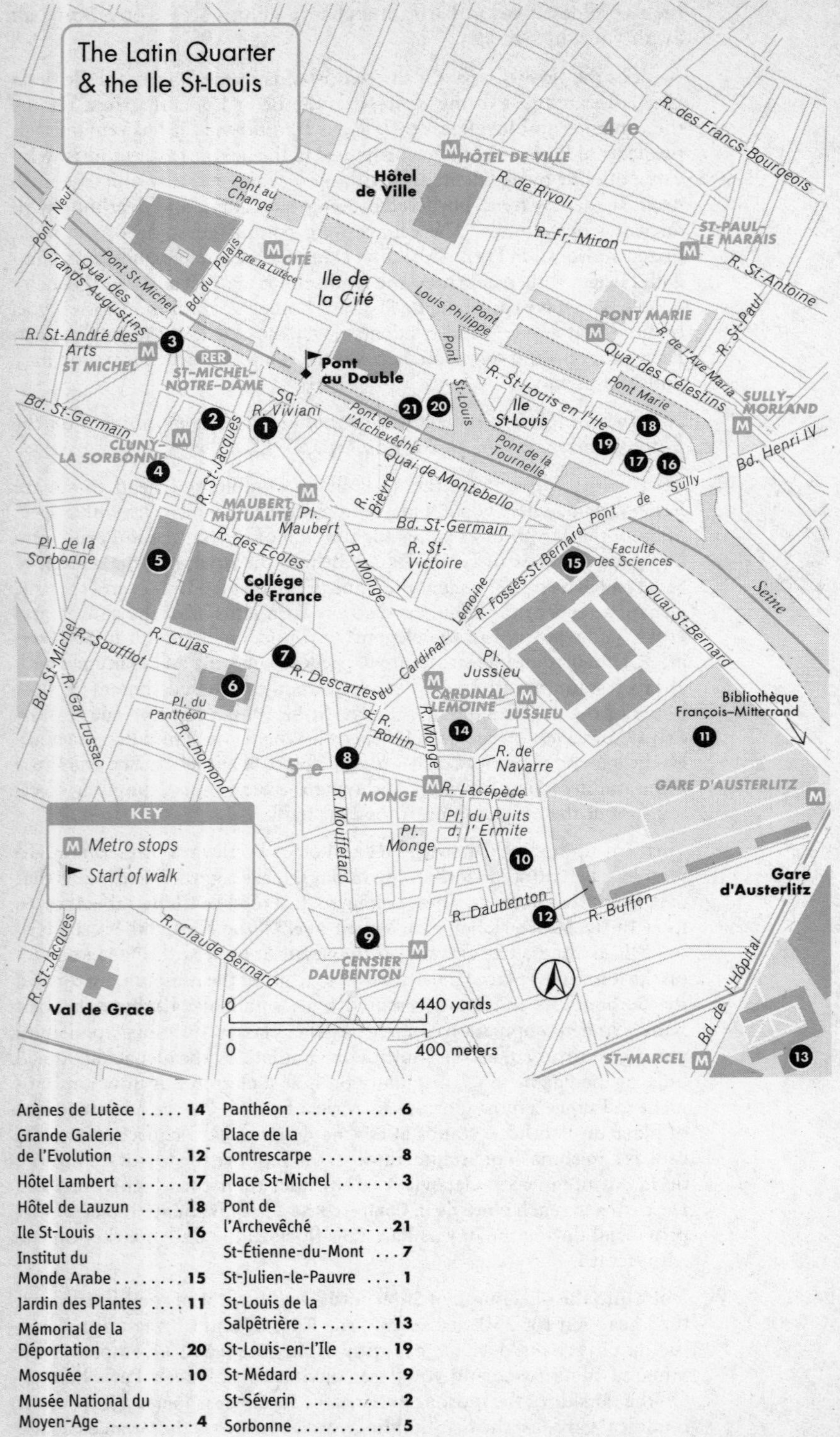

Arènes de Lutèce 14
Grande Galerie de l'Evolution 12
Hôtel Lambert 17
Hôtel de Lauzun 18
Ile St-Louis 16
Institut du Monde Arabe 15
Jardin des Plantes 11
Mémorial de la Déportation 20
Mosquée 10
Musée National du Moyen-Age 4
Panthéon 6
Place de la Contrescarpe 8
Place St-Michel 3
Pont de l'Archevêché 21
St-Étienne-du-Mont . . . 7
St-Julien-le-Pauvre 1
St-Louis de la Salpêtrière 13
St-Louis-en-l'Ile 19
St-Médard 9
St-Séverin 2
Sorbonne 5

many of extinct or endangered animals. The museums of entomology, paleontology, and mineralogy are on the south side of the park along rue Buffon; an old-fashioned zoo is on the other.

Although it's a bit out of the way, **St-Louis de la Salpêtrière** 13, the church of the Salpêtrière Hospital, is within walking distance of the Jardin des Plantes: take boulevard de l'Hôpital, at the far end of the park; the church is in the grounds of the hospital beyond Gare d'Austerlitz. Farther upriver, via quai d'Austerlitz and quai de la Gare, is the Bibliothèque Nationale François-Mitterrand, the French National Library, with its four huge, shiny glass towers.

If you forgo the distant pleasures of southeast Paris, take the northwest exit from the Jardin des Plantes up rue Lacépède then rue de Navarre to the **Arènes de Lutèce** 14, the remains of a Roman amphitheater. Rue des Arènes and rue Limé lead to place Jussieu and its hideous 1960s concrete campus; there's greater refinement around the corner down rue des Fossés-St-Bernard at the glass-facaded **Institut du Monde Arabe** 15, a center devoted to Arab culture.

Cross the Seine on Pont de Sully to the **Ile St-Louis** 16, the smaller of the city's two islands; it's a time capsule of old Paris and a tranquil place for taking a stroll back to the 17th and 18th centuries. The **Hôtel Lambert** 17 and the **Hôtel de Lauzun** 18, set near the eastern prow of the island, are two of the most majestic mansions on the island. Rue St-Louis-en-l'Ile runs the length of the island, dividing it in two. Walk down the street and admire the strange, pierced spire of **St-Louis-en-l'Ile** 19; stop off for an ice cream at Berthillon at No. 31. Then head down to the Pont St-Louis at the island's western tip to admire the celebrated views of Notre-Dame and the Hôtel de Ville and St-Gervais church on the Right Bank. Just across the bridge on Ile de la Cité lies the **Mémorial de la Déportation** 20, a starkly moving modern crypt dedicated to the French Jews who died in Nazi concentration camps. You may wish to linger in the quiet garden above before savoring the view of Notre-Dame from the **Pont de l'Archevêché** 21, which links the island to the Left Bank.

TIMING At just under 6 km (about 3½ mi), this walk can be done in a morning or afternoon, or serve as the basis for a leisurely day's exploring—given that several sites, notably the Musée de Cluny, deserve a lengthy visit. Note that the Grande Galerie d'Évolution stays open until 10 PM Thursday. You can easily make a brief excursion to St-Louis de la Salpêtrière as well as the Bibliothèque Nationale François-Mitterrand.

What to See

14 **Arènes de Lutèce** (Lutetia Amphitheater). This Roman arena was discovered only in 1869, and has since been excavated and landscaped to reveal parts of the original amphitheater. Designed as a theater and circus, the arena was almost totally destroyed by the barbarians in AD 280, though you can still see part of the stage and tiered seating. Along with the remains of the baths at the Cluny, this constitutes rare evidence of the powerful Roman city of Lutetia that flourished on the Left Bank in the 3rd century. Today it's a favorite spot for picnicking and *boule* playing. ✉ *Entrance at rue Monge or rue de Navarre, Latin Quarter* *Free* *Daily 8–sunset* Ⓜ *Place Monge.*

Fodor's Choice ★

12 **Grande Galerie de l'Evolution** (Great Hall of Evolution). This vast, handsome glass-and-iron structure in the Jardin des Plantes was built, like the Eiffel Tower, in 1889 but abandoned in the 1960s. It reopened amid popular acclaim in 1994 and now contains one of the world's finest collections of taxidermy, including a section devoted to extinct and endangered species. There's a reconstituted dodo—only a foot actually remains of

this clumsy, flightless bird from Mauritius—and a miniature South African zebra, the quagga, which disappeared early in the 20th century. Stunning lighting effects include push-button spotlighting and a ceiling that changes color to suggest storms, twilight, or hot savannah sun. ✉ *36 rue Geoffroy-St-Hilaire, Latin Quarter* ☎ *01–40–79–39–39* 🌐 *www.mnhn.fr/evolution* 🎫 *€7* ⏲ *Wed. and Fri.–Mon. 10–6, Thurs. 10–10* Ⓜ *Place Monge or Jussieu.*

⓱ **Hôtel Lambert.** Without this house—one of the most famous in Paris—Versailles probably wouldn't exist in all its glory. Sitting on the eastern end of the Ile St-Louis, it was created by the three great "Le"'s of the French Baroque: architect Louis Le Vau (1612–70), decorator Charles Le Brun, and painter Eustache Le Sieur. Built by the banker Lambert "le riche," the mansion was so impressive that Nicolas Fouquet ordered the team to build his château of Vaux-le-Vicomte, which, in turn, inspired Louis XIV to commission them to create Versailles. Voltaire was the most famous occupant of the Lambert, then owned by his lover, the Marquise du Châtelet. Here, in the Galerie d'Hercule, many of Paris's most famous costume balls were held; guests included everyone from Chopin to Empress Eugénie. Today, as through all of its privileged history, the house is private and has been lovingly restored by the Barons Rothschild. If you go around to the neighboring quay and bridge you can see part of the garden and, just possibly, the Galerie illuminated at night. ✉ *2 rue St-Louis-en-l'Ile, Ile St-Louis* Ⓜ *Pont Marie.*

⓲ **Hôtel de Lauzun.** Gilded and mirrored to within an inch of their lives, the salons here are some of the most important examples of the Baroque style in Paris and a must-see for art historians—others will be curious to visit this Ile St-Louis mansion because of the house's fascinating history. It was built by Louis Le Vau in 1657 and decorated in part by Charles Le Brun for Charles Gruyn, a supplier of goods to the French army who accumulated an immense fortune then landed in jail before the house was even completed. In the 19th century the revolutionary critic and visionary poet Charles Baudelaire (1821–67) had an apartment here, where he kept a cache of stuffed snakes and crocodiles, and wrote a large chunk of *Les Fleurs du Mal* (*The Flowers of Evil*), his masterpiece. In 1848 the poet Théophile Gautier (1811–72) moved in, making it the meeting place of the Club des Haschischines (Hashish Eaters' Club); novelist Alexandre Dumas and painter Eugène Delacroix were both members. The club came to represent more than just a den of drug takers and gossips, for these men believed passionately in the purity of art and the crucial role of the artist as sole interpreter of the chaos of life. Art for art's sake—the more refined and exotic the better—was their creed. Anything that helped the artist reach heightened states of perception was applauded. The building is closed for restoration until 2005. ✉ *17 quai d'Anjou, Ile St-Louis* ☎ *01–43–54–27–14* Ⓜ *Pont Marie.*

★ ⓰ **Ile St-Louis.** The smaller of the two Paris islands is linked to the Ile de la Cité by Pont St-Louis. The contrast between the islands is striking: whereas the Ile de la Cité is steeped in history and dotted with dignified public buildings, the Ile St-Louis is a discreet residential district. The island's most striking note is its architectural unity, which stems from the efforts of a group of early 17th-century property speculators. At that time, there were two islands here, the Ile Notre-Dame and Ile aux Vaches—Cow Island, a reference to its use as grazing land. The speculators, led by an energetic engineer named Christophe Marie (after whom the Pont Marie was named), bought the two islands, joined them together, and divided the newly formed Ile St-Louis into building plots. Baroque architect Louis Le Vau was commissioned to erect a series of imposing town houses, and by 1664 the project was largely complete. People still talk about the quaint, village-street feel of rue St-Louis-en-l'Ile, which runs the length of the island, dividing it neatly in two. From quai de Bourbon at the western end, facing the Ile de la Cité, there are attractive views of Notre-Dame, the Hôtel de Ville, and the church of St-Gervais. In summer, rows of baking bodies attest to the quay's enduring popularity as the city's favorite sunbathing spot, while crowds line up for a scoop from Berthillon's shop, the mecca of Parisian ice cream. You can savor your cone of *glace de Grande Marnier* by strolling along the isle's Seine-side streets—as Brassaï and other photographers proved, they are among Paris's most romantic sights. Ⓜ *Pont Marie.*

15 **Institut du Monde Arabe** (Institute of the Arab World). Jean Nouvel's striking glass-and-steel edifice adroitly fuses Arabic and European styles and was greeted with enthusiasm when it opened in 1988. Note the 240 shutterlike apertures that open and close to regulate light exposure. Inside, the institute tries to do for Arab culture what the Centre Pompidou does for modern art, with the help of a sound-and-image center; a vast library and documentation center; and an art museum containing Arab-Islamic art, textiles, and ceramics, plus exhibits on Arabic mathematics, astronomy, and medicine. Glass elevators whisk you to the ninth floor, where you can sip mint tea at the rooftop café and enjoy a memorable view of the Seine and Notre-Dame. ✉ *1 rue des Fossés-St-Bernard, Latin Quarter* ☎ *01–40–51–38–38* *Exhibitions €7, museum €4* ⏲ *Tues.–Sun. 10–6* Ⓜ *Cardinal Lemoine.*

11 **Jardin des Plantes** (Botanical Gardens). Bordered by the Seine, the drab Gare d'Austerlitz, and the utilitarian Jussieu campus (a branch of the Paris University system), this enormous swath of greenery contains botanical gardens, the Grande Galerie de l'Evolution, and three other natural history museums, opened in 1898. The **Grande Galerie de l'Evolution** is devoted to stuffed taxidermied animals; the **Musée Entomologique** (closed for renovation at press time) to insects; the **Musée Paléontologique** to fossils and skeletons dating back to prehistoric times; and the **Musée Minéralogique** to rocks and minerals. The stock of plants in the botanical gardens, dating from the first collections from the 17th century, has been enhanced by subsequent generations of devoted French botanists. The garden shelters what is claimed to be Paris's oldest tree, an *acacia robinia,* planted in 1636. There is also an alpine garden, an aquarium, a maze, a number of hothouses, and one of the world's oldest zoos, the Ménagerie, started by Napoléon. ✉ *Entrances on rue Geoffroy-St-Hilaire, rue Civier, and rue Buffon, Latin Quarter* ☎ *01–40–79–30–00* 🌐 *www.mnhn.fr* *Museums and zoo €5, hothouses €2.50* ⏲ *Museums Wed.–Mon. 10–5. Zoo June–Aug., daily 9–6; Sept.–May, daily 9–5. Hothouses Wed.–Mon. 1–5. Garden daily 7:30 AM–sunset* Ⓜ *Place Monge.*

20 **Mémorial de la Déportation** (Memorial of the Deportation). On the eastern tip of the Ile de la Cité, in what was once the city morgue, lies a starkly moving modern crypt dedicated to all the French men, women, and children who died in Nazi concentration camps. *Free* ⏲ *Apr.–Sept., daily 9–6; Oct.–Mar., daily 9 AM–dusk* Ⓜ *Maubert Mutualité.*

10 **Mosquée** (Mosque). This beautiful white mosque was built between 1922 and 1925, complete with arcades and minaret, and decorated in the style of Moorish Spain. Students from the nearby Jussieu and Censier universities pack themselves into the tea salon for cups of sweet mint tea at the café and for copious quantities of couscous at the restaurant.

The sunken garden and tiled patios are also open to the public (the prayer rooms are not), as are the *hammams*, or Turkish baths. ✉ *2 pl. du Puits-de-l'Ermite, Latin Quarter* ☎ *01–45–35–97–33* 🎫 *Guided tour €2.30, Turkish baths €13* ⏲ *Baths daily 10–9 (Tues. and Sun. men only, Mon. and Wed.–Sat. women only). Guided tours of mosque Sat.–Thurs. 9–noon and 2–6* Ⓜ *Place Monge.*

off the beaten path

Chinatown. If China, rather than Arabia, is your cup of tea, take the métro at nearby Censier Daubenton to Paris's Chinatown. Although not as ornamental as San Francisco's or New York's, Paris's Chinatown nevertheless has myriad electronics and clothing stores and dozens of restaurants with an exciting choice of Chinese *comestibles* (foods). Tang-Frères Chinese supermarket (✉ 48 av. d'Ivry, Chinatown) packs in a serious crowd of shoppers. The Temple de l'Association des Résidents d'Origine Chinoise (✉ 37 rue du Disque, Chinatown) is a small Buddhist temple that looks like a cross between a school cafeteria and an exotic Asian enclave filled with Buddha figures, fruit, and incense. Ⓜ *Tolbiac.*

★ 4 **Musée National du Moyen-Age** (National Museum of the Middle Ages). Devoted to the arts of the Middle Ages, this highly important museum—sometimes referred to as the Musée de Cluny—is housed in that precious relic of the 15th century, the **Hôtel de Cluny.** Adorned with purely decorative machicolations and turrets, the mansion was originally built by the Abbot of Jumièges; note the main *coquilles,* or shells, among the carved stone ornaments—rue St-Jacques (the Pilgrim's Way) is nearby. Gardens (nicely illuminated at night), an intricately vaulted chapel, and a cloistered courtyard with mullioned windows (that originally belonged to monks of the Cluny Abbey in Burgundy) are some pleasing attractions here, but almost immediately upon entering you encounter the stunning array of tapestries which heads the Cluny's vast collection of medieval decorative arts. There are numerous examples of the *mille-fleur* ("thousand-flower") styles, yet all eyes are attracted by the world-famous ***Dame à la Licorne*** (Lady and the Unicorn) series, woven in the 15th or 16th century, probably in Belgium, and depicting the five senses and the legend of the unicorn. Byzantine crosses, Romanesque architectural capitals, and medieval paintings round out the collection, stunningly augmented in 1977 by the spectacular collection of the heads of the ***Kings of Israel and Judah*** (originally thought Kings of France), unearthed in northern Paris and originally set upon the Gothic figures of the facade of Notre-Dame. Alongside the mansion are a reconstituted medieval garden with 58 species of flora depicted in the *Dame à la Licorne* tapestries, and remnants of the city's Roman baths—both hot (*caldarium*) and cold (*frigidarium*), the latter containing the *Boatmen's Pillar,* Paris's oldest sculpture. ✉ *6 pl. Paul-Painlevé, Latin Quarter* ☎ *01–53–73–78–00* 🌐 *www.musee-moyenage.fr* 🎫 *€5.50, free 1st Sun. of month* ⏲ *Wed.–Mon. 9:15–5:45* Ⓜ *Cluny La Sorbonne.*

6 **Panthéon.** Originally commissioned by Louis XV to mark his recovery from illness in 1744, Germain Soufflot's mighty domed church was not begun until 1764, or completed until 1790—whereupon the godless philosophers of the Revolution had its windows blocked and ordered it transformed into a national shrine. Puvis de Chavannes's giant frescoes in the nave, retracing the life of St. Genevieve, warrant appraisal. Today the Panthéon is a monument to France's most glorious historical figures; the crypt holds the remains of Voltaire, Zola, Rousseau, and dozens of other national heroes. Nobel Prize–winning scientist Marie Curie became the first woman to join their ranks, in 1995. ✉ *Pl. du*

Panthéon, Latin Quarter ☎ *01–44–32–18–00* 🌐 *www.monum.fr* €7 ⏲ *Apr.–Sept., daily 9:30–6:30; Oct.–Mar., daily 10–6:15* Ⓜ *Cardinal Lemoine; RER: Luxembourg.*

8 **Place de la Contrescarpe.** This intimate square behind the Panthéon doesn't start to swing until after dusk, when its cafés and bars fill up. During the day the square looks almost provincial, as Parisians flock to the daily market at the bottom of rue Mouffetard, a steeply sloping street that retains much of its bygone charm. (Ⓜ Monge).

3 **Place St-Michel.** This square on the Seine was named for Gabriel Davioud's grandiose 1860 fountain depicting St. Michael slaying the dragon. *Métro or RER: St-Michel.*

21 **Pont de l'Archevêché** (Archbishop's Bridge). This bridge, built in 1828, links Ile St-Louis to the Left Bank. The bridge offers a breathtaking view of the east end of the cathedral, ringed by flying buttresses, floating above the Seine like some vast stone ship. Ⓜ *Maubert Mutualité.*

7 **St-Étienne-du-Mont.** The ornate facade of this mainly 16th-century church combines Gothic, Baroque, and Renaissance elements. Inside, the curly, carved rood screen (1525–35), separating nave and chancel, is the only one of its kind in Paris. Note the uneven-floored chapel behind the choir, which can be reached via a cloister containing exquisite 17th-century stained glass. ✉ *Pl. de l'Abbé-Basset, Latin Quarter* Ⓜ *Cardinal Lemoine.*

1 **St-Julien-le-Pauvre.** This tiny church was built at the same time as Notre-Dame (1165–1220), on a site where a succession of chapels once stood. The church belongs to a Greek Orthodox order today but was originally named for St. Julian, bishop of Le Mans, nicknamed Le Pauvre (the Poor) after he gave all his money away. ✉ *Rue St-Julien-le-Pauvre, Latin Quarter* Ⓜ *St-Michel.*

13 **St-Louis de la Salpêtrière.** The church of the Salpêtrière Hospital stands next to the Gare d'Austerlitz, which it dominates with its unmistakable, lantern-topped octagonal dome. The church was built (1670–77) in the shape of a Greek cross from the designs of Libéral Bruant. ✉ *Bd. de l'Hôpital, Latin Quarter* Ⓜ *Gare d'Austerlitz.*

19 **St-Louis-en-l'Ile.** The only church on the Ile St-Louis, built from 1664 to 1726 to the Baroque designs of architect Louis Le Vau, is lavishly furnished and has two unusual exterior features: its original pierced spire and an iron clock, added in 1741. ✉ *Rue St-Louis-en-l'Ile, Ile St-Louis* Ⓜ *Pont Marie.*

need a break?

Cafés all over sell the haute couture of ice cream, but **Berthillon** (✉ 31 rue St-Louis-en-l'Ile, Ile St-Louis ☎ 01–43–54–31–61) itself is the place to come. More than 30 flavors are served; expect to wait in line. The shop is open Wednesday–Sunday.

9 **St-Médard.** This church at the bottom of rue Mouffetard contains the painting *St. Joseph with the Christ Child* by Spanish master Zurbarán. The nave and facade, with its large late-Gothic window, date from the late 15th century. The 17th-century choir is in contrasting classical style. ✉ *Rue Mouffetard, Latin Quarter* Ⓜ *Censier Daubenton.*

off the beaten path

Manufacture des Gobelins. Tapestries have been woven on this spot in southeastern Paris, on the banks of the long-covered Bièvre River, which once flowed into the Seine, since 1662. Guided tours—in French only—combine historical explanation with the chance to admire both old tapestries and today's weavers at work in their airy workshops.

✉ 42 av. des Gobelins, Latin Quarter ☎ 01–44–08–52–00 🌐 www.monum.fr 🎫 €8 ⏲ Tues.–Thurs., guided tours only at 2 and 2:45 Ⓜ Les Gobelins.

❷ **St-Séverin.** This unusually wide Flamboyant Gothic church dominates the Left Bank neighborhood filled with squares and pedestrian streets. In the 11th century the church that stood here was the parish church for the entire Left Bank. Louis XIV's cousin, a capricious woman known simply as the Grande Mademoiselle, adopted St-Séverin when she tired of St-Sulpice; she then spent vast sums getting court decorator Le Brun to modernize the chancel in the 17th century. Note the splendidly deviant spiraling column in the forest of pillars behind the altar. *✉ Rue des Prêtres-St-Séverin, Latin Quarter ⏲ Weekdays 11–5:30, Sat. 11–10 Ⓜ St-Michel.*

❺ **Sorbonne.** Named after Robert de Sorbon, a medieval canon who founded a theological college here in 1253 for 16 students, the Sorbonne is one of the oldest universities in Europe. For centuries it has been one of France's principal institutions of higher learning, as well as the hub of the Latin Quarter and nerve center of Paris's student population. The church and university buildings were restored by Cardinal Richelieu in the 17th century, and the maze of amphitheaters, lecture rooms, and laboratories, surrounding courtyards, and narrow streets, retains a hallowed air. You can visit the main courtyard on rue de la Sorbonne and peek into the main lecture hall, a major meeting point during the tumultuous student upheavals of 1968, and also of interest for a giant mural by Puvis de Chavannes, the *Sacred Wood* (1880–89). The square is dominated by the university church, the noble **Église de la Sorbonne,** whose outstanding exterior features are its cupola and Corinthian columns. Inside is the white marble tomb of that ultimate crafty cleric, Cardinal Richelieu himself. *✉ Rue de la Sorbonne, Latin Quarter Ⓜ Cluny La Sorbonne.*

off the beaten path

Centre de la Mer et des Eaux (Center for Sea and Waters). A spell of fish-gazing is a soothing, mesmerizing experience for young and old here at one of the principal aquariums in Paris. From the Sorbonne, go up rue de la Sorbonne, and then take the first left on rue Cujas, and a right on rue St-Jacques. *✉ 195 rue St-Jacques, Latin Quarter ☎ 01–44–32–10–90 🌐 www.oceano.org 🎫 €4.60 ⏲ Tues.–Fri. 10–12:30 and 1:15–5:30, weekends 10–5:30 Ⓜ RER: Luxembourg.*

FROM ORSAY TO ST-GERMAIN

This walk covers the western half of the Left Bank, from the Musée d'Orsay in the stately 7ᵉ arrondissement to the Faubourg St-Germain, a lively and colorful area in the 6ᵉ arrondissement. In its northern reaches, this district goes under the moniker of St-Germain-des-Prés, now a prized address for the rich and stylish. In the 19th century, Émile Zola depicted these environs as the backdrop for his sordid tale *Thérèse Raquin,* Claude Monet and Auguste Renoir shared a studio at No. 20 rue Visconti, and the young Picasso managed to eke out an existence in a flat on rue de Seine. Where artists go, millionaires follow. Today St-Germain-des-Prés is one of the chicest and most delightful neighborhoods in the city; with numerous hotels, it is also (surprise) one of the most tourist-friendly.

The headliner on this tour is the Musée d'Orsay, which houses a superb collection of Impressionist paintings in a spectacularly converted Belle Epoque rail station on the Seine. Farther along the river, the 18th-century Palais Bourbon, where the National Assembly convenes, sets the tone. Hereabouts is Edith Wharton territory—select, discreet *vieille France,* where all the aristocrats live in gorgeous, sprawling, old-fashioned apartments or *maisons particuliers* (town houses). Luxurious ministries and embassies—including the Hôtel Matignon, residence of the French prime minister—line the surrounding streets, their majestic scale completely in keeping with the Hôtel des Invalides, whose gold-leafed dome climbs heavenward above the regal tomb of Napoléon. The splendid Rodin Museum—one of the few houses here where you can explore the grand interior—is only a short walk away.

To the east, boulevard St-Michel slices the Left Bank in two: on one side the Latin Quarter, on the other the Faubourg St-Germain, named for St-Germain-des-Prés, the oldest church in Paris. The venerable church tower has long acted as a beacon for intellectuals, most famously during the 1950s, when Albert Camus, Jean-Paul Sartre, and Simone de Beauvoir ate and drank existentialism in the neighborhood cafés. Today most of the philosophizing is done by tourists, yet a wealth of bookshops, art stores, and luscious antiques galleries ensure that St-Germain retains its very highbrow appeal. A highlight of St-Germain is the Jardin du Luxembourg, the city's most famous and colorful park. The 17th-century palace overlooking the gardens houses the French Senate.

Numbers in the text correspond to numbers in the margin and on the Orsay to St-Germain map.

a good walk

Arrive at the **Musée d'Orsay** 1 early to avoid the crowds that flock to see the museum's outstanding works of art, including many of the most beloved Impressionist paintings in France. A good meeting point is the pedestrian square outside the museum, where huge bronze statues of an elephant and a rhinoceros disprove the notion that the French take their art too seriously. Across the square stands the **Musée de la Légion d'Honneur** 2, where you can find an array of French and foreign decorations. A stylish two-tiered footbridge, opened in 2000, crosses the Seine to the Tuileries, but opt instead to either cut south down rue de Bellechasse (if you're short of time) to the Hôtel Matignon or head west along rue de Lille to the **Palais Bourbon** 3, home of the Assemblée Nationale (the French Parliament). There's a fine view across the Seine to place de la Concorde and the church of the Madeleine.

Rue de l'Université leads from the Assemblée to the grassy Esplanade des Invalides and an encounter with the **Hôtel des Invalides** 4, founded by Louis XIV to house wounded (*invalide*) veterans. The most impressive dome in Paris towers over the church at the back of the Invalides—the Église du Dôme. From the church, turn left, then left again onto boulevard des Invalides, then right on rue de Varenne to reach the elegant Hôtel Biron, better known as the **Musée Rodin** 5. Here you can see a fine collection of Auguste Rodin's emotionally charged statues and some wonderful gardens. The quiet, distinguished 18th-century streets between the Rodin Museum and the Parliament are filled with embassies and ministries. The most famous, farther along rue de Varenne, is the **Hôtel Matignon** 6, residence of the French prime minister. Just before, at No. 51, is one of Paris's handful of private culs-de-sac. Next door at No. 53 you can pay your respects to American novelist Edith Wharton, who lived and worked here from 1910 to 1920. Take the next left onto rue du Bac, then right onto rue de Grenelle, past the **Musée Maillol** 7, ded-

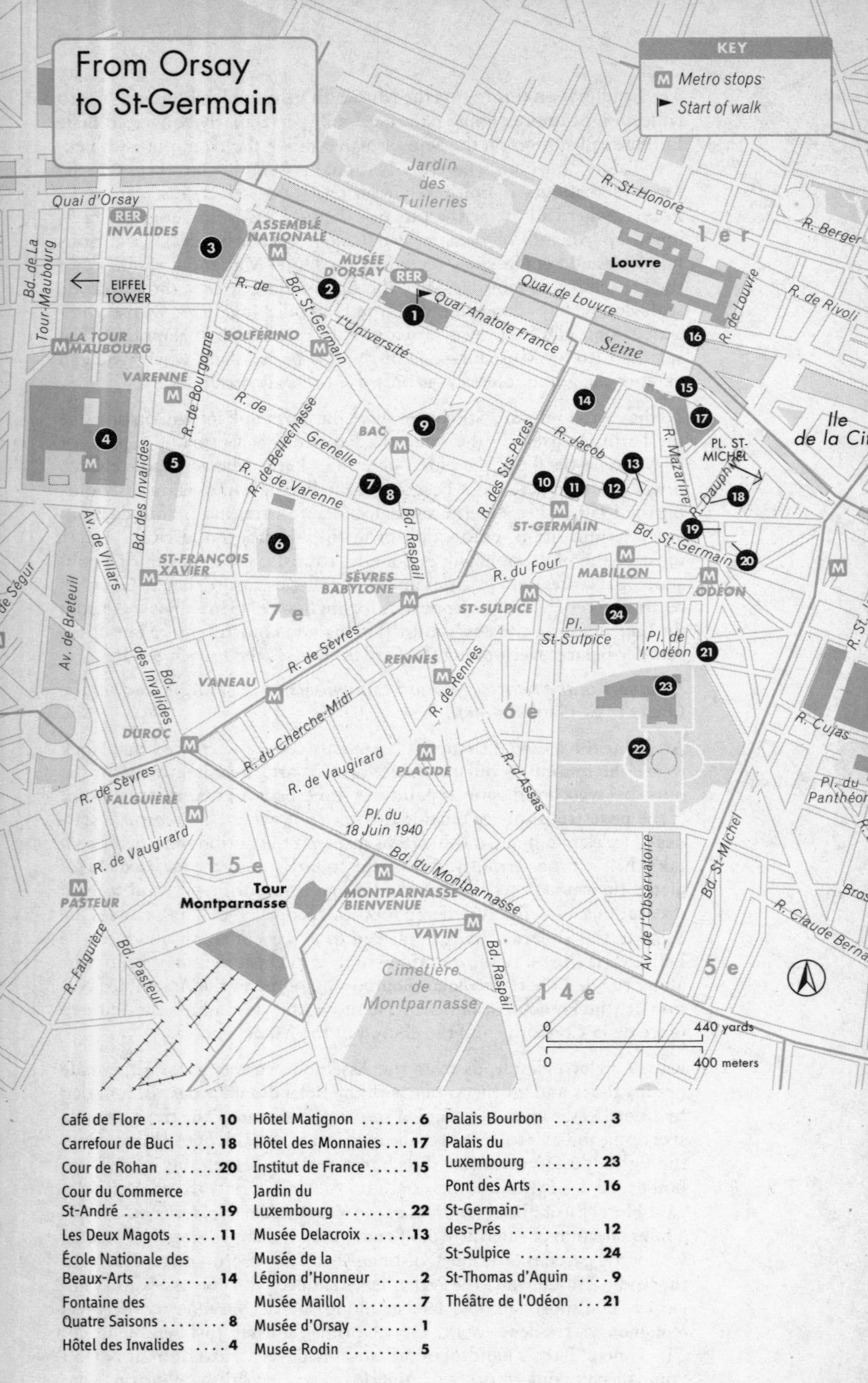

Café de Flore 10
Carrefour de Buci 18
Cour de Rohan 20
Cour du Commerce St-André 19
Les Deux Magots 11
École Nationale des Beaux-Arts 14
Fontaine des Quatre Saisons 8
Hôtel des Invalides 4
Hôtel Matignon 6
Hôtel des Monnaies . . . 17
Institut de France 15
Jardin du Luxembourg 22
Musée Delacroix 13
Musée de la Légion d'Honneur 2
Musée Maillol 7
Musée d'Orsay 1
Musée Rodin 5
Palais Bourbon 3
Palais du Luxembourg 23
Pont des Arts 16
St-Germain-des-Prés 12
St-Sulpice 24
St-Thomas d'Aquin 9
Théâtre de l'Odéon . . . 21

icated to the work of sculptor Aristide Maillol, and Bouchardon's monumental **Fontaine des Quatre Saisons** 8.

Turn left down boulevard Raspail and cross to rue de Luynes. Carry on across boulevard St-Germain to inspect the stately 17th-century church of **St-Thomas d'Aquin** 9; then double back and head east along boulevard St-Germain for 400 yards to the **Café de Flore** 10, one of the principal haunts of the intelligentsia after World War II. Another popular café, two doors down, is **Les Deux Magots** 11; politicians and showbiz types still wine and dine at the pricey Brasserie Lipp across the street. Looming above cobbled place St-Germain-des-Prés stands **St-Germain-des-Prés** 12, Paris's oldest church.

Follow rue de l'Abbaye, along the far side of the church, to rue de Furstenberg. The street opens out into place Furstenberg, an adorably picturesque square bedecked with white globe lamps and catalpa trees (one side now defaced by overly renovated town houses, reputedly among the most expensive lodgings on offer in today's Paris), where you'll find Eugène Delacroix's atelier, the **Musée Delacroix** 13. Take a left on rue Jacob and turn right down rue Bonaparte to the **École Nationale des Beaux-Arts** 14, whose students can often be seen painting and sketching on the nearby quays and bridges. Wander into the courtyard and galleries of the school to see the casts and copies of the statues stored here for safekeeping during the Revolution.

Continue down to the Seine and turn right along the quai, past the **Institut de France** 15. With its distinctive dome and commanding position overlooking the **Pont des Arts** 16—a footbridge affording delightful views of the Louvre and Ile de la Cité—the institute is one of the city's most impressive waterside sights. Farther along, on quai de Conti, you pass the **Hôtel des Monnaies** 17, the old national mint.

Head up rue Dauphine, the street that singer Juliet Greco put on the map when she opened the erstwhile Tabou jazz club here in the '50s. It's linked 150 yards up by the open-air passage Dauphine to rue Mazarine, which leads left to the **Carrefour de Buci** 18, a busy crossroad. Fanning out from the Carrefour are lively rue de Buci, with one of the best food markets in Paris; rue de l'Ancienne-Comédie, so named because it was the first home of the legendary Comédie Française, cutting through to busy place de l'Odéon; and rue St-André des Arts. Head left along the latter to swiftly find the historic **Cour du Commerce St-André** 19 (opposite No. 66), a magnificently cobbled pedestrian street where the 18th century seems preserved in amber, lined with cafés, including, halfway down on the left, Paris's oldest, Le Procope. Opposite this landmark stands the **Cour de Rohan** 20, which some people believe is the prettiest spot in Paris: one of the hidden treasures of the city, this series of tiny courtyards offers a trip back to storybook Renaissance France.

Head to the end of cour du Commerce St-André, cross boulevard St-Germain, and climb rue de l'Odéon to the colonnaded **Théâtre de l'Odéon** 21. Behind the theater, across rue de Vaugirard, lies the spacious **Jardin du Luxembourg** 22, one of the most stylish parks in the city. The large pond, usually animated by an armada of toy boats that can be hired alongside, enjoys the scenic backdrop of the rusticated 17th-century **Palais du Luxembourg** 23. Today the palace houses the French Senate and is not open to the public, but its adjacent art museum is.

Return to rue de Vaugirard and head west before turning right down pretty rue Férou to place St-Sulpice, a spacious square ringed with cafés; Yves Saint Laurent's famous Rive Gauche store is at No. 6. Looming over the square is the enormous church of **St-Sulpice** 24. If you wish to explore Montparnasse now, walk west down rue du Vieux-Colombier and take the métro three stops to Vavin.

TIMING Depending on how long you spend in the plethora of museums and shops along the way, this 6½-km (4-mi) walk could take anywhere from four hours to several days. Aim for an early start—that way you can hit the Musée d'Orsay early, when crowds are smaller, then get to the rue de Buci street market in full swing, in the late afternoon (the stalls are generally closed for lunch until 3 PM). Note that the Hôtel des Invalides is open daily, but Orsay is closed Monday. You might consider returning to one or more museums on another day or night—Orsay is open late Thursday evenings.

What to See

Fodor'sChoice ★ 10 **Café de Flore.** In the postwar years, Jean-Paul Sartre and Simone de Beauvoir would meet their friends and followers at this popular café. These days this quintessential slice of Paris is mostly filled with tourists on the outdoor terrace and locals inside. ✉ *172 bd. St-Germain, St-Germain-des-Prés* Ⓜ *St-Germain-des-Prés.*

18 **Carrefour de Buci.** This crossroads was once a notorious Left Bank landmark: during the 18th century it contained a gallows, an execution stake, and an iron collar used for punishing troublemakers. In September 1792 the revolutionary army used this daunting site to enroll its first volunteers, and many Royalists and priests lost their heads here during the bloody course of the Revolution. There's nothing sinister, however, about the carrefour today, as brightly colored flowers spill onto the sidewalk at the flower shop on the corner of rue Grégoire-de-Tours. A couple of the small (and highly congested) streets fanning out from the carrefour are of interest. **Rue de Buci** has a good outdoor food market, open Tuesday–Saturday 8–1 and 4–7, Sunday 9–1. **Rue de l'Ancienne-Comédie** got its name because it was the first home of the Comédie Française. Ⓜ *Mabillon.*

need a break? If you happen to arrive when the market on rue de Buci is closed, **La Vieille France** (✉ 14 rue de Buci, St-Germain-des-Prés ☎ 01–43–26–55–13) pâtisserie is the perfect place to help fill your hunger gap.

★ 19 **Cour du Commerce St-André.** Like an 18th-century engraving come to life, this exquisite, cobblestoned street-arcade is one of Paris's loveliest sights. While some faux cafés have taken up residence, its shop signs, awnings, and outdoor tables make it an authentic tableau, and Napoléon himself still wouldn't look too out of place taking his coffee here (as he did back when). The alleyway might also be called a very romantic sight, but before you abandon yourself to a tryst at a table here remember that at No. 9 Dr. Guillotin conceived the idea for a new, "humane" method of execution; among its many later victims was Charlotte Corday, who stabbed the famous journalist Jean-Paul Marat (who ran his revolutionary newspaper, *L'Ami du Peuple,* at No. 8) in his bath in his house just across boulevard St-Germain; that other great agitator of the French Revolution, Danton, lived at No. 20.

Marat's ashes were actually kept in a memorial at Paris's oldest café, **Le Procope** (☎ 01–40–46–79–00), halfway up the street, opened in 1686 by an Italian named Francesco Procopio. Many of Paris's most famous literary sons and daughters have imbibed here through the centuries, ranging from erudite academics like Denis Diderot to debauchees like Oscar Wilde, as well as Voltaire, Balzac, George Sand, Victor Hugo, and even Benjamin Franklin, who popped in whenever business brought him to Paris and probably rubbed shoulders with the fomenters of the Revolution. The café started out as the Sardi's of its day, because the Comédie-Française had opened nearby; Racine and Molière were regulars. The place is still going strong, so you, too, can enjoy its period (though now gussied-up) trimmings and haute cuisine menu. Just opposite Le Procope is that hidden treasure of the Cour du Commerce: the picturesque courtyard cul-de-sac Cour de Rohan. ✉ *Linking bd. St-Germain and rue St-André-des-Arts, St-Germain-des-Prés* Ⓜ *Odéon.*

★ 20 **Cour de Rohan** (Rohan Courtyard). The most magical hideaway in Paris, this series of three cloistered courtyards and passageways found Hollywood immortality when Cecil Beaton picked it as the locale of Gigi's home in the famed Lerner and Loewe 1958 musical film *Gigi*. Entered from the arcade of the Cour du Commerce St-André, it lies tucked beyond a fragment of medieval city walls and a turret remaining from the days of King Philippe-Auguste. Once part of the home of the archbishops of Rouen (over the years the name was transformed into Rohan), it remains a storybook stage set. As you enter, the steep staircase directly to your left leads to "chez Mamita" (Gigi's grandmother); beyond are two sloping courtyards, lined with lovely little apartment-ateliers (now the private property of the Foundation Giacometti). Before you leave, lift your eyes and take in the enchanting surrounding roofscape, much of which seems barely changed since the 17th century, including the back of the towering palace that was once the Paris pied-à-terre of Diane de Poitiers. ✉ *Entrance on cour du Commerce St-André, St-Germain-des-Prés* Ⓜ *Odéon.*

11 **Les Deux Magots.** This old-fashioned St-Germain café, named after the two Chinese figures, or *magots,* inside, still thrives on its post–World War II reputation as one of the Left Bank's prime meeting places for the intelligentsia. It remains crowded day and night, but these days you're more likely to rub shoulders with tourists than with philosophers. Still, if you are in search of the mysterious glamour of the Left Bank, you can do no better than to station yourself at one of the sidewalk tables—or at a window table on a wintry day—to watch the passing parade. ✉ *6 pl. St-Germain-des-Prés, St-Germain-des-Prés* ☎ *01–45–48–55–25* Ⓜ *St-Germain-des-Prés.*

14 **École Nationale des Beaux-Arts** (National Fine Arts College). Occupying three large mansions near the Seine, this school—today the breeding ground for painters, sculptors, and architects—was once the site of a convent founded in 1608 by Marguerite de Valois, the first wife of Henri IV. During the Revolution the convent was turned into a depot for works of art salvaged from the monuments that were under threat of destruction by impassioned mobs. Only the church and cloister remained by the time the Beaux-Arts school was established in 1816. ✉ *14 rue Bonaparte, St-Germain-des-Prés* ⏲ *Daily 1–7* Ⓜ *St-Germain-des-Prés.*

need a break?

The popular café, **La Palette** (✉ 43 rue de Seine, St-Germain-des-Prés ☎ 01–43–26–68–15), on the corner of rue de Seine and rue Callot, has long been a favorite haunt of Beaux-Arts students. One of them painted the ungainly portrait of the patron François that presides with mock authority.

8 **Fontaine des Quatre Saisons** (Four Seasons Fountain). This allegorical fountain, designed by Edme Bouchardon in 1739 to help boost the district's water supply, has a wealth of sculpted detail. Flanked by a majestic curved screen, the seated figure of Paris, framed by Ionic columns, surveys the rivers Seine and Marne, while bas-reliefs peopled by industrious cupids

represent the seasons. ✉ *57–59 rue de Grenelle, St-Germain-des-Prés* Ⓜ *Rue du Bac.*

★ 4 **Hôtel des Invalides.** Les Invalides, as it is widely known, is an outstanding monumental Baroque ensemble designed by architect Libéral Bruant in the 1670s at the behest of Louis XIV to house wounded (*invalid*) soldiers. Although no more than a handful of old soldiers live at the Invalides today, the military link remains in the form of the **Musée de l'Armée** (Army Museum), one of the world's foremost military museums, with a vast, albeit musty, collection of arms, armor, uniforms, banners, and military pictures down through the ages. Up in the attic in the same space is the **Musée des Plans-Reliefs** (Model Town Museum), with its fascinating collection of old scale models of French towns; the largest and most impressive is Strasbourg, which takes up an entire room. The main cobbled courtyard is a fitting scene for the parades and ceremonies still occasionally held at the Invalides.

Fodor's Choice ★

The 17th-century **Église St-Louis des Invalides,** the Invalides's original church, was the site of the first performance of Berlioz's *Requiem,* in 1837. The most impressive dome in Paris towers over Jules Hardouin-Mansart's **Église du Dôme** (Dome Church), built onto the end of Église St-Louis but blocked off from it in 1793—no great pity, perhaps, as the two buildings are vastly different in style and scale. Fittingly, for this military complex, **Napoléon's Tomb** is found here—his remains are kept in a series of no fewer than six coffins, one inside the next, within a bombastic memorial of red porphyry, ringed by low reliefs and a dozen statues symbolizing his campaigns. Among others commemorated in the church are French World War I hero Marshal Foch; Napoléon's brother Joseph, erstwhile king of Spain; and military architect Sébastien de Vauban. ✉ *Pl. des Invalides, Eiffel Tower/Trocadéro* ☎ *01–44–42–37–72 Army and Model museums* 🌐 *www.invalides.org* 🎫 €6 ⏲ *Dome Church, Army, and Model museums Apr.–Sept., daily 10–6; Oct.–Mar., daily 10–4:30* Ⓜ *La Tour-Maubourg.*

6 **Hôtel Matignon.** The most elegant residence of the French prime minister, built in 1721, is the Left Bank counterpart to the president's Élysée Palace. From 1888 to 1914 it was the embassy of the Austro-Hungarian Empire; only since 1958 has it housed heads of government. ✉ *57 rue de Varenne, Invalides* ⏲ *Not open to the public* Ⓜ *Varenne.*

17 **Hôtel des Monnaies** (Royal Mint). Louis XVI transferred the Royal Mint to this imposing mansion in the late 18th century. Although the mint was moved again, to Pessac, near Bordeaux, in 1973, weights and measures, medals, and limited-edition coins are still made here. The **Musée de la Monnaie** (Coin Museum) has an extensive collection of coins, documents, engravings, and paintings. On Tuesday and Friday at 2 PM you can catch the coin-metal craftsmen at work in their ateliers overlooking the Seine. ✉ *11 quai de Conti, St-Germain-des-Prés* ☎ *01–40–46–55–35* 🎫 €3 ⏲ *Tues.–Fri. 11–5:30, weekends noon–5:30* Ⓜ *Pont Neuf or Odéon.*

15 **Institut de France** (French Institute). The Institute is one of France's most revered cultural institutions, and its curved, dome-topped facade is one of the Left Bank's most impressive waterside sights. The Tour de Nesle, which formed part of Philippe-Auguste's wall fortifications along the Seine, used to stand here and, in its time, had many royal occupants, including Henry V of England. The French novelist Alexandre Dumas (1824–95) featured the stormy history of the Tour de Nesle—during which the lovers of a number of French queens were tossed from its windows—in a melodrama of the same name. In 1661 the wealthy Cardi-

nal Mazarin left 2 million French *livres* (pounds) in his will for construction of a college that would be dedicated to educating students from Piedmont, Alsace, Artois, and Roussillon, provinces that had been annexed to France during the years of his ministry. Mazarin's coat of arms is sculpted on the dome, and the library in the east wing, which holds more than 350,000 volumes, still bears his name.

At the beginning of the 19th century Napoléon stipulated that the Institute be transferred here from the Louvre. The Académie Française, the oldest of the five academies that compose the institute, was created by Cardinal Richelieu in 1635. Its first major task was to edit the definitive French dictionary (still unfinished); it is also charged with safeguarding the purity of the French language. Election to its ranks, subject to approval by the French head of state, is the highest literary honor in the land—there can only be 40 "immortal" lifelong members at any one time. ✉ *Pl. de l'Institut, St-Germain-des-Prés* ⏲ *Guided visits reserved for cultural associations only* Ⓜ *Pont Neuf.*

Fodor's Choice ★ 22 **Jardin du Luxembourg** (Luxembourg Gardens). Immortalized in countless paintings, the Jardin du Luxembourg possesses all that is unique and befuddling about Parisian parks: swarms of pigeons, cookie-cutter trees, ironed-and-pressed dirt walkways, and immaculate lawns meant for admiring, not touching. The tree- and bench-lined paths offer a reprieve from the incessant bustle of the Quartier Latin, as well as an opportunity to discover the dotty old women and smooching university students who once found their way into Doisneau photographs. Somewhat austere during the colder months, the garden becomes intoxicating as spring fills the flower beds with daffodils, tulips, and hyacinths; the pools teem with boats nudged along by children, and the paths with Parisians thrusting their noses toward the sun. The park's northern boundary is dominated by the Palais du Luxembourg, surrounded by a handful of well-armed guards; they are protecting the senators who have been deliberating in the palace since 1958. Feel free to move the green chairs around to create your own picnic area or people-watching site.

Although the garden may seem purely French, the original 17th-century planning took its inspiration from Italy. When Maria de' Medici acquired the estate of the deceased Duke of Luxembourg in 1612 she decided to turn his mansion into a version of the Florentine Medici home, the Palazzo Pitti. She ended up with something more Franco-Italian than strictly Florentine. The land behind the palace was loosely modeled on the Boboli Gardens. The landscapers, like the architects, didn't design a true version of the Florentine garden, opting for the emerging style of heavy-handed human manipulation of nature—linear vistas, box-trimmed trees, and color-coordinated flower beds—thereby further defining the "French" garden. A tiny corner of the park still has that nature-on-the-brink-of-overwhelming-civilization look that was the trademark of the Renaissance Italian garden—namely, the intentionally overgrown cluster of trees and bushes lining the 1624 Fontaine de Médicis. The park captured the hearts of Parisians when it became public after the Revolution; thousands turned out in the mid-1860s to prevent a Haussmann-directed boulevard from being built through its middle.

One of the great attractions of the park is the **Théâtre des Marionnettes,** where on Wednesday, Saturday, and Sunday at 3 and 4:15 PM you can catch one of the classic guignols (marionette shows) for a small admission charge. The wide-mouthed kiddies, though, are the real attraction; their expressions of utter surprise, despair, or glee have fascinated the likes of Henri Cartier-Bresson and François Truffaut. And finally, for those eager to burn off their pastry breakfasts: the Jardin de Luxembourg has a well-maintained trail around the perimeter, and it is one of the few public places the French will be seen in athletic clothes. It takes an average jogger 20 minutes to get all the way around, and water fountains are strategically placed along the way. Men of all ages are also strategically placed; their comments to female runners are irritating, but otherwise this is a great escape. ✉ *Bordered by bd. St-Michel and rues de Vaugirard, de Médicis, Guynemer, and Auguste-Comte, St-Germain-des-Prés* Ⓜ *Odéon; RER: Luxembourg.*

13 **Musée Delacroix.** The studio of artist Eugène Delacroix (1798–1863) contains only a small collection of his sketches and drawings, but it's a good place to visit if you want to pay homage to France's foremost Romantic painter. Another reason to pay a call: the atelier is set on rue Furstenberg, one of the tiniest, most romantic squares in Paris. ✉ *6 rue Furstenberg, St-Germain-des-Prés* ☎ *01–44–41–86–50* 🌐 *www.musee.delacroix.fr* 🎫 *€4* ⏲ *Wed.–Mon. 9:30–5* Ⓜ *St-Germain-des-Prés.*

2 **Musée de la Légion d'Honneur** (Legion of Honor Museum). French and foreign decorations are displayed in this mansion by the Seine, linked to the Tuileries by an elegant, two-tier footbridge. The original building, constructed in 1786, was one of the largest and grandest mansions in town. The Hôtel de Salm—as it is officially known—was burned down during the Commune in 1871, and rebuilt in 1878 in glittering neoclassical style. It was under renovation at press time and scheduled, call ahead to confirm if it has repopened. ✉ *2 rue de Bellechasse, St-Germain-des-Prés* ☎ *01–40–62–84–25* Ⓜ *Solférino; RER: Musée d'Orsay.*

7 **Musée Maillol.** Bronzes by Art Deco sculptor Aristide Maillol (1861–1944), whose sleek, stylized nudes adorn the Tuileries Gardens, can be admired at this handsome town house lovingly restored by his former muse, Dina Vierny. Maillol's drawings, paintings, and tapestries are also on show. Works by other artists include a roomful of Poliakoff abstractions and two sensuous Zitman nudes in the barrel-vaulted cellar café. ✉ *61 rue de Grenelle, St-Germain-des-Prés* ☎ *01–42–22–59–58* 🎫 *€6* ⏲ *Wed.–Mon. 11–6* Ⓜ *Rue du Bac.*

Fodor's Choice ★

1 **Musée d'Orsay.** Setting out to form a bridge between the classical collections of the Louvre and the modern collections of the Centre Pompidou, the collection of the Musée d'Orsay includes many of the most famous Impressionist and Postimpressionist paintings in the world. On top of that, the building itself—a spectacularly renovated Belle Epoque train station—is a work of art. Beginning in 1900, the building was used as a depot for routes between Paris and the southwest of France. By 1939 the Gare d'Orsay had become too small for mainline travel, and intercity trains were transferred to the Gare d'Austerlitz, with the d'Orsay becoming a suburban terminus until it closed in the 1960s. The building was temporarily used as a theater, an auction house, and a setting for Orson Welles's movie *The Trial,* based on Kafka's novel, before it was finally slated for demolition. However, the destruction of the 19th-century Les Halles (market halls) across the Seine provoked a furor among conservationists, and in the late 1970s former president Giscard d'Estaing ordered the d'Orsay to be transformed into a museum. Architects Pierre Colboc, Renaud Bardou, and Jean-Paul Philippon were commissioned to remodel the building; Gae Aulenti, known for her renovation of the Palazzo Grassi in Venice, was hired to reshape the interior. Aulenti's modern design in a building almost a century old provoked much controversy, but the museum's attributes soon outweighed any criticism shortly after its opening in December 1986.

The collection is devoted to the arts (mainly French) spanning the period 1848–1914. Exhibits take up three floors, but the immediate impression is of a single, vast, stationlike hall. While the chief artistic attraction is the Impressionists, whose works are displayed under the roof, the museum also prominently includes lesser-ranked academic and salon painters, many of whose names will be unfamiliar to most. Renoir, Sisley, Pissarro, and Monet do not, in other words, compose the entire history of French 19th-century art. Still, the highlights include Monet's *Les Coquelicots* (*Poppy Fields*) and Renoir's *Le Moulin de la Galette* (*Wafer Windmill*), which differs from many other Impressionist paintings in that Renoir worked from numerous studies and completed it in his studio rather than painting it in the open air. Nonetheless, its focus on the activities of a group of ordinary Parisians amusing themselves in the sun on a Montmartre afternoon is typical of the spontaneity and fleeting sense of moment that are the essence of Impressionism. Whereas Monet, the only one of the group to adhere faithfully to the tenets of Impressionism throughout his career, strove to catch the effects of light—for more of this great master, remember to also visit the Musée Marmottan—Renoir was more interested in the human figure.

The Postimpressionists—Cézanne, van Gogh, Gauguin, and Toulouse-Lautrec—are also represented on the top floor. You may find the intense, almost classical serenity of Cézanne the dominant presence here; witness his magnificent Mont Ste-Victoire series, in which he paints and repaints the same subject, in the process dissolving form until the step to Cubism and abstract painting seems an inevitability. Or you may be drawn by the vivid simplicity and passion of van Gogh or by the psychedelic, pagan rhythms of Gauguin.

On the first floor are the works of Manet and the delicate nuances of Degas. Be sure to see Manet's *Déjeuner sur l'Herbe* (*Lunch on the Grass*), the painting that scandalized Paris in 1863 at the Salon des Refusés, an exhibit organized by artists refused permission to show their work at the Academy's official annual salon. The painting shows a nude woman and two clothed men picnicking in a park. In the background, another girl bathes in a stream. Manet took the subject, poses and all, from a little-known Renaissance print in the Louvre but updated the clothing to mid-19th-century France. What would otherwise have been thought a respectable "academic" painting thus became deeply shocking: two clothed men with a naked woman in 19th-century France! The loose, bold brushwork, a far cry from the polished styles of the Renaissance, added insult to artistic injury. Another reworking by Manet of a classical motif is his reclining nude, *Olympia.* Gazing boldly out from the canvas, she was more than respectable 19th-century Parisian proprieties could stand, with her unfinished hands (they were described as monkey paws) and black cat (a symbol of female sexuality). These two Manet works all but ushered in the age of modern painting. American works are also on view, one of which, Whistler's iconic portrait of his mother, *Arrangement in Black and White,* might seem to be merely a dose of American spartan puritanism; its minimalist palette and striking sense of design, however, were almost as revolutionary as Manet's achievements.

If you prefer more academic paintings, look at Puvis de Chavannes's larger-than-life classical canvases. The pale, limpid beauty of his figures is enjoying renewed attention after years of neglect. For sheer spectacle, lose yourself in Thomas Couture's *Romans of the Decadence,* a Cinerama-screen-size depiction of ancient excess. If you are more excited by more modern developments, look for the early 20th-century Fauves (meaning "wild beasts," the name given them by an outraged critic in 1905)—particularly Matisse, Derain, and Vlaminck. Thought-provoking sculptures also litter the museum at every turn. Two further highlights are the faithfully restored Belle Epoque restaurant and the model of the entire Opéra quarter displayed beneath a glass floor, along with an extensive display of drawings and models given over to that 19th-century masterwork, the Opéra Garnier. ✉ *1 rue de la Légion d'Honneur, St-Germain-des-Prés* ☎ *01–40–49–48–14* 🌐 *www.musee-orsay.fr* 🎫 *€7, Sun. €5* ⏲ *Tues.–Wed. and Fri.–Sat. 10–6, Thurs. 10–9:45, Sun. 9–6* Ⓜ *Solférino; RER: Musée d'Orsay.*

need a break?

Find respite from the overwhelming collection of art in the gorgeous **Musée d'Orsay Café** (☎ 1–45–49–47–03), in the Musée d'Orsay behind one of the giant station clocks, close to the Impressionist galleries on the top floor. The interior is a white-on-white Belle Epoque dazzler, the luncheon is buffet, and the late afternoon *le goûter Orsay* offers a sumptuous high tea. From the rooftop terrace alongside there is a panoramic view across the Seine toward Montmartre and the Sacré-Coeur.

5 **Musée Rodin.** The splendid Hôtel Biron, with its spacious vestibule, broad staircase, and patrician salons lined with boiseries, retains much of its 18th-century ambience and makes a somewhat startling frame for the sculpture of Auguste Rodin (1840–1917). His funeral, at the height of World War I, drew the largest nonmilitary crowd of the time (26,000); while alive, however, Rodin was stalked by controversy. His career took off in 1876 with *L'Age d'Airain* (*The Bronze Age*), inspired by a pilgrimage to Italy and the sculptures of Michelangelo. Because the work was so realistic, some critics accused Rodin of having stuck a live boy in plaster, while others blasted him for what was seen as a sloppy sculpting and casting technique. His seeming messiness, though, was intentional; Rodin sought to capture the sculpting process through the imprints of fingers, rags used to keep the clay moist, and tools he left on his works.

Fodor's Choice ★

Four years later, Rodin was commissioned to create the doors for the newly proposed Musée des Arts Décoratifs (Museum of Decorative Arts). He set out to sculpt a pair of monumental bronze doors in the tradition of Italian Renaissance churches, calling his proposal *La Porte de l'Enfer* (*The Gate of Hell*). The Gate, a visual representation of stories from Dante's Divine Comedy, became his obsession: he spent the last 37 years of his life working on it. Possibly Rodin's most celebrated work is *Le Penseur* (*The Thinker,* circa 1880), the muscular man caught in a moment of deep thought and flex. The version here in the garden is the original—the city of Paris, its intended owner, refused to accept it. Before installing the permanent bronze statue on the steps of the Panthéon, Rodin set up a full-scale plaster cast. Its physicality horrified the public; crowds gathered around the statue, debates ensued, and Rodin was ridiculed in the press. A sad footnote in the collection is evidenced by works by Rodin's mistress Camille Claudel (1864–1943), a remarkable sculptor in her own right. Her torturous relationship with Rodin drove her out of his studio—and out of her mind. In 1913 she was packed off to an asylum, where she remained, barred from any artistic activities, until her death in 1943. As much a work of art as the sculptures on view, the gardens of the Musée Rodin are justly famous for their rosebushes (more than 2,000 of them, representing 100 varieties). Here, you'll find some prime Rodin pieces, such as the powerful *Balzac* and the mythic *Burghers of Calais.* ✉ *77 rue de Varenne, Eiffel Tower/Trocadéro*

☎ 01–44–18–61–10 ⊕ *www.musee-rodin.fr* 🎫 *€5; Sun. €3; gardens only, €1* ⏲ *Easter–Oct., Tues.–Sun. 9:30–5:45; Nov.–Easter, Tues.–Sun. 9:30–4:45* Ⓜ *Varenne.*

need a break?

Sure, they call it the **Cafétéria du musée Rodin** (✉ 77 rue de Varenne, Eiffel Tower/Trocadéro ☎ 01–44–18–61–10), but the stone path along the old wall and the pretty tables under the linden trees are more reminiscent of a Marcel Pagnol film than a high-school lunchroom. The trees are so thick with leaves the sun can't penetrate, which is just what you want on on a hot summer day. And while you munch on delicious tartines, sandwiches, salads, or the *plat du jour,* your children can run wild on the wide stretch of lush grass. Admission to the garden is €1 and it's closed Monday.

1

❸ **Palais Bourbon.** The most prominent feature of the Palais Bourbon—home of the Assemblée Nationale, the French Parliament since 1798—is its colonnaded facade, commissioned by Napoléon to match that of the Madeleine across the Seine. Cortot's sculpted pediment portrays France holding the tablets of law, flanked by Force and Justice. ✉ *Pl. du Palais-Bourbon, Eiffel Tower/Trocadéro* ⏲ *During temporary exhibits only* Ⓜ *Assemblée Nationale.*

off the beaten path

Basilique Ste-Clotilde. Once the most fashionable church in 19th-century Paris, this neo-Gothic church (built 1846–58) is notable for its imposing twin spires, visible from across the Seine. French composer César Franck was organist here from 1858 to 1890. From the Palais Bourbon, take rue Bourgogne south; then take a left on rue Las-Cases. ✉ *Rue Las-Cases, Eiffel Tower/Trocadéro* ⊕ *www.sainte-clotilde.com* Ⓜ *Solférino.*

㉓ **Palais du Luxembourg** (Luxembourg Palace). The gray, imposing, rusticated Luxembourg Palace was built, like the surrounding Luxembourg Gardens, for Maria de' Medici, widow of Henri IV, at the beginning of the 17th century. Maria was born and raised in Florence's Pitti Palace, and, having languished in the Louvre after the death of her husband, she was eager to build herself a new palace, where she could recapture something of the lively, carefree atmosphere of her childhood. In 1612 she bought the Paris mansion of the Duke of Luxembourg, tore it down, and built her palace. It was not completed until 1627, and Maria was to live there for just five years (the grand series of canvases Rubens painted to decorate the palace are now in the Louvre). In 1632 Cardinal Richelieu had her expelled from France, and she saw out her declining years in Cologne, Germany, dying there almost penniless in 1642. The palace remained royal property until the Revolution, when the state took it over and used it as a prison. Danton, the painter David, and Thomas Paine were all detained here. Today the French Senate meets here, so the building is not open to the public. However, adjacent to the palace is the venerable **Musée de Luxembourg.** Once home to many of the masterpieces now on view at the Musée d'Orsay, it is open occasionally for temporary exhibitions—currently on view for a loan of several years is the Rau Collection, amassed by an eccentric millionaire and studded with famous paintings which may be auctioned off for charity in 20 years' time. *Musée* ✉ *17 rue de Vaugirard, St-Germain-des-Prés* ☎ *01–42–34–25–95* Ⓜ *Odéon; RER: Luxembourg.*

⓰ **Pont des Arts** (Arts Footbridge). Immortalized in paintings by Renoir and Pissarro, this iron-and-wood footbridge linking the Louvre to the Institut de France is a favorite with painters, art students, and misty-eyed romantics moved by the delightful views of the Ile de la Cité. The bridge got its name because the Louvre was once called the Palais des Arts (Palace of Art). Ⓜ *Pont Neuf.*

12 **St-Germain-des-Prés.** Paris's oldest church was first built to shelter a relic of the true cross, brought back from Spain in AD 542. The chancel was enlarged and the church then consecrated by Pope Alexander III in 1163; the tall, sturdy tower—a Left Bank landmark—dates from this period. The colorful 19th-century frescoes in the nave by Hippolyte Flandrin, a pupil of the classical painter Ingres, depict vivid scenes from the Old Testament. The church stages superb organ concerts and recitals. ✉ *Pl. St-Germain-des-Prés, St-Germain-des-Prés* ⏲ *Weekdays 8–7:30, weekends 8 AM–9 PM* Ⓜ *St-Germain-des-Prés.*

24 **St-Sulpice.** Dubbed the Cathedral of the Left Bank, this enormous 17th-century church has entertained some unlikely christenings—the Marquis de Sade's and Charles Baudelaire's, for instance—and the nuptials of irreverent wordsmith Victor Hugo. The 18th-century facade was never finished, and its unequal towers add a playful touch to an otherwise sober design. The interior is baldly impersonal, despite the magnificent Delacroix frescoes—notably *Jacob Luttant avec l'Ange* (*Jacob Wrestling with the Angel*)—in the first chapel on your right. ✉ *Pl. St-Sulpice, St-Germain-des-Prés* Ⓜ *St-Sulpice.*

9 **St-Thomas d'Aquin.** This elegant, domed church designed by Pierre Bulet in 1683 was originally dedicated to St. Dominique and flanked by a convent—whose buildings now belong to the army. The east-end chapel was added in 1722 and the two-tier facade in 1768. Pope Pius VII popped in during his trip to Paris for Napoléon's coronation in December 1804. ✉ *Pl. St-Thomas-d'Aquin, St-Germain-des-Prés* Ⓜ *Rue du Bac.*

21 **Théâtre de l'Odéon.** At the north end of the Luxembourg Gardens, on place de l'Odéon, sits the colonnaded Odéon Theater—a masterpiece of the neoclassical style. It was established in 1792 to house the Comédie Française troupe; the original building was destroyed by fire in 1807. Since World War II it has specialized in 20th-century productions and was the base for Jean-Louis Barrault and Madeleine Renaud's theater company, the Théâtre de France, until they fell out of favor with the authorities for their alleged role in spurring on student revolutionaries in May 1968. Today the theater is the French home of the Theater of Europe and stages excellent productions by major foreign companies, sometimes in English. ✉ *1 pl. de l'Odéon, St-Germain-des-Prés* ☏ *01–44–41–36–36* Ⓜ *Odéon.*

MONTPARNASSE

About 15 blocks south of the Seine lies the Montparnasse district, named after Mount Parnassus, the Greek mountain associated with the worship of Apollo and the Muses. Montparnasse's cultural heyday came in the first four decades of the 20th century, when it replaced Montmartre as *the* place for painters and poets to live. Pablo Picasso, Amedeo Modigliani, Ernest Hemingway, Jean Cocteau, Man Ray, and Leon Trotsky were among the luminaries who spawned an intellectual café society—as can be seen at the just-opened Fondation Henri Cartier-Bresson—and prompted the launch of a string of arty brasseries along the district's main thoroughfare, the broad boulevard du Montparnasse.

The boulevard may lack poetic charm these days, but nightlife stays the pace as bars, clubs, restaurants, and cinemas crackle with energy beneath continental Europe's tallest high-rise, the 59-story Tour Montparnasse. Although the tower itself is a typically bland product of the early 1970s, of note only for the view from the top, several more adventurous buildings have risen in its wake. Ricardo Bofill's semicircular Amphithéâtre housing complex, with its whimsical postmodernist quotations of classical detail, is the most famous. The glass-cubed Cartier center for contemporary art and the Montparnasse train station, with its giant glass facade and designer garden above the tracks, are other outstanding examples.

If you have a deeper feel for history, you may prefer the sumptuous Baroque church of Val-de-Grâce or the quiet earth of Montparnasse cemetery, where Baudelaire, Sartre, Bartholdi (who designed the Statue of Liberty), and actress Jean Seberg slumber. The Paris Resistance had its headquarters nearby—in the Roman catacombs—during the Nazi occupation. After ignoring Hitler's orders to blow up the city, Governor von Choltitz signed the German surrender in Montparnasse in August 1944.

Numbers in the text correspond to numbers in the margin and on the Montparnasse map.

a good walk

Take the métro or walk to the Vavin station (only three stops from St-Sulpice), beneath Rodin's 10-ft statue of Balzac and alongside the café La Rotonde at the corner of boulevards Raspail and Montparnasse. Three other cafés, famous since Montparnasse's interwar heyday, are all within a stone's throw on boulevard du Montparnasse: Le Sélect at No. 99 and, across the street, the Café du Dôme (No. 108) and **La Coupole** 1, with its painted columns and restored Art Deco interior (No. 102). Head west along boulevard du Montparnasse to **place du 18-Juin-1940** 2. Towering above the square is the **Tour Montparnasse** 3. Behind the building is the huge, gleaming glass facade of Gare Montparnasse, the train station that is terminus for the 200-mph *TGV Atlantique,* serving western France.

Cross place Bienvenüe, to the right of Tour Montparnasse; then take avenue Maine, then your first left onto rue Antoine-Bourdelle. The sharp brick outlines of the **Musée Bourdelle** 4, full of the powerful sculpture of Antoine Bourdelle, loom halfway along. Continue to the end of the street and turn left onto rue Armand-Moissant; note the elegant beige-and-green brick facade of the École Commerciale on your left before turning right onto boulevard de Vaugirard. There's a fine view from here of Tour Montparnasse away to your left. A short way along the boulevard is the **Musée de la Poste** 5, a must if you're a stamp collector. Cross the boulevard and take the elevator by No. 25 to reach the **Jardin Atlantique** 6, a modern park laid over the rail tracks of Montparnasse station. Memories of World War II—notably the French Resistance and the Liberation of Paris—are evoked in a modern museum to the left.

Cross the Jardin Atlantique at the far end and turn left down to **place de Catalogne** 7, dominated by the monumental curves of the post-modern Amphithéâtre housing complex. Explore its arcades and circular forecourts, and compare its impersonal grandeur with the cozy charm of the small church of Notre-Dame du Travail behind. Rue Jean-Zay leads from place de Catalogne to the corner of the high-walled **Cimetière du Montparnasse** 8. Enter the cemetery down rue Froidevaux if you wish to pay homage to local and foreign worthies. Rue Froidevaux continues to place Denfert-Rochereau, where you can admire the huge bronze *Lion of Belfort* by Frédéric-Auguste Bartholdi, the sculptor of the Statue of Liberty (he, too, is buried in Montparnasse cemetery), and visit the extensive underground labyrinth of the **catacombs** 9, which tunnel under much of the Left Bank and the suburbs.

Walk up boulevard Raspail, past the eye-catching glass cube that houses the **Fondation Cartier** 10. Take the third right onto rue Campagne-Première, a handsome street once inhabited by Picasso, Miró, Kandinsky, and Modigliani. Note the tiled facade on the artists' residence at No. 31. Turn right at the bottom of the street onto boulevard du Montparnasse. At avenue de l'Observatoire stands perhaps the most famous bastion of Left Bank café culture, the **Closerie des Lilas** 11. Up avenue de l'Observatoire is the **Observatoire de Paris** 12, Louis XIV's astronomical observatory. In the other direction, the tree-lined avenue sweeps past the **Fontaine de l'Observatoire** 13. To the right of the fountain, at the bottom of rue du Val-de-Grâce, is the imposing Baroque dome of **Val de Grâce** 14. Straight ahead is the Jardin du Luxembourg.

TIMING This walk around Montparnasse is just under 5 km (3 mi) long and should comfortably take a morning or an afternoon if you choose to check out one of the historic cafés, the cemetery, and the catacombs along the way.

What to See

9 **Catacombs.** *"Arrête! C'est ici l'Empire de la Mort"* ("Halt! This is the Empire of Death"). This message scrawled at the entrance was enough to convince German troops in World War II to leave promptly before they guessed that Resistance fighters used the tunnels in the catacombs as a base. This dire warning now welcomes you after a winding descent through dark, clammy passages to Paris's principal ossuary and most disturbing collection of human remains. Bones from the notorious Cimetière des Innocents were the first to be transplanted here in 1786, when decomposing bodies started seeping into neighboring cellars, bringing swarms of ravenous rats with them. The legions of bones dumped here are arranged not by owner but by type—witness the rows of skulls, stacks of tibias, and piles of spinal disks. There are also some bizarre attempts at bone art, like skulls arranged in the shape of hearts. It's macabre and makes you feel quite . . . mortal. Among the bones in here are those of Mirabeau (1749–91), the revolutionary leader; 16th-century satirist and writer Rabelais (1490–1553), transplanted from the former cemetery at the Église St-Paul–St-Louis; and famous courtesan Madame de Pompadour (1721–64), mixed in with the rabble after a lifetime spent as the mistress to Louis XV. Be prepared to walk long distances when you come here—the tunnels stretch for miles, and the only light comes from your flashlight. ✉ *1 pl. Denfert-Rochereau, Montparnasse* ☎ *01–43–22–47–63* 🌐 *www.paris-france.org/musees* 🎫 *€5, guided tours €3 extra* ⏲ *Wed.–Sun. 9–4, Tues. 11–4. Guided tours Wed. at 2:45* Ⓜ *Métro or RER: Denfert-Rochereau.*

8 **Cimetière du Montparnasse** (Montparnasse Cemetery). High walls encircle this cemetery, a haven of peace in one of Paris's busiest shopping and business areas. It is not picturesque (with the exception of the towered rump of an old windmill that used to be a student tavern) but contains many of the quarter's most illustrious residents, buried only a stone's throw away from where they lived and loved: Charles Baudelaire, Bartholdi (who designed the Statue of Liberty), Alfred Dreyfus, Guy de Maupassant, Camille Saint-Saëns, Tristan Tzara, and, more recently, photographer Man Ray, playwright Samuel Beckett, philosopher Jean-Paul Sartre, actress Jean Seberg, and singer-songwriter Serge Gainsbourg. ✉ *Entrances on rue Froidevaux, bd. Edgar-Quinet, Montparnasse* Ⓜ *Raspail, Gaîté.*

11 **Closerie des Lilas.** Now a pricey bar-restaurant, the Closerie remains a staple of all literary tours of Paris. Commemorative plaques fastened to the bar mark the places where members of the literati such as Baudelaire, Verlaine, and Hemingway (who wrote pages of *The Sun Also Rises* here;

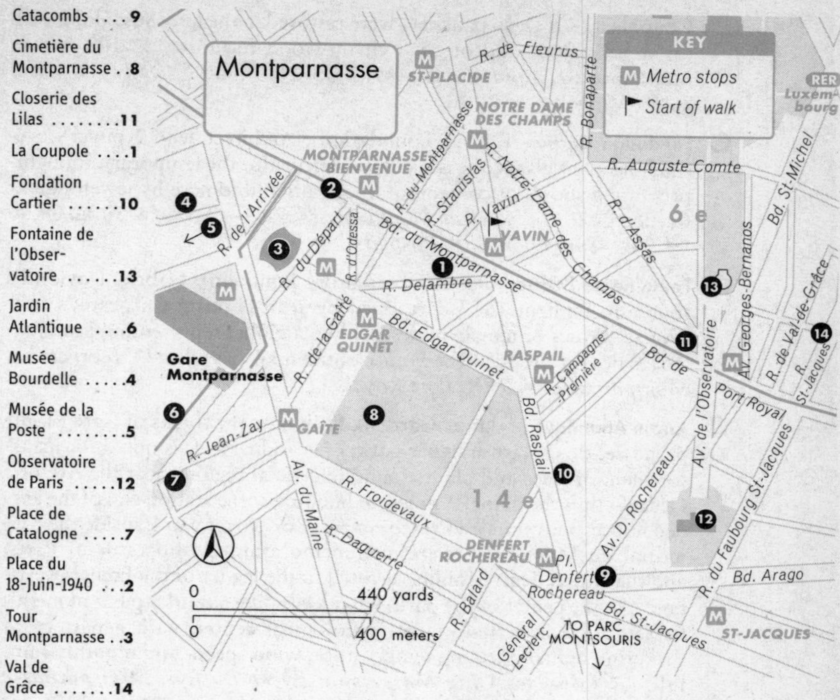

he lived around the corner at 115 rue Notre-Dame-des-Champs) used to station themselves. Although the lilacs that graced the garden are gone—they once shaded such habitués such as Ingres, Whistler, and Balzac—the terrace still opens onto a garden wall of luxuriant evergreen foliage and is as crowded in summer as it ever was. ✉ *171 bd. du Montparnasse, Montparnasse* ☎ *01–43–26–70–50* Ⓜ *Vavin; RER: Port Royal.*

off the beaten path

Le Ballon Eutelsat. As tall as a 12-story building, this is the largest outdoor balloon in the world. It's attached to the ground by sturdy cables and climbs up to 450 ft high to give you one of the most spectacular (and perfectly silent) views of the city; the ride takes about 10 minutes. Be sure to call to check the weather in advance, if it's too windy, it won't go up. ✉ *Parc Andre-Citroën, 2 rue de la Montagne-de-la-Fage, 15e, Montparnasse* ☎ *01–44–26–20–00* ⏲ *Daily 9–5* 🎫 *€10* Ⓜ *Balard.*

Musée Zadkine. Russian-born sculptor Ossip Zadkine (1890–1967) trained in London before setting up in Paris in 1909. The works on exhibit at this museum, in Zadkine's former house and studio, reveal the influences of Rodin, African art, and Cubism. ✉ *100 bis rue d'Assas, Montparnasse* ☎ *01–43–26–91–90* 🌐 *www.paris-france.org/musees* 🎫 *Permanent collection free, exhibitions €4* ⏲ *Tues.–Sun. 10–5:40* Ⓜ *Vavin.*

❶ **La Coupole.** One of Montparnasse's most famous brasseries, La Coupole opened in 1927 as a bar-restaurant and dance hall and soon became a home-away-from-home for Apollinaire, Max Jacob, Cocteau, Satie, Stravinsky, and Hemingway. It may not be quite the same draw these days, but it still pulls in a classy crowd. The columns painted by a host of Parisian artists, including Chagall and Brancusi, which lend La

Coupole its Art Deco panache, were restored in the late '80s, along with the mosaic floor and original citron-wood furniture. ✉ *102 bd. du Montparnasse, Montparnasse* ☎ *01–43–20–14–20* ⏲ *Daily 7:30 AM–2 AM* Ⓜ *Vavin.*

❿ **Fondation Cartier** (Cartier Foundation). Architect Jean Nouvel's eye-catching giant glass cube is a suitable setting for the temporary, thought-provoking shows of contemporary art organized here by jewelry giant Cartier. ✉ *261 bd. Raspail, Montparnasse* ☎ *01–42–18–56–50* 🎟 *€4.60* ⏲ *Tues.–Sun. noon–8* Ⓜ *Raspail.*

⓭ **Fontaine de l'Observatoire** (Observatory Fountain). Gabriel Davioud's fountain, built in 1873, is topped by Jean-Baptiste Carpeaux's four bronze statues of female nudes holding a globe, representing Les Quatre Parties du Monde (The Four Continents). ✉ *Av. de l'Observatoire, Montparnasse* Ⓜ *RER: Port Royal.*

❻ **Jardin Atlantique** (Atlantic Garden). Built over the tracks of Gare Montparnasse, this smart designer park, opened in 1994, is noted for its assortment of trees and plants found in coastal regions near the Atlantic Ocean—thus the name. A museum building at the station end of the garden houses souvenirs and video coverage of World War II inside the **Mémorial du Maréchal-Leclerc,** commemorating the liberator of Paris, and the **Musée Jean-Moulin,** devoted to the leader of the French Resistance. In the center of the park, what looks like a quirky piece of metallic sculpture is actually a meteorological center, with a battery of flickering lights reflecting temperature, wind speed, and monthly rainfall. ✉ *Pont des Cinq-Martyrs-du-Lycée-Buffon, Montparnasse* ☎ *01–40–64–39–44* 🌐 *www.paris-france.org/musees* 🎟 *Free* ⏲ *Musée Tues.–Sun. 10–5:40* Ⓜ *Montparnasse Bienvenüe.*

❹ **Musée Bourdelle** (Bourdelle Museum). Opened in 1949 in the studios and gardens where Rodin's pupil Antoine Bourdelle (1861–1929) lived and worked, and extended by Christian de Portzamparc in 1992, this spacious brick museum houses 500 works in plaster, marble, and bronze, including castings of Bourdelle's landmark works, the bombastic *Heracles the Archer* and the *Dying Centaur.* ✉ *18 rue Antoine-Bourdelle, Montparnasse* ☎ *01–49–54–73–73* 🌐 *www.paris-france.org/musees* 🎟 *Permanent collections free, exhibitions €4.50* ⏲ *Tues.–Sun. 10–6* Ⓜ *Falguière.*

❺ **Musée de la Poste** (Postal Museum). On display at this five-story museum of postal history are international and French stamps (dating as far back as 1849), postal carriers' uniforms and mailboxes, sorting and stamp-printing machines, and one of the balloons used to send mail out of Paris during the Prussian siege of 1870. ✉ *34 bd. de Vaugirard, Montparnasse* ☎ *01–42–79–24–24* 🌐 *www.laposte.fr/musee* 🎟 *€4.50* ⏲ *Mon.–Sat. 10–6* Ⓜ *Montparnasse Bienvenüe.*

⓬ **Observatoire de Paris** (Paris Observatory). The observatory was constructed in 1667 for Louis XIV by architect Claude Perrault. Its four facades are aligned with the four cardinal points—north, south, east, and west—and its southern wall is the determining point for Paris's official latitude, 48° 50′11″N. French time was based on this Paris meridian until 1911, when the country decided to adopt the international Greenwich Meridian. The interior is not open to the general public. ✉ *Av. de l'Observatoire, Montparnasse* Ⓜ *RER: Port Royal.*

❼ **Place de Catalogne** (Catalonia Square). This circular square is dominated by the monumental **Amphithéâtre,** a housing complex built in the 1980s by architect Ricardo Bofill. Its chunky reinvention of classical detail may

ARTISTS, WRITERS & EXILES

FOR THREE-QUARTERS OF A CENTURY—roughly from the 1880s to the 1950s—Paris enjoyed a reputation as Europe's most creative and bohemian capital, acting as a magnet for the international avant-garde.

*The decades before World War I saw the slopes of **Montmartre,** in north Paris, alive with the sound of Belle Epoque music. Whirling windmills and swirling petticoats set the tone, no more so than at the Moulin Rouge cabaret, whose dancers doing the cancan were immortalized in posters and paintings by Toulouse-Lautrec. Femmes fatales? Lautrec drank and drugged himself to premature death.*

Artists had moved into the district as early as the 1860s, when Monet and Manet pursued their interest in steam and rail at the Gare St-Lazare. New boulevards meant easier access to nearby Montmartre: cheap and pretty, with an abundance of shady nightlife, the area was an artist's dream. Van Gogh, Cézanne, Seurat, Signac, Degas, Vuillard, and Dufy all followed. Renoir painted his Moulin de la Galette; Picasso and Braque sighted Cubism in the Bateau-Lavoir on place Émile-Goudeau.

Montmartre lost its luster after World War I; Utrillo remained, his repetitive street scenes a weak postscript to the powerful austerity of his youthful "White Period."

*The Roaring '20s saw the Paris art scene shift south to another hill: **Montparnasse.** Picasso and Modigliani decamped to rue Campagne-Première, joined by Miró and Kandinsky; Braque worked nearby in rue du Douanier-Rousseau.*

Belle Epoque cabarets lost out to Art Deco bars and brasseries, a whole string of them along boulevard du Montparnasse: the Coupole, Dôme, Select, Rotonde, and the Closerie des Lilas, most of them assiduously frequented by Ernest Hemingway. Gertrude Stein held court for her "Lost Generation" near the Luxembourg Gardens, hosting Picasso and writers like Ezra Pound, Henry Miller, and Zelda and F. Scott Fitzgerald. Redevelopment, epitomized by the Tour Montparnasse, has long since exiled aesthetes.

*After World War II the literati went north to **St-Germain-des-Prés,** whose own cluster of cafés—Flore (where Sartre and de Beauvoir preached existentialism), Lipp, Les Deux Magots (once favored by Rimbaud and Gide)—became the beacon for left-wing intellectuals in the 1950s and 1960s.*

Picture and antiques dealers crowd the streets of St-Germain, rubbing shoulders with the publishing houses that have been here since before Joyce first published Ulysses *at Shakespeare & Company on rue de l'Odéon in 1922. Baudelaire, Voltaire, and Oscar Wilde (as well as Delacroix, Sibelius, and Wagner) all lived in the area; Voltaire died there in 1788, and Wilde expired around the corner at **13 rue des Beaux-Arts**—a plaque on the building commemorates the spot and the street is still home to a fine-arts school.*

These days, however, once they finish school, few art students stick around: Paris is no longer the thriving center for contemporary art that it once was. But intellectual ghosts still haunt the Left Bank: at the bouquinistes by the Seine, along the creaking floorboards of Shakespeare & Company on rue de la Bûcherie, or in the tiny Théâtre de la Huchette nearby, where Ionesco's bald soprano sings nightly for her supper to full houses.

strike you as witty—or as overkill. Behind is the turn-of-the-20th-century **Notre-Dame du Travail** church, which made a powerful statement when it was built: its riveted iron-and-steel framework was meant to symbolize the work ethos enshrined in the church's name. The Sebastopol Bell above the facade is a trophy from the Crimean War. ✉ *Pl. de Catalogne, Montparnasse* Ⓜ *Gaîté.*

❷ **Place du 18-Juin-1940.** Beneath the Tour Montparnasse, this square is named for the date of the radio speech Charles de Gaulle broadcast from London, urging the French to resist the Germans after the Nazi invasion of May 1940. It was here that German military governor Dietrich von Choltitz surrendered to the Allies in August 1944, ignoring Hitler's orders to destroy the city as he withdrew. A plaque on the wall of what is now a shopping center—originally the Montparnasse train station extended this far—commemorates the event. Ⓜ *Montparnasse Bienvenüe.*

❸ **Tour Montparnasse** (Montparnasse Tower). Continental Europe's tallest skyscraper, completed in 1973, this 680-ft building offers a stupendous view of Paris from its open-air roof terrace. It attracts 800,000 gawkers each year; on a clear day you can see for 40 km (25 mi). A glossy brochure, "Paris Vu d'en Haut" ("Paris from On High") explains just what to look for. It also claims to have the fastest elevator in Europe. Fifty-two of the 59 stories are taken up by offices, and a vast commercial complex, including a Galeries Lafayette department store, spreads over the first floor. Banal by day, the tower becomes Montparnasse's neon-lit beacon at night. ✉ *Rue de l'Arrivée, Montparnasse* ☎ *01–45–38–52–56* 🌐 *www.tourmontparnasse56.com* 🎫 *€7.60* ⏲ *Daily 9:30 AM–11 PM* Ⓜ *Montparnasse Bienvenüe.*

⓮ **Val de Grâce** This imposing 17th-century Left Bank church was commissioned by Anne of Austria and designed by François Mansart. Its powerfully rhythmic two-story facade rivals the Dôme Church at the Invalides as the city's most striking example of Italianate Baroque. Pierre Mignard's 1663 cupola fresco bursts with more than 200 sky-climbing figures. The church's original abbey buildings are now a military army hospital, with a small museum of army medical history. ✉ *1 pl. Alphonse-Laveran, Latin Quarter* ☎ *01–40–51–51–94* 🎫 *€4.60* ⏲ *Museum Tues.–Wed. noon–6, weekends 1:30–5* Ⓜ *RER: Port Royal.*

MONTMARTRE

Topped by its "sculpted cloud"—the famous Sacré-Coeur Basilica—and set on a dramatic rise above the city, Montmartre is the picturesque quarter that was once the haunt of Toulouse-Lautrec, Utrillo, and van Gogh. Although the fabled nightlife of old Montmartre has fizzled down to some glitzy nightclubs and porn shows, the neighborhood still exudes a sense of history, a timeless quality infused with that hard-to-define Gallic charm.

Windmills once dotted Montmartre (often referred to by Parisians as *La Butte,* meaning "the mound"). They were set up here not just because the hill was a good place to catch the wind—at more than 300 ft, it's the highest point in the city—but because Montmartre was covered with wheat fields and quarries right up to the end of the 19th century. Today only 2 of the original 20 windmills remain.

Visiting Montmartre means negotiating a lot of steep streets and flights of steps. The crown atop this urban peak, Sacré-Coeur, is something of an architectural oddity. It has been called everything from grotesque to sublime; its silhouette, viewed from afar at dusk or sunrise, looks more like that of a mosque than a cathedral.

There is a disputed story of how Montmartre got its name. Some say the name comes from the Roman temple to Mercury that was once here, called the Mound of Mercury, or *Mons Mercurii.* Others contend that it was an adaptation of *Mons Martyrum,* a name inspired by the burial here of Paris's first bishop, St. Denis. The popular version of his martyrdom is that he was beheaded by the Romans in AD 250 but arose to carry his severed head from rue Yvonne-Le-Tac to a place 6½ km (4 mi) to the north, an area now known as St-Denis. A final twist on the name controversy is that Montmartre briefly came to be known as Mont-Marat during the French Revolution. Marat was a leading revolutionary figure who was stabbed to death in his bath.

Numbers in the text correspond to numbers in the margin and on the Montmartre map.

a good walk

Take the métro to the Blanche stop and start your tour at one of Paris's least-known but most atmospheric cemeteries, the tumbling **Cimetière de Montmartre** 1 at the end of avenue Rachel (off boulevard de Clichy). Return to **place Blanche,** where all eyes are drawn to the **Moulin Rouge** 2, the windmill–turned–dance hall immortalized by Toulouse-Lautrec and the Baz Luhrmann/Nicole Kidman film. The Café Cyrano, next door to the Moulin Rouge, was once the haunt of Salvador Dalí and his fellow Surrealists. A few steps along the boulevard is the **Musée de l'Erotisme** 3, whose collection of erotic artifacts from around the world pays fulsome tribute to Montmartre's Sin City image.

Walk up lively rue Lepic from place Blanche. The tiny Lux Bar at No. 12 has a 1910 mosaic showing place Blanche at the beginning of the 20th century. Wind your way up to the **Moulin de la Galette** 4, on your left, atop its leafy hillock opposite rue Tholozé, once a path over the hill. Then turn right down rue Tholozé, past **Studio 28** 5, the first cinema built expressly for experimental films.

Continue down rue Tholozé to rue des Abbesses, and turn left toward the triangular **place des Abbesses** 6. Note the austere redbrick facade of **St-Jean l'Evangéliste** 7. Tiny rue André-Antoine, to the right of the popular Café St-Jean, leads to what was originally the **Théâtre Libre** 8, or Free Theater, at No. 37. Return to the square and take rue Yvonne-Le-Tac off to the right. Paris's first bishop, St. Denis, is commemorated by the 19th-century **Chapelle du Martyre** 9 at No. 9, built on the spot where he is said to have been beheaded.

Return to the square and follow rue Ravignan as it climbs, via place Émile-Goudeau, an enchanting little cobbled square, to the **Bateau-Lavoir** 10, or Boat Wash House, at its northern edge. Painters Picasso and Braque had studios in the original building; this drab concrete building was built in its place. Continue up the hill via rue de la Mire to **place Jean-Baptiste-Clément** 11, where Modigliani had a studio.

The upper reaches of rue Lepic lead to rue Norvins, formerly rue des Moulins (Windmill Street). At the end of the street, to the left, is stylish avenue Junot, site of the Cité Internationale des Arts (International Residence of the Arts), where the city authorities rent out studios to artists from all over the world. Continue right past the bars and tourist shops until you reach famous **place du Tertre** 12. Check out the restaurant **La Mère Catherine** 13, a favorite with the Russian Cossacks when they occupied Paris in 1814. Fight your way through to the southern end of

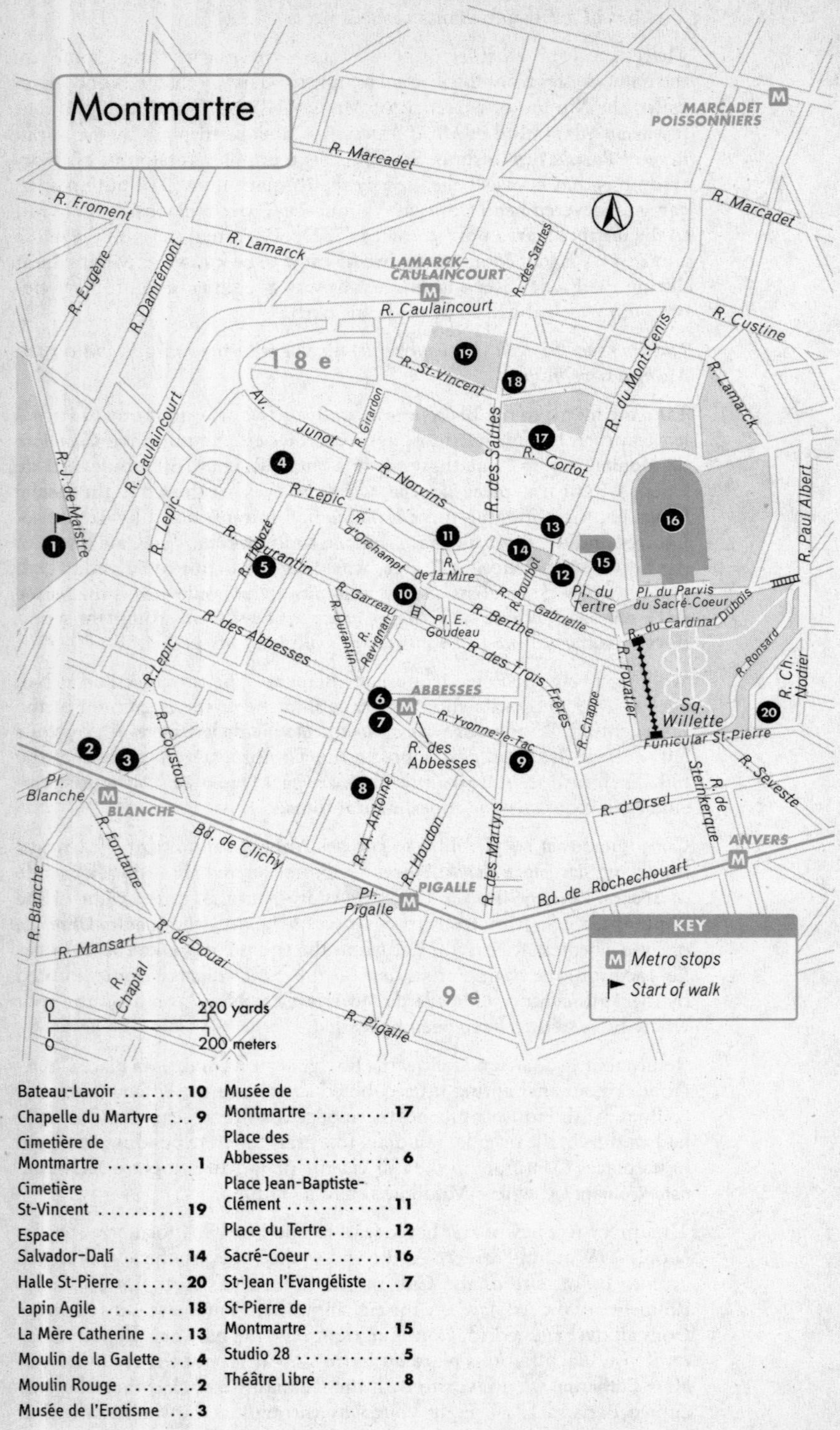

Bateau-Lavoir 10
Chapelle du Martyre . . . 9
Cimetière de Montmartre 1
Cimetière St-Vincent 19
Espace Salvador-Dalí 14
Halle St-Pierre 20
Lapin Agile 18
La Mère Catherine 13
Moulin de la Galette . . . 4
Moulin Rouge 2
Musée de l'Erotisme . . . 3
Musée de Montmartre 17
Place des Abbesses 6
Place Jean-Baptiste-Clément 11
Place du Tertre 12
Sacré-Coeur 16
St-Jean l'Evangéliste . . . 7
St-Pierre de Montmartre 15
Studio 28 5
Théâtre Libre 8

the square for a breathtaking view of the city. Around the corner on rue Poulbot, the **Espace Salvador-Dalí** 14 houses works by Salvador Dalí, who once had a studio in the area.

Return to place du Tertre. Just off the square is the tiny church of **St-Pierre de Montmartre** 15. Looming menacingly behind is the scaly white dome of the **Sacré-Coeur basilica** 16. The cavernous interior is worth visiting for its golden mosaics; climb to the top of the dome for the view of Paris, or just settle for the Cinerama-size vista seen from its entrance parterre.

Walk back toward place du Tertre. Turn right onto rue du Mont-Cenis and left onto rue Cortot, site of the **Musée de Montmartre** 17, which, like the Bateau-Lavoir, once sheltered an illustrious group of painters, writers, and assorted cabaret artists. One of the best things about the museum, however, is its view of the tiny vineyard on neighboring rue des Saules. Another famous Montmartre landmark is at No. 22: the bar-cabaret **Lapin Agile** 18, originally one of the raunchiest haunts in Montmartre and the subject of one of Picasso's most famous paintings. Opposite the Lapin Agile is the tiny **Cimetière St-Vincent** 19.

Return to Sacré-Coeur and head down the cascading staircases to place St-Pierre. On the corner to the left is the **Halle St-Pierre** 20, site of the Museum of Naive Art. The neighboring streets teem with fabric shops, which are good places to find inexpensive materials. From the top of rue de Steinkerque, one of the busiest shopping streets, you can take in the archetypal view of Sacré-Coeur soaring skyward atop its grassy mound, with the funicular railway to the left. Turn right at the bottom of rue de Steinkerque and head toward place Pigalle, still notorious as a center of sleazy nightlife, despite the classier bars and nightclubs that have been springing up.

If you still have the energy to see another illustrious church after you've walked around Montmartre, make the excursion to the Gothic **Basilique de St-Denis** in the nearby suburb of St-Denis. Take the métro at place de Clichy to St-Denis Basilique. Or get on at Anvers (near the Halle St-Pierre) and transfer at place de Clichy.

TIMING Reserve four to five hours for this 4-km (2½-mi) walk: many of the streets are steep and slow going. Include half an hour each at Sacré-Coeur and the museums (the Dalí museum is open daily, but the Montmartre museum is closed Monday). Leave about two hours for the excursion to St-Denis, including the métro ride there. From Easter through September, Montmartre is besieged by tourists. Two hints to avoid the worst of the rush: come on a gray day, when Montmartre's sullen-tone facades suffer less than most in the city; or during the afternoon, and return to place du Tertre (maybe via the funicular) by the early evening, once the tourist buses have departed. More festive times of the year are June 24, when fireworks and street concerts are staged around Montmartre, and the first weekend of October, when revelry accompanies the wine harvest at the vineyard on rue des Saules.

What to See

10 **Bateau-Lavoir** (Boat Wash House). Montmartre poet Max Jacob coined the name for the original building on this site, which burned down in 1970. He said it resembled a boat and that the warren of artists' studios within was perpetually paint-splattered and in need of a good hosing down. It was in the original Bateau-Lavoir that, early in the 20th century, Pablo Picasso and Georges Braque made their first bold stabs at Cubism—a move that paved the way for abstract painting. The poet Guillaume Apollinaire also had a studio here; his book *The Painters of Cubism* (1913) set the seal on the movement's historical acceptance. The

replacement building also contains art studios, but, if you didn't know its history, you'd probably walk right past it. ✉ *13 pl. Émile-Goudeau, Montmartre* Ⓜ *Abbesses.*

❾ **Chapelle du Martyre** (Martyr's Chapel). It was in the crypt of the original chapel—built over the spot where St. Denis is said to have been martyred around AD 250—that Ignatius of Loyola, Francis Xavier, and five other companions swore an oath of poverty, chastity, and service to the Church in 1534. This led to the founding of the Society of Jesus (the Jesuits) in Rome six years later—a decisive step in the efforts of the Catholic Church to reassert its authority in the face of the Protestant Reformation. ✉ *9 rue Yvonne-Le-Tac, Montmartre* Ⓜ *Abbesses.*

❶ **Cimetière de Montmartre** (Montmartre Cemetery). Although not as large as the better-known Père-Lachaise, this leafy split-level cemetery is just as moving and evocative. Incumbents include painters Jean-Baptiste Greuze, Jean-Honoré Fragonard, and Edgar Degas; Adolphe Sax, inventor of the saxophone; composers Hector Berlioz and Jacques Offenbach; and La Goulue, the Belle Epoque cabaret dancer who devised the French cancan. The florid Art Nouveau tomb of novelist Émile Zola (1840–1902), who died in nearby rue de Clichy, lords over a lawn near the entrance—though Zola's mortal remains were removed to the Panthéon in 1908. ✉ *Av. Rachel, Montmartre* Ⓜ *Blanche.*

⓳ **Cimetière St-Vincent** (St. Vincent Cemetery). It's a small graveyard, but if you're a serious student of Montmartre you may want to visit painter Maurice Utrillo's burial place. ✉ *Entrance on rue Lucien-Gaulard (via rue St-Vincent), behind the Lapin Agile, Montmartre* Ⓜ *Lamarck Caulaincourt.*

⓮ **Espace Salvador-Dalí** (Dalí Center). Some of Salvador Dalí's less familiar works are among the 25 sculptures and 300 signed etchings and lithographs housed in this museum. The "ambience" is meant to approximate the surreal experience, with black walls, low lighting, and a New Agey musical score—punctuated by recordings of Dalí's own voice. ✉ *11 rue Poulbot, Montmartre* ☎ *01–42–64–40–10* *€7* ⏲ *Daily 10–6:30* Ⓜ *Abbesses.*

⓴ **Halle St-Pierre** (St. Peter's Market Hall). This elegant iron-and-glass 19th-century market hall, at the foot of Sacré-Coeur, houses a children's play area, a café, a children's and outsider-art bookstore, and the **Musée de l'Art Naïf Max-Fourny** (Max Fourny Museum of Naive Art), with its psychedelic collection of contemporary international naive painters. ✉ *2 rue Ronsard, Montmartre* ☎ *01–42–58–72–89* *Museum €6* ⏲ *Daily 10–6* Ⓜ *Anvers.*

★ ⓲ **Lapin Agile.** This bar-cabaret is still one of the most picturesque spots in Montmartre. It got its curious name—the Nimble Rabbit—when the owner, André Gill, hung up a sign (now in the Musée du Vieux Montmartre) of a laughing rabbit jumping out of a saucepan clutching a bottle of wine. In those days the place was still tamely called *La Campagne* (The Countryside). Once the sign went up, locals rechristened it the Lapin à Gill, meaning Gill's Rabbit. When, in 1886, it was sold to cabaret singer Jules Jouy, he called it the *Lapin Agile,* which has the same pronunciation in French as *Lapin à Gill.* In 1903, the premises were bought by the most celebrated cabaret entrepreneur of them all, Aristide Bruand, portrayed by Toulouse-Lautrec in a series of famous posters, and soon thereafter Picasso painted his famous *Au Lapin Agile* (sold at auction in the 1980s for nearly $50 million and on view at New York City's Metropolitan Museum). Today the Lapin Agile manages to preserve at least something of its earlier flavor, unlike the Moulin Rouge. ✉ *22 rue* *des Saules, Montmartre* ☎ *01–46–06–85–87* 🎫 *€20* ⏲ *Tues.–Sun. 9 PM–2 AM* Ⓜ *Lamarck Caulaincourt.*

13 **La Mère Catherine.** This restaurant was a favorite with the Russian Cossacks who occupied Paris in 1814. Little did they know that when they banged on the tables and shouted "*bistro,*" the Russian word for "quickly," they were inventing a new breed of French restaurant. ✉ *6 pl. du Tertre, Montmartre* Ⓜ *Abbesses.*

4 **Moulin de la Galette** (Wafer Windmill). This windmill, on a hillock shrouded by shrubbery, is one of the remaining two in Montmartre. It was once the focal point of an open-air cabaret (made famous in a painting by Renoir, now part of the collection of the Musée d'Orsay), and rumor has it that the miller, Debray, was strung up on its sails and spun to death after striving vainly to defend it against invading Cossacks in 1814. Unfortunately, it is now privately owned and can only be admired from the street below. ✉ *Rue Tholozé, Montmartre* Ⓜ *Abbesses.*

2 **Moulin Rouge** (Red Windmill). Built originally as a windmill, this world-famous cabaret was transformed into a dance hall in 1889. Those wild, early days were immortalized by Toulouse-Lautrec in his posters and paintings. It still trades shamelessly on the notion of Paris as a city of sin: if you fancy a Vegas-style night out, with computerized light shows and troupes of bare-breasted Doriss Girls sporting feather headdresses, this is the place to go. The cancan, by the way—still a regular sight here—was considerably raunchier when Toulouse-Lautrec was around. ✉ *82 bd. de Clichy, Montmartre* ☎ *01–53–09–82–82* 🌐 *www.moulin-rouge.com* Ⓜ *Blanche.*

3 **Musée de l'Erotisme** (Museum of Eroticism). This seven-story museum at the foot of Montmartre claims to provide "a prestigious showcase for every kind of erotic fantasy." Its 2,000 works of art—you may find that this term is used rather loosely—include Peruvian potteries, African carvings, Indian miniatures, Nepalese bronzes, Chinese ivories, Japanese prints, and racy Robert Crumb cartoons. Three floors are devoted to temporary exhibitions of painting and photography. ✉ *72 bd. de Clichy, Montmartre* ☎ *01–42–58–28–73* 🎫 *€7* ⏲ *Daily 10 AM–2 AM* Ⓜ *Blanche.*

17 **Musée de Montmartre** (Montmartre Museum). In its turn-of-the-20th-century heyday, Montmartre's historical museum was home to an illustrious group of painters, writers, and assorted cabaret artists. Foremost among them were Renoir—he painted the *Moulin de la Galette,* an archetypal Parisian scene of sun-drenched revelers, while he lived here—and Maurice Utrillo, Montmartre painter par excellence. Utrillo was encouraged to paint by his mother, Suzanne Valadon, a model of Renoir's and a major painter in her own right. Utrillo's life was anything but happy, despite the considerable success his paintings enjoyed. He was an alcoholic continually in trouble with the police and spent most of his declining years in hospitals. He took the gray, crumbling streets of Montmartre as his subject matter, working more effectively from postcards than from the streets themselves. For all that, almost all his best works—from his "White Period"—were produced before 1916 (he died in 1955). They evoke the *parfum* of old Montmartre hauntingly: to help convey the decaying buildings of the area, he mixed plaster and sand in with his paints. The museum also provides a view of the tiny **vineyard**—the only one in Paris—on neighboring rue des Saules. A token 125 gallons of wine are still produced every year. It's hardly *grand cru* stuff, but there are predictably bacchanalian celebrations during the harvest on the first weekend of October. ✉ *12 rue Cortot, Montmartre* ☎ *01–46–06–61–11* 🎫 *€3.80* ⏲ *Tues.–Sun. 11–6* Ⓜ *Lamarck Caulaincourt.*

6 **Place des Abbesses.** This triangular square is typical of the picturesque, slightly countrified style that has made Montmartre famous. The entrance to the Abbesses métro station, designed by the great Hector Guimard as a curving, sensuous mass of delicate iron, is one of the two original Art Nouveau entrance canopies left in Paris. Ⓜ *Abbesses.*

Place Blanche. The name place Blanche—White Square—comes from the clouds of chalky dust that used to be churned up by the carts that carried wheat and crushed flour from the nearby windmills, including the Moulin Rouge. Ⓜ *Blanche.*

off the beaten path

Musée de la Vie Romantique. This tranquil, countrified town house, set in a little park at the foot of Montmartre (head down rue Blanche from place Blanche; the third left is rue Chaptal), was for years the site of Friday-evening salons hosted by the Dutch-born painter Ary Scheffer and including the likes of Ingres, Delacroix, Turgenev, Chopin, and Sand. The memory of author George Sand (1804–76)—real name Aurore Dudevant—haunts the museum. Portraits, furniture, and household possessions, right down to her cigarette box, have been moved here from her house in Nohant in the Loire Valley. There's also a selection of Scheffer's competent artistic output on the first floor. The salons are newly asparkle, thanks to the eye of Jacques Garcia, France's most fashionable interior decorator. Take a moment to enjoy a cup of tea in the garden café. ✉ *16 rue Chaptal, Montmartre* ☎ *01–48–74–95–38* 🌐 *paris-france.org/musees* 🎫 *Free for permanent collection, exhibitions €4.50* 🕙 *Tues.–Sun. 10–5:40* Ⓜ *St-Georges.*

11 **Place Jean-Baptiste-Clément.** Painter Amedeo Modigliani (1884–1920) had a studio here at No. 7. Some say he was the greatest Italian artist of the 20th century, fusing the genius of the Renaissance with the modernity of Cézanne and Picasso. He claimed that he would drink himself to death—and he eventually did, and chose the right part of town to do it in. Look for the octagonal tower at the north end of the square; it's all that's left of Montmartre's first water tower, built around 1840 to boost the area's feeble water supply. ✉ *Pl. Jean-Baptiste-Clément, Montmartre* Ⓜ *Abbesses.*

12 **Place du Tertre** (Mound Square). This tumbling square (*tertre* means hillock) regains its village atmosphere only in winter, when the branches of the plane trees sketch traceries against the sky. At any other time of year you'll be confronted by crowds of tourists and a swarm of artists clamoring to do your portrait. If one produces a picture of you without your permission, you're under no obligation to buy. Ⓜ *Abbesses.*

need a break?

There are few attractive snack options in this part of town, but **Patachou** (✉ 9 pl. du Tertre, Montmartre ☎ 01–42–51–06–06) sounds the one classy note on place du Tertre, serving exquisite, if expensive, cakes and teas.

★ 16 **Sacré-Coeur** (Sacred Heart Basilica). The white domes of this basilica patrol the Paris skyline from the top of Montmartre. The French government decided to erect Sacré-Coeur in 1873, as a sort of national guilt-offering in expiation for the blood shed during the Commune and Franco-Prussian War in 1870–71. It was meant to symbolize the return of self-confidence to late-19th-century Paris. Even so, the building was to some extent a reflection of political divisions within the country: it was largely financed by French Catholics fearful of an anticlerical backlash and determined to make a grandiloquent statement on behalf of the Church. Construction lasted until World War I; the basilica was not consecrated until 1919. In style the Sacré-Coeur borrows elements from Romanesque and Byzantine architecture. Built on a grand scale, the church is strangely disjointed and unsettling; architect Paul Abadie (who died in 1884, long before the church was finished) had made his name by sticking similar scaly, pointed domes onto the medieval cathedrals of Angoulême and Périgueux in southwest France. The gloomy, cavernous interior is worth visiting for its golden mosaics; climb to the top of the dome for the view of Paris. Grand vistas of the city can be seen from the entrance terrace *and* from the steps at the back of the basilica. ✉ *Pl. du Parvis-du-Sacré-Coeur, Montmartre* Ⓜ *Anvers.*

7 **St-Jean l'Evangéliste.** This redbrick church, built in 1904, was one of the first concrete buildings in France; despite its sinuous Art Nouveau curves, the bricks had to be added later to soothe offended locals. ✉ *Pl. des Abbesses, Montmartre* Ⓜ *Abbesses.*

need a break?

Le Sancerre (✉ 35 rue des Abbesses, Montmartre ☎ 01–42–58–08–20) is a raucous café/restaurant with large windows, loud music, and loads of true *montmartrois* charm. The tables outside offer quieter seating, and a good vantage point of the bustling Abbesses street scene.

15 **St-Pierre de Montmartre.** Sitting awkwardly beneath the brooding silhouette of Sacré-Coeur, just off place du Tertre, is this church—one of the oldest in Paris. Built in the 12th century as the abbey church of a substantial Benedictine monastery, it has been remodeled on a number of occasions through the years; thus the 18th-century facade, built under Louis XIV, clashes with the mostly medieval interior. ✉ *Off pl. du Tertre, Montmartre* Ⓜ *Anvers.*

5 **Studio 28.** What looks like no more than a generic little movie theater has a distinguished dramatic history: When it opened in 1928 it was the first one purposely built for *art et essai,* or experimental theater, in the world. Over the years, the movies of directors like Jean Cocteau, François Truffaut, and Orson Welles have been shown here before their official premieres. ✉ *10 rue Tholozé, Montmartre* ☎ *01–46–06–36–07* Ⓜ *Abbesses.*

8 **Théâtre Libre** (Free Theater). Founded in 1887 by director André Antoine (1858–1943), this theater was immensely influential in popularizing the work of iconoclastic young playwrights such as Ibsen and Strindberg. Antoine later became the director of the Odéon Theater in 1906. ✉ *37 rue André-Antoine, Montmartre* Ⓜ *Abbesses.*

PASSY, AUTEUIL & THE BOIS DE BOULOGNE

Passy and Auteuil were independent villages until Baron Haussmann soldered them together in 1860 and annexed them to Paris under the mundane title of the 16e arrondissement. Tumbling alleys and countrified culs-de-sac recall those bygone days, colliding with some of the city's finest 20th-century architecture, by Guimard, Perret, Le Corbusier, and Mallet-Stevens. One of the city's most overlooked museums is here—the Musée Marmottan, with its enormous Monet collection.

Not far away from those Monets is the sprawling Bois de Boulogne—an enormous park that also assumed its present form during the days of Haussmann and Napoléon III, when it became the Parisians' favorite day trip. The 16e is the largest arrondissement in Paris, and Le Bois, as it is known, is of almost equal size. Public transportation to the Bois is poor, and few Parisians ever get to know all its glades and pathways—but all know and love the Bois's Pré Catalan and Bagatelle gardens, two of Paris's prettiest spots. The photogenic Lac Supérieur, however, which anchors the Bois's eastern sector, is easy to reach on foot and by métro.

Numbers in the text correspond to numbers in the margin and on the Passy, Auteuil, and the Bois de Boulogne map.

a good walk

Start at the **Cimetière de Passy** 1, above place du Trocadéro. A map to the left of the entrance charts the tombs of the famous buried here. Leaving the cemetery, cross avenue Paul-Doumer, and veer left to a small garden (Square Yorktown) where there is a statue of Benjamin Franklin. Turn right down rue Benjamin-Franklin. Verdant gardens flank the curved wing of the Palais de Chaillot to your left. On the right, at No. 25 bis, note the huge-windowed Immeuble Perret—an innovative building for its time (1903), with a reinforced-concrete facade clad in floral-patterned ceramic tiles. Auguste Perret, then just 29, was to become one of the century's leading architects.

Cross place Costa-Rica, with its plummeting view of the aboveground métro as it shoots across the Seine, and take rue Raynouard. Opposite No. 12, turn left down rue des Eaux, a sinister-looking stone staircase flanked by barbed wire: the nearest Paris gets to urban hell, straight out of Dickens, and duly depositing you on rue Charles-Dickens at the bottom. You reemerge into daylight to be confronted by a templelike town house with huge Greek columns and, to your left, the quaint **Musée du Vin** 2, with exhibits on wine in its medieval cellars. After an excursion through bacchanalian pastures, big-city reality hits again as you retrace your steps along rue Charles-Dickens and venture right into avenue Marcel-Proust, in search of the time when the fortresslike walls on the right supported some of the fanciest flats in Paris and the majestic double staircase halfway along led down to the grand entrance of the Ministry of Public Works (relocated to La Défense) rather than, as is presently the case, the Parc de Passy housing complex.

A policeman generally lurks a hundred yards on, barring the leafy driveway to the Turkish embassy. You might have to consult him for advice as you search for rue Bertin, a cobbled, ivy-clad alley that sneaks off right, undisturbed by traffic, to a flight of stairs that leads back to rue Raynouard and the **Maison de Balzac** 3, a dachalike bungalow with trim lawns, once home to France's own Dickens. Rue Benjamin-Franklin returns at the corner of rues Raynouard and Singer where—says a tall, tapering plaque—the great man invented the lightning conductor between 1777 and 1785. Rue Raynouard tumbles down past the circular bulk of **Maison de Radio France** 4, the headquarters of state radio and television. If you'd like to see a miniversion of the **Statue of Liberty** 5, head left toward the Seine; it's at the end of the Allée des Cygnes, a striplike artificial island backed by the skyscrapers of the 1970s Front de Seine complex that cynical Parisians dub their mini-Manhattan.

Continue on rue Raynouard, which becomes rue La Fontaine, to inspect the **Castel-Béranger** 6 at No. 14, one of the city's earliest Art Nouveau buildings. If you're a fan of sculptor Auguste Rodin you may want to make a detour next right up avenue du Recteur-Poincaré to **place Rodin** 7 to see a small bronze casting of his male nude, *The Bronze Age.* Otherwise stay on rue La Fontaine, pass the **Orphelins d'Auteuil** 8—a still-functioning orphanage. Pause at No. 60, the **Hôtel Mezzara** 9, another fine Guimard mansion. Some 150 yards along, turn left onto rue des Perchamps. Note the bay-windowed, striped-tile Studio Building at No. 20—

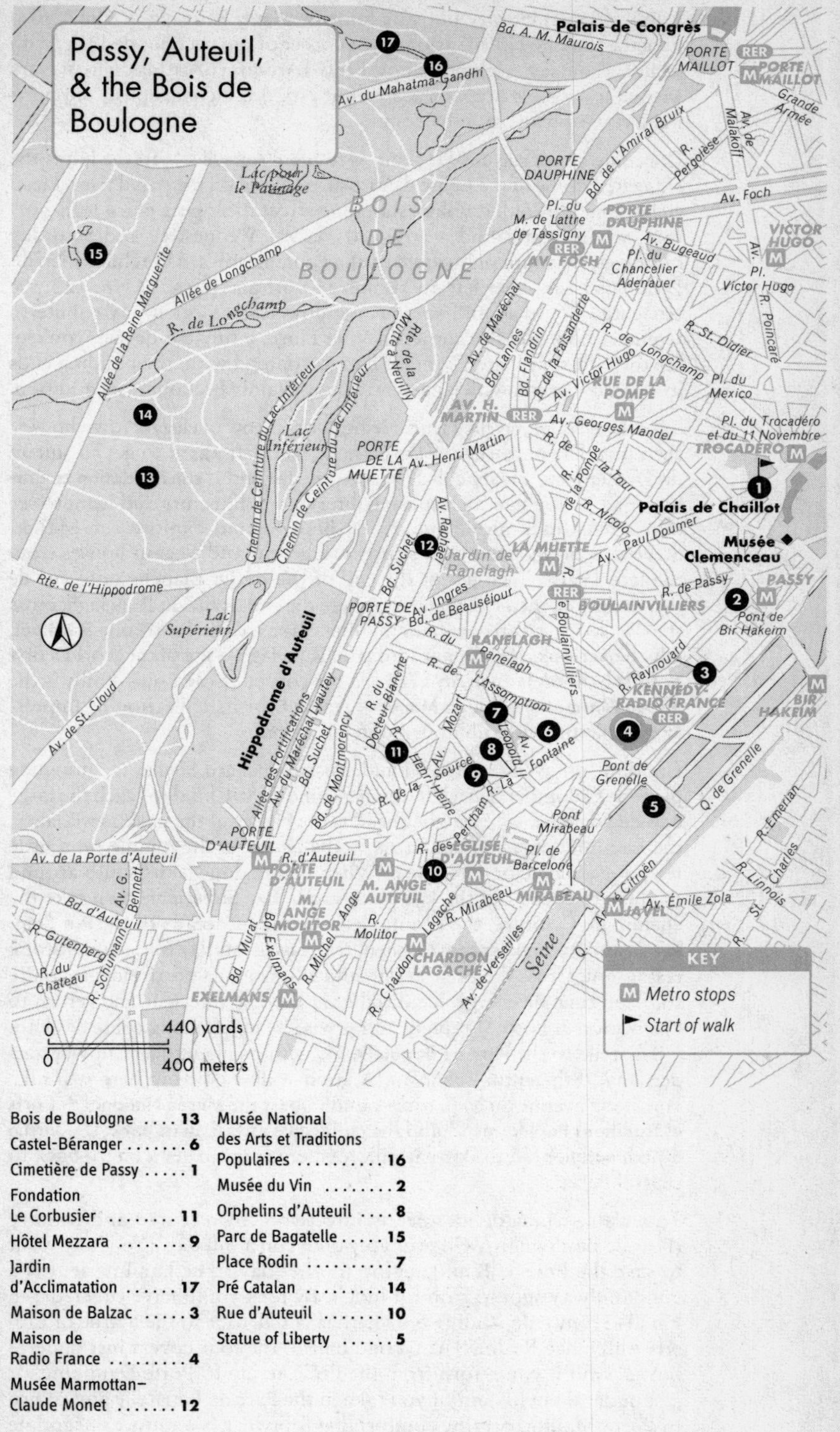

Bois de Boulogne 13
Castel-Béranger 6
Cimetière de Passy 1
Fondation Le Corbusier 11
Hôtel Mezzara 9
Jardin d'Acclimatation 17
Maison de Balzac 3
Maison de Radio France 4
Musée Marmottan–Claude Monet 12
Musée National des Arts et Traditions Populaires 16
Musée du Vin 2
Orphelins d'Auteuil 8
Parc de Bagatelle 15
Place Rodin 7
Pré Catalan 14
Rue d'Auteuil 10
Statue of Liberty 5

it looks contemporary but was built by Henri Sauvage in 1927. Also note the funky white mansion at the corner of rue Leconte-de-l'Isle, with its heavy, outsize triglyphs. Some beefy Baroque caryatids on loan from Vienna are visible across the street at No. 33, incongruously supporting a row of wafer-thin balconies.

Continue along rue des Perchamps to **rue d'Auteuil** 10. To the left is the elongated dome of the Église d'Auteuil, modeled on the papal tiara. Head right along this old, crooked shopping street to sloping place Jean-Lorrain, where you'll find a crowded market Wednesday and Saturday mornings; then turn right down rue La Fontaine toward the chunky Crédit Lyonnais bank. Veer left up avenue Mozart and pause at No. 122; the elongated doorway and sinuous window frames again pay tribute to Guimard. Around the corner in Villa Flore, a tiny cul-de-sac, you can see the odd-shape site Guimard had to contend with: the building ends in a narrow point, with jagged brickwork vainly beckoning an addition.

Take the next left up rue Henri-Heine, with its row of elegant town houses; then turn left onto rue du Dr-Blanche, and left again to get to square du Dr-Blanche, a leafy cul-de-sac. At the far end is the **Fondation Le Corbusier** 11. If you like such spartan interwar architecture and want to see more, backtrack along rue du Dr-Blanche and explore rue Mallet-Stevens, a mews lined with sturdy evergreens and elegant houses from the late 1920s. Turn left at the end of rue du Dr-Blanche onto rue de l'Assomption, then right, and, opposite the end of rue du Ranelagh, cross the disused St-Lazare-Auteuil rail line. Take a right on avenue Raphaël, which overlooks the elegant Jardin du Ranelagh—site of the world's first hot-air balloon launch, in 1783. At the corner of rue Louis-Boilly is the **Musée Marmottan–Claude Monet** 12, famed for its collection of Impressionist pictures and illuminated manuscripts.

Continue on avenue Raphaël and cross boulevard Suchet to sprawling place de Colombie. Turn left down avenue de St-Cloud to reach the large **Bois de Boulogne** 13. Straight ahead is the bigger of the park's two lakes, the Lac Inférieur; you can cross to the island in the middle on a little ferry for a picnic or café lunch. When you're done, skirt south around the lake to check out the less picturesque Lac Supérieur; then take the chemin de Ceinture, then route de la Grande-Cascade to the **Pré Catalan** 14 and its Shakespeare Garden, trim lawns, stately trees, and historic restaurant. Cross the Pré Catalan and exit from its north side. If you're short on time or energy, head right via the Lac Inférieur and return to civilization at Porte Dauphine; otherwise head left along route des Lacs à Bagatelle to the **Parc de Bagatelle** 15, with its magnificent flower garden and 18th-century château. A good walk east from here will take you along avenue du Mahatma-Gandhi, past the **Musée National des Arts et Traditions Populaires** 16 and the children's amusement park, the **Jardin d'Acclimatation** 17, to Porte Maillot, where you can get a métro back to central Paris.

TIMING This walk, which divides neatly into two—town (Paris) and country (Bois de Boulogne)—will probably take you a full day. (You may want to save the Bois de Boulogne for another day.) The Lac Inférieur is a good midway spot to stop for lunch. By then you'll have covered 5–6 km (3–3½ mi), depending on whether you detour to the Statue of Liberty and place Rodin. The second half of the tour covers just under 4 km (2½ mi) if you return from the Pré Catalan to Porte Dauphine, or just under 6 km (3½ mi) if you take in the Parc de Bagatelle and return to Porte Maillot. Sturdy, comfortable footwear is a must to negotiate the slopes and steps of the Paris sector and the gravelly pathways of the Bois de Boulogne.

What to See

13 **Bois de Boulogne.** Class and style have been associated with this 2,200-acre wood—known to Parisians simply as *Le Bois*—ever since it was landscaped into an upper-class playground by Baron Haussmann in the 1850s. Emphasizing that onetime glamour is Haussmann's approach road from the Arc de Triomphe: avenue Foch, Paris's widest boulevard (120 yards across), originally named avenue de l'Impératrice in honor of Empress Eugénie (wife of Napoléon III). The Porte Dauphine métro station at the bottom of avenue Foch retains its original Art Nouveau iron-and-glass entrance canopy, designed by Hector Guimard.

The wood, which lost thousands of trees during 100-mph wind storms in 1999, is crisscrossed by broad, leafy roads, is much favored by rowers, joggers, strollers, riders, *pétanque* (a sort of bowling game) players, picnickers, and lovers. Meetings at **Longchamp** and **Auteuil** racetracks are high up the social calendar and re-create something of its Belle Epoque heyday. The French Open tennis tournament at the beautiful **Roland Garros** stadium in late May is another occasion when Parisian style and elegance are on full display.

The manifold attractions of Le Bois include cafés, restaurants, lakes, waterfalls, gardens, and museums. Rowboats can be rented at both **Lac Inférieur** and **Lac Supérieur.** A cheap and frequent ferry crosses to the idyllic island in the middle of Lac Inférieur. The **Fête à Neu-Neu,** a giant carnival, takes place every September and October around the two lakes. Buses traverse the Bois de Boulogne during the day (take Bus 244 from Porte Maillot), but Le Bois becomes a distinctly adult playground after dark, when prostitutes of various genders come prowling for clients. ✉ *Main entrance at bottom of av. Foch, Bois de Boulogne* Ⓜ *Porte Maillot, Porte Dauphine, Porte d'Auteuil; Bus 244.*

6 **Castel-Béranger.** Dreamed up in 1895 by Hector Guimard (of métro fame) when he was 28, this building is considered the city's first Art Nouveau structure. The apartment building once housed Postimpressionist Paul Signac as well as Guimard himself. Today the place looks a little dowdy and its occupants are less illustrious—though this hasn't stopped them from posting a menacing sign on the asymmetrical iron doorway warning you to keep out. Rust-streaked pale green paint, however, fails to detract from the florid appeal of the iron doors and balconies, or from the eccentric use of colored brick. Cross the street to admire the mask-fronted iron balconies and quilt-patterned brown, red, and turquoise brickwork; then venture around the side into Hameau Béranger to see rampant ivy obliterating the original fancy iron fencing, beneath the dismayed gazes of stylized sea horses halfway up the walls. There's a cleaner, subtler display of Art Nouveau at the corner of rue Lafontaine and rue Gros, where a finely carved stone apartment building segues into the dainty rue Agar. Tucked away at the corner of rue Gros is a tiny café-bar with Art Nouveau glass front and furnishings. ✉ *14 rue la Fontaine, Passy-Auteuil* Ⓜ *Ranelagh; RER: Maison de Radio France.*

need a break?

It seats just 15, but the **Café-Bar Antoine** (✉ 17 rue la Fontaine, Passy-Auteuil ☎ 01–40–50–14–30) warrants a visit for its Art Nouveau facade, floor tiles, and carved wooden bar. Count on €30 for a meal or stick to a snack and coffee.

1 **Cimetière de Passy** (Passy Cemetery). Perched on a spur above place du Trocadéro in the shadow of the Eiffel Tower and Palais de Chaillot, this cemetery was opened in 1820 when Passy was a country village. Its handsome entrance—two sturdy pavilions linked by a colonnade—is a 1930s

Art Deco cousin to the nearby Palais de Chaillot. Precocious painter-poetess Marie Baskirtseff's tomb, with its pinnacles and stone Byzantine dome, dominates the cemetery; a Pietà behind Plexiglas mourns Hungarian peer Pierre Perenyi nearby. Just left of the main crossroads is a weathered bust of Impressionist Edouard Manet, buried with his wife, Berthe Morisot, next to the poignant figure of a girl in a hat—calling to mind Zola's novel *Une Page d'Amour* (*Love Episode*), which ends with the burial of the young heroine Jeanne in Passy Cemetery, "alone, facing Paris, forever." Claude Debussy is also among the incumbents. ⊠ *Rue du Commandant-Schloesing, Trocadéro/Eiffel Tower* ⏲ *Daily 9–8 or dusk* Ⓜ *Trocadéro.*

11 **Fondation Le Corbusier** (Le Corbusier Foundation). The Villa Laroche is less of a museum in honor of Swiss architect Charles-Edouard Jeanneret, better known as Le Corbusier (1887–1965), than a well-preserved 1923 example of his innovative construction techniques, based on geometric forms, recherché color schemes, and unblushing recourse to iron and concrete. The sloping ramp that replaces the traditional staircase is one of the most eye-catching features. ⊠ *10 sq. du Dr-Blanche, Passy-Auteuil* ☎ *01–42–88–41–53* 🎫 *€1.50* ⏲ *Weekdays 10–12:30 and 1:30–6* Ⓜ *Jasmin.*

9 **Hôtel Mezzara.** With its sumptuous wrought-iron staircase, Art Nouveau windows, and plaster molding, this Hector Guimard mansion, built in 1911 as a workshop for textile designer Paul Mezzara, has one of the finest 20th-century interiors in Paris. Unfortunately, it is only open during exhibitions, though a bit of curiosity and perseverance might get you through the door. ⊠ *60 rue la Fontaine, Passy-Auteuil* ☎ *01–45–27–02–29* Ⓜ *Jasmin.*

17 **Jardin d'Acclimatation** (Amusement Park). At this children's zoo and amusement park on the northern edge of the Bois de Boulogne you can see a mix of exotic and familiar animals, take a boat trip along an "enchanted river," ride a miniature railway, and enjoy various fairground booths that keep young and old entertained. The zoo and amusement park can be reached via the miniature railway—a surefire hit with children—that runs from Porte Maillot on Wednesday and weekends, beginning at 1:30; tickets cost €1. Many of the attractions have separate entry fees (except the zoo, which is spread throughout the park), notably the child-oriented art museum and workshop center, the **Musée en Herbe** (literally, Museum in the Grass); admission is €3. ⊠ *Bd. des Sablons, Bois de Boulogne* ☎ *01–40–67–97–66* 🎫 *€2.30, workshops €4.50* ⏲ *Daily 10–7* Ⓜ *Les Sablons.*

3 **Maison de Balzac** (Balzac's House). The Paris home of the great French 19th-century novelist Honoré de Balzac (1799–1850) contains exhibits charting his tempestuous life. ⊠ *47 rue Raynouard, Passy-Auteuil* ☎ *01–55–74–41–80* 🌐 *paris-france.org/musees* 🎫 *Free* ⏲ *Feb.–Dec., Tues.–Sun. 10–5:40* Ⓜ *Passy.*

4 **Maison de Radio France** (Radio France Building). Headquarters to France's state radio, this monstrous circular building, completed in 1962, is more than 500 yards in circumference and said to be the largest in France in terms of floor space; a 200-ft tower overlooks the Seine. You can explore the foyer, obtain tickets to attend recordings, or join a guided tour (in French) of the studios and the museum, with its notable collection of old radios. ⊠ *116 av. du Président-Kennedy, Passy-Auteuil* ☎ *01–56–40–15–16* 🎫 *Guided tours (at half past the hour) €5* ⏲ *Mon.–Sat. 10:30–11:30 and 2:30–4:30* Ⓜ *Ranelagh; RER: Maison de Radio France.*

★ 12 **Musée Marmottan–Claude Monet.** One of the most underestimated museums in town, the Marmottan is Paris's "other" Impressionist museum (after the Musée d'Orsay). A few years ago this museum, in an elegant 19th-century mansion, tacked "Claude Monet" onto its official name—and justly so, as this may be the best collection of the artist's works anywhere. Monet occupies a specially built basement gallery, where you'll find such spectacular works as the *Cathédrale de Rouen* series (1892–96) and *Impression: Soleil Levant* (*Impression–Sunrise,* 1872), the work that helped give the Impressionist movement its name. Other exhibits include letters exchanged by Impressionist painters Berthe Morisot and Mary Cassatt. There's a roomful of priceless illuminated medieval manuscripts on the ground floor, and impressive Empire furniture from Napoléon's time makes you feel as if you're at an actual salon, with comfortable couches and grand windows overlooking the Jardin de Ranelagh on one side and the hotel's private yard on the other. ✉ *2 rue Louis-Boilly, Passy-Auteuil* ☎ *01–42–24–07–02* 🌐 *www.marmottan.com* 🎫 *€6.50* 🕙 *Tues.–Sun. 10–6* Ⓜ *La Muette.*

16 **Musée National des Arts et Traditions Populaires** (National Museum of Folk Arts and Traditions). In a nondescript modern building next to the Jardin d'Acclimatation, this museum is an impressive pile of artifacts related principally to preindustrial rural life. Many exhibits have buttons to press and knobs to twirl; however, there are no descriptions in English. The museum is a favorite destination for school field trips, so avoid weekday afternoons. ✉ *6 av. du Mahatma-Gandhi, Bois de Boulogne* ☎ *01–44–17–60–00* 🎫 *€3.85, free 1st Sun. of month* 🕙 *Wed.–Mon. 9:30–5:15* Ⓜ *Les Sablons.*

2 **Musée du Vin** (Wine Museum). In the vaulted 15th-century cellars of a former abbey, this small museum is devoted to traditional wine-making artifacts. The premises double as a wine bar and the visit includes a wine tasting. ✉ *5 sq. Charles-Dickens, Passy-Auteuil* ☎ *01–45–25–63–26* 🎫 *€6* 🕙 *Tues.–Sun. 10–6* Ⓜ *Passy.*

8 **Orphelins d'Auteuil** (Auteuil Orphanage). This still-functioning orphanage, founded in 1866 by Abbé Roussel, has pretty, sloping gardens, a red-brick cloister, a crafts shop, and a tasteful neo-Gothic chapel (built 1927). ✉ *40 rue La Fontaine, Passy-Auteuil* ☎ *01–44–14–75–20* Ⓜ *Jasmin.*

15 **Parc de Bagatelle.** This beautiful floral garden counts irises, roses, tulips, and water lilies among its showstoppers; it is at its most colorful between April and June. The velvety green lawns and the bijou château (only open when hosting exhibitions) are fronted by a terrace with attractive views of the Seine. The white-walled château was built by the Comte d'Artois in 1777 on a bet with Marie-Antoinette that it could be finished within two months; 900 construction workers toiled day and night (by torchlight) to make it happen. ✉ *Rte. de Sèvres-à-Neuilly or Rte. des Lacs-à-Bagatelle, Bois de Boulogne* ☎ *01–40–67–97–00* 🎫 *Gardens €1.50, château entrance according to exhibition* 🕙 *Daily 9–6 or dusk* Ⓜ *Pont de Neuilly.*

7 **Place Rodin.** A half-size bronze casting of Rodin's virile *L'Age d'Airain* (*The Bronze Age*) nude, created in 1874, emerges unblushingly from rosebushes at the heart of this minor roundabout. Ⓜ *Ranelagh.*

14 **Pré Catalan.** This garden in the Bois de Boulogne contains one of Paris's largest trees: a copper beech more than 200 years old. The **Jardin Shakespeare** (Shakespeare Garden) on the west side has a sampling of the flowers, herbs, and trees mentioned in Shakespeare's plays. Nearby still stands the restaurant Le Pré Catalan, where *le tout Paris* in the Belle

Epoque era used to dine on its beautiful garden terrace. ✉ *Rte. de la Grande-Cascade, Bois de Boulogne* 🎫 *Pré Catalan free, Shakespeare Garden €1* ⏲ *Pré Catalan daily 8–dusk. Shakespeare Garden daily 3–3:30 and 4:30–5* Ⓜ *Porte Dauphine.*

⑩ **Rue d'Auteuil.** This narrow, crooked shopping street escaped the attentions of Baron Haussmann and retains a country feel. Molière once lived on the site of No. 2; Racine was on nearby rue du Buis; the pair met up to clink glasses and exchange drama notes at the Mouton Blanc Inn, now a brasserie at No. 40. Note some genuinely old buildings dating from the 17th and 18th centuries at Nos. 19, 21, 25, and 29; the elegant courtyard of the school at No. 11 bis; and the scaly dome of the **Église d'Auteuil** (built in the 1880s), an unmistakable small-time cousin of the Sacré-Coeur. Rue d'Auteuil is at its liveliest on Wednesday and Saturday mornings, when a much-loved street market crams onto place Jean-Barraud. Ⓜ *Michel-Ange Auteuil, Église d'Auteuil.*

off the beaten path

Musée National de la Céramique. Hundreds of the finest creations of the world-famous Sèvres porcelain works are displayed at the National Ceramics Museum at the southern end of the tumbling, wooded Parc de St-Cloud, a short métro ride from the Michel-Ange Auteuil stop. ✉ *Pl. de la Manufacture, Sèvres* ☎ *01–41–14–04–20* 🎫 *€3.50* ⏲ *Wed.–Mon. 10–5:15* Ⓜ *Pont de Sèvres; Tramway: Musée de Sèvres.*

Serres D'Auteuil. Tropical and exotic plants sweat it out in mighty hothouses just off place de la Porte-d'Auteuil, on the southern fringe of the Bois de Boulogne. A bewildering efflorescence of plants and flowers is grown here for use in Paris's municipal parks and for displays on official occasions. The surrounding gardens' leafy paths and well-tended lawns offer cooler places to admire floral virtuosity. ✉ *3 av. de la Porte-d'Auteuil, Bois de Boulogne* ☎ *01–40–71–76–07* 🎫 *€1* ⏲ *Daily 10–6* Ⓜ *Porte d'Auteuil.*

⑤ **Statue of Liberty.** Just in case you'd forgotten that the enduring symbol of the American dream is actually French, a reduced version of Frédéric-Auguste Bartholdi's matriarch brandishes her torch at the southern tip of the Allée des Cygnes. To Bartholdi's dismay, she originally faced the city and was only turned around to gaze across the waters of the Seine in 1937. The best view of her can be had during a Bateaux-Mouche river tour: boats usually make an obliging U-turn right in front. The original statue—the one in New York City—is known in French as *La Liberté Éclairant le Monde* (*Liberty Lighting Up the World*); it was made in Paris in 1886 with the help of a giant steel framework designed by Gustave Eiffel. ✉ *Allée des Cygnes, Passy-Auteuil* Ⓜ *Javel; RER: Maison de Radio France.*

OFF THE BEATEN TRACK

If you're in search of wide-open green spaces, skyscrapers, the church where Gothic architecture made its first appearance, or great Art Deco architecture, make a brief excursion to the city's peripheries.

What to See

★ **Basilique de St-Denis.** Built between 1136 and 1286, St. Denis Cathedral is in some ways the most important Gothic church in the Paris region. It was here, under dynamic prelate Abbé Suger, that Gothic architecture (typified by pointed arches and rib vaults) arguably made its first appearance. Suger's writings also show the medieval fascination with the bright, shiny colors that appear in stained glass. The kings of France soon chose St-Denis as their final resting place, and their richly sculpted tombs—along with what remains of Suger's church—can be seen in the choir area at the east end of the church. The vast 13th-century nave is a brilliant example of structural logic; its columns, capitals, and vault are a model of architectural harmony. The facade, retaining the rounded arches of the Romanesque that preceded the Gothic style, is set off by a small rose window, reputedly the earliest in France. ✉ *1 rue de la Légion d'Honneur, St-Denis* ☎ *01–48–09–83–54* *Choir and tombs €5.50* ⏲ *Easter–Sept., Mon.–Sat. 10–6:30, Sun. noon–6; Oct.–Easter, Mon.–Sat. 10–4:30, Sun. noon–4:30. Guided tours daily at 11:15 and 3* Ⓜ *St-Denis Basilique.*

La Défense. You may be pleasantly surprised by the absence of high-rise buildings and concrete towers in central Paris; one of the reasons for this is that French planners, with their usual desire to rationalize, ordained that modern high-rise development be restricted to the city's outskirts. Over the last 20 years, La Défense, just west of Paris across the Seine from Neuilly, has been transformed into a futuristic showcase for state-of-the-art engineering and architectural design. A few people actually live amid all this glass and concrete; most just come to work. The soaring high-rises are mainly taken up by offices—often the French headquarters of multinational companies—with no expense spared in the pursuit of visual ingenuity. Crowning the plaza is the **Grande Arche de La Défense,** an enormous open cube aligned with avenue de la Grande-Armée, the Arc de Triomphe, the Champs-Élysées, and the Louvre. Tubular glass elevators whisk you 360 ft to the top. ✉ *Parvis de La Défense, La Défense* ☎ *01–49–07–27–57* 🌐 *www.grandearche.com* *€7* ⏲ *Daily 10–7* Ⓜ *Métro or RER: Grande Arche de La Défense.*

Parc Andre-Citroën (Andre-Citroën Park). This innovative and lovely park in southwest Paris was built on the site of the former Citroën automobile factory. Now it has lawns, Japanese rock gardens, rambling wildflowers, and elegant greenhouses full of exotic plants and flowers. There's also a delightful, computer-programmed "dancing fountain" that you can play in. On a sunny day it's a great place to take a break from sightseeing. ✉ *Entrances on rue St-Charles and rue de la Montagne de l'Esperou, Passy-Auteuil* Ⓜ *Métro or RER: Javel.*

Parc Montsouris and Cité Universitaire (Montsouris Park and University City). The picturesque, English-style Montsouris Park and the University "City," or campus, are in the residential 14e arrondissement, south of Montparnasse. Parc Montsouris has cascades, a lake, and a meteorological observatory disguised as a Tunisian Palace. The Cité Universitaire, opposite Parc Montsouris and next to the futuristic Stade Charléty athletics stadium, houses 5,000 international students in buildings that date mainly from the 1930s and reflect the architecture of different countries. Le Corbusier designed the Swiss and Brazilian houses; John D. Rockefeller funded the Maison Internationale; and the Sacré-Coeur church recalls the simple, muscular confidence of buildings erected in Mussolini's Italy. ✉ *Parc Montsouris: entrances on av. Reille, bd. Jourdan, and rue Gazan; Cité Universitaire: entrance at 19 bd. Jourdan, Montparnasse* ☎ *01–44–16–64–00 Cité Universitaire information* Ⓜ *RER: Cité Universitaire.*

Parcours des Années Trente and Musée des Années 30 (1930s Trail and 1930s Museum). For a look at outstanding Art Deco buildings by such architects as Le Corbusier, Auguste Perret, Raymond Fisher, and Robert

Mallet-Stevens, follow the 1930s Trail in the suburb of **Boulogne-Billancourt.** The route is outlined in an illustrated booklet available at the magnificent Hôtel de Ville (av. André-Morizet), built by Tony Garnier in 1934. More Art Deco is to be found at the 1930s Museum, next to the Hôtel de Ville. This museum has a wealth of beautifully presented paintings and sculpture produced in France during the interwar period. There's also an intriguing section on "colonial art," which borders between the naive and the patronizing. The collection of furniture and objects is disappointingly sparse. ✉ *28 av. André-Morizet, Boulogne-Billancourt* ☎ *01–55–18–46–42* €4.60 ⏲ *Tues.–Sun. 11–6* Ⓜ *Marcel-Sembat.*

WHERE TO EAT

2

FODOR'S CHOICE

Alain Ducasse, Champs-Élysées
L'Astrance, Trocadéro/Eiffel Tower
Chez Savy, Champs-Élysées
Les Élysées du Vernet, Champs-Élysées
Le Grand Véfour, Louvre/Tuileries
Lapérouse, Latin Quarter
Les Pipos, Latin Quarter
La Régalade, Montparnasse
Taillevent, Champs-Élysées
Ze Kitchen Galerie, Latin Quarter

Revised and updated by Rosa Jackson

PARIS HAS WORKS OF ART OF VARIED KINDS. Some hang on the walls of the Louvre. Some smile up at you from a plate. Anyone who has ordered a dessert at Le Cinq and received a concoction that looks like a hat styled by Christian Lacroix knows that in Paris food is far more than fuel. The French regard gastronomy as essential to the art of living, the art of transforming the gross and humdrum aspects of existence into something witty, charming, gracious, and satisfying. Parisians, above all, feel that every meal is—if not a complete way of life—certainly an event that demands undivided attention. Happily, the city's chefs exist principally to please its citizens on that score, so it is no surprise that Paris is also a place where you come to experience full gastronomic rapture.

Even though a dramatic and widely heralded improvement in the restaurants of cities from Boston to Brisbane has narrowed the gap that once made Paris nonpareil, no other metropolis in the world has yet developed a food sensibility as refined, reasoned, and deeply rooted as that clinging to the French capital. From the edible genius of haute cuisine wizards Eric Frechon, Alain Ducasse, and Pierre Gagnaire—whose marriage of heated fois gras, pressed caviar, and Japanese seaweeds will make you purr—to brilliant bistro chef Yves Camdeborde's red mullet with chestnuts and cèpes, dining out in Paris can easily reduce you to a pleasurable stupor. For a change of pace, you can always slip away to a casual little place for an earthy, bubbling cassoulet; make a midnight feast of the world's silkiest oysters; or even opt out of Gaul altogether for superb paella, couscous, or an herb-bright Vietnamese stir-fry. Once you know where to go (and this is crucial), Paris is a city where perfection awaits at all stations of the food chain.

Paris is currently witnessing the rise of the ambitious female chef. Though Ghislaine Arabian, former chef of Ledoyen, threw in the towel just a few months after opening her eponymous restaurant in the 16e (she was last spotted in Japan), others are seeking to step into her considerable clogs. Flora Mikula, the Alain Passard-trained chef who made her name at the Provençal bistro Les Olivades, is now running a chic restaurant just off the Champs-Élysées. Similarly, Catherine Guerraz grew weary of running the soul-warming bistro Chez Catherine and is serving her cuisine bourgeoise classics in a sleek new setting.

Both Mikula and Guerraz seem to be emulating the style of Pascal Barbot's wildly popular L'Astrance—neither bistro nor haute cuisine, but something comfortably in between. Barbot continues to wow diners with his cleverly judged France-meets-Asia style, cultivated during his time in Australia, but now has stiff competition from the delicate Japanese-inspired cooking of Hiramatsu on the Ile St-Louis. Another restaurant that appears to be pointing the way forward is Chamarré, which gently fuses French and Mauritian cooking in sober surroundings.

The traditional bistro remains in good health thanks to two breeds of chef: those who take pride in cultivating the classics (think boeuf bourguignon or sole meunière), and members of a young, energetic set who offer ever-changing seasonal menus, usually influenced by their native regions. If you can't wait three weeks to secure one of the three evening sittings at Yves Camdeborde's La Régalade, try booking a few days in advance at Chez Michel, where Thierry Breton works with the finest ingredients to update hearty dishes from his native Brittany—a pumpkin soup served in the squash shell adorned with salted herring eggs and tiny, crunchy croutons is one example. Or head to Chez Savy, a sepia-tone bistro that defies the galloping fashionization of the 8e arrondissement with such hearty delights as its charred shoulder of lamb and mounds of crisp *frites* (fries). The bistro boom is so big, in fact, that it has now

Mealtimes

Generally, Paris restaurants are open from noon to about 2 and from 7:30 or 8 to about 11. Brasseries have longer hours and often serve all day and late into the evening; some are open 24 hours. The iconoclastic wine bars pretty much do as they wish, frequently serving hot food only through lunch, then cold assortments of charcuterie and cheese until a late-afternoon or early evening close. Assume a restaurant is open every day unless otherwise indicated. Surprisingly, many restaurants close on Saturday as well as Sunday, and Monday closings are also frequent. July and August are the most common months for annual closings, but Paris in August is no longer the total culinary wasteland it used to be.

Menus

All establishments must post menus outside, so study them carefully before deciding to enter. Most restaurants have two basic types of menu: à la carte and fixed price (prix-fixe, un menu, or la formule). The prix-fixe menu is usually the best value, though choices are more limited. Most menus begin with a first course (une entrée), often subdivided into cold and hot starters, followed by fish and poultry, then meat; it's rare today that anyone orders something from all three. However, outside of brasseries, wine bars, and other casual places, it's usually inappropriate to order a single dish, as you'll understand when you see the waiter's expression. If you feel like indulging more than usual, the menu dégustation (tasting menu), consisting of numerous small courses, allows for a wide sampling of the chef's offerings. In general, consider the season when ordering; daily specials are usually based on what's freshest in the market that day.

See the Menu Guide at the back of the book for guidance with menu items that appear frequently on French menus and throughout the reviews that follow.

Reservations

In the following reviews, the topic of reservations has been covered by indicating only where they are essential (and when booking weeks or months in advance is necessary), and where they are not accepted. Because restaurants are open for only a few hours for lunch and dinner, and because meals are long affairs here, it's always wisest to make reservations. To help you translate some of the needed phrases—"Hello/Good evening. I'd like to make a reservation for X people for today/tomorrow/day-of-week at X-time. The last name is . . . Thank you"—here are a few sentences to help out if needed: "Bonjour (Bonsoir after 6 PM). Je voudrais faire une reservation pour X (1, un/une; 2, deux; 4, quatre; 6, six) personnes pour le diner (evening); le déjeuner (lunch) aujourd'hui à X heures (today at X o'clock)/demain à X heures (tomorrow at X o'clock); lundi (Monday), mardi (Tuesday), mercredi (Wednesday), jeudi (Thursday), vendredi (Friday), samedi (Saturday), dimanche (Sunday) à X heures. Le nom est (your own name). Merci bien." Note that most wine bars do not take reservations; reservations are also unnecessary for brasserie and café meals at odd hours.

Smoking

You can count on it: Parisians smoke before, during, and after meals. Restaurants are supposed to have no-smoking sections—if you want to sit in one, make this clear at the outset—though these areas are often limited to a very few tables where the no-smoking policy is not strictly monitored.

What to Wear

Casual dress is acceptable at all but the fanciest restaurants. Be aware that in Paris, however, casual usually means stylish sportswear, which is often more dressed up than you may be used to. When in doubt, leave the blue jeans and sneakers behind. Most of all, use your judgment. If an establishment requires jacket and tie, it is noted in the reviews below.

Wine

No matter what restaurant you're heading to, try to enjoy a taste of the grape along the way, whether vin ordinaire (table wine) or a Romanée-Conti. As the French say, a day without wine is like a day without sunshine. The wine that suits your meal is the wine you like. The traditional rule of white with fish and red with meat no longer applies. If the restaurant has a sommelier, let him (yes, it's usually a man) help you. Most sommeliers are knowledgeable about their lists and will suggest what is appropriate after you've made your tastes and budget known. In addition to the wine list, informal restaurants will have a vin maison (house wine) that is less expensive. Simpler spots will have wines en carafe (in a carafe) or en pichet (in a pitcher). Many restaurants now sell wine by the glass but beware the price—you might save money by ordering a bottle. If you'd like something before the meal, consider ordering your wine for the meal ahead of time, or sample a typical French apéritif, such as a kir, chilled white wine with black-currant liqueur.

Prices

Although prices can be steep at luxury restaurants, an effort has been made to include a number of lower-priced establishments. By French law, prices must include tax and tip (service compris or prix nets), but pocket change left on the table in basic places, or an additional 5% in better restaurants, is always appreciated. Beware of bills stamped "Service Not Included" in English or restaurants slyly using American-style credit-card slips, hoping that you'll be confused and add the habitual 15% tip. In neither case should you tip beyond the guidelines suggested above.

WHAT IT COSTS In Euros*

	$$$$	$$$	$$	$	¢
AT DINNER	over €30	€23–€30	€17–€22	€11–€16	under €10

*per person for a main course only, including tax (19.6%) and service; note that if a restaurant offers only prix-fixe (set-price) meals, it has been given the price category that reflects the full prix-fixe price.

invaded the haunts of haute cuisine. Even the most luxurious kitchens are getting back to the bedrock of French culinary traditions—a.k.a. The Patrimony. Don't, therefore, be surprised to find *grandmère*'s lamb with white beans on the *carte* at the superexpensive Le Bristol. *Cuisine rassurante* ("cookery that reassures") is all the rage in Paris these days.

Given the fickle nature of Paris fashionistas, it's no surprise that the Champs-Élysées restaurant bubble has burst. The novelty of chicken in Coca-Cola sauce and lobster hot dogs wasn't enough to keep the crowds coming to Korova, which has been replaced by a Pierre Hermé tearoom. Nobu, despite its long-standing popularity in other world capitals, also flopped like a fish out of water. Still going strong, though, are Alain

Ducasse's fusion bistro Spoon, Food and Wine and the swish Maison Blanche, where the view across Paris is as splendid as the Pourcel brothers' modern cuisine.

The biggest change in Paris dining, though, has little to do with what's happening on the plate. Since the French bade farewell to the franc in 2002, the bargain meal has become increasingly rare. Restaurateurs seized the opportunity to bump up their prices, often by several euros, and today a puny bottle of mineral water can easily set you back five euros. This provides all the more reason to plan carefully when dining out in Paris, so as to make the most of your budget.

2

If money is no object—or if you've saved your centimes for a one-in-a-lifetime meal—it's hard to go wrong at Taillevent, Les Ambassadeurs at the Hôtel Crillon, or Guy Savoy. Gastronomads—those who travel to eat—won't want to miss the far-flung culinary acrobatics of Pierre Gagnaire, who is half mad scientist, half inspired artist. Budget-wise gourmands know that many of Paris's best restaurants have prix-fixe lunch menus which are dramatically more affordable (but much more limited) than ordering from their regular à la carte menus. You'll probably have to ask for the lunch menu, for obvious reasons—most restaurants would prefer that you order à la carte. So watch out for that chilly look if you do pipe up and ask to see the prix-fixe lunch menu.

For those who come to Paris looking for a dose of elegance in an increasingly Gap-dressed world, the revival of the dining rooms in the city's grande dame hotels provides an ideal opportunity to show off new Diors and Balmains in truly gilded surroundings. Decor, of course, is not always the key to great food: some of the best bistros in Paris look downright simple—a kind of reverse *snobbisme*. For regal ambience but no demand to wear jacket and tie, don't forget the restaurants to be found in some of the city museums, notably the Restaurant Musée d'Orsay—a gigantic Second Empire salon swimming in gilt, frescoes, chandeliers, and marble; the café at the Musée Jacquemart-André (where else can you munch on salads beneath a Tiepolo ceiling?); and the Café Marly, set in the main courtyard of the Louvre (in all, meals are more than decent and lovely afternoon teas are also offered).

Included in this listing are a wide range of restaurants and prices. More than half are in the 1er–8e arrondissements, within easy reach of hotels and sights; many others are in the 14^e^ and 16^e^, also popular visitor areas; and some are in the 11^e^–20^e^, outlying, often residential neighborhoods where cheaper rents allow young chefs to strike out on their own. Recognizing that even in Paris you may not want to eat French food at every meal, ethnic restaurants are also included. (One area worth exploring—especially at lunchtime—is Paris's Chinatown in the 13e arrondissement; the main streets are avenue d'Ivry and avenue du Choisy.)

Restaurants by Arrondissement

1er Arrondissement (Louvre/Les Halles)

See Where to Eat on the Right Bank: Ile de la Cité to Montmartre map.

CONTEMPORARY
$$$–$$$$

✕ **Cabaret.** The food isn't substantial enough to cause indigestion, but you might find other reasons to recline, literally, on a settee-bed at this hyper-trendy restaurant after your meal. Lunch is served in the cool white dining room, but dinner in the funky basement is where it's at—star-decorator Jacques Garcia has gone all-out with phosphorescent floors, silk cushions, an "African bar," and Indian-style beds, surrounded by veils, each with a table built into the center. Expect tongue-in-cheek comfort food such as slow-cooked ostrich and mashed potatoes with truffles. ✉ *2 pl. du Palais-Royal, Louvre/Tuileries* ☎ *01–58–62–56–25* ▭ *AE, DC, MC, V* ⊙ *Closed Sun.* Ⓜ *Palais-Royal.*

FRENCH $$$$ ✕ **Gérard Besson.** With its collection of ceramic and metallic roosters in lighted glass cases, pale pink fabrics, and carved-wood boiseries, this classic dining room feels old-fashioned and intimate, if slightly stuffy. Chef Besson has mastered a superb classical repertoire, subtly enlivened by creative touches such as his terrine of Bresse chicken with foie gras and oyster flan. In winter, his game menu is probably the best in town: try the perfectly executed *lièvre à la royale,* braised hare in a luscious truffled sauce. For dessert, sample the distinctive confit of fennel with vanilla ice cream. Other pluses include an excellent wine cellar and a good-value €49 lunch menu. ✉ *5 rue du Coq-Héron, Louvre/Tuileries* ☎ *01–42–33–14–74* *Jacket required* ▭ *AE, DC, MC, V* ⊙ *Closed Sun. No lunch Sat. and Mon.* Ⓜ *Les Halles.*

$$$$ Fodor'sChoice ★ ✕ **Le Grand Véfour.** Victor Hugo could stride in and still recognize this place—in his day, as now, a contender for the title of most beautiful restaurant in Paris. Originally built in 1784, set in the arcades of the Palais-Royal, it has welcomed everyone from Napoléon to Colette to Jean Cocteau—nearly every seat bears a plaque commemorating a famous patron. The mirrored ceiling and early 19th-century glass paintings of goddesses and muses create an air of restrained seduction. Foodies as well as the fashionable gather here to enjoy chef Guy Martin's unique blend of sophistication and rusticity. He hails from Savoie, so you'll find lake fish and mountain cheeses on the menu alongside such luxurious dishes as foie gras–stuffed ravioli. For dessert, try the house specialty, *palet aux noisettes* (meringue cake with milk-chocolate mousse, hazelnuts, and caramel ice cream). If you can't spring for the extravagantly priced dishes on the à la carte menu, try the lunchtime prix fixe for a mere €72. ✉ *17 rue Beaujolais, Louvre/Tuileries* ☎ *01–42–96–56–27* *Reservations essential* *Jacket and tie* ▭ *AE, DC, MC, V* ⊙ *Closed weekends and Aug. No dinner Fri.* Ⓜ *Palais-Royal.*

$$$ ✕ **Macéo.** If you want to enjoy classic French food with a modern spin, then Macéo delivers in eat-your-*gâteau*-and-still-have-it fashion. Run by the British owners of Willi's Wine Bar, the restaurant is bathed in natural light streaming in from both sides; a broad, curved staircase leads to a spacious upstairs room. With its reasonably priced set menus (€34 at lunch and €38 in the evening), this is an ideal spot for an elegant yet relaxed meal after a day at the Louvre and Palais-Royal gardens. Typical of Macéo's style are foie gras with chutney, duck breast with spices and chicory, and almond cake on a bed of mango marmalade—unusually for a French restaurant, it's also vegetarian-friendly. The only downside is the sometimes haughty service. ✉ *15 rue des Petits-Champs, Louvre/Tuileries* ☎ *01–42–97–53–85* ▭ *MC, V* ⊙ *Closed Sun. No lunch Sat.* Ⓜ *Palais-Royal.*

$$–$$$$ ✕ **Au Pied de Cochon.** Part of the Frères Blanc chain, this 24-hour classic is famous for its trademark dishes of breaded pig's trotters with béarnaise and cheesy onion soup (the latter said to cancel out the effects of a boisterous night on the town). The setting is Busby Berkleyesque—wall sconces are adorned with giant bunches of frosted-glass grapes. Though tourists make up the bulk of the clientele, Au Pied de Cochon also attracts a frisky crowd of night owls—club kids, off-duty cops, couples coming up for air—and the terrace is a good spot for people-watching. ✉ *6 rue Coquillière, Beaubourg/Les Halles* ☎ *01–40–13–77–00* ▭ *AE, DC, MC, V* Ⓜ *Les Halles.*

★ $$–$$$$ ✕ **Restaurant du Palais-Royal.** Tucked away in the northeast corner of the magnificent Palais-Royal garden, this pleasant bistro offers traditional cuisine with a few contemporary touches and—most appropriate for a

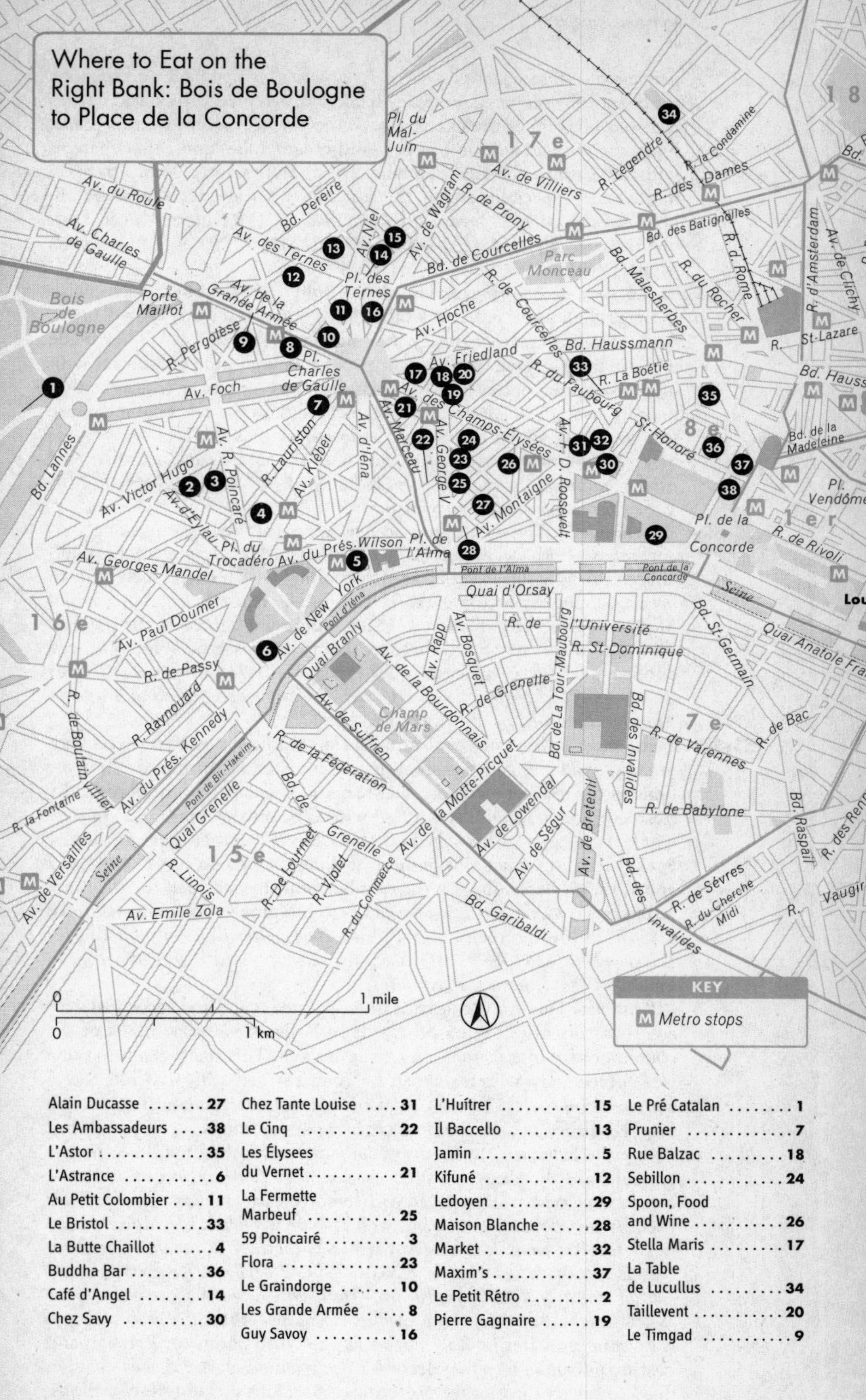

Alain Ducasse 27
Les Ambassadeurs 38
L'Astor 35
L'Astrance 6
Au Petit Colombier 11
Le Bristol 33
La Butte Chaillot 4
Buddha Bar 36
Café d'Angel 14
Chez Savy 30
Chez Tante Louise 31
Le Cinq 22
Les Élysees du Vernet 21
La Fermette Marbeuf 25
59 Poincairé 3
Flora 23
Le Graindorge 10
Les Grande Armée 8
Guy Savoy 16
L'Huîtrer 15
Il Baccello 13
Jamin 5
Kifuné 12
Ledoyen 29
Maison Blanche 28
Market 32
Maxim's 37
Le Petit Rétro 2
Pierre Gagnaire 19
Le Pré Catalan 1
Prunier 7
Rue Balzac 18
Sebillon 24
Spoon, Food and Wine 26
Stella Maris 17
La Table de Lucullus 34
Taillevent 20
Le Timgad 9

prime real-estate situation—a lovely summer terrace. Sole and scallops are beautifully prepared, but juicy steak with symmetrically stacked frites is also a favorite of the expense-account lunchers who love this place. Finish up with an airy puff pastry–and-cream mille-feuille that changes with the seasons—berries in summer, chestnuts in winter. Be sure to book in advance, especially during the summer, when the terrace tables are hotly sought after. ✉ *Jardins du Palais-Royal, 110 Galerie Valois, Louvre/Tuileries* ☎ *01–40–20–00–27* ▭ *AE, MC, V* ⊙ *Closed weekends* Ⓜ *Palais-Royal.*

$–$$$ ✕ **Aux Crus de Bourgogne.** This delightfully old-fashioned bistro, with its bright lights and red-check tablecloths, attracts a lively crowd. Open since 1905, it has been run by the same family since 1932. They made it popular by serving two luxury items—foie gras and cold lobster with homemade mayonnaise—at surprisingly low prices, a tradition that happily continues. Among the bistro classics on the seasonal menu are soul-warming winter dishes such as *boeuf au gros sel* (beef and vegetables in bouillon with rock salt) and confit *de canard* (duck confit). ✉ *3 rue Bachaumont, Beaubourg/Les Halles* ☎ *01–42–33–48–24* ▭ *AE, MC, V* ⊙ *Closed weekends* Ⓜ *Sentier.*

$$–$$$ ✕ **Le Poquelin.** The theater-like scenery gives this little restaurant a welcome that's both elegant and relaxed. Owners Maggie and Michel Guillaumin proudly serve classic French cooking with a twist, such as duck breast topped with foie gras. The popular, regularly changing *menu Molière* is excellent value at €31.25, offering a choice of six starters, six mains (three meat and three fish), and six desserts. Wines are well chosen and fairly priced. ✉ *17 rue Molière, Louvre/Tuileries* ☎ *01–42–96–22–19* ▭ *AE, DC, MC, V* ⊙ *Closed Sun. and 3 wks in Aug. No lunch Mon.* Ⓜ *Palais-Royal.*

$$–$$$ ✕ **Le Safran.** Passionate chef Caroll Sinclair works almost exclusively with organic produce, and her small menu changes according to what she finds in the market—creamy shellfish and spinach soup brightened by fresh coriander, red mullet stuffed with cèpe mushrooms, and *gigot de sept heures* (leg of lamb cooked for seven hours) are some signature dishes. Put yourself in her capable hands by asking for a menu surprise (€27.15 and €39.35, depending on the number of dishes), or ask for the vegetarian menu (€24). Sinclair also caters to budding young gourmets with a €15 children's menu. ✉ *29 rue d'Argenteuil, Louvre/Tuileries* ☎ *01–42–61–25–30* ▭ *MC, V* ⊙ *Closed Sun. and 2 wks in Sept. No lunch Sat.* Ⓜ *Tuileries, Pyramides.*

$ ✕ **L'Ardoise.** This minuscule storefront, painted white and decorated with enlargements of old sepia postcards of Paris, is the very model of the contemporary bistros making waves in Paris. This one's claim to fame is chef Pierre Jay, who trained at La Tour d'Argent. His first-rate three-course menu for €30 (you can also order à la carte) tempts with such original dishes as crab flan in a creamy parsley emulsion and fresh cod with grilled chorizo chips, served on a bed of mashed potatoes. Just as enticing are the desserts, such as a superb *feuillantine au citron*—caramelized pastry leaves filled with lemon cream and lemon slices. With friendly service and a small but well-chosen wine list, L'Ardoise would be perfect if it weren't often crowded and noisy. ✉ *28 rue du Mont Thabor, Beaubourg/Les Halles* ☎ *01–42–96–28–18* ✍ *Reservations essential* ▭ *MC, V* ⊙ *Closed Mon.–Tues. and Aug.* Ⓜ *Concorde.*

Fodor'sChoice ★

$ ✕ **Willi's Wine Bar.** Don't be fooled by the name—this British-owned spot is no modest watering hole but rather a stylish haunt for Parisian and visiting gourmands. The selection of reinvented classic dishes changes daily to reflect the market's offerings and might include fresh scallops, foie gras prepared on the premises, *andouillette* (chitterling sausage), and crème brûlée or a bitter chocolate *terrine* (pudding). Co-owner Mark

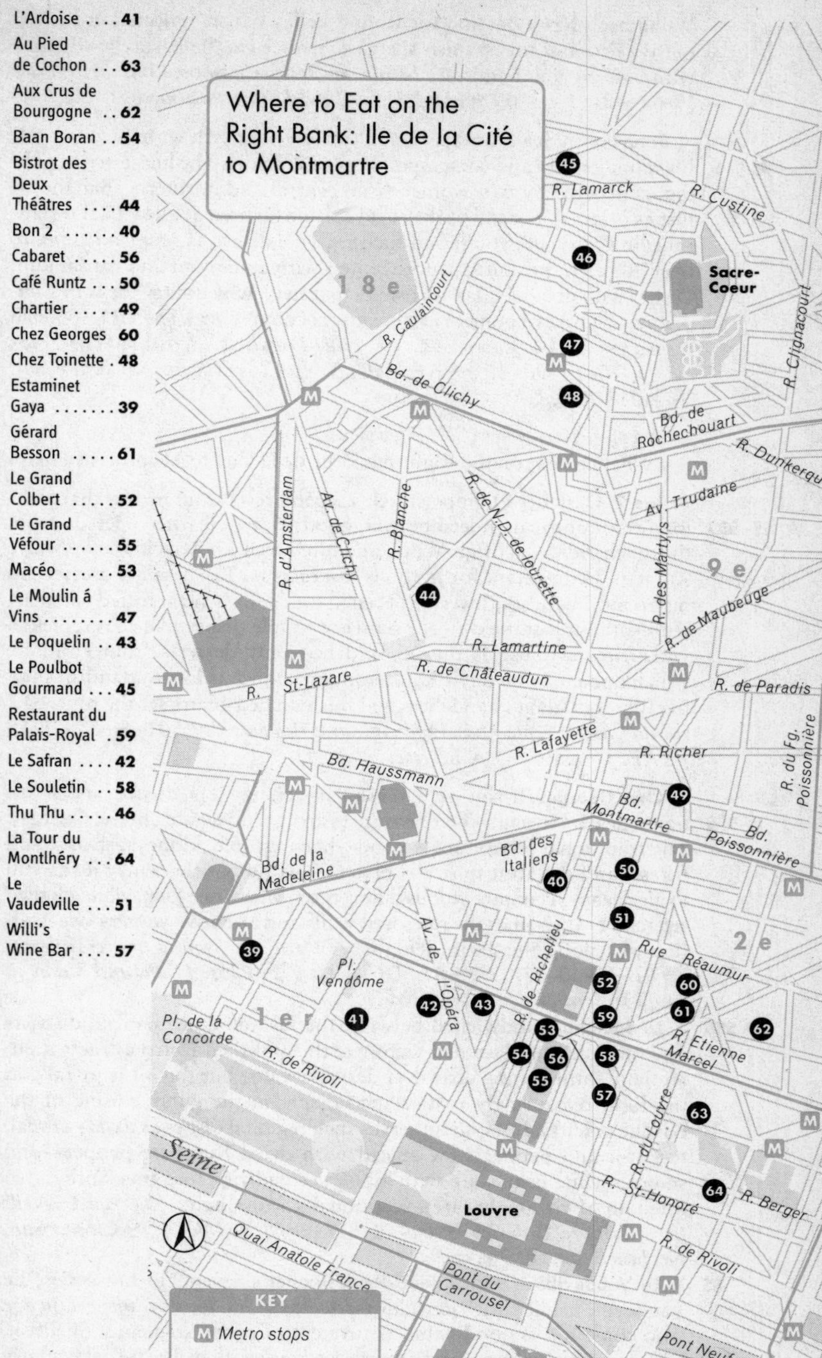

Where to Eat on the Right Bank: Ile de la Cité to Montmartre
L'Ardoise 41
Au Pied de Cochon . . . 63
Aux Crus de Bourgogne . . 62
Baan Boran . . 54
Bistrot des Deux Théâtres 44
Bon 2 40
Cabaret 56
Café Runtz . . . 50
Chartier 49
Chez Georges 60
Chez Toinette . 48
Estaminet Gaya 39
Gérard Besson 61
Le Grand Colbert 52
Le Grand Véfour 55
Macéo 53
Le Moulin á Vins 47
Le Poquelin . . 43
Le Poulbot Gourmand . . . 45
Restaurant du Palais-Royal . 59
Le Safran 42
Le Souletin . . 58
Thu Thu 46
La Tour du Montlhéry . . . 64
Le Vaudeville . . . 51
Willi's Wine Bar 57
R. Lamarck
R. Custine
Sacre-Coeur
18e
R. Caulaincourt
R. Clignacourt
Bd. de Clichy
Bd. de Rochechouart
R. Dunkerque
Av. Trudaine
R. d'Amsterdam
Av. de Clichy
R. Blanche
R. de N.D.-de-lourette
R. des Martyrs
9e
R. de Maubeuge
R. Lamartine
R. de Châteaudun
R. St-Lazare
R. de Paradis
R. Lafayette
R. Richer
Bd. Haussmann
R. du Fg. Poissonnière
Bd. Montmartre
Bd. Poissonnière
Bd. des Italiens
Bd. de la Madeleine
Av. de l'Opéra
R. de Richelieu
Rue Réaumur
2e
Pl. Vendôme
Pl. de la Concorde
1er
R. de Rivoli
R. Etienne Marcel
R. du Louvre
Seine
R. St-Honoré
R. Berger
Louvre
Quai Anatole France
Pont du Carrousel
R. de Rivoli
KEY
Metro stops
Pont Neuf
0 .5 mile
0 .5 km
Bd. St-Germain
Pl. St-Michel
Ile de la Cité

Williamson has a passion for Rhône Valley wines, reflected in the extensive list, and for Spanish sherries. Service can be leisurely, so come with time on your hands. ✉ *13 rue des Petits-Champs, Louvre/Tuileries* ☎ *01–42–61–05–09* ▭ *MC, V* ⊙ *Closed Sun.* Ⓜ *Bourse.*

THAI ★ ¢–$ ✕ **Baan Boran.** Baan Boran steers clear of Thai kitsch with its sunny yellow dining room and contemporary plastic chairs. The home-style cooking, concocted by two women from central and northern Thailand, is just as original. Instead of the royal cuisine favored at most Thai restaurants in Paris, here you'll find such regional dishes as *gaeng mussaman,* beef in a rich, peanutty sauce scented with cinnamon and cardamom. Dishes with no added fat are listed separately: why not try the *yam somo,* tangy chunks of pomelo in a creamy coconut sauce? The €11.50 lunch menu is a bargain. ✉ *17 rue Duphot, Louvre/Tuileries* ☎ *01–40–15–90–45* ▭ *AE, MC, V* ⊙ *Closed Sun. No lunch Sat.* Ⓜ *Palais-Royal.*

2e Arrondissement (La Bourse/Opéra)

See Where to Eat on the Right Bank: Ile de la Cité to Montmartre map.

CONTEMPORARY ★ $$–$$$ ✕ **Bon 2.** Designer Philippe Starck's second restaurant proves that fashion restaurants can indeed be *bon* (good). Starck learned a lesson from the much-ridiculed original Bon and hired well-known chef Jean-Marie Amat as a consultant for both his restaurants. The result is dressed-up bistro food with southwestern French touches, such as stuffed calamari with squid-ink-stained rice. Even very simple dishes like roast chicken with frites are just as they should be—only desserts from Ladurée, which appear to be day-old, disappoint. Bon 2 is less outlandish than the first, but giant chandeliers and mismatched chairs set the tone. ✉ *2 rue du Quatre Septembre, Opéra/Grands Boulevards* ☎ *01–44–55–51–55* ▭ *AE, DC, MC, V* Ⓜ *Bourse.*

FRENCH $$$ ✕ **Chez Georges.** If you were to ask Parisian bankers, aristocrats, or antiques dealers to name their favorite bistro, many would choose Georges. The traditional bistro fare is good—herring, sole, kidneys, steaks, and frites—and the atmosphere is better. A wood-paneled entry leads you to an elegant yet unpretentious dining room where one long, white-clothed stretch of tables lines the mirrored walls and attentive waiters sweep efficiently along the entire length. ✉ *1 rue du Mail, Louvre/Tuileries* ☎ *01–42–60–07–11* ▭ *AE, DC, MC, V* ⊙ *Closed Sun. and 3 wks in Aug.* Ⓜ *Sentier.*

$$–$$$ ✕ **Le Souletin.** Sandwiched between the fashion and financial districts on either side of place des Victoires, this polished bistro attracts a potentially intimidating crowd of designer suits, but the air is jovial and the food reassuringly rustic. Specializing in the gutsy cuisine of the Basque country, Le Souletin serves such regional dishes as *axua*—a veal, tomato, and pepper stew spiced with dried Espelette pepper—and smooth white bean soup with nibbles of panfried foie gras. Sorbets, so often an afterthought, are exceptionally fruity here. ✉ *6 rue La Vrillière, Louvre/Tuileries* ☎ *01–42–61–43–78* ▭ *MC, V* ⊙ *Closed Sun. No lunch Sat.* Ⓜ *Bourse.*

$$ ✕ **Le Vaudeville.** One of Jean-Paul Bucher's seven Flo brasseries, Le Vaudeville is filled with journalists, bankers, and locals *d'un certain âge* who come for its good-value assortment of prix-fixe menus. Shellfish, house-smoked salmon, and desserts such as profiteroles are particularly enticing. Enjoy the handsome 1930s decor—almost the entire interior of this intimate dining room is done in real or faux marble—and lively dining until 1 AM daily. ✉ *29 rue Vivienne, Opéra/Grands Boulevards* ☎ *01–40–20–04–62* ▭ *AE, DC, MC, V* Ⓜ *Bourse.*

L'As du Fallafel **72**
Astier **85**
Au Bourguignon du Marais . . . **77**
Au Camelot . . **88**
Au Trou Gascon **97**
Au Vieux Bistrot **66**
Baracane **89**
Barrio Latino . **95**
Bofinger **90**
La Boulangerie . **84**
Brasserie Flo **68**
Brasserie de L'Ile St-Louis . **76**
Chai 33 . . . . . **91**
Chez Casimir . **67**
Chez Jenny . . . **80**
Chez Marianne . . . **73**
Chez Michel . . **65**
Chez Omar . . . **78**
Les Fernandises . . **81**
Georges **71**
Les Grandes Marches **93**
Grizzli Café . . **70**
Hiramatsu . . . **75**
Julien **69**
Le Kitch **86**
L'Oulette **98**
Le Pamphlet . **79**
Le Passage des Carmagnoles . **94**
Le Pavillon Puebla **82**
Le Repaire de Cartouche . . . **87**
Sardegna a Tavola **99**
Le Square Trousseau . . . **96**
Trumilou **74**
Wok **92**
Le Zéphyr **83**

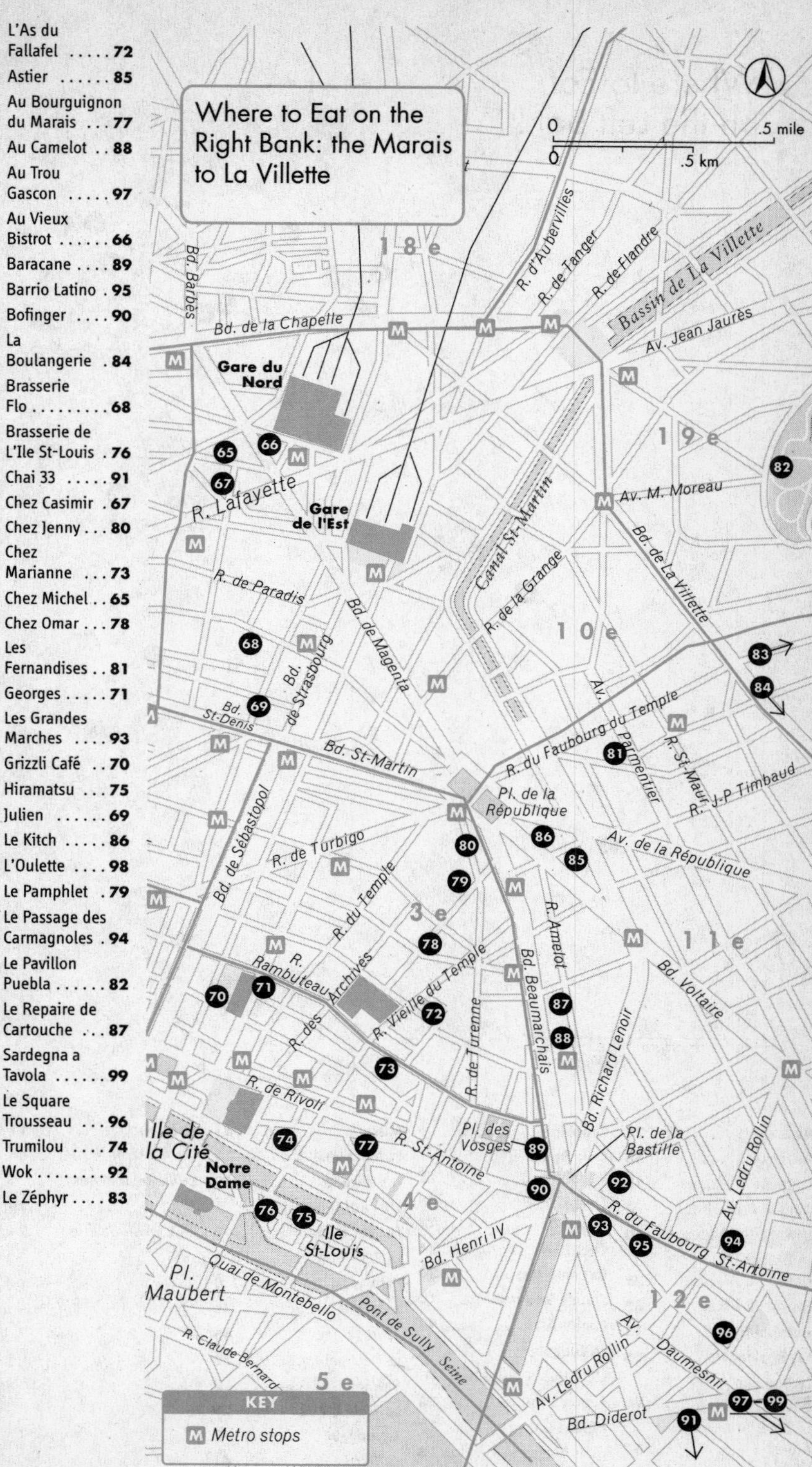

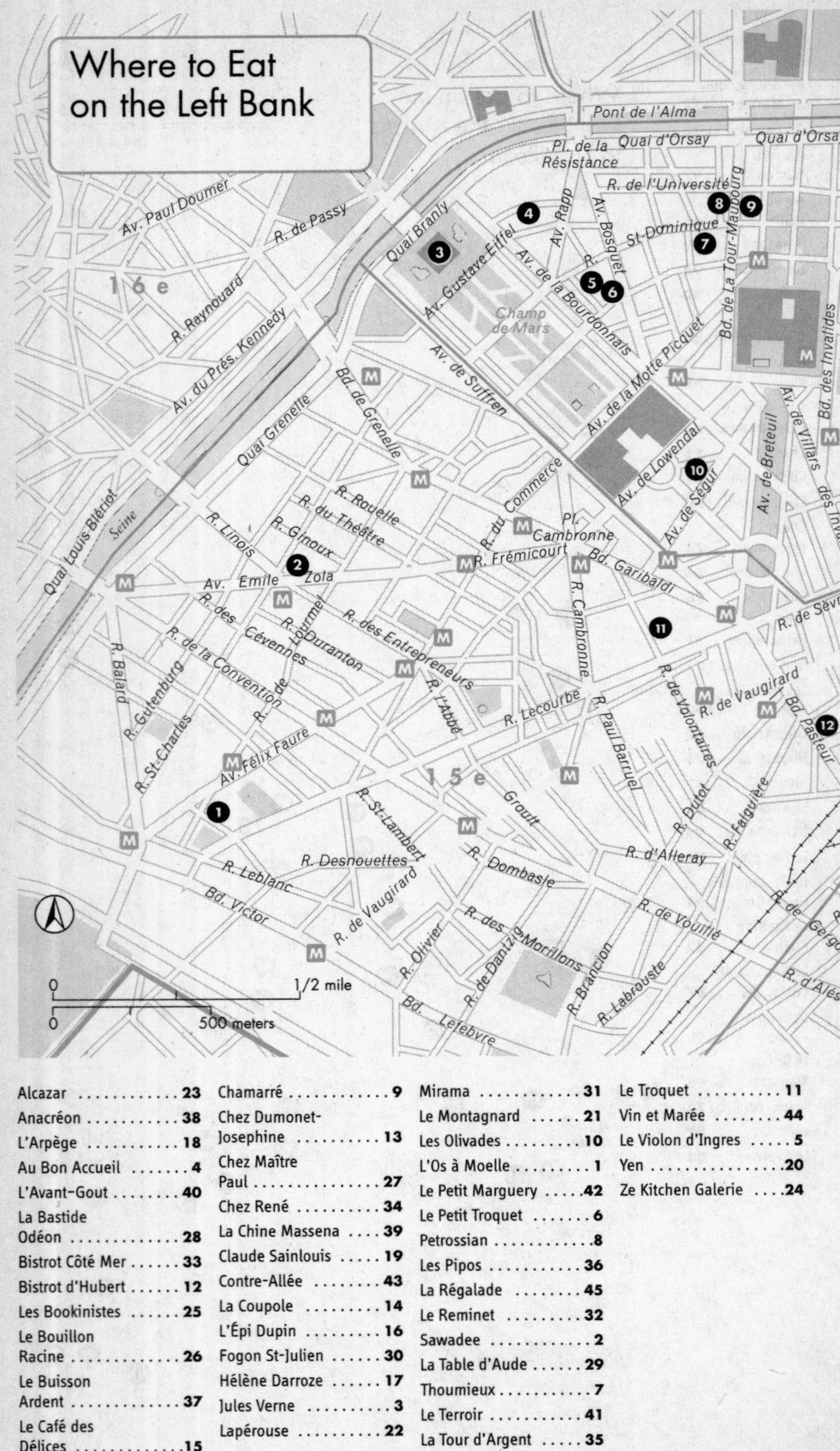

Alcazar 23
Anacréon 38
L'Arpège 18
Au Bon Accueil 4
L'Avant-Gout 40
La Bastide Odéon 28
Bistrot Côté Mer 33
Bistrot d'Hubert 12
Les Bookinistes 25
Le Bouillon Racine 26
Le Buisson Ardent 37
Le Café des Délices 15
Chamarré 9
Chez Dumonet-Josephine 13
Chez Maître Paul 27
Chez René 34
La Chine Massena 39
Claude Sainlouis 19
Contre-Allée 43
La Coupole 14
L'Épi Dupin 16
Fogon St-Julien 30
Hélène Darroze 17
Jules Verne 3
Lapérouse 22
Mirama 31
Le Montagnard 21
Les Olivades 10
L'Os à Moelle 1
Le Petit Marguery 42
Le Petit Troquet 6
Petrossian 8
Les Pipos 36
La Régalade 45
Le Reminet 32
Sawadee 2
La Table d'Aude 29
Thoumieux 7
Le Terroir 41
La Tour d'Argent 35
Le Troquet 11
Vin et Marée 44
Le Violon d'Ingres 5
Yen 20
Ze Kitchen Galerie 24

Louvre
Ile de la Cité
Notre Dame
Ile St-Louis
Jardin du Luxembourg
Jardin des Plantes
Cimetière de Montparnasse
R. St-Honore
R. de Rivoli
Quai de Louvre
Quai Anatole France
Quai de la Mégisserie
Bd. de Sébastapol
Bd. St-Germain
Bd. St-Michel
Bd. du Montparnasse
Bd. de Port Royale
Bd. Raspail
Bd. Arago
Bd. St-Jacques
Bd. Auguste Blanqui
Quai de Montebello
Quai de la Tournelle
Quai de l'Hôtel de Ville
R. de Rennes
R. de Vaugirard
R. du Cherche-Midi
R. de Sèvres
R. de Grenelle
R. de Varenne
R. Jacob
R. du Four
R. des Écoles
R. Mouffetard
R. Monge
R. Cujas
R. Gay Lussac
R. d'Assas
R. de la Santé
Pl. St-Michel
Pl. St-Sulpice
Pl. de l'Odéon
Pl. Maubert
Pl. du Panthéon
Pl. Monge
Pl. d'Italie
Pl. du 18 Juin 1940
1er
3e
4e
5e
6e
7e
13e
14e

CloseUp

RESTAURANT TYPES

*W**HAT'S THE DIFFERENCE** between a bistro and a brasserie? Can you order food at a café? Can you go to a restaurant just for a snack? The following definitions should help.*

*A **restaurant** traditionally serves a three-course meal (first, main, and dessert) at both lunch and dinner. Although this category includes the most formal, three-star establishments, it also applies to more casual neighborhood spots—the line can be fuzzy between bistros and restaurants. In general, restaurants are what you choose when you want a complete meal and have the time to linger over it; don't expect to grab a quick snack. Wine is typically ordered with restaurant meals. Hours are fairly consistent.*

*It has been said that **bistros** served the world's first fast food. After the fall of Napoléon, the Russian soldiers who occupied Paris were known to bang on zinc-topped café bars, crying* bistro*—"quickly" in Russian. In the past, bistros were simple places with minimal fixings and service. Although many nowadays are quite upscale, with beautiful interiors and chic clientele, most remain cozy establishments serving straightforward, frequently gutsy cooking; a wide variety of meats; and long-simmered dishes such as pot-au-feu and veal blanquette.*

***Brasseries**—ideal places for quick, one-dish meals—originated when Alsatians fleeing German occupiers after the Franco-Prussian War came to Paris and opened restaurants serving specialties from home. Pork-based dishes, choucroute (sauerkraut), and beer (brasserie also means brewery) were—and still are—mainstays here. The typical brasserie is convivial and keeps late hours. Some are open 24 hours a day—a good thing to know, since many restaurants stop serving at 10:30 PM.*

*Like bistros and brasseries, **cafés** come in a confusing variety. Often informal neighborhood hangouts, cafés may also be veritable showplaces attracting chic, well-heeled crowds. At most cafés, regulars congregate at the bar, where coffee and drinks are cheaper than at tables. At lunch, tables are set and a limited menu is served. Sandwiches, usually with* jambon *(ham),* fromage *(cheese, often Gruyère or Camembert), or* mixte *(ham and cheese), are served throughout the day. Cafés are for lingering, for people-watching, and for daydreaming; they are listed separately below.*

***Wine bars,** or* bistros à vins*, are a newer phenomenon. These informal places often serve very limited menus, perhaps no more than open-face sandwiches (*tartines*) and selections of cheeses and cold cuts (charcuterie). Owners concentrate on their wine lists, which often include less well-known, regional selections, many of them available by the glass. Like today's bistros and brasseries, some wine bars are very upscale indeed, with full menus and costly wine lists. Still, most remain friendly and unassuming places for sampling wines you might otherwise never have a chance to try.*

$–$$ ✕ **Café Runtz.** Next to the noted theater Salle Favart, in a neighborhood once filled with theaters, this friendly bistro is still gleaming from Jacques Garcia's stage-set makeover a few years ago. Old brass gas lamps on each table and rich *boiseries* (woodwork) create a cozy and Flaubertian mise-en-scène. Tasty, hearty Alsatian dishes include Gruyère salad, onion tart, choucroute, and fresh fruit tarts. Order a pitcher of Riesling or other Alsatian wine to accompany your meal. The two prix-fixe menus are a good value at €18 and €22.50; one of them, the "*Salé-Sucré,*" is served in the evening. ✉ *16 rue Favart, Opéra/Grands Boulevards* ☎ *01–42–96–69–86* ▭ *AE, MC, V* ⊙ *Closed Sun. and Aug.* Ⓜ *Richelieu Drouot.*

$–$$ ✕ **Le Grand Colbert.** One of the few independently owned brasseries remaining in Paris, Le Grand Colbert, with its globe lamps and ceiling moldings, feels grand yet not overpolished—old theater posters still line the walls. The high-ceilinged dining room attracts a wonderfully Parisian mix of elderly lone diners, business lunchers, tourists, and couples, who come for hearty nourishment in the form of steak with frites, robust stews, and well-prepared fish. It's best to stick to classics, though, as this is what the kitchen does best: finish with profiteroles (puff pastry filled with ice cream and smothered in chocolate) or a fluffy chocolate mousse. To aid digestion, stroll through the gorgeous Galerie Vivienne next door, which houses tempting clothing and gift shops. ✉ *2–4 rue Vivienne, Louvre/Tuileries* ☎ *01–42–86–87–88* ▭ *AE, DC, MC, V* Ⓜ *Bourse.*

3ᵉ Arrondissement (République/Marais)

See Where to Eat on the Right Bank: the Marais to La Villette map.

FRENCH ★ $$$ ✕ **Le Pamphlet.** Chef Alain Carrere's modern and very affordable take on the hearty cooking of the Basque and Béarn regions of southwestern France has made this Marais bistro popular with an artsy crowd. Beyond the delicious, homey food, what many Parisians love is the provincial feel, though with its fresh coat of paint and new chairs the beamed room has shed some of its old-fashioned air. The market-fresh prix-fixe menu, which changes daily, runs from first courses such as a carpaccio of duck breast or cream of lentil soup to a juicy pork chop with béarnaise sauce and hand-cut frites. Finish up with a slice of tangy sheep's cheese. ✉ *38 rue Debelleyme, Le Marais* ☎ *01–42–72–39–24* ✍ *Reservations essential* ▭ *MC, V* ⏲ *Closed Sun., 2 wks in Jan., and 2 wks in Aug. No lunch Mon. and Sat.* Ⓜ *St-Sébastien Froissart.*

$–$$$ ✕ **Chez Jenny.** Part of the Frères Blanc group, this classic two-story brasserie is famed for its infectious buzz and outstanding choucroute, delivered weekly by a private supplier in Alsace and served with a panoply of charcuterie and an oversize grilled ham knuckle. To finish, the perfectly aged Muenster cheese and homemade blueberry tart are fine choices. Staff in regional dress add a charming Alsatian touch. ✉ *39 bd. du Temple, République* ☎ *01–44–54–39–00* ▭ *AE, DC, MC, V* Ⓜ *République.*

NORTH AFRICAN $–$$ ✕ **Chez Omar.** Popular with a high-voltage fashion crowd—yes, that is Vivienne Westwood having dinner with Alexander McQueen—this is the place to come for couscous with all the succulent trimmings. Order it with grilled skewered lamb, spicy *merguez* sausage, a lamb shank, or chicken—portions are generous—and wash it down with robust Algerian or Moroccan wine. Proprietor Omar Guerida speaks English and is famously friendly. Since he doesn't take reservations, arrive early or be prepared for a mouthwatering wait. ✉ *47 rue de Bretagne, République* ☎ *01–42–72–36–26* ✍ *Reservations not accepted* ▭ *No credit cards* ⏲ *No lunch Sun.* Ⓜ *Filles du Calvaire.*

4ᵉ Arrondissement (Beaubourg/Marais/Ile St-Louis)

See Where to Eat on the Right Bank: the Marais to La Villette map.

CONTEMPORARY ★ $$$$ ✕ **Hiramatsu.** This jewel of a restaurant overlooking the Seine seats just 18 diners who know by the end of the meal just how lucky they are. Chef Hajime Nakagawa worked for 18 years with Hiroyuki Hiramatsu before being put in charge of this restaurant, one of several run by his boss in Tokyo and abroad. The food proves that Hiramatsu hasn't sacrificed quality to expand his empire—whether you choose the three-course lunch menu for €50 or the eight-course evening *dégustation* for €130, you're in for a rare treat with dishes such as panfried foie gras with an incredible eggplant-lemon confit; sea bass with artichokes and a tomato bouillon; venison with puff pastry, red cabbage, and chestnuts; and a *savarin* with orange cream and coffee granita. Though the food is not outrageously priced, beware the cost of drinks (a glass of wine costs €12 and coffee is €7). ✉ *7 quai de Bourbon, Ile St-Louis* ☎ *01–56–81–08–80* ✍ *Reservations essential* ▭ *AE, DC, MC, V* ⊙ *Closed Sun.–Mon., 3 wks in Aug., and 2 wks at Christmas* Ⓜ *Pont Marie.*

$$$–$$$$ ✕ **Georges.** One of those rooftop, showstopping venues so popular in Paris, Georges stands in stark contrast to its graceful city view from the top floor of the Centre Georges Pompidou. Staff are as sleek and angular as the furniture, and at night the terrace has distinct snob appeal: come snappily dressed or suffer the consequences (you may be relegated to something resembling a dentist's waiting room). Part of the Costes brothers' ever-expanding empire, the establishment trots out predictable fare such as macaroni with morel mushrooms, steak tartare, and raw tuna with a sesame crust. It's all considerably less dazzling than the view, except for desserts by star pâtissier Stéphane Secco, whose YSL (as in Yves St-Laurent, darling) bitter-chocolate cake is an event. ✉ *Centre Pompidou, 6th fl., rue Rambuteau, Beaubourg/Les Halles* ☎ *01–44–78–47–99* ▭ *AE, DC, MC, V* ⊙ *Closed Tues.* Ⓜ *Rambuteau.*

FRENCH $$–$$$ ✕ **Bofinger.** One of the oldest, most beautiful, and most popular brasseries in Paris has generally improved since brasserie maestro Jean-Paul Bucher (of the Flo group) took over. Settle in to one of the tables dressed in crisp white linen under the gorgeous Art Nouveau glass cupola—this part of the dining room is no-smoking—and enjoy classic brasserie fare such as oysters, grilled sole, or lamb fillet. The prix-fixe includes a decent half bottle of red or white wine. ✉ *5–7 rue de la Bastille, Bastille/Nation* ☎ *01–42–72–87–82* ▭ *AE, DC, MC, V* Ⓜ *Bastille.*

$–$$$ ✕ **Brasserie de l'Ile St-Louis.** Set on picturesque Ile St-Louis and opened in 1870—when Alsace-Lorraine was taken over by Germany and its chefs decamped to the capital—this outpost of Alsatian cuisine remains a cozy cocoon filled with stuffed animal heads, antique fixtures fashioned from barrels, and folk-art paintings. The food is gemütlich, too: *coq-au-Riesling,* omelets with Muenster cheese, onion tarts, and choucroutes *garni* (sauerkraut studded with ham, bacon, and pork loin—one variant is made with smoked haddock). Pots of cumin seeds (for sprinkling on Muenster cheese) accompany the salt and pepper shakers on the communal tables, and in warm weather the crowds move out to the terrace overlooking the Seine and Notre-Dame. ✉ *55 quai de Bourbon, Ile St-Louis* ☎ *01–43–54–02–59* ▭ *MC, V* ⊙ *Closed Wed. and Aug. No lunch Thurs.* Ⓜ *Pont Marie.*

$$ ✕ **Trumilou.** Crowds of students, artists, and others on a budget come here to eat bistro cuisine, such as leg of lamb, côte de boeuf for two, and apple tarts—most opt for the bargain prix-fixe at €13.50 or €16.50. The non-decor is somehow homey, the staff is friendly, and the location facing the Seine and the Ile St-Louis is especially pleasant in nice weather, when you can sit on the narrow though noisy terrace under the trees. ✉ *84 quai de l'Hôtel de Ville, Le Marais* ☎ *01–42–77–63–98* ▭ *MC, V* ⊙ *Closed 2 wks in Aug.* Ⓜ *Pont Marie.*

$–$$ ✕ **Au Bourguignon du Marais.** The handsome, contemporary look of this Marais bistro and wine bar is the perfect backdrop for the good traditional fare and excellent Burgundies served by the glass and bottle. Always on the menu are Burgundian classics such as *jambon persillé* (ham in parsleyed aspic jelly), escargots, and *oeufs en meurette* (eggs poached in a red-wine sauce); another favorite is the steak, served grilled or chopped and nicely seasoned in a tartare. ✉ *19 rue de Jouy, Beaubourg/Les Halles* ☎ *01–48–87–15–40* ▭ *AE, MC, V* ⊙ *Closed Sun. No dinner Sat.* Ⓜ *St-Paul.*

$–$$ ✕ **Grizzli Café.** The closing of this beloved 19th-century bistro for renovations sent shudders down the spines of its many French and foreign devotees. The result is, well, not disastrous—much of the historic main-floor dining room has been preserved, while the upstairs has been modernized (though the current owners wisely hung on to the bizarre bear tableau). New chef Eric Lawkang turns out a mix of hearty classics and sprightlier pastas and salads. All-day serving hours are good news—too bad about the thumping music, which sadly makes the place feel like just another trendy Marais bar. ✉ *7 rue St-Martin, Le Marais* ☎ *01–48–87–77–56* ▭ *AE, DC, MC, V* Ⓜ *Châtelet.*

$ ✕ **Baracane.** Come to this small, plain place for the decent food, not the atmosphere, which is scant. The menu is robust, with specialties from the owner's native southwestern France—roast lamb with thyme, cassoulet, and madeleine cakes with stewed rhubarb are three good bets. The reasonable dinner menus and the even cheaper lunch menus keep Baracane solidly affordable and one of the best values in the Marais. However, it's not a good bet for young children—staff suggested that the courtyard (where there are no tables) might be the best place for a baby in a stroller. ✉ *38 rue des Tournelles, Le Marais* ☎ *01–42–71–43–33* ▭ *MC, V* ⏲ *Closed Sun. No lunch Sat.* Ⓜ *Bastille.*

MIDDLE EASTERN ★ ¢–$$ ✕ **Chez Marianne.** You'll know you've found Marianne's place when you see the line of people reading the bits of wisdom and poetry painted across her windows. The restaurant-deli serves excellent Middle Eastern specialties such as hummus, fried eggplant, and soul-warming chopped liver. The sampler platter lets you try four, five, or six items—even the smallest plate makes a filling feast. Falafel is served only at lunch on weekdays in the restaurant, though you can get it every day at the take-out window. ✉ *2 rue des Hospitalières-St-Gervais, Le Marais* ☎ *01–42–72–18–86* ▭ *MC, V* Ⓜ *St-Paul.*

¢–$ ✕ **L'As du Fallafel.** Look no farther than the fantastic falafel stands on rue de Rosiers for some of the cheapest and tastiest meals in Paris. A falafel costs €5, but shell out a little extra money for the "spécial" with grilled eggplant, cabbage, hummus, tahini, and hot sauce. Though take-out is popular, you might find that it's quicker, easier, and more entertaining to eat off a plastic plate in the buzzy dining room. Wash it all down with a glass of fresh lemonade. ✉ *34 rue des Rosiers, Le Marais* ☎ *01–48–87–63–60* ▭ *MC, V* ⏲ *Closed dusk Fri. –dusk Sat. and Jewish holidays* Ⓜ *St-Paul.*

5ᵉ Arrondissement (Latin Quarter)

See Where to Eat on the Left Bank map.

CHINESE ¢–$$ ✕ **Mirama.** Regulars at this popular and rather chaotic Chinese restaurant order the soup, a rich broth with a nest of thick noodles garnished with dumplings, barbecued pork, or smoked duck. Main courses are generous—the best are made with shellfish, and the Peking duck is also excellent. Service is brisk, so plan on coffee in a nearby café. For dining alone, it's quick and easy. ✉ *17 rue St-Jacques, Latin Quarter* ☎ *01–43–29–66–58* ▭ *MC, V* Ⓜ *St-Michel.*

FRENCH ★ $$$$ ✕ **La Tour d'Argent.** Beyond the pretty wonderful food (the current chef is Jean-François Sicallac), many factors conspire to make a meal at this venerable landmark memorable: the extraordinary wine cellar, considerate service, and, of course, that privileged vista across the Seine and beyond. If the price of an à la carte meal makes you pause, you can't go wrong with the €65 lunch—you'll even be entitled to succulent slices of one of the restaurant's numbered ducks (the great duck slaughter began in 1919 and they are well past their millionth mallard, as your numbered certificate will attest). More elaborate prix-fixe menus cost €195 and €225. Don't get too daunted by the wine list—more of a Bible, really—for with the help of one of the famous sommeliers you can splurge a little (about €80) and perhaps taste a rare vintage Burgundy.

CloseUp

WITH CHILDREN?

EATING OUT IS A WAY OF LIFE for Parisians, including children. Although it might not occur to restaurateurs to provide luxuries such as high chairs and coloring books except in overtly child-friendly chains such as Hippopotamus, the French can be extraordinarily welcoming to budding gastronomes. Waiters have been known to give the best table to a group with a small baby, produce child portions of dishes on the menu, heat bottles of milk, and take time to play with youngsters.

You can help the experience by doing some pre-dining homework: If you have room in your suitcase, pack a folding booster seat for a toddler—in the rare cases where high chairs are provided (in some brasseries, such as La Coupole), they are usually missing pieces. Bring toys and coloring books in case your little one starts to get restless. Cigarette smoke is likely to be a problem, so ask for the no-smoking area if such a thing exists.

Where to eat is often as an important question as what to eat: Brasseries are one of the best choices for kids; they're lively and noisy, and provide safe options, such as pomme frites *(French fries), for fussy eaters. Don't feel obliged, though, to choose the most boring dish on the menu, your kids might surprise you and lap up escargots in garlic butter. Créperies are also fun, fast, and quintessentially French: what child can resist a crepe filled with steaming banana and smothered in chocolate sauce? A three-course bistro meal could be a bit tiresome for active kids, but in a slow moment the waiter might be happy to give your child a tour of the kitchen. Or you could try one of the big Chinese restaurants: the magical* **Dragons Elysées** *(✉ 11 rue de Berri ☎ 01–42–89–85–10) near the Arc de Triomphe has aquariums underfoot. For an unforgettable snack, head to the Ile St-Louis for sublime Berthillon ice cream (sold at several cafés with tables, as well as by the cone from the famous shop) or wicked hot chocolate at the fairy-tale tearoom La Charlotte en l'Ile.*

If your kids are older and relatively well-behaved, there is nothing wrong with taking them to a fancier restaurant. Children have often been seen having a fabulous lunch at La Tour d'Argent; this is the kind of meal that could turn your formerly finicky kid into a lifelong gourmet.

The lunch crowd is remarkably casual, while evenings are a more formal affair, attracting a mix of suited tycoons and smoochy couples. *✉ 15 quai de la Tournelle, Latin Quarter ☎ 01–43–54–23–31 Reservations essential Jacket and tie at dinner AE, DC, MC, V Closed Mon. No lunch Tues. M Cardinal Lemoine.*

$$$–$$$$ Fodor's Choice ★ ✕ **Lapérouse.** Émile Zola, George Sand, and Victor Hugo were regulars, and the restaurant's mirrors still bear diamond scratches from the days when mistresses didn't take jewels at face value. It's hard not to fall in love with this 17th-century Seine-side town house, whose warren of intimate, boiserie-graced salons breathes history. The latest chef, Alain Hacquard, has found the right track with a daring (for Paris) spice-infused menu: his lobster, Dublin Bay prawn, and crayfish bisque is flavored with Szechuan pepper and lemon. Game is prominent in fall, with a selection of southwestern wines to accompany dishes like Scottish grouse. For the ultimate romantic meal, reserve one of the legendary private salons where anything could happen (and probably has). ✉ *51 quai des Grands Augustins, Latin Quarter* ☎ *01–43–26–68–04* ✍ *Reservations essential* ▭ *AE, DC, MC, V* ⊙ *Closed Sun., 3 wks in July, and 1 wk in Aug. No lunch Sat.* Ⓜ *St-Michel.*

$$–$$$ ✕ **Bistrot Côte Mer.** Run by celebrated chef Michel Rostang's daughter Caroline, this reasonably priced fish house has become a local hit for the professionalism of its staff, warm decor, and very delicious food. Best bets include a celery and apple rémoulade with fresh scallops, shrimp cooked *à la plancha* (cooked on a stone, Spanish-style), and grilled sea bass with black-olive polenta. End it all with crepes flamboyantly flamed in Grand Marnier or the first-rate cocoa soufflé. The dining room can get a bit noisy when full; the summertime terrace is more peaceful. Good-value weekday lunch menus cost €17 and €22. ✉ *16 bd. St-Germain, Latin Quarter* ☎ *01–43–54–59–10* ▭ *AE, DC, MC, V* ⊙ *Closed 1 wk in Aug.* Ⓜ *Maubert Mutualité.*

★ $–$$$ ✕ **Chez René.** Cozy and appealingly shabby, this reliable address at the eastern end of boulevard St-Germain has satisfied three generations of Parisians who can't resist such Burgundian classics as boeuf bourguignon and coq au vin. As you sit on the red leatherette banquettes, be sure to enjoy some of the Mâconnais and Beaujolais wines available here. Prix-fixe menus cost €28 at lunch, €39.50 at dinner. ✉ *14 bd. St-Germain, Latin Quarter* ☎ *01–43–54–30–23* ▭ *MC, V* ⊙ *Closed Sun., Mon., Christmas wk, and Aug.* Ⓜ *Cardinal Lemoine.*

$–$$ ✕ **Le Buisson Ardent.** Just across the street from the ugly Jussieu campus of the University of Paris, this cozy spot is a good example of how the modern bistro genre is thriving in Paris. The airy front room is a pleasant place for a meal, with a solicitous proprietor, good waiters, and scrumptious food from chef Philippe Duclos. His style shows in such dishes as panfried scallops with vegetable strips, wild duck with spices, and a pork chop with lentils and foie gras. An intellectual set of regulars goes for the budget-smart set menus: €15 at lunch and €28 at dinner. ✉ *25 rue Jussieu, Latin Quarter* ☎ *01–43–54–93–02* ▭ *AE, MC, V* ⊙ *Closed weekends and Aug.* Ⓜ *Jussieu.*

★ $–$$ ✕ **Le Reminet.** Chandeliers and mirrors add an unexpected note of elegance at this relaxed and unusually good bistro set in a narrow salon with stone walls. The menu changes regularly and displays the young chef's talent with dishes like a salad of scallops, greens, and sesame seeds, and roasted guinea hen with buttered savoy cabbage. If it's available, try the luscious caramelized pear with cream. A prix-fixe lunch menu for €13 is served on Monday, Thursday, and Friday, while the dinner menu at €17 is available only on Monday and Thursday. ✉ *3 rue des Grands-Degrés, Latin Quarter* ☎ *01–44–07–04–24* ▭ *MC, V* ⊙ *Closed Tues.–Wed., 1 wk in Feb., and 3 wks in Aug.* Ⓜ *Maubert Mutualité.*

¢–$ ✕ **Les Pipos.** The tourist-traps along romantic rue de la Montagne Ste-
Fodor's Choice ★ Genevieve are enough to make you despair—and then you stumble across this bistro, bursting with chatter and laughter. Slang for students of the famous École Polytechnique nearby, Les Pipos is everything you could ask of a Latin Quarter bistro: the space is cramped, the food is substantial (the cheese comes from the Lyon market), and conversation flows as freely as the wine. Unfortunately, if it gets too crowded you may not be able to get a seat. ✉ *2 rue de L'École Polytechnique, Latin Quarter* ☎ *01–43–54–11–40* ▭ *No credit cards* ⊙ *Closed Sun. and 2 wks in Aug.* Ⓜ *Maubert Mutualité.*

SPANISH ✕ **Fogon St-Julien.** On one of Paris's oldest streets, this intimate, sunny
★ $–$$ yellow restaurant serves outstanding Spanish food. Begin, of course, with some tasty tapas selections; then make a beeline for one of the superb paellas (€18 per person), such as saffron with seafood, inky squid, or Valencia-style with rabbit, chicken, snails, and vegetables. Finish up with

the custardy crème Catalan, accompanied by a glass of Muscatel, or splurge on one of the excellent Riojas. ✉ *10 rue St-Julien-le-Pauvre, Latin Quarter* ☎ *01–43–54–31–33* ✍ *Reservations essential* ▭ *MC, V* ⊙ *Closed Mon. and 3 wks in Aug.* Ⓜ *St-Michel.*

6e Arrondissement (St-Germain-des-Prés/ Montparnasse)

See Where to Eat on the Left Bank map.

CONTEMPORARY
$–$$ ✕ **Le Bouillon Racine.** After a few years as a Belgian restaurant, Le Bouillon Racine has returned to its French roots under new owners. Originally a *bouillon*—one of the Parisian soup kitchens popular at the turn of the 20th century—this two-story restaurant is now a lushly renovated Belle Epoque oasis with a casual setting downstairs and a more lavish upstairs room. The chef has stayed on and now changes his menu every season: lamb knuckle with licorice, a wild boar *parmentier* (like a shepherd's pie, with a layer of mashed potatoes on top and meat underneath), and roast suckling pig were a few warming winter dishes, with chestnut cream spiked with Jack Daniels for dessert. The beer selection is less extensive than in the restaurant's Belgian days, but you'll still find 6 on tap and 10 by the bottle. ✉ *3 rue Racine, St-Germain-des-Prés* ☎ *01–44–32–15–60* ✍ *Reservations essential* ▭ *AE, MC, V* Ⓜ *Odéon.*

$–$$ Fodor'sChoice ★ ✕ **Ze Kitchen Galerie.** Baby bistros grow up so fast—now they're even spawning their own offshoots. William Ledeuil made his name at the popular Les Bookinistes (a Guy Savoy baby) before opening this pared-down contemporary bistro nearby. If the name isn't exactly inspired, the cooking shows unbridled creativity and a sense of fun: from a deliberately deconstructed menu featuring raw fish, soups, pastas, and "à la plancha" plates, expect dishes such as a chicken wing, broccoli, and artichoke soup with lemongrass or pork ribs with curry jus and white beans. Not for those who are set in their ways, this restaurant changes its menu every five weeks and its art exhibit every three months. ✉ *4 quai des Grands-Augustins, Latin Quarter* ☎ *01–44–32–00–32* ▭ *AE, DC, MC, V* ⊙ *Closed Sun. No lunch Sat.* Ⓜ *St-Michel.*

★ $ ✕ **Le Café des Délices.** There is a lot to like about this bistro, from the Art Nouveau facade and the warm and spacious Asia-meets-Africa decor (lots of dark wood and little pots of spices on each table), to the polished service and lip-smacking food. Drop in for the bargain €14 lunch (the plat du jour with a glass of wine and coffee), or indulge in à la carte dishes such as sea bream on white beans cooked with anchovy, lemon, coriander, and chili pepper. Tongue-in-cheek comfort-food desserts tout such ingredients such as Chupa Chups (lollipops) and sugary cereal. ✉ *87 rue d'Assas, Montparnasse* ☎ *01–43–54–70–00* ▭ *AE, MC, V* ⊙ *Closed Aug.* Ⓜ *Vavin.*

FRENCH
$$$–$$$$ ✕ **Hélène Darroze.** Hélène Darroze has won a lot of followers with her refined take on southwestern French cooking, from the lands around Albi and Toulouse. You know it's not going to be *la meme chanson*—the same old song—as soon as you see the contemporary Tse & Tse tableware, and her intriguingly modern touch comes through in such dishes as a sublime duck foie gras confit served with chutney of exotic fruits, or a blowout of roast wild duck stuffed with foie gras and truffles. The downstairs bistro offers similar food in (even) smaller, tapas-style portions, but you can still expect to pay €60–€65 per person with wine. ✉ *4 rue d'Assas, St-Germain-des-Prés* ☎ *01–42–22–00–11* ▭ *AE, DC, MC, V* ⊙ *Closed Sun.–Mon.* Ⓜ *Sèvres Babylone.*

$$$ ✕ **La Bastide Odéon.** A face-lift has breathed new life into this popular Provençal bistro near the Luxembourg Gardens, opening up the kitchen so diners in the freshly renovated room can admire the cooks at work.

Chef Gilles Ajuelos has a fine, loving hand with Mediterranean cuisine—expect fine fish dishes; wonderful pastas, such as tagliatelle in *pistou* (basil and pine nuts) with wild mushrooms; and heartwarming main courses such as roast suckling pig and cod with capers. ✉ *7 rue Corneille, St-Germain-des-Prés* ☎ *01–43–26–03–65* ▭ *AE, MC, V* ⊙ *Closed Sun.–Mon., 1st wk in Jan., and 3 wks in Aug.* Ⓜ *Odéon; RER: Luxembourg.*

$$–$$$ ✕ **Alcazar.** To take in the scene at Sir Terence Conran's brasserie—and quite a scene it is, as this place seats 300 under a skylight roof—opt for a table on the mezzanine, where a long, brushed-steel bar gives you a bird's-eye view. Chef Guillaume Lutard trained at Taillevent and Prunier, and it shows in the quality of the food, which ranges from "so British" fish-and-chips to contemporary French dishes. Lunch menus are available for €15–€25, and you can also snack in the bar. If you got carried away on Saturday night, brunch, served up with a soothing hand massage, is the perfect antidote. ✉ *62 rue Mazarine, St-Germain-des-Prés* ☎ *01–53–10–19–99* ▭ *AE, DC, MC, V* Ⓜ *Odéon.*

$$–$$$ ✕ **Les Bookinistes.** Now run by chef William Cosimo (who took over from William Ledeuil when he moved to Ze Kitchen Galerie next door), this is the most popular of Guy Savoy's "baby bistros." You can expect to hear more English than French in the cheery dining room looking out onto the Seine, but the food—such as mussel and pumpkin soup or baby chicken roasted in a casserole with root vegetables—is as authentic as you could hope for. Only the vegetarian option disappoints: unimaginative steamed vegetables drizzled with olive oil. The rather expensive wine list contrasts with the reasonable food prices. Service is friendly but erratic and occasionally overfamiliar. ✉ *53 quai des Grands-Augustins, St-Germain-des-Prés* ☎ *01–43–25–45–94* ▭ *AE, DC, MC, V* ⊙ *Closed Sun. and Christmas wk. No lunch Sat.* Ⓜ *St-Michel.*

$$–$$$ ✕ **Chez Dumonet–Josephine.** Stylish and convivial, this venerable bistro with amber walls, moleskin banquettes, and frosted glass lamps is popular with theater people and politicians. Generous portions of classic French cuisine are served; typical are the very good boeuf bourguignon and the roasted saddle of lamb with artichokes. The wine list is excellent but expensive. ✉ *117 rue du Cherche-Midi, St-Germain-des-Prés* ☎ *01–45–48–52–40* ▭ *AE, MC, V* ⊙ *Closed weekends, 3 wks in Aug., Christmas wk, and 1 wk in Feb.* Ⓜ *Duroc.*

$$–$$$ ✕ **Chez Maître Paul.** This calm, comfortable spot is a great place to discover the little-known cooking of the Jura and Franche-Comté regions of eastern France. Though sturdy, this cuisine appeals to modern palates, too, as you'll discover with the *montbéliard,* a smoked sausage served with potato salad, ample enough for two. Also try one of the succulent free-range chicken dishes, either in a sauce of *vin jaune*—a dry wine from the region that resembles sherry—or baked in cream and cheese. The walnut meringue is sinfully wonderful, and the regional Arbois wines are not the usual selection. ✉ *12 rue Monsieur-le-Prince, St-Germain-des-Prés* ☎ *01–43–54–74–59* ▭ *AE, DC, MC, V* ⊙ *Closed July–Aug. and Dec. 20–27* Ⓜ *Odéon.*

$$–$$$ ✕ **L'Épi Dupin.** Other bistros are more welcoming, but L'Épi Dupin's cramped, beamed dining room continues to attract an eager crowd of tourists and Gaultier-clad locals who don't seem to mind waiting in the rain for their reserved tables. The prix-fixe-only menu of updated French classics is revised regularly and might include an upside-down tart of caramelized Belgian endive and goat cheese, curried saddle of rabbit with sweet-potato chutney, and crisp, pyramid-shape pastry filled with apples and candied fennel for dessert. ✉ *11 rue Dupin, St-Germain-des-Prés* ☎ *01–42–22–64–56* ✍ *Reservations essential* ▭ *AE, MC, V* ⊙ *Closed weekends and Aug. No lunch Mon.* Ⓜ *Sèvres Babylone.*

$$ ✕ **Claude Sainlouis.** This cheerful spot has served the same dependable food for a very long time: côte de boeuf for two, lamb knuckle, pork with lentils, and salad. Most of the locals and tourists who add their own boisterous color to the discreetly lit red dining room come here to refuel on the €25 prix-fixe. ✉ *27 rue du Dragon, St-Germain-des-Prés* ☎ *01–45–48–29–68* ▭ *MC, V* ⊙ *Closed Sun.–Mon. and Aug.* Ⓜ *St-Germain-des-Prés.*

★ $$ ✕ **La Table d'Aude.** Rive Gauche students, senators, and book editors who dine here are on to a good thing, since this jolly restaurant serves some of the best *cuisine régionale* in Paris. Owner Bernard Patou and his wife Véronique take a contagious pleasure in serving up the best of their home turf—the Aude, a long, narrow region in the Languedoc-Roussillon. Almost everyone orders the cassoulet, bubbling hot in a small, high-sided ceramic dish and filled to the brim with white beans, sausage, and preserved duck. Of the house wines, go with the rich, cherry-color Corbières. Good-value prix-fixe menus are also available at lunch and dinner. ✉ *8 rue de Vaugirard, St-Germain-des-Prés* ☎ *01–43–26–36–36* ▭ *MC, V* ⊙ *Closed Sun. and Aug. No lunch Sat., no dinner Mon.* Ⓜ *Odéon.*

$–$$ ✕ **Le Montagnard.** This rustic little spot—"The Mountaineer"—attracts a hip, festive crowd that comes to dine on fondue and *raclette* (cheese melted on potatoes) before hitting the many local bars. Split an *assiette montagnard,* an appetizing assortment of Savoyard cold cuts such as *viande de Grisons* (air-dried beef), and then go for the cheese or beef fondue. And bear in mind a little tip from the mountains: fresh black pepper makes a cheese meal much more digestible. ✉ *24 rue des Canettes, St-Germain-des-Prés* ☎ *01–43–26–47–15* ▭ *AE, MC, V* ⊙ *Closed Aug.* Ⓜ *Mabillon.*

JAPANESE
★ $–$$ ✕ **Yen.** If you're having what is known in French as a *crise de foie* (liver crisis)—the result of overindulging in rich food—this Japanese noodle house offers the perfect antidote. The blond-wood walls soothe the senses, the staff are happy to explain the proper slurping technique, and the soba (buckwheat noodles), served in soup or with a restorative broth for dipping, will give you the courage to face another round of caramelized foie gras. ✉ *22 rue St-Benoît, St-Germain-des-Prés* ☎ *01–45–44–11–18* ▭ *AE, MC, V* ⊙ *Closed 2 wks in Aug. No lunch Sun.–Mon.* Ⓜ *St-Germain-des-Prés.*

7e Arrondissement (Invalides)

See Where to Eat on the Left Bank map.

CONTEMPORARY
$$$–$$$$ ✕ **Petrossian.** Twentysomething chef Sebastien Faré took over in late 2002 from Philippe Conticini, who had injected this swish and rather sober-looking Russian-theme restaurant with his wildly imaginative style. Conticini remains a consultant to Petrossian, which is good news for its *gauche caviar* clientele. Smoked fish and caviar star, but another of his winning concoctions is fried frogs' legs and snails in garlic sauce. Don't miss the "drinkable perfumes," an almost magical approach to palate-cleansing. ✉ *18 bd. de La Tour-Maubourg, Eiffel Tower/Trocadéro* ☎ *01–44–11–32–32* ▭ *AE, DC, MC, V* ⊙ *Closed Sun., Mon., and 3 wks in Aug.* Ⓜ *La Tour-Maubourg, Invalides.*

★ $$ ✕ **Chamarré.** Chamarré means "richly colored," and that perfectly describes the cooking at this classy, if slightly too formal restaurant run by two Alain Passard–trained cooks. Antoine Heerah is Mauritian and Jérôme Bodereau is French—the result is artfully presented food that draws on exotic ingredients such as combawa (a type of lime), green mango, and curry spices. At lunch, a three-course "business menu" for € 30 allows you to sample a limited selection of dishes available on the standard menu, where curry-infused cream enlivens a Jerusalem artichoke velouté and chicken cooked with curry leaves is bathed in a frothy sauce. A plate of cèpe mushrooms comes as a generous surprise interlude, and a beautiful poached pear with star anise and a red wine granité brings the unusual meal to a happy end. ✉ *13 bd. de La Tour-Maubourg, Invalides/Eiffel Tower* ☎ *01–47–05–50–18* ▭ *AE, MC, V* ⊙ *Closed Sun., Aug., and Dec. 22–28. No lunch Sat.* Ⓜ *La Tour-Maubourg, Invalides.*

FRENCH $$$$ ✕ **L'Arpège.** Alain Passard, one of the most respected chefs in Paris, famously shocked the French culinary world by declaring that he was bored with meat and fish. Though his vegetarianism is more theoretical than practical—L'Arpège still caters to carnivores—he does cultivate his own vegetables outside Paris, which are zipped into the city by high-speed train. His dishes elevate the humblest vegetables to sublime heights: beets are served with aged balsamic vinegar, leeks with black truffles, black radishes and cardoon with *Rarmigiano Reggiano.* Whether this justifies the shocking prices depends on how much disposable income you have to flambé. ✉ *84 rue de Varenne, Invalides/Eiffel Tower* ☎ *01–45–51–47–33* ▭ *AE, DC, MC, V* ⊙ *Closed weekends* Ⓜ *Varenne.*

$$$$ ✕ **Jules Verne.** Top-flight chef Alain Reix's cuisine, not to mention a location 400 ft high—on the second level of the Eiffel Tower—makes a table at the Jules Verne one of the hardest dinner reservations to get in Paris. Sautéed baby squid with foie gras and veal filet mignon cooked with preserved lemon and dried fruits are examples of Reix's cooking. A mere €49 will buy you the Jules Verne experience at lunch (weekdays only), though the food doesn't live up to the à la carte offerings. An evening menu at €110 is served every day. A table is easier to snag at lunch—arrive early for a prime seat near the window, and be prepared for the distinctive all-black decor, a rather strange and tired hybrid of *Star Trek* and '70s disco (where else in Paris can you still find octagonal black plates?). Though service has been variable in the past, on recent visits the waiters showed exceptional good humor and patience. ✉ *Eiffel Tower, Invalides/Eiffel Tower* ☎ *01–45–55–61–44* ✍ *Reservations essential* 👔 *Jacket and tie* ▭ *AE, DC, MC, V* Ⓜ *Bir-Hakeim.*

★ $$$$ ✕ **Le Violon d'Ingres.** Christian Constant, former head of the Hôtel Crillon's kitchens and mentor to many a successful bistro chef, runs his own dressed-up bistro in one of the quieter but elegant parts of the city. A suit-clad crowd comes to sample the regularly revised menu, which may include such dishes as cream of pumpkin soup with sheep's cheese, risotto with boned chicken wings, and guinea hen on a bed of diced turnips. Constant has revamped the sleek decor, and his reliable presence in the kitchen ensures a high standard. ✉ *135 rue St-Dominique, Invalides/Eiffel Tower* ☎ *01–45–55–15–05* ✍ *Reservations essential* ▭ *AE, DC, MC, V* ⊙ *Closed Sun. and 3 wks in Aug. No lunch Sat. and Mon.* Ⓜ *École Militaire.*

★ $$–$$$ ✕ **Au Bon Accueil.** To see what well-heeled Parisians like to eat these days, book a table at this extremely popular bistro as soon as you get to town. The excellent, reasonably priced *cuisine du marché* (a daily, market-inspired menu, €25 at lunch and €29 at dinner) has made it a hit: typical of the winter fare is roast suckling pig with thyme and endives. Desserts are homemade and delicious, from the fruit tarts to the superb *pistache,* a pastry curl filled with homemade pistachio ice cream. True to the bistro's name ("the good welcome"), the owners admirably chose not to bump up prices with the arrival of the euro. ✉ *14 rue de Montessuy, Invalides/Eiffel Tower* ☎ *01–47–05–46–11* ✍ *Reservations essential* ▭ *MC, V* ⊙ *Closed weekends and 2 wks in Aug.* Ⓜ *Métro or RER: Pont de l'Alma.*

$$–$$$ ✕ **Thoumieux.** Delightfully Parisian, this place charms with red-velour banquettes, yellow walls, and bustling waiters in white aprons. Budget prices for rillettes, duck confit, and cassoulet make Thoumieux—owned by the same family for three generations—popular. Don't come with lofty expectations but for a solid, gently priced meal (the prix-fixe menu costs €31 at lunch and dinner). ✉ *79 rue St-Dominique, Invalides/Eiffel Tower* ☎ *01–47–05–49–75* ▭ *AE, MC, V* ⊙ *Closed Christmas wk* Ⓜ *Invalides.*

$ ✕ **Le Petit Troquet.** In the shadow of the Eiffel Tower is this tiny, pleasant bistro filled with homey antiques like old tin signs for clocks and soda siphons. The prix-fixe-only menu for €27 changes daily, but may include such dishes as goat-cheese mousse with smoked salmon, roast chicken, and fruit crumble for dessert. It's popular with locals, so book ahead. ✉ *28 rue de l'Exposition, Invalides/Eiffel Tower* ☎ *01–47–05–80–39* ✍ *Reservations essential* ▭ *MC, V* ⊙ *Closed Sun. and 3 wks in Aug. No lunch Mon. and Sat.* Ⓜ *École Militaire.*

8e Arrondissement (Champs-Élysées)

See Where to Eat on the Right Bank: Bois du Boulogne to Place de la Concorde map.

CONTEMPORARY $$$$ ✕ **Maison Blanche.** The celebrated twin Pourcel brothers (Laurent and Jacques) of Le Jardin des Sens in Montpellier preside over this hip "White House," which basks in its show-off view across Paris from the top floor of the Théâtre du Champs- Élysées. The food offers a refreshing taste of the south: hot and iced tomatoes on a pumpkin puree with fresh truffles, scallop carpaccio with sea-urchin coral, and Swiss-chard ravioli with tomato confit. Desserts such as a caramel popsicle with pecan cake attest to the chefs' sense of humor, which doesn't seem to be shared by the stony-faced staff. ✉ *15 av. Montaigne, Champs-Élysées* ☎ *01–47–23–55–99* ▭ *AE, DC, MC, V* ⊙ *Closed Sun. and 3 wks in Aug. No lunch Sat.* Ⓜ *Franklin-D.-Roosevelt.*

★ $$$–$$$$ ✕ **Market.** Celebrated New York–based Alsatian chef Jean-Georges Vongerichten (think Vong, Mercer Kitchen, Jean-Georges, and JoJo) set up shop in this strategic neighborhood to much fanfare, as this is his first restaurant in France. Put together with deceptively simple raw materials—burnt pine and stone offset with African masks—the dining room makes a stylish and relaxed, if sometimes noisy arena for well-traveled dishes such as pizza with raw tuna and wasabi cream, Thai-style chicken-coconut soup with galangal, and duck fillet with sesame jus and tamarind confit. Politicians and power shoppers are delighted—the dining room has been packed since it opened. A meal here is most affordable at lunch, when menus are available for €32 and €39. ✉ *15 av. Matignon, Champs-Élysées* ☎ *01–56–43–40–90* ▭ *AE, MC, V* Ⓜ *Franklin-D.-Roosevelt.*

$$$–$$$$ ✕ **Spoon, Food and Wine.** Star chef Alain Ducasse's bistro may be the granddaddy of style-conscious restaurants around the Champs-Élysées, but its popularity shows no signs of waning. What draws the black-clad crowd are the playful, Asian- and American-inspired menu; the hyper-cool interior (white by day, plum by night); and the fact that it's so hard to get a reservation (you can always drop by for a snack at the bar). For a quick fashion hit, opt for the 40-minute "Speedy Spoon" menu (€37.35, or €46.50 with a glass of wine), which continent-hops every weekday: Africa on Monday, Europa on Tuesday, and so on. High-style vegetarians love this place for its many vegetable, pasta, and grain dishes. Come late for the models and movie stars. ✉ *14 rue de Marignan, Champs-Élysées* ☎ *01–40–76–34–44* ✍ *Reservations essential* ▭ *AE, MC, V* ⊙ *Closed weekends and 4 wks in July–Aug.* Ⓜ *Franklin-D.-Roosevelt.*

★ $$–$$$ ✕ **Flora.** Flora Mikula made her name at Les Olivades, a Provençal bistro in the 7e, before joining a gaggle of ambitious restaurateurs in this ultrachic neighborhood. Moving away from the bistro register, she is turning out refined food with Mediterranean and Asian twists in a setting that feels just a little too staid, despite the gorgeous plaster moldings—paintings instead of mirrors might warm up the rooms. Standout dishes in the €50 *dégustation* menu (lunch and dinner) are chorizo ravioli with *merguez* (spicy sausage) sauce, roasted tuna with zucchini-flower fritters, and *pain perdu* (French toast) with honey-sweet mirabelle plums. Service, like the food, is impeccable. ✉ *36 av. George V, Champs-Élysées* ☎ *01–40–70–10–49* ✍ *Reservations essential* 💳 *AE, MC, V* ⏲ *Closed Sun. No lunch Sat.* Ⓜ *Franklin-D.-Roosevelt.*

FRENCH $$$$ Fodor'sChoice ★ ✕ **Alain Ducasse.** You may need to set a steel trap outside his door actually to catch megastar chef Alain Ducasse in this kitchen—he now has restaurants around the globe (and never cooks on weekends)—but it would probably be worth the wait. The rosy Rococo salons in the Hôtel Plaza Athenée were updated by decorator Patrick Jouin, who draped metallic organza over the chandeliers and, in a symbolic move, made time stand still by stopping the clock. Overlooking the prettiest courtyard in Paris, this makes for a setting as delicious as Ducasse's roast lamb garnished with "crumbs" of dried fruit, or duckling roasted with fig leaves. When you sample the *bisque de homard* (lobster bisque) or the pork belly, you know you are getting the real thing—each is made from as many elements (shell, skin, juice, pan drippings) as possible and offers the absolute essence of the ingredients. At these prices, the level of presentation—there are few visual adornments on the plate—could be enhanced. To be on the safe side, reserve weeks in advance. ✉ *Hôtel Plaza Athenée, 27 av. Montaigne, Champs-Élysées* ☎ *01–53–67–66–65* *Jacket required* 💳 *AE, DC, MC, V* ⏲ *Closed weekends, Christmas wk, 2 wks in July, and 3 wks in Aug. No lunch Mon.–Wed.* Ⓜ *Alma-Marceau.*

★ $$$$ ✕ **Les Ambassadeurs.** Looking as if Madame de Pompadour might stroll in the door at any moment, Les Ambassadeurs is Paris in full ancien-régime dress. With its dramatic black-and-white diamond floor and honey-color marble walls, the place is polished and furnished to such a degree it would still make Louis XV (who had it built in 1758) proud. Chef Dominique Bouchet likes to mix luxe with more down-to-earth flavors: potato pancakes topped with smoked salmon, caviar-flecked scallops wrapped in bacon with tomato and basil, duck with rutabaga, turbot with cauliflower. The €62 lunch menu is well worth the splurge—especially in summer, when you can while away the rest of the afternoon on the gorgeous terrace. There is even a breakfast—talk about luxury—served from 7 to 10:30 AM. ✉ *10 pl. de la Concorde, Louvre/Tuileries* ☎ *01–44–71–16–16* *Jacket and tie* 💳 *AE, DC, MC, V* Ⓜ *Concorde.*

$$$$ ✕ **L'Astor.** Chef Eric Lecerf pays homage to his mentor, Joël Robuchon, by offering some classic Robuchon dishes such as cauliflower cream with caviar and spiced roasted lobster. But he also shows his own talent with sophisticated offerings like sole with baby squid and artichokes. The service and wine list are superb. Trendy interior designer Frédérique Méchiche is responsible for the spacious and attractive dining room, which takes a cue from the '30s with star appliqués on the walls and a checkerboard carpet. The €50 prix-fixe lunch menu is great value. ✉ *Hôtel Astor, 11 rue d'Astorg, Opéra/Grands Boulevards* ☎ *01–53–05–05–20* 💳 *AE, DC, MC, V* ⏲ *Closed weekends and Aug.* Ⓜ *Madeleine.*

★ $$$$ ✕ **Le Bristol.** After a rapid ascent at his own nouvelle-wave bistro that led to his renown as one of the more inventive young chefs in Paris, Eric

Frechon became head chef at the Bristol, that home-away-from-home of billionaires and power brokers. Frechon uses one of the grandest pantries in Paris to create masterworks—ravioli of foie gras in mushroom cream with truffles, or scallops on a bed of diced celery root in truffle juice—that never stray too far away from the comfort-food tastes found in bistro cooking: no wonder his tables are so coveted. Courtly service and two beautiful dining rooms—an oval oak-paneled one for fall and winter and a marble-floored pavilion overlooking the courtyard garden for spring and summer—make this a top destination for a memorable meal. Unusually for a luxury restaurant, Le Bristol has a not-extortionate evening menu for €60. ✉ *Hôtel Bristol, 112 rue du Faubourg St-Honoré, Champs-Élysées* ☎ *01–53–43–43–00* *Reservations essential* *Jacket and tie* ▭ *AE, DC, MC, V* Ⓜ *Miromesnil.*

★ $$$$ ✕ **Le Cinq.** The massive flower arrangement at the entrance proclaims the no-holds-barred luxury that is on offer here. Painted powder-blue, with stuccoed medallions worked into the ceiling trim, this beautiful though staid room makes a fitting stage set for chef Philippe Legendre. Formerly a legend at Taillevent, he is clearly thriving in these kitchens, where he has apparently been given carte blanche. His fricassee of Breton lobster is astounding as is his *amuse-bouche* of a single oyster sublimated by truffle and caviar. Occasionally, the luxe menu is brought back down to earth by such heady selections as *lièvre à la royale*—hare and mashed potatoes. ✉ *Hôtel Four Seasons George V, 31 av. George V, Champs-Élysées* ☎ *01–49–52–70–00* *Reservations essential* *Jacket and tie* ▭ *AE, DC, MC, V* Ⓜ *George V.*

$$$$ Fodor'sChoice ★ ✕ **Les Élysées du Vernet.** Eric Briffard found himself out in the cold when Alain Ducasse took over the Plaza Athenée's kitchens—he has now found a suitably grand setting for his talents in the form of this intimate dining room, whose gorgeous *verrière* (glass ceiling) was designed by none other than Gustave Eiffel. Bringing together prosaic and luxury ingredients, Briffard is making his mark with dishes such as truffled pig's trotter, foie gras on toast, monkfish with ginger and lime, and potato salad with truffles. This restaurant remains relatively affordable at lunch (€45 or €60 for a set menu), and the wine service is outstanding. ✉ *Hôtel Vernet, 25 rue Vernet, Champs-Élysées* ☎ *01–44–31–98–98* *Reservations essential* ▭ *AE, DC, MC, V* ⊙ *Closed weekends, Aug., and 2 wks in Dec.* Ⓜ *George V.*

$$$$ ✕ **Ledoyen.** This elegant restaurant tucked away in the quiet gardens flanking the Champs-Élysées was once a study in the grandiose style of Napoléon III (you'll find most of the historic rooms upstairs; avoid downstairs). Unfortunately, this aging beauty needs a face-lift, at least from the look of the upholstery. Still, whether you want to eat light or hearty, young chef Christian Le Squer's elegant, beautifully realized menu is a treat; especially the well-priced lunch prix-fixe at €58. He uses superb produce, as seen in *les coquillages* (shellfish), a delicious dish of herb risotto topped with lobster, langoustine, scallops, and grilled ham. The turbot with truffled mashed potatoes is excellent, too, and don't skip the first-rate cheese trolley. ✉ *1 av. Dutuit, on the Carré des Champs-Élysées, Champs-Élysées* ☎ *01–53–05–10–01* *Reservations essential* ▭ *AE, DC, MC, V* ⊙ *Closed weekends* Ⓜ *Concorde, Champs-Élysées–Clemenceau.*

$$$$ ✕ **Maxim's.** Count Danilo sang "I'm going to Maxim's" in Lehar's *The Merry Widow,* Leslie Caron was klieg-lit here by Cecil Beaton for *Gigi,* and Audrey Hepburn adorned one of its banquettes with Peter O'Toole in *How to Steal a Million.* In reality, Maxim's has lost some of its luster—the restaurant had its heyday 100 years ago during La Belle Epoque, when *le tout Paris* swarmed here—but this exuberant Art Nouveau sanc-

tuary still offers a taste of the good life under its breathtaking painted ceiling. Opened in 1893 by Maxime Gaillard, Maxim's has belonged to designer Pierre Cardin since 1981 (who proceeded to clone Maxim's around the world, greatly tarnishing the allure of this home base). It's just a shame that Maxim's is so jaw-droppingly expensive for food that would feel at home in a brasserie, and that—in a fit of cost-cutting not reflected in the menu prices—a lone singing pianist has replaced the orchestra. ✉ *3 rue Royale, Louvre/Tuileries* ☎ *01–42–65–27–94* ✍ *Reservations essential* ▭ *AE, DC, MC, V* ⏲ *Closed Sun.–Mon in July–Aug. and Sun. in Sept.–June* Ⓜ *Concorde.*

★ **$$$$** ✕ **Pierre Gagnaire.** Legendary chef Pierre Gagnaire's cooking is at once intellectual and poetic—in a single dish at least three or four often unexpected tastes and textures come together in a sensational experience—so if you want to venture to the frontier of luxe cooking today, a meal here is a must. Just taking in the menu requires concentration, so complex are descriptions such as "suckling lamb from Aveyron: sweetbreads, saddle and rack; green papaya and turnip velouté thickened with Tarbais beans." The "*Grand Dessert,*" a seven-dessert marathon, will leave you breathless. Though hardly stylish, the businesslike gray-and-wood dining room feels refreshingly informal. The uninspiring prix-fixe lunch, uneven service, and a scanty wine list linger as drawbacks, but the fact remains: there are few chefs as thrilling as Gagnaire today. ✉ *6 rue de Balzac, Champs-Élysées* ☎ *01–58–36–12–50* ✍ *Reservations essential* ▭ *AE, DC, MC, V* ⏲ *Closed Sat. and 2 wks in July. No lunch Sun. and Aug.* Ⓜ *Charles-de-Gaulle–Étoile.*

$$$$ Fodor's Choice ★ ✕ **Taillevent.** Perhaps the most traditional—for many diners this is only high praise—of all Paris luxury restaurants, this grande dame has been subtly modernized, first with the hiring of chef Michel Del Burgo and now with rising star Alain Solivères, who has taken his place. A passionate cook, Solivères draws inspiration from the Basque country, Bordeaux, and Languedoc with dishes that change daily. Classics such as the *boudin de homard*—an airy sausage-shape lobster soufflé—offer continuity with the fabled past. Service is flawless, the setting—19th-century paneled salons now accented with abstract paintings—is luxe, the well-priced wine list probably one of the top 10 in the world: all in all, a meal here comes as close to the classic haute-cuisine experience as you can find in Paris today. Not surprisingly, you must reserve your table for dinner three weeks in advance—lunch is more accessible. ✉ *15 rue Lamennais, Champs-Élysées* ☎ *01–44–95–15–01* ✍ *Reservations essential* 🧥 *Jacket and tie* ▭ *AE, DC, MC, V* ⏲ *Closed weekends and Aug.* Ⓜ *Charles-de-Gaulle–Étoile.*

$$$–$$$$ ✕ **Stella Maris.** A pretty Art Deco front window is the calling card for this spot near the Arc de Triomphe. An expense-account crowd mixes with serious French gourmands to dine on the very subtle cuisine of Japanese chef Taderu Yoshino, who trained with Joël Robuchon and rewrites his menu four times a year. You'll find nuances of Japan in delicious dishes—made with organic ingredients—such as eel *blanquette* (stew) with grilled cucumber, and rice pudding with white truffle. ✉ *4 rue Arsène-Houssaye, Champs-Élysées* ☎ *01–42–89–16–22* ✍ *Reservations essential* ▭ *AE, DC, MC, V* ⏲ *Closed Sun. No lunch Sat. and Mon.* Ⓜ *Étoile.*

$$–$$$ ✕ **Chez Tante Louise.** The late chef Bernard Loiseau's three Paris outposts—his original eponymous restaurant is in Saulieu in Burgundy—are appealing bastions of traditional Burgundian cooking. Here he wisely left the vintage '30s decor almost completely untouched. The food is pleasantly old-fashioned and hearty—like *oeufs en meurette à la bourguignonne* (poached eggs in red wine sauce with bacon) and sole Tante Louise, in which a fillet is served on a bed of *duxelles* (finely chopped mushrooms). Of course, there's a nice selection of Burgundies, and service is prompt and professional for the well-dressed crowd. ✉ *41 rue Boissy d'Anglas, Opéra/Grands Boulevards* ☎ *01–42–65–06–85* *Reservations essential* ▭ *AE, DC, MC, V* ⊙ *Closed weekends and Aug.* Ⓜ *Madeleine.*

$$–$$$ ✕ **La Fermette Marbeuf.** Graced with one of the most magically beautiful Belle Epoque rooms in town—accidentally rediscovered during renovations in the 1970s—this is a favorite haunt of French celebrities, who adore the sunflowers, peacocks, and dragonflies of the Art Nouveau mosaic and stained-glass mise-en-scène. The menu rolls out a solid, updated classic cuisine. Try the snails in puff pastry, saddle of lamb with *choron* (a tomato-spiked béarnaise sauce), and bitter-chocolate fondant—but ignore the rather depressing prix-fixe unless you're on a budget. Popular with tourists and businesspeople at lunch, La Fermette becomes truly animated around 9 PM. ✉ *5 rue Marbeuf, Champs-Élysées* ☎ *01–53–23–08–00* ▭ *AE, DC, MC, V* Ⓜ *Franklin-D.-Roosevelt.*

$–$$$ ✕ **Sébillon.** The original Sébillon has nurtured chic residents of the fashionable suburb of Neuilly for generations; this elegant, polished branch off the Champs-Élysées continues the tradition. The menu includes lobster salad, lots of shellfish, and—the specialty—roast leg of lamb sliced table-side and served until you beg the waiter to stop. Service is notably friendly. ✉ *66 rue Pierre Charron, Champs-Élysées* ☎ *01–43–59–28–15* ▭ *AE, DC, MC, V* Ⓜ *Franklin-D.-Roosevelt.*

$–$$ Fodor'sChoice ★ ✕ **Chez Savy.** Just off the glitzy avenue Montaigne, Chez Savy exists in its own circa-1930s dimension, oblivious to the area's galloping fashionization. The Art Deco cream-and-burgundy interior looks blissfully intact (avoid the back room unless you're in a large group) and the waiters show not a trace of attitude. Fill up on rib-sticking specialties from the Auvergne in central France—lentil salad with bacon, beautifully charred lamb with feather-light shoestring frites, poached peach with sorbet—order a celebratory bottle of Mercurey, and feel smug that you've found this place. ✉ *23 rue Bayard, Champs-Élysées* ☎ *01–47–23–46–98* ▭ *AE, MC, V* ⊙ *Closed weekends and Aug.* Ⓜ *Franklin-D.-Roosevelt.*

PAN-ASIAN **$$–$$$** ✕ **Buddha Bar.** The cavernous Buddha Bar has spawned many an imitator—and, even if some of the vogueish glamour has faded (celebrities being fickle creatures), it still makes for a big night out. Eye the scene wistfully from the bar upstairs, or splash out and book a table within reach of the giant gilt Buddha that reigns over the dining room. Japanese snacks are served at lunch and there is a separate sushi menu at night—or choose from a range of quite tasty Asian-Pacific dishes that will do more harm to your wallet than your waistline. Frankly, though, the opulent chinoiserie setting and sultry music by world-renowned DJs are more of a draw than the food. ✉ *8 rue Boissy d'Anglas, Louvre/Tuileries* ☎ *01–53–05–90–00* ▭ *AE, MC, V* ⊙ *No lunch weekends* Ⓜ *Concorde.*

9e Arrondissement (Opéra/Pigalle-Clichy)

See Where to Eat on the Right Bank: Ile de la Cité to Montmartre map.

FRENCH **$$$** ✕ **Bistrot des Deux Théâtres.** Quality is high and prices are low at this well-run restaurant in the Pigalle-Clichy area. The prix-fixe-only menu for €29 includes an apéritif, first and main dishes, a cheese or dessert course, half a bottle of wine, and coffee. The food—such as foie-gras salad, steak with morels, and apple tart flambéed with calvados—is far from banal. ✉ *18 rue Blanche, Montmartre* ☎ *01–45–26–41–43* ▭ *AE, DC, MC, V* Ⓜ *Trinité.*

¢–$ ✕ **Chartier.** People come here more for the bonhomie than the food, which is often stunningly ordinary. This cavernous 1896 restaurant enjoys a huge following among budget-minded students, solitary bachelors, and tourists. You may find yourself sharing a table with strangers as you study the long, old-fashioned menu of such favorites as hard-boiled eggs with mayonnaise, steak tartare, and roast chicken with fries. ✉ *7 rue du Faubourg-Montmartre, Opéra/Grands Boulevards* ☎ *01–47–70–86–29* ✍ *Reservations not accepted* ▭ *AE, DC, MC, V* Ⓜ *Montmartre.*

2

SEAFOOD $$$ ✕ **Estaminet Gaya.** Come here for affordable seafood in all its guises, from marinated anchovies to Basque tuna to bouillabaisse. The colorful Portuguese tiles on the ground floor are delightful; the upstairs dining room, decorated with photos, seems plain in comparison. Given the often exorbitant prices at fish restaurants in Paris, the prix-fixe menu at €29 (lunch and dinner) is an excellent value. Other prices vary with the day's catch. ✉ *17 rue Duphot, Opéra/Grands Boulevards* ☎ *01–42–60–43–03* ▭ *AE, MC, V* ⊗ *Closed weekends and Dec. 24–Jan. 1* Ⓜ *Madeleine.*

10ᵉ Arrondissement (Opéra/République)

See Where to Eat on the Right Bank: the Marais to La Villette map.

FRENCH ★ $$$ ✕ **Chez Michel.** Effusive chef Thierry Breton pulls in a stylish crowd with his wonderful market-inspired cooking, despite the out-of-the-way location in a pretty neighborhood near Gare du Nord. The prix-fixe-only menu changes constantly, but you'll start with a bowl of snails on the table and almost invariably find the Breton specialties *kig ha farz* (a robust pork stew with a bread stuffing) and *kouing aman* (the butteriest cake imaginable). In winter, don't miss Breton's succulent game dishes (for a €10.70 supplement) such as the surprisingly mild-tasting boar chops, served in a cast-iron pot with tiny potatoes and roasted garlic. The cheese course, served on a slate, is outstanding. There is a long, convivial table in the vaulted cellar. ✉ *10 rue Belzunce, Opéra/Grands Boulevards* ☎ *01–44–53–06–20* ✍ *Reservations essential* ▭ *MC, V* ⊗ *Closed weekends and Aug. No lunch Mon.* Ⓜ *Gare du Nord.*

★ $$–$$$ ✕ **Brasserie Flo.** The first of brasserie king Jean-Paul Bucher's many Paris addresses is hard to find down its passageway near the Gare de l'Est, but it's worth the effort, as much for its Alsatian rich woods and stained glass and conviviality as for its savory brasserie standards (such as shellfish, steak tartare, and choucroute). Order a carafe of Alsatian wine to go with your meal. It's open until 1:30 AM, with a special late-night menu for €21.50 from 10 PM. ✉ *7 cour des Petites-Écuries, Opéra/Grands Boulevards* ☎ *01–47–70–13–59* ▭ *AE, DC, MC, V* Ⓜ *Château d'Eau.*

$$–$$$ ✕ **Julien.** Famed for its 1879 decor—think Majorelle bar, Art Nouveau stained glass, *La-Bohème*-ish street lamps hung with vintage hats—this Belle Epoque dazzler certainly lives up to its oft-quoted moniker, "the poor man's Maxim's." Fare includes smoked salmon, foie gras, stuffed roast lamb, cassoulet, and its famous profiteroles. Diners are ebullient and lots of fun; this place has a strong following with the fashion crowd, so it's mobbed during the biannual fashion and fabric shows. The downside? Readers have complained about some lackluster dishes and even worse service (and the area is frankly not the safest in Paris). There's service until midnight, with a late-night menu for €21.50 from 10 PM. ✉ *16 rue du Faubourg St-Denis, Opéra/Grands Boulevards* ☎ *01–47–70–12–06* ▭ *AE, DC, MC, V* Ⓜ *Strasbourg St-Denis.*

$ ✕ **Chez Casimir.** Another project of chef Thierry Breton of Chez Michel, this (too) brightly lit, easygoing bistro is popular with stylish Parisian professionals for whom it serves as a sort of canteen—why cook when you can eat this well for so little money? The menu shows Breton's cooking style with dishes such as lentil soup with fresh croutons, braised endive and *andouille* (tripe sausage) salad, and roast lamb on a bed of Paimpol beans. Good desserts include *pain perdu,* a dessert version of French toast—here it's topped with a roasted pear or whole cherries. ✉ *6 rue de Belzunce, Opéra/Grands Boulevards* ☎ *01–48–78–28–80* ▭ *MC, V* ⏲ *Closed weekends and Aug.* Ⓜ *Gare du Nord.*

¢–$ ✕ **Au Vieux Bistrot.** If you're staying near the Gare du Nord or looking for a meal in the area before taking the train, this pleasant, old-fashioned neighborhood bistro is a good bet. From the big zinc bar to the steak with mushroom sauce and veal in cream, this place delivers a traditional bistro experience at prices that seem to belong to another era. Finish up with the fruit tart. ✉ *30 rue Dunkerque, Opéra/Grands Boulevards* ☎ *01–48–78–48–01* ▭ *MC, V* ⏲ *Closed Sun. No dinner Sat.* Ⓜ *Gare du Nord.*

11e Arrondissement (Bastille/République)

See Where to Eat on the Right Bank: the Marais to La Villette map.

CHINESE $–$$ ✕ **Wok.** Design-it-yourself Asian stir-fry in a slick, minimalist room has made this spot a hit with the penny-wise hipsters around party-hearty Bastille. You select the type of noodle you want and load up at a buffet with meats, seafood, and vegetables; then join the line to discuss your preferred seasoning with the chefs who man the woks in the open kitchen. The all-you-can-eat single-price tariff (€15.50–€20) lets you walk the wok as many times as you want. Otherwise, there are deep-fried spring rolls as starters and a signature dessert of caramelized fruit salad. Mobbed on weekends but unfortunately closed at lunch, this place is fun, nourishing, and cheap. ✉ *23 rue des Taillandiers, Bastille/Nation* ☎ *01–55–28–88–77* ▭ *MC, V* ⏲ *Closed Sun. No lunch* Ⓜ *Bréguet Sabin, Bastille, Ledru-Rollin.*

FRENCH ★ $$–$$$ ✕ **Astier.** The prix-fixe menu (there's no à la carte) at this popular, old-fashioned restaurant must be one of the best values in town, with a lunch menu for €20.50 and a second lunch menu and dinner menu for €25. Among the beautifully prepared seasonal dishes are baked eggs topped with truffled foie gras, fricassee of *joue de boeuf* (beef cheeks), rabbit in mustard sauce with fresh tagliatelle, and plum *clafoutis* (a fruit flan). This is a great place to come if you're feeling cheesy, since it's locally famous for having one of the best *plateaux de fromages* (cheese plates) in Paris—a giant wicker tray lands on the table and you help yourself. The lengthy, well-priced wine list is a connoisseur's dream. ✉ *44 rue Jean-Pierre Timbaud, République* ☎ *01–43–57–16–35* ✍ *Reservations essential* ▭ *MC, V* ⏲ *Closed weekends, Aug., Christmas wk, and Easter wk* Ⓜ *Parmentier.*

$$ ✕ **Le Repaire de Cartouche.** Between Bastille and République, this split-level, dark-wood '50s-style bistro offers excellent food for good-value prices. Young chef Rodolphe Paquin is a creative and impeccably trained cook who does a stylish take on earthy French regional dishes. The menu changes regularly, but typical are a salad of *haricots verts* (string beans) topped with tender slices of squid, scallops on a bed of diced pumpkin, and old-fashioned desserts like custard with tiny madeleine cakes. The wine list is very good, too, with bargains like a Cheverny from the Loire Valley for €17. ✉ *99 rue Amelot, Bastille/Nation* ☎ *01–47–00–25–86* ✍ *Reservations essential* ▭ *MC, V* ⏲ *Closed Sun.–Mon. and Aug.* Ⓜ *Filles du Calvaire.*

$–$$ ✕ **Les Fernandises.** The chef-owner of this neighborhood spot near place de la République is more concerned with his Normandy-inspired cuisine than with his restaurant's inconsequential decor. Fresh foie gras

A CHEESE PRIMER

THE COOKING MIGHT BE GETTING LIGHTER *in Paris restaurants, but the French aren't ready to relinquish their cheese. Nearly every restaurant, no matter how humble or haute, takes pride in its odorous offerings. Some present just a single, lovingly selected slice, while others wheel in an entire trolley of specimens aged on the premises. Always, though, cheese comes after the main course and before—or instead of—dessert. You're under no obligation to indulge, but nowhere else will you find such an astonishing variety—a recent cheese fair in Paris showcased some 1,000 variations on the theme.*

Being a cheese dunce is not necessarily an obstacle to enjoying this quintessentially French ritual. Armed with these phrases, you can wow the waiter and happily work your way through the most generous platter.

Avez-vous le Beaufort d'été? *(Do you have the summer Beaufort?) Beaufort—similar to Gruyère—is probably the king of French cheeses, and the best Beaufort is made with milk produced during the summer, when the cows munch on fresh grass and alpine flowers. Beaufort that has aged for more than a year is even more reminiscent of a mountain hike.*

Je voudrais un chèvre bien frais/bien sec. *(I'd like a goat cheese that's nice and fresh/nice and dry.) France produces many dozens of goat cheeses, some so fresh they can be scooped up with a spoon and some tough enough to use as doorstops. It's a matter of taste, but hard-core cheese eaters favor the drier specimens, which stick to the roof of the mouth and have a frankly goaty aroma.*

C'est un St-Marcellin de vache ou de chèvre? *(Is this St-Marcellin made with cow's or goat's milk?) St-Marcellin makes a more original choice than the ubiquitous crottin de chèvre (poetically named after goats' turds). It was originally a goat cheese but today is more often made with cow's milk. The best have a delightfully oozy center, though some people like it dry as a hockey puck.*

C'est un Brie de Meaux ou de Melun? *(Is this Brie from Meaux or Melun?) There are many kinds of Brie, all produced in the Paris region. Brie de Meaux is the best-known, with a smooth flavor and runny center, while the much rarer Brie de Melun is more pungent and saltier.*

Je n'aime pas le Camembert industriel! *(I don't like industrial Camembert!) Camembert might be a national treasure, but most of it is industrial. Real Camembert has a white rind with rust-color streaks and a yellow center. In Normandy, people prefer it a little firm, not runny.*

Avez-vous de la confiture pour accompagner ce brebis? *(Do you have any jam to go with this sheep's cheese?) In France's Basque region, berry jam is the traditional accompaniment for sharp sheep's milk cheeses, such as Ossau-Iraty from the Pyrenees.*

C'est la saison du Mont d'Or. *(It's Mont d'Or season.) This potent mountain cheese, also known as Vacherin, is produced only from September to March. So runny is the texture that it's traditionally eaten with a spoon—it can also be warmed and slathered on potatoes.*

Avez-vous du cheddar? *(Do you have any cheddar?) Ask this and you're asking for trouble—unless you happen to be at Willi's Wine Bar or Macéo, where the owners are British.*

— Rosa Jackson

sautéed in cider and scallops in cream sauce are examples of his varied style. Choose from at least six Camemberts at any given time, including one doused in calvados and another coated in hay. ✉ *17 rue Fontaine-au-Roi, République* ☎ *01–43–57–46–25* ▭ *MC, V* ⊙ *Closed Sun.–Mon. and Aug.* Ⓜ *République.*

★ $ ✕ **Au Camelot.** This minuscule bistro brings in the crowds with its excellent home-style cooking, consistently some of the best in Paris. Chef Didier Varnier trained with guru Christian Constant at the Crillon and it shows in such creative dishes as pumpkin soup with goat-cheese ravioli, squid-ink risotto with Dublin Bay prawns, sweet-and-sour duck with dried-fruit tabouleh, and spice bread pudding with lemon cream—the selection changes every day. In keeping with waist-conscious times, Varnier has dropped his five-course menu and now offers three courses for €30—you can also order à la carte. Though the place is noisy and very crowded, service is friendly, and the house Bordeaux is a treat. ✉ *50 rue Amelot, Bastille/Nation* ☎ *01–43–55–54–04* ✍ *Reservations essential* ▭ *AE, MC, V* ⊙ *Closed Sun.–Mon. and 3 wks in Aug. No lunch Sat.* Ⓜ *République.*

¢–$ ✕ **Le Kitch.** Fighting the good fight against ennui, this whimsically casual place attracts graphic designers, couturiers-in-training, and other denizens of its arty neighborhood. There's more than a touch of Pee-Wee's Playhouse here—faux-stucco walls, plastic children's furniture, naif paintings of cats, and scudding clouds across the ceiling make this a cute boutique restaurant. The food here is snappy if mainly snacky—expect pastas and sandwiches, such as a bagel with *tapenade* (olive paste)—and tasty enough to give a satisfied buzz to the room. ✉ *10 rue Oberkampf, Père Lachaise* ☎ *01–40–21–94–14* ▭ *No credit cards* ⊙ *No lunch weekends* Ⓜ *Oberkampf.*

¢–$ ✕ **Le Passage des Carmagnoles.** Not far from place de la Bastille, in the obscure passage de la Bonne Graine, is this friendly spot with a homey air. Though it bills itself as a wine bar, it has a full menu, including four kinds of *andouillette* (chitterling sausage). The initials AAAAA, by the way, mean the sausage has the stamp of approval from the French andouillette aficionados' association. Since the andouillette's pungent aroma makes it an acquired taste, other, less fragrant dishes are available such as duck leg with orange, rabbit with mustard, steak tartare flavored with mint, and game in season. Le Passage is also a delight for wine lovers, with many unusual bottles. ✉ *18 passage de la Bonne Graine (enter by 108 av. Ledru-Rollin), Bastille/Nation* ☎ *01–47–00–73–30* ▭ *AE, MC, V* ⊙ *Closed Sun.* Ⓜ *Ledru-Rollin.*

12e Arrondissement (Bastille/Gare de Lyon)

See Where to Eat on the Right Bank: the Marais to La Villette map.

CONTEMPORARY ★ $–$$$ ✕ **Chai 33.** Thierry Begué, one of the names behind the trendsetting Buddha Bar and Barrio Latino, has created something more personal with this forward-looking spot appropriately located in a neighborhood once dedicated to the wine trade. A restaurant, hip bar, and wine shop rolled into one, Chai 33 aims to make wine unintimidating—instead of the usual regional listings, wines are classified by style, and customers are invited into the cellar to choose their bottle with the help of an expert sommelier. Go for the funky wine cocktails or the perfectly fine food, such as white-bean salad with andouille or seared tuna with pistachio and cumin, served on a relaxing terrace in summer. ✉ *33 Cour Saint-Emilion, Bercy/Tolbiac* ☎ *01–53–44–01–01* ▭ *AE, MC, V* Ⓜ *Cour St-Emilion.*

FRENCH $$$–$$$$ ✕ **L'Oulette.** Chef-owner Marcel Baudis's take on the cuisine of his native southwestern France is original and delicious, and service here is effusive—qualities that will help you overlook the out-of-the-way location and out-of-date design. The menu changes with the seasons, but you'll always find his trademark dishes: marinated squid, braised oxtail with foie gras and a mousseline of Puy lentils, and *pain d'épices* (spice cake). The restaurant, in the rebuilt Bercy district, is a bit hard to find, so head out with your map. Prix-fixe menus are available at lunch (€28 or €45) and dinner (€45). ✉ *15 pl. Lachambeaudie, Bastille/Nation* ☎ *01–40–02–02–12* ▭ *AE, DC, MC, V* ⊙ *Closed weekends* Ⓜ *Dugommier.*

★ $–$$ ✕ **Au Trou Gascon.** This classy establishment with sumptuous ceiling moldings and contemporary furnishings off place Daumesnil—well off the beaten tourist track, but worth the trip—is overseen by celebrated chef Alain Dutournier, whose wife runs the dining room. He does a refined take on the cuisine of Gascony—a region of outstanding ham, foie gras, lamb, and duck (don't miss out on his classic white-chocolate mousse, too). The lunch menu is excellent value at €36; you can also order à la carte at lunch and dinner. Most popular with the regulars are the surprisingly light cassoulet and a superb duck confit, but you'll also find sophisticated dishes such as scallop carpaccio and an ethereal dessert of raspberries, ice cream, and meringue. ✉ *40 rue Taine, Bastille/Nation* ☎ *01–43–44–34–26* ▭ *AE, MC, V* ⊙ *Closed weekends and Aug. No lunch Sat.* Ⓜ *Daumesnil.*

$–$$ ✕ **Barrio Latino.** This megaseater restaurant has a rather speciously New York–goes–Puerto Rican theme, so don't come here expecting *West Side Story*—the place pulls a rather self-consciously trendy crowd to its theaterlike atrium (it used to be a furniture showroom). The food is passable, and there is a very cheap lunch menu (€10.50), but the raison d'être for this place is to make the scene and hang out over tropical cocktails. Reserve a table to avoid having to wait outside. ✉ *46–48 rue du Faubourg St-Antoine, Bastille/Nation* ☎ *01–55–78–84–75* ▭ *AE, DC, MC, V* Ⓜ *Bastille.*

★ $–$$ ✕ **Le Square Trousseau.** This beautiful Belle Epoque bistro is a favorite of the fashion set. You might see a supermodel—Claudia Schiffer often stops in when in town—while dining on the peppered country pâté, slow-cooked lamb, or tender baby chicken with mustard and bread-crumb crust. The food is reliably good, human scenery is never lackluster, and the staff is cheerful. Wines might seem a little pricey, but are lovingly selected from small producers—you can also buy them at the restaurant's boutique next door. ✉ *1 rue Antoine Vollon, Bastille/Nation* ☎ *01–43–43–06–00* ▭ *AE, MC, V* ⊙ *Closed Sun.–Mon. and Christmas wk* Ⓜ *Ledru-Rollin.*

ITALIAN ★ $ ✕ **Sardegna a Tavola.** Paris might have more Italian restaurants than you can shake a noodle at, but few smack of authenticity like this out-of-the-way Sardinian spot with peppers, braids of garlic, and cured hams hanging from the ceiling. Dishes are listed in Sardinian with French translations—*malloredus* is a small, gnocchilike pasta, while Sardinian ravioli are stuffed with cheese and mint. Perhaps best of all are the clams in a spicy broth with tiny pasta, and orange-scented Dublin Bay prawns with tagliatelle. If charcuterie *artisanale* sounds too tame, try the horse carpaccio. ✉ *1 rue de Cotte, Bastille/Nation* ☎ *01–44–75–03–28* ▭ *MC, V* ⊙ *Closed Sun. No lunch Mon.* Ⓜ *Ledru-Rollin.*

13e Arrondissement (Les Gobelins)

See Where to Eat on the Left Bank map.

FRENCH ★ $$$ ✕ **Le Petit Marguery.** As the diorama of a stuffed ferret amid a fairy-tale mushroom forest announces, this charming ruby-color bistro offers some of the earthiest dishes in the French canon. Thankfully, despite a change of owner and chef in 2002, its spirit remains intact. With its historic fin-de-siècle charm, this is the place to head for if you're hunting for game—catch it here in late fall, in such dishes as the deeply flavored *lièvre à la royale* (hare in a carnivorous wine-and-blood sauce). Some dishes are so *authèntique* they are even topped with pine needles. ✉ *9 bd. de Port Royal, St-Germain-des-Prés* ☎ *01–43–31–58–59* ▭ *AE, MC, V* ⊙ *Closed Sun.–Mon., Aug., and Christmas wk* Ⓜ *Les Gobelins.*

$$–$$$ ✕ **Anacréon.** André le Letty, who polished his cooking technique at La Tour d'Argent, has transformed a neighborhood café into a pleasant new-wave bistro. Inventive dishes such as pressed duck with red peppercorns and fresh cod with spices have been highlights on the regularly changing menu. Desserts are always good, too, and the St-Joseph is a perfect choice from the wine list. The menu is prix-fixe: €20 at lunch and €32 at dinner. ✉ *53 bd. St-Marcel, St-Germain-des-Prés* ☎ *01–43–31–71–18* ✍ *Reservations essential* ▭ *AE, DC, MC, V* ⊙ *Closed Sun.–Mon. and Aug. No lunch Wed.* Ⓜ *Les Gobelins.*

$–$$$ ✕ **Le Terroir.** A jolly crowd of regulars makes this little bistro festive. Based on first-rate ingredients from all over France, the menu is solidly classical—salads with chicken livers or fresh marinated anchovies, calves' liver or monkfish with saffron, and pears marinated in wine for dessert, for instance. There's also a well-balanced wine list. ✉ *11 bd. Arago, St-Germain-des-Prés* ☎ *01–47–07–36–99* ▭ *AE, MC, V* ⊙ *Closed weekends, Easter wk, 3 wks in Aug., and Christmas wk* Ⓜ *Les Gobelins.*

★ $ ✕ **L'Avant-Gout.** For excellent contemporary French cooking at very reasonable prices, it's worth seeking out this tiny, off-the-beaten-path bistro in a residential part of the city. Though "The Foretaste" can get crowded and noisy, you won't be disappointed by young chef Christophe Beaufront's appealing and unusual daily prix-fixe menu (you can also order à la carte), which might include dishes such as sea bass with creamy celery root and almonds, and steak with roasted shallots. Delicious homemade desserts and a good-value wine list round off the meal. ✉ *26 rue Bobillot, Bercy/Tolbiac* ☎ *01–53–80–24–00* ✍ *Reservations essential* ▭ *MC, V* ⊙ *Closed Sat.–Mon., 1st wk in Jan., 1st wk in May, and 3 wks in Aug.* Ⓜ *Place d'Italie.*

PAN ASIAN **¢–$** ✕ **La Chine Massena.** With wonderfully overwrought rooms that seem draped in what looks like a whole restaurant-supply catalog's worth of Asiana (plus four monitors showing the very latest in Hong Kong music videos), this is a fun place to come with friends. Not only is the Chinese-Vietnamese-Thai food good and moderately priced, but the place itself has a lot of entertainment value—wedding parties often provide a free floor show, and, on weekends, variety shows followed by Asian disco come as part of your meal. Steamed dumplings and lacquered duck are specialties, but for the best value come at noon on weekdays for the bargain lunch menus. ✉ *Centre Commercial Massena, 13 pl. de Venetie, Chinatown* ☎ *01–45–83–98–88* ▭ *MC, V* Ⓜ *Porte de Choisy.*

14e Arrondissement (Montparnasse)

See Where to Eat on the Left Bank map.

FRENCH **$$$** ✕ **Contre-Allée.** Left Bank students and professors crowd this large restaurant, stomach-upsettingly decorated with bullfighting posters. The menu has original selections such as squid salad with mussels and roast cod with Parmesan; homemade fresh pasta accompanies many dishes. A sidewalk terrace enlivens shady avenue Denfert-Rochereau in summer. ✉ *83 av. Denfert-Rochereau, Montparnasse* ☎ *01–43–54–99–86* ▭ *AE, DC, MC, V* ⊙ *No lunch weekends* Ⓜ *Denfert-Rochereau.*

$$$ Fodor's Choice ★ **La Régalade.** As the leading priest who marries bistro and nouvelle cookery—who can resist his soup of lentils and pureed chestnuts poured over a mound of fois gras?—Yves Camdeborde has to satisfy the hordes who trek to the edge of town for three dinner sittings (and you still have to book at least two weeks ahead). The crowded, no-frills rooms evokes the dullest provinces, but the food is worthy of a luxury restaurant: duck-confit ravioli in wine sauce, juicy roast capon with chestnuts, fresh foie gras panfried in spice-bread crumbs, and a bitter, adult dessert of grapefruit in Campari jelly. Portions are small, but the country pâté that begins each meal will take the edge off your appetite. If you don't like feeling rushed, book the last seating. ✉ *49 av. Jean-Moulin, Montparnasse* ☎ *01–45–45–68–58* *Reservations essential* *MC, V* *Closed Sun.–Mon. and Aug. No lunch Sat.* Ⓜ *Alésia.*

$–$$$ **La Coupole.** This world-renowned, cavernous spot with Art Deco murals practically defines the term brasserie. La Coupole might have lost its intellectual aura since the Flo group's restoration—that giant rotating sculpture was one of the "improvements"—but it has been popular since the days when Jean-Paul Sartre and Simone de Beauvoir were regulars and is still great fun. Today it attracts a mix of bourgeois families, tourists, and elderly lone diners treating themselves to a dozen oysters. Expect the usual brasserie menu—including perhaps the largest shellfish platter in Paris—choucroute, and some great over-the-top desserts. ✉ *102 bd. du Montparnasse, Montparnasse* ☎ *01–43–20–14–20* *AE, DC, MC, V* Ⓜ *Vavin.*

SEAFOOD $–$$ **Vin et Marée.** The third, lower-priced annex of the fancy Right Bank fish house La Luna is a one of the better bets around Montparnasse. Begin with a tasty bowl of baby clams in a creamy lemon-butter sauce, offered as an hors d'oeuvre; then have a generous plate of fresh red shrimp sautéed in thyme, followed by white tuna in shallot sauce or sautéed *rouget* (red mullet fish), if available—the menu changes depending on what's in the market that day. Nicely chosen wines come by the bottle, carafe, or glass. ✉ *108 av. du Maine, Montparnasse* ☎ *01–43–20–29–50* *AE, MC, V* Ⓜ *Montparnasse, Gaité.*

15e Arrondissement (Motte-Picquet/Balard)

See Where to Eat on the Left Bank map.

FRENCH $$$ **Bistrot d'Hubert.** In a studied environment that might have sprung from the pages of *Elle Decor,* this popular bistro draws a stylish crowd with food that perfectly expresses the countercurrents of the Parisian culinary landscape. The prix-fixe-only menu is split into two: "tradition" and "discovery." New chef Vincent Lourdelle's menu changes every two weeks—in winter you might choose scallops with caramelized endives and grainy mustard; duck foie gras with port, apple confit and chestnuts; and crepes with orange, Grand Marnier, and licorice. ✉ *41 bd. Pasteur, Montparnasse* ☎ *01–47–34–15–50* *Reservations essential* *AE, DC, MC, V* *No lunch Sat.* Ⓜ *Pasteur.*

★ $$$ **L'Os à Moelle.** This small, popular bistro has a good-value six-course dinner menu for €32 (there's no à la carte) that changes daily; portions are generous. A sample meal might include white-bean soup, sautéed foie gras, red mullet (rouget) fillets with red peppers, lamb with potato puree, cheese with a small salad, and a delicious roasted pear with cinnamon ice cream. At lunch there is a shorter, equally good prix-fixe. With an excellent list of fairly priced wines, your bill can stay comfortably low—but, if you're feeling broke, the restaurant's casual wine bar across the street is a tempting option. ✉ *3 rue Vasco-de-Gama, Invalides/Eiffel Tower* ☎ *01–45–57–27–27* *Reservations essential* *MC, V* *Closed Sun.–Mon. and Aug.* Ⓜ *Balard.*

★ $$–$$$ ✕ **Le Troquet.** On a quiet street in a residential neighborhood near the UNESCO headquarters, this contemporary, outstanding-value bistro feeds a crowd of lucky regulars. They come for chef Christian Etchebest's tasty, constantly changing prix-fixe menu of dishes from the Basque and Béarn regions of southwestern France. A typical meal might include vegetable soup with foie gras and cream, hot scallops on a bed of mixed vegetables, pan-roasted dove, sheep's cheese with cherry preserves, and a chocolate macaroon. The Béarn red wine cheerfully accompanies this food. Though the dining room looks a little fusty, the place is relaxed and the staff eager to please. ✉ *21 rue François-Bonvin, Invalides/Eiffel Tower* ☎ *01–45–66–89–00* ▭ *MC, V* ⏲ *Closed Sun.–Mon., Aug., and Christmas wk* Ⓜ *Ségur.*

THAI $ ✕ **Sawadee.** Once you've tried the delicious Thai food here you'll understand why this off-the-beaten-path spot is full every night. Statues and wood carvings dress up the warm dining room, while a casual atmosphere and friendly service add to the charm. A dizzying array of prix-fixe menus is available: start with the unusual fried-rice salad, or the delicate shrimp and pork ravioli, and then try the shrimp sautéed with salt and pepper or the chopped beef with basil. ✉ *53 av. Émile-Zola, Invalides/Eiffel Tower* ☎ *01–45–77–68–90* ▭ *AE, MC, V* ⏲ *Closed Sun. and 10 days in Aug.* Ⓜ *Charles Michel.*

16e Arrondissement (Trocadéro/Bois de Boulogne)

See Where to Eat on the Right Bank: Bois du Boulogne to Place de la Concorde map.

FRENCH ★ $$$$ ✕ **Jamin.** This intimate if rather frilly restaurant where Joël Robuchon made his name serves brilliant food well away from the media spotlight. The best value is the lunch prix-fixe at €53, which entitles you to an impeccable meal with generous extras such as the sorbet trolley. The evening menu has gone up to €95 (a €19 increase in one year), but this still compares favorably with other restaurants of Jamin's ilk. Benoît Guichard, Robuchon's second for many years, is a subtle and accomplished chef and a particularly brilliant *saucier* (sauce maker). The menu changes regularly, but Guichard favors such dishes as sea bass with pistachios in fennel sauce and braised beef with cumin-scented carrots. The seasonal gratin of rhubarb with a red-fruit sauce makes an excellent dessert. ✉ *32 rue de Longchamp, Eiffel Tower/Trocadéro* ☎ *01–45–53–00–07* ✍ *Reservations essential* ▭ *AE, DC, MC, V* ⏲ *Closed weekends and 3 wks in Aug.* Ⓜ *Iéna.*

$$$$ ✕ **Le Pré Catalan.** Dining beneath the chestnut trees on the terrace of this fanciful landmark *pavillon* in the Bois de Boulogne is a Belle Epoque fantasy. Among the winning dishes on chef Frédéric Anton's menu are spit-roasted baby pigeon in a caramelized sauce, sweetbreads with morels and asparagus tips, and roast pear on a caramelized waffle with bergamot ice cream. Unfortunately, some dishes are decidedly lackluster. Still, the opulent surroundings help you forget that limp turbot, especially if you order the more reasonably priced lunch menu (€55). ✉ *Bois de Boulogne, rue de Surèsnes, Champs-Élysées* ☎ *01–44–14–41–14* ✍ *Reservations essential* 👔 *Jacket and tie* ▭ *AE, DC, MC, V* ⏲ *Closed Mon., mid-Feb., and 1 wk in Nov. No dinner Sun.* Ⓜ *Porte Dauphine.*

$$$ Fodor's Choice ★ ✕ **L'Astrance.** Rarely have critics been so enthralled with a restaurant: *Le Point* has called L'Astrance "a miracle" while *Le Figaro*'s respected critic Francois Simon has described it as "perfect." What's all the fuss about? Well, this split-level gray dining room is probably the best place in Paris to part with your hard-earned euros for a special-occasion meal: you get the quality of haute cuisine without the pomposity or the crushing price tag. For a mere €29 at lunch you might feast on an av-

ocado-and-crab mille-feuille, a ballotine of quail and foie gras, spiced mackerel fillet on Asian-style spinach, and orange soufflé with marjoram ice cream (and that's not to mention the surprise extras). A more elaborate menu costs €65 at lunch and dinner—just don't forget to reserve weeks in advance. ✉ *4 rue Beethoven, Eiffel Tower/Trocadéro* ☎ *01–40–50–84–40* ✍ *Reservations essential* ▭ *AE, DC, MC, V* ⏲ *Closed Mon., 3 wks in Aug., and Dec. 22–Jan. 3. No lunch Tues.* Ⓜ *Passy.*

$$$ ✕ **Le 16 au 16.** Barely a year after having opened an eponymous restaurant decked out in glittering gold and mirrors at this location, chef Ghislaine Arabian threw in the towel—she was last spotted in Tokyo, where she has said she feels more appreciated than in her native France. Her longtime sous-chef Frederick Simonin has taken over—and since Arabian was the first to admit that she learned much of her technique from him, the result is as polished as the surroundings. This is one restaurant where there is no pressure to order a three-course meal—however, it might be hard to resist starters such as foie gras with red-onion jam and a lobster vol-au-vent, and desserts such as the *exotique* roasted mango with tea ice cream, or a caramel soufflé to complement your turbot in beer sauce or veal with sage jus and lemon "marmalade." ✉ *16 av. Bugeaud, Eiffel Tower/Trocadéro* ☎ *01–56–28–16–16* ▭ *MC, V* ⏲ *Closed Sun. and 2 wks in Aug. No lunch Mon. and Sat.* Ⓜ *Victor-Hugo.*

$$–$$$ ✕ **La Butte Chaillot.** A dramatic iron staircase connects two levels in turquoise and earth tones at one of the most popular of chef Guy Savoy's fashionable bistros. Dining here is part theater, as the à la mode clientele demonstrate, but it's not all show: the very good food includes tasty ravioli from the town of Royans, roast free-range chicken with mashed potatoes, and stuffed veal breast with rosemary. Recent renovations have expanded the dining room and made it feel more harmonious. A wide sidewalk terrace fronts tree-shaded avenue Kléber. ✉ *112 av. Kléber, Eiffel Tower/Trocadéro* ☎ *01–47–27–88–88* ▭ *AE, DC, MC, V* ⏲ *Closed 2 wks in Aug. No lunch Sat.* Ⓜ *Trocadéro.*

$$–$$$ ✕ **La Grande Armée.** The Costes brothers, who own the most stylish hotel in Paris (the Costes), are perpetually in the forefront of whatever's trendy in town. Their brasserie near the Arc de Triomphe is a great spot to check out their gig, since it's open daily, serves nonstop, and has knockout over-the-top Napoléon III decor dreamed up by superstar designer Jacques Garcia—black lacquered tables, leopard upholstery, Bordeaux velvet, and a carefully tousled clientele picking at salads, pastas, and soothing potato puree. Breakfast here for €18.50 is a stylish way to start your day. ✉ *3 av. de la Grande Armée, Champs-Élysées* ☎ *01–45–00–24–77* ▭ *AE, DC, MC, V* Ⓜ *Charles-de-Gaulle–Étoile.*

$$ ✕ **Le Petit Rétro.** Two different clienteles—men in expensive suits at noon and well-dressed locals in the evening—frequent this little bistro with Art Nouveau tiles and bentwood furniture. You can't go wrong with the daily special, which is written on a chalkboard presented by one of the friendly waitresses. Come in some night when you want a good solid meal, like the perfect *pavé de boeuf* (thick steak) in a ruddy red-wine and stock sauce, accompanied by potatoes au gratin and caramelized braised endive. ✉ *5 rue Mesnil, Eiffel Tower/Trocadéro* ☎ *01–44–05–06–05* ▭ *AE, MC, V* ⏲ *Closed weekends., 3 wks in Aug., and 1 wk at Christmas* Ⓜ *Victor-Hugo.*

SEAFOOD **$$$–$$$$** ✕ **Prunier.** Founded in 1925, this seafood restaurant is surely the prettiest in Paris—even more so following renovations (though the wood-paneled upstairs dining room does look a bit saunalike). Now a New York–style caviar house, Maison Prunier doesn't offer much in the way of cooking—a world-weary set from the blasé 16e comes here to feast

REFUELING

"LE FAST FOOD" *is not what Paris does best; you can easily spend two hours, albeit pleasantly, having lunch in a café. There's no point trying to make a Parisian waiter move faster than he wants to; instead, head to a new breed of snack shop that puts speed first without sacrificing quality.*

Le Pain Quotidien: *Part bakery, part café, this Belgian chain with locations throughout the city serves wonderfully fresh salads and sandwiches, plus tasty cakes. Avoid peak times, when it can be overrun with office workers.*

Cosi *(✉ 54 rue de Seine ☎ 01–46–33–36–36): Miles from the cardboard panini served at so many crepe stands, this Italian sandwich shop in St-Germain piles the fillings onto crusty bread. You order at the counter downstairs and carry your sandwich upstairs, where there is (oh, miracle) a no-smoking area.*

Nils *(✉ 36 rue Montorgueil ☎ 01–55–34–39–49 ✉ 10 rue de Buci ☎ 01–46–34–82–82): The Danes eat lunch in 15 minutes and live to be over 80, which is reason enough to eat at these Scandinavian delis. Try a rolled Swedish sandwich or a smoked fish plate, and save room for a blueberry tart.*

Be *(✉ 73 bd. de Courcelles ☎ 01–46–22–20–20): Star chef Alain Ducasse and bread whizz Eric Kayser have created this neighborhood deli for Parisians weary of endless jambon-beurre (ham and butter) baguettes. Try a luxury sandwich at one of the handful of tables and choose from condiments hand-selected by the great chef.*

Oh Poivrier! *Specializing in quirkily named open-faced sandwiches, this chain makes a good alternative to slower-paced cafés, with terraces in some scenic spots.*

on Aquitaine caviar (for a cool €100 a tablespoon), chilled oysters with hot, spiced sausages (a Bordeaux specialty), the so-chic "Christian Dior jellied egg," and French vodka or champagne. If you can't spring for caviar but want to soak up the setting, try the prix-fixe lunch menu (weekdays only) for €65. ✉ *16 av. Victor-Hugo, Champs-Élysées* ☎ *01–44–17–35–85* *Jacket and tie* *AE, DC, MC, V* *Closed Sun. and Aug.* Ⓜ *Étoile.*

17e Arrondissement (Monceau/Clichy/Champs-Élysées)

See Where to Eat on the Right Bank: Bois du Boulogne to Place de la Concorde map.

FRENCH ★ $$$$ ✕ **Guy Savoy.** Redecorated by Jean-Michel Wilmotte, who dressed up the space with dark African wood, rich leather, and cream-color marble, Guy Savoy's luxury restaurant has stepped gracefully into the 21st century. Come here for a perfectly measured, contemporary haute-cuisine experience, since Savoy's several bistros have not lured him away from his kitchen. The artichoke soup with black truffles, sea bass with spices, and veal kidneys in mustard-spiked jus reveal the magnitude of his talent, and his mille-feuille is a contemporary classic. Half portions allow you to graze your way through the menu—unless you choose the blow-out feast for €235—and reasonably priced wines are available. Best of all, the atmosphere is joyful—Savoy senses that having fun is just as important as eating well. ✉ *18 rue Troyon, Champs-Élysées* ☎ *01–43–80–40–61* *AE, MC, V* *Closed Sun.–Mon., Aug., and 2 wks at Christmas.* Ⓜ *Charles-de-Gaulle–Étoile.*

$$$–$$$$ ✕ **Au Petit Colombier.** This is a perennial favorite among Parisians, who come to eat comforting *cuisine bourgeoise* (traditional cuisine) in the warm dining rooms accented with wood and bright copper. Seasonal

specialties include milk-fed lamb chop *en cocotte* (in a small, enameled casserole), game in all its guises, and truffles. Service is friendly and unpretentious. ✉ *42 rue des Acacias, Champs-Élysées* ☎ *01–43–80–28–54* ▭ *AE, MC, V* ⏲ *Closed Sun. and Aug. No lunch Sat. and Mon.* Ⓜ *Charles-de-Gaulle–Étoile.*

★ $$–$$$ ✕ **La Table de Lucullus.** Working in a spot that could be politely described as modest—three gigantic menus now decorate the walls—Nicolas Vagnon has caused quite a stir in the Paris restaurant world with his iconoclastic, comfort-food-meets-haute-cuisine style. A meal here, though not cheap, is a full-on experience—the chef himself describes each dish (in excellent English, too) and his passion is evident. Try the *délice de Lucullus,* smooth foie gras sandwiched between thin slices of beet and white radish, and—in winter—such dishes as steamed scallops with endive salad or boned, long-cooked hare with mashed beet and crushed potatoes. This is that rarest of things in Paris, a no-smoking restaurant. ✉ *129 rue Legendre, Champs-Élysées* ☎ *01–40–25–02–68* ▭ *MC, V* ⏲ *Closed Sun.–Mon. No lunch Sat.* Ⓜ *La Fourche.*

$$ ✕ **Café d'Angel.** A trend-conscious yuppie crowd frequents this relaxed little bistro near the Arc de Triomphe, whose name is echoed in its angel-print tablecloths. The menu changes regularly but offers interesting modern bistro dishes and good value for the money. Try the seasonal fish dishes, rabbit compote with lentils, and intriguing upside-down millefeuille with apple, quince, and spice bread. ✉ *16 rue Brey, Champs-Élysées* ☎ *01–47–54–03–33* ▭ *MC, V* ⏲ *Closed weekends, 3 wks in Aug., and 2 wks at Christmas* Ⓜ *Charles-de-Gaulle–Étoile.*

$$ ✕ **Le Graindorge.** Formerly at the justly popular Au Trou Gascon, chef-owner Bernard Broux has thrived since he opened his own establishment. A recent renovation wisely left the vintage 1930s character intact, but the tables, chairs, and lighting are new and the paint is fresh. Broux prepares an original mix of the cuisines of southwestern France and his native Flanders: experience the succulent eel terrine in a delicious herb aspic (seasonal) and rouget with endive in beer sauce, followed by a small but judicious selection of potent northern cheeses. Madame Broux oversees the pleasant, provincial-style dining rooms and can help you select one of the many fine beers. ✉ *15 rue de l'Arc-de-Triomphe, Champs-Élysées* ☎ *01–47–54–00–28* ▭ *AE, MC, V* ⏲ *Closed Sun. and 2 wks in Aug. No lunch Sat.* Ⓜ *Charles-de-Gaulle–Étoile.*

ITALIAN

★ $$–$$$ ✕ **Il Baccello.** Young chef Raphael Bembaron is pulling crowds to this outpost with first-rate contemporary Italian food, inspired by his training at the top-draw vegetarian restaurant Joia in Milan. He works almost entirely with organic ingredients, whose quality shows in dishes such as tagliatelle with saffron and rouget, roast lamb with buckwheat-and-corn polenta, and iced cappuccino with coffee and cardamom. This is a good address for vegetarians. The dining room is done in sleek (if noisy) minimalist style. ✉ *33 rue Cardinet, Parc Monceau* ☎ *01–43–80–63–60* ✍ *Reservations essential* ▭ *AE, DC, MC, V* ⏲ *Closed Sun.–Mon. and 3 wks in Aug.* Ⓜ *Wagram.*

JAPANESE

$$–$$$ ✕ **Kifuné.** Removed from the Japanese hub of rue Ste-Anne near the Opéra, Kifuné attracts those with a yen for the real thing. It's rare to see a non-Japanese face in the modest dining room, where you can sit at the bar and admire the sushi chef's lightning-quick skills or opt for a more intimate table. Futo maki (inside-out seaweed rolls) is a popular choice among the Japanese customers; crab and shrimp salad makes a sublime starter, and the miso soup with clams is deeply flavored. A meal here will leave a dent in your wallet—consider it a minitrip to Japan. ✉ *44 rue St-Ferdinand, Champs-Élysées* ☎ *01–45–72–11–19* ✍ *Reserva-*

tions essential ▭ *MC, V* ⊗ *Closed Sun. and 2 wks in Aug. No lunch Mon.* Ⓜ *Argentine.*

NORTH AFRICAN
$$–$$$

✕ **Le Timgad.** For a stylish evening out and a night off from French food, head to this elegant, beautifully decorated North African restaurant. Start with a savory *brick* (crispy parchment pastry filled with meat, eggs, or seafood), followed by tasty couscous or succulent *tagine* (meat or poultry that's slowly braised inside a domed pottery casserole). The lamb tagine with artichokes is especially good. ✉ *21 rue de Brunel, Champs-Élysées* ☎ *01–45–74–23–70* ▭ *AE, DC, MC, V* Ⓜ *Argentine.*

SEAFOOD
$$–$$$

✕ **L'Huîtrier.** If you have a single-minded craving for oysters, this is the place for you. The friendly owner will describe the different kinds available; you can follow these with any of several daily fish specials. The excellent cheeses are from the outstanding shop of Roger Alléosse. Blond wood and cream tones prevail. Should you have trouble getting a table, L'Huîtrier also runs the Presqu'île next door. ✉ *16 rue Saussier-Leroy, Parc Monceau* ☎ *01–40–54–83–44* ▭ *AE, MC, V* ⊗ *Closed Aug. No lunch Mon.* Ⓜ *Ternes.*

18e Arrondissement (Montmartre)

See Where to Eat on the Right Bank: Ile de la Cité to Montmartre map.

FRENCH
$$

✕ **Le Poulbot Gourmand.** Engravings of Old Montmartre and discreet lighting create a relaxed, comfortable conviviality at this tiny neighborhood restaurant named after the chef and owner's favorite painter, Francisque Poulbot. Working in a mostly traditional register, Jean-Paul Langevin whips up dishes such as escargots on artichoke hearts and roast duckling with turnips. There's a well-chosen wine list and good-buy prix-fixe menus for €18 and €33. ✉ *39 rue Lamarck, Montmartre* ☎ *01–46–06–86–00* ▭ *MC, V* ⊗ *Closed Sun. June–Sept. and 2 wks in Aug. No dinner Sun. Oct.–May.* Ⓜ *Lamarck Caulaincourt.*

$–$$

✕ **Chez Toinette.** Between the red lights of Pigalle and the Butte Montmartre, this cozy, candlelit bistro seems too good to be true—even more so when you pay the unassuming bill. In autumn and winter, game features prominently—choose from *marcassin* (young wild boar), venison, and pheasant, or opt for a fish dish, such as red tuna. Regulars can't resist the crème brûlée and the raspberry tart. ✉ *20 rue Germaine Pilon, Montmartre* ☎ *01–42–54–44–36* ▭ *MC, V* ⊗ *Closed Sun.–Mon., Aug., and 2 wks at Christmas* Ⓜ *Pigalle.*

VIETNAMESE
¢–$

✕ **Thu Thu.** Just across the street from the town hall of the 18e arrondissement, this little spot is a great address for thrifty fans of Vietnamese cooking. The engaging owner, Julia Le Phuong, serves up first-rate *pho* (Vietnamese noodle soup); *nems* (deep-fried spring rolls); duck with ginger; and great pork spareribs simply roasted with salt and pepper. There's also a good choice of vegetarian dishes here, and the lunch menu is a real bargain. ✉ *51 bis rue Hermel, Montmartre* ☎ *01–42–54–70–30* ▭ *MC, V* ⊗ *Closed Mon. No lunch Sun. or Aug.* Ⓜ *Simplon.*

19e Arrondissement (Buttes-Chaumont/La Villette)

See Where to Eat on the Right Bank: the Marais to La Villette map.

FRENCH
$$$

✕ **Le Pavillon Puebla.** A bucolic setting and original, flavorful cuisine, such as squid sautéed in saffron and boned pigeon with chorizo-stuffed cabbage are the draw at this 1900s building in the spectacular Parc des Buttes-Chaumont. The elegant dining rooms are a romantic cold-weather lure, and the large terrace is extremely popular in summer. The restaurant feels wonderfully removed from the bustle of the city, but it's a bit hard to find. Seduction comes (relatively) cheaply here if you opt for the prix-fixe menus at €30 or €40. ✉ *In the Parc Buttes-Chaumont (entrance on rue Botzaris), La Villette* ☎ *01–42–08–92–62* ▭ *AE, MC, V* ⏲ *Closed Sun.–Mon., 3 wks in Aug., and Christmas wk* Ⓜ *Buttes-Chaumont.*

20e Arrondissement (Père Lachaise)

See Where to Eat on the Right Bank: the Marais to La Villette map.

FRENCH ★ $$–$$$ ✕ **Le Zéphyr.** Don't let the obscure location put you off—this restaurant is easy to get to from central Paris and well worth the small effort for its buzzy Art Deco dining room and inventive bistro food. The restaurant changed owners and chef in late 2002, but new chef Ludovic Enée continues to serve classic French dishes with unexpected twists, such as marbled foie gras with artichokes and balsamic vinegar; scallops with bay leaves, beet compote, and deep-fried beet strips; and a lemon crème brûlée with thyme sorbet made on the premises. Le Zéphyr's popular terrace allows you to take in the street theater while you dine. ✉ *1 rue du Jourdain, Père Lachaise* ☎ *01–46–36–65–81* ▭ *AE, DC, MC, V* ⏲ *Closed 3 wks in Aug.* Ⓜ *Jourdain.*

$ ✕ **La Boulangerie.** This friendly, incredibly good-value bistro—three courses cost €18—is a great bet if you're planning on a night out in the increasingly trendy Ménilmontant neighborhood or maybe hoping to bring yourself back to life after a visit to Père-Lachaise Cemetery. Occupying an old bakery, this place attracts a relaxed, young local crowd, which comes for the sincere and satisfying seasonal dishes. The menu changes daily but runs to dishes like tuna tartare, grilled rouget on a bed of spinach, pot au feu, and excellent desserts like the rhubarb-filled mille-feuille. ✉ *15 rue des Panoyaux, Père Lachaise* ☎ *01–43–58–45–45* ▭ *MC, V* ⏲ *Closed 2 wks in Aug. No lunch Sat.* Ⓜ *Père-Lachaise.*

Cafés & Salons de Thé

Along with air, water, and wine, the café remains one of the basic necessities of life in Paris. Though they continue to close in the face of changing work and eating habits, cafés can still be found on almost every corner. Many of them look alike—the unfortunate result of '60s and '70s renovations—and only if you stick around long enough and become a regular (or write entire books, as Simone de Beauvoir did) will you discover their true intrigue. The more modest establishments (look for nonchalant locals) will give you a cheaper cup of coffee and a feeling of what real French café life is like. Cafés are required to post a *tarif des consommations,* a list that includes prices for the basics ranging from *café* (espresso) to *vin rouge* (red wine) and list two prices, *au comptoir* (at the counter) and *à terrasse* or *à salle* (seated at a table). If you just need a quick cup of coffee, have it at the counter and save yourself money. If you have a rendezvous, take a table: remember you're paying rent on that little piece of wood, and hang out as long as you like.

1er & 2e Arrondissements (Les Halles/Palais-Royal)

A Priori Thé. Stop in for tea while browsing through the lovely Galerie Vivienne shopping arcade. ✉ *35–37 Galerie Vivienne, at 66 rue Vivienne, Louvre/Tuileries* ☎ *01–42–97–48–75* Ⓜ *Bourse.*

Au Père Tranquille. One of the best places in Paris for people-watching, this café also offers free entertainment from street artists and local performers. ✉ *16 rue Pierre Lescot, Beaubourg/Les Halles* ☎ *01–45–08–00–34* Ⓜ *Les Halles.*

Bernardaud. Decorated by interior-design star Olivier Gagnère, this quiet spot in a covered atrium serves good snacks on the company's own china. ✉ *11 rue Royale, Opéra/Grands Boulevards* ☎ *01–42–66–22–55* Ⓜ *Concorde.*

Café Marly. Run by the Costes brothers, this café overlooking the main courtyard of the Louvre and I. M. Pei's glass pyramid is one of chicest places in Paris to meet for a drink or a coffee. Note that ordinary café service shuts down during meal hours, when overpriced, mediocre food is served. ✉ *Cour Napoléon du Louvre (enter from the Louvre courtyard), 93 rue de Rivoli, Louvre/Tuileries* ☎ *01–49–26–06–60* Ⓜ *Palais-Royal.*

Café Verlet. Many Parisians think this compact spot serves the best coffee in town. You can also get sandwiches and delicious tarts. ✉ *256 rue St-Honoré, Louvre/Tuileries* ☎ *01–42–60–67–39* Ⓜ *Tuileries.*

Le Fumoir. From the same team that made the China Club one of the more enduringly hip addresses in Paris, this café-restaurant has passed over the curve of red-hot chic to become permanent and useful. Its location just across from the Louvre helps, but ultimately what makes it work is that the fashionable folks—press attachés with cell phones, sulky tattooed model-artists, and so on—actually like this place, with its salons that seem variously inspired by Vienna, Edward Hopper, and Scandinavia. The most intimate room is the book-lined library, where book exchanges take place. The modern bistro food is quite tasty and, of the (too) many brunches in Paris, this is one of the best. ✉ *Pl. du Louvre, 6 rue de l'Amiral-Coligny, Louvre/Tuileries* ☎ *01–42–92–00–24* Ⓜ *Louvre.*

Le Ruc Univers. Actors from the Comédie Française and young hipsters hang out at this sleekly modern café near the Louvre. ✉ *1 pl. André-Malraux, Louvre/Tuileries* ☎ *01–42–60–31–57* Ⓜ *Palais-Royal.*

4e Arrondissement (Marais/Beaubourg/Ile St-Louis)

Café Beaubourg. Near the Centre Pompidou, this slick, modern café, designed by architect Christian de Portzamparc, is one of the trendiest rendezvous spots for fashion and art types. Omelets and decent salads are served if you've missed lunch or want a light dinner. ✉ *43 rue St-Merri, Beaubourg/Les Halles* ☎ *01–48–87–63–96* Ⓜ *Hôtel de Ville.*

La Charlotte en l'Ile. The witch who baked gingerbread children in *Hansel and Gretel* might take a fancy to this place—set with fairy lights, carnival masques, and decoupaged detritus, it's a storybook nookery that offers more than 30 varieties of tea along with a sinfully good hot chocolate. ✉ *24 rue St-Louis-en-l'Ile, Ile St-Louis* ☎ *01–43–54–25–83* Ⓜ *Pont Marie.*

L'Etoile Manquante. Owned by Xavier Denamur, who runs several stylish cafés in this street, the "Missing Star" is a great spot for people-watching, but the real attraction is the rest rooms: an electric train is just one of the surprises in store. ✉ *34 rue Vieille-du-Temple, Le Marais* ☎ *01–42–72–48–34* Ⓜ *Hôtel de Ville, St-Paul.*

Le Flore en l'Ile. At this café on the Ile St-Louis you can find renowned Berthillon ice cream and a magnificent view of the Seine. ✉ *42 quai d'Orléans, Ile St-Louis* ☎ *01–43–29–88–27* Ⓜ *Pont Marie.*

Le Loir dans la Théière. This wonderful tearoom in the heart of the Marais has comfortable armchairs and delicious pâtisseries, most memorably a sky-high lemon-meringue tart that seems straight out of the film *Amélie.* ✉ *3 rue des Rosiers, Le Marais* ☎ *01–42–72–90–61* Ⓜ *St-Paul.*

Ma Bourgogne. On the exquisite place des Vosges, this is a calm oasis for a coffee or a light lunch away from the noisy streets. The specialty is steak tartare. ✉ *19 pl. des Vosges, Le Marais* ☎ *01–42–78–44–64* Ⓜ *St-Paul.*

Mariage Frères. This elegant salon de thé serves 500 kinds of tea, along with delicious tarts. ✉ *30 rue du Bourg-Tibourg, Le Marais* ☎ *01–42–72–28–11* Ⓜ *Hôtel de Ville.*

Petit Fer à Cheval. Great coffee is served in the perfect setting for watching the fashionable Marais locals saunter by; food such as a leathery *bavette* (beef skirt steak) however, leaves something to be desired. ✉ *30 rue Vieille-du-Temple, Le Marais* ☎ *01–42–72–47–47* Ⓜ *St-Paul.*

6e Arrondissement (St-Germain/Montparnasse)

Brasserie Lipp. This brasserie, with its turn-of-the-20th-century decor, was a favorite spot of Hemingway's; today television celebrities, journalists, and politicians come here for coffee on the small glassed-in terrace off the main restaurant. ✉ *151 bd. St-Germain, St-Germain-des-Prés* ☎ *01–45–48–53–91* Ⓜ *St-Germain-des-Prés.*

Café de Flore. Picasso, Chagall, Sartre, and de Beauvoir, attracted by the luxury of a heated café, worked and wrote here in the early 20th century. Today you'll find more tourists than intellectuals, but its outdoor terrace is still popular. ✉ *172 bd. St-Germain, St-Germain-des-Prés* ☎ *01–45–48–55–26* Ⓜ *St-Germain-des-Prés.*

Café de la Mairie. Preferred by Henry Miller and Saul Bellow to those on noisy boulevard St-Germain, this place still retains the quiet and unpretentious air of a local café—although Catherine Deneuve could easily be a passerby here. ✉ *8 pl. St-Sulpice, St-Germain-des-Prés* ☎ *01–43–26–67–82* Ⓜ *St-Sulpice.*

Café Orbital. Have a snack while you access your e-mail or the Internet. ✉ *13 rue de Médicis, Latin Quarter* ☎ *01–43–25–76–77* Ⓜ *RER: Luxembourg.*

Les Deux Magots. Dubbed the second home of the *élite intellectuelle,* this café counted Rimbaud, Verlaine, Mallarmé, Wilde, and the Surrealists among its regulars. These days it's overpriced and mostly filled with tourists. ✉ *170 bd. St-Germain, St-Germain-des-Prés* ☎ *01–45–48–55–25* Ⓜ *St-Germain-des-Prés.*

La Palette. In good weather, the terrace is as popular with local art students and gallery owners as it is with tourists. On a rainy afternoon, the interior, too, is cozy—it's decorated with works of art by its habitués. ✉ *43 rue de Seine, St-Germain-des-Prés* ☎ *01–43–26–68–15* Ⓜ *Odéon.*

La Rotonde. The café, a second home to foreign artists and political exiles in the '20s and '30s, has a less exotic clientele today. But it's still a pleasant place to have a coffee on the sunny terrace. ✉ *105 bd. Montparnasse, Montparnasse* ☎ *01–43–26–68–84* Ⓜ *Montparnasse.*

Le Sélect. Isadora Duncan and Hart Crane used to hang out here; now it's a popular spot for a post-cinema beer. ✉ *99 bd. Montparnasse, Montparnasse* ☎ *01–45–48–38–24* Ⓜ *Vavin.*

Le Vieux Colombier. Take a seat on the lovely wicker furniture in front of one of the big windows in this café just around the corner from St-Sulpice and the Vieux Colombier theater. ✉ *65 rue de Rennes, St-Germain-des-Prés* ☎ *01–45–48–53–81* Ⓜ *St-Sulpice.*

8e Arrondissement (Champs-Élysées)

Ladurée. Pretty enough to bring a tear to Proust's eye, this ravishing and famous salon de thé looks barely changed from 1862. Grandmother's grandmother, antiques dealers, and lovers of beauty make up the clientele, which dotes on the lemon and caramel signature macaroons, little tea sandwiches, and a slew of teas that will make you want to stick out your little pinky. A more recent branch, boasting a convincing faux-time-burnished look, is at 75 avenue des Champs-Élysées and there's a Left Bank location at 21 rue Bonaparte. ✉ *16 rue Royale, Opéra/Grands Boulevards* ☎ *01–42–60–21–79* Ⓜ *Madeleine.*

Le Paris. This buzzy little café with a hip crowd and decor is the latest outpost of the Costes brothers, local trendsetters and high-style mavens, and it reflects the fact that the famous avenue is coming back into fashion. Service can be chilly, but it's worth putting up with for the interesting crowd and good, light food. ✉ *93 av. des Champs-Élysées, Champs-Élysées* ☎ *01–47–23–54–37* Ⓜ *George V.*

11ᵉ Arrondissement (Bastille)

Café de l'Industrie. Have a late-afternoon coffee or beer in the warm yellow rooms of this Bastille hangout, where the walls are covered with photos of movie stars. ✉ *16 rue St-Sabin, Bastille/Nation* ☎ *01–47–00–13–53* Ⓜ *Bastille.*

Pause Cafe. This hip Bastille spot attracts a chic, artsy crowd for coffee, cheap beer, and tasty, inexpensive chili and quiche at its red-and-yellow Formica tables. ✉ *41 rue de Charonne, Bastille/Nation* ☎ *01–48–06–80–33* Ⓜ *Ledru-Rollin.*

14ᵉ Arrondissement (Montparnasse)

Café du Dôme. Now a fancy brasserie—though you can still just have a cup of coffee or a drink here—this place began as a dingy meeting place for exiled artists and intellectuals such as Lenin, Picasso, and Chaim Soutine. ✉ *108 bd. Montparnasse, Montparnasse* ☎ *01–43–35–25–81* Ⓜ *Vavin.*

Café de la Place. This café is a charming wood-paneled spot that is perfect for watching the activity inside and out. ✉ *23 rue d'Odessa, Montparnasse* ☎ *01–42–18–01–55* Ⓜ *Montparnasse.*

18ᵉ Arrondissement (Montmartre)

La Crémaillère. Alphonse Mucha frescoes decorate the walls at this veritable monument to 19th-century fin-de-siècle art in Montmartre. ✉ *15 pl. du Tertre, Montmartre* ☎ *01–46–06–58–59* Ⓜ *Anvers.*

Le Sancerre. Sit on the terrace sipping a coffee or a beer and watch the artists, hipsters, and tourists all pass by on their way through Montmartre. ✉ *35 rue des Abbesses, Montmartre* ☎ *01–45–58–08–20* Ⓜ *Abbesses.*

19ᵉ Arrondissement (Buttes-Chaumont/La Villette)

Café de la Musique. This vast, stylishly postmodern café is adjacent to the Cité de la Musique in the Parc de La Villette. In the evenings it's primarily filled with people attending concerts, but the free jazz on Wednesday night and the interesting crowd make it worth the excursion. ✉ *214 av. Jean-Jaurès, La Villette* ☎ *01–48–03–15–91* Ⓜ *Porte de Pantin.*

Wine Bars

Paris wine bars are the perfect place to enjoy a glass (or bottle) of wine with a plate of cheese, charcuterie, or a simple but delicious hot meal. Bar owners are often true wine enthusiasts ready to dispense expert advice. Hours vary widely, so it's best to check ahead if your heart is set on a particular place; many, however, close around 10 PM.

Au Sauvignon. A stylish but jolly Left Bank crowd frequents this homey, friendly spot with an ideally placed terrace. Delicious *tartines* (open-face sandwiches) are served. ✉ *80 rue des Sts-Pères, 7ᵉ, St-Germain-des-Prés* ☎ *01–45–48–49–02* Ⓜ *Sèvres Babylone.*

Aux Bons Crus. This cramped, narrow venue has an authentic Parisian feel (it dates from 1905). ✉ *7 rue des Petits-Champs, 1ᵉʳ, Louvre/Tuileries* ☎ *01–42–60–06–45* Ⓜ *Bourse.*

Le Baron Bouge. Formerly known as Le Baron Rouge, this wine bar near the Place d'Aligre market has changed in name only. In winter months you'll often find an oyster feast in mid-swing outside its door; inside, expect the regulars to welcome you with the same frosty suspicion as cowboys at their local saloon. ✉ *1 rue Théopile-Roussel, 12e, Bastille/Nation* ☎ *01–43–43–14–32* Ⓜ *Ledru-Rollin.*

Le Comptoir. Glasses of Burgundy and Bordeaux, as well as more unusual selections such as wines from Corsica, are served. ✉ *5 rue Monsieur-Le-Prince, 6e, St-Germain-des-Prés* ☎ *01–43–29–12–05* Ⓜ *Odéon.*

Jacques Mélac. This wine bar is named after the jolly owner who harvests grapes from the vine outside and bottles several of his own wines—he even hosts a harvest festival every September. Nonsmokers, make your way through the tiny kitchen to the fume-free back room. ✉ *42 rue Léon-Frot, 11e, Bastille/Nation* ☎ *01–43–70–59–27* Ⓜ *Charonne.*

La Robe et le Palais. Come here for the more than 120 wines from all over France, served *au compteur* (according to the amount consumed), as well as a daily selection of good bistro-style dishes for lunch and dinner. ✉ *13 rue des Lavandières-Ste-Opportune, 1er, Beaubourg/Les Halles* ☎ *01–45–08–07–41* Ⓜ *Châtelet Les Halles.*

Le Rouge Gorge. This sophisticated Marais wine bar attracts discriminating locals who come for unusual wines by the glass and the hearty food. ✉ *8 rue St-Paul, 4e, Le Marais* ☎ *01–48–04–75–89* Ⓜ *Bourse.*

Le Rubis. This resolutely old-time bar specializes in Burgundies. It's most crowded during the day; from 7 to 9:30 PM it's best to be smoke-resistant. ✉ *10 rue du Marché St-Honoré, 1er, Louvre/Tuileries* ☎ *01–42–61–03–34* Ⓜ *Tuileries.*

La Tartine. Inexpensive wine and tartines in a tatty, almost seedy, late-19th-century bar have given this place antihero status among the rebel cognoscenti. ✉ *24 rue de Rivoli, 4e, Le Marais* ☎ *01–42–72–76–85* Ⓜ *St-Paul.*

WHERE TO STAY

FODOR'S CHOICE

Ermitage Hôtel, Montmartre
L'Hôtel, St-Germain-des-Prés
Hôtel du Champ de Mars, Eiffel Tower/Trocadéro
Hôtel des Grands Hommes, Latin Quarter
Hôtel Langlois, Opéra/Grands Boulevards
Hôtel du Lys, Latin Quarter
Hôtel Montalembert, St-Germain-des-Prés
Hôtel de Nesle, St-Germain-des-Pres
Hôtel Relais Saint-Sulpice, St-Germain-des-Prés
Port-Royal Hôtel, Bercy/Tolbiac

HIGHLY RECOMMENDED

Artus Hôtel, St-Germain-des-Prés
Étoile-Péreire, Parc Monceau
Four Seasons Hôtel George V Paris, Champs-Élysées
Hôtel d'Aubusson, St-Germain-des-Prés
Hôtel Beaumarchais, Oberkampf
Hôtel Caron de Beaumarchais, Le Marais
Hôtel Le Clos Médicis, St-Germain-des-Prés
Hôtel de Crillon, Louvre/Tuileries
Hôtel des Jardins du Luxembourg, Latin Quarter
Hôtel Meurice, Louvre/Tuileries
Hôtel Le Saint-Grégoire, St-Germain-des-Prés
Hôtel Saint-Jacques, Latin Quarter
Hôtel Saint Merry, Beaubourg/Les Halles
Park Hyatt Paris Vendôme, Beaubourg/Les Halles
Pavillon de la Reine, Le Marais
Pershing Hall, Champs-Élysées
Relais Christine, St-Germain-des-Prés
Ritz, Louvre/Tuileries

Revised and updated by Ethan Gilsdorf

MORE PEOPLE VISIT FRANCE than any other country—some 77 million each year, or 50% more than runners-up Spain and the United States. Paris itself hosts 26 million, making it one of the top three destination cities on the planet (alongside London and New York). Faced with this ongoing influx, the city has generally risen to the housing challenge with style and grace, offering more than 1,450 different hotels and 73,600 rooms at every conceivable price. More beds spring up each year, feeding the 2.8 billion euro annual Parisian hotel sales juggernaut.

Despite the scales being tipped in favor of the well-heeled, overall there's good news for travelers of all budgets. Increased competition means the bar for service and amenities has been raised everywhere. Many good-value establishments in the lower-to-middle price ranges have updated their funky '70s wallpaper and "Why should I care, Madame?" attitudes, while still keeping their prices in check. Virtually every hotel is equipped with cable TV to meet the needs of international guests, and it's not uncommon for mid-range hotels to have a no-smoking floor, for inexpensive hotels to offer air-conditioning, and even for budget places to have planted an Internet terminal in their little lobbies. Whatever price you're looking for, compared to most other cities Paris is still a paradise for the weary traveler tired of dreary, out-of-date, or cookie-cutter rooms. The best hotels still emanate an unmistakable Paris vibe: weathered beamed ceilings, vaulted stone breakfast crypts, tall windows overlooking zinc rooftops, and leafy courtyards where you can sit and linger over your daily croissant and café (when it's not raining, *bien sûr*).

Generally, there are more hotels on the Right Bank offering luxury—at any rate, formality—than on the Left Bank, where the hotels are frequently smaller and richer in old-fashioned charm. The Right Bank's 1er and 8e arrondissements are still the most exclusive, and prices here reflect this. Less-expensive alternatives on the Right Bank may be found in the fashionable Marais quarter (3e and 4e arrondissements) and the 11e and 12e, near the Opéra Bastille.

Despite widespread improvement, many Paris hotels (especially budget-level accommodations) still have idiosyncrasies—some endearing, others less so. Hotel rooms in Paris's oldest quarters are generally much smaller than their American counterparts. The French double bed is slightly smaller than the American standard. Although air-conditioning has become de rigueur in mid- to higher-priced hotels, as room prices go down it is not always available. (In any case, air-conditioning is not a prerequisite for comfort except during the hottest summer days, which are rare.) Reviews indicate the number of rooms with private bathrooms (which may include a shower or a tub, but not necessarily both). Tubs don't always have stand-up showers, curtains, or full dividers. It's rare to find moderately priced places that expect guests to share toilets or bathrooms, but be sure you know what facilities you are getting when you book a budget hotel. If unsure, ask.

Almost all Paris hotels charge extra for breakfast, with per-person prices ranging from €5 to more than €30 at the luxury establishments. Occasionally breakfast is truly included in the hotel rate. We denote this with a CP, for Continental Plan. You may find the standard Continental breakfast of café au lait, baguette, croissant, jam, and butter neither a good value nor sufficiently robust for your high-energy Parisian adventures. If you do decide to eat elsewhere, it's prudent to inform the desk staff and make sure the breakfast hasn't been charged to your bill. That said, in response to client demand many hotels now offer pricier buffet breakfasts with cheese, cereal, fruit, meat, and eggs made to order. Some hotels have especially pleasant breakfast areas (listed as "dining rooms" in this guide), typically in a stone basement *cave.* Full-fledged hotel restaurants that serve lunch and dinner are common only at luxury establishments.

Unless otherwise stated, hotel rooms have elevators, air-conditioning, TV, telephones, and private bathrooms. Many hotels now have second phone lines with modem plugs installed in each room for Internet connection; we use "in-room data ports" to designate genuine high-speed lines (otherwise, expect escargot-paced surfing).

1er Arrondissement (Louvre/Tuileries)

See Where to Stay on the Right Bank: Ile de la Cité to Montmartre Lodging map.

$$$$ **Hôtel Costes.** Jean-Louis and Gilbert Costes's eponymous hotel is the darling of decorating magazines and a magnet for the sunglasses-at-night set. Nearly every room is swathed in enough pomegranate-red, $400-a-yard fabrics, swagging, and braided trim to choke a runway of supermodels. The bathrooms continue the Second Empire luxury theme. A seductive bar with its labyrinth of little rooms and secluded nooks is *the* place in Paris to be seen trying not to be seen. For taste, many consider this the top Paris hotel, but better wear thick skin: unless you're an off-duty celeb, the army of perfectly coiffed hosts and hostesses has a knack for making you feel underdressed and unimportant. ✉ *239 rue St-Honoré, Louvre/Tuileries, 75001* ☎ *01–42–44–50–00* 🖷 *01–42–44–50–01* 🌐 *www.hotelcostes.com* *77 rooms, 5 suites* *Restaurant, room service, in-room data ports, in-room safes, minibars, cable TV, in-room VCRs, indoor pool, gym, sauna, bar, laundry service, meeting rooms, parking (fee), some pets allowed* 💳 *AE, DC, MC, V* Ⓜ *Tuileries.*

★ $$$$ **Hôtel Meurice.** One of the finest hotels in the world is now even finer, thanks to the Sultan of Brunei's extravagant largesse. The rooms—furnished with Persian carpets, marble mantelpieces, and ormolu clocks—are grandly elegant (book well in advance for one overlooking the Tuileries Gardens). The bathrooms, in red and ocher marble from the Pyrénées and white and gray marble from Italy, are truly elaborate affairs. The winter garden has a stunning Art Nouveau glass roof. At the Restaurant le Meurice, the decor of chandeliers and gilt-boiserie seems as precious as jewelry, with food appropriately priced, as most entrées hover around €35 to €45: for Paris splendor in excelsis, there are few equals to this famous salon. ✉ *228 rue de Rivoli, Louvre/Tuileries, 75001* ☎ *01–44–58–10–10* 🖷 *01–44–58–10–15* 🌐 *www.meuricehotel.com* *160 rooms, 36 suites* *2 restaurants, room service, in-room data ports, in-room safes, minibars, cable TV, health club, bar, laundry service, concierge, business services, meeting rooms, no-smoking rooms* 💳 *AE, DC, MC, V* Ⓜ *Tuileries, Concorde.*

$$$$ **Hôtel Régina.** On handsome place des Pyramides, this 100-year-old Art Nouveau gem oozes old-fashioned grandeur in both its public spaces and guest rooms, where fine antiques abound. There's also a sublime Belle Epoque lounge. Request a room on rue de Rivoli, facing the Louvre and the Tuileries Gardens. ✉ *2 rue des Pyramides, Louvre/Tuileries, 75001* ☎ *01–42–60–31–10* 🖷 *01–40–15–95–16* 🌐 *www.regina-hotel.com* *105 rooms, 15 suites* *Restaurant, room service, in-room data ports, in-room safes, minibars, cable TV, bar, laundry service, concierge, Internet, meeting rooms, some pets allowed (fee), no-smoking rooms* 💳 *AE, DC, MC, V* Ⓜ *Tuileries.*

$$$$ **InterContinental Paris.** This exquisite, late-19th-century hotel, with period details sumptuously restored in 1998, was designed by the architect of the Paris Opéra, Charles Garnier, and three of its gilt-and-stuccoed

Hotel Reservations

It's always a good idea to make hotel reservations in Paris as far in advance as possible, especially in late spring, summer, and fall. E-mailing is probably the easiest way to contact a hotel if the hotel has Internet connections; faxing is another convenient way to contact the hotel (the staff is probably more likely to read English than to understand it over the phone long-distance), though calling also works. Specify the exact dates that you want to stay at the hotel (when you will arrive and when you will check out); the size of the room you want (single or double), and how many people will be sleeping there; what size bed you want (twin beds or double or larger, etc.); and whether you want a bathroom with a shower or bathtub (or both). You might also ask if a deposit (or your credit card number) is required and, if so, what happens if you cancel. Request that the hotel fax you back so that you have a written confirmation of your reservation in hand when you arrive at the hotel.

Here are some French words that can come in handy when booking a room: air-conditioning (*climatisation*); private bath (*salle de bain privée*); bathtub (*baignoire*); shower (*douche*).

If you arrive in Paris without a reservation, one of the two tourist offices may be able to help you. You may be able to get a better rate per night if you are staying a week or longer; ask. Note that the quality of accommodations, particularly in older properties and even in luxury hotels, can vary from room to room; **if you don't like the room you're given, ask to see another.** You'll often see a sign outside a hotel with a painted shield bearing one to four stars based on a government rating system. At the bottom end are one-star hotels, where you might have to share a bathroom and do without an elevator. Two- and three-star hotels generally have private bathrooms, elevators, and in-room televisions. The ratings are sometimes misleading, however, since many hotels prefer to be understarred for tax reasons.

Prices

Hotels are listed by neighborhood and then by price. Often a hotel in a certain price category will have a few less-expensive rooms; it's worth asking about. In the off-season—mid-July, August, November, early December, and late January—tariffs can be considerably lower. It helps to inquire about promotional specials and weekend deals. Rates must be posted in all rooms (usually on the back of the door), with all extra charges clearly shown. There is a nominal city taxe de séjour ranging between €.15 and €1.07 per person, per night, based on the hotel's star rating. Sometimes this tax is included in the room price, sometimes not. (This issue is confused by many rate cards stating that other taxes and services are compris, but then still adding the city tax to your bill. Ask to be certain.)

WHAT IT COSTS IN EUROS*

	$$$$	$$$	$$	$	¢
FOR 2 PEOPLE	over €180	€120–€180	€80–€120	€50–€80	under €50

*Prices are for two people in a standard double room in high season, including tax (19.6%) and service charge.

salons are historic monuments. Guest rooms, more sedate than the public areas, nevertheless have Empire-style furnishings and rich period fabrics. The most coveted and spacious guest rooms overlook quiet inner courtyards. In summer, breakfast on the patio is a delicious experience. *3 rue de Castiglione, Louvre/Tuileries, 75001 01–44–77–11–11; 800/327–0200 in the U.S. 01–44–77–14–60 www.interconti.com 351 rooms, 87 suites Restaurant, room service, in-room data ports, in-room safes, minibars, cable TV with movies and video games, gym, health club, piano bar, baby-sitting, laundry service, concierge, Internet, business services, meeting rooms, no-smoking floors AE, DC, MC, V Concorde.*

★ $$$$ **Ritz.** Festooned with Napoléonic gilt and ormolu, sparkling with crystal chandeliers, and adorned with *qualité de Louvre* antiques, it was founded in 1896 by Cesar Ritz. Be warned, however, that there really are two Ritz spheres. The first is the gilded place Vendôme wing which houses suites named after former high-profile residents, such as Marcel Proust and Coco Chanel. The newer wing, off the back of the building, remains surprisingly intimate. Still, every room is highly comfortable and furnished with all the latest gimmickry (many have a control panel hidden in the nightstand). The lack of a bona-fide lobby discourages sightseers, so you'll have to hang out in the wood-paneled bars, including one that Papa Hemingway "liberated" in 1944. The hotel's Espadon restaurant's terrace patio is swooningly pretty. To work off any extra calories, lucky guests can then repair to the basement health club and pool—a splendid spa that looks like a Louis XIV temple of sweat. *15 pl. Vendôme, Louvre/Tuileries, 75001 01–43–16–30–30 01–43–16–36–68 www.ritz.com 107 rooms, 55 suites 3 restaurants, room service, in-room data ports, in-room safes, minibars, cable TV, indoor pool, hair salon, health club, squash, 2 bars, shops, baby-sitting, laundry service, concierge, business services, meeting rooms, parking (fee) AE, DC, MC, V Opéra.*

$$$–$$$$ **Hôtel de Vendôme.** Formerly the 19th-century embassy of the Republic of Texas, this hotel offers every conceivable luxury. Though the entrance is less than grand, and the restaurant closed as of this writing, the rooms are handsomely done in Second Empire style, with walls and furnishings in muted earth tones and hand-carved wood detailing throughout, not to mention fax machines. Corner rooms have huge picture windows facing two directions, letting in a bath of natural light. Bathrooms are over the top: brass, marble, and silver bathtubs; waterproof telephones; and toiletries from Guerlain. Besides a videophone for checking out callers at the door is the fully automated bedside console straight out of *Star Trek* that controls the lights, curtains, and electronic do-not-disturb sign. *1 pl. Vendôme, Louvre/Tuileries, 75001 01–55–04–55–00 01–49–27–97–89 www.hoteldevendome.com 20 rooms, 9 suites Room service, in-room safes, minibars, cable TV, piano bar, laundry service, Internet, some pets allowed (fee) AE, DC, MC, V Concorde, Opéra.*

$$$ **Hôtel Britannique.** Open since 1870, and just a stone's throw from the Louvre, the Britannique blends courteous English service with old-fashioned French elegance. It has a handsome winding staircase and soundproof rooms appointed in mahogany, antiques, bookcases, and warm-color tones (which the staff likes to compare to the hues of a Turner painting). During World War I, the hotel served as headquarters for a Quaker mission. *20 av. Victoria, Beaubourg/Les Halles, 75001*

☎ 01–42–33–74–59 ⎙ 01–42–33–82–65 ⊕ www.hotel-britannic.com ⇨ 39 rooms, 1 suite ♨ Dining room, in-room data ports, in-room safes, minibars, cable TV, bar, laundry service, no-smoking rooms; no a/c ▭ AE, DC, MC, V Ⓜ Châtelet.

$$–$$$ **Hôtel Brighton.** Many of Paris's most prestigious palace hotels are found facing the Tuileries or Place de la Concorde. The Brighton breathes the same rarified air under the arcades, for a fraction of the price. Inside, you'll find stone columns, chandeliers, and a palatial ambience. Smaller rooms with showers look onto a courtyard; street-facing chambers have balconies and a royal view onto the gardens and Left Bank in the distance. Renovations will update a third of the older rooms—ask for one if you prefer the 21st century to the 19th. *✉ 218 rue de Rivoli, Louvre/Tuileries, 75001 ☎ 01–47–03–61–61 ⎙ 01–42–60–41–78 ⊕ www.esprit-de-france.com ⇨ 65 rooms ♨ Dining room, in-room data ports, in-room safes, minibars, cable TV, laundry service, some pets allowed ▭ AE, DC, MC, V Ⓜ Tuileries.*

$–$$ **Hôtel Londres St-Honoré.** An appealing combination of character and comfort distinguishes this small, inexpensive hotel a five-minute walk from the Louvre. Exposed oak beams, statues in niches, and rustic stone walls give this place an old-fashioned air, with new carpets and paint throughout after a touch-up. Though rooms have floral bedspreads and standard hotel furniture, they are pleasant and the price is right. Note that the elevator only starts on the second floor. *✉ 13 rue St-Roch, Louvre/Tuileries, 75001 ☎ 01–42–60–15–62 ⎙ 01–42–60–16–00 ⇨ 21 rooms, 4 suites ♨ Dining room, in-room data ports, minibars, cable TV, some pets allowed ▭ AE, DC, MC, V Ⓜ Pyramides.*

$–$$ **Hôtel Louvre Forum.** This hotel is a find: smack in the center of Paris, it has reasonably priced, clean, comfortable, well-equipped rooms and a friendly feel. What it lacks in time-burnished appeal it makes up for in location, amenities, and low rates. Breakfast is served in a homey vaulted cellar. *✉ 25 rue du Bouloi, Louvre/Tuileries, 75001 ☎ 01–42–36–54–19 ⎙ 01–42–33–66–31 ⊕ www.hotellouvreforum.com ⇨ 27 rooms ♨ Dining room, minibars, cable TV, bar; no a/c ▭ AE, DC, MC, V Ⓜ Louvre.*

¢–$ **Hôtel Henri IV.** Over on Ile de la Cité, the "other" island that's skipped by most tourists looking for lodging, this 400–year-old building once housed King Henri IV's printing presses. These days it's the site of one of the city's most beloved budget sleeps. The lobby is drab, the narrow staircase (five flights, no elevator) creaks, and the rooms wear their age with pride. But the location overlooking the oasis-like place Dauphine, just a few steps from Pont Neuf and the Seine, means you can use a park bench under the plane trees as your salon. Bathrooms are in the hallway; pay a little extra and get a room with private shower. *✉ 25 pl. Dauphine, Ile de la Cité, 75001 ☎ 01–43–54–44–53 ⇨ 17 rooms, 4 with bath ♨ Dining room; no a/c, no room phones, no room TVs ▭ No credit cards 🍽 CP Ⓜ Cité, St-Michel, Pont Neuf.*

2e Arrondissement (La Bourse/Opéra)

See Where to Stay on the Right Bank: Ile de la Cité to Montmartre map.

$$$$ **Hôtel Westminster.** This former inn and coach stop on an elegant street between the Opéra and place Vendôme was built in the mid-19th century and happily retains the requisite quasi-royal period furniture,

Oriental rugs, marble fireplaces, crystal chandeliers, parquet floors, and piped-in classical music. The pleasant Duke's piano bar is a popular rendezvous spot, and the hotel's Michelin one-star restaurant, Le Céladon, serves outstanding French cuisine. A glass-enclosed fitness center has views over the rooftops. ✉ *13 rue de la Paix, Opéra/Grands Boulevards, 75002* ☎ *01–42–61–57–46* 📠 *01–42–60–30–66* 🌐 *www.hotelwestminster.com* ⇨ *80 rooms, 22 suites* ♨ *Restaurant, room service, in-room data ports, in-room safes, minibars, cable TV with movies and video games, health club, spa, piano bar, baby-sitting, laundry service, business services, meeting rooms, parking (fee), no-smoking rooms* ▭ *AE, DC, MC, V* Ⓜ *Opéra.*

★ $$$$ **Park Hyatt Paris Vendôme.** Five connecting Haussmann-era buildings were converted into the Hyatt, upping the ante in an already luxury hotel–laden neighborhood. Whereas neighbors like the Ritz and Vendôme are gilded and curlicued to the max, the Hyatt paints a sleeker, more youthful picture. Beige and pale pink schemes complement the unadorned limestone of the vast museum-like lobby—a 350-plus-piece collection of contemporary art is scattered throughout the hotel. Sun beams in through a massive glass-roofed Salon Verrière. Rooms continue the minimal jazzy coolness, with Bang and Olufsen TVs and DVD players and Japanese-inspired bathrooms. American designer Ed Tuttle's most romantic decorative flourishes are the Roseline Granet–designed door handles and Giacometti-like bronze lamp sconces of arching human figures found everywhere except the 300-place parking lot, miraculously occupying the bowels below. ✉ *3–5 rue de la Paix, Beaubourg/Les Halles, 75002* ☎ *01–58–71–12–34* 📠 *01–58–71–12–35* 🌐 *www.paris.vendome.hyatt.com* ⇨ *159 rooms, 29 suites* ♨ *2 restaurants, room service, in-room data ports, in-room safes, minibars, cable TV, health club, massage, spa, bar, baby-sitting, laundry service, concierge, Internet, business services, meeting rooms, free parking, no-smoking floors* ▭ *AE, DC, MC, V* Ⓜ *Concorde, Opéra.*

$$$ **Hôtel de Noailles.** With a nod to the work of postmodern designers like Putman and Starck, this nouveau-wave inn (part of the Tulip Inn group) is near the top of Paris's short list of well-priced, style-driven boutique hotels. Though not to everyone's taste, rooms are imaginatively decorated with funky, almost Japanese-inspired furnishings and contemporary Deco details such as frosted glass, veneer paneling, and skinny, antenna-like lamps; the look is either fun and very hip or, depending on your outlook, extremely dated. A spacious outdoor terrace connects to the breakfast lounge. ✉ *9 rue de Michodière, Opéra/Grands Boulevards, 75002* ☎ *01–47–42–92–90* 📠 *01–49–24–92–71* 🌐 *www.hoteldenoailles.com* ⇨ *59 rooms, 2 suites* ♨ *Dining room, room service, in-room safes, minibars, cable TV, health club, bar, laundry service, meeting rooms, some pets allowed, no-smoking rooms* ▭ *AE, DC, MC, V* Ⓜ *Opéra.*

$$$ **Hôtel Victoires Opéra.** This terrific hotel is an oasis of calm amid the colorful bustle of Montorgueil, a very popular pedestrian-only market street near Les Halles, the Centre Pompidou, and the Marais. In 2001 it was renovated and renamed (formerly the Besançon). Now the lobby, corridors, and rooms exude a minimalist, streamlined aesthetic, with plenty of plum, mustard, and Burgundy-color fabrics and highly polished surfaces. ✉ *56 rue Montorgueil, Beaubourg/Les Halles, 75002* ☎ *01–42–36–41–08* 📠 *01–45–08–08–79* 🌐 *www.paris-hotel-opera.com* ⇨ *20 rooms* ♨ *Dining room, room service, in-room data ports, in-room safes, minibars, cable TV, baby-sitting, laundry service, business services, no-smoking rooms* ▭ *AE, DC, MC, V* Ⓜ *Étienne Marcel, Les Halles.*

¢ **Hôtel Tiquetonne.** Just off marché Montorgueil and a short hoof from Les Halles, this is one of the least expensive hotels in the city center. The

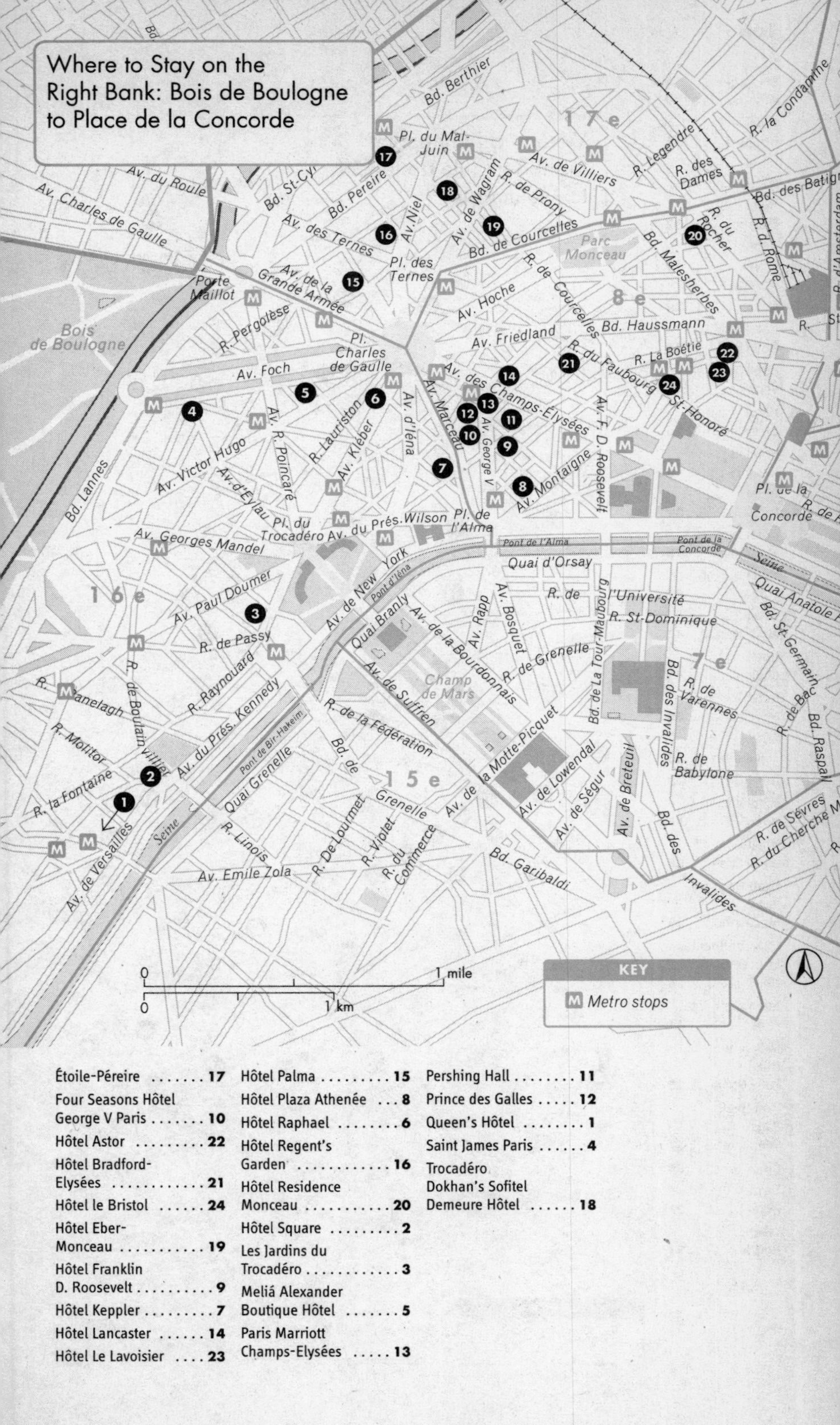

Where to Stay on the Right Bank: Bois de Boulogne to Place de la Concorde
Bd. Berthier
17e
R. la Condamine
Pl. du Mal-Juin
Av. de Villiers
R. Legendre
R. des Dames
Bd. des Batignolles
Av. du Roule
Av. Charles de Gaulle
Bd. St-Cyr
Bd. Pereire
Av. Niel
Av. de Wagram
R. de Prony
Av. des Ternes
Bd. de Courcelles
Parc Monceau
R. du Rocher
R. d. Rome
Bd. Malesherbes
Porte Maillot
Av. de la Grande Armée
Pl. des Ternes
Av. Hoche
R. de Courcelles
8e
Bd. Haussmann
Bois de Boulogne
R. Pergolèse
Pl. Charles de Gaulle
Av. Friedland
R. du Faubourg St-Honoré
R. La Boétie
Av. Foch
Av. des Champs-Élysées
Av. Marceau
Av. d'Iéna
R. Lauriston
Av. Kléber
Av. R. Poincaré
Av. Victor Hugo
Av. d'Eylau
Av. George V
Av. Montaigne
Av. F. D. Roosevelt
Bd. Lannes
Pl. du Trocadéro
Av. du Prés. Wilson
Pl. de l'Alma
Pl. de la Concorde
Av. Georges Mandel
Pont de l'Alma
Pont de la Concorde
Quai d'Orsay
Seine
Quai Anatole France
16e
Av. Paul Doumer
Av. de New York
Pont d'Iéna
Quai Branly
Av. Rapp
Av. Bosquet
R. de l'Université
R. St-Dominique
Bd. St-Germain
R. de Passy
Av. de la Bourdonnais
R. de Grenelle
7e
R. Ranelagh
R. de Boulainvilliers
R. Raynouard
Champ de Mars
Av. de Suffren
Bd. de La Tour-Maubourg
Bd. des Invalides
R. de Varennes
R. du Bac
Bd. Raspail
R. Molitor
Av. du Prés. Kennedy
R. de la Fédération
Av. de la Motte-Picquet
R. de Babylone
R. la Fontaine
Pont de Bir-Hakeim
Quai Grenelle
Bd. de Grenelle
15e
Av. de Lowendal
Av. de Ségur
Av. de Breteuil
Av. de Versailles
R. Linois
R. De Lourmel
R. Violet
R. du Commerce
Bd. Garibaldi
R. de Sèvres
R. du Cherche Midi
Av. Emile Zola
Bd. des Invalides
0 1 mile
0 1 km
KEY
M Metro stops
Étoile-Péreire 17
Four Seasons Hôtel George V Paris 10
Hôtel Astor 22
Hôtel Bradford-Elysées 21
Hôtel le Bristol 24
Hôtel Eber-Monceau 19
Hôtel Franklin D. Roosevelt 9
Hôtel Keppler 7
Hôtel Lancaster 14
Hôtel Le Lavoisier 23
Hôtel Palma 15
Hôtel Plaza Athenée . . . 8
Hôtel Raphael 6
Hôtel Regent's Garden 16
Hôtel Residence Monceau 20
Hôtel Square 2
Les Jardins du Trocadéro 3
Meliá Alexander Boutique Hôtel 5
Paris Marriott Champs-Elysées 13
Pershing Hall 11
Prince des Galles 12
Queen's Hôtel 1
Saint James Paris 4
Trocadéro Dokhan's Sofitel Demeure Hôtel 18

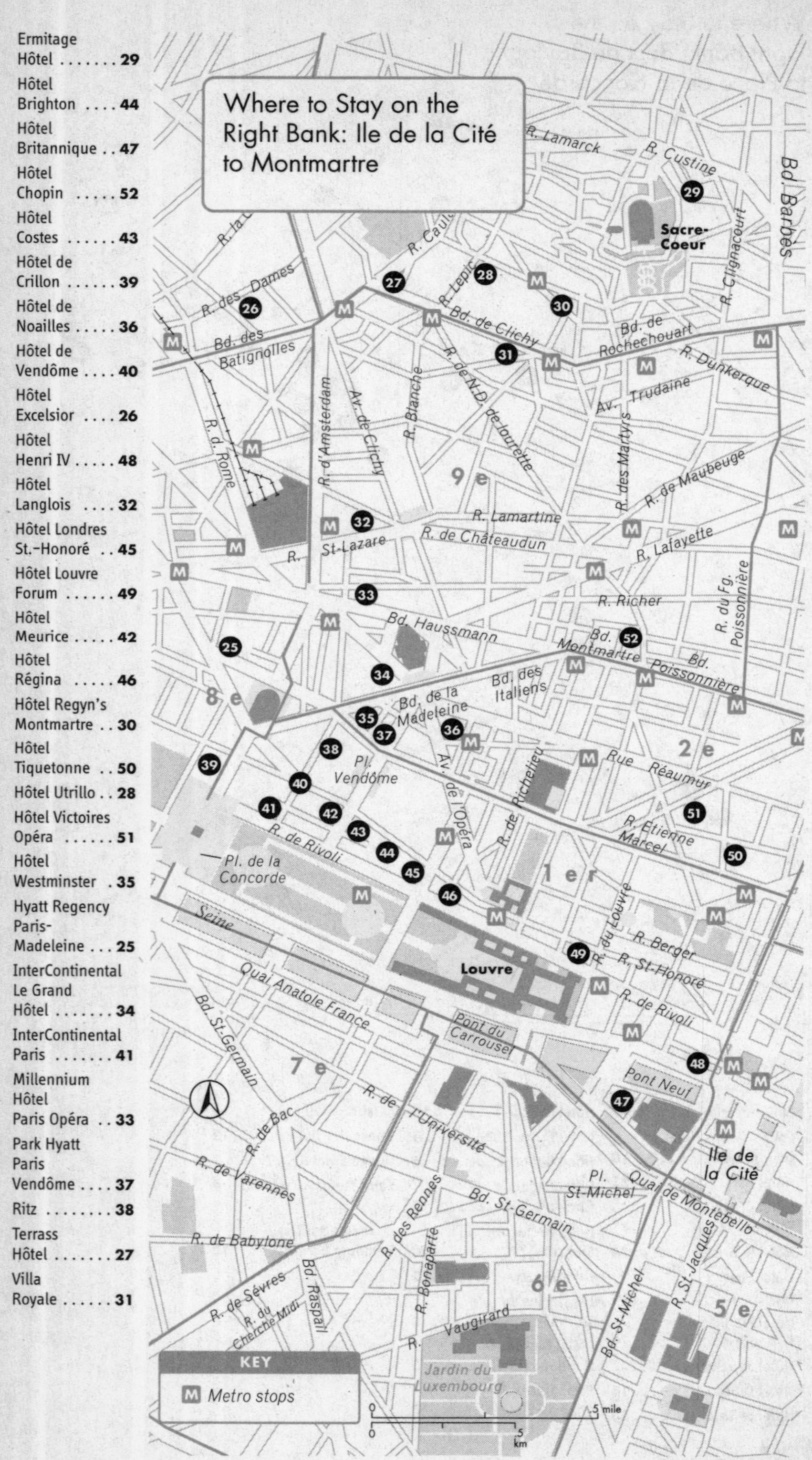
Ermitage Hôtel 29
Hôtel Brighton 44
Hôtel Britannique . . 47
Hôtel Chopin 52
Hôtel Costes 43
Hôtel de Crillon 39
Hôtel de Noailles 36
Hôtel de Vendôme 40
Hôtel Excelsior 26
Hôtel Henri IV 48
Hôtel Langlois 32
Hôtel Londres St.-Honoré . . 45
Hôtel Louvre Forum 49
Hôtel Meurice 42
Hôtel Régina 46
Hôtel Regyn's Montmartre . . 30
Hôtel Tiquetonne . . 50
Hôtel Utrillo . . 28
Hôtel Victoires Opéra 51
Hôtel Westminster . 35
Hyatt Regency Paris-Madeleine . . . 25
InterContinental Le Grand Hôtel 34
InterContinental Paris 41
Millennium Hôtel Paris Opéra . . 33
Park Hyatt Paris Vendôme 37
Ritz 38
Terrass Hôtel 27
Villa Royale 31
Where to Stay on the Right Bank: Ile de la Cité to Montmartre
R. Lamarck
R. Custine
Bd. Barbès
Sacre-Coeur
R. Clignacourt
R. des Dames
Bd. des Batignolles
Bd. de Clichy
Bd. de Rochechouart
R. Dunkerque
Av. Trudaine
R. d'Amsterdam
Av. de Clichy
R. Blanche
R. de N.-D. de Lourette
R. des Martyrs
R. de Maubeuge
R. d. Rome
9e
R. Lamartine
R. de Châteaudun
R. Lafayette
R. St-Lazare
R. Richer
R. du Fg. Poissonnière
Bd. Haussmann
Bd. Montmartre
Bd. Poissonnière
Bd. des Italiens
Bd. de la Madeleine
8e
2e
Rue Réaumur
Pl. Vendôme
Av. de l'Opéra
R. de Richelieu
R. Etienne Marcel
R. de Rivoli
Pl. de la Concorde
1er
R. du Louvre
R. Berger
R. St-Honoré
Seine
Louvre
Quai Anatole France
Pont du Carrousel
Bd. St-Germain
Pont Neuf
7e
R. de l'Université
R. de Bac
Ile de la Cité
R. de Varennes
Pl. St-Michel
Quai de Montebello
R. des Rennes
Bd. St-Germain
R. de Babylone
R. St-Jacques
R. de Sèvres
R. du Cherche Midi
Bd. Raspail
R. Bonaparte
6e
R. Vaugirard
Bd. St-Michel
5e
Jardin du Luxembourg
KEY
M Metro stops
0 .5 mile
0 .5 km

rooms aren't much to look at, but they're always clean and some are downright spacious. Book on one of the top two floors facing the quiet, pedestrian rue Tiquetonne, not the loud, car-strangled rue Turbigo. ✉ *6 rue Tiquetonne, Beaubourg/Les Halles, 75002* ☎ *01–42–36–94–58* 📠 *01–42–36–02–94* *45 rooms, 33 with bath* *Some pets allowed; no a/c, no room TVs* 💳 *AE, MC, V* Ⓜ *Étienne Marcel, Châtelet.*

3e Arrondissement (Marais)

See Where to Stay on the Right Bank: The Marais to La Villette map.

★ $$$$ **Pavillon de la Reine.** This gorgeous place des Vosges mansion dating from 1612 competes with Ritz-level luxury but on a more intimate scale, sans the pomp or potentially intimidating service. *Entrez* through a cobblestone courtyard into a luscious lobby that recalls a royal hunting lodge: massive beams overhead, tapestries, stone walls, and a salon with the original 300-year-old fireplace. You can reserve a room in the older section, decorated in classy Louis XIII style and perhaps with a canopy bed, or opt for the modern yet reserved wing that has parquet bathroom floors and plush eggplant-color sofas and padded headboards. For an absolutely royal feeling, ask for a duplex with French windows overlooking the flower-filled courtyards. ✉ *28 pl. des Vosges, Le Marais, 75003* ☎ *01–40–29–19–19; 800/447–7462 in the U.S.* 📠 *01–40–29–19–20* 🌐 *www.pavillon-de-la-reine.com* *31 rooms, 24 suites* *Dining room, room service, in-room data ports, in-room safes, minibars, cable TV, bar, laundry service, concierge, Internet, free parking, some pets allowed* 💳 *AE, DC, MC, V* Ⓜ *Bastille, St-Paul.*

4e Arrondissement (Marais/Ile St-Louis)

See Where to Stay on the Right Bank: The Marais to La Villette map.

$$$ **Hôtel du Jeu de Paume.** Set off the street by heavy doors and a small courtyard, the showpiece of this lovely 17th-century hotel on the Ile St-Louis is the stone-walled, vaulted lobby–cum–breakfast room. It stands on an erstwhile court where French aristocrats once played *jeu de paume,* an early version of tennis using palm fronds. The bright rooms are nicely done up in butter yellow with beamed ceilings and damask upholstery; however, some rooms are quite small. The little garden is a haven of sun-drenched tranquillity. ✉ *54 rue St-Louis-en-l'Ile, Ile-St-Louis, 75004* ☎ *01–43–26–14–18* 📠 *01–40–46–02–76* 🌐 *www.jeudepaumehotel.com* *26 rooms, 4 suites* *Dining room, in-room data ports, in-room safes, minibars, cable TV, exercise equipment, sauna, billiards, bar, baby-sitting, laundry service, meeting rooms, some pets allowed; no a/c* 💳 *AE, DC, MC, V* Ⓜ *Pont Marie.*

$$$ Fodor'sChoice ★ **Hôtel Saint Merry.** Due south of the Pompidou Center is this small and stunning Gothic hideaway, once the presbytery of the adjacent Saint Merry church. This enchanting hotel has been carefully restored, and in its 17th-century stone interior you can gaze through stained glass, relax on a church pew, or lean back on a headboard recycled from an old Catholic confessional. The hotel's lack of an elevator is also in keeping with its ascetic past. With a massive hardwood table, fireplace, and high ceiling, the suite is fit for a royal council. Room nine is bisected by stone buttresses still supporting the church. ✉ *78 rue de la Verrerie, Beaubourg/Les Halles, 75004* ☎ *01–42–78–14–15* 📠 *01–40–29–06–82* 🌐 *www.hotelmarais.com* *11 rooms, 1 suite* *In-room safes, laundry service, some pets allowed; no TV in some rooms* 💳 *MC, V* Ⓜ *Châtelet.*

$$–$$$ **Hôtel Axial Beaubourg.** A solid bet in the Marais, this hotel in a 16th-century building has beamed ceilings in the lobby and in the six first-floor rooms. In 2002 a top-to-bottom reworking resulted in a sleeker,

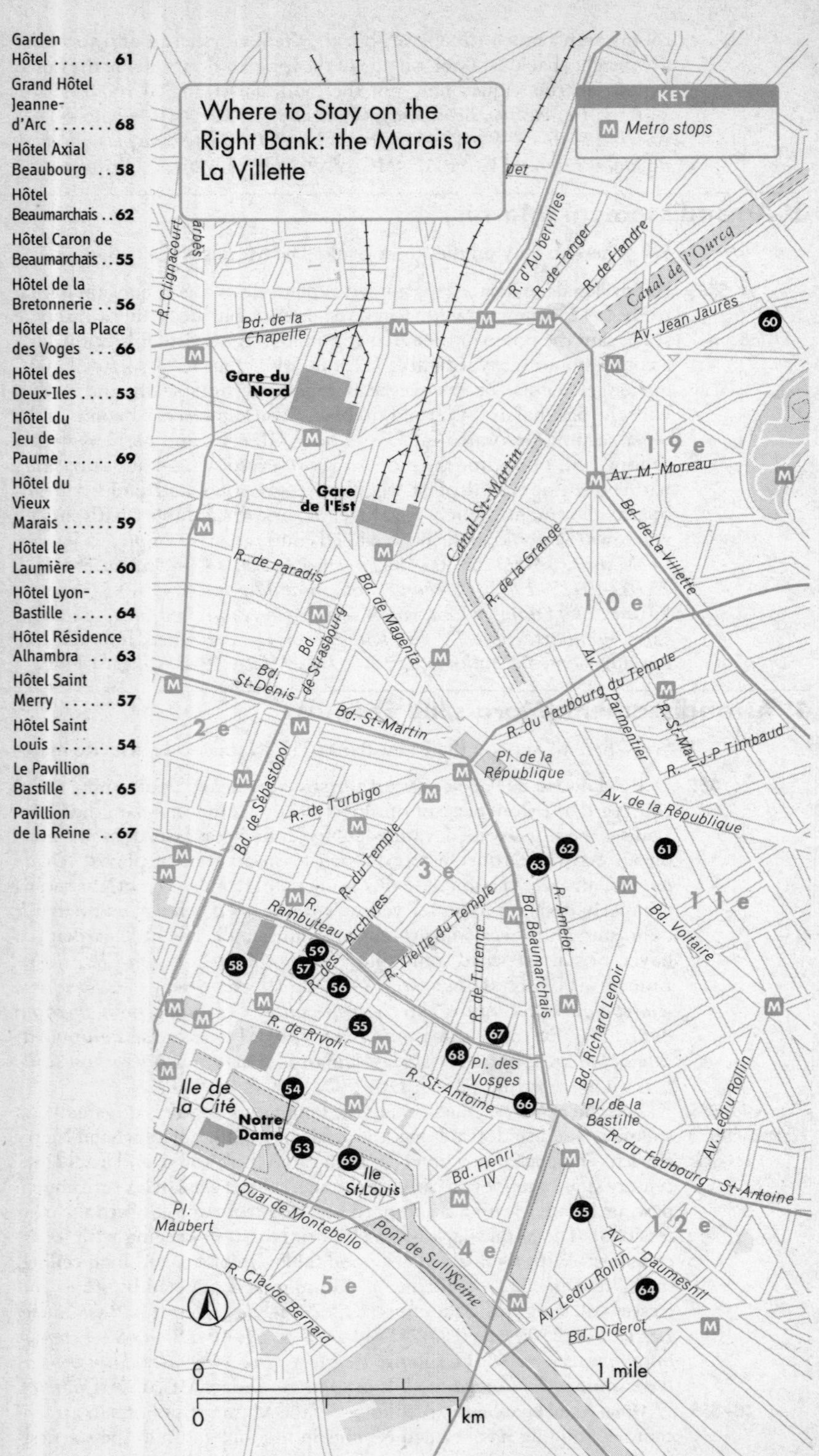
Where to Stay on the Right Bank: the Marais to La Villette
KEY
Metro stops
R. Clignacourt
Bd. de la Chapelle
Gare du Nord
Gare de l'Est
R. d'Au bervilles
R. de Tanger
R. de Flandre
Canal de l'Ourcq
Av. Jean Jaurès
19e
Av. M. Moreau
Bd. de La Villette
Canal St-Martin
R. de la Grange
R. de Paradis
Bd. de Magenta
Bd. de Strasbourg
Bd. St-Denis
10e
Av. Parmentier
R. du Faubourg du Temple
R. St-Maur
R. J-P Timbaud
Bd. St-Martin
2e
Pl. de la République
Av. de la République
Bd. de Sébastopol
R. de Turbigo
R. du Temple
3e
R. Rambuteau
R. des Archives
R. Vieille du Temple
R. de Turenne
Bd. Beaumarchais
R. Amelot
Bd. Voltaire
11e
R. des
R. de Rivoli
Pl. des Vosges
R. St-Antoine
Bd. Richard Lenoir
Av. Ledru Rollin
Ile de la Cité
Notre Dame
Pl. de la Bastille
R. du Faubourg St-Antoine
Ile St-Louis
Bd. Henri IV
Pl. Maubert
Quai de Montebello
Pont de Sully
Seine
4e
12e
Av. Daumesnil
R. Claude Bernard
5e
Av. Ledru Rollin
Bd. Diderot
0
1 mile
0
1 km

hipper interior and new, higher prices to match the fancy Burgundy and brown fabrics and added amenities. The bright lobby has big, street-facing picture windows, and the Centre Pompidou and the Picasso Museum are only a five-minute walk away. ✉ *11 rue du Temple, Le Marais, 75004* ☎ *01–42–72–72–22* 🖷 *01–42–72–03–53* 🌐 *www.axialbeaubourg.com* ⇨ *39 rooms* ♖ *Dining room, in-room data ports, in-room safes, minibars, cable TV, laundry service* 💳 *AE, DC, MC, V* Ⓜ *Hôtel de Ville.*

★ **$$–$$$** 🏨 **Hôtel Caron de Beaumarchais.** The theme of this intimate hotel is the work of former next-door neighbor Pierre-Augustin Caron de Beaumarchais, supplier of military aid to American revolutionaries and author of *The Marriage of Figaro*. First-edition copies of his books adorn the public spaces and the salons faithfully reflect the taste of 18th-century French nobility, right down to the wallpaper and upholstery. Rooms have Nordic-style wood tables and chairs, hand-painted bathroom tiles, and gilded mirrors. Street-side rooms on the second through fifth floors are the largest, while smaller sixth-floor garrets under the mansard roof have beguiling views across Right Bank rooftops. ✉ *12 rue Vieille-du-Temple, Le Marais, 75004* ☎ *01–42–72–34–12* 🖷 *01–42–72–34–63* 🌐 *www.carondebeaumarchais.com* ⇨ *19 rooms* ♖ *Dining room, in-room data ports, minibars, cable TV, laundry service* 💳 *AE, DC, MC, V* Ⓜ *Hôtel de Ville.*

$$ 🏨 **Grand Hôtel Jeanne-d'Arc.** If you're on a budget, you'll get your money's worth at this hotel in an unbeatable location off the tranquil place St-Catherine, one of the city's lesser-known pedestrian squares. The 17th-century building has been a hotel for more than a century, and while rooms are on the spartan side they are well maintained, fairly spacious, and done in cheery pastel colors (some rooms facing the back are dimmer). The welcoming staff is informal and happy to recount the history of this former market quartier, now home to café life and boutique shopping. ✉ *3 rue de Jarente, Le Marais, 75004* ☎ *01–48–87–62–11* 🖷 *01–48–87–37–31* 🌐 *www.hoteljeannedarc.com* ⇨ *36 rooms* ♖ *Dining room, cable TV, some pets allowed; no a/c* 💳 *MC, V* Ⓜ *St-Paul.*

$$ 🏨 **Hôtel de la Bretonnerie.** This small hotel is in a 17th-century *hôtel particulier* (town house) on a tiny street in the Marais, a few minutes' walk from the Centre Pompidou and the bars and cafés of rue Vieille du Temple. Rooms are classified as either *chambres classiques* or *chambres de charme,* the latter being more spacious, and naturally pricier, but with more elaborate furnishings like Louis XIII–style four-poster canopy beds and marble-clad bathtubs. Overall, the establishment is spotless. Breakfast is served in the vaulted cellar. ✉ *22 rue Ste-Croix-de-la-Bretonnerie, Le Marais, 75004* ☎ *01–48–87–77–63* 🖷 *01–42–77–26–78* 🌐 *www.labretonnerie.com* ⇨ *22 rooms, 7 suites* ♖ *Dining room, in-room data ports, in-room safes, minibars, cable TV, laundry service; no a/c* 💳 *MC, V* ⏲ *Closed Aug.* Ⓜ *Hôtel de Ville.*

$$ 🏨 **Hôtel des Deux-Iles.** A tiny Ile St-Louis hotel, it's best used for taking advantage of the lovely neighborhood setting. With red-and-gold floral fabrics and contemporary art on the walls, the rooms unsuccessfully try to blend modern fashion with the 17th-century neighborhood. At least beams are exposed and some rooms have blue-and-white tiled bathrooms. Ask for one overlooking the little garden courtyard. The lobby's better at showing off its charms: flowers and plants are scattered throughout the main hall, and tapestries cover the restored stone walls. In winter a roaring fire warms the basement lounge. ✉ *59 rue St-Louis-en-l'Ile, Ile-St-Louis, 75004* ☎ *01–43–26–13–35* 🖷 *01–43–29–60–25* 🌐 *www.hotel-ile-saintlouis.com* ⇨ *17 rooms* ♖ *Dining room, in-room safes, cable TV, baby-sitting, Internet* 💳 *AE, MC, V* Ⓜ *Pont Marie.*

$$ 🏨 **Hôtel de la Place des Vosges.** A loyal, eclectic clientele swears by this small, historic Marais hotel on a delightful street just south of place des

Vosges. The Louis XIII–style reception area and rooms with oak-beamed ceilings, rough-hewn stone, and a mix of rustic finds from secondhand shops evoke the Old Marais. Ask for the top-floor room, the hotel's largest, for its view over Right Bank rooftops; others the size of walk-in closets are less expensive. Five rooms have showers with multijet massage sprayers. ✉ *12 rue de Birague, Le Marais, 75004* ☎ *01–42–72–60–46* 🖷 *01–42–72–02–64* *16 rooms* *Dining room, in-room safes, minibars, cable TV, laundry service; no a/c* ▭ *AE, DC, MC, V* Ⓜ *Bastille.*

$$ **Hôtel Saint Louis.** Louis XIII–style furniture, oil paintings, exposed beams, bare stone, and various antiques invite speculation about which duke may have owned this 17th-century building on the coveted Ile St-Louis. It's best to request the remodeled rooms on the fourth and fifth floors. Mini balconies on the upper levels also have Seine views. Number 51 has a tear-shape tub and a peek at the Panthéon. Breakfast is served in the atmospheric cellar. ✉ *75 rue St-Louis-en-l'Ile, Ile St-Louis, 75004* ☎ *01–46–34–04–80* 🖷 *01–46–34–02–13* 🌐 *www.hotelsaintlouis.com* *19 rooms* *Dining room, in-room safes, cable TV* ▭ *MC, V* Ⓜ *Pont Marie.*

$$ **Hôtel du Vieux Marais.** This pleasingly minimalist hotel with a turn-of-the-20th-century facade is on a quiet street in the heart of the Marais. Rooms are bright and impeccably clean, with oak and burgundy-leather seating by the Italian interior designer Poltrona Frau; try to get one overlooking the courtyard. The renovated, sparkling bathrooms have recessed lighting and tile-work designs. Breakfast is served in the modish lounge. The staff is exceptionally courteous. ✉ *8 rue du Plâtre, Le Marais, 75004* ☎ *01–42–78–47–22* 🖷 *01–42–78–34–32* 🌐 *www.vieuxmarais.com* *30 rooms* *Dining room, in-room safes, cable TV* ▭ *AE, MC, V* Ⓜ *Hôtel de Ville.*

5e Arrondissement (Latin Quarter)

See Where to Stay on the Left Bank map.

$$$ Fodor'sChoice ★ **Hôtel des Grands Hommes.** The "Great Men" this hotel has in mind are busy resting in peace within the nearby Panthéon, which the Grands Hommes overlooks. Remodeled top to bottom, the hotel's look is Empire-style neo-Greek and Roman, combining plaster busts of writers and statesmen, urns, and laurel-wreath motifs with plush and impeccably selected beige, eggplant, and burgundy fabrics. The gamble succeeds as a sumptuous classical knock-off. Top-floor rooms have balconies with tables and chairs and fantastic north-facing views of the cityscape. Even if your room has no grand view, you'll still be happily distracted by the designer's obsessive attention to detail. ✉ *17 pl. du Panthéon, Latin Quarter, 75005* ☎ *01–46–34–19–60* 🖷 *01–43–26–67–32* 🌐 *www.hoteldesgrandshommes.com* *31 rooms* *Dining room, in-room data ports, in-room safes, minibars, cable TV, baby-sitting, laundry service, Internet, meeting room, some pets allowed* ▭ *AE, DC, MC, V* Ⓜ *RER: Luxembourg.*

★ **$$$** **Hôtel des Jardins du Luxembourg.** Blessed with a personable staff and a smart, stylish look, this hotel, on an unbelievably calm cul-de-sac just a block from the Luxembourg Gardens, is an oasis for contemplation—even Freud stayed here in winter 1885–86. A cheery hardwood-floor lobby with fireplace leads to smallish rooms furnished with wrought-iron beds, pastel bathroom tiles, and contemporary Provençal fabrics. Ask for one with a balcony overlooking the street; the best room, No. 25, has dormer windows with a peekaboo view of the Eiffel Tower. Two rooms have separate street-level entrances for ultimate privacy. It's an easy commute to either airport or the Eurostar via a direct train that stops at the end of the street. ✉ *5 impasse Royer-Collard, Latin Quar-*

ter, 75005 ☎ 01–40–46–08–88 📠 01–40–46–02–28 🌐 www.pariserve.com/jardin-luxembourg/english.htm ⇨ 26 rooms ♢ Dining room, in-room safes, minibars, sauna, laundry service ▭ AE, DC, MC, V Ⓜ RER: Luxembourg.

$$$ **Libertel Quartier Latin.** The flagship of the Libertel chain combines sleek design with intellectual rigor. It takes its cues from the nearby Sorbonne university, with a reading room in the lobby and photos and portraits of celebrated writers on the walls. Mixing robin's-egg blue, beige, and lilac color schemes, the classy, contemporary rooms are furnished with ebony veneer furniture and quilted cotton duvets. Ask for one on the sixth floor, preferably No. 602 or 603, which have beautiful views of Notre-Dame from their balconies. If this doesn't inspire you finally to write that novel, maybe the carpets will: they're inscribed with quotations from Balzac and Baudelaire. ✉ *9 rue des Écoles, Latin Quarter, 75005 ☎ 01–44–27–06–45 📠 01–43–25–36–70 🌐 www.libertel-hotels.com ⇨ 23 rooms, 6 suites ♢ Dining room, room service, in-room safes, minibars, cable TV, laundry service, some pets allowed, no-smoking rooms ▭ AE, DC, MC, V Ⓜ Cardinal Lemoine.*

$$ **Hôtel Grandes Écoles.** *Propriétaire* Madame Lefloch takes no chances with security: massive wooden doors protect her castle from invaders while cameras patrol the premises. Distributed among a trio of three-story buildings, her baby-blue-and-white guest rooms and their flowery, Louis-Philippe furnishings and lace bedspreads create a grandmotherly vibe, which may not be to everyone's taste. But the Grandes Écoles is legendary for its stunning interior cobbled courtyard and garden, your second living room and a perfect breakfast spot when *il fait beau.* Rooms 29 and 30 open directly into the greenery and calm. ✉ *75 rue du Cardinal Lemoine, Latin Quarter, 75005 ☎ 01–43–26–79–23 📠 01–43–25–28–15 🌐 www.hotel-grandes-ecoles.com ⇨ 51 rooms ♢ Dining room, room service, baby-sitting, parking (fee), some pets allowed; no a/c, no room TVs ▭ MC, V Ⓜ Cardinal Lemoine.*

$$ **Fodor's Choice ★** **Hôtel du Lys.** To conjure up an inexpensive Parisian fantasy, just climb the convoluted stairway to your room (there's no elevator) in this former 17th-century royal residence, one of city's oldest. Well-maintained by Madame Steffen, the hotel's rooms reveal unique quirks and nooks, weathered antiques, and exposed beams throughout. The lobby with its wee sitting nook can also be dated to the Renaissance. It may be modest, but it's extremely atmospheric. ✉ *23 rue Serpente, Latin Quarter, 75006 ☎ 01–43–26–97–57 📠 01–44–07–34–90 🌐 www.hoteldulys.com ⇨ 22 rooms ♢ In-room safes, cable TV, some pets allowed; no a/c ▭ MC, V 🍽 CP Ⓜ St-Michel, Odéon.*

★ $$ **Hôtel Saint-Jacques.** In a location convenient to universities, bookshops, and repertory cinemas, this bargain hotel is impressively decorated, nearly every wall bedecked with faux-marble and trompe-d'oeil murals. As in many old and independent Paris hotels, each room has unique features, furnishings, and layout, but the overall emphasis is on your comfort, with generous amenities for the price, such as an Internet kiosk, in-room safes, and fax service. About half the rooms have tiny step-out balconies that give a glimpse of Notre-Dame and the Panthéon. Room 25 has a long round-the-corner balcony; also popular is the all-yellow room, No. 31, set right under the roof. The Saint-Jacques' chirpy staff rewards repeat guests with souvenir knickknacks, the most loyal with T-shirts. ✉ *35 rue des Écoles, Latin Quarter, 75005 ☎ 01–44–07–45–45 📠 01–43–25–65–50 🌐 www.hotel-saintjacques.com ⇨ 35 rooms ♢ Dining room, in-room safes, cable TV, baby-sitting, Internet; no a/c ▭ AE, DC, MC, V Ⓜ Maubert Mutualité.*

$$ **Familia Hôtel.**As the name suggests, the Familia is family-run show. The snug lobby has reproduction antique tapestries and hardwood fur-

Where to Stay on the Left Bank

Artus Hôtel 21
Best Western Aramis-St-Germain . . . 27
Best Western Manoir St-Germain 15
Familia Hôtel 45
Grand Hôtel de l'Univers 19
Grand Hôtel Lévêque . . . 3
L'Hôtel 12
Hôtel de l'Abbaye 28
Hôtel d'Aubusson 17
Hôtel des Bains 25
Hôtel Bel-Ami 14
Hôtel Bonaparte 13
Hôtel de Buci 20
Hôtel du Cadran 4
Hôtel du Champ de Mars 5
Hôtel Le Clos Médicis 40
Hôtel Eiffel Rive Gauche 2
Hôtel Esméralda 42
Hôtel de Fleurie 22
Hôtel Grandes Écoles 47
Hôtel des Grandes Hommes 38
Hôtel Istria 32
Hôtel des Jardins du Luxembourg 39
Hôtel Latour Maubourg 7
Hôtel Le Tourville 6
Hôtel Lenox-Montparnasse 31
Hôtel du Lys 41
Hôtel Marignan 43
Hôtel du Midi 34
Hôtel Montalembert 10
Hôtel de Nesle 18
Hôtel d'Orsay 8
Hôtel du Parc Montsouris 33
Hôtel Pont Royal 9
Hôtel Raspail-Montparnasse 30
Hôtel Relais Saint-Germain 23
Hôtel Relais Saint-Sulpice 24
Hôtel le Sainte-Beuve 29
Hôtel le Saint-Grégoire 26
Hôtel Saint-Jacques . . .44
Hôtel de l'Université 11
Libertel Quartier Latin 46
Port-Royal Hôtel 37

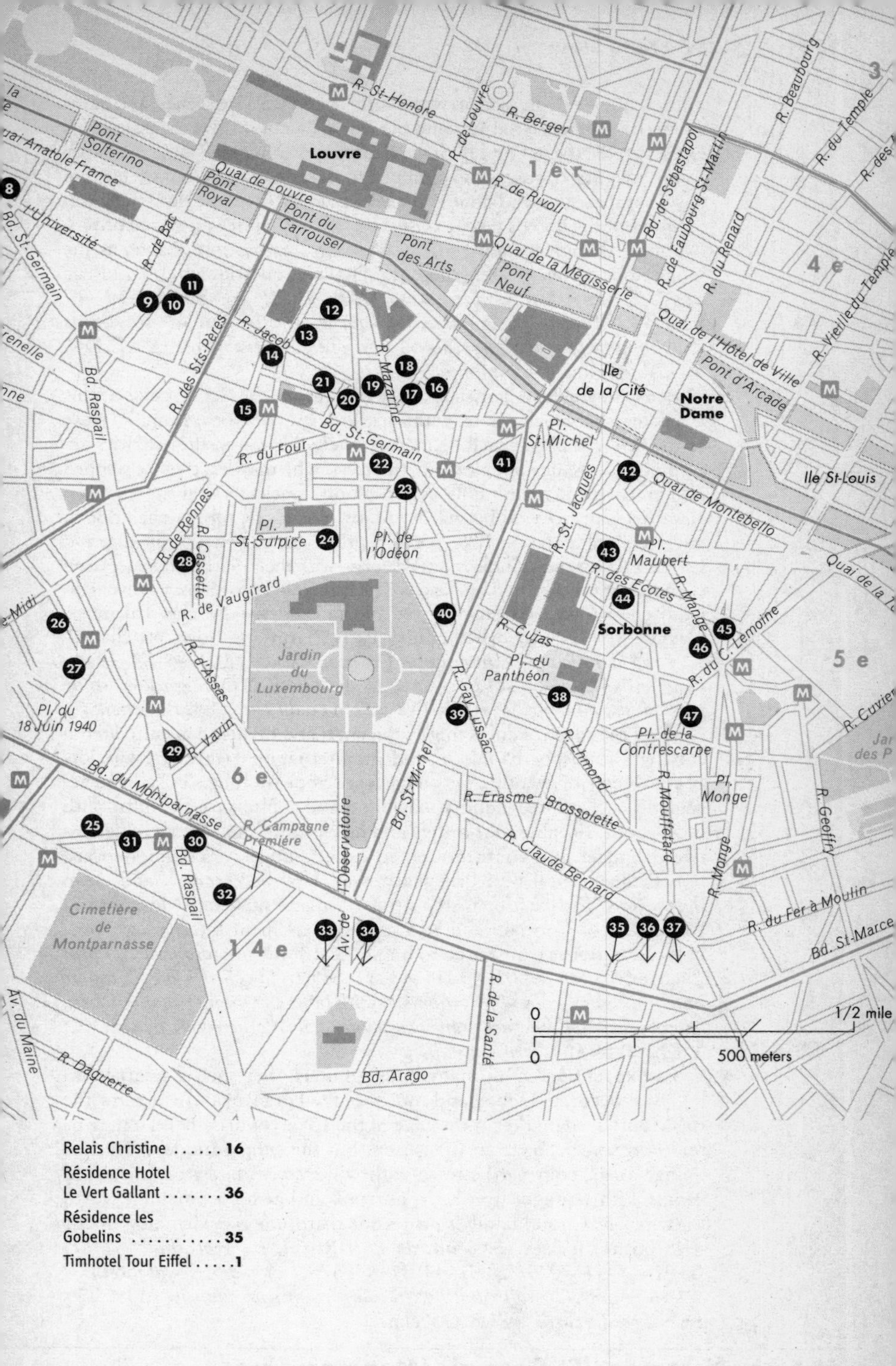

Relais Christine **16**

Résidence Hotel Le Vert Gallant **36**

Résidence les Gobelins **35**

Timhotel Tour Eiffel **1**

niture; rooms are snazzed up with murals of typical city scenes; and bathrooms have modern fixtures and tile work. Balconies give several rooms extra space; Nos. 61 and 62 have clear views to Notre-Dame. Cheaper rooms may strike you as too cramped for large suitcases, but each room has soundproofing and double-paned windows. Owner Eric Gaucheron is proud of his hotel's nearly obsessive level of service and pace of renovations (though the authenticity of some "restorations," such as the mock stone facing in some rooms and halls, is questionable). ✉ *11 rue des Écoles, Latin Quarter, 75005* ☎ *01–43–54–55–27* 🖷 *01–43–29–61–77* 🌐 *www.hotel-paris-familia.com* *30 rooms* *Dining room, minibars, cable TV, meeting rooms; no a/c* 💳 *AE, DC, MC, V* Ⓜ *Cardinal Lemoine.*

$ **Hôtel Esméralda.** A Parisian flea market meets the Renaissance at this legendary shabby-chic hotel with superior views of Notre-Dame so close to the Seine it may as well be moored there. However, these quirky accommodations may not please all travelers, who may feel they've stepped into an eccentric hobbit hole. A vertiginous, ancient spiral staircase (no elevator) leads to a rabbit warren of low corridors, mismatched doors, and even funkier decor. Take Room 7: green carpet, veneer paneling, and garage-sale antiques. Some rooms surprise with their marble fireplaces and chandeliers; others could be cleaner. The Esméralda's foyer may be its highlight: chapel-like, strewn with art and tapestries, with classical music playing. You'll decide whether it's "Paris charm" or "low-cost chaos." ✉ *4 rue St-Julien-le-Pauvre, Latin Quarter, 75005* ☎ *01–43–54–19–20* 🖷 *01–40–51–00–68* *19 rooms, 15 with bath* *Dining room, some pets allowed; no a/c, no room TVs* 💳 *No credit cards* Ⓜ *St-Michel.*

$ **Hôtel Marignan.** Paul Keniger, the energetic owner, has cultivated a convivial atmosphere for independent, international travelers, with lots of conveniences awaiting the budget conscious—a fully stocked and accessible kitchen, free laundry machines, and copious tourist info. With most rooms sleeping four or five and no elevator, the Marignan lies between budget and youth hostel, so expect modest accommodations; nonetheless, you'll find firm mattresses, new bed frames, and clean bathrooms. The location is steps from the medieval Cluny Museum and Boulevards St-Germain and St-Michel. A basement Internet café provides an in-house connection to home. ✉ *13 rue du Sommerard, Latin Quarter, 75005* ☎ *01–43–54–63–81* 🖷 *01–43–25–16–69* 🌐 *www.hotel-marignan.com* *30 rooms, 6 with bath* *Dining room, kitchen, laundry facilities, Internet, some pets allowed; no a/c, no room TVs* 💳 *MC, V* 🍽 *CP* Ⓜ *Maubert Mutualité.*

$ **Port-Royal Hôtel.** Not many budget hotels offer such a smart-looking, well-decorated lobby and rooms as the Port-Royal. Just below the rue Mouffetard market at the edge of the 13e arrondissement, it may be removed somewhat from the action, but the snug antiques-furnished lounge areas, courtyard strewn with white stone, and freshly painted rooms with wrought-iron beds, mirrors, and armoires make it worth the trip. The Giraud family's professional attitude is evident despite the rock-bottom prices. ✉ *8 bd. de Port-Royal, Bercy/Tolbiac, 75005* ☎ *01–43–31–70–06* 🖷 *01–43–31–33–67* 🌐 *www.portroyalhotel.fr.st* *46 rooms, 20 with bath* *Dining room; no a/c, no room TVs* 💳 *No credit cards* Ⓜ *Les Gobelins.*

Fodor's Choice ★

6e Arrondissement (St-Germain/Montparnasse)

See Where to Stay on the Left Bank map.

$$$$ **L'Hôtel.** Baroque mirrors, gold-leaf peacock murals, sinfully plush robes, and hidden fax machines in the closets are just a few of the highlights at this eccentric and opulent boutique hotel. Once an 18th-century

Fodor's Choice ★

pavilion d'amour (inn for trysts), as a hotel it welcomed Oscar Wilde, who in 1900 permanently checked out in Room 16. Designed by Jacques Garcia, the rooms deliver Empire Age pipe dreams, their sole downside being their snug size. In the grotto are a dipping pool and steam room; the spectacular six-story circular atrium is topped by a skylight. If you can't book a room, stop by for a cocktail in the Oriental-theme restaurant-lounge. ✉ *13 rue des Beaux-Arts, St-Germain-des-Prés, 75006* ☎ *01–44–41–99–00* 🖷 *01–43–25–64–81* 🌐 *www.l-hotel.com* *16 rooms, 4 suites* *Restaurant, room service, in-room data ports, in-room safes, cable TV, indoor pool, steam room, bar, baby-sitting, laundry service, concierge, Internet, some pets allowed* *AE, DC, MC, V* Ⓜ *St-Germain-des-Prés.*

3

$$$$ **Hôtel Bel-Ami.** While this property is less an "affordable chic" choice than it used to be, it's still refreshingly casual for a swank hotel. Just a stroll from Les Deux Magots and the Café Flore, the Bel-Ami fills up when the fashion circus come to town. The Conran Shop–meets–sushi bar lobby, done up in a spirit of minimalist eclecticism, has club music to match. Naive-art prints are hung around Internet terminals, a copper and glass-mosaic bar, and fireplace lounge. The rooms in gentle brown, cream, and olive palettes exemplify pared-down luxury. Service is efficient and amiable. To its credit, the hotel feels more intimate than its 115 rooms would suggest. ✉ *7–11 rue St-Benoît, St-Germain-des-Prés, 75006* ☎ *01–42–61–53–53* 🖷 *01–49–27–09–33* 🌐 *www.hotel-bel-ami.com* *113 rooms, 2 suites* *Dining room, room service, in-room data ports, in-room safes, minibars, cable TV with movies, bar, shop, baby-sitting, laundry service, concierge, Internet, meeting rooms, some pets allowed, no-smoking rooms* *AE, DC, MC, V* Ⓜ *St-Germain-des-Prés.*

$$$$ **Hôtel Relais Saint-Germain.** With a gracious staff and all the countrified flowers, beams, and flea-market finds you could dream of, the Relais St-Germain oozes with traditional 17th-century flavor. The rooms, done in bright yellow and red printed fabrics and paints, are at least twice the size of what you find at other hotels for the same price. Top-floor rooms have balconies and either kitchenettes or kitchens, and all have generously sized bathrooms. Doubles have separate sitting areas; four have kitchenettes. An adjacent café and former hangout of Hemingway, Picasso, Joyce, and Matisse is exclusive to hotel guests for the complimentary breakfast of coffee, croissants, and tartines. ✉ *9 carrefour de l'Odéon, St-Germain-des-Prés, 75006* ☎ *01–43–29–12–05* 🖷 *01–46–33–45–30* 🌐 *www.hotel-rsg.com* *21 rooms, 1 suite* *Room service, some kitchenettes, in-room safes, minibars, cable TV, bar, baby-sitting, laundry service, some pets allowed* *AE, DC, MC, V* *CP* Ⓜ *Odéon.*

★ **$$$$** **Relais Christine.** Like its romantic mate the Pavillon de la Reine, Relais Christine excels at dreaming up an opulent yet homey environment. The exquisite building was once a 13th-century abbey; the roots of its *Moyen Âge* past can be found in the stone basement breakfast room. The spacious rooms (particularly the duplexes)—accessible via convoluted halls and a heavy-duty banistered stairway—are elegant without being over-the-top. Expect overhead beams, parquet bathrooms, deep colors, rich fabrics, and antiques. The hard-to-reserve ground-level rooms (11 through 17) open onto an ideal garden with private patios and heaters. ✉ *3 rue Christine, St-Germain-des-Prés, 75006* ☎ *01–40–51–60–80; 800/525–4800 in the U.S.* 🖷 *01–40–51–60–81* 🌐 *www.relais-christine.com* *33 rooms, 18 suites* *Dining room, room service, in-room safes, minibars, cable TV, bar, baby-sitting, laundry service, concierge, Internet, meeting rooms, free parking, some pets allowed, no-smoking rooms* *AE, DC, MC, V* Ⓜ *Odéon.*

LODGING ALTERNATIVES

Apartment Rentals

If you want a home base that's roomy enough for a family and comes with cooking facilities, consider a furnished rental. These can save you money, especially if you're traveling with a group. Home-exchange directories sometimes list rentals as well as exchanges. You might also look in the bimonthly journal France-USA Contacts *(known as FUSAC), which lists rentals as well as apartment exchanges.*

Policies differ from company to company, but you can generally expect a minimum required stay of one week; a refundable deposit (expect to pay $200–$500) payable on arrival; and weekly or biweekly maid service.

Following is a list of good-value residence hotels and apartment services, each with multiple properties in Paris: ***Citadines Résidences Hôtelières*** *(☎ 08–25–33–33–32 🌐 www.citadines.fr).* ***Mercure*** *(☎ 08–25–88–33–33; 800/MERCURE in the U.S. 🌐 www.mercure.com).* ***Paris Apartments Services*** *(✉ 20 rue Bachaumont, Beaubourg/Les Halles, 75002 ☎ 01–40–28–01–28 📠 01–40–28–92–01 🌐 www.paris-apts.com) has upscale, fully furnished studio and one-bedroom apartments from €92 to €214 per night, minimum five-night rental.* ***Rothray*** *(✉ 10 rue Nicolas Flamel, Beaubourg/Les Halles, 74004 ☎ 01–48–87–13–37 📠 01–42–78–17–72 🌐 rothray.free.fr/) has pretty apartments for short- or long-term rental in stylish neighborhoods like the Marais for about €100–€200 per day*

Agencies based in the United States can also help you find an apartment in Paris: ***New York Habitat*** *(✉ 307 7th Ave., Suite 306, New York, NY 10001 ☎ 01–42–36–78–70 in France; 212/255–8018 in the U.S. 📠 212/627–1416 in the U.S. 🌐 www.nyhabitat.com) rents 1,500 furnished apartments for individuals who need tenants for a few days, a month, or longer. They also have apartment shares. Every property has multiple photos on their Web site. Other U.S.-based agencies include:* ***At Home Abroad*** *(✉ 405 E. 56th St., Suite 6H, New York, NY 10022 ☎ 212/421–9165 📠 212/752–1591 🌐 member.aol.com/athomabrod/index.html).* ***Drawbridge to Europe*** *(✉ 102 Granite St., Ashland, OR 97520 ☎ 541/482–7778 or 888/268–1148 📠 541/482–7779 🌐 www.drawbridgetoeurope.com).* ***Hideaways International*** *(✉ 767 Islington St., Portsmouth, NH 03801 ☎ 603/430–4433 or 800/843–4433 📠 603/430–4444 🌐 www.hideaways.com ☞ membership $129).* ***Hometours International*** *(📭 Box 11503, Knoxville, TN 37939 ☎ 865/690–8484 or 800/367–4668 🌐 thor.he.net/~hometour).* ***Interhome*** *(✉ 1990 N.E. 163rd St., Suite 110, N. Miami Beach, FL 33162 ☎ 305/940–2299 or 800/882–6864 📠 305/940–2911 🌐 www.interhome.com).* ***Vacation Home Rentals Worldwide*** *(✉ 235 Kensington Ave., Norwood, NJ 07648 ☎ 201/767–9393 or 800/633–3284 📠 201/767–5510 🌐 www.vhrww.com).* ***Villanet*** *(✉ 1251 N.W. 116th St., Seattle, WA 98177 ☎ 206/417–3444 or 800/964–1891 📠 206/417–1832 🌐 www.rentavilla.com).* ***Villas and Apartments Abroad*** *(✉ 370 Lexington Ave, Suite 1401, New York, NY 10017 ☎ 212/897–5045 or 800/433–3020 📠 212/897–5039 🌐 www.vaanyc.com).* ***Villas International*** *(✉ 950 Northgate Dr., Suite 206, San Rafael, CA 94903 ☎ 415/499–9490 or 800/221–2260 📠 415/499–9491 🌐 www.villasintl.com).*

Home Exchanges

If you would like to exchange your home for someone else's, join a home-exchange organization, which will send you its updated listings of available exchanges for a year and will include your own listing in at least one of them. It's up to you to make specific arrangements with the party interested in an exchange deal.

Two U.S.-based home exchange organizations are: ***HomeLink International*** *(📭 Box 47747, Tampa, FL 33647 ☎ 813/975–9825 or 800/638–3841 📠 813/910–8144 🌐 www.homelink.org*

☞ $98 per year), and **Intervac U.S.** (✉ 30 Corte San Fernando, Tiburon, CA 94920 ☎ 800/756–4663 🖷 415/435–7440 🌐 www.intervacus.com ☞ $90 yearly fee for a listing, on-line access, and a catalog; $50 without catalog).

Hostels

No matter what your age, you can save on lodging costs by staying at hostels. In some 5,000 locations in more than 70 countries around the world, Hostelling International (HI), the umbrella group for a number of national youth-hostel associations, offers single-sex, dorm-style beds and, at many hostels, rooms for couples and family accommodations. Membership in any HI national hostel association, open to travelers of all ages, allows you to stay in HI-affiliated hostels at member rates; one-year membership is about $25 for adults (C$35 for a two-year minimum membership in Canada, £13 in the United Kingdom, A$52 in Australia, and NZ$40 in New Zealand); hostels run about $10–$30 per night. Members have priority if the hostel is full; they're also eligible for discounts around the world, even on rail and bus travel in some countries.

Most of Paris's hostels and foyers (student hostels) are bargains at €20–€30 a night for a bed with free showers and a baguette-and-coffee wake-up call; some are even set near top city locales. In summer you should reserve in writing a month in advance (deposits are often taken via credit card, usually MasterCard and Visa, for advance reservations); if you don't have a reservation, it's a good idea to check in as early as 8 AM. Some foyers have age restrictions and tend to house young workers and students in dormlike accommodations, but other foyers accommodate travelers of all ages. Paris's major public hostels are run by the Féderation Unie des Auberges de Jeunesse (FUAJ)—for about €20, a bed, sheets, shower, and breakfast are provided, with beds usually three to four to a room. Maisons Internationales des Jeunes Étudiants (MIJE) have the plushest hostels, sometimes in historic mansions. Private hostels have accommodations that run from pleasant, if spartan, double rooms to dormlike arrangements.

The best hostel options in Paris include: In the Latin Quarter: **Young and Happy Youth Hostel** (✉ 80 rue Mouffetard, 75005 ☎ 01–45–35–09–53 🌐 www.youngandhappy.fr). In the Marais: **Hôtel Le Fauconnier MIJE** (✉ 11 rue de Fauconnier, 75004 ☎ 01–42–74–23–45 🖷 01–42–74–08–93). Near the Eiffel Tower: **Aloha Hostel** (✉ 1 rue Borromée, 75015 ☎ 01–42–73–03–03 🖷 01–42–73–14–14 🌐 www.aloha.fr). Near Montmartre: **Le Village** (✉ 20 rue d'Orsel, 75018 ☎ 01–42–64–22–02 🖷 01–42–64–22–04 🌐 www.villagehostel.fr). Near Père-Lachaise: **Auberge de Jeunesse d'Artagnan FUAJ** (✉ 80 rue Vitruve, 75003 ☎ 01–40–32–34–56 🖷 01–40–32–34–55).

For more information about hosteling, contact your local youth hostel office: **Australian Youth Hostel Association** (✉ 10 Mallett St., Camperdown, NSW 2050, Australia ☎ 02/9565–1699 🖷 02/9565–1325 🌐 www.yha.com.au). **Féderation Unie des Auberges de Jeunesse** (FUAJ/Hostelling International; FUAJ Beaubourg ✉ 9 rue Brantôme, 3e, Paris 🌐 www.fuaj.org 🖂 Centre National ✉ 27 rue Pajol, 18e, Paris ☎ 01–44–89–87–27). **Hostelling International—American Youth Hostels** (✉ 733 15th St. NW, Suite 840, Washington, DC 20005 ☎ 202/783–6161 🖷 202/783–6171 🌐 www.hiayh.org). **Hostelling International—Canada** (✉ 400–205 Catherine St., Ottawa, Ontario K2P 1C3, Canada ☎ 613/237–7884 🖷 613/237–7868 🌐 www.hostellingintl.ca). **Youth Hostel Association of England and Wales** (✉ Trevelyan House, Dimple Rd., Matlock, Derbyshire DE4 3YH, U.K. ☎ 0870/870–8808 🖷 0169/592–702 🌐 www.yha.org.uk). **Youth Hostels Association of New Zealand** (📭 Box 436, Level 3, 193 Cashel St., Christchurch, New Zealand ☎ 6403/379–9970 🖷 6403/365–4476 🌐 www.yha.org.nz).

★ $$$ **Artus Hôtel.** You'll find modern artwork on the walls, a graffiti-strewn stairwell, and zebra-pattern upholstered chairs in the lobby at this small, modern hotel formerly known as the Buci Latin. Each room's door is inspired by the work of a famous artist—Magritte, Léger, Monet, or Basquiat—done by local painters. Rooms are small, but clean and neat with ocher walls, open-weave armoires, and contoured tables. The more spacious duplex suite on the top floor, right under the roof, has a small bathroom loft with a shower, makeup table, and freestanding bathtub. The amazingly amenable English-speaking staff makes a stay here extra special. ✉ *34 rue de Buci, St-Germain-des-Prés, 75006* ☎ *01–43–29–07–20* 🖷 *01–43–29–67–44* 🌐 *www.artushotel.com* *25 rooms, 2 suites* *Dining room, room service, in-room data ports, minibars, cable TV, laundry service, Internet, some pets allowed* 💳 *AE, DC, MC, V* 🍽 *CP* Ⓜ *Mabillon.*

$$$ **Best Western Manoir St-Germain.** Part of the Best Western chain, this stylish hotel is right next to the Brasserie Lipp and across from the Café de Flore. The smallish rooms are done up in traditional 18th-century luxe, with wainscoting and rich upholsteries. There are Jacuzzis and soundproofing in every room, as well as thirsty terry robes and well-stocked minibars. ✉ *153 bd. St-Germain-des-Prés, St-Germain-des-Prés, 75006* ☎ *01–42–22–21–65* 🖷 *01–45–48–22–25* 🌐 *www.bestwestern.com* *32 rooms* *Dining room, in-room data ports, in-room safes, in-room hot tubs, minibars, cable TV, laundry service, some pets allowed* 💳 *AE, DC, MC, V* 🍽 *CP* Ⓜ *St-Germain-des-Prés.*

$$$ **Grand Hôtel de l'Univers.** In the heart of Paris's festive, adorable, vacation-friendly St-Germain-des-Prés quarter, this hotel is on a quiet side street, yet only steps away from numerous restaurants. The house dates back to the 15th century, which explains the dimensions of some rooms; if snug, they are so stylishly and delightfully decorated ("La Bonbonniere" is a *toile de Jouy*–fabric wonder), you won't notice. The staff is lovely. ✉ *6 rue Gregoire-de-Tours, St-Germain-des-Prés, 75006* ☎ *01–43–29–37–00* 🖷 *01–40–51–06–45* 🌐 *www.hotel-paris-univers.com* *34 rooms* *Dining room, in-room data ports, in-room safes, minibars, cable TV, bar, laundry service, Internet, some pets allowed, no-smoking floors* 💳 *AE, DC, MC, V* Ⓜ *Odéon.*

$$$ **Hôtel de l'Abbaye.** This delightful hotel near St-Sulpice welcomes you with a cobblestone ante-courtyard and vaulted stone entrance. Paneled in bright wood after an update and makeover, the rooms are spotless, if a little impersonal. The collision of modern art and country design—fruit baskets and flat-screen TVs—may not be to everyone's taste, but it's all redeemed by the lobby's many-nooked salons, the vestiges of the original 18th-century convent, and the spacious garden out back with a fountain that some first-floor rooms face. Upper-floor accommodations have oak beams and sitting alcoves, and duplexes have lovely private terraces. ✉ *10 rue Cassette, St-Germain-des-Prés, 75006* ☎ *01–45–44–38–11* 🖷 *01–45–48–07–86* 🌐 *www.hotel-abbaye.com* *37 rooms, 7 suites* *Dining room, room service, in-room data ports, in-room safes, cable TV, bar, baby-sitting, laundry service* 💳 *AE, MC, V* 🍽 *CP* Ⓜ *St-Sulpice.*

★ $$$ **Hôtel d'Aubusson.** Well-groomed in their pin-striped suits, the staff greets you with a hearty welcome at this 17th-century town house and former literary salon that clings to its "country in the city" past. The showpiece is the stunning salon spanned by massive beams and headed by a gigantic fireplace. Decked out in rich burgundies, greens, or blues, the bedrooms are filled with Louis XV- and Regency-style antiques; even the smallest rooms are a good size by Paris standards. Behind the paved courtyard (where in warmer weather you can have your breakfast or pre-dinner drink) there's a second structure with three apartments handy for families. The Café Laurent piano bar hosts live music every week. ✉ *33 rue Dauphine, St-Germain-des-Prés, 75006* ☎ *01–43–29–43–43* 🖷 *01–43–29–12–62* 🌐 *www.hoteldaubusson.com* *50 rooms* *Dining room, room service, in-room data ports, in-room safes, minibars, cable TV, piano bar, shop, baby-sitting, laundry service, concierge, Internet, meeting rooms, parking (fee), no-smoking floors* ▭ *AE, DC, MC, V* Ⓜ *Odéon.*

$$$ **Hôtel de Buci.** The eager-to-please staff adds to the luxurious feeling of this small hotel on the lively and crammed rue de Buci market street. Rooms, which vary in size from cozy to spacious, have armoires and reproductions of 18th-century fabrics in warm, regal patterns; bathrooms are done in marble. Ask for a room overlooking the rear for a quieter night's sleep, or one in front for a glimpse of Paris. The lobby, filled with club chairs and fresh flowers, and the cellar breakfast room are good spots to rendezvous. ✉ *22 rue de Buci, St-Germain-des-Prés, 75006* ☎ *01–55–42–74–74* 🖷 *01–55–42–74–44* 🌐 *www.hotelbuci.fr* *20 rooms, 4 suites* *Dining room, in-room data ports, minibars, cable TV, bar, baby-sitting, laundry service, Internet, business services, some pets allowed* ▭ *AE, DC, MC, V* Ⓜ *Odéon.*

★ $$$ **Hôtel Le Clos Médicis.** Contemporary style meets 17th-century tradition at this classy little hotel built for the Médicis family and still baring the scars of WWII-era bullets. An impressive sunken fireplace lounge with sun-color beams and low armchairs greets your entrance; the staff is equally as warm. The airy rooms come in various styles and configurations: modern with gray and burgundy, or gold-tinged Provençal; so-called "classic" rooms with shower; "supérieure" and "deluxe" rooms with bigger beds plus tub and shower combos; and even triples, split-level duplexes, and suites. Overall, a mix of modern pieces, painted country furnishings, and wrought iron sets the tone. The small open-air courtyard is perfect for tea or breakfast. ✉ *56 rue Monsieur-le-Prince, St-Germain-des-Prés, 75006* ☎ *01–43–29–10–80* 🖷 *01–43–54–26–90* 🌐 *www.closmedicis.com* *38 rooms* *Dining room, in-room data ports, in-room safes, minibars, cable TV, bar, laundry service, Internet, no-smoking floors* ▭ *AE, DC, MC, V* Ⓜ *Luxembourg.*

$$$ **Hôtel de Fleurie.** On a quiet side street near place de l'Odéon, this spiffy, family-run hotel has pretty, pastel-color rooms and many modern luxury amenities, including beautifully tiled bathrooms with heated towel racks. Antiques, Oriental rugs, and rich upholsteries fill the 18th-century building. The staff is helpful. ✉ *32–34 rue Grégoire-de-Tours, St-Germain-des-Prés, 75006* ☎ *01–53–73–70–00* 🖷 *01–53–73–70–20* 🌐 *www.hotel-de-fleurie.tm.fr* *29 rooms* *Dining rooms, in-room data ports, in-room safes, minibars, cable TV, bar, baby-sitting, laundry service, Internet* ▭ *AE, DC, MC, V* Ⓜ *Odéon.*

$$$ **Hôtel Le Sainte-Beuve.** Smack between the Jardin de Luxembourg and Boulevard de Montparnasse's timeless cafés and brasseries, tucked into a tiny, tranquil street, is the pleasant Saint-Beuve. A spacious lobby bathed in light has a wood-fire hearth and is ringed by Greek Revival columns. Whites and pastels predominate in the conservatively decorated rooms designed by the Brit David Hicks, who prefers antiques and a clean, uncluttered look. Each floor has two rooms that can be booked individually or as adjoining suites. ✉ *9 rue Sainte-Beuve, Montparnasse, 75006* ☎ *01–45–48–20–07* 🖷 *01–45–48–67–52* 🌐 *www.paris-hotel-charme.com* *22 rooms* *Room service, in-room safes, minibars, cable TV, bar, laundry service, Internet, some pets allowed* ▭ *AE, DC, MC, V* Ⓜ *Vavin.*

$$$ Fodor'sChoice ★ **Hôtel Relais Saint-Sulpice.** A savvy clientele with discerning taste frequents this fashionable little hotel sandwiched between place St-Sulpice and the Luxembourg Gardens. Eclectically selected art objects and fur-

nishings, some with an Asian theme, oddly pull off a unified look. A zebra-print stuffed fauteuil sits beside a Deco desk, while an African mud cloth hangs above a neo-Roman pillar. The rooms themselves, set around an ivy-clad courtyard, are understated, with simple colors and comfortable furnishings. There's a sauna downstairs, right off the atrium breakfast salon, whose glass roof shoots right through the courtyard. Room 11 has a terrific view of St-Sulpice. ✉ *3 rue Garancière, St-Germain-des-Prés, 75006* ☎ *01–46–33–99–00* 🖷 *01–46–33–00–10* *26 rooms* *Dining room, in-room safes, minibars, cable TV, sauna, laundry service, meeting rooms* ▭ *AE, DC, MC, V* Ⓜ *St-Germain-des-Prés, St-Sulpice.*

★ $$$ **Hôtel Le Saint-Grégoire.** On a calm street off bustling rue de Rennes, this discreet little luxury spot provides quiet and comfortable refuge from the hectic pace of Paris, feeling more like a private home than a hotel. Rooms, done in muted pinks, yellows, and beiges, have simple antique furnishings, bucolic prints on the walls, and big tubs. The sitting room–lobby is especially cozy, with a rustic fireplace and flowery wallpaper. Particularly romantic are Rooms 14 and 16, which have enclosed, ivy-covered terraces. The patient receptionist gracefully manages myriad guest requests with courtesy and grace. Private parking is available at the Holiday Inn across the street. ✉ *43 rue de l'Abbé-Grégoire, St-Germain-des-Prés, 75006* ☎ *01–45–48–23–23* 🖷 *01–45–48–33–95* 🌐 *www.hotelsaintgregoire.com* *19 rooms, 1 suite* *Dining room, in-room data ports, bar, baby-sitting, laundry service, some pets allowed (fee)* ▭ *AE, DC, MC, V* Ⓜ *St-Placide.*

$$ **Best Western Aramis-St-Germain.** You get great value for your money at this hotel. Although part of the Best Western chain, it still manages to be classically French. Rooms have damask bedspreads and sturdy cherrywood armoires. All are soundproof and equipped with cable TV; about half have air-conditioning, and nine have whirlpool baths. There are American-style extras like tea and coffee machines and radios in all rooms. Harvey's Piano Bar, on the ground floor, is popular with the smart business set. ✉ *124 rue de Rennes, St-Germain-des-Prés, 75006* ☎ *01–45–48–03–75; 800/528–1234 in the U.S.* 🖷 *01–45–44–99–29* 🌐 *www.hotel-aramis.com* *42 rooms* *In-room safes, minibars, some in-room hot tubs, cable TV, bar, laundry service, Internet, no-smoking floors; no a/c in some rooms* ▭ *AE, DC, MC, V* Ⓜ *St-Placide.*

$$ **Hôtel Bonaparte.** The congeniality of the staff only makes a stay in this intimate place more of a treat. Old-fashioned upholsteries, 19th-century furnishings, and paintings create a quaint feel in the relatively spacious rooms. And the location in the heart of St-Germain is nothing short of fabulous. ✉ *61 rue Bonaparte, St-Germain-des-Prés, 75006* ☎ *01–43–26–97–37* 🖷 *01–46–33–57–67* *29 rooms* ▭ *MC, V* Ⓜ *St-Germain-des-Prés.*

$–$$ Fodor'sChoice ★ **Hôtel de Nesle.** The services are bare-bones—no elevator, phones, or breakfast—but if you're on the lookout for a low-cost, one-of-a-kind spot as wondrous as a doll's house, the Hotel de Nesle will enchant you. The payoff is in the petite rooms cleverly decorated by theme. Sleep in Notre-Dame de Paris, lounge in an Oriental boudoir, spend the night with writer Molière, or steam it up in le Hammam. Decorations include colorful murals, canopy beds, custom lamps, and clay tiles. Most rooms overlook an interior garden oasis. Its dead-end street location keeps the Nesle quiet, despite its being a short walk from boulevard St-Germain in one direction and the Seine in the other. ✉ *7 rue de Nesle, St-Germain-des-Pres, 75006* ☎ *01–43–54–62–41* 🖷 *01–43–54–31–88* 🌐 *www.hoteldenesle.com* *20 rooms, 10 with bath* *Some pets allowed, no-smoking floors; no a/c, no room phones, no room TVs* ▭ *MC, V* Ⓜ *Métro: Odéon.*

7ᵉ Arrondissement (Eiffel Tower/Trocadéro)

See Where to Stay on the Left Bank map.

$$$$ Fodor'sChoice ★ **Hôtel Montalembert.** Highly in demand by stylish business and fashion-show travelers, the Montalembert has just completed an update that is all about receptionists in plum-color ties, made-to-order bronze lighting fixtures, and gentle club-trance Muzak. Rooms are dressed in either minimal hip or French royalty flavors, with CD-player alarm clocks and double-thick sound- and light-proof curtains. Square-footage is on the minimal side, except in suites. The restaurant serves its funky menu of dishes classified as Earth, Sea, Vegetable, or Sun nonstop from noon to 10:30. DVD players, flat-screen TVs, and in-room wireless Internet access are being installed. ✉ *3 rue de Montalembert, St-Germain-des-Prés, 75007* ☎ *01–45–49–68–68* 🖷 *01–45–49–69–49* 🌐 *www.montalembert.com* *50 rooms, 6 suites* *Restaurant, room service, in-room data ports, in-room safes, minibars, cable TV, in-room VCRs, massage, bar, baby-sitting, laundry service, concierge, meeting room* 💳 *AE, DC, MC, V* Ⓜ *Rue du Bac.*

$$$$ **Hôtel Pont Royal.** Once a favorite watering hole of everyone in the literary world from T. S. Eliot to Gabriel Garcia Marquez, this sumptuous hotel now attracts more businessmen than writers; the only recognizable authors you'll see are the ones whose photographs line the lobby. Color schemes in the rather spacious and generously appointed rooms are contemporary: earth tones, coral, and plum. The views from the top floors are magnificent, especially from Suite 801. The library-theme bar resembles a British reading room. In its 2003 incarnation as the Atelier Joël Robuchon, the restaurant has become a popular luncheon spot among well-heeled locals. ✉ *7 rue de Montalembert, St-Germain-des-Prés, 75007* ☎ *01–42–84–70–00* 🖷 *01–42–84–71–00* 🌐 *www.hotel-pont-royal.com* *65 rooms, 10 suites* *Restaurant, room service, in-room data ports, in-room safes, minibars, cable TV with movies, health club, bar, library, baby-sitting, concierge, business services, meeting rooms, some pets allowed, no-smoking rooms* 💳 *AE, DC, MC, V* Ⓜ *Rue du Bac.*

$$$ **Hôtel du Cadran.** Colorful window boxes lend a welcoming touch to this cheerful hotel in a handsome corner building near the market on rue Cler. The charming Madame Chaine and her gracious staff go out of their way to ensure that you enjoy your stay, from recommending a bistro to booking theater tickets. A fireplace and grandfather clock make the lobby pleasant for sitting. Rooms have coordinating drapes and bedspreads in cheery colors and are very comfortable; some have views of the Eiffel Tower. Ask about special weekend rates. ✉ *10 rue du Champ de Mars, Eiffel Tower/Trocadéro, 75007* ☎ *01–40–62–67–00* 🖷 *01–40–62–67–13* 🌐 *www.cadranhotel.com* *42 rooms* *Dining room, in-room data ports, in-room safes, minibars, cable TV, bar, baby-sitting, laundry service, no-smoking floors* 💳 *AE, DC, MC, V* Ⓜ *École Militaire.*

$$$ **Hôtel Latour Maubourg.** Part hotel, part private residence, with a city B&B feel, this small converted town house is homey and unpretentious, with a very helpful staff. Its simply furnished rooms have antique armoires and suitcase holders, marble fireplaces, high ceilings, and high-quality beds with either wool blankets or duvets. Proud owners Victor and Maria Orsenne and their dog Faust are especially welcoming to honeymooners and couples celebrating anniversaries. There's even a fridge at your disposal for keeping market purchases and late-night snacks. There's no elevator, but Latour Maubourg has just three levels. ✉ *150 rue de Grenelle, Eiffel Tower/Trocadéro, 75007* ☎ *01–47–05–16–16*

01–47–05–16–14 *www.latour-maubourg.fr* *9 rooms, 1 suite* *Dining room, in-room data ports, minibars, cable TV, laundry service, Internet, some pets allowed; no a/c in some rooms* *MC, V* *CP* *La Tour-Maubourg.*

$$$ **Hôtel de l'Université.** Staying at this hotel in a 17th-century town house between boulevard St-Germain and the Seine feels like going back in time. Guest rooms have English and French antiques and original fireplaces. Ask for one with a terrace on the fifth floor. Note that the cheapest guest rooms have showers—no tubs—in the bathrooms. *22 rue de l'Université, St-Germain-des-Prés, 75007* *01–42–61–09–39* *01–42–60–40–84* *www.hoteluniversite.com* *27 rooms* *Dining room, room service, in-room data ports, in-room safes, minibars, cable TV, laundry service, meeting rooms* *AE, MC, V* *Rue du Bac.*

$$ **Hôtel d'Orsay.** Across the street from the Musée d'Orsay, the Orsay (formerly the Solférino) is a cheerful little hotel made up of two 18th-century buildings. The atmosphere throughout is upbeat, with attentive service, bright color schemes, and flower-filled window boxes. The lobby faces a huge picture window and garden courtyard. The skylighted breakfast room is a pleasant place to greet the day. Rooms are comfortable; some have peaked ceilings and weathered beams. *93 rue de Lille, St-Germain-des-Prés, 75007* *01–47–05–85–54* *01–45–55–51–16* *www.esprit-de-france.com* *39 rooms, 2 suites* *Dining room, in-room safes, minibars, cable TV, Internet, meeting rooms; no a/c* *AE, DC, MC, V* *Solférino.*

$$ **Hôtel Le Tourville.** Here is a rare find: a cozy, upscale hotel that doesn't cost a fortune. Each room has crisp, virgin-white damask upholstery set against pastel or ocher walls, a smattering of antique bureaus and lamps, original artwork, and fabulous old mirrors. The hotel attracts a young, fashionable crowd, especially in the dishy Art Deco bar. The junior suites have hot tubs. The staff couldn't be more helpful. *16 av. de Tourville, Eiffel Tower/Trocadéro, 75007* *01–47–05–62–62* *01–47–05–43–90* *www.hoteltourville.com* *27 rooms, 3 suites* *Dining room, in-room data ports, some in-room safes, cable TV, bar, laundry service, some pets allowed, no-smoking rooms* *AE, DC, MC, V* *École Militaire.*

$ **Grand Hôtel Lévêque.** The Eiffel Tower is just around the corner, but the real draw here is the picturesque street market just outside the hotel's front door. This immaculate hotel has an eager-to-please staff, comfortable if slightly sterile rooms, and a bistro-style breakfast room. Make sure to get a room facing the street and reserve early—this is a very popular address among French and American foodies. *29 rue Cler, Eiffel Tower/Trocadéro, 75007* *01–47–05–49–15* *01–45–50–49–36* *www.hotel-leveque.com* *50 rooms, 45 with bath* *Dining room, in-room data ports, in-room safes, cable TV* *AE, MC, V* *École Militaire.*

★ $ **Hôtel du Champ de Mars.** If you'd like an affordable, B&B-theme, but fully modern room near the Eiffel Tower and Les Invalides, this is an excellent choice. Françoise and Stéphane Gourdal's comfortable hotel has an appealing down-home feel. Chippie, their faithful old dog, can be found lounging in the vibrant Provençal lobby. Rooms include custom wall stenciling and chair covers, and are named for flowers such as *tornesol*, *lilas* and *mimosa*; the two on the ground floor open onto a private leafy courtyard. The triple room is a split-level duplex, with a small flight of stairs leading up to a sitting room. *7 rue du Champ de Mars, Eiffel Tower/Trocadéro, 75007* *01–45–51–52–30* *01–45–51–64–36* *www.hotel-du-champ-de-mars.com* *25 rooms* *Dining room, in-room data ports, in-room safes, cable TV; no a/c* *MC, V* *École Militaire.*

$ **Hôtel Eiffel Rive Gauche.** On a quiet side street just a couple of blocks from the Eiffel Tower, this modern hotel with a leafy patio is a great budget find. The look is functional, but rooms are spacious and comfortable; some have red-and-gold wall fabrics and hardwood furniture. The owner, Monsieur Chicheportiche, is a walking multilingual encyclopedia of Paris. Bonuses include rooms with Eiffel Tower views, alarm clocks, and radios, and an attractive lobby and breakfast room ✉ *6 rue du Gros Caillou, Eiffel Tower/Trocadéro, 75007* ☎ *01–45–51–24–56* 📠 *01–45–51–11–77* 🌐 *www.hotel-eiffel.com* *30 rooms* *Dining room, in-room safes, cable TV, laundry service, Internet, some pets allowed; no a/c* 💳 *MC, V* Ⓜ *École Militaire.*

8e Arrondissement (Champs-Élysées)

See Where to Stay on the Right Bank: Bois du Boulogne to Place de la Concorde map.

★ **$$$$** **Four Seasons Hôtel George V Paris.** General Eisenhower's headquarters in 1945 is now owned by a Saudi prince (who gets first dibs on the Royal Suite) and managed by the Four Seasons group. The hotel is as bright and shiny as the day it opened in 1928: the original Art Deco detailing and 17th-century tapestries have been restored; the bas-reliefs regilded; the marble-floor mosaics rebuilt tile by tile. Rooms are decked in yards of fabrics and Louis XV trimmings with crystal chandeliers, marble bathrooms, and soaking tubs. The Le Cinq restaurant is one of Paris's hottest tables, thanks to the legendary Philippe Legendre of Taillevent fame. ✉ *31 av. George V, Champs-Élysées, 75008* ☎ *01–49–52–70–00* 📠 *01–49–52–70–10* 🌐 *www.fourseasons.com* *185 rooms, 60 suites* *2 restaurants, room service, in-room data ports, in-room safes, minibars, cable TV with video games, indoor pool, hair salon, health club, massage, bar, shop, baby-sitting, laundry service, business services, meeting rooms, some pets allowed, no-smoking floors* 💳 *AE, DC, MC, V* Ⓜ *George V.*

$$$$ **Hôtel Astor.** Part of the Sofitel hotel group, the Astor is a bastion of highly stylized, civilized chic. The Art Deco lobby is decked out in boldly patterned armchairs, huge mirrors, and clever ceiling frescoes. There's also a cozy bar; a small, neoclassic-inspired library; and a stunning trompe-l'oeil dining room. Guest rooms are testimonials to the sober Regency style, with weighty marble fireplaces and mahogany furnishings, yet have modern touches such as CD hi-fis. Several suites have walk-out balconies with superb vistas. The hotel's restaurant is supervised by the celebrated chef Joël Robuchon. ✉ *11 rue d'Astorg, Champs-Élysées, 75008* ☎ *01–53–05–05–05; 800/763–4385 in the U.S.* 📠 *01–53–05–05–30* 🌐 *www.hotel-astor.net* *129 rooms, 5 suites* *Restaurant, room service, some in-room data ports, in-room safes, minibars, cable TV, health club, bar, baby-sitting, laundry service, concierge, business services, no-smoking floors* 💳 *AE, DC, MC, V* Ⓜ *Miromesnil, St-Augustin.*

$$$$ **Hôtel Le Bristol.** The understated facade on rue du Faubourg St-Honoré might mislead the unknowing, but the Bristol ranks among Paris's most exclusive hotels and has the prices to prove it. Many billionaires and celebrities refuse to stay anywhere else, attracted by the tasteful luxe and the staff's finishing-school discretion. Some of the spaciously elegant rooms have authentic Louis XV and Louis XVI furniture and magnificent marble bathrooms in pure 1920s Art Deco; others have a more relaxed 19th-century style. The public salons are palatially stocked with old-master paintings, sculptures, sumptuous carpets, and tapestries. ✉ *112 rue du Faubourg St-Honoré, Champs-Élysées, 75008* ☎ *01–53–43–43–00* 📠 *01–53–43–43–01* 🌐 *www.lebristolparis.com* *127 rooms, 48 suites* *Restaurant, room service, in-room data* *ports, in-room safes, minibars, cable TV with video games, indoor pool, health club, hair salon, spa, bar, baby-sitting, laundry service, concierge, business services, meeting rooms, free parking* ▭ *AE, DC, MC, V* Ⓜ *Miromesnil.*

★ $$$$ **Hôtel de Crillon.** To anyone with a taste for history, the name Crillon produces a whole carillon's worth of chimes. In 1758, Louis XV commissioned the architect Jacques-Angė Gabriel to build two facades of the mansion which sits on the north side of the place de la Concorde. In 1909 it became a hotel and since then has played host to generations of diplomats and refined travelers (movie stars prefer the rooms that face the square). Three salons are national historic landmarks. Most rooms are lavishly decorated with rococo and Directoire antiques, crystal-and-gilt wall sconces, and gilt fittings. In tune with the times, more rooms were converted to suites and all were renovated in 2002. The sheer quantity of marble in the highly praised Michelin two-star Les Ambassadeurs is staggering. ✉ *10 pl. de la Concorde, Louvre/Tuileries, 75008* ☎ *01–44–71–15–00; 800/888–4747 in the U.S.* 📠 *01–44–71–15–02* 🌐 *www.crillon.com* *90 rooms, 57 suites* *2 restaurants, room service, in-room data ports, in-room safes, minibars, cable TV with movies, gym, spa, 2 bars, baby-sitting, children's programs, laundry service, concierge, Internet, business services, meeting rooms, no-smoking rooms* ▭ *AE, DC, MC, V* Ⓜ *Concorde.*

$$$$ **Hôtel Lancaster.** Another jewel in hotelier Grace Leo-Andrieu's crown, the Lancaster, one of Paris's most venerable institutions, has been transformed by her legion of star designers into a stellar and modish luxury hotel. The overall feel—a seamless blend of traditional with contemporary—is one of timeless elegance. Every detail speaks of quality, from the hotel's own line of bath products to the Porthault linens. Many of the suites pay homage to the hotel's colorful regulars, from Garbo to John Huston to Sir Alec Guinness. Marlene Dietrich's is decorated in lilac (her favorite color) and is adorned with superb Louis XV antiques. ✉ *7 rue de Berri, Champs-Élysées, 75008* ☎ *01–40–76–40–76; 877/757–2747 in the U.S.* 📠 *01–40–76–40–00* 🌐 *www.hotel-lancaster.fr* *49 rooms, 11 suites* *Restaurant, room service, in-room data ports, in-room safes, minibars, cable TV, in-room VCRs, health club, bar, baby-sitting, laundry service, concierge, meeting rooms, parking (fee), some pets allowed (fee)* ▭ *AE, DC, MC, V* Ⓜ *George V.*

$$$$ **Hôtel Plaza Athenée.** Restoration of the Art Deco Le Relais Plaza restaurant and the addition of a May to September dining option in the red parasoled La Cour Jardin help this avenue Montaigne palace continue to attract a Blahnik-heeled crowd. The legends surrounding the Plaza Athenée began because this was the favorite Paris hotel of both Grace Kelly and Jackie Kennedy. It's also only a croissant lob from the city's top couture and luxury shops. Most rooms have Regènce- and Louis Seize–style accent pieces, while the top two floors go Art Deco and are adorned with historic sketches by Dior himself. ✉ *25 av. Montaigne, Champs-Élysées, 75008* ☎ *01–53–67–66–65; 866/732–1106 in the U.S.* 📠 *01–53–67–66–66* 🌐 *www.plaza-athenee-paris.com* *145 rooms, 43 suites* *2 restaurants, room service, in-room safes, minibars, cable TV, health club, massage, bar, baby-sitting, laundry service, concierge, business services, meeting rooms, some pets allowed, no-smoking rooms* ▭ *AE, DC, MC, V* Ⓜ *Alma-Marceau.*

$$$$ **Hyatt Regency Paris-Madeleine.** This Haussmannesque building near the Opéra Garnier feels more like a boutique hotel than an international chain, thanks to stylized details like cherry paneling and mismatched bedside tables. You can also expect the usual plush carpeting and luxurious upholsteries. Book a room on the seventh or eighth floor facing boulevard Malesherbes for a view of the Eiffel Tower. ✉ *24 bd.*

Malesherbes, Opéra/Grands Boulevards, 75008 ☎ 01–55–27–12–34; 800/223–1234 in the U.S. 🖷 01–55–27–12–35 ⊕ www.paris.hyatt.com ⇌ 81 rooms, 5 suites ♁ Restaurant, room service, in-room data ports, in-room safes, minibars, cable TV with movies, health club, spa, bar, laundry service, concierge, business services, meeting rooms, some pets allowed (fee), no-smoking floors ▭ AE, DC, MC, V Ⓜ St-Augustin.

$$$$ **Paris Marriott Champs-Élysées.** Take a ground-zero locale, a stylish atrium lobby, and a chic, 19th-century style, and you've got the Paris Marriott. Ebony furnishings and antique prints are some of the nice touches that make you forget this is a chain, and state-of-the-art soundproofing shuts out the cacophonous Champs. The hotel restaurant specializes in high-end *cuisine americaine.* *✉ 70 av. des Champs-Élysées, Champs-Élysées, 75008 ☎ 01–53–93–55–00; 800/228–9290 in the U.S. 🖷 01–53–93–55–01 ⊕ www.marriott.com ⇌ 174 rooms, 18 suites ♁ Restaurant, room service, in-room data ports, in-room safes, minibars, cable TV with movies, gym, sauna, 2 bars, baby-sitting, laundry service, concierge, business services, meeting rooms, no-smoking floors ▭ AE, DC, MC, V Ⓜ George V.*

★ **$$$$** **Pershing Hall.** Formerly an American Legion hall, the hotel opened in 2000 and is a must-see, must-stay address. Designed by Andrée Putman, the grande dame of French interior architecture, this boutique hotel exudes an almost masculine minimalism, with smooth surfaces of marble, wood, and stone accented by muted colors. Rooms have gauzy curtains, slate-gray bathrooms, designer bedside tables, and soaking tubs that sit on round marble bases. In the central courtyard is a spectacular jungle garden with 300 varieties of plants. The stylish lounge bar serves drinks, dinner, and DJ-driven music until 2 AM. There's also a spa and health club, necessary after the sublime food by chef Erwan Louaisil. *✉ 49 rue Pierre-Charron, Champs-Élysées, 75008 ☎ 01–58–36–58–00 🖷 01–58–36–58–01 ⊕ www.pershinghall.com ⇌ 20 rooms, 6 suites ♁ Restaurant, room service, in-room data ports, in-room safes, minibars, cable TV, in-room VCRs, health club, bar, baby-sitting, laundry service, concierge, meeting rooms, some pets allowed ▭ AE, DC, MC, V Ⓜ George V, Franklin-D.-Roosevelt.*

$$$$ **Prince de Galles Hôtel.** At this Art Deco palace, the 1920s don't so much roar as purr. Rooms and suites are spacious and bright, with crystal chandeliers in every room and marble bathrooms. The restaurant, with its summer patio of Moorish blue-and-gold mosaics, is a quiet, sane refuge from the frenzied interplay of boulevards and business just outside. Le Regency, a cigar-friendly, club-style bar with a wall of single-malts, is the perfect *entente cordiale* between English sobriety and French culinary expertise. *✉ 33 av. George V, Champs-Élysées, 75008 ☎ 01–53–23–77–77 🖷 01–53–23–78–78 ⊕ www.luxurycollection.com ⇌ 138 rooms, 30 suites ♁ Restaurant, room service, in-room data ports, in-room safes, minibars, hair salon, health club, bar, baby-sitting, laundry service, concierge, Internet, business services, meeting rooms, no-smoking floors ▭ AE, DC, MC, V Ⓜ George V.*

$$$ **Hôtel Bradford-Élysées.** That this turn-of-the-20th-century hotel conserves its old-fashioned past is obvious, considering its chandelier-hung entry and airy, glass-roofed dining room with herringbone parquet floor. An old wooden elevator carries you from the flower-filled lobby to the spacious, luxurious rooms equipped with Louis XVI–style furniture, brass beds, and marble fireplaces. *✉ 10 rue St-Philippe-du-Roule, Champs-Élysées, 75008 ☎ 01–45–63–20–20 🖷 01–45–63–20–07 ⊕ www.astotel.com ⇌ 50 rooms ♁ Dining room, room service, in-room data ports, in-room safes, minibars, cable TV, baby-sitting, laundry service, some pets allowed, no-smoking rooms ▭ AE, DC, MC, V Ⓜ St-Philippe-du-Roule.*

$$$ **Hôtel Franklin D. Roosevelt.** One of the last family-run boutique hotels in the area, this is an intimate alternative to grander establishments in the same price category. The hotel has the look and feel of a London club, with hunting scenes on the walls and a fire crackling in the smoking salon. It's just as stylish upstairs—rooms and suites have mahogany doors and antiques, Oriental carpets and ceramics, cashmere draperies and printed calico wall coverings. Book a room on the fifth floor if you want to breakfast on a balcony. Ongoing renovations are transforming standard rooms into something more upscale. ✉ *18 rue Clément Marot, Champs-Élysées, 75008* ☎ *01–53–57–49–50* 🖷 *01–53–57–49–59* 🌐 *www.hroosevelt.com* *45 rooms, 3 suites* *Dining room, in-room data ports, in-room safes, minibars, cable TV, meeting room, some pets allowed* 💳 *AE, DC, MC, V* Ⓜ *Marbeuf.*

$$$ **Hôtel Le Lavoisier.** On a side street off the Champs-Élysées, this is a high-class hotel with small-town charm. The staff—from housekeeper to manager—is friendly, easygoing, and attentive, though not overly so. Six-foot windows seem huge in the small rooms with 9-ft ceilings. Everything in the neoclassical hotel is immaculate—linens are crisp and ultrawhite, headboards and chairs are slipcovered in white, dark-wood furniture and marble bathrooms gleam. Each room contains at least one antique furniture piece. One room has a terrace, two have balconies. Most rooms have original paintings. ✉ *21 rue Lavoisier, Champs-Élysées, 75008* ☎ *01–53–30–06–06* 🖷 *01–53–30–23–00* 🌐 *www.hotellavoisier.com* *30 rooms, 1 suite* *Dining room, in-room data ports, some in-room hot tubs, cable TV, lounge, library, dry cleaning, laundry service, Internet, business services, some pets allowed, parking (fee); no smoking rooms* 💳 *AE, MC, V* Ⓜ *St-Augustin.*

$$$ **Hôtel Résidence Monceau.** Within a stone's throw of the elegant Parc Monceau, this friendly and fashionable hotel is an oasis of refined tranquillity. Warm tones make rooms cozy; the efficient and professional staff makes your stay easy. The breakfast garden, surrounded by ivy-covered trellises, is a lovely place to start the day. The management also runs the equally smart and stylish Relais Saint-Sulpice and Jardins du Luxembourg hotels over on the Left Bank. ✉ *85 rue du Rocher, Parc Monceau, 75008* ☎ *01–45–22–75–11* 🖷 *01–45–22–30–88* *50 rooms, 1 suite* *Dining room, minibars bar, laundry service, no-smoking rooms; no a/c* 💳 *AE, DC, MC, V* Ⓜ *Villiers.*

9e Arrondissement (Opéra)

See Where to Stay on the Right Bank: Ile de la Cité to Montmartre map.

$$$$ **InterContinental Le Grand Hôtel.** Opened by Napoléon III and his empress Eugénie in 1862, Paris's largest luxury hotel received a major makeover and reopened in April 2003, after being closed for more than two years. New sitting areas, larger bedrooms, 20 meeting rooms, and an entire floor devoted to the Club InterContinental (with private lounge) are among the additions. Naturally, the dome of the stunningly lush Second Empire grand ballroom, the Grand Salon Opéra, and the restaurant's splendidly painted ceilings remain registered landmarks. The spacious guest rooms combine semiclassical furnishings and fabrics with quasi–Art Deco minimalism. As in the days of the Impressionists, the hotel's famed Café de la Paix is one of the city's great people-watching spots. ✉ *2 rue Scribe, Opéra/Grands Boulevards, 75009* ☎ *01–40–07–32–32; 800/327–0200 in the U.S.* 🖷 *01–42–66–12–51* 🌐 *www.interconti.com* *482 rooms* *2 restaurants, room service, in-room data ports, in-room safes, minibars, cable TV with movies, in-room VCRs, health club, sauna, bar, shop, baby-sitting, laundry service,*

WITH CHILDREN

MOST HOTELS IN PARIS ALLOW *children under a certain age to stay in their parents' room at no extra charge. Also, ask if small hotels have adjoining rooms; this is often the case at older Left Bank properties. You may also want to consider renting a furnished apartment (⇨ Apartment Rentals, above).*

Hôtel Meridien Montparnasse *(✉ 19 rue de Commandant-Mouchotte ☎ 01–44–36–44–00) offers games, and face painting (fee) for children up to 12 as well as a Sunday brunch where kids have their own buffet. The* ***Four Season George V*** *(✉ 31 ave George V ☎ 1–49–52–7000) has in-room cookies and milk and videos and games plus special kids' toiletries and free cribs. There's also a pool. The* ***Novotel*** *(☎ 800/221–4542 reservations) chain allows two children under 15 to stay free in their parents' room; many properties have playgrounds.* ***Sofitel*** *(☎ 800/221–4542 reservations) hotels offer a free second room for children July, August, and Christmas time.*

concierge, business services, meeting rooms, some pets allowed (fee), no-smoking floors ▭ *AE, DC, MC, V* Ⓜ *Opéra.*

$$$$ **Millennium Hôtel Paris Opéra.** This grande dame in a big Haussmann-era stone-block building includes checkerboard marble floors, chunky pillars, and chandeliers. Crane your neck at the Art Nouveau stained-glass ceiling of the Hall de Réception, connecting the library bar to the bright, shiny brasserie with its regal oyster bar. The glass Belle Epoque elevator still sweeps guests to their plush chambers that all have thoughtful touches such as coffee and tea makers and trouser presses. ✉ *12 bd. Haussmann, Opéra/Grands Boulevards, 75009* ☎ *01–49–49–16–00* 🖷 *01–49–49–17–00* 🌐 *www.millenniumhotels.com* *152 rooms, 11 suites* *Restaurant, room service, in-room data ports, in-room safes, minibars, cable TV with movies, bar, baby-sitting, laundry service, Internet, concierge, business services, meeting rooms, some pets allowed, no-smoking floors* ▭ *AE, DC, MC, V* Ⓜ *Le Peletier.*

$$$$ **Villa Royale.** On Place Pigalle, within view of Sacré-Coeur and just a catcall from all the sleazy sex-shop action, the Villa Royale design is inspired by the Moulin Rouge's bygone days. Every square foot of lobby, lounge, corridor and room is draped in blood-red satin, circus-tent stripes, or deep-blue velvet; flat-screen TVs hide behind gilt picture frames, and gas fireplaces light up the love nests. Bathrooms are over-the-top gold, brass, marble, some with Jacuzzis. You'll feel like you're sleeping inside a plush jewelry box; for four-star theatrical luxury, it's the best, and only, show in this part of town. ✉ *2 rue Duperré, Montmartre, 75009* ☎ *01–55–31–78–78* 🖷 *01–55–31–78–70* 🌐 *www.leshotelsdeparis.com* *34 rooms, 5 suites* *Dining room, room service, in-room data ports, in-room safes, minibars, some in-room hot tubs, cable TV with movies, bar, laundry service, business services, meeting rooms, some pets allowed, no-smoking floors* ▭ *AE, DC, MC, V* Ⓜ *Pigalle.*

$$ **Hôtel Langlois.** Fodor'sChoice ★ After starring in *The Truth About Charlie* (a remake of *Charade*), this darling hotel, formerly the Hôtel des Croisés, gained a reputation as one of the most atmospheric budget sleeps in the city. An impressive Art Nouveau building, the former circa-1870 bank retains its beautiful wood-paneled reception area and vintage wrought-iron elevator. The spacious rooms are fabulously decked out with elegant period furniture and original fixtures such as glazed-tile fireplaces. Rooms on the lower floors have the largest bathrooms, but those on the fifth and sixth have wonderful views of Paris rooftops. Nos. 63 and

64 look out upon Sacré-Coeur. ✉ *63 rue Saint-Lazare, Opéra/Grands Boulevards, 75009* ☎ *01–48–74–78–24* 📠 *01–49–95–04–43* *24 rooms, 3 suites* *Dining room, cable TV, minibars, some pets allowed; no a/c* 💳 *AE, MC, V* Ⓜ *Trinité.*

$ **Hôtel Chopin.** At the end of the passage Jouffroy—one of the many glass-roofed shopping arcades built in Paris in the early 19th century—the Chopin, with its creaky-floored lobby and old wooden trim still recalls its 1846 birth date. The basic but comfortable rooms overlook the arcade's quaint toy shops and bookstores, though plastic plants, salmon walls, green carpets, and modern reproduction furniture don't quite blend with the antique setting. The best rooms are Nos. 409, 310, and 412, while the cheapest are the darker, smaller rooms ending with a 7. Blissful silence reigns throughout, however: the passage gates are closed at dusk, making this possibly the quietest hotel in the city. ✉ *10 bd. Montmartre (46 passage Jouffroy), Opéra/Grands Boulevards, 75009* ☎ *01–47–70–58–10* 📠 *01–42–47–00–70* *36 rooms* *Dining room, in-room safes, cable TV; no a/c* 💳 *AE, MC, V* Ⓜ *Grands Boulevards.*

11e Arrondissement (Bastille)

See Where to Stay on the Right Bank: The Marais to La Villette map.

★ $$ **Hôtel Beaumarchais.** This bold hotel serves as a gateway to the hip student and artist neighborhood of Oberkampf and the 11e and 20e arrondissements. Brightly colored vinyl armchairs, an industrial metal staircase, and glass tables mark the lobby. Out back, a small courtyard is decked in hardwood, a choice you'll rarely see in Paris. The rooms are quite contemporary, splashed with primary reds and yellows, some with Keith Haring prints on the walls. Refurbished bathrooms are tiled with kaleidoscopes of ceramic fragments. The Beaumarchais is gradually being discovered by artsy budget travelers; for the price and attention to décor, the popularity is justified. ✉ *3 rue Oberkampf, République, 75011* ☎ *01–53–36–86–86* 📠 *01–43–38–32–86* 🌐 *www.hotelbeaumarchais.com* *31 rooms* *Dining room, in-room safes, cable TV, some pets allowed; no a/c in some rooms* 💳 *AE, MC, V* Ⓜ *Filles du Calvaire, Oberkampf.*

$ **Garden Hôtel.** This family-run hotel is on a pretty garden just out of earshot of Oberkampf. Rooms are basically functional, but spotless; those in front have lovely views of the verdant square, and all have double-glazed windows to ensure quiet. The staff speaks little English. Bathtubs are half size. ✉ *1 rue du Général-Blaise, République, 75011* ☎ *01–47–00–57–93* 📠 *01–47–00–45–29* *42 rooms* *Dining room, cable TV, some pets allowed; no a/c* 💳 *AE, MC, V* Ⓜ *St-Ambroise.*

$ **Hôtel Résidence Alhambra.** The white facade, rear garden, and flower-filled window boxes brighten an otherwise lackluster neighborhood. Inside, the look is more spartan, with smallish, modern rooms, some overlooking the flowery garden. A major face-lift upgraded the furniture and bathroom fixtures—perhaps not to everyone's taste, but the best reason to stay here is that prices are rock-bottom and the hotel is near the Marais and accessible to five métro lines at place de la République. ✉ *13 rue de Malte, République, 75011* ☎ *01–47–00–35–52* 📠 *01–43–57–98–75* 🌐 *www.hotelalhambra.fr* *58 rooms* *Dining room, cable TV, some pets allowed; no a/c* 💳 *MC, V* Ⓜ *Oberkampf.*

12e Arrondissement (Bastille/Gare de Lyon)

See Where to Stay on the Right Bank: The Marais to La Villette map.

$$ **Hôtel Lyon-Bastille.** Just a block from the Gare de Lyon is this cozy, congenial, family-run hotel, open since 1903. Rooms done up in blues

and lavenders give the place a French-country feel, with some turn-of-the-20th-century curves and alcoves. ✉ *3 rue Parrot, Bastille/Nation, 75012* ☎ *01–43–43–41–52* 📠 *01–43–43–81–16* 🌐 *www.bastille-paris-hotel.com* *47 rooms, 1 suite* *Dining room, in-room safes, minibars, cable TV; no a/c* 💳 *AE, DC, MC, V* Ⓜ *Gare de Lyon.*

$$ **Le Pavillon Bastille.** Here's a smart address (across from the Opéra Bastille) for savvy travelers who appreciate getting perks for less. The transformation of this 19th-century hôtel particulier into a colorful, high-design hotel garnered architectural awards. A fiercely loyal, hip clientele loves its bright blue and yellow interior and whimsical touches. Every detail is pitch-perfect, from the friendly staff right down to the 17th-century fountain in the garden. ✉ *65 rue de Lyon, Bastille/Nation, 75012* ☎ *01–43–43–65–65; 800/233–2552 in the U.S.* 📠 *01–43–43–96–52* 🌐 *www.pavillon-bastille.com* *24 rooms, 1 suite* *Dining room, room service, in-room data ports, in-room safes, minibars, cable TV, bar, laundry service, Internet, some pets allowed, no-smoking floors* 💳 *AE, DC, MC, V* Ⓜ *Bastille.*

13e Arrondissement (Les Gobelins)

See Where to Stay on the Left Bank map.

$$ **Résidence Hôtelière Le Vert Gallant.** In a little-known neighborhood just west of Place d'Italie awaits a sincere welcome from proprietor Madame Laborde. More like her own house, this plain but proper hotel encloses a peaceful green space. One fantastic feature of the Vert Gallant: six of the rooms are equipped with kitchenettes, allowing you to reduce dining-out costs. That is, unless you patronize the L'Auberge Etchegorry (where authors Victor Hugo and Chateaubriand used to drink and sing), the outstanding Pays Basque restaurant run by Monsieur Laborde, a 40-year veteran chef who will tempt you with southwestern French confit and foie gras. ✉ *41–43 rue Croulebarbe, Bercy/Tolbiac, 75013* ☎ *01–44–08–83–50* 📠 *01–44–08–83–69* *15 rooms* *Restaurant, dining room, in-room data ports, in-room safes, some kitchenettes, minibars, cable TV, laundry service, parking (fee); no a/c* 💳 *AE, DC, MC, V* Ⓜ *Les Gobelins.*

$ **Résidence Les Gobelins.** Jennifer Poirier is the Jamaican side of this couple (her husband Philippe is French); *ensemble* they run Résidence Les Gobelins, remarkable for the level of welcome and the price; for 20 years Jennifer has personally made sure her guests enjoy their stay in Paris. Wicker furniture and warm colors create a cozy touch at this small, simple hotel on a quiet side street between place d'Italie and the Latin Quarter, not far from the medieval market street rue Mouffetard. Some rooms overlook a small, flower-filled garden, as does the lounge where breakfast is served. ✉ *9 rue des Gobelins, Les Gobelins, 75013* ☎ *01–47–07–26–90* 📠 *01–43–31–44–05* 🌐 *www.hotelgobelins.com* *32 rooms* *Dining room, in-room data ports, cable TV, no-smoking rooms; no a/c* 💳 *AE, MC, V* Ⓜ *Les Gobelins.*

14e Arrondissement (Montparnasse)

See Where to Stay on the Left Bank map.

$$ **Hôtel du Midi.** Don't be put off by the facade and the reception area, which might make you think you're in a chain hotel. Rooms are French-provincial style—rich colors, stenciled furniture, and lots of wrought iron—and have large floor-to-ceiling windows. Some have air-conditioning, others have whirlpool baths or showers with jets, and those facing the street are quite spacious. ✉ *4 av. Réné-Coty, Montparnasse, 75014* ☎ *01–43–27–23–25* 📠 *01–43–21–24–58* 🌐 *www.midi-hotel.com* *45*

rooms, 1 suite ♘ Dining room, some in-room hot tubs, minibars, cable TV, parking (fee), some pets allowed; no a/c in some rooms ▭ AE, MC, V Ⓜ Métro or RER: Denfert-Rochereau.

$$ **Hôtel Istria.** This small, family-run hotel on a quiet side street was a Montparnasse artists' hangout in the '20s and '30s. It has a flower-filled courtyard and simple, clean, comfortable rooms with soft, pastel-tone Japanese wallpaper and light-wood furnishings. Breakfast is served in a pretty, vaulted cellar. ✉ *29 rue Campagne-Première, Montparnasse, 75014* ☎ *01–43–20–91–82* 🖷 *01–43–22–48–45* ⇨ *26 rooms* ♘ *Dining room, in-room safes, minibars, cable TV, laundry service, no-smoking floors; no a/c* ▭ *AE, DC, MC, V* Ⓜ *Raspail.*

$$ **Hôtel Lenox-Montparnasse.** The hotel may be modern, '60s-era, but it's in the heart of Montparnasse, just around the corner from the famous Dôme and Coupole brasseries, and close to the Luxembourg Gardens. The best rooms have fireplaces, old mirrors, and exposed beams; others follow a more functional, contemporary style. ✉ *15 rue Delambre, Montparnasse, 75014* ☎ *01–43–35–34–50* 🖷 *01–43–20–46–64* 🌐 *www.hotellenox.com* ⇨ *52 rooms, 6 suites* ♘ *Dining room, room service, in-room data ports, cable TV, bar, laundry service, parking (fee), no-smoking rooms; no a/c* ▭ *AE, DC, MC, V* Ⓜ *Vavin.*

$$ **Hôtel Raspail-Montparnasse.** Guest rooms here are named after the artists who made Montparnasse the art capital of the world in the '20s and '30s—Picasso, Chagall, and Modigliani, to name a few. Pastels are the dominant shades here, complemented by contemporary blond-wood furniture and crisp cotton upholstery. Most rooms are at the low end of this price category; five have spectacular panoramic views of Montparnasse and the Eiffel Tower. All are soundproofed. ✉ *203 bd. Raspail, Montparnasse, 75014* ☎ *01–43–20–62–86* 🖷 *01–43–20–50–79* 🌐 *www.charming-hotel-paris.com* ⇨ *38 rooms* ♘ *Dining room, in-room safes, minibars, cable TV, bar* ▭ *AE, DC, MC, V* Ⓜ *Vavin.*

$ **Hôtel des Bains.** A charming neighborhood, tastefully decorated rooms, satellite TV, friendly staff: can anyone explain why this hotel has only one government-ranked star? The price can't be beat, especially for the family-friendly two-room suites (€91–€137), one with a terrace, in a separate building off the courtyard garden. ✉ *33 rue Delambre, Montparnasse, 75014* ☎ *01–43–20–85–27* 🖷 *01–42–79–82–78* ⇨ *35 rooms, 8 suites* ♘ *Dining room, in-room safes, cable TV, some pets allowed; no a/c* ▭ *MC, V* Ⓜ *Vavin or Edgar Quinet.*

$ **Hôtel du Parc Montsouris.** This modest hotel in a 1930s villa is on a quiet residential street next to one of the city's lesser-known green spaces, Parc Montsouris. The small but clean rooms are embellished with attractive oak pieces and high-quality French fabrics. Those with showers are very inexpensive; suites sleep four. Adjoining double rooms are available. Ask for a room at the front; the views onto the park are lovely. Though out of the way, this is a fantastic deal, especially considering the impressive list of services and amenities. ✉ *4 rue du Parc-Montsouris, Montparnasse, 75014* ☎ *01–45–89–09–72* 🖷 *01–45–80–92–72* 🌐 *www.hotel-parc-montsouris.com* ⇨ *28 rooms, 7 suites* ♘ *Dining room, in-room data ports, minibars, cable TV, baby-sitting, laundry service, Internet, some pets allowed, no-smoking rooms* ▭ *AE, MC, V* Ⓜ *Montparnasse Bienvenüe.*

15e Arrondissement (Champ de Mars)

See Where to Stay on the Left Bank map.

$$ **Timhotel Tour Eiffel.** Inside this '70s-era hotel, within walking distance of the Eiffel Tower, are inexpensive, comfortable rooms with modern bathrooms, cable TV, and double-glazed windows that block out street noise.

Though part of the Timhotel chain, the light-wood furniture and crisp damask give rooms a clean if simple feel; some of them have great views of the Eiffel Tower. The buffet breakfast is one of the city's least expensive. ✉ *11 rue Juge, Eiffel Tower/Trocadéro, 75015* ☎ *01–45–78–29–29* 📠 *01–45–78–60–00* 🌐 *www.timhotel.com* *39 rooms* *Dining room, cable TV, laundry service, some pets allowed, no-smoking floors; no a/c in some rooms* 💳 *AE, DC, MC, V* Ⓜ *Dupleix.*

16e Arrondissement (Trocadéro/Bois de Boulogne)

See Where to Stay on the Right Bank: Bois du Boulogne to Place de la Concorde map.

3

$$$$ **Hôtel Raphael.** The Raphael was built in 1925 to cater to high-society travelers spending a season in Paris. Closets are thus spacious enough to hold wardrobes of ball gowns and plume hats. The large rooms are filled with 18th- and early 19th-century antiques and have 6-ft windows, Oriental rugs, silk damask wallpaper, chandeliers, and ornately carved wood paneling. Most rooms have massive king-size beds. Bathrooms are remarkably large; most have natural light, whirlpool tubs, and separate showers. The rooftop terrace, where meals are served in warm weather, has a panoramic view of the city. Construction is ongoing, so request a room away from the action. ✉ *17 av. Kléber, Eiffel Tower/Trocadéro, 75116* ☎ *01–53–64–32–00* 📠 *01–53–64–32–01* 🌐 *www.raphael-hotel.com* *54 rooms, 41 suites* *Restaurant, room service, in-room data ports, in-room safes, some in-room hot tubs, minibars, cable TV with movies, gym, sauna, bar, baby-sitting, dry cleaning, laundry service, concierge, Internet, business services, parking (fee), some pets allowed, no-smoking floors* 💳 *AE, MC, V* 🍽 *CP* Ⓜ *Kléber.*

$$$$ **Melià Alexander Boutique Hôtel.** This classy old hotel, formerly known just as the Alexander, reemerged in 2002 after a head-to-toe revamping. Now it's a "boutique hotel" (a fact plainly stated in its new name), refitted with plush draperies and carpeting and a higher price to match. But it still retains the Old Europe feel, from the room chandeliers and old-fashioned cage elevator to the 20-ft-high corniced ceilings and period wall sconces that bathe all in warm, rosy hues. It's also on one of Paris's finest shopping avenues. ✉ *102 av. Victor Hugo, Eiffel Tower/Trocadéro, 75116* ☎ *01–56–90–61–00* 📠 *01–45–53–12–51* 🌐 *www.meliaalexander.activehotels.com* *60 rooms, 2 suites* *Dining room, room service, in-room data ports, in-room safes, minibars, cable TV, bar, baby-sitting, laundry service, no-smoking rooms* 💳 *AE, DC, MC, V* Ⓜ *Victor-Hugo.*

$$$$ **Saint James Paris.** Called "the only château-hôtel in Paris," this gracious, late-19th-century mansion is surrounded by a lush private park. Ten rooms—done in the neoclassical mode—on the third floor open onto a winter garden; the poshest option is booking one of the two duplex gatehouses. The magnificent bar-library is lined with floor-to-ceiling oak bookcases. The restaurant is reserved for guests; in warm weather, meals are served in the garden. ✉ *43 av. Bugeaud, Trocadéro/Eiffel Tower, 75116* ☎ *01–44–05–81–81* 📠 *01–44–05–81–82* 🌐 *www.saint-james-paris.com* *18 rooms, 30 suites* *Restaurant, room service, in-room data ports, in-room safes, minibars, cable TV, health club, bar, baby-sitting, laundry service, concierge, Internet, meeting room, free parking, some pets allowed* 💳 *AE, DC, MC, V* Ⓜ *Porte Dauphine.*

$$$$ **Trocadéro Dokhan's Sofitel Demeure Hôtel.** Popular among fashionistas, the hotel has an idiosyncratic style. Its attention to detail is what truly sets it apart from other posh addresses in this very upscale neighborhood: a Louis Vuitton steamer-trunk elevator; an elegant bar stocked with 50 varieties of bubbly; a tea salon; and overequipped marble bathrooms with Roger et Gallet toiletries in every room and suite. The best rooms are the deluxe doubles; only the suites have views of the Eiffel Tower. It's part of the Sofitel chain. ✉ *117 rue Lauriston, Trocadéro/Eiffel Tower, 75016* ☎ *01–53–65–66–99* 🖷 *01–53–65–66–88* 🌐 *www.sofitel.com* *41 rooms, 4 suites* *Dining room, room service, in-room data ports, in-room safes, minibars, cable TV, bar, baby-sitting, laundry service, concierge, Internet, some pets allowed, no-smoking floors* 💳 *AE, DC, MC, V* Ⓜ *Porte Dauphine.*

$$$ **Hôtel Square.** There's little that's "square" about this very hip boutique hotel. Rooms are bright and spacious, decorated in what is best described as extravagant minimalism. Curved doors, walls, and furniture break up a hard-edged design dominated by stripes and squares, while flowers, designer lamps, and enormous beds soften the Zen aesthetic. Large desks, plus three phone lines and a fax-answering machine in each room make it ideal for business travelers. But the reading room, art gallery, and very sleek bar make it a good choice for pleasure-seekers as well. Note: The hotel offers a discount to readers who mention this guide at booking and show a copy at check-in. ✉ *3 rue de Boulainvilliers, Trocadéro/Eiffel Tower, 75016* ☎ *01–44–14–91–90* 🖷 *01–44–14–91–99* 🌐 *www.hotelsquare.com* *18 rooms, 4 suites* *Restaurant, room service, in-room data ports, in-room safes, minibars, cable TV, bar, laundry service, meeting rooms, parking (fee)* 💳 *AE, DC, MC, V* Ⓜ *Passy.*

$$$ **Les Jardins du Trocadéro.** This good-value hotel near the Trocadéro and the Eiffel Tower seamlessly blends old-style French elegance (period antiques, Napoléonic draperies, classical plaster busts) with modern conveniences (soundproofing, satellite TV, VCRs, modem lines). Beds are huge: either king- or queen-size. Marble bathrooms come complete with terry robes and whirlpool baths. ✉ *35 rue Benjamin-Franklin, Trocadéro/Eiffel Tower, 75116* ☎ *01–53–70–17–70; 800/246–0041 in the U.S.* 🖷 *01–53–70–17–80* 🌐 *www.jardintroc.com* *18 rooms, 5 suites* *Dining room, room service, in-room data ports, in-room safes, minibars, cable TV, hot tub, bar, laundry service, parking (fee), no-smoking rooms* 💳 *AE, DC, MC, V* Ⓜ *Trocadéro.*

$–$$ **Queen's Hôtel.** One of only a handful of hotels in the tony residential district near the Bois de Boulogne, Queen's is a small, comfortable, old-fashioned hotel with a high standard of service. Each room focuses on a different 20th-century French artist. Renovated rooms have hot tubs and new beds. ✉ *4 rue Bastien-Lepage, Bois de Boulogne, 75016* ☎ *01–42–88–89–85* 🖷 *01–40–50–67–52* 🌐 *www.queens-hotel.fr* *21 rooms, 1 suite* *Dining room, in-room safes, minibars, cable TV, some hot tubs, Internet, some pets allowed, no-smoking rooms; no a/c in some rooms* 💳 *AE, DC, MC, V* Ⓜ *Michel-Ange Auteuil.*

$ **Hôtel Keppler.** On the border of the 8e and 16e arrondissements, near the Champs-Élysées, is this small, modern hotel in a 19th-century building offering bargain prices in a chic neighborhood. The spacious, airy rooms have simple furnishings and floral upholstery, and more upscale amenities—such as room safes and room service—than you'd expect for the price. Upper-floor rooms face the Eiffel Tower. A big lounge and dining room provide plenty of hangout space. ✉ *12 rue Keppler, Champs-Élysées, 75016* ☎ *01–47–20–65–05* 🖷 *01–47–23–02–29* 🌐 *www.hotelkeppler.com* *49 rooms* *Dining room, room service, in-room safes, cable TV, bar, no-smoking rooms; no a/c* 💳 *AE, MC, V* Ⓜ *George V.*

17e Arrondissement (Monceau/Clichy)

See Where to Stay on the Right Bank: Bois du Boulogne to Place de la Concorde map.

★ $$$ Étoile-Péreire. The extremely congenial owner here has created a unique, intimate hotel set behind a quiet, leafy courtyard. It consists of two parts: a fin-de-siècle building on the street and a 1920s annex overlooking an interior courtyard. There's an air of fantasy at the Étoile-Péreire, since all of the rooms have individually decorated period or cultural themes. Travel in time to Regency or Deco days, or travel across continents to Africa, China, India, or a tropical beach. Only the duplex suites have air-conditioning. The copious breakfast is legendary, featuring 40 assorted jams and jellies. *146 bd. Péreire, Parc Monceau, 75017 01–42–67–60–00 01–42–67–02–90 www.etoileper.com 21 rooms, 5 suites Dining room, in-room safes, room service, minibars, cable TV, bar, laundry service, Internet, no-smoking rooms; no a/c in some rooms AE, DC, MC, V Péreire.*

$$–$$$ Hôtel Eber-Monceau. This small hotel—part of the Relais du Silence group—is just one block from Parc Monceau. It attracts a stylish media and fashion set, though the engaging owner, Jean-Marc Eber, delights in welcoming all first-time guests. Rooms are tastefully done in bright, cheerful colors; ask for one overlooking the courtyard. *18 rue Léon-Jost, Parc Monceau, 75017 01–46–22–60–70 01–47–63–01–01 13 rooms, 5 suites Dining room, in-room data ports, minibars, cable TV, bar, laundry service AE, DC, MC, V Courcelles.*

$$ Hôtel Excelsior. Owner Xavier Chateauvieux took over this circa 1890 hotel in 2001 and has been gradually replacing baths and fabrics. With the feeling of a private house, this endearing place is only a five-minute walk from Montmartre and near more than a dozen bus and métro lines. Rustic antiques and heavy armoires in the small, spotless rooms add a warm, cozy feel. Request a room overlooking the little garden. *16 rue Caroline, Montmartre, 75017 01–45–22–50–95 01–45–22–59–88 22 rooms Dining room, cable TV; no a/c AE, MC, V Place de Clichy.*

$$ Hôtel Palma. This modest hotel in a small 19th-century building between the Arc de Triomphe and Porte Maillot is an exceptional deal considering its rather aristocratic neighbors. Cheerful and homey, if not luxurious, rooms have basic wood furnishings and bright floral wallpaper; ask for one on the top floor with a view across Right Bank rooftops. There's air-conditioning on the sixth (top) floor only. *46 rue Brunel, Champs-Élysées, 75017 01–45–74–74–51 01–45–74–40–90 37 rooms Dining room, cable TV, some pets allowed; no a/c in some rooms AE, MC, V Argentine.*

$$ Hôtel Regent's Garden. Built in the mid-19th century by Napoléon III for his doctor, this Best Western hotel near the Arc de Triomphe is adorned, as you might imagine, with marble fireplaces, mirrors, gilt furniture, and cornicing. Ask for a room overlooking the gorgeous garden, where breakfast is served in summer. *6 rue Pierre-Demours, Champs-Élysées, 75017 01–45–74–07–30 01–40–55–01–42 www.hotel-paris-garden.com 39 rooms Dining room, in-room data ports, in-room safes, minibars, cable TV, Internet, parking (fee), no-smoking rooms AE, DC, MC, V Charles-de-Gaulle–Étoile, Ternes.*

18e Arrondissement (Montmartre)

See Where to Stay on the Right Bank: Ile de la Cité to Montmartre map.

$$$ Terrass Hotel. The hulking Terrass, known for its commanding location overlooking the city, dwarfs its rather humble Montmartre neighbors, which include the graves of the adjacent cemetery. The hotel excels at offering posh amenities for a demanding clientele, but does come off with somewhat of a business vibe. There's a mix of French-country color schemes and special touches such as tea kettles and complementary cos-

metics. Superior rooms have two sinks, shower, and bathtub or Jacuzzi bathtub, and some juniors suites have big wood-deck balconies. An impressive seventh-floor restaurant has an outdoor terrace (open April to September) with panoramic views. ✉ *12–14 rue Joseph de Maistre, Montmartre, 75018* ☎ *01–44–92–34–14* 🖷 *01–42–52–29–11* 🌐 *www.terrass-hotel.com* *86 rooms, 14 suites* *Restaurant, room service, some in-room safes, minibars, cable TV with movies, bar, laundry service, concierge, Internet, meeting rooms, no-smoking floors* 💳 *AE, DC, MC, V* *CP* Ⓜ *Place de Clichy.*

★ $ **Ermitage Hôtel.** Resembling a squat, modest mansion, the Ermitage is, in fact, a former residence converted into accommodations in the 1970s by legendary hosts Monsieur and Madame Canipel. Now their daughter Maggie runs the show, and the same genuine tranquillity and one-of-the-family welcome awaits. The hotel dates from Napoléon III's time and is filled with mirrored armoires, chandeliers, and other antiques. There's a private terrace for the two ground-level rooms; second-floor windows open wide toward north Paris. Rooms are have funky flowery interiors throughout. The building is only two stories high (no elevator), and the highest-tech item is the fax machine. ✉ *24 rue Lamarck, Montmartre, 75018* ☎ *01–42–64–79–22* 🖷 *01–42–64–10–33* *12 rooms* *Dining room, some pets allowed; no a/c, no room TVs* 💳 *No credit cards* *CP* Ⓜ *Lamarck Caulaincourt.*

$ **Hôtel Regyn's Montmartre.** The lobby is cramped, the plain dining room tiny, and the staircase skinny, but folks book the Regyn's for the *Amélie Poulain* neighborhood and the expansive views, not spacious digs or a gourmet breakfast. Despite the small and basic rooms, this owner-run hotel on Montmartre's evocative place des Abbesses provides comfortable accommodations. Bathrooms are modern with rare old-style ceramic pedestal sinks. Ask to stay on one of the two top floors for great views of either the Eiffel Tower or Sacré-Coeur; those on the lower floors are darker and less inviting. Overall, courteous service and a relaxed charm make this an attractive choice. ✉ *18 pl. des Abbesses, Montmartre, 75018* ☎ *01–42–54–45–21* 🖷 *01–42–23–76–69* 🌐 *www.regynsmontmartre.com* *22 rooms* *Dining room, cable TV with movies, in-room safes, some pets allowed* 💳 *AE, MC, V* Ⓜ *Abbesses.*

$ **Hôtel Utrillo.** This very likable hotel is on a quiet side street at the foot of Montmartre, near colorful rue Lepic. Reproduction prints and marble-top breakfast tables in every room make them feel charmingly old-fashioned, while the white-and-pastel color scheme makes them appear brighter and more spacious than they actually are. Two rooms (Nos. 61 and 63) have views of the Eiffel Tower. ✉ *7 rue Aristide-Bruant, Montmartre, 75018* ☎ *01–42–58–13–44* 🖷 *01–42–23–93–88* 🌐 *www.hotel-paris-utrillo.com* *30 rooms* *Dining room, minibars, cable TV, sauna, some pets allowed; no a/c* 💳 *AE, DC, MC, V* Ⓜ *Abbesses, Blanche.*

19e Arrondissement (Buttes-Chaumont)

See Where to Stay on the Right Bank: The Marais to La Villette map.

¢–$ **Hôtel Le Laumière.** Though it's some distance from the city center, the rock-bottom rates of this family-run hotel near the rambling Buttes-Chaumont park make it hard to resist. The staff, too, is exceptionally helpful. Unfortunately, the modern, modular furniture is less inspiring, though some of the larger rooms overlook a garden and lawn and have balconies. Ask about special rates. ✉ *4 rue Petit, Buttes-Chaumont, 75019* ☎ *01–42–06–10–77* 🖷 *01–42–06–72–50* 🌐 *www.hotel-lelaumiere.com* *54 rooms* *Dining room, cable TV, parking (fee), some pets allowed, no-smoking rooms; no a/c* 💳 *MC, V* Ⓜ *Laumière.*

NIGHTLIFE AND THE ARTS

4

FODOR'S CHOICE

Au Lapin Agile, Montmartre
Au Pied de Cochon, Beaubourg/Les Halles
New Morning, Opéra/Grands Boulevards
Opéra Garnier, Opéra/Grands Boulevards
La Pagode, Invalides
Le Pulp, Opéra/Grands Boulevards
The Ritz's Hemingway Bar, Louvre/Tuileries

HIGHLY RECOMMENDED

Bar d'Art/Le Duplex, Beaubourg/Les Halles
Batofar, Chinatown
Comédie Française, Louvre/Tuileries
Crazy Horse, Champs-Élysées
La Favela Chic, République
La Flèche d'Or, Charonne
Le Fumoir, Louvre/Tuileries
Galerie 213, Montparnasse
Harry's New York Bar, Opéra/Grands Boulevards
Paradis Latin, Latin Quarter
La Perla, Le Marais
Le Rex, Opéra/Grands Boulevards
Sainte-Chapelle, Ile de la Cité
Salle Cortot, Parc Monceau
Thaddaeus Ropac, Le Marais

Revised and updated by Christopher Mooney

THE CITY OF LIGHT TRULY BECOMES ILLUMINATED AFTER DARK. So, if you want to paint the town *rouge* after dutifully pounding the parquet in museums all day, there's a dazzling array of options to partake of. Whether you're a jazz fiend or a dance freak, a patron of the arts or a lounge lizard seeking refuge in a bar where the model count is high, Paris provides ample destinations for nocturnal creatures. From opulent opera houses to low-key bars, dance floors in 17th-century cellars, or just the light-splintered Seine, you can find it all in Paris after dark. The hottest nightspots are near Menilmontant and Parmentier, the Bastille, and the Marais. By comparison, the Left Bank is definitely a minor happening scene. The Champs-Élysées is making a comeback, especially with stylish singles bars on its side streets, though the clientele on the main drag itself remains predominantly foreign. Midweek, people are usually home after closing hours, around 2 AM, but weekends mean late-night partying. Take note: the last métro runs between 12:30 and 1 AM (you can take a cab, though they can be hard to find between midnight and 2 AM on weekends); you may just have to stay out until the métro starts running again at 5:30 AM.

Bars

The best of the bars in Paris have character, witty waiters, local color, and inventive cocktails at prices that permit consuming without counting. The variety of bar ambiences is also impressive—there are bars serving light food, moody late-night bars, bars with DJs, and bars with live music. Other options include cafés, many of which become bars at night, and wine bars. If you want to hit bars at a relatively quiet hour, try them during the *apéritif* (around 6 PM). That's when Parisians congregate to decide where they want to meet up later. In many bars you'll find two different tariffs—*au comptoir* (cheap prices if you stand with your drink at the bar) and *à salle* (more expensive rates if you sit down at at table).

BASTILLE & THE EASTERN RIGHT BANK

In the early 1990s, the Bastille was the hottest nightlife area in town. Though the scene for those in the know has moved to the adjacent Belleville sector, the Bastille still remains popular. The block-long rue de Lappe has more bars per foot than any other street in Paris; nearby rue de la Roquette and rue de Charonne also have many options.

Barrio Latino (✉ 46–48 rue du Faubourg St-Antoine, 12ᵉ, Bastille/Nation ☎ 01–55–78–84–75 Ⓜ Bastille) is a lush cross of casbah, Old Havana, and SoHo loft that pulls a very mixed crowd of hipsters, including everyone from threadbare art students to ambitious young lawyers. Though pricey, it can be a fun scene; it could be more so if the drinks were better. Alas, the food is even worse.

Café Charbon (✉ 109 rue Oberkampf, 11ᵉ, République ☎ 01–43–57–55–13 Ⓜ St-Maur, Parmentier) is a beautifully restored 19th-century café whose trendsetting clientele converses to a jazz background. The vibe gets livelier after 10 PM, when a DJ takes over.

Café de la Musique (✉ 213 av. Jean Jaurès, 19ᵉ, La Villette ☎ 01–48–03–15–91 Ⓜ Porte de Pantin) has a large and enticing selection of cocktails and limited brasserie offerings in a comfortable setting recently renovated by Parc de la Villette architect Christian Potzamparc.

Chez Prune (✉ 36 rue Beaurepaire, 10ᵉ, République ☎ 01–42–41–30–47 Ⓜ Jacques Bonsergent) is a lively bar with a terrace overlooking one of the footbridges crossing the Canal St-Martin. The area has become one of the hottest in Paris, yet, while you're more than likely to spot some hip fashion designer, celebrity photographer Mario Testino, and lots of beautiful people, the neighborhood mood is refreshingly more relaxed that poseurish.

TABLE-HOPPING IN TRENDY OBERKAMPF

*THE MOOD IS THE THING in the trendy nightlife area of the Oberkampf (between boulevard Voltaire and boulevard de Ménilmontant, midway between Bastille and Belleville, on rue Oberkampf, rue St-Maur, and rue Jean-Pierre-Timbaud)—not just the mood music that plays after sundown but the shabby, down-to-earth feel of narrow streets, largely unmolested by developers, that exude vague nostalgia for quintessential, lived-in, dyed-in-the-wool Paris. These streets still crackle with energy, none more than rue d'Oberkampf between the Ménilmontant and Parmentier métro stations, whose long stretch of bars and restaurants have taken their cue from **Café Charbon** (No. 109; ☎ 01–43–57–55–13), a converted turn-of-the-20th-century dance hall ostentatiously proud of its huge mirrors, smoke-stained ceilings, and ultratrendy dance club the Nouveau Casino (in the back room). The district plays on its image as a working-class antidote to the designer bars of Bastille and Beaubourg: **Café Mercerie** (No. 98; ☎ 01–43–38–81–30), across from Café Charbon, takes its name—and painted sign—from the draper's shop that used to be here. Looking back, the first wave of bars and boutiques hereabouts looked like they had been thrown together by impoverished art students during a particularly drunken weekend; many of those, sadly, are long gone, replaced by more conventionally cool joints. Still funky and fun, the rue is losing some of its street credo as a better-heeled clientele pushes out the pioneering boho crowd that first claimed the district as its own.*

*But while rue Oberkampf itself looks destined to be Bastilled into bobo (bourgeois bohemian) complacency, its neighboring streets still have their edges intact, especially rue Jean-Pierre-Timbaud, home to many hot haunts: **L'Auberge** (No. 4; ☎ 01–48–06–15–29), **Le Vestiaire** (No. 64; ☎ 01–43–55–42–50), **L'Autre Café** (No. 62; ☎ 01–40–21–03–07), and the friendly **Café Cannibale** (No. 93; ☎ 01–49–29–95–59). Rue de la Folie-Méricourt, lined with food shops and restaurants on its way south to the twin-spired neo-Gothic church of St-Ambroise, still epitomizes the area's unpretentious charm, with discreet, leafy courtyards sharing sidewalks with upmarket bars and working-class canteens.*

*A little farther south, near métro Charonne, is one of the city's most famous wine bars, **Jacques Mélac**, at 42 rue Léon Frot (☎ 01–43–70–59–27), where genial Jacques displays the largest mustache in town and grows his own grapes on a vine along the front of the building. The area is changing fast, however. Used to be that the nearest you'd come to a tourist site were the five unphotogenic granite blocks at the angle of rue de la Roquette and rue de la Croix-Faubin that served as the base for Paris's last public guillotine through 1899. Soon, neck-craners and camera-toters will have investigated every corner of the quartier. So make haste—faites vite!*

China Club (✉ 50 rue de Charenton, 12e, Bastille/Nation ☎ 01–43–43–82–02 Ⓜ Ledru-Rollin) has three floors of bars and a restaurant with lacquered furnishings and a colonial-Asia theme. During happy hour (7–9), all cocktails are €5.30. There are also free jazz concerts at 10 PM in the basement club on Friday and Saturday. Concerts on Thursday at 9 PM have an admission fee of €10.

La Fabrique (✉ 53 rue du Faubourg St-Antoine, 11e, Bastille/Nation ☎ 01–43–07–67–07 Ⓜ Bastille) is a bar and restaurant that brews its own beer (look for the huge copper vats by the entrance). It really gets going every evening after 9 PM, when a DJ hits the turntables.

★ **La Favela Chic** (✉ 18 rue du Faubourg du Temple, 11e, République ☎ 01–40–21–38–14 Ⓜ République) was one of the bars that made Oberkampf into the hippest area in Paris a few years back. A couple of years ago, however, it decamped to this new, large space hidden in a courtyard behind iron gates. It offers an organic juice bar, caipirinhas and mojitos, guest DJs, and an almost nonstop Latino party atmosphere.

★ **La Flèche d'Or** (✉ 102 bis rue de Bagnolet, 20e, Charonne ☎ 01–43–72–04–23 Ⓜ Alexandre Dumas), housed in a former railway station, is one of the best places in Paris to take in some live music. There are concerts Tuesday through Sunday at 9 PM and on Sunday at 7 PM, plus "Throw Mama off the Train" electronic DJ soirees on Wednesday. The music runs the gamut from reggae to rock to world music, and there's an open stage on Tuesday for any budding stars.

Le Gast (✉ 5 rue Crespin-du-Gast, 11e, République ☎ 01–43–55–53–34 Ⓜ Ménilmontant) is a rarity—a quiet, friendly neighborhood bar in the bustling Oberkampf district. There is a curvaceous wooden counter, cocktails such as Ti punch and piña colada, and Polaroids of regulars stuck on the walls.

Le Piston Pélican (✉ 15 rue de Bagnolet, 20e, Charonne ☎ 01–43–70–35–00 Ⓜ Alexandre Dumas), with its pewter bar and Belle Epoque trimmings, is one of those quintessential Parisian places. Often packed with a vibrant crowd, it plays host to DJs and live music on Friday and Saturday.

Sanz Sans (✉ 49 rue du Faubourg St-Antoine, 11e, Bastille/Nation ☎ 01–44–75–78–78 Ⓜ Bastille) has added a new twist to bar life—the "actors" performing on the upstairs lounge's gilt-framed video screen are really the habitués of the downstairs bar.

Wax (✉ 15 rue Daval, 11e, Bastille/Nation ☎ 01–40–21–16–16 Ⓜ Bastille) would be worth a visit simply for its psychedelic-moderne interior—check out the orange and pink walls, multicolor squiggles on the columns, and molded plastic banquettes by the window. It is also one of the most happening places in the city music-wise, with DJs spinning techno and house every evening.

CHAMPS-ÉLYSÉES/OPÉRA/LOUVRE

The Champs-Élysées ("Les Champs" to the initiated) and the streets branching off from it have seen many glitzy bars open and quickly gain a reputation by inviting models and stars. After the first few weeks, however, the model count goes down and the slicked-back hair, sharp suits, and mobile phones crowd moves in.

Barramundi (✉ 3 rue Taitbout, 9e, Opéra/Grands Boulevards ☎ 01–47–70–21–21 Ⓜ Richelieu Drouot) is one of Paris's hubs of nouveau-riche chic. The lighting is dim, the copper bar is long, and the walls are artfully textured. During the week, chill-out and world music is piped through to the bar. By the weekend, however, things get moving with a program of regular soirees, with names like "Super Nature," "Reelax," and "Corpus Noctem."

Buddha Bar (✉ 8 rue Boissy d'Anglas, 8e, Champs-Élysées ☎ 01–53–05–90–00 Ⓜ Concorde) has one of the most glittery settings in Paris, with a towering gold-painted Buddha contemplating enough Dragon Empress screens and colorful chinoiserie for five MGM movies. The crowd ranges from camera-friendly faces—*Vogue* did a big fashion spread here—to suburban trendsetters, with groups of office ladies out on the town now making the scene. A spacious mezzanine bar overlooks the dining room, where cuisines East and West meet somewhere between Blandsville and California.

★ **Le Fumoir** (✉ 6 rue Amiral-de-Coligny, 1er, Louvre/Tuileries ☎ 01–42–92–00–24 Ⓜ Louvre) is a fashionable spot for a late-afternoon beer or early evening cocktail (dinner is also served). There's a large bar in front, a library with shelves of books in back, and leather couches throughout.

★ **Harry's New York Bar** (✉ 5 rue Daunou, 2e, Opéra/Grands Boulevards ☎ 01–42–61–71–14 Ⓜ Opéra), a cozy, wood-paneled hangout decorated with dusty college pennants and popular with expatriates, is haunted by the ghosts of Ernest Hemingway and F. Scott Fitzgerald. This place claims to have invented the Bloody Mary, and one way or another, the bartenders here do mix a mean one.

Man Ray (✉ 34 rue Marbeuf, 8e, Champs-Élysées ☎ 01–56–88–36–36 Ⓜ Franklin-D.-Roosevelt) is one of the hottest places in town, which is not surprising given that it is owned by Johnny Depp, Sean Penn, and Simply Red's Mick Hucknall. May Ray becomes Woman Ray on Monday—an exclusive networking club for women. The ravishing Asian–Art Deco style is reminiscent of a slightly Disneyesque 1930s supper club in Chinatown. The bar is open until 2 AM and serves cocktails, tapas, and sushi.

Polo Room (✉ 3 rue Lord Byron, 8e, Champs-Élysées ☎ 01–40–74–07–78 Ⓜ George V), on the first floor of a building in a sleepy street off the Champs-Élysées, is the very first martini bar in Paris. The American owner's target clientele is the world of business (35- to 45-year-olds), and his aim is to give this space a very New York feel. There are polo photos on the wall, a 36-ft bar, and a selection of 28 different martinis (who can resist the Martini Chocolat?). There are also regular live jazz concerts and DJs every Friday and Saturday night.

LATIN QUARTER/ ST-GERMAIN-DES-PRÉS

In the heart of expensive (and touristy) Paris, bars here can't afford to be too cutting-edge. While the price you may pay for your beer can be high, the good news is that you'll probably meet a lot of other English-speaking travelers out on the town.

Alcazar (✉ 62 rue Mazarine, 6e, St-Germain-des-Prés ☎ 01–53–10–19–99 Ⓜ Odéon), Sir Terence Conran's first makeover of a Parisian landmark, has a stylish bar on the first floor, where you can sip a glass of wine under the huge glass roof. From Wednesday to Saturday a DJ spins either lounge or Latin music.

Chez Georges (✉ 11 rue de Canettes, 6e, St-Germain-des-Prés ☎ 01–43–26–79–15 Ⓜ Mabillon) has been serving glasses of red wine, pastis, and beer for the past 60-odd years. Down in the basement, young folk crowd around tiny tables, but don't be intimidated if the place looks packed—there's always room to squeeze in somewhere, and the regulars are more than willing to make new friends.

Le Comptoir (✉ 5 rue Monsieur-Le-Prince, 6e, Latin Quarter ☎ 01–43–29–12–05 Ⓜ Odéon) is a wine bar serving Burgundies and Bordeaux by the glass, as well as more unusual wines, such as vintages from Corsica.

Les Etages (✉ 5 rue de Buci, 6e, St-Germain-des-Prés ☎ 01–46–34–26–26 Ⓜ Odéon) is a laid-back, student-y type of place occupying three floors of a building near St-Germain-des-Prés. The walls are rustic red and ocher, the decor is simple, and the terrace is the perfect place to sit in summer.

Oya (✉ 25 rue de la Reine Blanche, 13e, Latin Quarter ☎ 01–47–07–59–59 Ⓜ Les Gobelins) is a haven for fans of board games. The owners have assembled more than 200 from around the world, which you can play for €5 a game.

Le Piano Vache (✉ 8 rue Laplace, 5e, Latin Quarter ☎ 01–46–33–75–03 Ⓜ Cardinal Lemoine) has music that is sufficiently angst-inspiring and a bar sufficiently dark to keep you from getting too optimistic. The place is wallpapered with '70s posters, is super-smoky, and has a Goth party every Wednesday eve.

Wagg (✉ 62 rue Mazarine, 6e, St-Germain-des-Prés ☎ 01–55–42–22–00 Ⓜ Odéon), is Sir Terence Conran's first foray into nightclub land. Jim Morrisson's hangout, the old Whiskey-a-Go-Go, in the vaulted stone cellar beneath Conran's popular Alcazar restaurant, has been turned into this Saint Germain-des-Prés nightspot. Run by the über-trendy London club Fabric, Wagg is a small, sleek club with state-of-the-art sound and lighting, guest DJs, and large helpings of house techno music.

MARAIS Creative souls tend to live in Le Marais, so the neighborhood bars are very welcoming and pleasant.

Le Café du Trésor (✉ 5 rue Trésor, 4e, Le Marais ☎ 01–44–78–06–60 Ⓜ St-Paul) is a lively, sophisticated bar, where every night except Sunday DJs spin a mixture of house and funk. There's also a next-door restaurant.
La Chaise au Plafond (✉ 10 rue du Trésor, 4e, Le Marais ☎ 01–42–76–03–22 Ⓜ St-Paul) has the feel of a traditional bistro with a few offbeat contemporary touches. Never overcrowded, it's the perfect place for an excellent glass of wine.
★ **La Perla** (✉ 26 rue François Miron, 4e, Le Marais ☎ 01–42–77–59–40 Ⓜ Hôtel de Ville, St-Paul) is one of the chicest spots in town for Latin lovers. Sit back, sip a margarita, munch on a few tapas, and take in all the lovely people.
La Tartine (✉ 24 rue de Rivoli, 4e, Le Marais ☎ 01–42–72–76–85 Ⓜ St-Paul) serves inexpensive glasses of wine and *tartines* (open-face sandwiches) in a tatty, almost seedy turn-of-the-20th-century bar that has earned antihero status among the cognoscenti.
Le Web Bar (✉ 32 rue de Picardie, 3e, Le Marais ☎ 01–42–72–66–55 Ⓜ Temple) is a lively, eclectic place where you can surf the Net or take in a photo exhibition or short film. There are also musical brunches on Saturday and Sunday and a whole host of soirees. For detailed information of events, check out the Web site (www.webbar.fr).

MONTMARTRE Amid the tourist trappings are some distinctive options for imbibing.

Café Carmen (✉ 22 rue de Douai, 9e, Montmartre ☎ 01–45–26–21–17 Ⓜ Pigalle) bears a name that is homage to Georges Bizet, whose opera set Paris ablaze in the early 19th century. The building once belonged to the composer's widow, then became a soup kitchen, then a high-class brothel. Today it maintains its magnificent Napoléon III–era molded ceilings, chandeliers, and gilt mirrors. In the basement is a cozy bar, where there are regular operetta concerts given by a distant relative of Toulouse-Lautrec and evenings dominated by deep lounge music.
Le Jungle Montmartre (✉ 32 rue Gabrielle, 18e, Montmartre ☎ 01–46–06–75–69 Ⓜ Abbesses) is a gem of a place in a very sleepy, off-the-beat street in Montmartre. Upstairs is an African restaurant; downstairs is a small bar with Senegalese sculptures and tiger and leopard designs on the tabletops. There are DJs every evening from 9 PM—music ranges from reggae and funk to techno and drum and bass—who are often joined by traditional African musicians.
Moloko (✉ 26 rue Fontaine, 9e, Montmartre ☎ 01–48–74–50–26 Ⓜ Blanche), a smoky late-night bar with several rooms, a mezzanine, a jukebox, and a small dance floor, is a popular spot with a trendy, fun-loving crowd.
Le Sancerre (✉ 35 rue des Abbesses, 18e, Montmartre ☎ 01–42–58–08–20 Ⓜ Abbesses), a café by day, turns into a lively watering hole for jovial Montmartrois and artist types at night.

MONTPARNASSE Raise a glass to the resident spirits of long-gone writers, artists, and poets.

American Bar at La Closerie des Lilas (✉ 171 bd. du Montparnasse, 6e, Montparnasse ☎ 01–40–51–34–50 Ⓜ Montparnasse) lets you drink in the swirling action of the adjacent restaurant and brasserie and do it at a bar hallowed by plaques honoring such former habitués as Man Ray, Jean-Paul Sartre, and Samuel Beckett. Happily, many Parisians still call this watering hole their home away from home.

Hotel Bars

Elegant and upscale, with a classic Parisian feel, the city's hotel bars are quiet spots to meet for a drink. Following are some of the best: **L'Hôtel** (✉ 10 rue des Beaux-Arts, 6e, St-Germain-des-Prés ☎ 01–44–41–99–00 Ⓜ St-Germain-des-Prés) had stylemeister Jacques Garcia revamp the historic decor.**Hôtel Le Bristol** (✉ 112 rue du Faubourg St-Honoré, 8e, Champs-Élysées ☎ 01–53–43–43–42 Ⓜ Miromesnil) attracts the rich and powerful. **Hôtel Costes** (✉ 239 rue St-Honoré, Louvre/Tuileries, 75001 ☎ 01–42–44–50–50) draws many many big names in the fashion world during Collections weeks. **Hôtel de Crillon** (✉ 10 pl. de la Concorde, 8e, Champs-Élysées ☎ 01–44–71–15–39 Ⓜ Concorde) allures with creamy elegance. **Hôtel Lutétia** (✉ 45 bd. Raspail, 6e, Montparnasse ☎ 01–49–54–46–09 Ⓜ Sèvres Babylone) has three bars, one of which, the Saint Germain, is a seductive boîte with red table lamps, seminude bronze statues, and live jazz four nights a week: no wonder legend Catherine Deneuve like to chill out here. **Hôtel Meurice** (✉ 228 rue de Rivoli, 1er, Louvre/Tuileries ☎ 01–44–58–10–66 Ⓜ Tuileries) has converted its ground-floor Fontainbleu library into a small, intimate bar with dark wood and delicious cocktails. **Hôtel Plaza Athenée** (✉ 25 av. Montaigne, 8e, Champs-Élysées ☎ 01–53–67–66–00 Ⓜ Champs-Élysées–Clemenceau) is Paris' perfect chill-out spot; the bar was designed by Starck protegé Patrick Jouin. Try the Jello shooters. **Hotel Vernet** (✉ 25 rue Vernet, 8e, Champs-Élysées ☎ 01–44–31–98–06 Ⓜ George V) is where you'll find Le Jaipur, a bit of the old Raj in Paris, and wonderful fresh herb-based cocktails. **Inter-Continental Grand Hotel** (✉ 3 rue Castiglione, 1er, Louvre/Tuileries ☎ 01–44–77–10–47 Ⓜ Tuileries) comes replete with 19th-century grandeur. Fodor's Choice ★ The **Ritz's Hemingway Bar** (✉ 15 pl. Vendôme, 1er, Louvre/Tuileries ☎ 01–43–16–33–65 Ⓜ Opéra) has Colin Field, the best barman in Paris, and Papa memorabilia (this is where the writer drank to the liberation of Paris) but with a dress code and cognac aux truffes on the menu, Hemingway might now stay away; the Ritz's Vendôme bar is far prettier, as it overlooks the Espadon restaurant garden terrace. **Trocadéro Dokhan's Sofitel Demeure Hôtel** (✉ 117 rue Lauriston, 16e, Eiffel Tower/Trocadéro ☎ 01–53–65–66–99 Ⓜ Trocadéro) has a bar decorated by top Parisian designer Frédéric Méchiche (emerald velvet walls and gilt Empire-style wainscoting make for a very soigné setting) that serves nothing but champagne. Every week there is a different champagne by the glass, and there are special musical evenings once a month.

Cabarets

Paris's cabarets range from boîtes once haunted by Picasso and Piaf to those sinful showplaces where tableaux vivants offer acres of bare female flesh (so much so that one critic recently exclaimed, "I'm not going to look anymore unless somebody has three of them"). These extravaganzas—sadly more Las Vegas than the petticoat vision recreated by Hollywood in Baz Lurmann's *Moulin Rouge*—are often shunned by Parisians but loved by tourists. You can dine at many of them, but come with tempered expectations, since the food is more about mass catering than providing gourmand pleasure: prices range from €30 (simple admission plus one drink) to more than €115 (dinner plus show). For €61–€77, you get a seat plus half a bottle of champagne.

L'Âne Rouge (✉ 3 rue Laugier, 17e, Champs-Élysées ☎ 01–43–80–79–97 Ⓜ Ternes) is a typical French cabaret playing to a mixed Parisian and foreign crowd, where the emphasis is on laughs and entertainment, with a host of singers, magicians, comedians, and ventriloquists.

Fodor's Choice ★ **Au Lapin Agile** (✉ 22 rue des Saules, 18e, Montmartre ☎ 01–46–06–85–87 Ⓜ Lamarck Caulaincourt), in Montmartre, considers itself the doyen of cabarets, and is a miraculous survivor from the 19th century. Founded in 1860, it is still housed in a fetchingly picturesque maison-cottage, once a favorite subject of painter Maurice Utrillo. At one point owned by Aristide Bruant (immortalized in many Toulouse-Lautrec posters), it became the home away from home for Braque, Modigliani, Apollinaire, and Vlaminck. The most famous habitué, however, was Picasso, who once paid for a meal with one of his paintings, then promptly went out and painted another, which he named after this place—today, after being purchased for nearly $50 million, it hangs in New York's Metropolitan Museum. Happily, this glamour hasn't entirely affected the Nimble Rabbit—prices are lower than elsewhere, as it is more of a large bar than a full-blown cabaret. If you want to commune with the spirit of the past (and any visiting ghosts), the best time to come is during the early morning hours.

Au Pied de la Butte (✉ 62 bd. Rochechouart, 18e, Montmartre ☎ 01–46–06–02–86 Ⓜ Anvers) played host in the past to Edith Piaf, Jacques Brel, and Maurice Chevalier. Today it has three shows per evening with modern-day songsters interpreting the traditional French repertoire and magicians performing tricks.

Le Caveau de la Bolée (✉ 25 rue de l'Hirondelle, 6e, Latin Quarter ☎ 01–43–54–62–20 Ⓜ St-Michel) was a prison in the 14th century, but these days you are free to sing along to Edith Piaf melodies or be entertained by magicians, comics, and mind readers.

★ **Crazy Horse** (✉ 12 av. George V, 8e, Champs-Élysées ☎ 01–47–23–32–32 Ⓜ Alma-Marceau) is where strip tease has been honed to an art. Founded by Alain Bernardin in 1951, it is renowned for pretty dancers and raunchy routines characterized by lots of humor and few clothes.

Éléphant Bleu (✉ 49 rue de Ponthieu, 8e, Champs-Élysées ☎ 01–42–25–17–61 Ⓜ Franklin-D.-Roosevelt) is a cabaret-cum-restaurant with an exotic (often Asian) touch to most of its shows.

Lido (✉ 116 bis av. des Champs-Élysées, 8e, Champs-Élysées ☎ 01–40–76–56–10 Ⓜ George V) stars the famous Bluebell Girls; the owners claim no show this side of Las Vegas can rival it for special effects. The extravaganza comes with dinner (€130–€160) or champagne only (€90).

Le Limonaire (✉ 21 rue Bergère, 9e, Opéra/Grands Boulevards ☎ 01–45–23–33–33 Ⓜ Grands Boulevards) is a small restaurant that simply oozes with Parisian charm. This is the kind of place where you could imagine Edith Piaf belting out "*Je ne regrette rien,*" and, in fact, imagination is often not required at 10 PM, Tuesday to Sunday, when the service stops and a singer takes to the floor. The house specialty is *la chanson française,* and one of its finest guest artists is the modern-day Little Sparrow, Kalifa. There are also traditional *bals musettes* (popular dances with accordion music) at 6 PM the first Sunday of every month and silent-film screenings the third Sunday.

Madame Arthur (✉ 75 bis rue des Martyrs, 18e, Montmartre ☎ 01–42–64–48–27 Ⓜ Pigalle) stages a wacky burlesque drag show—men dressed as famous French female vocalists—that's not for the fainthearted. Boys, as they say, will be girls.

Michou (✉ 80 rue des Martyrs, 18e, Montmartre ☎ 01–46–06–16–04 Ⓜ Pigalle) is owned by the always blue-clad Michou, famous in Paris circles. The men on stage wear extravagant drag—high camp and parody are the order of the day.

Moulin Rouge (✉ 82 bd. de Clichy, 18e, Montmartre ☎ 01–53–09–82–82 Ⓜ Blanche), that old favorite at the foot of Montmartre, mingles the Doriss Girls, the cancan, and a horse in an extravagant spectacle. Two shows a night are offered, with tickets ranging from €130 to €160.

★ **Paradis Latin** (✉ 28 rue du Cardinal Lemoine, 5e, Latin Quarter ☎ 01–43–25–28–28 Ⓜ Cardinal Lemoine) is perhaps the liveliest, busiest, and trendiest cabaret on the Left Bank. Show and dinner run from €125 to €200, €75 for show and champagne.

Clubs

Paris's *boîtes de nuit* (nightclubs) tend to be both expensive and exclusive—if you know someone who is a regular or your face graces the cover of *Vogue*, you'll have an easier time getting through the door. If you don't come up to the standards of the "model-friendly" door policy, stay happy: it would be a stretch to call Paris's club scene really "happening," as it's really just an outlet for a scrambling crowd of rich, spoiled teens. Many clubs are closed Monday and some on Tuesday. The best soirees tend to take place on Thursday and are generally more intimate and elitist than at the weekend. Nowadays, specific soirees are hosted at many different venues, so the party-hearty crowd is no longer faithful to just one club; on Monday they may go to Disco Night at the Queen, on Friday to "Automatik" at the Rex, on Saturday to "Scream" at the Elysée Montmartre. Many of these, such as "Scream" and "TGV," take place either just once or twice a month. For information about dates, keep an eye out for flyers in bars.

BASTILLE & THE EASTERN RIGHT BANK

Les Bains (✉ 7 rue du Bourg-l'Abbé, 3e, République ☎ 01–48–87–01–80 Ⓜ Étienne Marcel), opened in 1978 and often (back in the disco era) featured in the pages of French *Vogue*, is very much a Parisian institution. The upstairs bar and restaurant is generally packed wall-to-wall with stars, while downstairs house music rules on the dance floors. First, however, you have to get past the particularly selective door policy: if you don't look like Claudia Schiffer or Brad Pitt's double, this could prove more difficult than you might imagine.

Le Balajo (✉ 9 rue de Lappe, 11e; Bastille/Nation ☎ 01–47–00–07–87 Ⓜ Bastille), in an old Java ballroom, offers a bit of everything: salsa, techno, and retro. On Thursday and on Sunday afternoon, there are even *bals musettes,* which headline the accordion music so evocative of oldtime Montmartre street balls.

★ **Batofar** (✉ 11 quai François Mauriac, 13e, Chinatown ☎ 01–56–29–10–00 Ⓜ Bibliothèque) is an old Port of Paris lighthouse tug, now refitted to include a bar, a club, and a concert venue that's become one of the hippest spots in town. Star DJs from other European capitals often arrive to animate the dance floor.

Les Étoiles (✉ 61 rue Château d'Eau, 10e, Opéra/Grands Boulevards ☎ 01–47–70–60–56 Ⓜ Château d'Eau), open Thursday–Saturday, is the place for salsa (with a live band). Dinner, highlighting South American specialties, is served 9–11.

Le Gibus (✉ 18 rue du Faubourg du Temple, 11e, République ☎ 01–47–00–78–88 Ⓜ République) is one of Paris's most famous music venues. In more than 30 years there have been upwards of 6,500 concerts and more than 3,000 performers (including The Police, Deep Purple, and Billy Idol). Today the Gibus's cellars are *the* place for trance, techno, and jungle. There are also regular Latino house parties on Saturday.

La Java (✉ 105 rue du Faubourg du Temple, 10e, République ☎ 01–42–02–20–52 Ⓜ Belleville), where Edith Piaf and Maurice Chevalier made their names, has live Latin music and Cuban jam sessions on Thursday, Friday, and Saturday night that go from dusk to dawn. Before the party proper gets under way, there are also salsa lessons.

CHAMPS-ÉLYSÉES & GRANDS BOULEVARDS

Le Cabaret (✉ 68 rue Pierre-Charron, 8e, Champs-Élysées ☎ 01–58–62–56–25 Ⓜ Franklin-D.-Roosevelt), once just that, still delights with its original red velvet and flocked wallpaper. Nowadays it's a hip, chic club. Princess Caroline of Monaco, Liza Minnelli, and Naomi Campbell have all been spotted here.

Maxim's (✉ 3 rue Royale, 8e, Louvre/Tuileries ☎ 01–42–65–27–94 Ⓜ Concorde) used to be the most stylish restaurant in the city. However, although the restaurant is legendary, its worn-out Belle Epoque cake frosting interior was attracting mostly tourists until recently. Now party organizer Leo Chabot has turned it into the hottest spot in the city on Friday evenings. Young designers, models, and lots of beautiful people, dressed head-to-toe in designer frocks, flock here to groove to the trip-hop and trance in the bar or the funk, salsa, and rock in the blue-lit Jardin d'Hiver.

Niel's (✉ 27 av. Ternes, 17e, Champs-Élysées ☎ 01–47–66–45–00 Ⓜ Ternes) attracts a well-off set of regulars, as well as top models and showbiz glitterati. Music runs the gamut from salsa to house.

Nirvana (✉ 3 av. Matignon, 8e, Champs-Élysées ☎ 01–53–89–19–91 Ⓜ Champs-Élysées–Clemenceau) is Claude Challe of Buddha Bar fame's latest offering on the nightlife altar. A lounge/restaurant where the old Villa Barclay's used to be. Nirvana is a haven of mauve and sequins, with "Spiri'tea" in the afternoons presided over by tai-chi and yogi masters.

Queen (✉ 102 av. des Champs-Élysées, 8e, Champs-Élysées ☎ 01–53–89–08–90 Ⓜ George V), the mythic gay club of the '90s, celebrated its 10th year in 2003. Though not quite as monumental as it once was, its doors are still some of the hardest to get through, and it boasts a fantastic roster of house DJs. Known for soirees such as "Pure," "Sublime," and "Disco Inferno," Queen is gay on Friday, Saturday, and Sunday, but mixed the rest of the week.

★ **Le Rex** (✉ 5 blvd. Poissonnière, 2e, Opéra/Grands Boulevards ☎ 01–42–36–10–96 Ⓜ Grands Boulevards), open Thursday through Saturday, is the Paris temple of techno and house. On Thursday you'll often find France's most famous DJ, Laurent Garnier, at the turntables. The techno "Automatik" soirees on Friday are particularly popular.

Le VIP Room (✉ 76 av. des Champs-Élysées, 8e, Champs-Élysées ☎ 01–56–69–16–66 Ⓜ Franklin-D.-Roosevelt), located under Planet Hollywood, is owned by Jean Roch, the ringleader of nightlife in St-Tropez. If you like spending your evenings with young women dressed in micromini dresses and men sporting shades (even in the dark), then this is the place for you. You may even spot a few stars. Leonardo DiCaprio, George Michael, and French rocker Johnny Hallyday have all put in appearances. Beware: the club is frequently booked for private parties and film premieres (call ahead to check availability).

MONTMARTRE

Bus Palladium (✉ 6 rue Fontaine, 9e, Montmartre ☎ 01–53–21–07–33 Ⓜ Blanche) invites women free on Tuesday; on other nights it caters to a fashionable but relaxed crowd. Fear no techno; it serves up a mixture of rock, funk, and disco.

L'Élysée Montmartre (✉ 72 bd. de Rochechouart, 18e, Montmartre ☎ 01–55–07–06–00 Ⓜ Pigalle) holds extremely popular *bals* (balls) every other Saturday, where the music runs the gamut of hits from the '40s to the '80s and the DJ is backed up by a 10-piece orchestra.

Les Folies Pigalle (✉ 11 pl. Pigalle, 9e, Montmartre ☎ 01–48–78–55–25 Ⓜ Pigalle) is a former cabaret decorated like a '30s bordello. The ambience is decadent; the music varies according to the day of the week—hip-hop on Wednesday and Sunday, a mixture of house and techno at other times—and on Saturday from 9 to 11 PM there's a male strip show (for women only).

MONTPARNASSE **Dancing La Coupole** (✉ 100 bd. du Montparnasse, 14e, Montparnasse ☎ 01–43–27–56–00 Ⓜ Vavin) has retro disco on Friday and Saturday night; and on Tuesday, salsa, preceded at 8:30 by an optional refresher course—an idea that seems to have breathed new life into this monument. There are also popular tea dances at 3 PM on Sunday.

L'Enfer (✉ 34 rue du Départ, 14e, Montparnasse ☎ 01–42–79–94–53 Ⓜ Montparnasse Bienvenüe) has been given a second lease on life in recent years, with the organization of a number of regular, predominantly gay soirees. It has inherited "Scream," which used to be at the Élysée Montmartre.

Gay & Lesbian Bars & Clubs

Gay and lesbian bars and clubs are mostly concentrated in the Marais and include some of the hippest addresses in the city. Keep in mind, however, that clubs fall in and out of favor at lightning speed. The best way to find out what's hot is by picking up a copy of the free weekly *e.m@le* in one of the bars listed below.

For Men & Women

Amnésia Café (✉ 42 rue Vieille-du-Temple, 4e, Le Marais ☎ 01–42–72–16–94 Ⓜ Rambuteau, St-Paul) has an under-lit bar and Art Deco ceiling paintings that attract a young, professional gay and lesbian crowd.

Banana Café (✉ 13 rue de la Ferronnerie, 1er, Beaubourg/Les Halles ☎ 01–42–33–35–31 Ⓜ Châtelet Les Halles) has a trendy, energetic, and scantily clad mixed crowd; dancing on the tables is the norm.

Le Dépôt (✉ 10 rue aux Ours, 3e, République ☎ 01–44–54–96–96 Ⓜ Étienne Marcel) is a bar, club, and backroom. The ever-popular Gay Tea Dance on Sunday (from 5 PM) is held here.

Mostly Men

★ **Bar d'Art/Le Duplex** (✉ 25 rue Michel-Le-Comte, 3e, Beaubourg/Les Halles ☎ 01–42–72–80–86 Ⓜ Rambuteau) is frequented by young, tortured-artist types who enjoy the frequent art exhibitions, alternative music, and dim lighting.

Café Cox (✉ 15 rue des Archives, 4e, Le Marais ☎ 01–42–72–08–00 Ⓜ Hôtel de Ville) is a prime gay pickup joint. Behind the smoked-glass windows men line the walls and check out the talent.

L'Open Café (✉ 17 rue des Archives, 4e, Le Marais ☎ 01–42–72–26–18 Ⓜ Hôtel de Ville) is more convivial than neighboring Café Cox, with sunny yellow walls. In summer the crowd spills out onto the street.

Le Scorp (✉ 25 bd. Poissonnière, 9e, Opéra/Grands Boulevards ☎ 01–40–26–01–50 Ⓜ Montmartre) is one of Paris's longest-standing gay nightclubs. Wednesday is disco night, Thursday is devoted to French pop, Friday to house, Saturday to techno, and Sunday to New Wave.

Mostly Women

Alcantara Café (✉30 rue du Roi de Sicile, 4e, Le Marais ☎01–42–74–45–00 Ⓜ St-Paul) is a cool and friendly bar in the heart of the Marais. There is happy hour every evening from 6 to 8 PM, regular events (flamenco, tap, or salsa dancers), and a DJ in the tiny bar in the basement on Friday and Saturday evenings. Men are allowed in small numbers on weekdays.

Champmeslé (✉ 4 rue Chabanais, 2e, Opéra/Grands Boulevards ☎ 01–42–96–85–20 Ⓜ Bourse) is the hub of lesbian nightlife (open until dawn). Thursday night (starting at 10) is a cabaret of traditional French songs. There are also regular painting exhibitions and a *voyante* (fortune-teller) on hand every Friday.

Fodor'sChoice ★ **Le Pulp** (✉ 25 bd. Poissonnière, 2e, Opéra/Grands Boulevards ☎ 01–40–26–01–93 Ⓜ Grands Boulevards), one of the rare lesbian clubs in Paris, is housed in a space which hosts tea dances for retirees in the afternoon. On Thursday the music is house and guys are admitted in small numbers. On Friday and Saturday it's strictly women-only.

Les Scandaleuses (✉ 8 rue des Écouffes, 4e, Le Marais ☎ 01–48–87–39–26 Ⓜ St-Paul) is probably Paris's hippest lesbian hangout. Men are also allowed in (in small numbers), as long as they are accompanied by "scandalous women."

Jazz Clubs

Remember Audrey Hepburn scatting to "Basil Metabolism" in that dark and smoky jazz club in *Funny Face*? Sorry—you won't find many of those cellar places left, but Paris remains the celebrated home of *le jazz hot,* and its performing calendar offers plenty of variety, including some fine, distinctive local talent. Most jazz clubs are in the Latin Quarter or around Les Halles. For nightly schedules, consult the specialty magazines, *Jazz Hot, Jazzman,* or *Jazz Magazine*. Note that nothing gets going until 10 or 11 PM and that entry prices vary widely from about €7 to more than €16. The A Fleur de Jazz Festival also offers free concerts at 4:30 PM on Saturday and Sunday at the Parc Floral in the Bois de Vincennes from early March to the end of July. Also look out for the annual **Villette Jazz Festival** (☎ 01–40–03–75–75), held at La Villette at the end of June.

CHAMPS-ÉLYSÉES

Lionel Hampton Jazz Club (✉ Méridien Hotel, 81 bd. Gouvion–St-Cyr, 17e, Champs-Élysées ☎ 01–40–68–30–42 Ⓜ Porte Maillot), named for the zingy vibraphonist loved by Parisians, hosts a roster of international jazz musicians in a spacious, comfortable set of rooms.

LES HALLES/GARE DU NORD

Au Duc des Lombards (✉ 42 rue des Lombards, 1er, Beaubourg/Les Halles ☎ 01–42–33–22–88 Ⓜ Châtelet Les Halles) has modern, contemporary jazz in an ill-lit, romantic bebop venue with decor inspired by the Paris métro.

Le Baiser Salé (✉ 58 rue des Lombards, 1er, Beaubourg/Les Halles ☎ 01–42–33–37–71 Ⓜ Châtelet Les Halles) attracts a younger crowd with salsa, rhythm and blues, fusion, and funk.

Fodor'sChoice ★ **New Morning** (✉ 7 rue des Petites-Écuries, 10e, Opéra/Grands Boulevards ☎ 01–45–23–51–41 Ⓜ Château d'Eau) is a premier spot for serious fans of avant-garde jazz, folk, and world music; the look is spartan, the mood reverential.

Le Petit Opportun (✉ 15 rue des Lavandières–Ste-Opportune, 1er, Beaubourg/Les Halles ☎ 01–42–36–01–36 Ⓜ Châtelet Les Halles), in a converted bistro, always has French artists and sometimes headlines top-flight American soloists with French backup.

Le Sunset (✉ 60 rue des Lombards, 1er, Beaubourg/Les Halles ☎ 01–40–26–46–60 Ⓜ Châtelet Les Halles) delivers jazz from both French and American musicians, with an accent on jazz fusion and groove. Concerts start at 10 PM.

Le Sunside (✉ 60 rue des Lombards, 1er, Beaubourg/Les Halles ☎ 01–40–26–21–25 Ⓜ Châtelet Les Halles) is at the same address as Le Sunset. It specializes in more classic, traditional jazz and swing. There is also a featured vocalist on Monday night. Concerts start at 9 PM.

LATIN QUARTER/ST-GERMAIN/MONTPARNASSE

Le Bilboquet (✉ 13 rue St-Benoît, 6e, St-Germain-des-Prés ☎ 01–45–48–81–84 Ⓜ St-Germain-des-Prés) is the place to find primarily French musicians playing mainstream jazz in a faded Belle Epoque salon.

Le Petit Journal (✉ 71 bd. St-Michel, 5e, Latin Quarter ☎ 01–43–26–28–59 Ⓜ Cluny La Sorbonne ✉ 13 rue du Commandant-Mouchotte, 14e, Montparnasse ☎ 01–43–21–56–70 Ⓜ Montparnasse Bienvenüe), with two locations, has long attracted the greatest names in French and international jazz. It now specializes in Dixieland jazz and also serves dinner 8:30–midnight.

Pubs

Pubs wooing English-speaking clients with a selection of beers are becoming increasingly popular with Parisians. They are also good places to find reasonably priced food at off hours.

Auld Alliance (✉ 80 rue François Miron, 4e, Le Marais ☎ 01–48–04–30–40 Ⓜ St-Paul) has walls adorned with Scottish shields and a bar staff dressed in kilts. There are more than 120 malt whiskies to choose from, true Scottish beers, darts and pool competitions, and the odd evening of bagpipe music.

Connolly's Corner (✉ 12 rue Mirbel, 5e, Latin Quarter ☎ 01–43–31–94–22 Ⓜ Place Monge) is a convivial Irish pub with Guinness on tap and live music on Tuesday, Thursday, Saturday, and Sunday. Just make sure you don't wear a tie—it will be snipped off and stuck on the wall (though you'll be compensated with a free pint).

The Cricketer (✉ 41 rue des Mathurins, 8e, Opéra/Grands Boulevards ☎ 01–40–07–01–45 Ⓜ St-Augustin) is the British reply to the virtual Irish monopoly on Paris pubs. There's Newcastle Brown Ale on tap, and cricket memorabilia adorns the walls.

Finnegan's Wake (✉ 9 rue des Boulangers, 5e, Latin Quarter ☎ 01–46–34–23–65 Ⓜ Jussieu) is a wonderfully quiet and charming Irish pub on a steep cobbled street. Guinness, Kilkenny, and Murphys are on tap. Traditional Irish music is occasionally presented on Tuesday, and live music on Friday. Happy hour runs from 6 to 8 PM every evening.

Frog and Rosbif (✉ 116 rue St-Denis, 2e, Beaubourg/Les Halles ☎ 01–42–36–34–73 Ⓜ Étienne Marcel) has everything you could want from an English "local." Beers are brewed on premises, and rugby and football matches are shown on the giant-screen TV.

Rock, Pop & World Music Venues

Unlike jazz, French rock is generally not considered to be on a par with its American and British cousins. Even so, Paris is a great place to catch some of your favorite groups, because concert halls tend to be smaller and tickets can be less expensive. It's also a good spot to see all kinds of world music. Most places charge about €14–€18 and get going around 11 PM. The best way to find out about upcoming concerts is to consult the bulletin boards in FNAC stores.

Le Bataclan (✉ 50 bd. Voltaire, 11e, République ☎ 01–43–14–35–35 Ⓜ Oberkampf) is a legendary venue for live rock, rap, and reggae in an intimate setting.

Casino de Paris (✉ 16 rue de Clichy, 9e, Opéra/Grands Boulevards ☎ 01–49–95–99–99 Ⓜ Trinité), once a favorite with Serge Gainsbourg, has a horseshoe balcony and a cramped, cozy, music-hall feel.

La Cigale (✉ 120 bd. Rochechouart, 18e, Montmartre ☎ 01–49–25–89–99 Ⓜ Pigalle) often plays host to up-and-coming French rock bands.

Divan du Monde (✉ 75 rue des Martyrs, 18e, Montmartre ☎ 01–44–92–77–66 Ⓜ Pigalle) attracts a varied crowd, depending on the music of the evening: reggae, soul, funk, or salsa. Most nights after the concert, a DJ takes over.

L'Élysée Montmartre (✉ 72 bd. Rochechouart, 18e, Montmartre ☎ 01–55–07–06–00 Ⓜ Anvers) dates from Gustave Eiffel, its builder, who, it is hoped, liked a good concert. It's one of the prime venues for emerging French and international rock groups.

Olympia (✉ 18 rue Caumartin, 9e, Opéra/Grands Boulevards ☎ 01–47–42–25–49 Ⓜ Madeleine), a legendary venue once favored by Jacques Brel and Edith Piaf, still hosts leading French singers. Rather strangely, the original hall was demolished to make way for an underground car park and an identical theater constructed in the same building.

L'Opus Café (✉ 167 quai de Valmy, 10e, Canal-St-Martin ☎ 01–40–34–70–00 Ⓜ Louis Blanc), on the picturesque Canal St-Martin, has jazz and soul concerts.

Palais Omnisports de Paris-Bercy (✉ 8 bd. de Bercy, 12e, Bastille/Nation ☎ 08–25–03–00–31 Ⓜ Bercy) is the largest venue in Paris and where English and American pop stars perform.

Zenith (✉ Parc de La Villette, 211 av. Jean-Jaurès, 19e, La Villette ☎ 01–42–08–60–00 Ⓜ Porte de Pantin) is a large concert hall that primarily stages rock shows; check posters and listings for details. The neighboring Grande Halle de La Villette organizes lively world music festivals in June.

After-Hours Dining

Chances are that some of your nocturnal forays will have you looking for sustenance at an unlikely hour. If so, you might find it handy to know that there are restaurants open around the clock.

L'Alsace (✉ 39 av. des Champs-Élysées, 8e, Champs-Élysées ☎ 01–53–93–97–00 Ⓜ Franklin-D.-Roosevelt) is a smart, if characterless, brasserie-restaurant, serving seafood and sauerkraut around the clock.

Au Chien Qui Fume (✉ 33 rue du Pont-Neuf, 1er, Louvre/Tuileries ☎ 01–42–36–07–42 Ⓜ Les Halles), open until 2 AM, is filled with witty paintings (in the style of old masters) of smoking dogs. Traditional French cuisine and seafood platters are served.

Fodor's Choice ★ **Au Pied de Cochon** (✉ 6 rue Coquillière, 1er, Beaubourg/Les Halles ☎ 01–40–13–77–00 Ⓜ Les Halles), near St-Eustache church, once catered to the all-night workers at the adjacent Paris food market. Its Second Empire carvings and gilt have been restored, and traditional dishes like pig's trotters and chitterling sausage still grace the menu.

Le Bienvenu (✉ 42 rue d'Argout, 2e, Louvre/Tuileries ☎ 01–42–33–31–08 Ⓜ Louvre) certainly doesn't look like much (check out the slightly kitsch mural on the back wall), but it serves up a welcome couscous in the early hours of the morning. Open until 7 AM, it also has simple French food, such as pâté and niçoise salad.

La Cloche d'Or (✉ 3 rue Mansart, 9e, Montmartre ☎ 01–48–74–48–88 Ⓜ Place de Clichy) is a Paris institution where the likes of the late François Mitterrand, Depêche Mode, and the dancers from the Moulin Rouge have all dined on its traditional French cuisine. It's open until 4 AM every day except Sunday, when it closes at 1 AM.

Les Coulisses (✉ 5 rue du Mont-Cenis, 18e, Montmartre ☎ 01–42–62–89–99 Ⓜ Lamarck Caulaincourt), in Montmartre, near picturesque place du Tertre, has the most character of all the late-night restaurants: its red banquettes and 18th-century Venetian mirrors make it look like an Italian theater. The food—traditional French—is served until 4 AM. In the basement is a club, open Thursday–Saturday.

Grand Café des Capucines (✉ 4 bd. des Capucines, 9e, Montmartre ☎ 01–43–12–19–00 Ⓜ Opéra), whose exuberant pseudo–Belle Epoque dining room matches the mood of the neighboring Opéra, serves excellent oysters, fish, and meat dishes at hefty prices. It's open around the clock. **Le Tambour** (✉ 41 rue Montmartre, 2e, Montmartre ☎ 01–42–33–06–90 Ⓜ Étienne Marcel, Les Halles) is full of old-fashioned flea-market charm. The owner has one of those quintessentially Parisian moustaches, there is an old métro map on the wall, and advertising signs from yesteryear catch the eye. Le Tambour calls itself a "*bistrot de l'urbain bucolique*" (a "bistro for the bucolic city dweller") and serves up traditional French fare of onion soup, foie gras, steak tartare, and confit de canard. It's open around the clock.

THE ARTS

Without a doubt, Paris has been one of the 20th century's greatest capitals of the arts. In 1909 Sergey Diaghilev arrived in the city with his Ballets Russes. In the '20s Josephine Baker charmed audiences at the Théâtre des Champs-Élysées. And in the '40s Jean-Paul Sartre and Simone de Beauvoir wrote masterpieces at the Café de Flore. Nowadays, despite lavish government subsidies, the city's artistic life doesn't have the avant-garde edge it once did, but Parisians are still proud of being intellectual and passionate about all things cultural. The city has an impressive number of venues and regularly attracts international theater, dance, and opera companies. In addition, the phenomenal number of movie theaters makes Paris a cinephile's heaven.

The music and theater season runs September to June; in summer most productions are found at festivals elsewhere in France. There is, however, an excellent festival in Paris during July and August called Paris–Quartier d'Eté, which attracts international stars of dance, classical music, and jazz. Detailed entertainment listings can be found in the weekly magazines ***Pariscope*** (which has an English-language section produced by *Time Out* magazine), ***L'Officiel des Spectacles, Zurban,*** and ***Figaroscope*** (a supplement to *Le Figaro* newspaper). Tickets can be purchased at the theater itself (try to get them in advance, as many of the more popular performances sell out quickly). The 24-hour hot line and the Web site of the **Paris Tourist Office** (☎ 08–36–68–31–12 in English 🌐 www.paris-touristoffice.com) are other good sources of information about activities in the city.

Your hotel or a travel agency such as **Opéra Théâtre** (✉ 7 rue de Clichy, 9e, Opéra/Grands Boulevards ☎ 01–40–06–01–00 🌐 www.operatheatre.com Ⓜ Trinité) may be able to help you get tickets. They take a 20% commission on each ticket and also have a Web site. Tickets can be purchased at **FNAC stores** (Forum des Halles ✉ 1–5 rue Pierre Lescot, 3rd level down, 1er, Beaubourg/Les Halles ☎ 01–49–87–50–50 Ⓜ Châtelet Les Halles), especially the one in the Forum des Halles. **Virgin Megastore** (✉ 52 av. des Champs-Élysées, 8e, Champs-Élysées ☎ 08–03–02–30–24 Ⓜ Franklin-D.-Roosevelt) also sells theater and concert tickets. Half-price tickets for same-day theater performances are available at the **Kiosques Théâtre** (✉ Across from 15 pl. de la Madeleine, Opéra/Grands Boulevards Ⓜ Montparnasse Bienvenüe ✉ Outside the Gare Montparnasse, pl. Raoul Dautry, 15e, Montparnasse Ⓜ Montparnasse Bienvenüe), open Tuesday–Saturday 12:30–8 and Sunday 12:30–4. Expect to pay a €2.44 commission per ticket and stand in line. Half-price tickets are also available in numerous private theaters during the first week of each new show. Check the weekly guides for details.

Circus

You don't need to know French to enjoy the circus. Venues change frequently, so it is best to check one of the weekly guides; tickets range €6–€35. **Cirque Alexis Gruss** (✉ Pelouse de Madrid, Allée de la Reine Marguerite, Bois de Boulogne ☎ 01–45–01–71–26 Ⓜ Porte Maillot, then Bus 244 to the Route des Lacs stop) is in Paris five months of the year and remains an avowedly old-fashioned production with showy horsemen. From tigers to yaks, dogs, and clowns, **Cirque Diana Moreno Bormann** (✉ rue de la Haie Coq, 9e, Porte de La Chapelle ☎ 01–64–05–36–25 Ⓜ Porte de la Chapelle) is good for all ages; performances are on Saturday, Sunday, and Wednesday at 3 PM. **Cirque d'Hiver Bouglione** (✉ 110 rue Amelot, 11e, République ☎ 08–92–68–08–92 Ⓜ Filles du Calvaire), brings together two famous circus institutions. The beautiful Cirque d'Hiver hall, constructed in 1852, is now home to the Bouglione troupe, known for their rousing spectacle of acrobats, jugglers, clowns, contortionists, trapeze artist, snakes, and doves. **Cirque de Paris** (✉ 115 bd. Charles-de-Gaulle, Villeneuve-la-Garenne ☎ 01–47–99–40–40 Ⓜ Porte de Clignancourt, then Bus 137) offers "A Day at the Circus": a peek behind the scenes in the morning, lunch with the artists, and a performance in the afternoon.

Classical Music

Cité de la Musique (✉ in the Parc de La Villette, 221 av. Jean-Jaurès, 19e, La Villette ☎ 01–44–84–44–84 Ⓜ Porte de Pantin) presents a varied program of classical, experimental, and world music concerts in a postmodern setting.

IRCAM (✉ 1 pl. Igor-Stravinsky, 4e, Beaubourg/Les Halles ☎ 01–44–78–48–16 Ⓜ Châtelet Les Halles, Hôtel de Ville) organizes concerts of contemporary classical music on the premises, at the Centre Pompidou next door, or at the Cité de la Musique.

Maison de Radio France (✉ 116 av. du Président-Kennedy, 16e, Passy-Auteuil ☎ 01–56–40–15–16 Ⓜ RER: Maison de Radio France), the base for countless radio and TV stations, also often hosts the Orchestre National de France. The Orchestre Philharmonique de Radio France often performs in the smallish, modern Salle Olivier Messiaen.

L'Opéra Royal (✉ Château de Versailles, Versailles ☎ 01–30–83–78–88 Ⓜ RER: Versailles–Rive Gauche) was built in 20 months for the marriage of the future Louis XVI and Marie-Antoinette. In the 18th century, performances of both *Castor et Pollux* by Rameau and *Iphigénie* by Glück were given here. Today it plays host to a season of chamber and orchestral concerts, vocal recitals, dance, and theater called "Les Nouveaux Plaisirs" (March–September).

★ **Salle Cortot** (✉ 78 rue Cardinet, 17e, Parc Monceau ☎ 01–47–63–85–72 Ⓜ Malesherbes) is an acoustic gem, built by Auguste Perret in 1918. At the time, he promised to construct "a hall that sounds like a violin." Today jazz and classical concerts are held here. There are also free recitals at 12:30 PM on Tuesday and Thursday by the students of the adjoining École Normale de Musique.

Salle Gaveau (✉ 45 rue de la Boétie, 8e, Champs-Élysées ☎ 01–49–53–05–07 Ⓜ Miromesnil) is a small hall of only 1,200 seats with a distinctly faded Parisian allure and fantastic acoustics. Its original gold-and-white decoration was restored during renovation work. It plays host to chamber music, piano, and vocal recitals.

Salle Pleyel (✉ 252 rue du Faubourg St-Honoré, 8e, Champs-Élysées ☎ 08–25–00–02–52 Ⓜ Ternes) has been Paris's principal home of classical music since it opened in 1927. The Orchestre de Paris and other leading international orchestras play here regularly, and there's a fine series of recitals by international stars. After major renovations, it is slated to reopen in mid-2004.

Théâtre des Champs-Élysées (✉ 15 av. Montaigne, 8e, Champs-Élysées ☎ 01–49–52–50–50 Ⓜ Alma-Marceau) was the scene of the famous Battle of the Rite of Spring in 1913, when police had to be called in after the audience started ripping up the seats in outrage at Stravinsky's *Le Sacre du Printemps* and Nijinsky's choreography. Today this elegantly restored, plush Art Deco temple is worthy of a visit if only for its architecture. It also hosts top-quality concerts and ballet performances.

Théâtre du Palais-Royal (✉ 38 rue Montpensier, 1er, Louvre/Tuileries ☎ 01–48–24–16–97 Ⓜ Palais-Royal) is a sparkling 750-seat Italian theater bedecked in gold and purple. From January until June it's the setting for "*Les Concerts du Palais-Royal*": a series of performances of Baroque music, vocal recitals, and opera bouffe.

Church & Museum Concerts

Paris has a never-ending stream of free or inexpensive lunchtime and evening church concerts, ranging from organ recitals to choral music and orchestral works. Some are scheduled as part of the **Festival d'Art Sacré** (☎ 01–44–70–64–10 for information) between mid-November and Christmas. Check the weekly listings for information; telephone numbers for most church concerts vary with the organizer.

★ Here are the main venues for church concerts. **Sainte-Chapelle** (✉ 4 bd. du Palais, 1er, Ile de la Cité ☎ 01–42–77–65–65 Ⓜ Cité) holds memorable candlelit concerts April through mid-October; make reservations well in advance. **Notre-Dame** (✉ Ile de la Cité, 4e, Ile de la Cité Ⓜ Cité). **St-Eustache** (✉ Rue du Jour, 1er, Beaubourg/Les Halles Ⓜ Les Halles). **St-Germain-des-Prés** (✉ Pl. St-Germain-des-Prés, 6e, St-Germain-des-Prés Ⓜ St-Germain-des-Prés). **St-Julien-Le-Pauvre** (✉ 23 quai de Montebello, 5e, Latin Quarter Ⓜ St-Michel). **St-Louis-en-l'Ile** (✉ 19 bis rue St-Louis-en-l'Ile, 4e, Ile-St-Louis Ⓜ Pont Marie). **St-Roch** (✉ 296 rue St-Honoré, 1er, Louvre/Tuileries Ⓜ Tuileries).

Some of the best classical concerts are held in the **Auditorium du Louvre** (✉ Palais du Louvre, Louvre/Tuileries ☎ 01–40–20–84–00 Ⓜ Palais-Royal, Louvre) on Wednesday evening and Thursday at lunchtime. The **Musée d'Orsay** (✉ 1 rue de Bellechasse, 7e, St-Germain-des-Prés ☎ 01–40–49–47–57 Ⓜ RER: Musée d'Orsay) regularly holds small-scale concerts (song cycles, piano recitals, or chamber music) at lunchtime or in the early evening. The **Musée du Moyen Age** (✉ 6 pl. Paul Painlevé, 5e, Latin Quarter ☎ 01–53–73–78–16 Ⓜ Cluny La Sorbonne) stages early music concerts between October and July.

There is also a fine Chopin Festival at the delightfully picturesque **Orangerie de Bagatelle** (✉ Parc de Bagatelle, av. de Longchamp, Bois de Boulogne ☎ 01–45–00–22–19 Ⓜ Sablons) in late June and early July. In August and September there are also free classical concerts in the Parc Floral of the Bois de Boulogne on Saturday and Sunday at 4:30 PM.

Dance

As a rule, more avant-garde or up-and-coming choreographers show their works in the smaller performance spaces in the Bastille and the Marais and in theaters in nearby suburbs. Classical ballet is found in places as varied as the opera house and the sports stadium. Check the weekly guides for listings.

Maison des Arts et de la Culture (✉ 1 pl. Salvador Allende, 94000 ☎ 01–45–13–19–19 Ⓜ Créteil Préfecture), just outside Paris, is a fine venue for dance, which often attracts top-flight international and French companies, such as Blanca Li, Mikhail Baryshnikov's White Oak Project, and Philippe Decouflé.

Fodor's Choice ★ **Opéra Garnier** (✉ Pl. de l'Opéra, 9e, Opéra/Grands Boulevards ☎ 08–92–69–78–68 🌐 www.opera-de-paris.fr Ⓜ Opéra) is the sumptuous Napoléon III home of the well-reputed Ballet de l'Opéra National de Paris, and rarely hosts other dance companies. When performing, it offers the same program—a full-length ballet like *Sylvia* or *La Sylphide* or an evening of shorter works—for six or so consecutive performances. Special events (offered in multiple performances)—such as an evening devoted to works featuring the choreography of Maurice Béjart or the music of Stravinsky—are often interspersed among the regular performances. Seat prices range €6–€55; note that many of the cheaper seats have obstructed views, more of an obstacle than in opera performances.

Théâtre de la Bastille (✉ 76 rue de la Roquette, 11e, Bastille/Nation ☎ 01–43–57–42–14 Ⓜ Bastille) merits mention as an example of the innovative activity in the Bastille area; it has an enviable record as a launching pad for tomorrow's modern-dance stars.

Théâtre de la Cité Internationale (✉ 21 bd. Jourdan, 14e, Parc Montsouris ☎ 01–43–13–50–50 Ⓜ RER: Cité Universitaire) is a complex of three theaters at the heart of the international student residence, the Cité Universitaire. It often stages young, avant-garde companies, and is also the main venue for the Presqu'Iles de Danse festival in February.

Théâtre de la Ville (✉ 2 pl. du Châtelet, 4e, Beaubourg/Les Halles Ⓜ Châtelet ✉ 31 rue des Abbesses, 18e, Montmartre Ⓜ Abbesses ☎ 01–42–74–22–77 for both) is *the* place for contemporary dance. Troupes like La La La Human Steps and Anne-Teresa de Keersmaeker's Rosas company are presented here. The queen of modern European dance, Pina Bausch, also performs every June.

Film

Paris has hundreds of cinemas showing contemporary and classic French and American movies, as well as a tempting menu packed with independent, international, and documentary films. A number of theaters, especially in principal tourist areas such as the Champs-Élysées, boulevard des Italiens near the Opéra, St-Germain-des-Prés, and Les Halles, run English-language films. Check the weekly guides for a movie of your choice. The initials "v.o." mean *version originale,* or not dubbed; films that are dubbed are indicated by the initials "v.f." (*version française*). Cinema admission runs €5–€8; some cinemas have reduced rates on certain days (normally Monday, sometimes Wednesday) or for early shows; others offer reductions with the purchase of a multiple-entry card. Most theaters post two show times: the *séance,* when the commercials, previews, and, sometimes, short films begin; and the feature presentation, which usually starts 10–25 minutes later. Other than the Cinémathèque Française, Paris has many other theaters showing classic and independent films, often found in the Latin Quarter (with some notable exceptions). Showings are often organized around retrospectives (check "Festivals" in weekly guides). Following is a list of some of the noteworthy independent cinemas.

Gaumont Grand Écran (✉ 30 pl. d'Italie, 13e, Chinatown ☎ 01–40–30–30–31 Ⓜ Place d'Italie) boasts the biggest screen in Paris. **Grand Rex** (✉ 1 bd. Poissonnière, 2e, Opéra/Grands Boulevards ☎ 08–36–68–05–96 Ⓜ Bonne Nouvelle) opened in 1932 with a mammoth house of 2,800 seats. **Max Linder Panorama** (✉ 24 bd. Poissonnière, 9e, Opéra/Grands Boulevards ☎ 01–40–30–30–31 Ⓜ Grands Boulevards) opened in 1932 and was named after French burlesque actor

Max Linder; check out the marble floors and Florentine stucco on the walls. **MK2 Quai de Seine** (✉ 14 quai de Seine, 19e, Canal-St-Martin ☎ 01–40–30–30–31 Ⓜ Stalingrad), a restaurant–cinema complex showing major releases, is well worth a visit for its location on the Bassin de la Villette. **UGC Ciné Cité Les Halles** (✉ Pl. de la Rotonde, Forum des Halles, Level 3, access by the Porte du Jour near St-Eustache church, 1er, Beaubourg/Les Halles ☎ 08–92–70–00–00 Ⓜ Les Halles) is a huge complex of 19 theaters in the underground Les Halles shopping complex.

Fodor'sChoice ★ Unique in all the world is **La Pagode** (✉ 57 bis rue de Babylone, 7e, Eiffel Tower/Trocadéro ☎ 01–45–55–48–48 Ⓜ St-François Xavier)—where else but in Paris would you find movies screened in an antique pagoda? A Far East fantasy, this structure was built in 1896 for the wife of the owner of the Au Bon Marché department store. By the 1970s it had become a cinema slated for demolition, but was then saved by director Louis Malle. Though the fare is standard, the surroundings are enchanting—who can resist seeing a flick in the silk-and-gilt Salle Japonaise? After the film, repair to the historic little tea salon on site.

For the *cinéaste* (movie lover) brought up on Fellini, Bergman, and Resnais, the main mecca is the famed **Cinémathèque Française** (✉ 42 bd. de Bonne-Nouvelle, 10e, Opéra/Grands Boulevards ☎ 01–56–26–01–01 Ⓜ Bonne Nouvelle) and **Palais de Chaillot** (✉ 7 av. Albert-de-Mun, 16e, Eiffel Tower/Trocadéro ☎ 01–56–26–01–01 Ⓜ Trocadéro). This venerable institution pioneered the preservation of early films. Today its schedules often pay homage to major film directors, with the main programs scheduled for the Palais de Chaillot venue Wednesday–Sunday.

Accatone (✉ 20 rue Cujas, 5e, Latin Quarter ☎ 01–46–33–86–86 Ⓜ Cluny La Sorbonne, Luxembourg) shows mainly European art films. **Action Écoles** (✉ 23 rue des Écoles, 5e, Latin Quarter ☎ 01–43–29–79–89 Ⓜ Maubert Mutualité) specializes in old American classics. **Champo** (✉ 51 rue des Écoles, 5e, Latin Quarter ☎ 01–43–54–51–60 Ⓜ Cluny La Sorbonne) often programs Hitchcock films. **Grande Action** (✉ 5 rue des Écoles, 5e, Latin Quarter ☎ 01–43–29–44–40 Ⓜ Cardinal Lemoine, Jussieu) usually runs American classics. **Quartier Latin** (✉ 9 rue Champollion, 5e, Latin Quarter ☎ 01–43–26–84–65 Ⓜ Cluny La Sorbonne) is one of a number of cinemas near the Sorbonne. **St-André-des-Arts** (✉ 30 rue St-André-des-Arts, 6e, Latin Quarter ☎ 01–43–26–48–18 Ⓜ St-Michel) is one of the best cinemas in Paris, and generally has a festival devoted to one director, such as Bergman or Tarkovski.

Le Balzac (✉ 1 rue Balzac, 8e, Champs-Élysées ☎ 01–45–61–10–60 Ⓜ George V) often holds talks by directors before screenings. **Centre Pompidou** (✉ Pl. Georges-Pompidou, Beaubourg/Les Halles ☎ 01–44–78–12–33) hosts regular themed film festivals. **Cinéma des Cinéastes** (✉ 7 av. de Clichy, 17e, Montmartre ☎ 01–40–30–30–31 Ⓜ Place de Clichy) shows previews of feature films, as well as documentaries, short subjects, and rarely shown movies; it's in an old cabaret transformed into a movie theater and wine bar. **Dôme Imax** (✉ La Défense, La Défense ☎ 08–36–67–06–06 Ⓜ RER: La Défense) shows 3-D flicks. **L'Entrepôt** (✉ 7 rue Francis-de-Pressensé, 14e, Montparnasse ☎ 08–36–68–05–87 Ⓜ Pernety) screens films and has a café, bar, restaurant, and bookstore. **Le Forum des Images** (✉ Forum des Halles, Porte St-Eustache entrance, 1er, Beaubourg/Les Halles ☎ 01–44–76–62–00 Ⓜ Les Halles) organizes thematic viewings from its archive of films and videos on the city of Paris. For €5.50 you can watch up to four films, two hours of video, and surf the Web for 30 minutes. **La Géode** (✉ At the Cité des Sciences et de l'Industrie, Parc de La Villette, 26 av. Corentin-Cariou, 19e, La Villette ☎ 01–40–05–12–12 Ⓜ Porte de La Villette) screens wide-angle Omnimax films—usually documentaries—on a gigantic spherical surface. In summer at the **Parc de La Villette** (Ⓜ Porte de Pantin, Porte de La Villette), movies are shown outdoors on a large screen. Most people take along a picnic. You can also rent deck chairs by the entrance; check the weekly guides for film listings.

Galleries

Art galleries are scattered throughout the city, but those focusing on the same aesthetic period are often clustered in one neighborhood. There are many contemporary art galleries, for instance, near the Centre Pompidou, the Picasso Museum, and the Bastille Opéra. More recently, several avant-garde galleries have moved to rue Louise Weiss near the Bibliothèque François-Mitterrand in the 13e. (Note that it's not uncommon for galleries to be hidden away in courtyards, with the only sign of their presence a small plaque on the front of the building; take these as invitations to push through the doors.) Around St-Germain, the galleries are generally more traditional, and works by old masters and established modern artists dominate the galleries around rue du Faubourg St-Honoré and avenue Matignon. To help you plot your gallery course, get a free copy of the map published by the Association des Galeries; it's available at many of the galleries listed below. For listings of antiques galleries, *see* the Chapter 6.

The Parisian art world is abuzz because the main French auctioneers, most based at the **Hôtel Drouot** (✉ 9 rue Drouot, 9e, Opéra/Grands Boulevards ☎ 01–48–00–20–00 Ⓜ Richelieu Drouot), have lost their monopoly on art auctions in Paris. **Christie's** (✉ 9 av. Matignon, 8e, Champs-Élysées ☎ 01–40–76–85–85 Ⓜ Champs-Élysées Clémenceau) opened shop with lavish showrooms and a calendar of auctions. **Sotheby's** (✉ 76 rue du Faubourg St-Honoré, 8e, Champs-Élysées ☎ 01–53–05–53–05 Ⓜ St-Philippe-du-Roule), Christie's arch rival, has an ambitious calendar of sales scheduled.

Agathe Gaillard (✉ 3 rue Pont Louis-Philippe, 4e, Le Marais ☎ 01–42–77–38–24 Ⓜ Hôtel de Ville) was the first person to open a photo gallery in Paris way back in 1975. Since then she has exhibited many of the great names of the genre, from Kertesz and Cartier-Bresson to Edouard Boubat. Today she also represents a stable of up-and-coming stars.

Artcurial (✉ 61 av. Montaigne, 8e, Champs-Élysées ☎ 01–42–99–16–16 Ⓜ Franklin-D.-Roosevelt) has the feel of a museum shop. It sells artist-designed decorative objects and exhibits works by such artists as Bram van Velde and Zao Wou-Ki.

Carré Rive Gauche (Ⓜ St-Germain-des-Prés, Rue du Bac) is an area sheltering dozens of art and antiques galleries on its narrow lanes.

Galerie Arnoux (✉ 27 rue Guénégaud, 6e, St-Germain-des-Prés ☎ 01–46–33–04–66 Ⓜ Odéon), one of many galleries on this street, specializes in abstract painting of the '50s, as well as in the works of young painters and sculptors.

Galerie Camera Obscura (✉ 12 rue Ernest Cresson, 14e, Montparnasse ☎ 01–45–45–67–08 Ⓜ Mouton Duvernet) is a small photography gallery with a very Zen-like atmosphere. The work on show is top quality, and the photographers represented include Lucien Hervé, Willy Ronis, and Yasuhiro Ishimoto.

Galerie Claude Bernard (✉ 5 rue des Beaux-Arts, 6e, St-Germain-des-Prés ☎ 01–43–26–97–07 Ⓜ St-Germain-des-Prés) is very well established in the domain of traditional figurative work.

Galerie Dina Vierny (✉ 36 rue Jacob, 6e, St-Germain-des-Prés ☎ 01–42–60–23–18 Ⓜ St-Germain-des-Prés) was set up after the war by the former muse of sculptor Aristide Maillol. Since then, she has discovered artists such as Serge Poliakoff, Vladimir Yankelevsky, and Ilya Kabakov.

Galerie Laage-Salomon (✉ 57 rue du Temple, 4e, Le Marais ☎ 01–42–78–11–71 Ⓜ Hôtel de Ville) shows a well-known, very international group of artists such as Per Kirkeby, Georg Baselitz, and Candida Höfer.

Galerie Lelong (✉ 13 rue de Téhéran, 8e, Miromesnil ☎ 01–45–63–13–19 Ⓜ Miromesnil), which also has galleries in New York and Zurich, represents a mix of contemporary artists.

Galerie Louis Carré (✉ 10 av. de Messine, 8e, Miromesnil ☎ 01–45–62–57–07 Ⓜ Miromesnil) has a long history of promoting French artists, including Bazaine, but it is not lost in the past.

Galerie Maeght (✉ 42 rue du Bac, 7e, St-Germain-des-Prés ☎ 01–45–48–45–15 Ⓜ Rue du Bac) is the Paris branch of the Fondation Maeght in St-Paul-de-Vence. You can find paintings as well as books, prints, and reasonably priced posters.

Galerie Templon (✉ In courtyard of 30 rue Beaubourg, 3e, Beaubourg/Les Halles ☎ 01–42–72–14–10 Ⓜ Rambuteau) was the first to bring American artists to Paris in the '60s; now it represents many artists, including French star Jean-Pierre Raynaud.

★ **Galerie 213** (✉ 213 bd. Raspail, 14e, Montparnasse ☎ 01–43–22–83–23 Ⓜ Raspail) is owned by Marion de Beaupré, former agent of top photographers such as Peter Lindbergh and Paolo Roversi. Today she runs this gallery, which has a bookstore on the ground floor, in a magnificent early Art Nouveau space. On the first floor is a white gallery salon, where she exhibits work by the likes of Elger Esser, Gueorgui Pinkhassov, and Guido Mocafico.

Galerie Yvon Lambert (✉ 108 rue Vieille-du-Temple, 3e, Le Marais ☎ 01–42–71–09–33 Ⓜ St-Sébastien Froissart) is run by the man known to the French as "the discoverer of minimalism and Conceptual Art"—indeed, one of his more famous exploits was his sale of a painting to a blind man. Over the years, he has exhibited everyone from Daniel Buren and Christo to Sol Lewitt and Julian Schnabel. Today he exhibits artists like Jenny Holzer, Douglas Gordon, and Christian Boltanski.

Joyce (✉ Palais-Royal, 9 rue de Valois, 1er, Louvre/Tuileries ☎ 01–40–15–03–72 Ⓜ Palais-Royal) is a gallery and boutique set up by successful Asian retailer Joyce Ma, who regularly invites Asian artists to show their work.

Louvre des Antiquaires (✉ 2 pl. du Palais-Royal, 1er, Louvre/Tuileries ☎ 01–42–97–27–00 Ⓜ Palais-Royal) is an elegant multifloor complex where 250 of Paris's leading dealers showcase their rarest objects, including Louis XV furniture, tapestries, and antique jewelry. The center is open Tuesday–Sunday 11 AM–7 PM; it is closed Sunday in July and August.

★ **Thaddaeus Ropac** (✉ 7 rue Debelleyme, 3er, Le Marais ☎ 01–42–72–99–00 Ⓜ St-Sébastien Froissart) is at the cutting-edge crossover between fashion and art. Ropac, who also has a gallery in Salzburg, represents some of the contemporary scene's hippest artists, including Tom Sachs, Sylvie Fleury, and Yasumasa Morimura.

Opera

Paris offers some of the best opera in the world—and thousands know it. Consequently, getting tickets to the two main venues, the **Opéra de la Bastille** and the **Opéra Garnier,** can be difficult on short notice, so it is a good idea to plan ahead. Review a list of performances by getting a copy of the Paris Tourist Office's "*Saison de Paris*" booklet or by writing to the **Opéra de la Bastille** (✉ 120 rue de Lyon, Bastille/Nation, 75576 Paris, Cedex 12) well in advance. Make your selection and send back the booking form, giving several choices of nights and performances. If the response is affirmative, just pick up and pay for your tickets before the performance (you can also pay for them by credit card in advance). A word of caution: buying from a scalper is not recommended, as there have been reports of people selling counterfeit tickets.

Opéra de la Bastille (✉ Pl. de la Bastille, 12e, Bastille/Nation ☎ 08–92–69–78–68 🌐 www.opera-de-paris.fr Ⓜ Bastille), the ultramodern facility built in 1989 and designed by architect Carlos Ott, has taken over the role of Paris's main opera house from the Opéra Garnier; tickets for the Opéra de Paris productions range €10–€109 and go on sale at the box office two weeks before any given show or a month ahead by phone. The opera season usually runs September through July and the box office is open Monday–Saturday 11–6:30 (the Web site is very informative and complete and allows you to order tickets).

Opéra Comique (✉ 5 rue Favart, 2e, Opéra/Grands Boulevards ☎ 08–25–00–00–58 Ⓜ Richelieu Drouot) is a jewel of an opera house run by France's *enfant terrible* theater director Jérôme Savary. As well as staging operettas, the hall also plays host to modern dance, classical concerts, and vocal recitals.

Fodor's Choice ★ **Opéra Garnier** (✉ Pl. de l'Opéra, 9e, Opéra/Grands Boulevards ☎ 08–36–69–78–68 🌐 www.opera-de-paris.fr Ⓜ Opéra), the magnificent and magical former haunt of the Phantom, the painter Edgar Degas, and any number of legendary opera stars, still hosts occasional performances of the Opéra de Paris, along with a fuller calendar of dance performances, as the auditorium is the official home of the Ballet de l'Opéra National de Paris. The grandest opera productions are usually mounted at the Opéra de la Bastille, while the Garnier now presents smaller-scale opera, such as Mozart's *La Clemenza di Tito* and *Così fan tutte*. Gorgeous though the Garnier is, its tiara-shape theater means that many seats have limited sight lines, so it's best to ask specifically what the sight lines are when booking (partial-view in French is *visibilité partielle*). Needless to say, the cheaper seats are often those with partial views—of course, views of Garnier's house could easily wind up being much more spectacular than any sets on stage, so it's not really a loss. Budget-minded American and British operagoers will be surprised to learn there is no standing room at either opera house. Ticket prices for opera range €7–€109. Seats go on sale at the box office two weeks before any given show or a month ahead by phone; you must go in person to buy the €7 tickets. Sometimes rush tickets, if available, are offered 15 minutes before a performance. The box office is open 11 to 6:30 daily.

Théâtre Musical de Paris (✉ Pl. du Châtelet, 1er, Beaubourg/Les Halles ☎ 01–40–28–28–40 Ⓜ Châtelet), better known as the Théâtre du Châtelet, puts on some of the finest opera productions in the city and regularly attracts international divas like Cecilia Bartoli and Anne-Sofie von Otter. It also plays host to classical concerts, dance performances, and the occasional play.

Puppet Shows

On most Wednesday, Saturday, and Sunday afternoons, the Guignol—the French equivalent of Punch and Judy—can be seen going through their ritualistic battles in a number of Paris's parks. All but the Champ de Mars have weatherproof performance spaces. **Champ de Mars**

(☎ 01–48–56–01–44 Ⓜ École Militaire); **Jardin d'Acclimatation** (✉ Bois de Boulogne ☎ 01–45–01–53–52 Ⓜ Sablons); **Jardin du Luxembourg** (☎ 01–43–26–46–47 Ⓜ Vavin);**Jardins du Ranelagh** (☎ 01–45–83–51–75 Ⓜ La Muette).

Theater

A number of theaters line the Grands Boulevards between the Opéra and République, but there is no Paris equivalent to Broadway or the West End. Shows are mostly in French, with a few notable exceptions. Information about performances can be obtained on a Web site 🌐 www.theatreonline.fr, which lists 170 different theaters, offers critiques, and provides an on-line reservation service. A genre that has become particularly popular in France is the "Broadway musical." Parisians had shunned most all-singing-and-dancing shows, but then came the smash hit *Notre-Dame-de-Paris,* which launched the fashion for Broadway-style musicals (and went on to be produced in Las Vegas and London's West End). Numerous other Gallic musicals have since debuted; most are staged at either the Palais des Sports or the Palais des Congrès.

Bouffes du Nord (✉ 37 bis bd. de la Chapelle, 10e, Stalingrad/La Chapelle ☎ 01–46–07–34–50 Ⓜ La Chapelle) is the wonderfully atmospheric, slightly decrepit home of English director Peter Brook, who regularly delights with his wonderful experimental French-language productions.
Café de la Gare (✉ 41 rue du Temple, 4e, Le Marais ☎ 01–42–78–52–51 Ⓜ Hôtel de Ville) is a fun spot to experience a particularly Parisian form of theater, the *café-théâtre*—a mixture of satirical sketches and variety show riddled with slapstick humor, performed in a café salon. You need a good grasp of French.
La Cartoucherie (✉ In the Bois de Vincennes, Bois de Vincennes ☎ 01–43–74–24–08 or 01–43–28–36–36 Ⓜ Château de Vincennes, then shuttle bus), a complex of five theaters in a former munitions factory, turns cast and spectators into an intimate theatrical world. The resident director is the revered Ariane Mnouchkine. Go early for a simple meal; the cast often helps serve "in character."
Comédie des Champs-Élysées (✉ 15 av. Montaigne, 8e, Champs-Élysées ☎ 01–53–23–99–19 Ⓜ Alma-Marceau) offers fine productions in a theater neighboring the larger Théâtre des Champs-Élysées. This is where Yasmina Reza's international hit *Art* first came to the public's attention.
★ The **Comédie Française** (✉ Pl. Colette, 1er, Louvre/Tuileries ☎ 01–44–58–15–15 🌐 www.comedie-francaise.fr Ⓜ Palais-Royal) dates back to 1680 and is the most hallowed institution in French theater. It specializes in classical French plays by the likes of Racine, Molière, and Marivaux. Reserve seats in person about two weeks in advance, or turn up an hour beforehand and wait in line for cancellations.
MC93 Bobigny (✉ 1 bd. Lénine, Bobigny ☎ 01–41–60–72–72 Ⓜ Bobigny–Pablo-Picasso), in a suburb northeast of Paris, often stages top-flight English and American productions.
Théâtre de la Huchette (✉ 23 rue de la Huchette, 5e, Latin Quarter ☎ 01–43–26–38–99 Ⓜ St-Michel) is a highlight for Ionesco admirers; this tiny Left Bank theater has been staging *The Bald Soprano* every night since 1950! (Note that the box office is open only Monday–Saturday 5–9 PM.)
Théâtre de Marigny (✉ Carré Marigny, 8e, Champs-Élysées ☎ 01–53–96–70–00 Ⓜ Champs-Élysées–Clemenceau) is a private theater, where you're likely to find a big French star topping the bill.
Théâtre Mogador (✉ 25 rue de Mogador, 9e, Opéra/Grands Boulevards ☎ 01–53–32–32–00 Ⓜ Trinité), one of Paris's most sumptuous theaters, is the place for musicals and other productions with popular appeal.

Théâtre National de Chaillot (✉ 1 pl. du Trocadéro, 16e, Eiffel Tower/ Trocadéro ☎ 01–53–65–30–00 Ⓜ Trocadéro) is a cavernous place with two theaters dedicated to drama and dance. The program ranges from Shakespeare to cabaret shows and tango festivals. Top-flight dance companies like the Ballet Royal de Suède and William Forsythe's Ballet Frankfurt are also regular visitors.

Théâtre de l'Odéon (✉ Pl. de l'Odéon, 6e, St-Germain-des-Prés ☎ 01–44–41–36–36 Ⓜ Odéon) has made pan-European theater its primary focus and offers some of the finest productions in Paris.

Théâtre de la Renaissance (✉ 20 bd. St-Martin, 10e, Opéra/Grands Boulevards ☎ 01–42–08–18–50 Ⓜ Strasbourg St-Denis) was put on the map by Belle Epoque star Sarah Bernhardt (she was manager from 1893 to 1899). Big French stars often perform in plays here.

OUTDOOR ACTIVITIES AND SPORTS

5

FODOR'S CHOICE

French Open, Bois de Boulogne
Mike's Bike Tours, Eiffel Tower
Ritz Health Club, Louvre/Tuileries
32 rue Montorgueil, Les Halles

HIGHLY RECOMMENDED

Aquaboulevard, Montparnasse
Cinq Mondes, Grands Boulevards
Club Quartier Latin, Latin Quarter
Patinoire Sonja Henie, Bercy
Pilates Studio, Le Marais
Piscine St-Germain, St-Germain-des-Prés
Stade de France, Paris
Tour de France, Paris

Revised and updated by Nicola Keegan

IT IS DIFFICULT TO PERCEIVE how Parisians maintain their slender chic—you don't see them on the streets in a pair of sweats on their way to the gym and you certainly don't see them power walking to work in suits and sneakers with a pair of office shoes in their bag. Parisians have famously considered sweating something you didn't do on purpose. But all that is changing as city residents finally discover the stress-reducing benefits of a good workout, though they exercise as only the French can—in subdued designer outfits with matching Gucci baseball caps and full, waterproof, makeup.

Sleek gyms and chic day spas have taken over the city, in fact, even the most exclusive palace-hotels have opened their gilded arms to luxurious spa treatments and access to their architectural dream pools. There are also a number of gardens and wooded areas in Paris that offer a variety of activities for children such as trampoline jumping and pony rides in the Tuileries or pony rides, go-carts, and a large playground complex in the Luxembourg gardens. The Buttes-Chaumont is a park with enough space for soccer and other games and a rather hilly jog. Paris's two largest parks—the Bois de Boulogne, on the western fringe of the city, and the Bois de Vincennes, on the eastern side—have wide-open spaces that allow for an array of activities. There are more than 200 km (124 mi) of bike lanes within the city as well as tennis courts, six professional-level climbing walls, and 34 municipal pools.

The French passion for sport is amazing—the daily sports paper ***L'Equipe*** is actually the country's best-selling national newspaper. Paris often hosts major international sporting events; it is the location for the French Open every May. Information on upcoming events can be found on posters around the city or in the weekly guide ***Pariscope.***

Your best bet for information in English about all athletic activities in Paris is to consult the official Web site 🌐 www.paris.org, which lists every major sporting possibility within the city limits plus all of the practical information such as opening hours, prices, exact locations, and current activities. You can also pick up a free copy of the booklet ***Le Guide du Sport à Paris,*** available from the Paris Tourist Office or in any of the city halls or *mairies* located in each arrondissement. It lists, in simple French, sports facilities in each arrondissement, has a map of all bike lanes, and contains a calendar of major sporting events.

Aerobics

From 9 to noon on Sunday the Paris town authorities organize free aerobics and stretch classes in 11 venues dotted throughout the city. Left Bank devotees head to the Pavillon des Gardes in the **Jardin du Luxembourg** (Ⓜ RER: Luxembourg). For the Montparnasse area, classes are offered at the Mire de l'Observatoire in the **Parc Montsouris** (✉ Bd. Jourdan, 14e, Montparnasse Ⓜ RER: Cité Universitaire). At the **Parc des Buttes-Chaumont,** the meeting place is the music kiosk on place Armand Carrel in front of the town hall of the 19e arrondissement. Note that there are no classes at any of these venues during July and August.

Athletics

The annual **Paris Marathon** (☎ 01–41–33–15–94 Athlétisme Organization) takes place in early April and attracts more than 20,000 participants. It sets off from the Champs-Élysées and finishes at the top of avenue Foch, near the Arc de Triomphe. Along the route, in spots like place de la Concorde and place de la République, there are groups who play live music to create a more festive atmosphere. The Paris track-and-field **Grand Prix** meeting is held at the Stade de France (⊠St-Denis ☎01–55–93–00–00 Ⓜ RER: La Plaine–Stade de France) in June and generally attracts a host of top international stars.

Bicycling

★ The amazingly popular **Tour de France** (🌐 www.letour.fr) consists of a grueling three weeks of pure physical torture as the world's best cyclists cover more than 2,000 mi of French terrain that includes, among other things high-speed chases, uphill climbing, downhill falling, and the sometimes extreme weather conditions of July. The athletes finish in a blaze of adulation, as tradition requires and the winner no doubt merits, on the Champs-Élysées with the president of the Republic, the mayor of Paris, live music, and hundreds of thousands of fans in attendance ready to celebrate. The race usually begins the end of June or beginning of July and finishes in Paris sometime in July.

Maps of Paris's main cycle paths can be found in the free brochure *Paris A Vélo,* available in any city hall or at one of the tourist offices. Paris's two large parks are the best places for biking. Bike enthusiasts on the western side of Paris tend to flock to the **Bois de Boulogne** (Ⓜ Porte Maillot, Porte Dauphine, Porte d'Auteuil; Bus 244). On the east side of Paris, the largest number of bike trails can be found in the vast **Bois de Vincennes** (Ⓜ Château de Vincennes, Porte Dorée).

The city also has more than 200 km (124 mi) of **bike lanes,** and there are plans to develop even more. Unfortunately, most bike routes are along the main axes of the city, which means that you may find yourself riding in traffic. Cars, however, have been banned from certain scenic routes altogether on Sunday and on the numerous national holidays. These include the banks of the Seine from 9 to 5 and the picturesque **Canal St-Martin** from noon to 6 year-round.

The following places rent bikes, and many of these establishments also organize guided excursions. **Bike 'n Roller** (⊠38 rue Fabert, 7e, Eiffel Tower/Trocadéro ☎ 01–45–50–38–27 🌐 www.bikenroller.fr Ⓜ La Tour-Maubourg) hires bikes for €12 for three hours and €17 for the day

FodorsChoice ★ **Mike's Bike Tours** (⊠ 24 rue Edgar Faure, 15e, Eiffel Tower/Trocadéro ☎01–56–58–10–54 🌐 www.MikesBikeToursParis.com Ⓜ Dupleix) organizes fun guided tours of Paris daily from March to November and by appointment from December to February. Tours are peppered with historical information and give a great overview of the city. Day tours run €22, night tours €26. **Pariscyclo** (⊠ Rond Point de Jardin d'Acclimatation, in the Bois de Boulogne, 16e, Bois de Boulogne ☎01–47–47–76–50 Ⓜ Les Sablons) is the perfect place for bike rentals if you want to explore the Bois de Boulogne. **Paris à Vélo, C'est Sympa** (⊠ 37 bd. Bourdon, 4e, Bastille/Nation ☎01–48–87–60–01 🌐 www.parisvelosympa.com Ⓜ Bastille) rents bikes for €10 for a half day and €13 a full day and also organizes three-hour excursions of both the heart of Paris and lesser-known sites. Times vary according to season, so either call ahead for information or consult the organization's Web site. Tours cost €30 (€25 for under-26s). A security deposit of €307 is also required, so do take along a credit card. **Paris Vélo Rent a Bike** (⊠ 2 rue Fer à Moulin, 5e, Latin Quarter ☎01–43–37–59–22 Ⓜ Censier Daubenton) charges €12 for half-day and €14 for full-day bike rental (with an additional security deposit of €300).

Health Clubs

Short-term passes are available from the following health clubs.

Club Jean de Beauvais (✉ 5 rue Jean-de-Beauvais, 5e, Latin Quarter ☎ 01–46–33–16–80 🌐 www.clubjeandebeauvais.com Ⓜ Maubert Mutualité) has an entire floor of exercise equipment and classes, as well as a sauna. A one-day pass costs €38; a week is €95. There is also the possibility of balneotherapy treatments at an additional cost. It's open Monday, Tuesday, and Thursday 7 AM–10:30 PM; Wednesday and Friday 7 AM–10 PM; Saturday 8:30–7; and Sunday 9:30–6. For more information, consult the Web site.

★ **Club Quartier Latin** (✉ 19 rue de Pontoise, 5e, Latin Quarter ☎ 01–55–42–77–88 Ⓜ Maubert Mutualité) has a skylighted pool, squash courts, and exercise equipment. For €13 per day you can use the gym and pool (the pool only is €4); add another €12 per 40 minutes for squash (€2.30 racket rental). It's open weekdays 9 AM–midnight, weekends 9:30–7.

Espace Vit'Halles (✉ Pl. Beaubourg, 48 rue Rambuteau, 3e, Beaubourg/Les Halles ☎ 01–42–77–21–71 Ⓜ Rambuteau) has a broad array of aerobics classes (€15.30 per class), exercise machines, sauna, and steam room (€15.30 a day). It's open Monday, Wednesday, and Friday 8 AM–10 PM; Tuesday and Thursday 8 AM–11 PM; Saturday 10–7; and Sunday 10–6.

★ **Pilates Studio** (✉ 39 rue du Temple, 4e, Le Marais ☎ 01–42–72–91–74 Ⓜ Hôtel de Ville) is run by Philippe Taupier, who studied in New York with one of the pupils of the technique's founder, Joseph Pilates. It may be based in just a three-room apartment but it attracts numerous celebrities, such as actress Kristin Scott Thomas and former French *Vogue* editor Joan Juliet Buck. One-hour solo classes cost €58. Duo classes are €46 per person and group classes €23.

Hotel Health Clubs

The hotels with the best fitness facilities are generally the newer ones around the perimeter of the city center.

Fodor's Choice ★ **Ritz Health Club** (✉ Pl. Vendôme, 1er, Louvre/Tuileries ☎ 01–43–16–30–60 Ⓜ Opéra), as fancy as the hotel, has a swimming pool, sauna, steam room, hot tub, exercise machines, and aerobics classes (free for hotel guests; €95 on weekdays, €107 on weekends). It's open daily 7 AM–10 PM.

Sofitel Paris Club Med Gym (✉ 8 rue Louis-Armand, 15e, Montparnasse ☎ 01–45–54–79–00 Ⓜ Balard) has a 15-m pool, a sauna, a steam room, and a hot tub, plus a stunning view of the Paris skyline (€40 per day, free to hotel guests). It's open Monday and Wednesday–Friday 8 AM–10 PM, Tuesday 8 AM–midnight, Saturday 9–7, and Sunday 9–3.

Horse Racing

Paris and its suburbs are remarkably well furnished with *hippodromes* (racetracks). Admission is between €2.30 and €7.63. Details of meetings can be found in the daily newspaper ***Le Parisien*** or the specialist racing paper ***Paris Turf.*** The easiest racetrack to get to is the **Hippodrome d'Auteuil** (✉ Bois de Boulogne, 16e, Bois de Boulogne ☎ 01–40–71–47–47 Ⓜ Porte d'Auteuil) in the Bois de Boulogne. Also in the Bois de Boulogne is the city's most beautiful track, the **Hippodrome de Longchamp** (✉ Rte. des Tribunes, Bois de Boulogne, 16e, Bois de Boulogne ☎ 01–44–30–75–00 Ⓜ Porte d'Auteuil, then free shuttle), the stage for the prestigious (and glamorous) Prix de l'Arc de Triomphe in October. The **Hippodrome de Vincennes** (✉ Rte. Ferme, Bois de Vincennes ☎ 01–49–77–17–17 Ⓜ RER: Joinville-Le-Pont) is a cinder track used for trotting races. The French Derby (Prix du Jockey-Club) and the very chic French Oaks (Prix de Diane-Hermès) are held at the beginning of June at **Chantilly,** north of Paris; direct trains from the Gare du Nord take about 40 minutes. Other racetracks near Paris are in **Enghien-les-Bains, Évry,** and **St-Cloud.**

Ice-Skating

From mid-December through the end of February, weather permitting, the city of Paris transforms three outdoor sites into spectacular ice-skating rinks with pretty Christmas lights, music, and on-site instructors. The rinks are free to the public; skate rental for adults costs €5 but is free for the little ones. Don't forget to take advantage of the antique merry-go-rounds near the rinks—they're free as well. The **Place de l'Hôtel de Ville** (the square in front of the Hôtel de Ville); is transformed into a 1,200-m (3,960-ft) rink. **Patinoire Montparnasse** (✉ Pl. Raoul Dantry, 15e, Montparnasse Ⓜ Montparnasse Bienvenüe) has an 800-m (2,624-ft) rink in a heavily built-up neighborhood. **Bassin de La Villette**'s (✉ Pl. de la Bataille de Stalingrad, 19e, La Villette Ⓜ Stalingrad) 800-m (2,624-ft) rink is in a somewhat undesirable neighborhood.

★ The **Patinoire Sonja Henie** (✉ 8 bd. de Bercy, 12e, Bercy/Tolbiac ☎ 01–40–02–60–60 Ⓜ Bercy) is a 500-m (1,650-ft) indoor rink, open year-round. Admission ranges from €4 during the day to €14 at night. Friday and Saturday nights it turns into a huge ice-skating nightclub with giant screens, disco lights, and loud music.

In-Line Skating

Where once it was rare to see people with a pair of skates on their feet, now it seems like almost every other Parisian is an adept of *le roller.* To avoid pedestrians and road crossings, they often use the city's cycle paths. You'll also see them doing their tricks on **place du Palais-Royal** and the esplanade at the **Musée d'Art Moderne de la Ville de Paris** on avenue du Président-Wilson. On Sunday, when cars are banned, **quai de la Tournelle,** along the Seine (9–5), and the **Canal St-Martin** (noon–6) are also ideal in-line skating spots.

Every Friday night starting at 10, thousands of in-line skaters gather at **place de l'Italie** to take a different weekly three-hour route through Paris (roads are blocked off). The pace is pretty hairy, so novices are discouraged. For details, check the Web site, www.pari-roller.com. A more leisurely three-hour route is organized on Sunday at 2:30 PM and leaves from **Roller Location Nomades** near place de la Bastille. For those who want to practice their acrobatics, there are two ramps in the **Stade Boutroux** (✉ 1 av. Boutroux, 13e, Chinatown ☎ 01–45–84–08–46 Ⓜ Porte d'Ivry).

In-line skates can be rented from **Bike 'n Roller** (✉ 6 rue St-Julien-le-Pauvre, 5e, Latin Quarter ☎ 01–44–07–35–89 Ⓜ St-Michel ✉ 137 St-Dominique, 7e, Eiffel Tower/Trocadéro ☎ 01–44–18–30–39 Ⓜ École Militaire ✉ 38 rue Fabert, 7e, Eiffel Tower/Trocadéro ☎ 01–45–50–38–27 Ⓜ La Tour-Maubourg) for €10 for three hours and €12.50 per day. **Roller Location Nomades** (✉ 37 bd. Bourdon, 4e, Bastille/Nation ☎ 01–44–54–07–44 Ⓜ Bastille) rents skates for about €10 per day. **Vertical Line** (✉ 60 av. Raymond Poincaré, 16e, Trocadéro/Eiffel Tower ☎ 01–47–27–21–21 Ⓜ Victor-Hugo) rents skates for 30–60 minutes for €5–€10.

Jogging

Running through the streets of Paris may sound romantic, but it can be quite unpleasant if you don't go early in the day: there's just too much traffic on the narrow streets. Exceptions are quai de la Tournelle, along the Seine, and along the Canal St-Martin. The city's parks are better places to run. The **Champ de Mars** (Ⓜ École Militaire), next to the Eiffel Tower, measures 2½ km (1½ mi) around the perimeter. Many jogging fans prefer the pleasant route—though shorter and more crowded that the Champ de Mars—that is the 1½-km (1-mi) loop just inside the fence around the **Jardin du Luxembourg** (Ⓜ Odéon; RER: Luxembourg). The **Jardin des Tuileries** (Ⓜ Concorde, Tuileries) measures about 1½ km (1 mi) around. The **Bois de Boulogne** has miles of trails through woods, around lakes, and across grassy meadows. There are 1.8-km (1.1-mi) and 2½-km (1½-mi) loops. The especially bucolic **Bois de Vincennes** has a 14½-km (9-mi) circuit or a 1½-km (1-mi) loop around the Château de Vincennes itself. Maps of routes in both bois can be found in *Le Guide du Sport à Paris*. Those who prefer track running can have access to Paris's athletics facilities during times when they have not been booked by schools or clubs. Try any of the following, but make sure to call ahead to check availability. In the 12e district, head to the **Centre Sportif Léo-Lagrange** (✉ 68 bd. Poniatowski, Bastille/Nation ☎ 01–46–28–31–57 Ⓜ Porte de Charenton). In the 15e district, try the **Centre Sportif Suzanne-Lenglen** (✉ 2 rue Louis-Armand, Montparnasse ☎ 01–45–54–72–85 Ⓜ Balard). In the 16e district, check out **Stade Porte-de-la-Muette** (✉ 60 bd. Lannes, Eiffel Tower/Trocadéro ☎ 01–45–04–54–85 Ⓜ RER: Av. Henri-Martin).

There are a number of annual running races that are open to the public. The **Paris Marathon** takes place in April. Subscription details are available from the Athlétisme Organisation (☎ 01–41–33–15–94). A lesser-known event is the **20 km de Paris** (✉ Atalante, 9–11 rue Letellier, 15e, Montparnasse ☎ 01–45–75–67–12), held in October. **Le Cross du Figaro** (☎ 01–42–21–60–00 for information) is a cross-country race organized each December by the French national daily *Le Figaro*.

Rugby

The Paris Université Club plays home matches on Sunday in winter at 3 PM at the **Stade Charléty** (✉ 99 bd. Kellermann, 13e, Cité Universitaire ☎ 01–44–16–62–69 club Ⓜ RER: Cité Universitaire); tickets are €5. For information and game dates, call the club directly. France's national rugby team plays at the **Stade de France** (✉ St-Denis ☎ 01–55–93–00–00 Ⓜ RER: La Plaine–Stade de France). Admissions range from €8 to €95; your best bet is to get tickets from FNAC or Virgin Megastore in advance or contact the Fédération Française de Rugby (☎ 01–53–21–15–15). The Racing Club de France has games Saturday or Sunday afternoon at the **Stade Charléty** (☎ 01–45–67–55–86 Racing Club). Paris's top team, Le Stade Français, usually plays home matches on Saturday or Sunday afternoon at the **Stade Jean Bouin** (✉ 26 av. du Général Sarrail, 16e, Eiffel Tower/Trocadéro ☎ 01–46–51–51–11 🌐 www.stade.fr Ⓜ Porte d'Auteuil).

Soccer

As in most other European cities, *football* (soccer) is the sport that pulls in the biggest crowds. **Paris St-Germain** (✉ 24 rue du Commandant Guilbaud, 16e, Passy-Auteuil ☎ 01–42–88–02–76 🌐 www.psg.fr Ⓜ Porte d'Auteuil), the city's main club, was founded in 1970 and has won various titles. It plays at the Parc des Princes stadium in southwest Paris. Most matches are on Saturday evening at 8 PM, although times do vary.

It is best to check ahead on the club's official Web site. Admission is €16–€55; your best bet is to get tickets from FNAC in advance.

★ The **Stade de France** (✉ St-Denis ☎ 01–55–93–00–00 Ⓜ RER: La Plaine–Stade de France) was built for the World Cup in 1998 and is now home to the wildly popular French national soccer team.

Spectator Sports

A far-ranging calendar of sporting events, including indoor athletics, ice-skating, horse shows, gymnastics, and stock-car racing, take place at the **Palais Omnisports de Paris-Bercy** (✉ 8 bd. de Bercy, 12e, Bastille/Nation ☎ 08–03–03–00–31 🌐 www.bercy.com Ⓜ Bercy, Gare de Lyon). Details of events are also on their Web site.

Swimming

There are certain rules you should know about swimming in Paris–everyone must wear a swimming cap, men aren't allowed to wear swim trunks or cutoffs (only those tight Lycra swimming briefs are accepted), and most people wear flip-flops around the pool and the shower area to protect their feet from *French fungi*. Once you have that down, swimming in the capital is quite easy—every arrondissement has its own public *piscine* (pool); the Paris Tourist Office's *Le Guide du Sport à Paris* lists addresses. One of the biggest and best is the **Piscine des Halles** (✉ Pl. de la Rotonde, Forum des Halles, 1er, Beaubourg/Les Halles ☎ 01–42–36–98–44 Ⓜ Châtelet Les Halles), a 50-m pool inside the shopping mall in the center of Paris. It's open Monday 11:30–8; Wednesday 10–7; Tuesday, Thursday, and Friday 11:30–10; and weekends 9–5. Admission is €4 and you can stay as long as you like. ★ The **Piscine St-Germain** (✉ 12 rue de Lobineau, 6e, St-Germain-des-Prés ☎ 01–43–29–08–15 Ⓜ Mabillon), one of the nicest pools in Paris, is open Tuesday 7 AM–8 AM, 11:30 AM–1 PM, and 5 PM–7:30 PM; Wednesday 7 AM–8 AM and 11:30 AM–5:30 PM; Thursday and Friday 7 AM–8 AM and 11:30 AM–1 PM; Saturday 7 AM–5:30 PM; and Sunday 8 AM–5:30 PM. Admission is €3. If you want to take in a bit of architectural heritage with your laps, swim at the registered historic monument **Piscine Butte-aux-Cailles** (✉ 5 pl. Paul-Verlaine, 13e, Buttes-aux-Cailles ☎ 01–45–89–60–05 Ⓜ Place d'Italie). Classed as a historic monument, the **Piscine des Amiraux** (✉ 6 rue Hermann-Lachapelle, 18e, Montmartre ☎ 01–46–06–46–47 Ⓜ Simplon, Marcadet-Poissonniers) is a picturesque venue. In summer many Parisians head off to the open-air **Piscine de la Grenouillère** (✉ Parc d'Antony, 146 bis av. du Général-de-Gaulle ☎ 01–46–60–75–30 Ⓜ RER: Croix-de-Berny), which is open daily 9–7 from mid-May to mid-September.

★ **Aquaboulevard** (✉ 4 rue Louis-Armand, 15e, Montparnasse ☎ 01–40–60–10–00 Ⓜ Balard), the best place to take kids in summer, has an enormous indoor wave pool with water slides and in summer a simulated outdoor beach. It's open Monday–Thursday 9 AM–11 PM, Friday 7 AM–8 AM, Saturday 7 AM–8 AM, and Sunday 7 AM–8 AM. Last admission each day is at 9 PM. Adults can stay for six hours for €19. The **Club Quartier Latin** (✉ 19 rue de Pontoise, 5e, Latin Quarter ☎ 01–55–42–77–88 Ⓜ Maubert Mutualité) has a very nice, skylighted, 33-m pool that you can use for €4.

Tennis

Fodor'sChoice ★ One of the highlights of the international tennis circuit is the action on the dusty red-clay courts at the **French Open**, held during the last week of May and the first in June at **Roland-Garros Stadium** (✉ 2 av. Gordon Bennett, 16e, Bois de Boulogne ☎ 01–47–43–48–00 Ⓜ Porte d'Auteuil).

Center-court tickets are often difficult to obtain; try your hotel's concierge or turn up early in the morning (matches start at 11 AM) and buy a general grounds ticket to see early round matches. Tickets range from €13 to €55. The **Bercy Indoor Tournament** in November at the Palais Omnisports de Paris-Bercy awards one of the largest prizes in the world and attracts most of the top players. The **Open Gaz de France** (Stade Pierre de Coubertin ✉ 82 av. Georges-Lafont, 16e, St-Cloud ☎ 01–45–27–79–12 Ⓜ Porte de St-Cloud) every February is one of the official tournaments on the women's tour. Tickets for both events can be purchased at FNAC or Virgin Megastore, or at the stadium.

Paris has a number of municipal courts, but getting to play on them is not so easy. Normally, you must apply for a special card from the local *mairie* (town hall; each arrondissement has one), which takes one month to process, and then reserve a court in advance. You can, however, take a chance, turn up at the public courts, and, if there is one available, play (the best time to go is the middle of the day during the week); the cost is €6 an hour per court, which you pay there. The most central, and most crowded, courts are in the **Jardin du Luxembourg.**

Well-Being

Walk through Paris and you'll notice that on almost every street corner, sandwiched between the butchers and the bakers, stands the local *institut de beauté* a veritable haven of skin care, beauty products, various magic potions, and home to those special secret beauty rituals—steaming, waxing, massaging, plucking, wrapping—French women have been practicing since Marie-Antoinette took lukewarm milk baths. All the posh palace-hotels—The Ritz, Meurice, and George V—have luxurious spa treatments of their own and are readily available to those of you who know no budget. But you actually don't have to spend more than your plane ticket being royally pampered in Paris; there are a number of great locations where you can escape the grind of museums, cafés, restaurants, and shops and just lie back and enjoy. Please note though, due to the incredibly high demand, you should try and reserve your day in paradise at least one month in advance.

Les Bains du Marais (✉ 31-33 rue des Blancs Manteaux, 4e, Le Marais ☎ 01–44–61–02–02 Ⓜ Rambuteau) is on the site of ancient bathing spots that now provide facial care, massages, saunas, nail treatments, and traditional steam rooms for both men (Thursday to Saturday) and women (Monday to Wednesday). Your €30 fee allows you to spend as long as you want in the steam rooms and includes bathrobe, slippers, and a towel. You can also get a massage and body scrub as you steam away the jet lag for another €30.

★ **Cinq Mondes** (✉ 6 Square Louis Jouvet, 9e, Opera/Grands Boulevards ☎ 01–55–37–93–83 Ⓜ Opéra) blends traditional techniques from five ancient schools in a lush, Zen atmosphere that has all Paris clamoring to get in. Try the "urban ritual" for two hours of pure relaxation including a ceremonial Japanese bath in an oval cedarwood tub afloat with rose petals and essential oils. Prices range from €45 to €400 for a full day.

Daniel Jouvance Espace Mer (✉ 91 av. des Champs-Élysées, 8e, Champs-Élysées ☎ 01–47–23–48–00 Ⓜ George V) brings the benefits of *thalassotherapie* (healing with ocean water) to the city. This sleek, glass-encased complex blends the serious science of marine biology and dermatology with classic beauty treatments. Try the *Aquaprima* body treatment—an hour and a half of exfoliation, hydromassage, massage and seaweed wrap for €110, or the *Aquanova* facial with shiatsu massage for €40.

Nickel (✉ 48 rue des Francs-Bourgeois, 4ᵉ, Le Marais ☎ 01–42–77–41–10 🌐 www.nickel.fr Ⓜ St-Paul) is a silver-and-dark-blue spa that offers no-frills service for men in the heart of the Marais. Here you can get massaged, manicured, waxed, and all around pampered in a no-nonsense, nonfussy, busy-guy kind of way that French men love.

Fodor'sChoice ★ **32 rue Montorgeuil** (✉ 32 rue Montorgeuil, 1ᵉ Beaubourg/Les Halles ☎ 01–55–80–71–40 Ⓜ Les Halles) is the hip spa by the creators of the Nuxe line of skin care products. Parisian starlets flock to this ancient cellar with its arched corridors, exposed cream stone, and hush-hush atmosphere smack in the middle of one of the busiest areas in Paris. Try the anti-age treatment; a spectacular 1½ hours of pure luxury for €100. Jean Norell, star hairdresser to *tout* Paris, is on hand to take expert care of your locks after one of your treatments.

Villa Thalgo (✉ 218-220 rue du Faubourg St-Honoré, 8ᵉ, Champs-Élysées ☎ 01–45–62–00–20 Ⓜ Charles-de-Gaulle–Étoile) is where Isabelle Adjani comes to treat the cellulite she doesn't and absolutely will never have. There is a heated saltwater swimming pool with specialized aquagym lessons and massages to relaunch the lymphatic system, eliminate toxins, and stimulate circulation. There are also facials and body packs filled with trace sea minerals to promote rejuvenation.

SHOPPING

FODOR'S CHOICE

Au Bon Marché, St-Germain-des-Prés
Dary's, Louvre/Tuileries
Jean-Paul Gaultier, Champs-Élysées
Le Marché aux Puces St-Ouen, Clignancourt
Les Salons du Palais-Royal Shiseido, Louvre/Tuileries
Vanessa Bruno, Louvre/Tuileries

HIGHLY RECOMMENDED

Anouschka, Opéra/Grands Boulevards
Bonpoint, Trocadéro
Chanel, Champs-Élysées
Christian Louboutin, Beaubourg/Les Halles
Colette, Louvre/Tuileries
Didier Ludot, Louvre/Tuileries
Les Folies d'Elodie, Trocadéro/Eiffel Tower
Hermès, Louvre/Tuileries
La Hune, St-Germain-des-Prés
Isabel Marant, Bastille/Nation
Jamin Puech, Opéra/Grands Boulevards
Kiliwatch, Beaubourg/Les Halles
Ladurée, Latin Quarter
Marni, Champs-Élysées
Le Monde Sauvage, Latin Quarter
Rodolphe Menudier, Louvre/Tuileries
Sabbia Rosa, St-Germain-des-Prés

Revised and updated by Nicola Keegan

DON'T BE SURPRISED TO SEE SPEED-WALKING PARISIANS slow to a crawl as their eyes lock on an attractive store window. Window-shopping is one of this city's greatest spectator sports, and the French have come up with a wonderful expression for this highly cultivated art. They call it *lèche-vitrine*—literally, "licking the windows"—which is quite fitting because many of the displays are good enough to eat. Sonia Rykiel always fills her windows with the latest literary releases, Dior has commissioned artwork for its windows, and a coffee-table book has even been dedicated to those at Hermès, whose windows are sometimes like diminutive theaters, small masterpieces of fantasy whose presentation is almost as worthy a sight as the Eiffel Tower. In the most beautiful city in the world it's no surprise to discover that the local greengrocer displays his tomatoes as artistically as Cartier does its rubies. The capital of style, Paris has endless delights to tempt shop-till-you-droppers, from grand couturiers to the funkiest flea markets. Happily, Paris chic is often about pairing a vintage Dior jacket with a casual crew-neck T-shirt, so whether you're *fauché*—broke—or want to buy up a storm, this city can be the most rewarding of hunting grounds.

Truth is, shopping here can be contagious, and if you don't buy something—bottles of fruit-flavor *eaux-de-vie* that Hemingway and Fitzgerald loved so much, antique brooches from the 1930s, modern vases crafted from Parisian rooftop-tile zinc, rare artwork, or lacy lingerie (this *is* Paris)—you're missing out on a truly Parisian experience, a chance to mix with the natives and feel the heartbeat of the city.

The shopping options in Paris are endless and geared to every taste. You can price emerald earrings at Cartier, spend an afternoon browsing through bookstalls along the Seine, tour the high-gloss department stores, or haggle over the price for one of those flea-market "Souvenir de Paris" bracelets, which clank with tin Arc de Triomphes and poodles. But no matter where you head, you'll find scores of special boutiques that sell the Parisian staple: chic. Style, after all, is one of the things the French do best. No matter if a waitress or a countess, all *Parisiennes* seem to share a common denominator: that elusive chic that depends less on the way they choose their clothes than on their manner of wearing them. It is this unique sense of style that inspires all those foreign-born couturiers and tastemakers to this day—if you get your inspiration from the catwalk, the couturiers often get their ideas from the streets. Today every neighborhood seems to reflect a different attitude and style: designer extravagance and haute couture characterize avenue Montaigne and rue du Faubourg St-Honoré; classic sophistication pervades St-Germain; avant-garde style dresses up the Marais; while a hip feel suffuses the area around the place des Victoires.

Most stores in Paris—excepting department stores and flea markets—stay open until 6 or 7 PM, but many take a lunch break sometime between noon and 2 PM. Although shops traditionally close on Sunday, regulations have been greatly relaxed in the past decade, and you'll find a number of stores open then, too, most especially in the Marais.

Duty-Free Shopping

A value-added tax of 19.6%, known in France as the TVA, is imposed on most consumer goods. Non–European Union residents ages 15 and over who stay in France and/or the EU for less than six months can reclaim the part of this tax known as the *détaxe*. To qualify, your purchases in a single shop in a single day need to total €185 or more. The refund ranges between 13% and 16%. Department stores offer special détaxe desks where the *bordereaux* (export sales invoices) help streamline the process, while high-profile shops often offer détaxe forms but are not required to do paperwork. If the discount will be a sizable one, ask if the détaxe is available before purchasing. Note that there is no refund for food, wine, and tobacco. Invoices and bordereaux forms are to be shown to French customs upon leaving the country, with purchases in question available for inspection. The customs official will stamp your form, and then you'll need to seal it in the envelope provided and drop it into any of the mailboxes at the airport. Your refund will arrive either as a check in U.S. dollars or a credit to your credit card (the faster and easier of the two options.

Shopping by Neighborhood

Avenue Montaigne & Surroundings

Avenue Montaigne is one of the most elusive, exclusive shopping streets in the galaxy—it just doesn't get much more *haute* than this, darling. They're all here, all those incredibly expensive luscious, luxurious, yummy boutiques that strike fear in the heart of even the most well-padded wallet: **Chanel, Dior, Nina Ricci, Celine, Valentino, Max Mara, Genny, Krizia, Escada, Marni, Emanuel Ungaro, Prada, Pucci, Calvin Klein,**and **Dolce & Gabbana.** You'll also find accessories by **S. T. Dupont, Loewe,** and **Louis Vuitton.** Many of the boutiques are housed in exquisite mansions with wrought-iron gates in front. On the sidewalks, princess-cum-model-cum-super-rich-girl types canter along in tiny heeled boots with lacquered packages dangling off their bird-thin wrists. The boutiques, as you can imagine, are very, very *nice* and, as in all pinnacles of luxury in France, the sales staff are well trained in the evil eye, but, as they say, "when in Rome." Here one must play by the stringent rules of the purely superficial world; dress to the nines (this is **not** a jeans-and-sneakers day), ignore as you are being ignored, and shop away; and, as any great shopper knows, you don't have to actually *buy* anything to enjoy the experience. Oh, and don't forget neighboring rue François and avenue George V which also have their share of fine boutiques: **Armani, Versace, Fendi, Givenchy, Balenciaga,** and the must-see **Jean-Paul Gaultier** fantasy.

Champs-Élysées

Cafés and movie theaters keep the once-chic Champs-Élysées active 24 hours a day, but the invasion of exchange banks, car showrooms, and fast-food chains has certainly lowered the tone. Nowadays, galleries filled with overpriced finds and shops like the **Virgin Megastore, Gap,** and **Disney Store** capture most of the retail action. Meriting a stop, however, are the cosmetic wonder store **Sephora,** the French perfumer **Guerlain,** and the quintessentially fashionable **Louis Vuitton** boutique, whose partnership with American designer Marc Jacobs has turned this bourgeois institution into the epitome of cool.

The Faubourg St-Honoré & Place Vendôme

Prime shopping ground for the rich and beautiful, this residential and political hub—you'll find the the Élysée Palace here, as well as the official residences of the American and British ambassadors—contains some of the most famous shops in the world. Renowned antiques galleries such as **Didier Aaron** add artistic flavor. Boutiques include **Hermès, Lanvin, Gucci, Chloé, Yves Saint Laurent, Prada,** and **Christian Lacroix.** Head a bit north to find the place Vendôme, home to many of the world's most elegant jewelers, such as **Cartier, Boucheron, Chaumet,** and **Jar's.**

Left Bank

After decades of clustering on the Right Bank's venerable shopping avenues, the high-fashion houses have stormed the Rive Gauche. The first to arrive were **Sonia Rykiel** and **Yves Saint Laurent** in the late '60s. Forty years later **Christian Dior, Louis Vuitton, Emporio Armani,** and **Cartier** have

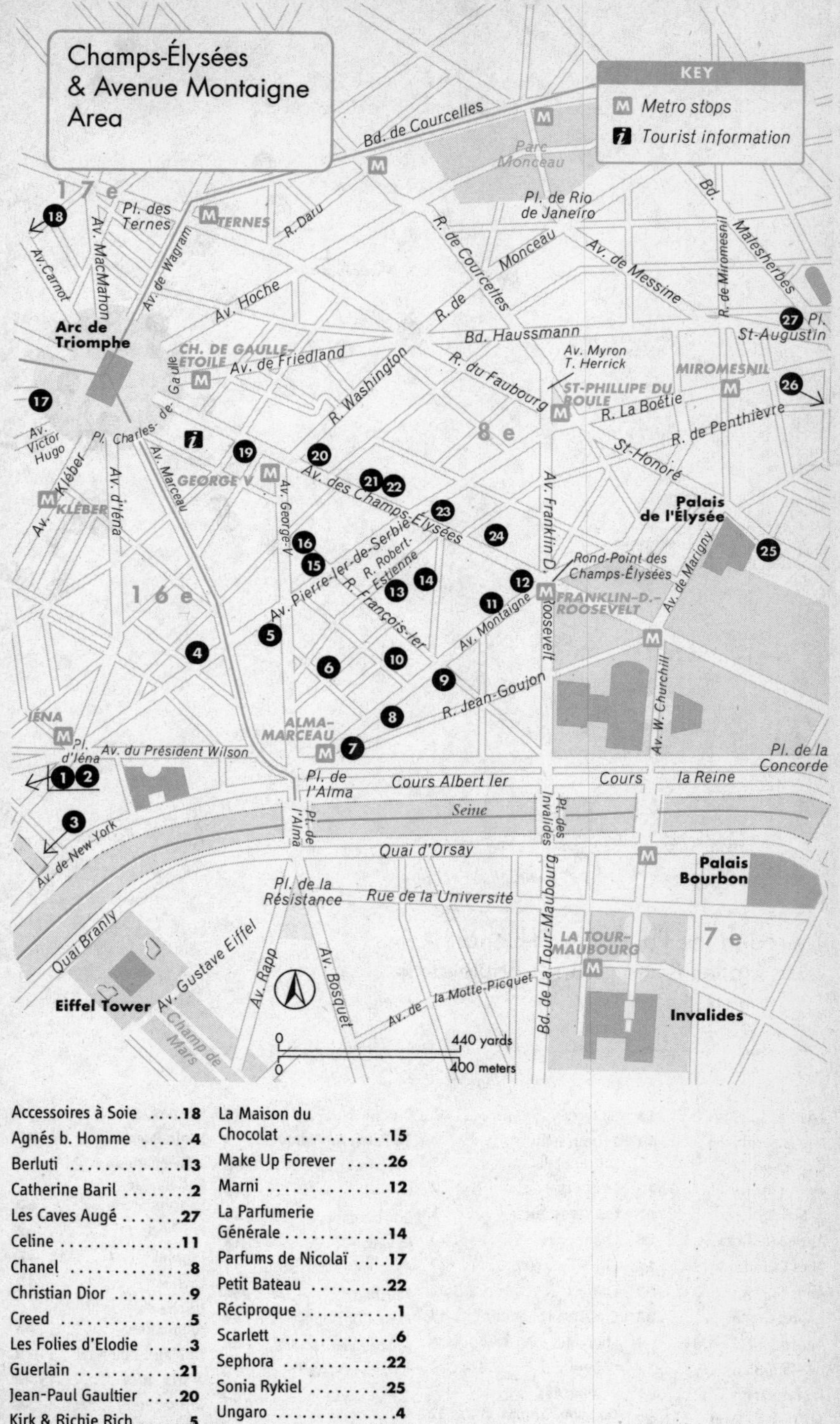

Accessoires à Soie 18	La Maison du Chocolat 15
Agnés b. Homme 4	Make Up Forever 26
Berluti 13	Marni 12
Catherine Baril 2	La Parfumerie Générale 14
Les Caves Augé 27	Parfums de Nicolaï 17
Celine 11	Petit Bateau 22
Chanel 8	Réciproque 1
Christian Dior 9	Scarlett 6
Creed 5	Sephora 22
Les Folies d'Elodie 3	Sonia Rykiel 25
Guerlain 21	Ungaro 4
Jean-Paul Gaultier 20	Virgin Megastore 23
Kirk & Richie Rich 5	Zara 24
Louis Vuitton 20	

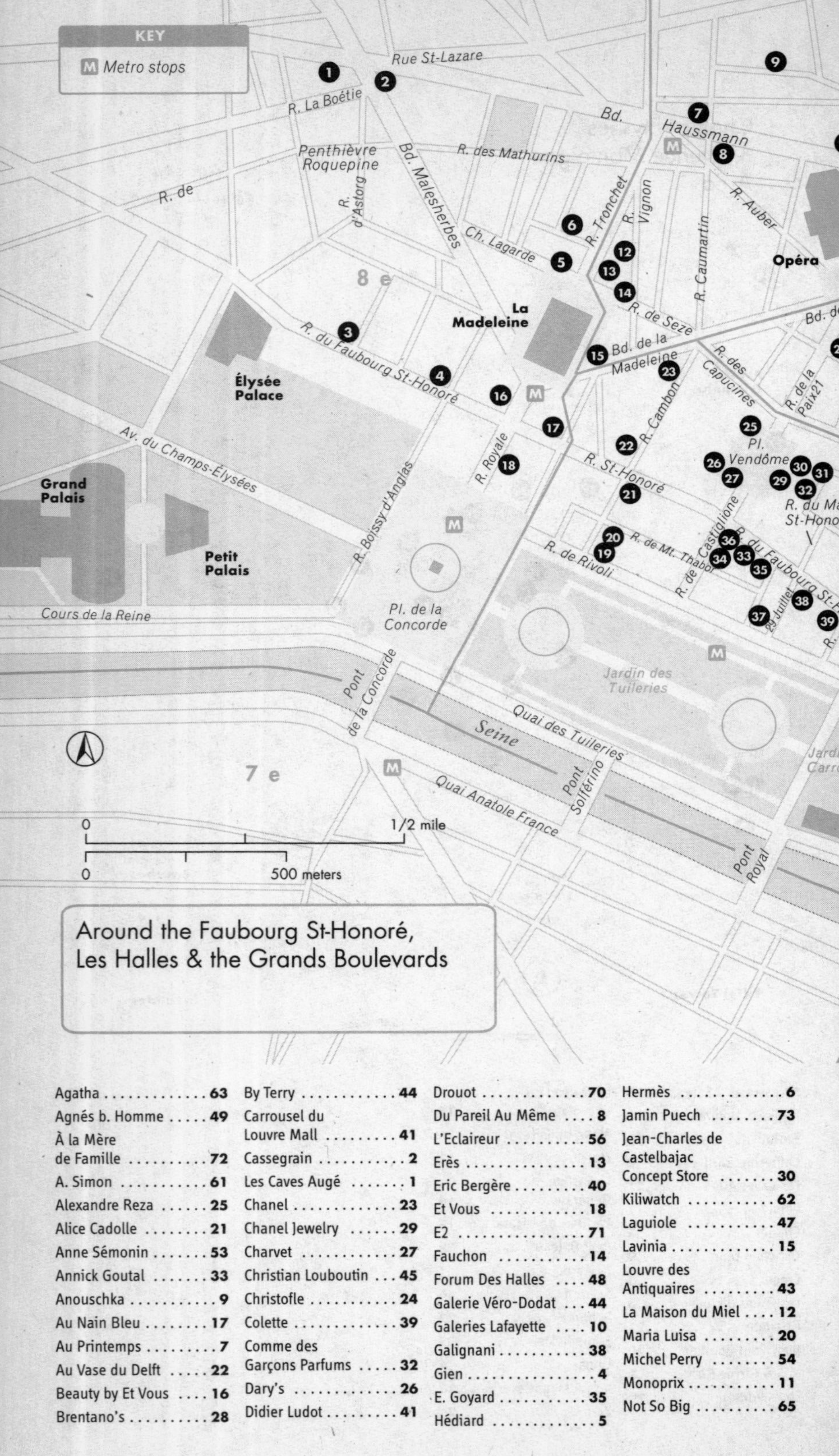
KEY
Metro stops
Rue St-Lazare
R. La Boétie
Bd. Haussmann
Penthièvre
Roquepine
Bd. Malesherbes
R. des Mathurins
R. de
R. d'Astorg
Ch. Lagarde
R. Tronchet
R. Vignon
R. Caumartin
R. Auber
Opéra
8e
La Madeleine
R. de Seze
Bd. de la Madeleine
Bd. des
R. du Faubourg St-Honoré
Élysée Palace
R. des Capucines
R. de la Paix
R. Cambon
Av. du Champs-Élysées
R. Royale
Pl. Vendôme
R. St-Honoré
R. du Marché St-Honoré
Grand Palais
R. Boissy d'Anglas
R. de Mt. Thabor
R. de Castiglione
R. de Rivoli
Petit Palais
29 Juillet
Cours de la Reine
Pl. de la Concorde
Jardin des Tuileries
Pont de la Concorde
Seine
Quai des Tuileries
Jardin Carrou
7e
Pont Solférino
Quai Anatole France
0
1/2 mile
0
500 meters
Pont Royal
Around the Faubourg St-Honoré, Les Halles & the Grands Boulevards
Agatha 63
Agnés b. Homme 49
À la Mère de Famille 72
A. Simon 61
Alexandre Reza 25
Alice Cadolle 21
Anne Sémonin 53
Annick Goutal 33
Anouschka 9
Au Nain Bleu 17
Au Printemps 7
Au Vase du Delft 22
Beauty by Et Vous 16
Brentano's 28
By Terry 44
Carrousel du Louvre Mall 41
Cassegrain 2
Les Caves Augé 1
Chanel 23
Chanel Jewelry 29
Charvet 27
Christian Louboutin . . . 45
Christofle 24
Colette 39
Comme des Garçons Parfums 32
Dary's 26
Didier Ludot 41
Drouot 70
Du Pareil Au Même 8
L'Eclaireur 56
Erès 13
Eric Bergère 40
Et Vous 18
E2 71
Fauchon 14
Forum Des Halles 48
Galerie Véro-Dodat . . . 44
Galeries Lafayette 10
Galignani 38
Gien 4
E. Goyard 35
Hédiard 5
Hermès 6
Jamin Puech 73
Jean-Charles de Castelbajac Concept Store 30
Kiliwatch 62
Laguiole 47
Lavinia 15
Louvre des Antiquaires 43
La Maison du Miel 12
Maria Luisa 20
Michel Perry 54
Monoprix 11
Not So Big 65

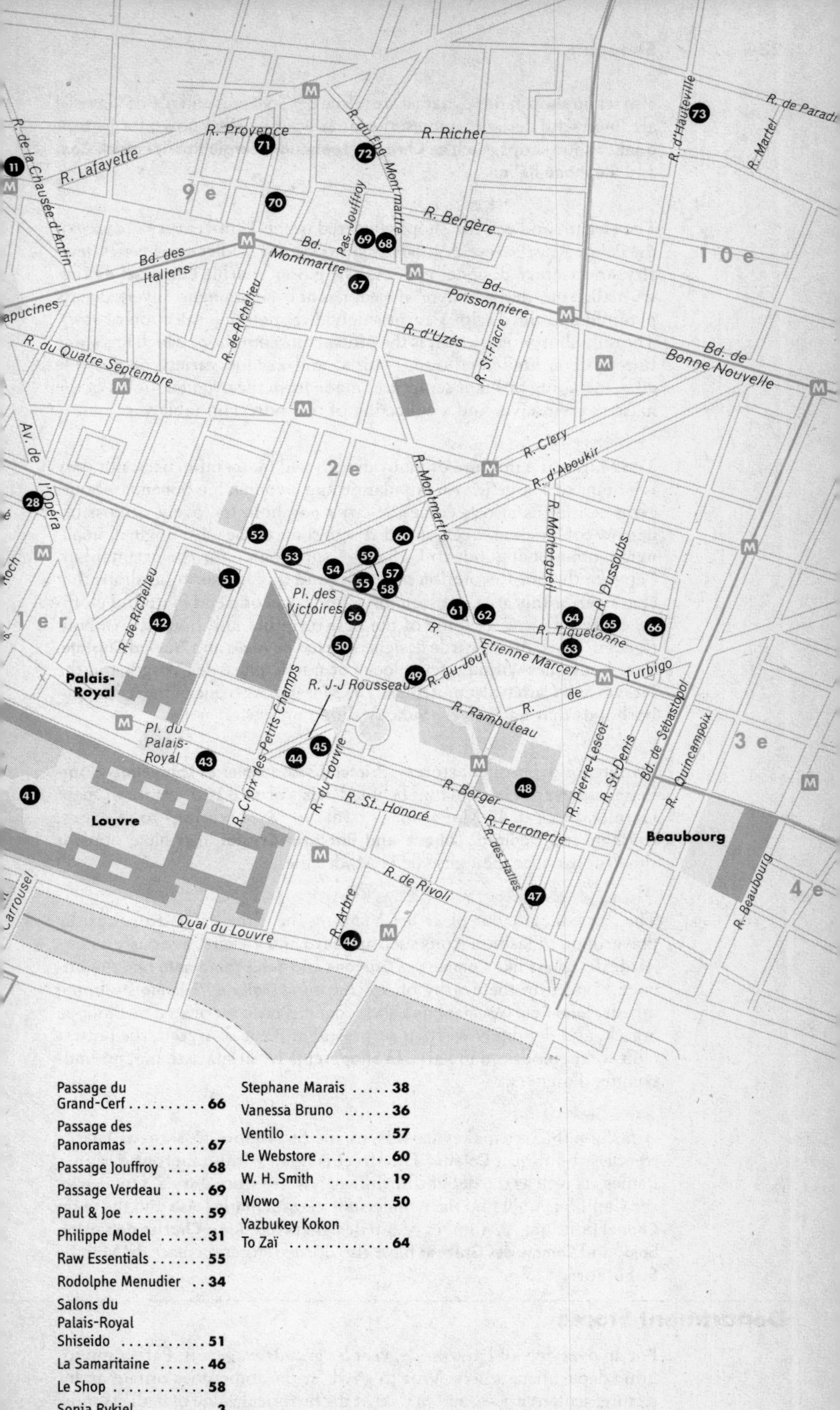

- Passage du Grand-Cerf 66
- Passage des Panoramas 67
- Passage Jouffroy 68
- Passage Verdeau 69
- Paul & Joe 59
- Philippe Model 31
- Raw Essentials 55
- Rodolphe Menudier . . 34
- Salons du Palais-Royal Shiseido 51
- La Samaritaine 46
- Le Shop 58
- Sonia Rykiel 3
- Stephane Marais 38
- Vanessa Bruno 36
- Ventilo 57
- Le Webstore 60
- W. H. Smith 19
- Wowo 50
- Yazbukey Kokon To Zaï 64

also set up shop in this dynamic area. Rue des Sts-Pères and rue de Grenelle are lined with designer names; the latter is especially known for its top-quality shoe shops, such as **Christian Louboutin, Sergio Rossi, Patrick Cox,** and **Stéphane Kélian.**

Louvre–Palais-Royal

The elegant and eclectic shops clustered in the 18th-century arcades of the Palais-Royal sell such goods as antiques, toy soldiers, cosmetics, jewelry, and vintage designer dresses. The glossy, marble **Carrousel du Louvre** mall, beneath the Louvre Museum, is lit by an immense inverted glass pyramid and filled with a surprisingly disappointing selection of *stuff*. The only shop worth a visit is the official museum shop, which has some fine posters, limited-edition T-shirts, and a wide variety of possible gifts, including brilliant sculptures made from the original molds of the masters themselves and a collection of fine porcelain tableware.

Le Marais

The Marais is a mixture of many moods and many influences; not only is it home to a large Jewish population and a young, hip bohemian-bourgeois set; it has also become the city's gay hub. Its lovely, impossibly narrow cobblestone streets are filled with some of the most original, small-name, nonglobal goods to be had—a sure source for the original gift. Between the pre-Revolution mansions and tiny kosher food shops that characterize this area are seemingly hundreds of trendy gift and clothing stores, as well as some of the best furniture and housewares boutiques in Paris. Avant-garde designers **Azzedine Alaïa** and **Tsumori Chistato,** have boutiques within a few blocks of stately place des Vosges and the Picasso and Carnavalet museums. The Marais is also one of the few neighborhoods that has a lively Sunday shopping scene.

Opéra to Madeleine

Two major department stores—**Printemps** and **Galeries Lafayette**—dominate boulevard Haussmann, behind Paris's ornate 19th-century Opéra Garnier. Place de la Madeleine is home to two luxurious food stores, **Fauchon** and **Hédiard. Lalique** and **Baccarat Crystal** also have opulent showrooms near the Église de la Madeleine.

Place des Victoires & Rue Étienne Marcel

The graceful, circular place des Victoires, near the Palais-Royal, is the playground of fashion icons such as **Kenzo** and **Victoire.** Seriously avant-garde designers like **Comme des Garçons** and **Yohji Yamamoto** line rue Étienne Marcel. In the nearby oh-so-charming **Galerie Vivienne** shopping arcade, **Jean-Paul Gaultier** has a shop that has been renovated by Philippe Starck, and definitely worth a stop. And at 3 rue d'Argout, the hottest club-wear emporium in Paris, **Le Shop,** rents retail space to hip, up-and-coming designers.

Rue St-Honoré

A fashionable set makes its way to rue St-Honoré to shop at Paris's trendiest boutique, **Colette.** The street is lined with numerous designer names, as well as the delightful vintage jewelry store **Dary's.** On nearby rue Cambon you'll find the wonderfully elegant **Maria Luisa** and the main **Chanel** boutique. A number of hip designers like **Jean-Charles de Castelbajac** and **Comme des Garçons** have also opened stores on place du Marché St-Honoré.

Department Stores

For an overview of Paris *mode,* visit *les grands magasins,* Paris's monolithic department stores. Visit to gawk at the sometimes ornate architecture, scoff at prices, and marvel at the historical value of it all, as some

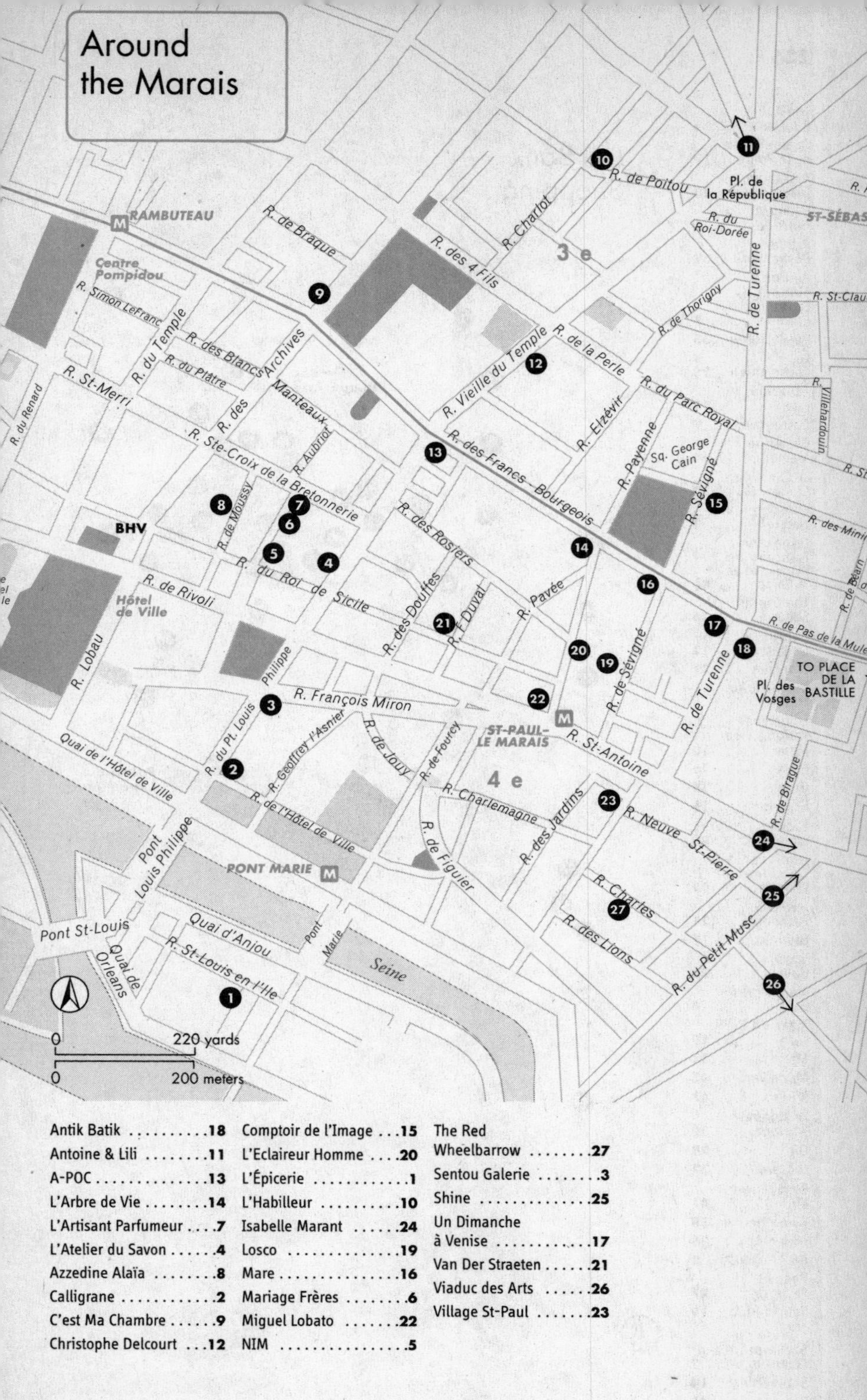

- Antik Batik **18**
- Antoine & Lili **11**
- A-POC **13**
- L'Arbre de Vie **14**
- L'Artisant Parfumeur **7**
- L'Atelier du Savon **4**
- Azzedine Alaïa **8**
- Calligrane **2**
- C'est Ma Chambre **9**
- Christophe Delcourt . . . **12**
- Comptoir de l'Image . . . **15**
- L'Eclaireur Homme **20**
- L'Épicerie **1**
- L'Habilleur **10**
- Isabelle Marant **24**
- Losco **19**
- Mare **16**
- Mariage Frères **6**
- Miguel Lobato **22**
- NIM **5**
- The Red Wheelbarrow **27**
- Sentou Galerie **3**
- Shine **25**
- Un Dimanche à Venise **17**
- Van Der Straeten **21**
- Viaduc des Arts **26**
- Village St-Paul **23**

The Abbey Bookstore 26
Agathe Ruize de la Prade . . .19
Alexandre Biaggi 23
L'Angelot par Gilles Neveu . .16
Arthus-Bertrand 39
Au Bon Marché/ La Grande Épicerie 7
Avant-Scène . .33
Le Cachemirien . .25
Capucine Puerari 13
Cassegrain 9
Catherine Memmi 34
La Chambre Claire 30
Christian Liaigre 3
Compagnie Française de l'Orient et de la Chine 40
The Conran Shop 6
Debauve & Gallais 11
Diptyque 29
Du Pareil Au Même 8
Editions de Parfums Frédéric Malle 10
FNAC 46
Guerlain 38
La Hune 15
Isabel Marant 20
Jean-Charles de Castelbajac Concept Store .42
Jewels & Pashminas . . .21
Ladurée 17
Lagerfeld Gallery 22
Madeleine Gely 4
Make Up By Terry 19
Marie Mercié .31
Marie Papier .43
Mi-Prix 47
Le Monde Sauvage 32
Ofr 28
Onward 37
Peggy Huynh Kinh 41
Pierre Hermé .18
Pom d'Api . . .36
R&Y Augousti . .5
Renaud Pellegrino 27
Sabbia Rosa . .12
7L 1
Shakespeare and Company 2
Sonia Rykiel . .14
Tati 45
Tea and Tattered Pages 44
Village Voice .35

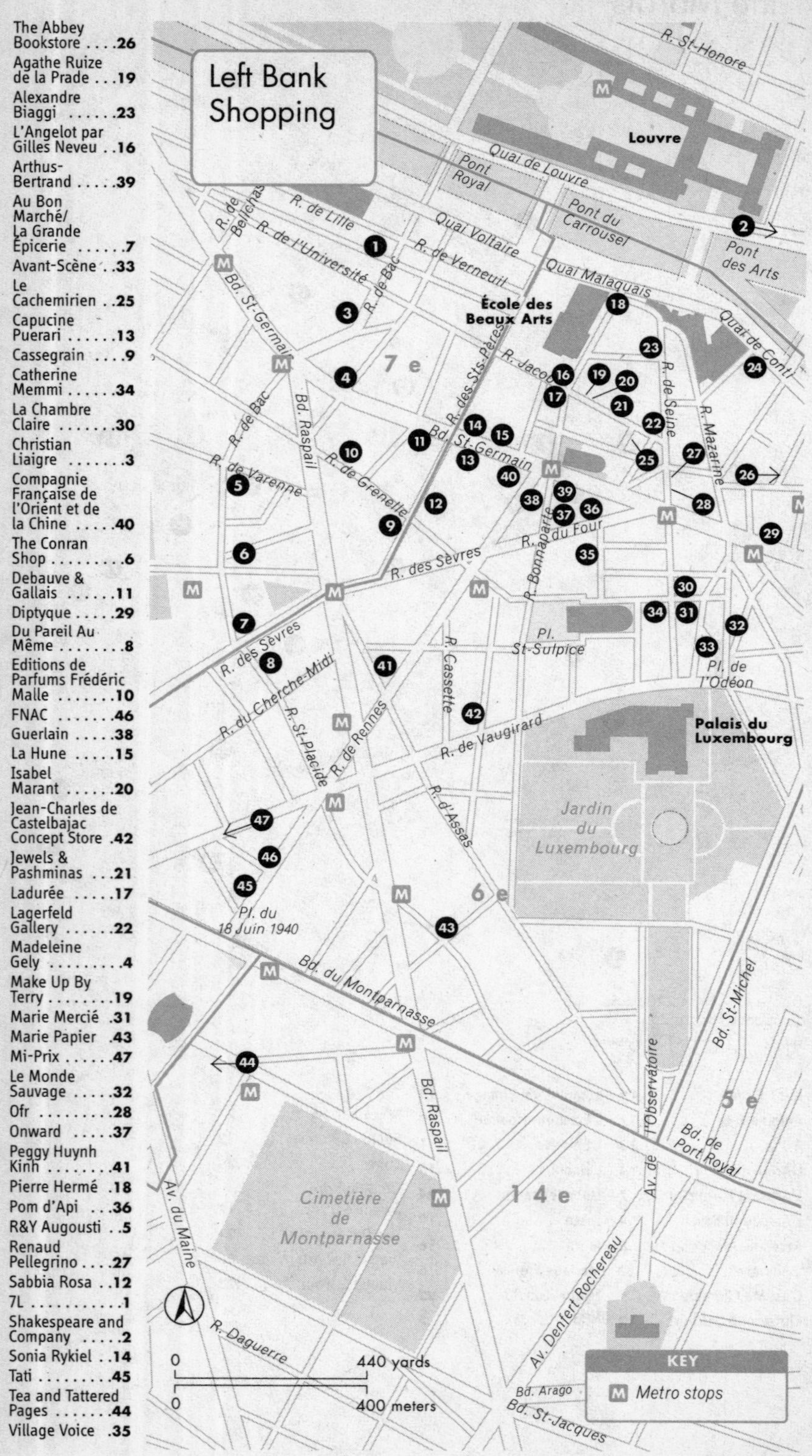

of these stores have been around since 1860. Most are open Monday through Saturday from about 9:30 AM to 7 PM, and some are open until 10 PM one weekday evening. All five major stores listed below have multilingual guides, international welcome desks, détaxe offices, and restaurants. Most are on the Right Bank, near the Opéra and the Hôtel de Ville; the notable exception is Au Bon Marché, on the Left Bank.

Fodor's Choice ★ **Au Bon Marché** (✉ 24 rue de Sèvres, 7e, St-Germain-des-Prés ☎ 01–44–39–80–00 Ⓜ Sèvres Babylone), founded in 1852, is an excellent hunting ground on the Left Bank for linens, table settings, and high-quality furniture. In the last few years it has undergone a complete face-lift and is now incontestably Paris's chicest department store, with an impressive array of designers represented for both men and women. You can find anything from inexpensive Comptoir du Coton to trendy Chloé to designer Balenciaga. La Grande Épicerie is one of the largest groceries in Paris and a gourmand's home away from home, and the basement is a great place for books, records, classy stationery, and arty gifts.

Au Printemps (✉ 64 bd. Haussmann, 9e, Opéra/Grands Boulevards ☎ 01–42–82–50–00 Ⓜ Havre Caumartin, Opéra, and RER: Auber) spent a whopping €30 million in revamping its three major stores: Printemps de la Maison (home furnishings), Printemps de l'Homme (menswear—six floors no less), and the brilliant Printemps de la Mode (fashion, fashion, fashion), which is cool, happening, and has everything from cutting-edge Helmut Lang to glitzy-gold Jeremy Scott, from the mid-range Zara line to the teenage Free. Fashion shows are held on Tuesday (all year) and Friday (April–October) at 10 AM under the cupola on the seventh floor of La Mode and are free. (Reservations can be made in advance by calling 01–42–82–63–17; tickets can also be obtained on the day of show at the service desk on the first floor.)

Bazar de l'Hôtel de Ville (✉ 52–64 rue de Rivoli, 4e, Beaubourg/Les Halles ☎ 01–42–74–90–00 Ⓜ Hôtel de Ville), better known as BHV, houses an enormous basement hardware store that sells everything from doorknobs to cement mixers and has to be seen to be believed. The fashion offerings are minimal, but BHV is noteworthy for quality household goods, home-decor materials, and office supplies.

Galeries Lafayette (✉ 40 bd. Haussmann, 9e, Opéra/Grands Boulevards ☎ 01–42–82–34–56 Ⓜ Chaussée d'Antin, Opéra, Havre Caumartin ✉ Centre Commercial Montparnasse, 14e, Montparnasse ☎ 01–45–38–52–87 Ⓜ Montparnasse Bienvenüe) is one of those places that you wander into unawares, leaving hours later a poorer and humbler person. It has everything (over 75,000 brand names). Along with the world's largest perfumery, the main store has the "Espace Lafayette Maison," a huge Yves Taralon–designed emporium dedicated to the art of living *à la française.* There is fashion for every style and then some. Free **fashion shows** (☎ 01–48–74–02–30 reservations) are held Wednesday at 11:30 AM and Friday (April–October) at 2:30 PM. Don't miss the delectable comestibles department, stocked with the best of everything from herbed goat cheese to Iranian caviar. The Montparnasse branch is a pale shadow of its sister store.

La Samaritaine (✉ 19 rue de la Monnaie, 1er, Louvre/Tuileries ☎ 01–40–41–20–20 Ⓜ Pont Neuf, Châtelet), a sprawling five-store complex, has everything from designer fashions to a free climbing wall, but is especially known for kitchen supplies, housewares, and furniture. Its most famous asset is the Toupary restaurant in Building 2, from which there's a marvelous view of Notre-Dame and the Left Bank.

Budget

Monoprix (✉ 21 av. de l'Opéra, 1er, Opéra/Grands Boulevards ☎ 01–42–61–78–08 Ⓜ Opéra ✉ 6 av. de la Plaine, 20e, Bastille/Nation

☎ 01–43–73–17–59 Ⓜ Nation ✉ 50 rue de Rennes, 6e, St-Germain-des-Prés ☎ 01–45–48–18–08 Ⓜ St-Germain-des-Prés), with branches throughout the city, is *the* French dime store par excellence, stocking everyday items like toothpaste, groceries, toys, typing paper, and bath mats—a little of everything. It also has a line of relatively inexpensive basic wearables for the whole family and is, on the whole, not a bad place to stock up on good wines and fine French liqueurs at a reasonable price.

Tati (✉ 2–28 bd. Rochechouart, 18e, Montmartre ☎ 01–55–29–50–00 Ⓜ Barbès Rochechouart) is one of Paris's most iconic stores. The ultimate haven for bargain-basement prices, it is certainly not for the faint-hearted or claustrophobic. On an average day it is jam-packed with people of all colors, classes, and sizes, rifling through the jumbled trays in search of a great buy, which they always succeed in finding, since the key word here is cheap, utterly, unabashedly cheap. One of its most famous scoops was to offer underwear for just €.15 a pair (they sell 5 million pairs a year). You can also get panty hose for €1 or a cotton T-shirt for €2. It is also well known for its pink-and-white Vichy shopping bags, ridiculously inexpensive bridal store, and chain of cheap jewelry shops, **Tati Or**.

Markets

Flea Markets

Fodor's Choice ★ The venerable **Le Marché aux Puces St-Ouen** (Ⓜ Porte de Clignancourt), also referred to as Clignancourt, on Paris's northern boundary, still attracts the crowds when it opens—Friday from 6 AM to 2 PM, Saturday from 7 AM to 5 PM, and Sunday and Monday from 10:30 AM to 6 PM—-but its once-unbeatable prices are now a relic of the past. This century-old labyrinth of alleyways packed with antiques dealers' booths and junk stalls spreads for more than a square mile. Arrive early to pick up the most worthwhile loot (like old prints). But be warned—if there's one place in Paris where you need to know how to bargain, this is it! For lunch, stop for mussels and fries in one of the rough-and-ready cafés.

On the southern and eastern sides of the city—at **Porte de Vanves** (Ⓜ Porte de Vanves) and Porte de Montreuil—are other, smaller flea markets. Vanves is a hit with the fashion set and specializes in smaller objects—mirrors, textiles, handbags, clothing, and glass. It's open on weekends only from 8 AM to 5 PM, but you have to arrive early if you want to find a bargain: the good stuff goes fast and stalls are liable to be packed up before noon.

Flower & Bird Markets

Paris's main flower market is in the heart of the city on the Ile de la Cité (Cité), between Notre-Dame and the Palais de Justice. It's open every day from 8 AM until 7:30 PM. On Sunday it also hosts to a bird market. Other colorful flower markets are held beside the Madeleine church (Madeleine, open Monday–Saturday 9 AM–9 PM and alternate Sundays 9:30 AM–8:30 PM), and on place des Ternes (Ternes, open Tuesday–Sunday).

Food Markets

Many of the better-known markets are in areas you'd visit for sightseeing–most are open from 8 AM to 1 PM three days a week (usually the weekend and one weekday) on a rotating basis—to get a list of market days in your area, ask your concierge. There are more than 84 markets in Paris—here is a list of the top bets: **Rue de Buci** (✉ 6e, St-Germain-des-Prés Ⓜ Odéon), in the chic and lively St-Germain-des-Prés quarter, is closed Sunday PM and Monday. **Rue Mouffetard** (✉ 5e, Latin Quarter Ⓜ Monge), near the Jardin des Plantes, is best on weekends. **Rue Mon-**

torgueil (✉ 1er, Beaubourg/Les Halles Ⓜ Châtelet Les Halles) is closed Monday. **Rue Lepic** (✉ 18e, Montmartre Ⓜ Blanche or Abbesses) is best on weekends. **Rue Lévis** (✉ 17e, Parc Monceau Ⓜ Villiers), near Parc Monceau, is closed Sunday PM and Monday. **Boulevard Richard Lenoir** (✉ 11e, Bastille/Nation Ⓜ Bastille). The **Marché d'Aligre** (✉ Rue d'Aligre, 12e, Bastille/Nation Ⓜ Ledru-Rollin), open until 1 PM every day except Monday, is a bit farther out but is the cheapest market in Paris; on weekends a small flea market is also held here.

Stamp Market

Philatelists (and fans of the Audrey Hepburn–Cary Grant 1963 thriller *Charade*) will want to head for Paris's unique **stamp market** (Ⓜ Champs-Élysées–Clemenceau) at the intersection of avenue Marigny and avenue Gabriel overlooking the gardens at the bottom of the Champs-Élysées. On sale are vintage postcards and stamps from all over the world. It is open Thursday, weekends, and public holidays from 10 AM until 5 PM.

Shopping Arcades

Paris's 19th-century commercial arcades, called *passages,* are the forerunners of the modern shopping mall. Glass roofs, decorative pillars, and inlaid mosaic floors make these spaces real architectural gems. In 1828 they numbered 137, of which only 24 are left. The major arcades are in the 1er and 2e arrondissements on the Right Bank.

Galerie Véro-Dodat (✉ 19 rue Jean-Jacques Rousseau, 1er, Louvre/Tuileries Ⓜ Louvre) was built in 1826. At what is now the Café de l'Epoque, the French writer Gérard de Nerval took his last drink before heading to Châtelet to hang himself. The gallery has painted ceilings and slender copper pillars, and shops selling old-fashioned toys, contemporary art, stringed instruments, and leather goods. It is best known, however, for its antiques stores.

Galerie Vivienne (✉ 4 rue des Petits-Champs, 2e, Opéra/Grands Boulevards Ⓜ Bourse), between the Stock Exchange (Bourse) and the Palais-Royal, is home base for a range of interesting and luxurious shops; a quite delicious tearoom, A Priori Thé; and Cave Legrand, a quality wine shop.

Passage du Grand-Cerf (✉ 145 rue St-Denis, 2e, Beaubourg/Les Halles Ⓜ Étienne Marcel) is now certainly the hippest of all of Paris's shopping arcades. Take a look at the design showroom, Haute Definition, at No. 4, check out the African objects and furniture at As'Art and the Zen-like furnishings at PM Style, or pop into the boutiques of milliner Jean-Louis Pinabel and jewelers Marie-Lise Goëlo, Eric & Lydie, and Didier Guillemin.

Passage Jouffroy (✉ 12 bd. Montmartre, 9e, Montmartre Ⓜ Montmartre) is full of shops selling toys, antique canes, Oriental furnishings, and cinema books and posters. Try Pain d'Épices at No. 29 and Au Bonheur des Dames at No. 39.

Passage des Panoramas (✉ 11 bd. Montmartre, 2e, Montmartre Ⓜ Métro: Opéra or Grands Boulevards), opened in 1800, is the oldest arcade; it's especially known for its stamp shops.

Passage Verdeau (✉ 4–6 rue de la Grange Batelière, 9e, Opéra/Grands Boulevards Ⓜ Montmartre) is across the street from passage Jouffroy and has shops carrying antique cameras, comic books, and engravings.

Specialty Shops

Arts & Antiques

Antiques dealers proliferate in the **Carré Rive Gauche** (✉ Between St-Germain-des-Prés and the Musée d'Orsay, 6e, St-Germain-des-Prés Ⓜ St-Germain-des-Prés, Rue du Bac)—head to the area around the rue de Bac, rue de l'Université, rue de Lille, and rue des Sts-Pères to find a cluster of more than 120 stylish shops. Several antiques dealers are around the **Drouot auction house** (✉ Corner of rue Rossini and rue Drouot, 9e, Opéra/Grands Boulevards Ⓜ Richelieu Drouot) near the Opéra. The **Louvre des Antiquaires** (✉ Pl. du Palais-Royal, 1er, Louvre/Tuileries Ⓜ Palais-Royal) is a stylish mall devoted primarily to antiques. The **Viaduc des Arts** (✉ 9–147 av. Daumesnil, 12e, Bastille/Nation Ⓜ Ledru-Rollin) houses dozens of art galleries, artisans' boutiques, and upscale shops under the arches of a stone viaduct that once supported train tracks. **Village St-Paul** (✉ Enter from rue St-Paul, 4e, Le Marais Ⓜ St-Paul) is a clutch of streets with many antiques shops.

Bags, Scarves & Accessories

Le Cachemirien (✉ 13 rue de Tournon, 6e, St-Germain-des-Prés ☎ 01–43–29–93–82 Ⓜ Odéon) is exclusively dedicated to the fabrics of the Kashmir region of India. Decorated with silk rugs and Anglo-Indian armchairs, the store is also flocked with exquisitely embroidered shawls, pashminas, scarves, and elegantly pared-down clothing made from materials like pashmina and silk.

E. Goyard (✉ 233 rue St-Honoré, 1er, Louvre/Tuileries ☎ 01–42–60–57–04 Ⓜ Tuileries) has been making the finest luggage since 1853. Clients in the past included Arthur Conan Doyle, Gregory Peck, and the Duke and Duchess of Windsor. Today Karl Lagerfeld and Madonna are both Goyard fans. Check out the house's signature chevron monogram, which can be found on everything from polo chests and hatboxes to suitcases and wallets.

★ **Hermès** (✉ 24 rue du Faubourg St-Honoré, 8e, Louvre/Tuileries ☎ 01–40–17–47–17 Ⓜ Concorde) was established as a saddlery in 1837, and went on to create the famous, eternally chic Kelly bag, for Grace Kelly. The magnificent silk scarves—truly fashion icons—are legendary for their rich colors and intricate designs, which change yearly (and men, don't overlook the sumptuous ties). The pared-down women's-wear collection is created by avant-garde Belgian designer Martin Margiela. Bags start at a mere €2,300. During semiannual sales, in January and July, prices are slashed by up to 50% and the crowds line up for blocks.

★ **Jamin Puech** (✉ 61 rue d'Hauteville, 10e, Opéra/Grands Boulevards ☎ 01–40–22–08–32 Ⓜ Poissonière) is where you'll find the entire collection of bags from this happening duo. What makes the bags of Benoit Jamin and Isabelle Puech so unique and desirable are the soft classic shapes and witty details. They do beaded bags in every shade of the rainbow with thin link chains, dark embossed leather bags with fringe, small evening bags in shell, or hand-dyed crochet numbers—all whimsical, unusual, and fun.

Losco (✉ 20 rue de Sévigné, 4e, Le Marais ☎ 01–48–04–39–93 Ⓜ St-Paul ✉ 5 rue de Sèvres, 6e, Latin Quarter ☎ 01–42–22–77–47 Ⓜ Sèvres Babylone) allows customers to design their own high-quality, reasonably priced belts by mixing and matching buckles and straps.

Louis Vuitton (✉ 101 av. des Champs-Elysées, 8e, Champs-Elysées ☎ 01–53–27–24–00 Ⓜ George V ✉ 6 pl. St-Germain-des-Prés, 6e, St-Germain-des-Prés ☎ 01–45–49–62–32 Ⓜ St-Germain-des-Prés) is one of the most recognizable names in luxury luggage and handbags. In addition to its signature line of brown and tan initial bags, there are now sophisticated women's shoes and clothing, and bright, modern, child-like takes on their classic handbags.

Madeleine Gely (✉ 218 bd. St-Germain, 7e, St-Germain-des-Prés ☎ 01–42–22–63–35 Ⓜ Rue du Bac) is the queen of walking sticks. Late president François Mitterrand used to buy his at this tiny shop also filled with an amazing range of umbrellas.

Miguel Lobato (✉ 6 rue Malher, 4e, Le Marais ☎ 01–48–87–68–14 Ⓜ St-Paul) is a sweet little boutique filled with stylish accessories for the girl who wants it all: beautiful avant-garde shoes by Rodolphe Menudier, Bruno Frisoni, and Alain Tondowski; bags and nifty little coin purses by Jamin Puech; mod belts by Paris 75000; and beaded bracelets by Azuni. Most thankfully, the charming Miquel is on hand to help you sort it all out.

Peggy Huynh Kinh (✉ 11 rue Coëtlogon, 6e, Latin Quarter ☎ 01–42–84–83–82 Ⓜ St-Sulpice), a former architect who made her name designing accessories for the prestigious Parisian houses of Balmain and Celine, is now behind the structural line of bags at Cartier. In this boutique she presents her own line of accessories; chicly pared-down totes, shoulder bags, wallets, and belts in quality leather, as well as a line of office accessories.

Renaud Pellegrino (✉78 rue de Seine, 6e, Latin Quarter ☎01–43–54–62–25 Ⓜ Odéon) sells his creations under his own name in this discreet boutique at the back of a courtyard. Inspiration for his shoulder bags and totes comes from artists like Matisse and Braque; fans include Catherine Deneuve and model Laetitia Casta. Recently, Pellegrino has also successfully turned his hand to shoes.

DISCOUNT **Accessoires à Soie** (✉ 21 rue des Acacias, 17e, Champs-Élysées ☎ 01–42–27–78–77 Ⓜ Argentine) is where savvy Parisians buy superb silk scarves and ties in all shapes and sizes. The wide selection includes many big-name designers, and everything costs about half of what you'd pay elsewhere.

Books (English-Language)

The scenic open-air *bouquinistes* bookstalls along the Seine sell secondhand books (mostly in French), prints, and souvenirs. Numerous French-language bookshops—specializing in a wide range of topics including art, film, literature, and philosophy—are found in the scholarly Latin Quarter and the publishing district, St-Germain-des-Prés. For English-language books and magazines, try the following.

The Abbey Bookstore (✉ 29 rue Parcheminerie, 5e, Latin Quarter ☎ 01–46–33–16–24 Ⓜ Cluny La Sorbonne) is Paris's Canadian bookstore. It sells Canadian newspapers (*La Presse* and the *Toronto Globe & Mail*), books on Canadian history, as well as new and secondhand Québecois and English-language novels. The Canadian Club of Paris also organizes regular poetry readings and literary conferences here.

Brentano's (✉ 37 av. de l'Opéra, 2e, Opéra/Grands Boulevards ☎ 01–42–61–52–50 Ⓜ Opéra) is stocked with everything from classics to children's titles. It also has a slightly haphazardly arranged international magazine section.

La Chambre Claire (✉ 14 rue St-Sulpice, 6e, Latin Quarter ☎ 01–46–34–04–31 Ⓜ Odéon) is chock-a-block with photography books by everyone from Edward Weston to William Wegman. It even stocks instruction manuals and is a favorite with fashion folk, including designer Martine Sitbon.

Comptoir de l'Image (✉ 44 rue de Sévigné, 3e, Le Marais ☎ 01–42–72–03–92 Ⓜ St-Paul) is where designers John Galliano, Marc Jacobs, and Emanuel Ungaro stock up on old copies of *Vogue, Harper's Bazaar,* and *The Face*. It also sells trendy magazines like *Dutch, Purple,* and *Spoon,* designer catalogs from the past, and rare photo books.

Galignani (✉ 224 rue de Rivoli, 1er, Louvre/Tuileries ☎ 01–42–60–76–07 Ⓜ Tuileries) stocks both French- and English-language books and is especially known for its extensive shelves filled with art books and coffee-table tomes.

★ **La Hune** (✉ 170 bd. St-Germain, 6e, St-Germain-des-Prés ☎ 01–45–48–35–85 Ⓜ St-Germain-des-Prés), sandwiched between the Café de Flore and Les Deux Magots, is a landmark for intellectuals. French literature is downstairs, but the main attraction is the comprehensive collection of international books on art and architecture upstairs. Stay here until midnight with all the other genius-insomniacs.

Ofr (✉ 30 rue Beaurepaire, 10e, République ☎ 01–42–45–72–88 Ⓜ République) gets magazines from the most fashionable spots in the world before anyone else. In this messy store you can rub shoulders with photo and press agents and check out the latest in underground, art, and alternative monthlies.

The Red Wheelbarrow (✉ 13 rue Charles, 4e, Le Marais ☎ 01–42–77–42–17 Ⓜ St-Paul) is *the* anglophone bookstore—if it was written in English, they can get it. It also has a complete academic section and every literary review you can think of. Ask owner Penelope for gift ideas—she has a wonderful collection of special-edition historical reads. At least once a month there are readings in English with local artists and visiting authors.

7L (✉ 7 rue de Lille, 7e, St-Germain-des-Prés ☎ 01–42–92–03–58 Ⓜ St-Germain -des-Prés) is a rather minimalist space owned by the book-addicted Karl Lagerfeld. The fashion designer has a personal library of more than 240,000 volumes, and in this store he chooses to display and sell a selection of his favorite new releases, as well as the books he edits himself.

Shakespeare and Company (✉ 37 rue de la Bûcherie, 5e, Latin Quarter ☎ 01–43–26–96–50 Ⓜ St-Michel), the sentimental Left Bank favorite, is named after the publishing house that first edited James Joyce's *Ulysses*. Nowadays it specializes in expatriate literature. The staff tends to be rather pretentious, but the shelves of secondhand books hold real bargains. Poets give readings upstairs on Monday at 8 PM; there are also tea-party talks on Sunday at 4 PM.

Tea & Tattered Pages (✉ 24 rue Mayet, 6e, St-Germain-des-Prés ☎ 01–40–65–94–35 Ⓜ Duroc) sells cheap secondhand paperbacks, plus new books (publishers' overstock) at low prices. Tea and brownies are served, and browsing is encouraged.

Village Voice (✉6 rue Princesse, 6e, St-Germain-des-Prés ☎01–46–33–36–47 Ⓜ Mabillon), known for its selection of contemporary authors, hosts regular literary readings.

W. H. Smith (✉248 rue de Rivoli, 1er, Louvre/Tuileries ☎01–44–77–88–99 Ⓜ Concorde) carries a multitude of travel and language books, cookbooks, and fiction for adults and children. It also has the best selection of foreign magazines and newspapers in Paris (which you are allowed peruse without interruption—many magazine dealers in France aren't so kind).

Clothing (Children's)

Almost all the top designers make minicouture, but you can expect to pay unearthly prices for each wee outfit. Following is where mere mortal Parisian parents shop to keep their kids looking chic.

L'Angelot par Gilles Neveu (✉28 rue Bonaparte, 6e, St-Germain-des-Prés ☎ 01–56–24–21–22 Ⓜ St-Germain-des-Prés) has everything the newborn to one-year-old baby could desire: clothes in white and beige, bed linen, cuddly teddy bears and rabbits, and jewelry in solid gold. Personalized embroideries and engravings are available upon request, as are deliveries to foreign destinations.

★ **Bonpoint** (✉ 64 av. Raymond Poincaré, 16e, Eiffel Tower/Trocadéro ☎ 01–47–27–60–81 Ⓜ Trocadéro ✉ 229 bd. St-Germain, 7e, St-Germain-des-Prés ☎ 01–40–26–76–20 Ⓜ Rue du Bac) is for the prince or princess in your life (as it is, royalty *does* shop here). Yes, the prices are high, but the quality is truly exceptional—the clothing lasts generations and you can't say that very often nowadays. The style ranges from sturdy play clothes—think a weekend at the chateau—to the perfect pink dress lined in black silk with tiny rosebuds hand sewn across the bodice or a midnight-blue velvet suit for Little Lord Fauntleroy. Don't even think about just browsing through the collection for newborns—it's irresistible.

Du Pareil Au Même (✉ 15 and 23 rue des Mathurins, 8e, Opéra/Grands Boulevards ☎ 01–42–66–93–80 Ⓜ Havre Caumartin ✉ 14 rue St-Placide, 6e, St-Germain-des-Prés ☎ 01–45–44–04–40 Ⓜ St-Placide) is *the* address for French children from toddlers to preteens. Clothes have a decided French twist, with strict attention to details: Peter Pan collars, wool coats with velvet insets, and white shirts embroidered with sweet things.

Not So Big (✉ 38 rue Tiquetonne, 1er, Beaubourg/Les Halles ☎ 01–42–33–34–26 Ⓜ Étienne Marcel) has a great selection of original clothes, toys, and accessories for both children and mom. Favorites include a line of fun T-shirts, funky winter coats, fur caps, sweet slippers, and the Mexican bola, a sterling silver necklace made for pregnant women that falls low on the belly and is said to sing the baby to sleep.

Petit Bateau (✉ 116 av. des Champs-Élysées, 8e, Champs-Élysées ☎ 01–40–74–02–03 Ⓜ George V ✉ 81 rue Sèvres, 6e, St-Germain-des-Prés ☎ 01–45–49–48–38 Ⓜ Sèvres Babylone) completes a fundamental part of the classic French wardrobe from cradle to teen and beyond (the fashion set are wild about the perfectly cut T-shirts they wear under their vintage Chanel). The clothes are made of high-grade cotton cut in classic designs that haven't changed in decades—onesies and pajamas for the newborn, T-shirts for every season in every color, leggings, sweet underwear sets, dresses with tiny straps for summer. Stock up while you're here—if you can find this French classic back home, the prices are sure to be high.

Pom d'Api (✉28 rue du Four, 6e, St-Germain-des-Prés ☎01–45–48–39–31 Ⓜ St-Germain-des-Prés) stocks medium to pricey footwear for babies and preteens in quality leathers and wonderfully vivid colors. Expect well-made, eye-catching fashion—bright gold sneakers, sandals with feathers and beads, and fringed suede boots as well as the classic Mary Janes in shades of silver, pink, and gold. There are also standard utility boots for boys and sturdy rain gear.

Wowo (✉ 4 rue Hérold, 1er, Beaubourg/Les Halles ☎ 01–53–40–84–80 Ⓜ Châtelet Les Halles) is an original line of well-made clothes for children from three months to the preteen. Designer Elizabeth Relin blends her fashion sensibility and love of color with her respect for the world of childhood—no baby Spice Girls here. The clothes are high quality, wearable, and fun.

Clothing (Discount)

L'Habilleur (✉ 44 rue Poitou, 3e, Le Marais ☎ 01–48–87–77–12 Ⓜ St-Sébastien Froissart) is a favorite with the fashion press and anyone else looking for a great deal. For women there's a great selection from designers like Prada, Barbara Bui, and Martine Sitbon. Men can find suits from Mugler, Strelli, and Paul Smith at slashed prices.

Rue d'Alésia (Ⓜ Alésia), in the 14e arrondissement, is the main place to find shops selling last season's fashions at a discount. Be forewarned: most of these shops are much more downscale than their elegant sister shops, and dressing rooms are not always provided.

CloseUp

BARGAIN HUNTING

THERE ARE A NUMBER OF BOUTIQUES *that specialize in bargains and are every savvy Parisian's secret for maintaining incredible style without breaking the bank.* Soldéries *offer stacks of low-priced designer labels permanently on sale, while* stocks *are stores that specialize in one label and sell last season's leftovers with prices slashed at least in half.* Dépôts-Vente *are consignment shops that carry barely worn designer outfits in great condition at killer prices. Fashionable* friperies *stock clothes and accessories from the '50s to the '80s and are a constant inspiration to the international design teams that come to Paris during the collections.* Surplus *sell army surplus jackets, pants, and great lace-up boots for nearly nothing. Watch for the word* soldes *(sales). By law, the two main sale seasons are January and July, when the average discount is 30%–50% off regular prices. Sales last six weeks. Also look for goods marked* dégriffé*—designer labels, often from last year's collection, for sale at a deep discount.*

In addition, there are the delightful flea markets and brocantes *(secondhand shops) where you'll always have the chance of finding a stray bit of Quimper faiënce, Art Deco brooches, or evocative old copies of* Paris-Match*. At such markets, or in antiques stores, bargaining is accepted. So if you're thinking of buying several articles, you've nothing to lose by cheerfully suggesting to the proprietor, "*Vous me faites un prix?*" ("How about a discount?"). Other bits of lingo to keep in mind:* braderie *or* fin de série *(clearance);* occasions *or* brocante *(secondhand); and* nouveautés *(new arrivals).*

Clothing (Men's)

Agnés b. Homme (✉ 25 av. Pierre 1er de Serbie, 16e, Eiffel Tower/Trocadéro ☎ 01–47–23–36–69 Ⓜ Iéna ✉ 3 rue de Jour, 1er, Beaubourg/Les Halles ☎ 01–42–33–04–13 Ⓜ Châtelet Les Halles) is famed for her modern easy pieces for men. Those elegant, slouchy, cigarette-smoking, scarf-clad men you see on the streets in boxy velour or corduroy suits with the square pockets in shades of gray and black? Agnés b.

Charvet (✉ 28 pl. Vendôme, 1er, Opéra/Grands Boulevards ☎ 01–42–60–30–70 Ⓜ Opéra) is the Parisian equivalent of a Savile Row tailor: a conservative, aristocratic institution famed for made-to-measure shirts, exquisite ties, and accessories, for garbing John F. Kennedy, Charles de Gaulle, and the Duke of Windsor, and for its regal address.

L'Eclaireur (✉ 12 rue Mahler, 4e, Le Marais ☎ 01–44–54–22–11 Ⓜ St-Paul) has opened this loft-style menswear store, just a stone's throw from its flagship store on rue des Rosiers. At the front of the boutique is a counter selling Diptyque candles and scents; at the back are fashions by designers like Jil Sander, Helmut Lang, and Dirk Schönberger.

Le Printemps de L'Homme (✉ Au Printemps department store, 61 rue Caumartin, 9e, Opéra/Grands Boulevards ☎ 01–42–82–50–00 Ⓜ Havre Caumartin, Opéra) is Paris's menswear fashion leader: six floors of suits, sportswear, coats, ties, and accessories in all price ranges. The funkiest designers, such as Paul Smith, Comme des Garçons, and Martin Margiela, can be found on the third floor, more classic labels like Christian Dior and Burberry on the sixth floor. Make sure you check out the megacool Helmut Lang corner, as well as the rocking World Bar, whose walls are covered with newspapers from around the globe.

Clothing (Resale)

★ **Anouschka** (✉6 av. Coq, 9e, Opéra/Grands Boulevards ☎01–48–74–37–00 Ⓜ St-Lazare, Trinité) has set up shop in her apartment (open Monday noon–7; Saturday by appointment) and has rack upon rack of vintage clothing dating from the '30s to the '70s. It is the perfect place to find a '50s cocktail dress in perfect condition or a mod jacket for him. A former model herself, she calls it a "designer laboratory," and teams from top fashion houses often pop by looking for inspiration.

Catherine Baril (✉ 14 rue de la Tour, 16e, Eiffel Tower/Trocadéro ☎ 01–45–20–95–21 Ⓜ Passy) specializes in barely worn designer ready-to-wear from all the big names including Chanel, Saint Laurent, Lacroix, Ungaro, and Rykiel. Few shoppers can pass up one of last season's outfits at one-third the price, or forget to linger over the vast selection of accessories: bags, belts, scarves, shoes, and costume jewelry.

★ **Didier Ludot** (✉ Jardins du Palais-Royal, 20 Galerie Montpensier, 1er, Louvre/Tuileries ✉ 24 Galerie Montpensier, 1er, Louvre/Tuileries ✉ 125 galérie de Valois, 1er, Louvre/Tuileries ☎ 01–42–96–06–56 Ⓜ Palais-Royal) is one of the world's most famous vintage clothing dealers and an incredibly charming man to boot. His clientele ranges from model Stephanie Seymour to fashion designer Azzedine Alaïa. Check out the French couture from the '20s to the '70s on the racks: wonderful old Chanel suits, Balenciaga dresses, and Hermès scarves. He has three boutiques: No. 20 houses his amazing collection of vintage couture, No. 24 his collection of ready-to-wear, and across the way at No. 125 you'll find his collection of vintage black dresses and his coffee-table book aptly titled *The Little Black Dress*.

Guerrisold (✉17 bis bd. Rochechouart, 9e, Montmartre ☎01–42–80–66–18 Ⓜ Barbès Rochechouart) is for that sturdy race of shoppers willing to sift through rack upon rack of cheap (often musty) clothing from the 1970s and 1980s to find that heart-stopping treasure, made even more precious by the fact that it will probably cost a mere €10.

★ **Kiliwatch** (✉ 64 rue Tiquetonne, 2e, Beaubourg/Les Halles ☎ 01–42–21–17–37 Ⓜ Étienne Marcel) is a large concrete cavern that houses one of Paris's hottest places to shop. Everyone comes here: designers, models, journalists, musicians, funky Parisians, and anyone else who loves to shop for stylish vintage pieces, here renovated, dry-cleaned, and slapped with a fairly high price tag. More affordable and fun are the racks upon racks of secondhand finds called "fripes" that are organized according to color and style to ease the immensity of the task of sifting through each and every item (as most of the shop's fans do).

Réciproque (✉ 88, 89, 92, 95, 101, and 123 rue de la Pompe, 16e, Eiffel Tower/Trocadéro ☎ 01–47–04–30–28 Ⓜ Rue de la Pompe) is Paris's largest and most exclusive swap shop. Savings on designer wear—Hermès, Dior, Chanel, and Louis Vuitton—are significant, but prices are not as cheap as you might expect, and there's not much in the way of service or space. The shop at No. 89 specializes in leather goods. The store is closed Sunday and Monday.

Scarlett (✉ 10 rue Clément-Marot, 8e, Eiffel Tower/Trocadéro ☎ 01–56–89–03–00 Ⓜ Alma-Marceau) offers exceptional vintage couture by the likes of Givenchy, Poiret, Schiaparelli, and Vionnet.

Clothing (Women's)

CHIC & CASUAL **Celine** (✉ 36 av. Montaigne, 8e, Champs-Élysées ☎ 01–56–89–07–91 Ⓜ Franklin-D.-Roosevelt) was venerable and dusty before designer Michael Kors showed up with his version of Jackie Oh—"the Greek magnate years." Slim-fitting white jeans, wide-ribbed cashmere sweaters, skintight T-shirts in Saint-Tropez stripes, and other Park Avenue must-haves have put this king of casual elegance on the map.

Et Vous (✉ 6 rue des Francs-Bourgeois, 3e, Le Marais ☎ 01–42–71–75–11 Ⓜ St-Paul) takes its cue from the catwalk; turning out affordable, extremely well-cut clothing: pants (low waist/slim hip), knee-skimming skirts, chunky sweaters, and classic work wear with individual details.

★ **Marni** (✉ 57 av. Montaigne, 8e, Champs-Élysées ☎ 01–56–88–08–08 Ⓜ Franklin-D.-Roosevelt) is the address par excellence for the girl in the know—those sparkly bolero jackets Sarah Jessica Parker is wearing? *Marni.* It's an Italian label with the coolest take on boho chic ever—wonderful mixtures of texture and retro design with an ethnic twist and a collection of the most copied accessories for every season.

Fodor's Choice ★ **Vanessa Bruno** (✉ 12 rue de Castiglione, 1er, Louvre/Tuileries ☎ 01–42–61–44–60 Ⓜ Pyramides ✉ 25 rue St-Sulpice, 6e, Latin Quarter ☎ 01–43–54–41–04 Ⓜ Odéon) is home to one of the best-selling, most accessible collections in recent years. This is where you can pick up one of those large canvas bags with the sparkles and the patchwork boots everyone seems to be wearing. The clothes are well cut, feminine, and very, very pretty—a high-collared Victorian blouse in dusty pink, a low-on-the-hip skirt, a great cape with tassels . . . and they won't break your bank.

Ventilo (✉ 27 bis rue du Louvre, 2e, Louvre/Tuileries ☎ 01–44–76–83–00 Ⓜ Louvre) brings cool ethnic style to the classy city girl. Who else would need a bright-orange silk shantung ball skirt with mirror appliqué or a modern Mongol leather coat lined in fur? There is also room for classics to mix and match, such as handmade wool turtlenecks and zippered riding pants that fit perfectly.

Zara (✉ 44 av. des Champs-Élysées, 8e, Champs-Élysées ☎ 01–45–61–52–80 Ⓜ Franklin-D.-Roosevelt ✉ 109 rue St-Lazare, 9e, Opéra/Grands Boulevards ☎ 01–53–32–82–95 Ⓜ St-Lazare) is hyped as the most reasonable place to go for the latest trends. While they do have everything copied and on the racks in record time, the prices aren't as low as one would expect for this type of quality. Choose wisely: check the seams, feel the fabric, and whatever you do, try it on before deciding if it's worth the investment. Oh, and don't worry—it's *not* you; the tops are cut small, the pants smaller.

CLASSIC CHIC

No matter, say the French, that fewer and fewer of their top couture houses are still headed by compatriots. It's the chic elegance, the classic ambience, the *je ne sais quoi,* that remains undeniably Gallic. Most of the high-fashion shops are on avenue Montaigne, avenue George-V, and rue du Faubourg St-Honoré on the Right Bank, though St-Germain-des-Prés has also become a stomping ground for renowned designers. Following are just a few of Paris's haute couture highlights.

★ **Chanel** (✉ 42 av. Montaigne, 8e, Champs-Élysées ☎ 01–47–23–74–12 Ⓜ Franklin-D.-Roosevelt ✉ 31 rue Cambon, 1er, Louvre/Tuileries ☎ 01–42–86–28–00 Ⓜ Tuileries) is helmed by a newly svelte Karl Lagerfeld, who lost more than 80 pounds in a year and is now so skinny his ears look fleshy. Collections at Chanel have followed Karl's descent into skeleton: dresses and jackets have that tiny schoolgirl arm and skirts caress pencil-thin legs. The historic center is at the rue Cambon and is the best place to visit to get the full Chanel effect. Great investments include all of Coco's favorites—one perfect navy-blue suit with the signature white piping, a quilted bag with the gold chain, or you can indulge in one small guiltless pleasure—the always fashionable camellia brooch in your favorite color.

Christian Dior (✉ 30 av. Montaigne, 8e, Champs-Élysées ☎ 01–40–73–54–44 Ⓜ Franklin-D.-Roosevelt) installed flamboyant John Galliano as head designer after his triumphant run at Givenchy and, since then, nothing but nothing has been the same. His catwalks are always the most talked-about *evenements* (events) of the fashion season: opulent, crazy shows with sheer evening gowns grazing the floor outfitted on a new species of Amazonian nomad, hundreds of floating butterflies, bottles of iced champagne, and some of the most beautiful women in the world in attendance (not to mention the men). Despite the theatrical staging and surreal hijinks, his full-length body-skimming evening dresses cut on the bias are brilliantly beautiful in whatever fabric he chooses . . . so what if he pairs them with high-tops and a Davy Crockett raccoon hat? It's just fashion, darling.

Fodor'sChoice ★ **Jean-Paul Gaultier** (✉ 44 av. George V, 8e, Champs-Élysées ☎ 01–44–43–00–44 Ⓜ George V ✉ 6 Galerie Vivienne, 2e, Opéra/Grands Boulevards ☎ 01–42–86–05–05 Ⓜ Bourse) first made headlines with his celebrated corset with the ironic i-conic breasts for Madonna, but now sends fashion editors into ecstasy with his supersumptuous haute couture creations. This past year Jean-Paul moved up in the world, leaving street-smart Bastille for haute George V, where designer Philippe Starck created an *Alice in Wonderland* fantasy. There you'll find quilted cream walls, Murano mirrors, and a giant perfume bottle for that just-fell-down-the-hatch feel. Make no mistake though, it's all about the clothes, dazzling creations considered to be among the finest in France, that make Gaultier a must-see.

Sonia Rykiel (✉ 175 bd. St-Germain, 6e, St-Germain-des-Prés ☎ 01–49–54–60–60 Ⓜ St-Germain-des-Prés ✉ 70 rue du Faubourg St-Honoré, 8e, Louvre/Tuileries ☎ 01–42–65–20–81 Ⓜ Concorde) has been designing fabulous knitwear since the '60s, and is a French icon in her own right. Her velvet ensembles, sexy keyhole sweaters, and hot accessories line maintain her incredible popularity. Her line of bags—huge leather satchels with battered copper coins for example—are always a good buy; but if you're looking for a simple little gift, pick up a green-leather sequinned flower for the perfect chignon or a bottle of the house fragrance *Rose*.

Ungaro (✉ 2 av. Montaigne, 8e, Champs-Élysées ☎ 01–53–57–00–00 Ⓜ Alma-Marceau) is the master of the sexy diva look with his floor-length fluid dresses in sheer florals and his famed draped mousseline cocktail dresses that skim the knee in shades of butterfly. His dresses grace the most beautiful women in the world (Sharen Stone, Jennifer Lopez, Sophie Marceau). Check out his line of boho-chic accessories.

TRENDSETTERS **Antik Batik** (✉ 18 rue de Turenne, 4e, Le Marais ☎ 01–48–87–95–95 Ⓜ St-Paul ✉ 8 rue de Foin, 4e, Le Marais ☎ 01–40–29–49–93 Ⓜ St-Paul) has a wonderful line of ethnically inspired clothes popular with models and other hip Parisians. There are row upon row of embroidered velvet dress coats, Chinese silk tunics, short fur jackets, fringed printed shawls, and some of Paris's most popular handbags. Children have their own boutique around the corner on the rue de Foin.

Antoine & Lili (✉ 95 quai de Valmy, 10e, République ☎ 01–40–37–41–55 Ⓜ Jacques-Bonsergent) is a bright fuchsia store packed with eclectic objects from the East and its own line of clothing. The fantasy seems to work for the French because these boutiques are always hopping. There is an ethnic rummage-sale feel, with old Asian posters, small lanterns, and basket upon basket of cheap little doodads, baubles, and trinkets for sale. Oddly, the clothing is on the austere side.

A-POC (✉ 47 rue des Francs-Bourgeois, 4e, Le Marais ☎ 01–44–54–07–05 Ⓜ St-Paul) stands for "A Piece of Cloth" (also a play on the word "epoch") and is Japanese designer Issey Miyake's latest adventure. The concept is the intellectual side of avant garde; a fabrication technique that allows for hundreds of clothes to be cut from one piece of tubular cloth, resulting in an incredibly interesting line of clothing that you can customize at will. Miyake has an almost religious following and, contrary to first impressions, his clothes are eminently stylish and wearable. There are even adorable styles for children.

Azzedine Alaïa (✉ 7 rue de Moussy, 4e, Le Marais ☎ 01–42–72–19–19 Ⓜ Hôtel de Ville) is one of the darlings of the fashion set with his perfectly proportioned "king of cling" dresses. You don't have to be under 20 to look good in one of his dresses; Tina Turner wears his clothes well as does every other beautiful woman with the courage and the curves. His boutique/workshop/apartment is covered with artwork by Julian Schnabel and is not the kind of place you casually wander into out of curiosity; the sales staff immediately makes you feel awkward in that distinctive Parisian way.

Beauty by Et Vous (✉25 rue Royale, 8e, Louvre/Tuileries ☎01–55–25–30–30 Ⓜ Madeleine) is a concept store filled with exclusive one-of-a-kind creations from the best of the newest young designers, a beauty counter for both men and women with helpful friendly service, the ubiquitous video installation no one pays attention to, wonderful clothes from Et Vous' less expensive diffusion line *EV,* and a whole floor devoted to menswear featuring Mandarina Duck and Trace.

★ **Colette** (✉ 213 rue St-Honoré, 1er, Louvre/Tuileries ☎ 01–55–35–33–90 Ⓜ Tuileries) is the address for fashion par excellence, and because it is the address for fashion par excellence it's also the least consumer-friendly. But who cares! There are ultramodern trinkets and trifles of all kinds; perfumes, world-famous cosmetics, creams, and potions of all sorts, including Aesop, Kiehls, and François Nars; plus Marie-Hélène de Taillac's jewelry "bar" . . . and that's just the ground floor. The first floor has beautiful clothing from every internationally known and unknown designer (clothes, shoes, and accessories) that oozes trendiness and street cred, and a small library for the ultramod hipster in the know. The basement has a water bar (because that's what the models eat) and a small restaurant that's actually quite good for a quick bite.

E2 (✉ 2 rue de Provence, 9e, Opéra/Grands Boulevards ☎01–47–70–15–14 Ⓜ Grands Boulevards) houses, by appointment only, three lines created by designers Michèle and Olivier Chatenet: their own label of ethnic-influenced fashion inspired by the '30s to the '70s; impeccable vintage couture finds like Pucci, Lanvin, and Hermès; plus clothing created with their own special method of customizing fashion (they take tired fashion and cut it up or sew it into a whole new outfit; for example, sewing emerald-green sequins into the pleats of an ordinary gray kilt). With one of these creations in tow you will be dressed like no one else, as fashion friends Madonna and Gwyneth would tell you (if you were their fashion friend).

L'Eclaireur (✉ 3 rue des Rosiers, 4e, Le Marais ☎ 01–48–87–10–22 Ⓜ St-Paul) has been on the cutting edge of fashion for years and stocks avant-garde favorites such as Martin Margiela, Anne Demeulemeester, and Carpe Diem, plus a taste of most other ready-to-wear icons like Prada and Dolce & Gabbana.

Eric Bergère (✉ 16 rue de la Sourdière, 1er, Louvre/Tuileries ☎ 01–47–03–33–19 Ⓜ Tuileries) is a rare species in Paris these days: a *French* designer. Not only that, he's one of the best. His clothes are timeless, not trendy—witness his take on the perfect trench. Contemporary basics that flatter with interesting details often borrowed from folklore, sheer black flouncy saloon skirts, and Anna Karenina flowing cowl capes are just some of the delights here.

★ **Isabel Marant** (✉ 16 rue de Charonne, 11e, Bastille/Nation ☎ 01–49–29–71–55 Ⓜ Ledru-Rollin ✉ 1 rue Jacob, 6e, St-Germain-des-Prés ☎01–43–26–04–12 Ⓜ St-Germain-des-Prés) is a young designer who wowed the fashion world with her bohemian rock-star line for women. This is sexy and fun fashion that skims the body without constricting it: great wide-legged pants in tweed, long corduroy skirts cut on the bias, tight little knitwear sets in cool colors (prune, green, and taupe). Night is devoted to the diva.

Jean-Charles de Castelbajac Concept Store (✉ 26 rue Madame, 6e, St-Germain-des-Prés ☎ 01–45–48–40–55 Ⓜ St-Sulpice ✉ 31 pl. du Marché St-Honoré, 1er, Louvre/Tuileries ☎ 01–42–60–41–55 Ⓜ Tuileries) carries the quirkily cerebral yet memorably elegant designs of the designer's own clothing collection, along with furniture, candles, blankets, and luggage. There is also jewelry by different young designers each season; cool books and magazines like *Dutch, Crash,* and *Very*; and Keith Haring–designed dominoes.

Lagerfeld Gallery (✉ 40 rue de Seine, 6e, St-Germain-des-Prés ☎ 01–55–42–75–51 Ⓜ Mabillon) sells Karl's own signature Lagerfeld line, as well as the collection he designs for Italian fur house Fendi. On the first floor are accessories, perfumes, magazines, and exhibitions of Lagerfeld's own photography.

Maria Luisa (✉ 38 rue du Mont-Thabor, 1er, Louvre/Tuileries ☎ 01–42–96–47–81 Ⓜ Concorde) is one of the most important names in town for cutting-edge fashion. The store at No. 38 is considered a "style laboratory" for young designers for both him and her; No. 2 is the woman's shop stocked by an army of established designers (like Lang and Demeulemeester); No. 4 houses one of the few places in Paris to get übercool shoes by Manolo Blahnik and chichi bags by Lulu Guinness; No. 19 is the address for *monsieur.*

NIM (✉ 16 rue du Bourg-Tibourg, 4e, Le Marais ☎ 01–42–77–19–79 Ⓜ Hôtel de Ville) is the name of Levi's Parisian concept store. The simple concrete boutique has 501s and customized vintage jeans hanging on hooks on the walls, as well as limited-edition accessories and an exhibition space for avant-garde art installations.

Onward (✉ 147 bd. St-Germain, 6e, St-Germain-des-Prés ☎ 01–55–42–77–55 Ⓜ St-Germain-des-Prés), formerly known as Kashiyama, stocks fashion-forward clothes and accessories by the likes of Ann Demeulemeester, Martin Margiela, Martine Sitbon, Véronique Branquinho, and A. F. Vandevorst. It also gives over a space each season to up-and-coming labels, like Luella, Viktor & Rolf, and Alexandre Mathieu.

Paul & Joe (✉ 46 rue Étienne Marcel, 2e, Beaubourg/Les Halles ☎ 01–40–28–03–34 Ⓜ Étienne Marcel) is designer Sophie Albou's eclectic mix of modern trends for the fashionable girl who hasn't yet decided where she fits in. There is a decidedly retro feeling to the crisp poplin shirts, A-line skirts with matching fitted jackets, and wonderfully swingy felt coats. In summer she likes to mix in a little hippie chic.

Raw Essentials (✉ 46 rue Étienne-Marcel, 2e, Beaubourg/Les Halles ☎ 01–42–21–44–33 Ⓜ Étienne Marcel) is a haven for fans of raw denim. It uniquely stocks the designs of the Dutch-based label G-Star, whose highly desirable jeans have replaced those of Levi's as the ones to be seen in. There are also military-inspired clothing, bags, and T-shirts.

Shine (✉ 30 rue de Charonne, 11e, Bastille/Nation ☎ 01–48–05–80–10 Ⓜ Ledru-Rollin) travels the world to find clothes and accessories that embody the store's spirit: chic, glamorous, and rock and roll. As well as taking in the fashions, also check out the fabulous floral wallpaper and sparkly, gold wall displays.

Le Shop (✉ 3 rue d'Argout, 2e, Louvre/Tuileries ☎ 01–40–28–95–94 Ⓜ Louvre) is the Parisian address for fans of street wear and techno. The industrial-style shop rocks to the beat of resident DJs and carries numerous hip designers as well as skateboards, sports shoes, and flyers for raves and parties. The whole experience is rather like shopping in a nightclub.

Le Webstore (✉29 rue du Louvre, 2e, Louvre/Tuileries ☎01–40–26–92–77 Ⓜ Louvre) is the showcase for the Web site www.le-webstore.com. Created by brothers Jean-Yves and Hubert Lanvin (great-nephews of the famed couturiere Jeanne), it sells everything from funky T-shirts and scented bracelets to designer radiators and miniature cameras.

Yazbukey Kokon To Zaï (✉ 48 rue Tiquetonne, 2e, Beaubourg/Les Halles ☎ 01–42–36–92–41 Ⓜ Étienne Marcel) is a Japanese expression to sum up the concept of opposing extremes (such as hot and cold, young and old). It is also a hip boutique, selling the creations of more than 40 young designers, including Jeremy Scott, Bernard Wilhelm, and Viktor & Rolf.

Cosmetics

When it comes to *maquillage* (makeup), many Parisian women head directly to **Monoprix,** an urban supermarket/dime store and a gold mine for inexpensive, good-quality cosmetics. Brand names to look for are Bourjois, whose products are made in the Chanel factories, and Arcancil. For a great bargain on the best French products, check out the host of "parapharmacies" that have sprung up throughout the city. The French flock here to stock up on brilliant cosmetics, pharmaceutical skin-care lines, hair-care basics, and great baby-care necessities normally sold in the more expensive pharmacies. Look for the Roc line of skin products, hair care by Réné Furterer or Phytologie, the popular Caudelie line of skin care made with grape extracts, or the Nuxe line of body oils and creams infused with a slight gold hue that French actresses swear by, all of which are several times the price if you can find them back home.

Anne Sémonin (✉ 2 rue des Petits-Champs, 2e, Beaubourg/Les Halles ☎ 01–42–60–94–66 Ⓜ Palais-Royal ✉ 108 rue du Faubourg St-Honoré, 8e, Champs-Élysées ☎ 01–42–66–24–22 Ⓜ Champs-Élysées–Clemenceau) sells exceptional skin-care products made out of seaweed and trace elements, as well as essential oils that are popular with fashion models.

By Terry (✉21 Galerie Véro-Dodat, 1er, Louvre/Tuileries ☎01–44–76–00–76 Ⓜ Louvre, Palais-Royal ✉ 1 rue Jacob, 6e, St-Germain-des-Prés ☎01–46–34–00–36 Ⓜ St-Germain-des-Prés) is the brainchild of Yves Saint Laurent's former director of makeup, Terry de Gunzberg. This small and refined jewel of a store offers her own brand of "ready-to-wear" makeup that is a favorite of French actresses and socialites. Upstairs there is a team of specialists that creates what de Gunzberg calls *haute couleur,* an exclusive made-to-measure makeup line created specifically for each client (very expensive and to be booked way in advance.

Make Up for Ever (✉ 5 rue de la Boétie, 8e, Champs-Élysées ☎ 01–42–66–01–60 Ⓜ St-Augustin), at the back of a courtyard, is a must-stop for makeup artists, models (Kate Moss is a regular), and actresses (Madonna has dropped in, too). The ultrahip selection spans 100 shades of foundation, 100 different lipsticks, 125 eye shadows, 24 glittering powders, and scores of fake eyelashes.

La Parfumerie Générale (✉ 6 rue Robert-Estienne, 8e, Champs-Élysées ☎ 01–43–59–10–62 Ⓜ Franklin-D.-Roosevelt) is the concept of Victoire de Taillac (of boutique Colette fame) who wanted to create a cutting-edge address with the most innovative cosmetics in the world—makeup by Chantecaille; Territoire, a line of perfumes and essential oils from Morocco; Nirvana Naturel for perfect hair; Ebaviva skin care for pregnant women; a makeup bar with an in-house artist; and a small corner of the shop with products for men with an in-house barber for the perfect shave.

Sephora (✉ 70 av. des Champs-Élysées, 8e, Champs-Élysées ☎ 01–53–93–22–50 Ⓜ Franklin-D.-Roosevelt ✉ 1 rue Pierre Lescot, in the Forum des Halles, 1er, Beaubourg/Les Halles ☎ 01–40–13–72–25 Ⓜ Châtelet Les Halles), the leading chain of perfume and cosmetics megastores in France, sells its own makeup as well as all the big brands. Choose from 365 colors of lipstick, browse through the "Cultural Gallery" at the Champs-Élysées store, and even send e-mails for free from the in-store computers.

Stephane Marais (✉ 217 rue St-Honoré, 1er, Louvre/Tuileries ☎ 01–42–61–73–22 Ⓜ Tuileries), is the boutique from hot-off-the-runway makeup superstar Stephane Marais. Look for mascaras with fine combs and wonderful eye glosses in every shade—the makeup is picture perfect, affordable, and as discrete or as crazy as you may wish. His team of professional makeup artists, known for their magazine and top runway work, offers makeup lessons—€120 for a 1½-hour session—but must be booked well in advance.

Food & Wine

À la Mère de Famille (✉ 35 rue du Faubourg-Montmartre, 9e, Opéra/Grands Boulevards ☎ 01–47–70–83–69 Ⓜ Cadet) is an enchanting shop well versed in French regional specialties and old-fashioned bonbons, sugar candy, and more.

Les Caves Augé (✉ 116 bd. Haussmann, 8e, Opéra/Grands Boulevards ☎ 01–45–22–16–97 Ⓜ St-Augustin), one of the best wine shops in Paris since 1850, is just the ticket whether you're looking for a rare vintage for an oenophile friend or a seductive Bordeaux for a tête-à-tête. English-speaking Marc Sibard is a knowledgeable and affable adviser.

Debauve & Gallais (✉ 30 rue des Sts-Pères, 7e, St-Germain-des-Prés ☎ 01–45–48–54–67 Ⓜ St-Germain-des-Prés) was founded in 1800 by two former chemists to Louis XVI who decided to start making chocolates. Today their delectable recipes can still be found here.

L'Épicerie (✉ 51 rue St-Louis-en-L'Ile, 4e, Ile St-Louis ☎ 01–43–25–20–14 Ⓜ Pont Marie) sells 90 types of jam (such as figs with almonds and cinnamon), 70 kinds of mustard (including one with chocolate and honey), numerous olive oils, and flavored sugars.

Fauchon (✉ 26 pl. de la Madeleine, 8e, Opéra/Grands Boulevards ☎ 01–47–42–60–11 Ⓜ Madeleine) is the most famous and iconic of all Parisian food stores. Established in 1886, it sells renowned pâté, honey, jelly, and private-label champagne. Hard-to-find foreign foods (U.S. pancake mix, British lemon curd) are also stocked, and delectable pastries and chocolates are served in the café. Prices can be eye-popping—chocolates for €70 a pound, marzipan fruits for €95 a pound—but who can nay-say that soigné, top-of-the-line Fauchon chocolate box, whose cover bears an antique engraving of place de la Madeleine.

La Grande Épicerie (✉ 38 rue de Sèvres, 7e, St-Germain-des-Prés ☎ 01–44–39–81–00 Ⓜ Sèvres Babylone), on the ground floor of Au Bon Marché, stocks a veritable cornucopia of fine French foodstuffs.

Hédiard (✉ 21 pl. de la Madeleine, 8e, Opéra/Grands Boulevards ☎ 01–43–12–88–88 Ⓜ Madeleine), established in 1854, was famous in the 19th century for its high-quality imported spices. These—along with rare teas and beautifully packaged house brands of jam, mustard, and cookies—are still sold.

★ **Ladurée** (✉ 21 rue Bonaparte, 6e, Latin Quarter ☎ 01–44–07–64–87 Ⓜ Odéon), founded in 1862, is a French institution and a great place to stock up on some delicious chocolates, pastries, and macaroons in flavors such as violet, cassis, amaretto, salty caramel, tea, and bitter lime, to name just a few. They sell more than 800 macaroons a day, upwards of 60,000 hazelnut croissants per year, and use approximately 30 tons of chocolate a year—just to give you an idea of how popular they are. Stop in for a taste in the tearoom and bring some of your faves home—if they make it that far, they'll love you for it.

Lavinia (✉ 3 –5 bd de la Madeleine, 8e, Opéra/Grands Boulevards ☎ 01–42–97–20–20 Ⓜ St-Augustin) has the largest selection of wine in one spot in Europe—a choice of more than 6,000 wines and spirits from all over the world, ranging in quality and caliber from the simple to the sublime. On-site there are expert sommeliers to help you sort it all out. A wine-tasting bar, a bookshop, and a restaurant are also here.

La Maison du Chocolat (✉ 56 rue Pierre-Charron, 8e, Champs-Élysées ☎ 01–47–23–38–25 Ⓜ Franklin-D.-Roosevelt ✉ 8 bd. de la Madeleine, 9e, Louvre/Tuileries ☎ 01–47–42–86–52 Ⓜ Madeleine ✉ 225 rue du Faubourg St-Honoré, 8e, Louvre/Tuileries ☎ 01–42–27–39–44 Ⓜ Ternes) is heaven if you love chocolate: take some home or have a treat in the tearooms at the stores on rue Pierre-Charron or Madeleine.

La Maison du Miel (✉ 24 rue Vignon, 9e, Louvre/Tuileries ☎ 01–47–42–26–70 Ⓜ Madeleine) takes *miel* (honey) seriously—more than 30 varieties are in stock, many sweetly packaged for delicious gift-giving.

Mariage Frères (✉ 30 rue du Bourg-Tibourg, 4e, Le Marais ☎ 01–42–72–28–11 Ⓜ Hôtel de Ville), with its colonial *charme* and wooden counters, is the place to get tea in Paris. You can choose from more than 450 blends from 32 different countries and purchase teapots, teacups, books about tea, and tea-flavor biscuits and candies. There is also an on-site tearoom that serves high tea or a light lunch.

Pierre Hermé (✉ 72 rue Bonaparte, 6e, Latin Quarter ☎ 01–43–54–47–77 Ⓜ Odéon), is the first boutique from Pierre Hermé, whom the French refer to as the "Picasso of pastry." It's all about his pastries—even notoriously impatient Parisians line outside waiting for them—most notably his exotic macaroons in a flavors from rose cream to hazelnut, passion fruit, milk chocolate, white truffle, or the standard bitter raspberry, lemon, and mandarine. Sweet but not *too,* the perfect high-tea treat and a great gift—they travel well.

Verlet (✉ 256 rue St-Honoré, 1er, Louvre/Tuileries ☎ 01–42–60–67–39 Ⓜ Palais-Royal) is *the* place in Paris to buy coffee. There are more than 20 varieties, from places as far flung as Hawaii and Papua New Guinea (you can also sample the brews on the premises). Also on sale are teas, jams from the Savoie region, and (during winter months) a stunning assortment of candied fruits.

Hats

Marie Mercié (✉ 23 rue St-Sulpice, 6e, St-Germain-des-Prés ☎ 01–43–26–45–83 Ⓜ Mabillon, St-Sulpice) is one of Paris's most fashionable hatmakers. Her husband, Anthony Peto, makes men's hats and has a store at 58 rue Tiquetonne.

Philippe Model (✉ 33 pl. du Marché St-Honoré, 1er, Louvre/Tuileries ☎ 01–42–96–89–02 Ⓜ Tuileries) has been confecting amazing hats for *haute société* for many years, and has more recently expanded his creative energy into a successful line of shoes and unusual objects for the home.

Housewares

Agatha Ruiz de la Prada (✉ 9 rue Guénégaud, 6e, Latin Quarter ☎ 01–43–25–86–88 Ⓜ Odéon) is nothing if not prolific. She designs clothing and accessories for the Spanish department store El Corte Inglès, watches for Swatch, and furniture for Amat. In this small store she also sells her own creations, from bags and children's fashions to yo-yos and notebooks. All are typified by naive motifs in primary colors.

Alexandre Biaggi (✉ 14 rue de Seine, 6e, St-Germain-des-Prés ☎ 01–44–07–34–73 Ⓜ St-Germain-des-Prés) is one of the best addresses for 20th-century furniture. He specializes in the period 1910–50 and also commissions the occasional design from such talented contemporary designers as Nicolas Aubagnac and Hervé van der Straeten.

A. Simon (✉ 48 rue Montmartre, 2e, Beaubourg/Les Halles ☎ 01–42–33–71–65 Ⓜ Étienne Marcel) is one of the places where all those wonderful Parisian chefs come to acquire everything they need in the kitchen—from plates and glasses to pans, dishes, and wooden spoons. The quality is excellent and the prices pleasantly reasonable.

Avant-Scène (✉ 4 pl. de l'Odéon, 6e, Latin Quarter ☎ 01–46–33–12–40 Ⓜ Odéon) has been selling original, poetic furniture for the past 15 years. Owner Elisabeth Delacarte commissions limited-edition pieces from artists like Mark Brazier-Jones, Franck Evennou, and Hubert Le Gall.

Catherine Memmi (✉ 32–34 rue St-Sulpice, 6e, St-Germain-des-Prés ☎ 01–44–07–22–28 Ⓜ Mabillon, St-Sulpice ✉ 43 rue Madame, 6e, St-Germain-des-Prés ☎ 01–45–48–18–34 Ⓜ St-Sulpice) sells wonderfully chic bed linens, bath products, lamps, table settings, furniture, and cashmere sweaters—all in elegantly neutral colors and minimalist designs. Cheaper items in cotton are sold at the rue Madame address.

Christian Liaigre (✉ 42 rue du Bac, 7e, St-Germain-des-Prés ☎ 01–53–63–33–66 Ⓜ Rue du Bac) is one of the most fashionable interior decorators at the moment. He designed the Mercer Hotel in New York and the homes of designer Kenzo and French actress Carole Bouquet. His fashionably simple furniture is sold in this flagship boutique.

Christofle (✉ 24 rue de la Paix, 2e, Opéra/Grands Boulevards ☎ 01–42–65–62–43 Ⓜ Opéra ✉ 9 rue Royale, 8e, Louvre/Tuileries ☎ 01–55–27–99–00 Ⓜ Concorde, Madeleine), founded in 1830, is *the* name to know in French silver. Come here for perfectly elegant table settings, vases, cigarette holders, jewelry boxes, and more.

Christophe Delcourt (✉ 125 rue Vieille-du-Temple, 3e, Le Marais ☎ 01–42–78–44–97 Ⓜ Rambuteau, St-Paul) is one of France's most sought-after interior designers. Fashion designers and film stars flock to this store to snap up his lamps based on old-fashioned drawing tools, waxed-steel furniture, and sleek, wooden tables.

Compagnie Française de l'Orient et de la Chine (✉ 163 bd. St-Germain, 6e, St-Germain-des-Prés ☎ 01–45–48–00–18 Ⓜ St-Germain-des-Prés) imports ceramics and furniture from China and Mongolia. On the first floor are vases, teapots, and table settings; in the basement are straw hats, raffia baskets, and bamboo footstools.

Conran Shop (✉ 117 rue du Bac, 7e, St-Germain-des-Prés ☎ 01–42–84–10–01 Ⓜ Sèvres Babylone ✉ 30 bd. des Capucines, 9e, Opéra/Grands Boulevards ☎ 01–53–43–29–00 Ⓜ Madeleine) is the brainchild of British entrepreneur Terence Conran. Here you can find expensive contemporary furniture, beautiful bed linens, glassware, kitchen utensils, vases, lamp shades, and bathroom accessories.

Diptyque (✉ 34 bd. St-Germain, 5e, St-Germain-des-Prés ☎ 01–43–26–45–27 Ⓜ Maubert Mutualité) is famous for its scented candles and *eaux de toilettes* in sophisticated scents—Elton John requests that his favorite candles be lit when he makes his grand entrance into his suite at the Ritz. All that aside, Diptyque has also introduced some decadent bath products like the shower gel Three Waters that smell heavenly.

Gien (✉ 18 rue de l'Arcade, 8e, Louvre/Tuileries ☎ 01–42–66–52–32 Ⓜ Madeleine) has been making fine china since 1821. As well as traditional designs, you'll also find place settings especially designed by contemporary artists.

Laguiole (✉ 1 pl. Ste-Opportune, 1er, Beaubourg/Les Halles ☎ 01–40–28–09–42 Ⓜ Châtelet) is the name of the country's most famous knife. Today designers like Philippe Starck and Sonia Rykiel have created special models for the company. Starck also designed this striking boutique (note the animal horn sticking out of the wall).

★ **Le Monde Sauvage** (✉ 11 rue de l'Odéon, 6e, Latin Quarter ☎ 01–43–25–60–34 Ⓜ Odéon) is a must-visit address for home accessories—reversible silk bedspreads in rich colors, scrumptious velvet throws, hand-quilted bed linens, silk floor cushions, and the best selection of ready-made, hand-embroidered curtains in silk, cotton, linen, or velvet. There is also a great collection of crystal chandeliers, rice-paper lanterns, silk shades in fuchsia and yellow, beaded lamp shades, mirrors in zinc, bathroom fixtures, and kitchen tables in weathered wood.

R & Y Augousti (✉ 103 rue du Bac, 7e, St-Germain-des-Prés ☎ 01–42–22–22–21 Ⓜ Sèvres Babylone) are two Paris-based designers who make furniture and objects for the home in materials like coconut, bamboo, fish skin, palm wood, and parchment. Also on sale is their line of textiles inspired by peacock feathers. Treat yourself to one of their cushions in pashmina, raffia, leather, or printed cotton.

Sentou Galerie (✉ 24 rue du Pont Louis-Philippe, 4e, Le Marais ☎ 01–42–71–00–01 Ⓜ St-Paul) knocked the Parisian world over the head with the huge success of its original, playful designs. Lamps by artists, avant-garde furniture, spiral staircases, rugs, and a variety of home accessories line this cool boutique. Look for the Spring Vase, old test tubes linked together to form different shapes, or the oblong suspended crystal vases that look great hanging above the dinner table or in front of a mirror. Be sure to stop by No. 18, a small shop devoted to the art of the table, with charming hand-painted plates, salt and pepper shakers, candleholders, and such.

Van Der Straeten (✉ 11 rue Ferdinand Duval, 4e, Le Marais ☎ 01–42–78–99–99 Ⓜ St-Paul) is the lofty gallery-cum-showroom of Paris designer Hervé van der Straeten. He started out creating jewelry for Saint Laurent and Lacroix, designed a perfume bottle for Christian Dior, and also moved into making rather baroque and often wacky furniture. On show are necklaces, rugs, chairs, and startling mirrors.

Jewelry

Most of the big names are on or near place Vendôme. Designer semiprecious and costume jewelry can generally be found in boutiques on avenue Montaigne and rue du Faubourg St-Honoré.

Agatha (✉ 32 rue Étienne Marcel, 2e, Beaubourg/Les Halles ☎ 01–45–08–04–56 Ⓜ Étienne Marcel ✉ 45 rue Bonaparte, 6e, St-Germain-des-Prés ☎ 01–46–33–20–00 Ⓜ St-Germain-des-Prés) is the perfect place to buy a moderately priced piece of jewelry just for fun. Agatha's line of earrings, rings, hair accessories, bracelets, necklaces, watches, brooches, and pendants are ever popular with Parisians. Styles change quickly, but classics include nifty charm bracelets and fine gold necklaces with whimsical pendants.

Alexandre Reza (✉ 23 pl. Vendôme, 1er, Opéra/Grands Boulevards ☎ 01–42–96–64–00 Ⓜ Opéra), one of Paris's most exclusive jewelers, is first and foremost a gemologist. He travels the world looking for the finest stones and then works them into stunning pieces, many of which are replicas of jewels of historical importance.

Arthus-Bertrand (✉ 6 pl. St-Germain-des-Prés, 6e, St-Germain-des-Prés ☎ 01–49–54–72–10 Ⓜ St-Germain-des-Prés), which dates back to 1803, carries vitrines full of designer jewelry and numerous objects to celebrate births.

Au Vase de Delft (✉ 19 rue Cambon, 1er, Louvre/Tuileries ☎ 01–42–60–92–49 Ⓜ Concorde) specializes in fine vintage jewelry, ivory sculptures from China and Japan, gold boxes, watches, and Russian-made silverware (some by Fabergé).

Chanel Jewelry (✉ 18 pl. Vendôme, 1er, Opéra/Grands Boulevards ☎ 01–55–35–50–00 Ⓜ Tuileries, Opéra) spent a year renovating the building that houses its jewelry boutique. The interior is extremely refined, with beige sofas, animal sculptures, and Coromandel screens like the famous ones the designer used to have in her apartment. On offer are a selection of Chanel watches, rings, earrings, and bracelets with semiprecious stones, and some extra-special pieces with diamonds, sapphires, and pearls. Prices range from €770 to €2,307,690.

Fodor'sChoice ★ **Dary's** (✉ 362 rue St-Honoré, 1er, Louvre/Tuileries ☎ 01–42–60–95–23 Ⓜ Tuileries) is what shopping in Paris is all about—a wonderful cavern of Ali Baba popular with artists, actors, models, and jewelry lovers. It's run by the Dary family, with Katherine—a gemologist and author of a book on collecting jewelry—on hand to help. You'll need to take your time though, because the walls are filled with row upon row of antique jewels from every era, more modern secondhand jewelry, and drawer upon drawer of antique one-of-a-kinds.

Christian Dior (✉ 28 av. Montaigne, 8e, Champs-Élysées ☎ 01–47–23–52–39 Ⓜ Franklin-D.-Roosevelt ✉ 8 pl. Vendôme, 1er, Opéra/Grands Boulevards ☎ 01–42–96–30–84 Ⓜ Opéra) got a big dollop of wit and panache when they signed on young designer Victoire de Castellane to create Dior's first line of fine jewelry. She has taken much inspiration from the life of Christian Dior himself, and has come up with lucky charms as a nodding reference to the designer's superstition and earrings in the form of his favorite flowers—roses and lilies of the valley. All the stones used are the real McCoy, so don't expect to get anything for cheap. Indeed, prices go up to €462,500 for a necklace.

Jewels & Pashminas (✉ 12 rue Jacob, 6e, St-Germain-des-Prés ☎ 01–43–25–84–85 Ⓜ St-Germain-des-Prés) is composed of two stores, discreetly situated in a leafy courtyard. The jewelry store is the only outlet in Europe for the sublime creations made in the legendary Gem Palace in Jaipur. In the neighboring pashmina boutique you'll find Nepalese clothing and hand-embroidered shawls.

Lingerie

Alice Cadolle (✉ 14 rue Cambon, 1er, Louvre/Tuileries ☎ 01–42–60–94–94 Ⓜ Concorde) has been selling the finest lingerie to Parisians since 1889. In the first-floor boutique are ready-to-wear bras, corsets, and sleepwear. Upstairs, Madame Cadolle offers a made-to-measure service, popular with couture clients from nearby Chanel.

Erès (✉ 2 rue Tronchet, 8e, Opéra/Grands Boulevards ☎ 01–47–42–24–55 Ⓜ Madeleine) has the most modern line of swimwear and lingerie in town, no chichi here; just pure streamline shapes in classic colors. The lingerie masters the art of soft sheer tones and is comfortable, flattering, and subtly sexy.

★ **Les Folies d'Elodie** (✉ 56 av. Paul Doumer, 16e, Eiffel Tower/Trocadéro ☎ 01–45–04–93–57 Ⓜ Trocadéro) is the address in Paris for elegant, feminine lingerie. In this large, lush boutique you can find anything from a 1950s-style cotton bra and panties in pale pink vichy *à la Bardot* to a risqué sheer-silk nightgown with Calais lace insets. Famous lovers seem to feel at home here, too—Warren Beatty stops by when he's in town and Bill popped in to pick out a champagne-color confection for Senator Clinton.

★ **Sabbia Rosa** (✉ 73 rue des Sts-Pères, 6e, St-Germain-des-Prés ☎ 01–45–48–88–37 Ⓜ St-Germain-des-Prés) is a discreet, boudoirlike boutique you could easily walk straight past. It is, however, probably the finest lingerie store in the world and the place where actresses Sharon Stone, Catherine Deneuve, and Isabelle Adjani buy their underwear in the finest French silk.

Miscellaneous

Kirk & Richie Rich (✉ 9 rue de La Trémoille, 8e, Champs-Élysées ☎ 01–47–23–81–00 Ⓜ Alma-Marceau) has an abundance of objects that owner Gisela Trigano brings back from her travels. Among her *coups de coeur* are shoes and Murano glass from Italy, pashminas from India, blankets from England, wooden sculptures from Nepal, and ancestor paintings from China.

Nature et Découvertes (✉ In the Carrousel du Louvre, 99 rue de Rivoli, 1er, Louvre/Tuileries ☎ 01–47–03–47–43 Ⓜ Palais-Royal) has a large selection of children's toys as well as objects linked to nature—telescopes, birdseed, gardening equipment, hiking gear, crystals, aromatherapy diffusers, and little Zen gardens.

Music

Born Bad (✉ 17 rue Keller, 11e, Bastille/Nation ☎ 01–49–23–98–05 Ⓜ Bastille ✉ 11 rue St-Sabin, 11e, Bastille/Nation ☎ 01–49–23–98–05 Ⓜ Bastille) is the place to go for rare underground finds—stop by the branch **Born Bad Exotica** on the rue Saint-Sabin if you'd like to listen to a sound track of every James Bond movie ever made, or check out a host of old records with dancing Hawaiian hula girls on the cover—in other words, you'll find all that is kitsch and underground and otherwise unfindable and rather fun to look at to boot.

FNAC (✉ Forum des Halles, 1er, Beaubourg/Les Halles ☎ 01–40–41–40–00 Ⓜ Les Halles ✉ 74 av. des Champs-Élysées, 8e, Champs-Élysées ☎ 01–53–53–64–64 Ⓜ Franklin-D.-Roosevelt ✉ 136 rue de Rennes, 6e, Montparnasse ☎ 01–49–54–30–00 Ⓜ St-Placide) is a high-profile French chain selling music and books, and photo, TV, and audio equipment at good prices, by French standards.

Virgin Megastore (✉ 52 av. des Champs-Élysées, 8e, Champs-Élysées ☎ 01–49–53–50–00 Ⓜ Franklin-D.-Roosevelt ✉ In the Carrousel du Louvre, 99 rue de Rivoli, 1er, Louvre/Tuileries ☎ 01–49–53–52–90 Ⓜ Palais-Royal) has acres of CDs and tapes; the Champs-Élysées store has a large book section and a trendy café upstairs.

Perfumes

Annick Goutal (✉ 14 rue de Castiglione, 1er, Louvre/Tuileries ☎ 01–42–60–52–82 Ⓜ Concorde) sells its own exclusive line of 18 signature scents, which come packaged in gilded gauze purses.

L'Artisanat Parfumeur (✉ 32 rue du Bourg Tibourg, 4e, Le Marais ☎ 01–48–04–72–75 Ⓜ Hôtel de Ville) sells its own brand of scents for the home and perfumes with names like Méchant Loup (Big Bad Wolf) and Riviera Palace.

L'Atelier du Savon (✉ 29 rue Vieille-du-Temple, 4e, Le Marais ☎ 01–44–54–06–10 Ⓜ St-Paul) is a soap addict's delight. There are blocks of chocolate and lime soap, mint and lemon soap, and others that look strangely like brownies. Fizzy balls for the bath have rose petals and sequins inside of them, and shampoos come in solid blocks.

Comme des Garçons (✉ 23 pl. du Marché St-Honoré, 1er, Louvre/Tuileries ☎ 01–47–03–60–72 Ⓜ Tuileries) is the very first boutique in the world devoted to the trendy Japanese label's perfumes, scented candles, and body creams. The shop is worth a visit simply to admire the whiter-than-white store design with pink-tinted lighting.

Creed (✉ 38 av. Pierre 1er de Serbie, 8e, Champs-Élysées ☎ 01–47–20–58–02 Ⓜ George V) was founded in 1760 and was the official perfume supplier to Queen Victoria and numerous European courts. Today it sells a selection of its own scents and makes personalized perfumes.

Editions de Parfums Frédéric Malle (✉ 37 rue de Grenelle, 7e, St-Germain-des-Prés ☎ 01–42–22–77–22 Ⓜ Rue du Bac) is based on a simple concept: take the nine most famous noses in France and have them edit one singular perfume. The result? Nine fragrances of exceptional quality to be had nowhere else. Le Parfum de Therese for example, was created by famous Dior nose Edmond Roudnitska for his wife, and is available to the public here for the first time ever. The perfumes are highly concentrated and stored in refrigerated glass cases in this innovative boutique designed by Andrée Putman. You can test the scents like the professionals do—in crystal olfactory cases (rather *Star Trek* but quite effective) where the essences are stored.

Guerlain (✉ 68 av. des Champs-Élysées, 8e, Champs-Élysées ☎ 01–45–62–52–57 Ⓜ Franklin-D.-Roosevelt ✉ 47 rue Bonaparte, 6e, St-Germain-des-Prés ☎ 01–43–26–71–19 Ⓜ Mabillon) boutiques are the only authorized Paris outlets for legendary perfumes like Shalimar, Jicky, Vol de Nuit, Mitsouko, Chamade, Champs-Élysées, and their collection of light toilet waters. They also have an extremely popular makeup and skin-care line and Terra Cotta, their bronzing powder, is an eternal French favorite.

Parfums de Nicolaï (✉ 69 av. Raymond Poincaré, 16e, Eiffel Tower/Trocadéro ☎ 01–47–55–90–44 Ⓜ Victor-Hugo) is run by a member of the Guerlain family, Patricia de Nicolaï. Children's, women's, and men's perfumes are on offer, as well as sprays for the home and scented candles. Celebrity clients include Isabelle Adjani and Elton John.

Fodor'sChoice ★ **Les Salons du Palais-Royal Shiseido** (✉ Jardins du Palais-Royal, 142 Galerie de Valois, 25 rue de Valois, 1er, Louvre/Tuileries ☎ 01–49–27–09–09 Ⓜ Palais-Royal) is a magical boutique with marble floors and lilac walls that open to contain the entire Shiseido cosmetic and skin-care line. But that's not why people flock here. They come because every year Shiseido's creative genius Serge Lutens dreams up two new scents, which are then sold exclusively in this boutique. There are now 18 parfums and each is wonderfully different from the over-marketed scents out there. Sample the latest, Vetiver Oriental, or classics like Chergui, named after a desert wind in Tunisia, the sweet almond and vanilla scent of Ralat Loukoum, or the classic Rose de Nuit.

DISCOUNT The airport duty-free shops are your best bet for minor purchases. But if you're going to spend more than €185, it's worthwhile to seek out the top discounters. Don't forget to claim your détaxe!

Les Halles Montmartre (✉ 85 rue Montmartre, 2e, Opéra/Grands Boulevards ☎ 01–42–33–11–13 Ⓜ Bourse) routinely discounts its great selection of perfumes and cosmetics by up to 20%.

Michel Swiss (✉ 16 rue de la Paix, 2nd fl., 2e, Opéra/Grands Boulevards ☎ 01–42–61–61–11 Ⓜ Opéra ✉ 24 av. de l'Opéra, 1er, Louvre/Tuileries ☎ 01–47–03–49–11 Ⓜ Pyramides) offers savings of up to 25% on perfumes, designer jewelry, and fashion accessories.

Shoes

Berluti (✉ 26 rue Marbeuf, 8e, Champs-Élysées ☎ 01–53–93–97–97 Ⓜ Franklin-D.-Roosevelt) has been making fantastically exquisite and expensive men's shoes for more than a century. "Nothing is too beautiful for feet," is Olga Berluti's motto. She even exposes her creations to the moonlight to give them an extra-special patina! One model is named after Andy Warhol, and other famous clients of the past have included the Duke of Windsor, Fred Astaire, and James Joyce.

★ **Christian Louboutin** (✉ 19 rue Jean-Jacques Rousseau, 1er, Beaubourg/Les Halles ☎ 01–42–36–05–31 Ⓜ Palais-Royal ✉ 38-40 rue de Grenelle, 7e, St-Germain-des-Prés ☎ 01–42–22–33–07 Ⓜ Sèvres Babylone) is famous for his wacky but elegant creations and his trademark blood-red soles; Madonna, Gwyneth, Catherine Deneuve, J-Lo, Tina Turner, Celine Dion, and Donatella Versace shop here.

Un Dimanche A Venise (✉ 7 rue Francs Bourgeois, 4e, Le Marais ☎ 01–42–76–02–65 Ⓜ St-Paul ✉ 318 rue St-Honoré, 1er, Louvre/Tuileries ☎ 01–40–20–47–37 Ⓜ Concorde) has the best collection of mid-range shoes, sandals, and boots in the city. These shoes are *hot*. From the worn brown-leather boots with the perfect tooling, the classic pointy-toed two-tone pump, to the high-heeled evening fantasies with sequins and feathers and beads—you just can't go wrong.

Mare (✉ 23 rue des Francs-Bourgeois, 4e, Le Marais ☎ 01–48–04–74–63 Ⓜ St-Paul ✉ 4 rue du Cherche-Midi, 6e, St-Germain-des-Prés ☎ 01–45–44–55–33 Ⓜ St-Sulpice) has stylish, trendy shoes made from fine Italian leather.

Michel Perry (✉ 4 rue des Petits-Pères, 2e, Louvre/Tuileries ☎ 01–42–44–10–07 Ⓜ Palais-Royal) is famous for his elegant, slender, high-heeled shoes. The rose-color boudoir-style store also stocks many hip labels, including Chloé, Colette Dinnigan, and Guy Laroche.

★ **Rodolphe Menudier** (✉ 14 rue de Castiglione, 1er, Louvre/Tuileries ☎ 01–42–60–86–27 Ⓜ Tuileries) is a gem of a boutique, which sells some of the most beautiful shoes in the world. As well as creating his own mules and stilettos, he also creates the footwear for Christian Dior. The interior design—think sleek black windows, metal cupboards, and a wall covered in white crocodile leather—is the creation of hip interiors star Christophe Pillet.

DISCOUNT In the know Parisians flock to the République *quartier* to check out the luxury-shoe-lover-on-a-slender-budget boutiques on the **rue Meslay.** The eight discount stores are often jam-packed and the service rather dodgy, but for over 50% off on last season's collections from the biggest names it's well worth the visit.

Dina Brice (✉ 13 rue Meslay, 3e, République ☎ 01–48–87–57–78 Ⓜ République) has been selling last season's Jourdan and Clergerie for men and women at half the price for more than 25 years.

Mi-Prix (✉ 27 bd. Victor-Hugo, 15e, Montparnasse ☎ 01–48–28–42–48 Ⓜ Porte de Versailles) is an unruly jumble of end-of-series designer shoes and accessories from the likes of Gucci, Philippe Model, Walter Steiger, Prada, Michel Perry, and Azzedine Alaïa, priced at up to 70% below retail.

Patashoes (✉ 25 rue de Meslay, 3e, République ☎ 01–48–04–30–04 Ⓜ République) is not the most beautiful boutique in the world but they do have good shoes. They carry a great line of evening shoes from Lolita Lempika and handmade Italian moccasins for men for little or nearly nothing.

Stationery

Calligrane (✉ 4-6 rue Pont Louis Philippe, 4e, Le Marais ☎ 01–48–04–31–89 Ⓜ St-Paul ✉ 68 rue de Grenelle, 7e, St-Germain-des-Prés ☎ 01–45–49–96–02 Ⓜ Sèvres Babylone) has three adjacent stores in the 4e arrondissement. Only one sells an Italian paper called Fabriano, another designer office equipment (pens, staplers, and unusual notebooks covered in ostrich skin), and the third accents its different types of paper from India, Japan, and Mexico.

Cassegrain (✉ 422 rue St-Honoré, 8e, Louvre/Tuileries ☎ 01–42–60–20–08 Ⓜ Concorde ✉ 81 rue des Sts-Pères, 6e, St-Germain-des-Prés ☎ 01–42–22–04–76 Ⓜ Sèvres Babylone) is the last word on beautifully engraved cards and elegant French stationery. The desk accessories and inexpensive glass-nib writing pens make great gifts.

Marie Papier (✉ 26 rue Vavin, 6e, Montparnasse ☎ 01–43–26–46–44 Ⓜ Vavin) sells extraordinary colored, marbled, and Japanese writing paper and notebooks, plus every kind of stylish writing accessory. One fan is fashion designer Donna Karan, who stocks part of the range in her Madison Avenue store.

Toys

L'Arbre de Vie (✉ 21 rue de Sevigne, 3e, Le Marais ☎ 01–48–87–05–43 Ⓜ St-Paul) is one of those boutiques that's been around for over 30 years and hasn't changed one bit. The window is packed with everything from metal windup toys (some are collector's items) to wooden puppets to snow globes from all over the world. Inside there is a collection of hand-knit clothes for children and every kind of toy you could possibly imagine, except for those of the modern or plastic variety.

Au Nain Bleu (✉ 408 rue St-Honoré, 8e, Louvre/Tuileries ☎ 01–42–60–39–01 Ⓜ Concorde) is a high-priced wonderland of elaborate dollhouses, miniature sports cars, and enchanting hand-carved rocking horses.

C'est Ma Chambre (✉45 rue des Archives, 3e, Le Marais ☎01–48–87–26–67 Ⓜ Rambuteau) is the place to spoil your kids; it sells beautiful wooden toys and gorgeous furniture for kids' rooms.

SIDE TRIPS FROM PARIS

FODOR'S CHOICE

Cathédrale de Chartres, Chartres
Château de Chantilly, Chantilly
Château de Versailles, Versailles

HIGHLY RECOMMENDED

RESTAURANTS

Auberge Ravoux, Auvers-sur-Oise
Château d'Esclimont, Chartres
Les Trois Marches, Versailles

SIGHTS

Château de Vaux-le-Vicomte, Maincy
Grandes Écuries, Chantilly
Maison et Jardin de Claude Monet, Giverny
Parc de Versailles, Versailles
Petit Trianon, Versailles
Voyage au Temps des Impressionnistes, Auvers-sur-Oise

Revised and updated by Simon Hewitt

EVEN THOUGH PARIS ITSELF HAS SO MUCH TO SEE, you should plan on taking a short trip outside the city, for just beyond its gates lies the fabled region known as Ile-de-France, the ancient heartland of France—the core from which the French kings gradually extended their power over the rest of a rebellious, individualistic nation. Though Ile-de-France is not really an island (*île*), it is figuratively isolated from the rest of France by three rivers—the Seine, the Marne, and the Oise—that weave majestic, meandering circles around its periphery. Remarkably, this fairly confined region contains 10 million people—one-sixth of France's population. This type of statistic conjures up visions of a never-ending suburban sprawl, but nothing could be further from the truth. There are lovely villages here—notably Auvers-sur-Oise, immortalized by Vincent van Gogh, and Giverny, site of Monet's home and garden.

Grand cathedrals and stately châteaux dot the lush, gently rolling landscape: the kings and clerics who ruled France liked to escape from the capital now and then. The region never lost favor with the powerful, partly because its many forests—large chunks of which still stand—harbored sufficient game to ensure even the most indolent monarch an easy kill. First Fontainebleau, in humane Renaissance proportions, then Versailles, on a minion-crushing, Baroque scale, reflected the royal desire to transform hunting lodges into palatial residences.

In 1992 Disney wrought its own kind of kingdom here: Disneyland Paris. Since then, the park has emerged as France's leading tourist attraction, with 11 million tickets sold a year and a second park, Walt Disney Studios, opened in 2002. Getting from the capital to the sights in this region is easy: almost all are within an hour of central Paris, and most are easily accessible by train.

Contact the Espace du Tourisme d'Ile-de-France (open Wednesday–Monday 10–7, www.pidf.com), under the inverted pyramid in the Carrousel du Louvre, in the center of Paris, for general information on the area.

Pleasures & Pastimes

Culinary Delights

Ile-de-France's fanciest restaurants can be just as pricey as their Parisian counterparts; little wonder as the cuisine here mirrors that of the big capital. Look for sumptuous game and asparagus in season in the south of the region and the soft, creamy cheese of Meaux and Coulommiers to the east. In smaller towns or if you venture off the beaten tourist path, well-priced meals are not hard to find. Reservations are a must at all restaurants in summer.

WHAT IT COSTS IN EUROS*

	$$$$	$$$	$$	$	¢
AT DINNER	over €30	€23–€30	€17–€22	€11–€16	under €10

*per person for a main course only, including tax (19.6%) and service; note that if a restaurant offers only prix-fixe (set-price) meals, it has been given the price category that reflects the full prix-fixe price.

AUVERS-SUR-OISE

Cézanne, Pissarro, Corot, Daubigny, and Berthe Morisot all painted in Auvers in the second half of the 19th century. But it is Vincent van Gogh whose memory haunts every nook and cranny of this pretty riverside village. Van Gogh moved here from Arles in 1890 to be with his brother, Theo. Little has changed since the summer of 1890, which coincided with the last 10 weeks of van Gogh's life, when he painted no fewer than 70 pictures, then shot himself behind the village château. He is buried in the village cemetery next to his brother in a simple, ivy-covered grave. The whole village is peppered with plaques marking the spots that inspired van Gogh's art; the plaques bear reproductions of his paintings, enabling you to compare his final works with the scenes as they are today. After years of indifference and neglect, van Gogh's last abode has been turned into a shrine. The château is now home to a stunning high-tech exhibit on the Impressionist era. You can also visit the medieval village church, subject of one of van Gogh's most famous paintings, *L'Église d'Auvers,* and admire Ossip Zadkine's powerful statue of van Gogh in the village park.

The Auberge Ravoux, the inn where van Gogh stayed, is now the **Maison de van Gogh** (Van Gogh House). A dingy staircase leads up to the tiny, spartan wood-floor attic where van Gogh stored some of modern art's most famous pictures under his bed. A short film retraces van Gogh's time at Auvers, and there is a well-stocked souvenir shop. Stop for a drink or for lunch in the ground-floor restaurant. ✉ *8 rue de la Sansonne* ☎ *01–30–36–60–60* 🌐 *maison-de-van-gogh.com* 🎫 *€5* ⏲ *Tues.–Sun. 10–6.*

★ The elegant 17th-century village château, set above split-level gardens, now houses the **Voyage au Temps des Impressionnistes** (Journey Through the Impressionist Era). You'll receive a set of infrared headphones (English available), with commentary that guides you past various tableaux illustrating life during the Impressionist years. Although there are no Impressionist originals—500 reproductions pop up on screens interspersed between the tableaux—this is one of France's most imaginative, enjoyable, and innovative museums. Some of the special effects—talking mirrors, computerized cabaret dancing girls, and a simulated train ride past Impressionist landscapes—are worthy of Disney. ✉ *Rue de Léry* ☎ *01–34–48–48–40* 🌐 *www.chateau-auvers.fr* 🎫 *€10* ⏲ *May–Oct., Tues.–Sun. 10–8; Nov.–Apr., Tues.–Sun. 11–4:30.*

The landscape artist Charles-François Daubigny, a precursor of the Impressionists, lived in Auvers from 1861 until his death in 1878. You can visit his studio, the **Maison-Atelier de Daubigny,** and admire the remarkable mural and roof paintings by Daubigny and fellow artists Camille Corot and Honoré Daumier. ✉ *61 rue Daubigny* ☎ *01–34–48–03–03* 🎫 *€4.50* ⏲ *Thurs.–Sun. 2–6:30.*

Where to Eat

★ $–$$ ✕ **Auberge Ravoux.** For total van Gogh immersion, have lunch in the restaurant he patronized regularly more than 100 years ago and where, in fact, he finally expired. The €30, three-course menu changes regularly, but it's the genius loci that makes eating here special, with glasswork, lace curtains, and wall blandishments carefully modeled on the original designs. A magnificently illustrated book, *Van Gogh's Table,* by culinary historian Alexandra Leaf and Fred Leeman, recalls Vincent's stay at the Auberge and describes in loving detail the dishes served there at the time. ✉ *52 rue Général-de-Gaulle* ☎ *01–30–36–60–63* ✍ *Reservations essential* 💳 *AE, DC, MC, V* ⏲ *Closed Jan. and Tues. Oct.–Mar. No dinner Sun.–Mon.*

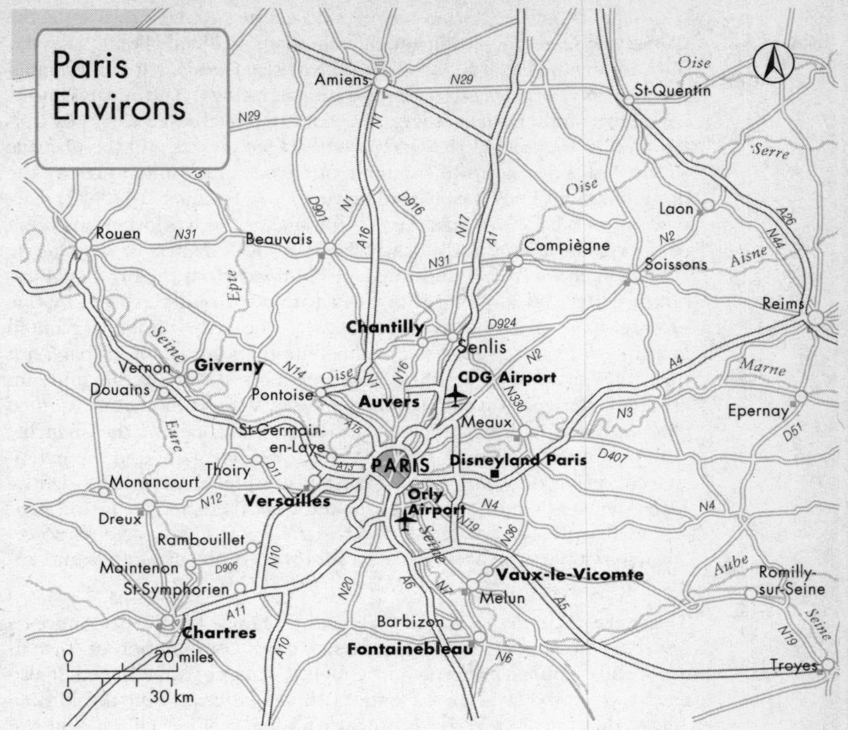

Auvers-sur-Oise A to Z

To research prices, get advice from other travelers, and book travel arrangements, visit www.fodors.com.

CAR TRAVEL

Auvers is 38 km (24 mi) northwest of Paris. Take highway A1, then A15 toward Pontoise; then head east along N184 to Méry-sur-Oise and pick up the N328, which crosses the river to Auvers.

TRAIN TRAVEL

Two trains depart every hour for Auvers from Paris's Gare du Nord; a change is necessary, usually at St-Ouen-l'Aumône, and the journey time varies from 60 to 90 minutes. A quicker (53 minutes) but more infrequent train leaves from Paris's Gare St-Lazare and involves a change at Pontoise.

VISITOR INFORMATION

Auvers-sur-Oise Office de Tourisme ✉ Rue de la Sansonne, opposite the Maison de van Gogh, 95430 Auvers-sur-Oise ☎ 01-30-36-10-06, 🌐 www.auvers-sur-oise.com.

CHANTILLY

Celebrated for lace, cream, and the most beautiful medieval manuscript in the world—*Les Très Riches Heures du Duc de Berry*—romantic Chantilly has a host of other attractions: a faux Renaissance château with an eye-popping art collection, splendid Baroque stables, a classy racecourse, and a 16,000-acre forest.

Fodor's Choice ★ Although its lavish exterior may be 19th-century Renaissance-style, the **Château de Chantilly,** sitting snugly behind an artificial lake, houses the outstanding medieval collections of the **Musée Condé,** with illuminated manuscripts, tapestries, furniture, and paintings. The most famous room, the **Santuario** (sanctuary), contains two celebrated works by Italian painter Raphael (1483–1520)—the *Three Graces* and the *Orleans Virgin*—plus an exquisite ensemble of 15th-century miniatures by the most illustrious French painter of his time, Jean Fouquet (1420–81). Farther on, in the ***Cabinet des Livres*** (library), is the world-famous book of hours whose title translates as *The Very Rich Hours of the Duc de Berry,* which was richly decorated, or illuminated, by the Brothers Limbourg with magical pictures of early 15th-century life as lived by one of Burgundy's richest lords (unfortunately, due to their fragility, painted facsimiles of the celebrated calendar illuminations are on display, not the actual pages of the book). Other highlights of this unusual museum are the **Galerie de Psyché** (Psyche Gallery), with 16th-century stained glass and portrait drawings by Flemish artist Jean Clouet II; the **Chapelle,** with sculptures by Jean Goujon and Jacques Sarrazin; and the extensive collection of paintings by 19th-century French artists, headed by Jean-Auguste-Dominique Ingres. In addition, there are grand and petit salons, all stuffed with palace furniture, family portraits, and Sèvres porcelains, making this an absolute must for lovers of the decorative and applied arts.

The château's park, designed by Versailles's famed landscaper André Le Nôtre, is based on that familiar French royal combination of formality—neatly planned parterres and a mighty, straight-banked canal. It also has a romantic eccentricity: a waterfall and a *hameau,* a mock-Norman village that inspired Marie-Antoinette's version at Versailles. You can take a tour on an electric train (daily July–August, weekends only May–June and September–October) or board a **Hydrophile,** an electric-powered boat, for a 30-minute glide down the Grand Canal. ☎ *03–44–62–62–62* 🌐 *www.chateaudechantilly.com* 🎫 *€7 including park; park only €3, with boat €8, with boat and train €10; €15 joint ticket including château, park, boat, and train* ⏲ *Château and park Mar.–Oct., daily 10–6; château Nov.–Feb., Wed.–Mon. 10:30–12:45 and 2–5; park Nov.–Feb., daily 10:30–12:45 and 2–5.*

★ The palatial 18th-century **Grandes Écuries** (Great Stables) by the racetrack, built by Jean Aubert in 1719 to accommodate 240 horses and 500 hounds for stag and boar hunts in the forests nearby, are the grandest stables in France. They're still in use as the home of the **Musée Vivant du Cheval** (Living Horse Museum), with 30 breeds of horses and ponies housed in straw-lined comfort—in between dressage performances in the courtyard or beneath the awe-inspiring central dome. Half-hour demonstrations are held at 11:30, 3:30, 4:15; special shows are held throughout the year. The 31-room museum has a comprehensive collection of equine paraphernalia: everything from saddles, bridles, and stirrups to rocking horses, anatomy displays, and old postcards. There are explanations in English throughout. ✉ *7 rue du Connétable* ☎ *03–44–57–40–40* 🌐 *www.musee-vivant-du-cheval.fr* 🎫 *€8* ⏲ *Apr.–Oct., Wed.–Mon. 10:30–5:30; Nov.–Mar., Wed.–Fri. and Mon. 2–5, weekends 10:30–5:30.*

Where to Eat

¢–$ ✕ **Capitainerie.** Adorned with old kitchen utensils, this scenic restaurant in the Château de Chantilly's vaulted medieval basement has an extensive buffet with salads, cheeses, and desserts, along with a choice of hot dishes. There are set-price menus at €14 and €31. ✉ *In Château de Chantilly* ☎ *03–44–57–15–89* 💳 *MC, V* ⏲ *Closed Tues.*

Chantilly A to Z

To research prices, get advice from other travelers, and book travel arrangements, visit www.fodors.com.

CAR TRAVEL

Take highway A1 from Paris (Porte de la Chapelle) to Senlis, 50 km (31 mi) away; Chantilly is 10 km (6 mi) west along pretty D924.

TRAIN TRAVEL

Chantilly is about 30 minutes from Paris's Gare du Nord; at least one train departs every hour.

VISITOR INFORMATION

Chantilly Office de Tourisme ✉ 60 av. du Maréchal-Joffre ☎ 03-44-57-08-58 🌐 www.ville-de-chantilly.fr.

CHARTRES

The noble, soaring spires of Chartres are among the most famous sights in Europe. Try to catch a glimpse of them surging out of the vast, golden grain fields of the Beauce as you approach from the northeast. Although you're probably visiting Chartres chiefly for its magnificent Gothic cathedral and its world-famous stained-glass windows, the whole town is also worth leisurely exploration. Ancient streets tumble down from the cathedral to the Eure River; the view of the rooftops beneath the cathedral from rue du Pont-St-Hilaire is particularly appealing. Like the cathedral, the old part of town, studded with picturesque houses and streets, has been preserved in its cloak of mellowing old stone; other sectors have been slapped with modern apartment buildings and whizzing traffic.

Fodor's Choice ★ The **Cathédrale de Chartres** is the sixth church to occupy the same spot. It dates mainly from the 12th and 13th centuries; the previous 11th-century structure burned down in 1194. A well-chronicled outburst of religious fervor followed the discovery that the relic kept in the church, the Virgin Mary's tunic, had miraculously survived unsinged. Reconstruction went ahead at a breathtaking pace. In only 25 years Chartres Cathedral rose again, and it has remained substantially unchanged ever since.

Worship on the site of the cathedral goes back to before the Gallo-Roman period; the crypt contains a well that was the focus of Druid ceremonies. With the arrival of Christianity, the original cult of the fertility goddess merged into that of the Virgin Mary. In the late 9th century King Charles the Bold presented Chartres with what was believed to be the tunic of the Virgin Mary. This precious relic attracted hordes of pilgrims, and Chartres swiftly became—and has remained—a prime destination for the faithful. To this day, pilgrims trek to Chartres from Paris on foot.

The lower half of the facade is all that survives from the 11th-century Romanesque church. (The Romanesque style is evident in the use of round, rather than pointed, arches.) The main door—the **Portail Royal** (Royal Portal)—is richly sculpted with scenes from the life of Christ. The flanking towers are also Romanesque, though the upper part of the taller of the two **spires** (380 ft versus 350 ft) dates from the start of the 16th century, and its fanciful flamboyance contrasts with the stumpy solemnity of its Romanesque counterpart. The **rose window** above the main portal dates from the 13th century. The three windows below it contain some of the finest examples of 12th-century stained glass in France.

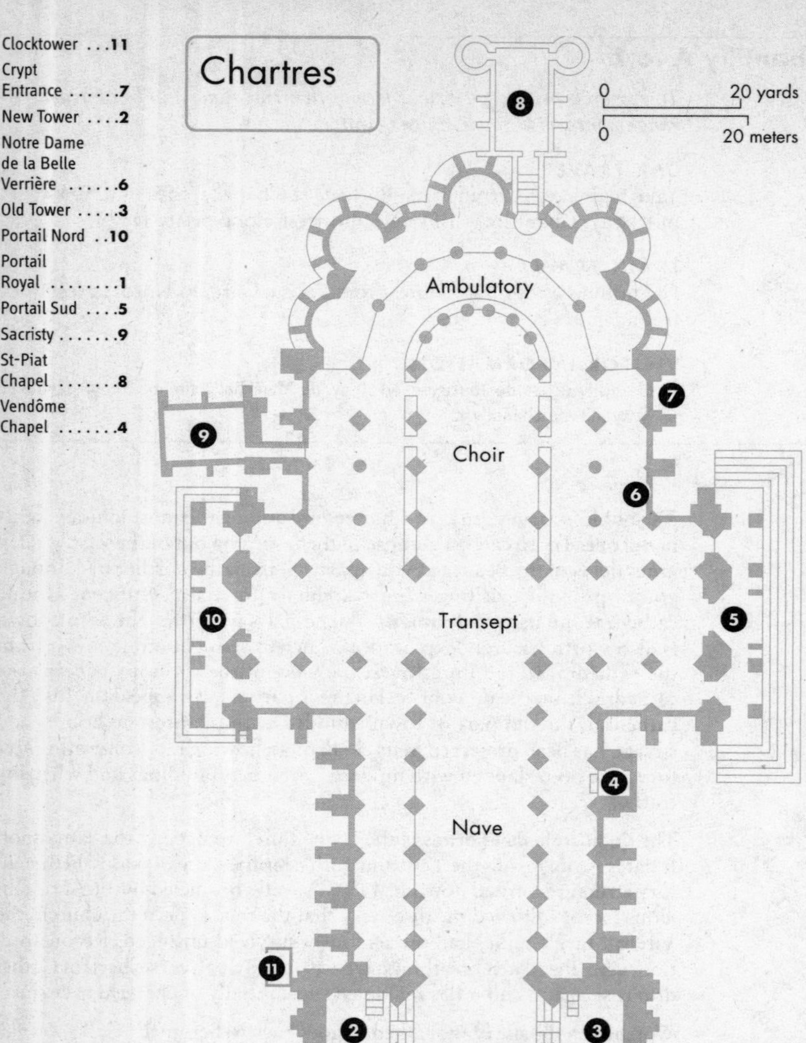

The interior is somber, so you'll need time to adjust to the dark. Your reward will be a view of the gemlike richness of the stained glass, dominated by the famous deep "Chartres blue." The oldest window, and perhaps the most stunning, is **Notre-Dame de la Belle Verrière** (Our Lady of the Lovely Window), in the south choir. It is well worth bringing binoculars to pick out the details. If you wish to know more about stained-glass techniques and the motifs used, visit the small exhibit in the gallery opposite the north porch. The vast black-and-white medieval pattern on the floor of the nave is one of the few to have survived from the Middle Ages. The faithful were expected to crawl along its entire length (some 300 yards) on their knees. A longtime Chartres aficionado, Malcolm Miller, knows more than most art historians and gives fabulous tours in English most days at noon and 2:45 PM, providing information on the narrative stained glass for a fee (call ahead to make sure he's on duty).

Otherwise, you can head out the cathedral's south door to the crypt across the street and rent a Walkman and a (vastly inferior) tape-recorded tour in English.

Guided tours of the crypt start from the **Maison de la Crypte** (Crypt House) opposite the south porch. You'll see the Romanesque and Gothic chapels that run around the crypt, along with a 4th-century Gallo-Roman wall and some 12th-century wall paintings. ✉ *16 cloître Notre-Dame* ☎ *02–37–21–56–33* *Towers €3, English guided tour €5.50* ⏲ *Guided tours of crypt Easter–Oct., daily at 11, 2:15, 3:30, 4:30, and 5:15; Nov.–Easter, daily at 11 and 4.*

The **Musée des Beaux-Arts** (Fine Arts Museum) is a handsome 18th-century building just behind the cathedral—it used to serve as the bishop's palace. Its varied collection includes Renaissance enamels, a portrait of Erasmus by Holbein, tapestries, armor, and some fine, mainly French paintings of the 17th, 18th, and 19th centuries. There is also a room devoted to the forceful 20th-century works of painter Maurice de Vlaminck, who lived in the region. ✉ *29 cloître Notre-Dame* ☎ *02–37–36–41–39* *€2.50* ⏲ *May–Oct., Wed.–Mon. 10–noon and 2–6; Nov.–Apr., Wed.–Mon. 10–noon and 2–5.*

The Gothic **Église St-Pierre** (✉ Rue St-Pierre) near the Eure River has magnificent medieval windows from a period (circa 1300) not represented at the cathedral. The oldest stained glass here, portraying Old Testament worthies, is to the right of the choir and dates from the late 13th century. There is more fine stained glass (17th century) to admire at the **Église St-Aignan** (✉ Rue des Grenets), around the corner from St-Pierre.

Where to Eat

★ $$$–$$$$ ✕ **Château d'Esclimont.** One of the most photogenic of all châteaux-hotels in France, this magnificently restored Renaissance estate—part of the Relais & Châteaux group—is frequented by high-profile Parisian businesspeople. Lamb with asparagus, hare fricassee (in season), and lobster top the menu. After dining on the rich cuisine, take a stroll through the luxuriant grounds, embellished with regal lawns and lake. ✉ *2 rue du Château-d'Esclimont, St-Symphorien-le-Château (6 km [4 mi] west of Ablis exit on A11 and about 24 km [15 mi] from Chartres and Rambouillet)* ☎ *02–37–31–15–15* *Reservations essential* *Jacket and tie* *AE, DC, MC, V.*

$$$ ✕ **La Vieille Maison.** Close to Chartres Cathedral, in the same narrow street as Le Buisson Ardent, this intimate spot with a flower-filled patio has a regularly changing menu. Invariably, however, it includes regional specialties such as truffles and asparagus with chicken. Prices, though justified, can be steep; the €27 prix-fixe lunch menu is a good bet. ✉ *5 rue au Lait* ☎ *02–37–34–10–67* *AE, MC, V* ⏲ *Closed Mon. No dinner Sun.*

$–$$ ✕ **Le Buisson Ardent.** This wood-beamed restaurant on a quaint old street near Chartres Cathedral has two prix-fixe menus, imaginative food, and attentive service. Some of the excellent dishes include chicken ravioli with leeks and rolled beef with spinach. ✉ *10 rue au Lait* ☎ *02–37–34–04–66* *AE, DC, MC, V* ⏲ *Closed Wed. No dinner Sun.*

Chartres A to Z

To research prices, get advice from other travelers, and book travel arrangements, visit www.fodors.com.

CAR TRAVEL

The A10/A11 expressways link Paris to Chartres, 88 km (55 mi) away.

GUIDED TOURS

Cityrama organizes half-day trips to Chartres (€48) and combined excursions to Chartres and Versailles (€85).

Cityrama ✉ 4 pl. des Pyramides, Paris ☎ 01-44-55-61-00 🌐 graylineparis.com.

TRAIN TRAVEL

Trains depart hourly from Paris's Gare Montparnasse to Chartres (travel time is 50–70 minutes, depending on service).

VISITOR INFORMATION

Chartres Office de Tourisme ✉ Pl. de la Cathédrale, 28000 Chartres ☎ 02-37-18-26-26 🌐 www.ville-chartres.fr.

DISNEYLAND PARIS

In 1992 American pop culture secured a mammoth outpost just 32 km (20 mi) east of Paris in the form of Disneyland Paris. On 1,500 acres in Marne-la-Vallée, Disneyland Paris has a convention center, sports facilities, an entertainment and shopping complex, restaurants, thousands of hotel rooms, and, of course, the theme park itself. The park is made up of five "lands": Main Street U.S.A., Frontierland, Adventureland, Fantasyland, and Discoveryland. The central theme of each land is relentlessly echoed in every detail, from attractions to restaurant menus to souvenirs.

Main Street U.S.A. is the scene of the Disney Parades held every afternoon and—during holiday periods—every evening, too. Top attractions at **Frontierland** are the chilling Phantom Manor, haunted by holographic spooks, and the thrilling runaway mine train of Big Thunder Mountain, a roller coaster that plunges wildly through floods and avalanches in a setting meant to evoke Monument Valley. Whiffs of Arabia, Africa, and the West Indies give **Adventureland** its exotic cachet; the spicy meals and snacks served here rank among the best food in the theme park. Don't miss the Pirates of the Caribbean, an exciting mise-en-scène populated by eerily human computer-driven figures, or Indiana Jones and the Temple of Doom, a breathtaking ride that relives some of our luckless hero's most exciting moments.

Fantasyland charms the youngest park visitors with familiar cartoon characters from such Disney classics as *Snow White, Pinocchio, Dumbo,* and *Peter Pan.* The focal point of Fantasyland, and indeed Disneyland Paris, is Le Château de la Belle au Bois Dormant (Sleeping Beauty's Castle), a 140-ft, bubble gum–pink structure topped with 16 blue- and gold-tipped turrets. The castle design was allegedly inspired by illustrations from a medieval Book of Hours. In the dungeon is a scaly, green 2-ton dragon who rumbles and grumbles in his sleep and occasionally rouses to roar—an impressive feat of engineering that terrifies every tot in the crowd! **Discoveryland** is a futuristic spin for high-tech Disney entertainment. Robots on roller skates welcome you to Star Tours, a pitching, plunging, sense-confounding ride through intergalactic space. Space Mountain's star-bejeweled roller coaster ride catapults you through the Milky Way.

Walt Disney Studios opened next to the Disneyland park in March 2002, and is divided into four "production zones" behind imposing entrance gates. **Front Lot,** with its 100-ft water-tower based on the one erected in 1939 for Disney Studios in Burbank, California, contains shops, a restaurant, and a studio recreating the atmosphere of Sunset Boulevard. **Animation Courtyard** has Disney artists demonstrating the various phases of character animation; Animagique brings to life scenes from

Pinocchio and *The Lion King*, while Aladdin's Genie hosts Flying Carpets over Agrabah.

Production Courtyard incorporates the Walt Disney Television Studios; Cinemagique, a special-effects tribute to U.S. and European cinema; and a behind-the-scenes Studio Tram tour of location sites, movie props, studio design, and costuming, ending with a visit to *Catastrophe Canyon* in the heart of a film shoot. Highlights of **Back Lot** are Armageddon Special Effects, where you'll fly through a flaming meteor shower aboard the Mir space station; and a Stunt Show Spectacular, involving cars, motorbikes and Jet Skis, at a 3,000-seater, giant-screen, outdoor arena.

For entertainment outside the theme parks, check out **Disney Village** (☎ 01–60–45–68–04 information), a vast pleasure mall designed by celebrated American architect Frank Gehry. Featured are American-style restaurants (crab shack, diner, deli, steak house), a disco, and a dinner theater where Buffalo Bill stages his Wild West Show twice nightly. An 18-hole golf course is open to the public. ✉ *Marne-la-Vallée* ☎ *01–60–30–60–30* 🌐 *www.disneylandparis.com* 🎫 *Disneyland Paris and Walt Disney Studios (prices vary according to season) each €29–€38* ⏲ *Disneyland Paris mid-June–mid-Sept., daily 9 AM–10 PM; mid-Sept.–mid-June, daily 10–8; Walt Disney Studios daily 10 AM–6 PM (tickets for Walt Disney Studios are valid for Disneyland Paris for the last 3 hrs before closing).*

Where to Stay & Eat

$–$$$ ✕ **Disneyland Restaurants.** Disneyland Paris is peppered with places to eat, ranging from snack bars and fast-food joints to five full-service restaurants—all with a distinguishing theme. In addition, Disney Village and Disney Hotels have restaurants open to the public. But since these are outside the park, it is not recommended that you waste time traveling to them for lunch. Disneyland Paris has relaxed its no-alcohol policy and now serves wine and beer in the park's sit-down restaurants, as well as in the hotels and restaurants outside the park. ☎ *01–60–45–65–40* 💳 *AE, DC, MC, V accepted at sit-down restaurants.*

$$–$$$$ 🏨 **Disneyland Hotels.** The resort has 5,000 rooms in six hotels, all a short distance from the park, ranging from the luxurious Disneyland Hotel to the not-so-rustic Camp Davy Crockett. Free transportation to the park is available at every hotel. Packages including Disneyland lodging, entertainment, and admission are available through travel agents in Europe. ✉ *Centre de Réservations, B.P. 100, 77777 Marne-la-Vallée Cedex 4* ☎ *01–60–30–60–30; 407/934–7639 in U.S.* 📠 *01–49–30–71–00* ♿ *Restaurant, café, indoor pool, exercise facilities, sauna, bar, Internet, free parking* 💳 *AE, DC, MC, V.*

Disneyland Paris A to Z

To research prices, get advice from other travelers, and book travel arrangements, visit www.fodors.com.

BUS TRAVEL

Shuttle buses link Disneyland Paris to Roissy (56 km [35 mi]) and Orly (50 km [31 mi]) airports. Each trip lasts around 45 minutes and the fare is €14 one-way.

CAR TRAVEL

The Strasbourg-bound A4 expressway leads from Paris to Disneyland Paris, at Marne-la-Vallée, a journey of 32 km (20 mi) that in normal traffic takes about 30 minutes. The 4-km (2½-mi) route from the expressway to the entrance of the theme park is clearly marked. Day visitors must head for the PARKING VISITEURS, which costs €8 per car and is 600 yards from the theme-park entrance.

TRAIN TRAVEL

Disneyland Paris's suburban train station (Marne-la-Vallée–Chessy) is just 100 yards from the entrance to both the theme park and Festival Disney. Trains run every 10 to 20 minutes from RER-A stations in central Paris: Charles-de-Gaulle–Étoile, Auber, Châtelet Les Halles, Gare de Lyon, and Nation. The trip takes about 40 minutes and costs €13 round-trip (including the métro to the RER). A TGV station next to the RER station at Disneyland Paris offers direct train service to and from Lille, Lyon, and Marseille.

VISITOR INFORMATION

Disneyland Paris S.C.A. ✉ Central Reservations Office, B.P. 104, 77777 Marne-la-Vallée, Cedex 4, France ☎ 01-60-30-60-30 📠 01-49-30-71-00 🌐 www.disneylandparis.com. **Walt Disney World Central Reservations** 📫 Box 10,100, Lake Buena Vista, FL 32830-0100 ☎ 407/934-7639 🌐 disneyworld.disney.go.com.

FONTAINEBLEAU & VAUX-LE-VICOMTE

Fontainebleau, with its historic château—favored retreat of King François I and Napoléon—is a favorite destination for excursions, especially since the superb Baroque château of Vaux-le-Vicomte is close by.

Fontainebleau

Like Chambord in the Loire Valley and Compiègne to the north of Paris, Fontainebleau earned royal esteem as a hunting base. As at Versailles, a hunting lodge once stood on the site of the current château, along with a chapel built in 1169 and consecrated by exiled (later murdered and canonized) English archbishop Thomas à Becket.

The **Château de Fontainebleau** you see today dates from the 16th century, although additions were made by various royal incumbents over the next 300 years. The palace was begun under flamboyant Renaissance King François I, the French contemporary of England's Henry VIII.

The king hired Italian artists Il Rosso (a pupil of Michelangelo) and Primaticcio to embellish his château. In fact, they did much more: by introducing the pagan allegories and elegant lines of Mannerism to France, they revolutionized the realm of French decorative art. Their extraordinary frescoes and stuccowork can be admired in the **Galerie François-I** (Francis I Gallery) and the crown jewel of the interior, the **Salle de Bal.** Here in the ceremonial ballroom, which is nearly 100 ft long, you can admire the dazzling 16th-century frescoes and gilding. Completed under Henri II, François's successor, it is luxuriantly wood paneled, with a parquet floor whose gleaming finish reflects the patterns on the ceiling above. Like the château as a whole, the room exudes a sense of elegance and style—but on a more intimate, human scale than at Versailles: this is Renaissance, not Baroque.

Napoléon's apartments occupied the first floor. You can see a lock of his hair, his Légion d'Honneur medal, his imperial uniform, the hat he wore on his return from Elba in 1815, and one bed in which he definitely did spend a night (almost every town in France boasts a bed in which the emperor supposedly snoozed). There is also a throne room—Napoléon spurned the one at Versailles, a palace he disliked—and the Queen's Boudoir, known as the Room of the Six Maries (occupants included ill-fated Marie-Antoinette and Napoléon's second wife, Marie-

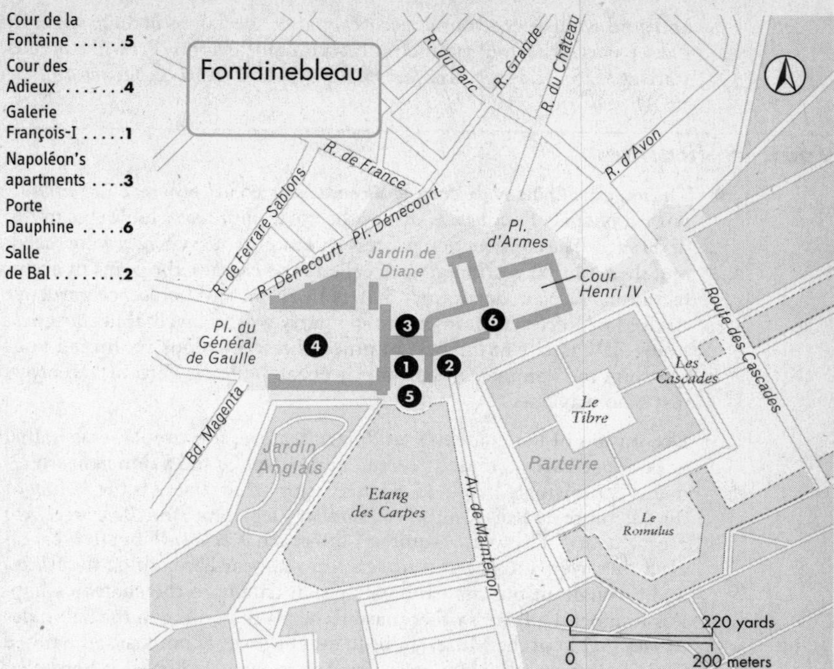

Louise). Highlights of other salons include 17th-century tapestries, marble reliefs by Jacquet de Grenoble, and paintings and frescoes by the versatile Primaticcio.

Although Louis XIV's architectural fancy was concentrated on Versailles, he commissioned Mansart to design new pavilions and had André Le Nôtre replant the gardens at Fontainebleau, to which the king and his court returned every fall for the hunting season. But it was Napoléon who made a Versailles out of Fontainebleau, as it were, by spending lavishly to restore it. He held Pope Pius VII prisoner here in 1812, signed the second Church-State Concordat here in 1813, and, in the cobbled **Cour des Adieux** (Farewell Courtyard), said good-bye to his Old Guard in 1814 as he began his brief exile on the Mediterranean island of Elba. The famous Horseshoe Staircase that dominates the Cour des Adieux, once the Cour du Cheval Blanc (White Horse Courtyard), was built by Androuet du Cerceau for Louis XIII (1610–43).

Another courtyard—the **Cour de la Fontaine** (Fountain Courtyard)—was commissioned by Napoléon in 1812 and adjoins the Étang des Carpes (Carp Pond). Ancient carp are alleged to swim here, although Allied soldiers drained the pond in 1915 and ate all the fish, and, in the event they missed some, Hitler's hordes did likewise in 1940.

The **Porte Dauphine** is the most beautiful of the various gateways that connect the complex of buildings; its name commemorates the fact that the Dauphine—the heir to the throne, later Louis XIII—was christened under its archway in 1606. ✉ *Pl. du Général-de-Gaulle* ☎ *01–60–71–50–70* 🎫 *Château €5.50, Napoleon's Apartments €3 extra, gardens free* ⏲ *Château Wed.–Mon. 9:30–5, gardens daily 9* AM*–dusk.*

Where to Eat

$$ ✕ **Table des Maréchaux.** Close to the château, in the Napoléon hotel, this restaurant serves classic French fare in a plush salon, with red-velvet seats

and gold wallpaper, around a central patio; specialties include snails in flaky pastry, fried mullet, and rabbit with mushrooms. Prix-fixe menus start at €25. ✉ *9 rue Grande* ☎ *01–60–39–50–50* *Jacket and tie* *AE, DC, MC, V.*

Vaux-le-Vicomte

★ The majestic **Château de Vaux-le-Vicomte,** started in 1656 by court finance wizard Nicolas Fouquet, is one of the most impressive buildings in Ile-de-France. The construction process was monstrous: villages were razed, and then 18,000 workmen were called in to execute the plans of architect Louis Le Vau, decorator Charles Le Brun, and landscape gardener André Le Nôtre. The housewarming party was so lavish that star guest Louis XIV, tetchy at the best of times, threw a jealous fit, hurled Fouquet into the slammer, and promptly began building Versailles to prove just who was boss.

Decoration of the château's landmark feature, the **cupola,** was halted at Fouquet's arrest, and the ceiling of the oval **Grand Salon** beneath remains depressingly blank. Le Brun's major achievement is the ceiling of the **Chambre du Roi** (King's Bedchamber) depicting *Time Bearing Truth Heavenward*. The word "squirrel" in French is *écureuil,* but in local dialect they were known as *fouquets*; they appear here (along the frieze) and throughout the château, a sly visual tribute to the château's hapless founder. Le Brun's other masterwork is the ceiling in the **Salon des Muses** (Salon of the Muses), a brilliant allegorical composition painted in glowing, sensuous colors surpassing anything he achieved at Versailles. A clever **exhibit,** complete with life-size wax figures, explains the rise and fall of Nicolas Fouquet. Although accused by Louis XIV and subsequent historians of megalomania and shady financial dealings, he was apparently condemned on little evidence by a court eager to please the jealous, irascible monarch.

Le Nôtre's stupendous, studiously restored **gardens** contain statues, waterfalls, and fountains that play afternoons on the second and last Saturday of each month (Apr.–Oct.). There is also a **Musée des Équipages** (Carriage Museum)—stocked with carriages, saddles, and a smithy—near the entrance. Check with the château office or Web site to see if there are any special events scheduled around the time of your visit—candlelight tours, concerts, and other delights sometimes adorn the Vaux-le-Vicomte schedule. ✉ *Domaine de Vaux-le-Vicomte, 77950 Maincy* ☎ *01–64–14–41–90* *www.vaux-le-vicomte.com* *€10; candlelight visits €13* *Château Easter–Nov. 11, daily 10–6. Candlelight visits May–Oct., Sat. 8–midnight.*

Where to Eat

¢–$ ✕ **L'Écureuil.** An imposing barn to the right of the château entrance has been transformed into this self-service cafeteria, where you can enjoy fine steaks (insist yours is cooked enough), coffee, or a snack beneath the ancient rafters of a wood-beam roof. The restaurant is open daily for lunch and tea, and for dinner during candlelight visits. ✉ *Château de Vaux-le-Vicomte* ☎ *01–60–66–95–66* *MC, V.*

Fontainebleau & Vaux-le-Vicomte A to Z

To research prices, get advice from other travelers, and book travel arrangements, visit www.fodors.com.

CAR TRAVEL

From Paris's Porte d'Orléans or Porte d'Italie, take A6, then N7 to Fontainebleau (total distance 72 km [45 mi]). Vaux-le-Vicomte is 21 km

(13 mi) north of Fontainebleau. Take N6 to Melun, then N36 northeast (direction Meaux), turning right after 1½ km (1 mi) or so along D215.

GUIDED TOURS

Cityrama and Paris Vision run half-day trips to Fontainebleau (including a visit to the nearby painters' village of Barbizon). The cost is €54.

Cityrama ✉ 4 pl. des Pyramides, Paris ☎ 01-44-55-61-00 🌐 graylineparis.com. **Paris Vision** ✉ 214 rue de Rivoli Paris ☎ 01-42-60-30-01 🌐 www.parisvision.com.

TRAIN TRAVEL

Fontainebleau is about 50 minutes from Paris's Gare de Lyon; take a bus to complete the 3-km (2-mi) trip from the station (Fontainebleau-Avon) to the château. You can buy a *forfait* (fixed price) pass including train and bus tickets plus château admission, for €20 at Gare de Lyon. Vaux-le-Vicomte is a 7-km (4-mi) taxi ride from the nearest station at Melun, served by regular trains from Paris and Fontainebleau. The taxi ride costs about €15.

VISITOR INFORMATION

Fontainebleau Tourism ✉ 4 rue Royale, 77300 Fontainebleau ☎ 01-60-74-99-99 🌐 www.tourisme.fr/office-de-tourisme/fontainebleau.htm.

GIVERNY

The village of Giverny has become a place of pilgrimage for art lovers. It was here that Claude Monet lived, for 43 years, until his death in 1926 at the age of 86, adorning his house with a water-lily garden that many feel resembles a three-dimensional Impressionist painting. After decades of neglect, his pretty pink house with green shutters, his studios, and ★ his garden with its famous lily pond, the **Maison et Jardin de Claude Monet** (Claude Monet House and Garden), were lovingly restored thanks to gifts from around the world and, in particular, from the United States. Late spring is perhaps the best time to visit, when the apple trees are in blossom and the garden is a riot of color. Try to avoid summer weekends and afternoons in July and August, when the limited capacity of Monet's home and gardens is pushed to the limit by busloads of tourists.

Monet was brought up in Normandy and, like many of the other Impressionists, was attracted by the soft light of the Seine Valley. After several years at Argenteuil, just north of Paris, he moved downriver to Giverny in 1883 along with his two sons, his mistress Alice Hoschedé (whom he later married), and her six children. By 1890, a prospering Monet was able to buy the house outright. Three years later, he purchased another plot of land across the lane to continue his gardening experiments, diverting the Epte River to make a pond.

Monet's house has a warm family feeling that may come as a welcome break after visiting stately French châteaux. The rooms have been restored to Monet's original designs: the kitchen with blue tiles, the buttercup-yellow dining room, and Monet's bedroom on the second floor. Reproductions of his own works, as well as some of the Japanese prints Monet avidly collected, are displayed around the house. The garden, with flowers spilling out across the paths, is as cheerful and natural as the house—quite unlike formal French gardens. The enchanting water garden, with its water lilies, bridges, and rhododendrons, is across the lane that runs to the side of the house and can be reached through a tunnel. The lilies and Japanese bridges became signature touches of his garden and now help to conjure up an image of a grizzly bearded Monet dabbing cheerfully at his canvases—capturing changes in light and weather in a way that was to have a major influence on 20th-century art. ✉ *84 rue Claude-Monet* ☎ *02–32–51–28–21* 🌐 *www.giverny.org* 🎫 *€5.50; gardens only, €4* ⏲ *Apr.–Oct., Tues.–Sun. 10–6.*

The spacious, airy **Musée d'Art Américain** (American Art Museum), endowed by Chicago art patrons Daniel and Judith Terra, displays works by American Impressionists who were influenced by—and often studied with—Claude Monet. ✉ *99 rue Claude-Monet* ☎ *02–32–51–94–65* 🎫 *€5* ⏲ *Apr.–Nov., Tues.–Sun. 10–6.*

Where to Stay & Eat

$$ ✕ **Baudy.** Back in Monet's day, this pretty-in-pink villa was the hotel of the American painters colony. Today the dining room and terrace are more modern than historic, but parts of this old *épicerie-buvette* are still so enchanting (notably, the luscious rose gardens and the studio hut where Cézanne once took up residence) that a recent art book was devoted to La Maison Baudy. This enchanting mise-en-scène makes it easier to forgive the very simple cuisine and busloads of tour groups. ✉ *81 rue Claude-Monet* ☎ *02–32–21–10–03* 💳 *MC, V* ⏲ *Closed Mon. and Nov.–Mar. No dinner Sun.*

$$ ✕ **Les Jardins de Giverny.** This restaurant, with a tile-floor dining room overlooking a rose garden, is a few minutes' walk from Monet's house. Enjoy the €20 menu or choose from a repertoire of inventive dishes such as foie gras spiked with calvados, duck in cider, or scallops with wild mushrooms. ✉ *Rue du Roy* ☎ *02–32–21–60–80* 💳 *AE, MC, V* ⏲ *Closed Mon. and Dec.–Feb. No dinner Sun.–Fri.*

$–$$$ 🏨 **Giverny B&Bs.** Giverny's dire shortage of hotels is made up for by a plethora of enticing, stylish, and affordable bed-and-breakfasts set up in many of the town's homes. Particularly notable are **Le Clos Fleuri** (✉ 5 rue de la Dîme ☎📠 02–32–21–36–51), a Norman manor house set in a lovely garden and run by Claude and Danielle Fouche; **La Réserve** (✉ Rue Blanche-Hoschedé ☎📠 02–32–21–99–09), about a mile outside town, an expansive residence surrounded by orchards and with gorgeous, antiques-adorned and wood-beamed guest apartments, some of which have fireplaces and canopy beds; and the residence of **Marie-Claire Boscher** (✉ 1 rue du Colombier ☎📠 02–32–51–39–70), that used to be a hotel-restaurant that Monet frequented. (🌐 www.giverny.org/hotels).

$$ 🏨 **La Musardière.** Just a short stroll from chez Monet, this manor house has a cozy lobby, guest rooms with views overlooking a park, and its own restaurant-crêperie (closed December–February, no lunch Monday). ✉ *123 rue Claude-Monet, 27620 Giverny* ☎ *02–32–21–03–18* 📠 *02–32–21–60–00* 🛏 *25 rooms, 5 suites* 🛎 *Restaurant, tennis court, pool; no a/c* 💳 *AE, DC, MC, V.*

Giverny A to Z

To research prices, get advice from other travelers, and book travel arrangements, visit www.fodors.com.

CAR TRAVEL

Take expressway A13 from Paris to the Vernon exit (D181). Cross the Seine in Vernon and follow D5 to Giverny (total distance just over 80 km [50 mi]).

GUIDED TOURS

Cityrama runs afternoon tours to Giverny, lasting about five hours, Tuesday–Saturday; the cost is €60.

ℹ Cityrama ✉ 4 pl. des Pyramides, Paris ☎ 01–44–55–61–00.

TRAIN TRAVEL

Take the train from Paris's Gare St-Lazare to Vernon (50 minutes). Giverny is 5½ km (3½ mi) away by bus or taxi, which you can get at the train station. Call the Vernon Tourist Office for information.

VISITOR INFORMATION

Vernon Tourist Office ☎ 02-32-51-39-60.

VERSAILLES

Numbers in the text correspond to numbers on the Versailles map.

Paris in the 17th century was a rowdy, rabble-ridden city. Louis XIV hated it and set about in search of an alternative power base. He settled on Versailles, 20 km (12 mi) west of Paris, where his father had a small château–hunting lodge.

1 Fodor's Choice ★ Today the **Château de Versailles** seems monstrously big, but it wasn't large enough for the army of 20,000 noblemen, servants, and hangers-on who moved in with Louis. A new city—a new capital, in fact—had to be constructed from scratch to accommodate them. Tough-thinking town planners promptly dreamt up vast mansions and avenues broader than the Champs-Élysées—all in biceps-flexing Baroque.

It was hardly surprising that Louis XIV's successors rapidly felt out of sync with their architectural inheritance. The Sun King's successors, Louis XV and Louis XVI, preferred to cower in small retreats in the gardens, well out of the mighty château's shadow. The two most famous of these structures are the Petit Trianon, a model of classical harmony and proportion built by Louis XV; and the Hameau, where Marie-Antoinette could play at being a shepherdess amid the ersatz rusticity of her Potemkin hamlet. The contrast between the majestic and the domesticated is an important part of Versailles's appeal. But pomp and bombast dominate the mood here, and you won't need reminding that you're in the world's grandest palace—or one of France's most popular tourist attractions. The park and gardens outside are a great place to stretch your legs while taking in details of formal landscaping that you'll also see at Versailles.

The château was built under court architects Le Vau and Mansart between 1662 and 1690; the entrance is through the gilt-and-iron gates from huge place d'Armes. In the center of the building, across the sprawling cobbled forecourt, are the rooms that belonged to the king and queen. The two wings were occupied by the royal children and princes; attendants were up in the attics.

One of the highlights of the tour is the **Galerie des Glaces** (Hall of Mirrors), fully restored to its original dazzle. It was here that Bismarck proclaimed the unified German Empire in 1871, and the controversial Treaty of Versailles, asserting Germany's responsibility for World War I, was signed in 1919. The **Grands Appartements** (State Apartments) are formal; the **Petits Appartements** (Private Apartments), where royal family and friends lived, are on a more human scale. The intimate **Opéra Royal,** the first oval hall in France, was designed for Louis XV. Touch the "marble" loges—they're actually painted wood. The chapel, built by Mansart, is a study in white-and-gold solemnity. The former state rooms and the sumptuous debate chamber of the **Aile du Midi** (South Wing) are also open to the public, with infrared headphone commentary (available in English) explaining Versailles's parliamentary history. ☎ *01–30–83–77–88* 🌐 *www.chateauversailles.fr* 🎫 *Château €7.50, par-*

Château de Versailles 1
Grandes Écuries 5
Grand Trianon 3
Parc de Versailles 2
Petit Trianon 4

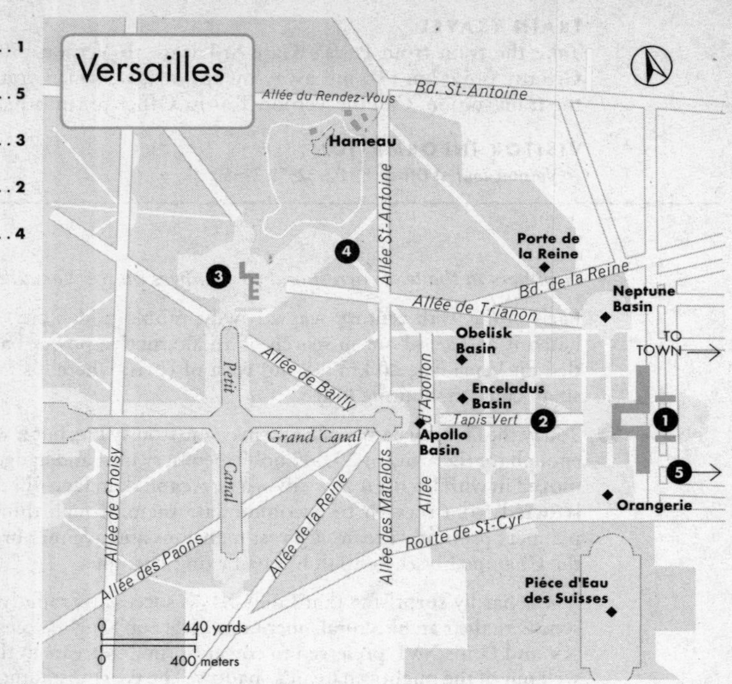

liament exhibition €4 extra ⏲ *May–Sept., Tues.–Sun. 9–6:30; Oct.–Apr., Tues.–Sun. 9–5:30.*

★ ❷ After the awesome feast of interior pomp, the **Parc de Versailles** (Versailles Park) is an ideal place to catch your breath. The gardens were designed by André Le Nôtre, whose work here represents classical French landscaping at its most formal and sophisticated. The 250-acre grounds include woods, lawns, flower beds, statues, artificial lakes, and fountains galore (for a guided tour of the groves, call 01–30–83–77–88). An extensive tree-replacement scheme—necessary once a century—was launched in 1998 to recapture the full impact of Le Nôtre's artful vistas; replantings became all the more necessary after 10,000 trees were uprooted by a hurricane in 1999. The cost of that damage came to some $35 million, and American donors contributed 40% of that amount. The distances are vast—the Trianons themselves are more than a mile from the château—so you might want to climb aboard a horse-drawn carriage (round-trip from the château to Trianon, €7), take the electric train (€3.20 single trip, €5.10 round-trip), or rent a bike from the **Grille de la Reine** near the Trianon Palace Hotel (€4.40 per hour) or from the **Petite-Venise** building at the top of the Grand Canal (€5.10 per hour, or €25 for six hours, ☎ 01–39–66–97–66). You can also drive to the Trianons and Canal through the Grille de la Reine (€5.50 per car). The park is at its golden-leafed best in fall but is also enticing in summer—especially on Sunday afternoons from mid-April through mid-October, when the fountains are in full flow. You can hire a rowing boat (€8.30 for four) from the start of the Grand Canal; there is a popular restaurant nearby. 🎫 *Park free; €5 for Sun. fountain displays* ⏲ *Daily 7 AM–8 PM or dusk.*

At one end of the Petit Canal, about 1½ km (1 mi) from the château, stands
3 the **Grand Trianon,** a pink-marble pleasure palace built by Jules Hardouin-Mansart in the late 1680s. *€5 (joint ticket with Petit Trianon) May–Sept., Tues.–Sun. noon–6:30; Oct.–Apr., Tues.–Sun. noon–5:30.*

★ 4 The **Petit Trianon,** close to the Grand Trianon, is a sumptuously furnished neoclassical mansion erected in the 1760s by architect Jacques Gabriel. Louis XV had a superb botanical garden planted here; some of the trees from that era survive today. Louis XVI presented the Petit Trianon to Marie-Antoinette, who spent lavish sums creating an idealized world nearby, the charming **Hameau,** a hamlet of thatched-roof cottages, complete with water mill, lake, and pigeon loft. Here the tragic queen played out her happiest days pretending to be a shepherdess tending a flock of perfumed sheep, and here, today, her spirit is stronger than anywhere else in France, making this a must-do for fans of the hapless queen. *€5 (joint ticket with Grand Trianon) May–Sept., Tues.–Sun. noon–6:30; Oct.–Apr., Tues.–Sun. noon–5:30.*

5 Facing the château are the Trojan-size royal stables, the **Grandes Écuries** (Great Stables). Nowadays the **Musée des Carosses** (Carriage Museum) is housed here, with its distinguished array of royal and imperial carriages. *1 av. de Paris 01–30–21–54–82 €2 Apr.–Oct., weekends 12:30–6:30.*

The **town of Versailles** is often overlooked. Although you may be tired from exploring the palace and park, it's worth strolling along the town's broad, leafy boulevards. The majestic scale of many buildings is a reminder that this was, after all, the capital of France from 1682 to 1789 (and again from 1871 to 1879). Visible to the right, as you look toward the town from the palace, is the dome of the austere **Cathédrale St-Louis** (Pl. St-Louis), built from 1743 to 1754; it has a fine organ loft and two-tiered facade.

To the left of place d'Armes, beyond elegant, octagonal place Hoche, is the sturdy Baroque church of **Notre-Dame** (At rue Hoche and rue de la Paroisse), built from 1684 to 1686 by Jules Hardouin-Mansart as the parish church for Louis XIV's brand-new town. The street in front of Notre-Dame, rue de la Paroisse, leads up to **place du Marché,** site of a magnificent morning market every Tuesday, Friday, and Sunday. The **Musée Lambinet** (54 bd. de la Reine 01–39–50–30–32 €5 Tues.–Sun. 2–5) behind Notre-Dame church, is an imposing 18th-century mansion with a maze of cozy rooms furnished with paintings, weapons, fans, and porcelain.

Where to Eat

★ $$$$ **Les Trois Marches.** One of the best-known restaurants in the Paris area, in the Trianon Palace hotel near an entrance to the château park, serves chef Gérard Vié's creative dishes such as duckling roasted with vinegar and honey. The prix-fixe (€49) weekday lunch is the most affordable option. *1 bd. de la Reine 01–39–50–13–21 Reservations essential Jacket and tie AE, DC, MC, V Closed Aug.*

$–$$ **Quai No. 1.** Barometers, sails, and model boats fill this small seafood restaurant. In summer you can enjoy your meal outside on the terrace. Fish with sauerkraut and home-smoked salmon are specialties; any dish on the two prix-fixe menus is a good value. *1 av. de St-Cloud 01–39–50–42–26 MC, V Closed Mon. No dinner Sun.*

Versailles A to Z

To research prices, get advice from other travelers, and book travel arrangements, visit www.fodors.com.

CAR TRAVEL

From Paris, head west on highway A13 from Porte d'Auteuil (a total distance of 20 km [12 mi]). Allow 15–30 minutes, depending on traffic.

GUIDED TOURS

Many guided-tour companies offer excursions to Versailles. Paris Vision arranges a variety of half- and full-day guided tours of Versailles costing between €34 and €87. Cityrama is another popular Versailles tour-company option.

Cityrama ✉ 4 pl. des Pyramides, Paris ☎ 01-44-55-61-00. **Paris Vision** ✉ 214 rue de Rivoli, Paris ☎ 01-42-60-30-01.

TRAIN TRAVEL

Three train routes travel between Paris and Versailles (20–30 minutes away). The RER-C to Versailles Rive-Gauche takes you closest to the château (600 yards away via avenue de Sceaux). An all-inclusive forfait pass including return train fare plus château admission costs €15. The other trains run from Paris's Gare St-Lazare to Versailles Rive-Droite (closer to the Trianons and town market but 1 km (½ mi) from the château via rue du Maréchal-Foch and avenue de St-Cloud) and from Paris's Gare Montparnasse to Versailles-Chantiers (1 km [½ mi] from the château via rue des États-Généraux and avenue de Paris). From Versailles-Chantiers, some trains continue on to Chartres.

VISITOR INFORMATION

Versailles Office du Tourisme ✉ 2 bis av. de Paris, 78000 Versailles ☎ 01-39-24-88-88 🌐 www.versailles-tourisme.com.

UNDERSTANDING PARIS

PORTRAIT OF PARIS

PARIS AT A GLANCE

BOOKS & MOVIES

VOCABULARY

MENU GUIDE

PARIS À LA PARISIENNE

IT IS MIDNIGHT at the neighborhood brasserie. Waiters swathed in starchy white glance discreetly at their watches as a family—mother, son, and wife—sip the last of a bottle of Chiroubles and scrape up the remains of their steak tartare with silverware dexterously poised with arched wrists. They are all wearing scarves: the mother's is a classic silk *carré,* tastefully folded at the throat; the wife's is Indian gauze and glitters; the son's is wool and hangs like a prayer shawl over his black turtleneck. Finished, they stir their coffee without looking. They smoke: the mother, Gitanes; the son, Marlboros; the wife rolls her own from a silver case. Alone, they act out their personal theater, uncontrived and unobserved, their Doisneauesque tableau reflected only in the etched-glass mirrors around them, enhanced by the sobriety of their dress and the pallor of their Gallic skin.

Whoever first said that "God found Paris too perfect, so he invented the Parisians" had it wrong. This extraordinary maquette of a city, with its landscape of mansards and chimneys, its low-slung bridges and vast boulevards, is nothing but a rough-sketched stage set that drinks its color from the lifeblood of those infamous Parisians whom everyone claims to hate but whom everyone loves to emulate.

Mythologized for their arrogance, charm, and savoir faire—as well as their disdain for the foreigners they find genetically incapable of sharing these characteristics—the Parisians continue to mesmerize. For the generations of American and English voyeurs who have ventured curiously, enviously into countless mirrored brasseries, downed numerous bottles of *cuvée maison,* fumbled at nautical knots in newly bought scarves, even suffered squashed berets and unfiltered Gauloises, the Parisians remain inimitable—and infinitely fascinating.

Alternately patronizing and self-effacing, they move through their big-city lives with enviable style and urban grit. They are chronically thin, despite the truckloads of beef stew, pâté, and tarte Tatin they consume without blushing. They still make the cigarette look glamorous—and a graceful bit of stage business indispensable to good talk—in spite of the gas-mask levels of smoke they generate. They stride over bridges aloof to the monuments framed in every sweeping perspective, yet they discourse—lightly, charmingly—on Racine, NATO, and the latest ruling of the Académie Française. They are proud, practical, often witty, and always chic, from the thrift-shop style of the Sorbonne student to the Chanel suit on the thin shoulders of a well-boned *dame d'un certain âge.*

Ferociously (with some justice) in love with their own culture—theater, literature, film, art, architecture, haute cuisine, and haute couture—Parisians worship France as ardently as New Yorkers dismiss the rest of America. While Manhattanites berate the nonentities west of the Hudson, Parisians romanticize the rest of France, making an art of the weekend foray and the regional vacation: why should we go *à l'étranger* (abroad) when we have the Dordogne, the Auvergne, and Bretagne?

And for all their vulnerability to what they frame as the "American Assault," for every Disney store, action film, and McDonald's in Paris (not to mention Benetton and Laura Ashley, and France's own Celio, Orcade, and Descamps chains), there is a plethora of unique shops selling all-white blouses, African bracelets, dog jackets, and Art Deco jewelry.

And for every commercial bookstore chain there are five tiny *librairies* selling tooled-leather encyclopedias, collections of out-of-print plays, and yellow paperbacks lovingly pressed in waxed paper. The famous *bouquinistes* hover like squatters along the Seine, their folding metal boxes opening to showcase a trove of old magazines, scholarly journals, and hand-colored botanical prints that flap from clothespins in the wind. Yet they are not nomads, these bouquinistes: dormant through winter, their metal stands are fixtures as permanent and respectable as those of the medieval merchants that built shops along the cobbled streets of the city. They are determinedly Parisian—individual, independent, and one-of-a-kind.

But in spite of their fierce individuality, Parisians also demand that certain conformities be followed. And here the gap between native and visitor widens. If Parisians treat tourists a bit like occupying forces—disdainfully selling them Beaujolais Nouveau in July, seating them by the kitchen doors, refusing to understand honest attempts at French—they have formed their opinions based on bitter experience. The waiter who scorches tourists with flared nostrils and firmly turned back was trained to respect his métier—meaning not pouring Coke with foie gras or bringing the check with dessert. The meal is a sacred ritual here, and diverging from the norm is tantamount to disgrace.

Doing as the Parisians do, you can go a long way toward closing the gap of disdain. When dining, for example, give yourself over to the meal. Order a kir as an aperitif instead of a whiskey or beer. Drink wine or mineral water with your meal. Order coffee *after* dessert, not with it. And accept the fact that diet sodas are rarely available in restaurants.

The wine will come chilled, aired, and ready for tasting with the respect usually reserved for a holy relic. Enjoy each course, sipping, discussing, digesting leisurely; the waiter will not be pressed by hurried tourists. When you're done eating, align your silverware on the plate (a sign for the waiter to clear). Cheese can be the climax of the meal, well worth skipping dessert if necessary, and a magnificent way to finish the wine. Have your coffee after dessert and, without exception, black with sugar; a milky froth will not do on a full stomach. The art of stirring *un express* in Paris rivals the art of scarf-tying.

Ask for *l'addition*; the waiter will not commit the gaffe of bringing the check uninvited. And no matter how deeply you enter into your role as Parisian manqué, avoid saying "*Garçon*!" (Say "*S'il vous plait*" instead.) These are rules that apply at the most unassuming corner bistro and the grandest three-star restaurant; following them can thaw the waiterly chill that can render a meal unforgettable—for all the wrong reasons—and can make for meals that are as memorable as an evening at the Opéra de la Bastille, complete with sets and choreography.

It is this fixed attention to experience and detail that sets the Parisians apart. Desk-eaters they are not: when they work, they work without a coffee break. When they eat, business still grinds to a halt. Weekends are sacred. And oh, do they vacation, all of them at once, all of them abandoning Paris in August with a fierceness of purpose that mirrors their commitment to food—an all-night drive, a rental booked months in advance.

By matching that Parisian passion for the complete, the correct, the *comme il faut,* your own experience will be all the more authentic. Having eaten with proper reverence, keep your sightseeing agenda at the same lofty level. If you go to the Louvre, spend the day; do not lope through the wide corridors in search of *La Joconde* (*Mona Lisa*). You can leave for a three-hour lunch, if you choose, and come back with the same ticket, even avoiding the lines by reentering via the Passage Richelieu. If time won't allow an all-day survey, do as the locals do: choose an era and immerse yourself. Then take a break and plunge into another. Eavesdrop on a guided tour. Go back and look at a painting again. And take the time to stare at the ceilings: the architecture of this historic monument alone merits a day's tour.

As you apply yourself to the Parisian experience in spirit, diverge in fact: walk. The natives may prefer to sit in a café or even hurry straight home by métro ("*métro, boulot, dodo*"—"métro, work, sleep"—as the saying goes). You, as a visitor, are obliged to wander down tortuous medieval streets; up vast boulevards so overscaled you seem to gain no ground; over bridges that open up broad perspectives on illuminated monuments that outnumber even those in Rome.

They are all there, the clichés of Paris romance: the moon over the Seine reflected in the wakes of the Bateaux Mouches (river barges); the steps Leslie Caron blushed down in *An American in Paris*; the lovers kissing under the lime tree pollards. But there are surprises, too: a troop of hunting horns striking unearthly sonorities under a resonant bridge; flocks of wild geese flying low over the towers of Notre-Dame; and a ragged expatriate writer leaving a well-scraped plat du jour on the table as he bolts away from the bill.

(*C'est dommage*: he would have been well fed by Ragueneau, the baker-writer in *Cyrano de Bergerac* who opened his Paris pastry shop to starving poets.)

The more resourceful you are, the more surprises you will unearth in your Paris wanderings. Follow the strains of Lully into a chamber orchestra rehearsal in St-Julien-le-Pauvre; if you're quiet and still, you may not be asked to leave. Brave the smoking lounge at intermission at the Comédie-Française and you'll find the battered leather chair that the young actor Molière sat in as *L'Invalide Imaginaire*. Take the métro to *L'Armée du Salut* (Salvation Army) in the 13e *arrondissement* (ward), and you'll not only find Art Deco percolators and hand-knit stockings but you'll also be inside the futuristic curves of a 1933 Le Corbusier masterwork.

Tear yourself away from the big-name museums and you'll discover a world of small galleries. Go in: you don't have to press your nose to the glass. The exhibits are constantly changing and you can always find one relating to Paris—Frank Horvat's photos of Pigalle or a Christo retrospective, including the Pont Neuf wrappings. It is worth buying one of the weekly guides—*Pariscope, L'Officiel des Spectacles, Figaroscope*—and browsing through it over your *café crème* and croissant.

Resourcefulness, after all, is a sign of enthusiasm and appreciation—for when you are well informed and acutely tuned in to the nuances of the city, you can approach it as a connoisseur. Then you can peacefully coexist with Parisians, partaking, in their passion for this marvelous old city, of the same plate of cultural riches. Hemingway, as usual, put it succinctly: "It was always pleasant crossing bridges in Paris." Cultural bridges, too.

Bon séjour à Paris.

—Nancy Coons

PARIS AT A GLANCE

ca. 200 BC The Parisii—Celtic fishermen—live on the Ile de la Cité.

52 Romans establish a colony, Lutetia, on the Ile de la Cité, which soon spreads to both Seine banks. Under the Romans, Paris becomes a major administrative and commercial center, its situation on the Seine at a low, defensible crossing point making it a natural communications nexus.

ca. AD 250 St. Denis, the first bishop of Paris and France's patron saint, is martyred in Christian persecutions.

451 The hordes of Attila the Hun are said to be halted before reaching Paris by the prayers of St. Geneviève (died 512); in fact they are halted by an army of Romans and mercenaries. Traces of the Roman era remaining in Paris include the catacombs of Montparnasse and the baths that form part of the National Museum of the Middle Ages.

The Merovingian Dynasty (486–751)

507 Clovis, King of the Franks and founder of the Merovingian Dynasty, makes Paris his capital. Many churches are built, including the abbey that will become St-Germain-des-Prés. Commerce is active; Jewish and Asian communities are founded along the Seine.

The Carolingian Dynasty (751–987)

Under the Carolingians, Paris ceases to be the capital of France but remains a major administrative, commercial, and ecclesiastical center—and, as a result, one of the foremost centers of culture and learning west of Constantinople.

845–87 Parisians restore the fortifications of the city, which is repeatedly sacked by Vikings (up to 877).

The Capetian Dynasty (987–1328)

987 Hugh Capet, Count of Paris, becomes king. Paris, once more the capital, grows in importance. The Ile de la Cité is the seat of government, commerce makes its place on the right bank, and a university develops on the left bank.

1140–63 The Gothic style of architecture appears at St-Denis: Notre-Dame, begun in 1163, sees the style come to maturity. In the late 12th century streets are paved.

1200 Philippe-Auguste charters a university, builds walls around Paris, and constructs a fortress, the first Louvre.

1243–46 The Sainte-Chapelle is built to house the reputed crown of thorns brought by Louis IX (St. Louis) from Constantinople.

1253 The Sorbonne is founded, to become a major theological center.

The Valois Dynasty (1328–1589)

1348–49 The Black Death and the beginning of the Hundred Years' War bring misery and strife to Paris.

1364–80 Charles V works to restore prosperity to Paris. The Bastille is built to defend the new city walls. The Louvre is converted into a royal palace.

1420–37 After the Battle of Agincourt, Henry V of England enters Paris. Joan of Arc leads an attempt to recapture the city (1429). Charles VII of France drives out the English (1437).

1469 The first printing house in France is established at the Sorbonne.

1515–47 François I imports Italian artists, including Leonardo da Vinci, to work on his new palace at Fontainebleau, bringing the Renaissance to France. François resumes work on the Louvre and builds the Hôtel de Ville in the new style. The Tour St-Jacques (bell tower) is completed (all that now remains of the church of St-Jacques-de-la-Boucherie).

1562–98 In the Wars of Religion, Paris remains a Catholic stronghold. On August 24, 1572, Protestant leaders are killed in the St. Bartholomew's Day massacre.

The Bourbon Dynasty (1589–1789)

1598–1610 Henri IV begins his reign after converting to Catholicism, declaring "Paris is worth a mass." He embellishes Paris, laying out the Renaissance Place des Vosges, the first square in a new style of town planning that will last until the 19th century. In 1610, Henri is assassinated. His widow, Maria de' Medici, begins the Luxembourg Palace and Gardens.

1624 Cardinal Richelieu is appointed minister to Louis XIII and concludes the ongoing religious persecution by strictly imposing Catholicism on the country. In 1629 he begins construction of the Palais-Royal.

1635 The Académie Française is founded.

1643–1715 Reign of Louis XIV, the Sun King. Paris rebels against him in the Fronde uprisings (1648–52). Early in his reign he creates a new palace at Versailles, away from the Paris mobs. His minister of finance, Colbert, establishes the Gobelins factory-school for tapestries and furniture (1667). André le Nôtre transforms the Jardin de Tuileries (Tuileries Gardens) and lays out the Champs-Élysées (1660s). Louis founds the Hôtel des Invalides (1670). Cultural activity abounds, with Molière, Racine, Fragonard, and Rameau reaffirming Paris's reputation as a center of artistic production.

1715–89 During the reigns of Louis XV and Louis XVI, Paris becomes the European center of culture and style.

1765 The Western world's first restaurant opens in what is now the Rue du Louvre, serving a single dish: sheep's feet simmered in wine.

1783 New outer walls of Paris are begun, incorporating customs gatehouses to control the flow of commerce into the city. The walls, which include new parks, triple the area of Paris.

The Revolution, Empire, and Restoration (1789–1814)

1789–99 The French Revolution begins as the Bastille is stormed on July 14, 1789. The First Republic is established. Louis XVI and his queen, Marie-Antoinette, are guillotined in Place de la Concorde. Almost 2,600 others perish in the same way during the Terror (1793–94).

1799–1814 Napoléon begins to convert Paris into a neoclassical city—the Empire style. The Arc de Triomphe and the first iron bridges across the Seine are built. In 1805 he orders the completion of the Louvre museum.

1815 The Congress of Vienna ensures the restoration of the Bourbon Dynasty following the fall of Napoléon.

1828–42 Urban and political discontent causes riots and demonstrations in the streets. An uprising replaces Charles X with Louis-Philippe's liberal monarchy in 1830. Napoléon's remains are returned to Paris in 1840.

The Second Republic and Second Empire (1848–70)

1852 Further additions to the Louvre are made. Under Napoléon III, the Alsatian town planner Baron Haussmann guts large areas of medieval Paris to lay out broad boulevards linking important squares. Railroad stations and the vast covered markets at Les Halles are built. Au Bon Marché, the first department store in Paris, opens its doors.

1857 Charles-Pierre Baudelaire (1821–67) ignites a literary scandal with the publication of his *Fleurs de Mal.*

1858 Englishman Charles Worth establishes the first haute-couture fashion house in Paris.

1862 Victor Hugo's *Les Misérables* is published in Paris while the liberal author remains in exile by order of Napoléon III.

1870–71 Franco-Prussian War; Paris is besieged by Prussian troops; starvation is rampant—each week during the winter 5,000 people die. The Paris Commune, an attempt by the citizens to take power in 1871, results in bloody suppression and much property damage (the Tuileries Palace is razed). Hugo returns to Paris.

The Third Republic (1871–1944)

1875 The Paris Opéra is inaugurated after 14 years of construction.

1889 The Eiffel Tower is built for the Paris world exhibition. The Moulin Rouge opens. The Paris exhibition opens, showcasing the Eiffel Tower.

1894–1900 The Dreyfus Affair bitterly divides French society, showing that the hundred-year-old wound of the French Revolution hadn't yet healed.

1895 The Lumière Brothers introduce their Cinématographe to a paying public, screening a series of 10 short films in the basement of the Grand Café on December 28.

1900 The international exhibition in Paris popularizes the curving forms of Art Nouveau with the entrances for the newly opened Paris métro.

1914–18 World War I. The Germans come within 15 km (9 mi) of Paris (so close that Paris taxis are used to carry troops to the front).

1915 The cabaret singer Edith Piaf, known as the Little Sparrow, is born under a gaslight on the rue de Belleville.

1919 The Treaty of Versailles is signed, formally ending World War I.

1925 International decorative art exhibition consecrates the restrained, sophisticated design style now known as Art Deco.

1918–39 Between the wars Paris attracts artists and writers, including Americans Ernest Hemingway and Gertrude Stein. Paris nourishes existentialism, a philosophical movement, and major modern art movements—Constructivism, Dadaism, Surrealism.

1939–45 World War II. Paris falls to the Germans in 1940. The French Government moves to Vichy and collaborates with the Nazis. The resistance movement uses Paris as a base. The Free French Army, under Charles de Gaulle, joins with the Allies to liberate Paris after D-Day, in August 1944.

The Fourth and Fifth Republics (1944–Present)

1944–46 De Gaulle moves the provisional government to Paris.

1946 With the arrival of the Fourth Republic, women acquire the right to vote.

1958–69 De Gaulle is President of the Fifth Republic.

1959 The European Economic Community, a precursor of the European Union, is established, with France a founding member.

1960s–70s Paris undergoes physical changes: dirty buildings are cleaned, beltways are built around the city, and expressways are driven through the heart of it. Major new building projects (especially la Défense) are banished to the outskirts.

1962 De Gaulle grants Algeria independence; growing tensions with immigrant workers in Paris and other cities.

1968 Parisian students declare the Sorbonne a commune in riots that lead to De Gaulle's resignation.

1969 Les Halles market is moved and its buildings are demolished.

1977 The Centre Pompidou opens to controversy, marking a high point in modern political intervention in the arts and public architecture.

1981 François Mitterrand (1916–96) is elected president, and embarks on a major building program throughout the city.

1986 The Musée d'Orsay opens in the former Gare d'Orsay train station.

1989 Paris celebrates the bicentennial of the French Revolution. The Louvre's glass pyramid, the Grande Arche of la Défense, and the Opéra Bastille are completed.

1994 Paris–London rail link via Channel tunnel becomes operational.

1995 Paris mayor Jacques Chirac replaces François Mitterrand as the president of France.

1998 Amid scenes of popular fervor in Paris not seen since the Liberation in 1944, France hosts and wins the soccer World Cup.

1999 Opening of the Bibliothèque Nationale de France François Mitterrand in southeast Paris, containing 12 million books.

2000 Paris marks the new millennium with a new lighting scheme for the Eiffel Tower, a giant wheel on Place de la Concorde, and a huge statue of Charles de Gaulle on the Champs-Élysées. The facade of the Opéra is cleaned and the Centre Pompidou reopens after major renovation. A new pedestrian bridge links the Musée d'Orsay to the Tuileries.

2001 To repair the damage caused by a storm at the end of 1999, nine new parks and gardens are planned. The Mediterranean TGV line connecting Paris and Marseille opens.

2002 On February 17, the franc ceases to be legal tender and is officially replaced by the euro. On May 5, Jacques Chirac is reelected president in a landslide victory.

BOOKS & MOVIES

Books

Books on Paris can fill several libraries. For a look at American expatriates in Paris between the wars, read *Sylvia Beach and the Lost Generation* by Noel R. Fitch or *A Moveable Feast* by Ernest Hemingway. Flaubert's *Sentimental Education* includes excellent descriptions of Paris and its environs, as do many Zola novels. Other recommended titles are Charles Dickens's *A Tale of Two Cities,* Henry James's *The Ambassadors,* Colette's *The Complete Claudine,* Hemingway's *The Sun Also Rises,* and Gertrude Stein's *Paris, France.* George Orwell's *Down and Out in Paris and London* gives an account of life on a shoestring in these two European capitals. More essays about Paris are excerpted in *A Place in the World Called Paris.* Other anthologies of essays on Paris include the *Travelers' Tales Guides: Paris* and *The Collected Traveller: Paris.*

Jules Verne's *Paris in the Twentieth Century* provides a view from the past of Paris in the future. A history of Paris from the Revolution to the Belle Epoque is found in Johannes Willms's *Paris: Capital of Europe. A Traveller's History of Paris* by Robert Cole is a good overview. Tyler Stovall's *Paris Noir: African-Americans in the City of Light* examines black American writers', artists', and performers' affection for Paris during the 20th century. *Inside Paris* is a photography book of Paris interiors. Two unconventional guides to Paris are Karen Elizabeth Gordon's witty and surreal *Paris Out of Hand* and Lawrence Osborne's *Paris Dreambook.*

Three memoirs by Americans who have lived in Paris are Art Buchwald's *I'll Always Have Paris,* Edmund White's *Our Paris: Sketches with Memory,* with illustrations by Hubert Sorin, and Stanley Karnow's *Paris in the Fifties. Paris Notebooks* by Mavis Gallant is her observations on Paris life. *Between Meals* by A. J. Liebling looks at the art of eating in Paris. *A Corner in the Marais: Memoir of a Paris Neighborhood* combines Alex Karmel's personal impressions with a history of the neighborhood. More recently, Adam Gopnik, the distinguished Paris-based correspondent of the *New Yorker,* hit the best-seller lists with his collection of essays *Paris to the Moon.*

Movies

For a glimpse of Paris before you go, rent one of the following films: *Gigi* (1958; in English), Hollywood's most opulent valentine to Paris won the Best Picture Oscar, thanks to its memorable Lerner and Loewe musical score and magnificent sets designed by Cecil Beaton; *An American in Paris* (1951; in English), a Hollywood musical with a great Gershwin score stars Gene Kelly and Leslie Caron and is another Best Picture Oscar winner; *Charade* (1963; in English) is a comic thriller starring Cary Grant and Audrey Hepburn; *How to Steal a Million* (1966; in English) is a chic art-theft caper starring Peter O'Toole, Audrey Hepburn, and many soigné Paris settings; *À Bout de Souffle* (*Breathless,* 1960; in French), by Jean-Luc Godard, is about a car thief who flees with his American girlfriend. Others to try are *Diva* (1981; in French), about a singer in Paris who becomes involved in murder and drug smuggling; *Funny Face* (1957; in English), a Roger Edens musical with Audrey Hepburn and Fred Astaire immortalizing the high-fashion world of 1950s Paris; *Last Tango in Paris* (1972; in English), a Bertolucci film starring Marlon Brando; *Ready to Wear* (1994; in English), a Robert Altman film about the fashion industry; *Zazie Dans le Métro* (1960; in French), a Louis Malle film about the adventures of a 10-year-old girl in Paris; and *The Red Balloon* (in French), the Oscar-winning short film of 1956, unforgettably filmed in the district of Ménilmontant. Finally, in 2001 the elfin charms of *Amélie* (in French) captured the hearts of moviegoers worldwide.

VOCABULARY

One of the trickiest French sounds to pronounce is the nasal final *n* sound (whether or not the *n* is actually the last letter of the word). You should try to pronounce it as a sort of nasal grunt—as in "huh." The vowel that precedes the *n* will govern the vowel sound of the word, and in this list we precede the final *n* with an *h* to remind you to be nasal.

Another problem sound is the ubiquitous but untransliterable *eu,* as in *bleu* (blue) or *deux* (two), and the very similar sound in *je* (I), *ce* (this), and *de* (of). The closest equivalent might be the vowel sound in "put," but rounded.

Words and Phrases

Basics

English	French	Pronunciation
Yes/no	Oui/non	wee/nohn
Please	S'il vous plaît	seel voo play
Thank you	Merci	mair-**see**
You're welcome	De rien	deh ree-**ehn**
That's all right	Il n'y a pas de quoi	eel nee ah pah de kwah
Excuse me, sorry	Pardon	pahr-**dohn**
Sorry!	Désolé(e)	day-zoh-**lay**
Good morning/ afternoon	Bonjour	bohn-**zhoor**
Good evening	Bonsoir	bohn-**swahr**
Goodbye	Au revoir	o ruh-**vwahr**
Mr. (Sir)	Monsieur	muh-**syuh**
Mrs. (Ma'am)	Madame	ma-**dam**
Miss	Mademoiselle	mad-mwa-**zel**
Pleased to meet you	Enchanté(e)	ohn-shahn-**tay**
How are you?	Comment allez-vous?	kuh-mahn-tahl-ay **voo**
Very well, thanks	Très bien, merci	tray bee-ehn, mair-**see**
And you?	Et vous?	ay voo?

Numbers

English	French	Pronunciation
one	un	uhn
two	deux	deuh
three	trois	twah
four	quatre	**kaht**-ruh
five	cinq	sank
six	six	seess
seven	sept	set
eight	huit	wheat
nine	neuf	nuf

ten	dix	deess
eleven	onze	ohnz
twelve	douze	dooz
thirteen	treize	trehz
fourteen	quatorze	kah-torz
fifteen	quinze	kanz
sixteen	seize	sez
seventeen	dix-sept	deez-**set**
eighteen	dix-huit	deez-**wheat**
nineteen	dix-neuf	deez-**nuf**
twenty	vingt	vehn
twenty-one	vingt-et-un	vehnt-ay-**uhn**
thirty	trente	trahnt
forty	quarante	ka-**rahnt**
fifty	cinquante	sang-**kahnt**
sixty	soixante	swa-**sahnt**
seventy	soixante-dix	swa-sahnt-**deess**
eighty	quatre-vingts	kaht-ruh-**vehn**
ninety	quatre-vingt-dix	kaht-ruh-vehn-**deess**
one hundred	cent	sahn
one thousand	mille	meel

Colors

black	noir	nwahr
blue	bleu	bleuh
brown	brun/marron	bruhn/mar-**rohn**
green	vert	vair
orange	orange	o-**rahnj**
pink	rose	rose
red	rouge	rouge
violet	violette	vee-o-**let**
white	blanc	blahnk
yellow	jaune	zhone

Days of the Week

Sunday	dimanche	dee-**mahnsh**
Monday	lundi	luhn-**dee**
Tuesday	mardi	mahr-**dee**
Wednesday	mercredi	mair-kruh-**dee**
Thursday	jeudi	zhuh-**dee**
Friday	vendredi	vawn-druh-**dee**
Saturday	samedi	sahm-**dee**

Months

January	janvier	zhahn-vee-**ay**
February	février	feh-vree-**ay**
March	mars	marce
April	avril	a-**vreel**
May	mai	meh
June	juin	zhwehn
July	juillet	zhwee-**ay**
August	août	ah-**oo**
September	septembre	sep-**tahm**-bruh
October	octobre	awk-**to**-bruh

November	novembre	no-**vahm**-bruh
December	décembre	day-**sahm**-bruh

Useful Phrases

Do you speak English?	Parlez-vous anglais?	par-lay **voo ahn-**glay
I don't speak . . . French	Je ne parle pas . . . français	zhuh nuh parl pah frahn-**say**
I don't understand	Je ne comprends pas	zhuh nuh kohm-**prahn** pah
I understand	Je comprends	zhuh kohm-**prahn**
I don't know	Je ne sais pas	zhuh nuh say **pah**
I'm American/ British	Je suis américain/ anglais	zhuh sweez a-may-ree-**kehn**/ahn-**glay**
What's your name?	Comment vous appelez-vous?	ko-mahn voo za-pell-ay-**voo**
My name is . . .	Je m'appelle . . .	zhuh ma-**pell** . . .
What time is it?	Quelle heure est-il?	kel air eh-**teel**
How?	Comment?	ko-**mahn**
When?	Quand?	kahn
Yesterday	Hier	yair
Today	Aujourd'hui	o-zhoor-**dwee**
Tomorrow	Demain	duh-**mehn**
This morning/ afternoon	Ce matin/cet après-midi	suh ma-**tehn**/ set ah-pray-mee-**dee**
Tonight	Ce soir	suh **swahr**
What?	Quoi?	kwah
What is it?	Qu'est-ce que c'est?	kess-kuh-**say**
Why?	Pourquoi?	**poor**-kwa
Who?	Qui?	kee
Where is . . .	Où est . . .	oo ay
the train station?	la gare?	la gar
the subway station?	la station de métro?	la sta-**syon** duh may-**tro**
the bus stop?	l'arrêt de bus?	la-**ray** duh **booss**
the terminal (airport)?	l'aérogare?	lay-ro-**gar**
the post office?	la poste?	la post
the bank?	la banque?	la bahnk
the . . . hotel?	l'hôtel . . .?	lo-**tel**

the store?	le magasin?	luh ma-ga-**zehn**
the cashier?	la caisse?	la **kess**
the . . . museum?	le musée . . .?	luh mew-**zay**
the hospital?	l'hôpital?	lo-pee-**tahl**
the elevator?	l'ascenseur?	la-sahn-**seuhr**
the telephone?	le téléphone?	luh tay-lay-**phone**
Where are the restrooms?	Où sont les toilettes?	oo sohn lay twah-**let**
Here/there	Ici/là	ee-**see**/la
Left/right	A gauche/à droite	a goash/a draht
Straight ahead	Tout droit	too drwah
Is it near/far?	C'est près/loin?	say pray/lwehn
I'd like . . .	Je voudrais . . .	zhuh voo-**dray**
a room	une chambre	ewn **shahm**-bruh
the key	la clé	la clay
a newspaper	un journal	uhn zhoor-**nahl**
a stamp	un timbre	uhn **tam**-bruh
I'd like to buy . . .	Je voudrais acheter . . .	zhuh voo-**dray ahsh**-tay
a cigar	un cigare	uhn see-**gar**
cigarettes	des cigarettes	day see-ga-**ret**
matches	des allumettes	days a-loo-**met**
dictionary	un dictionnaire	uhn deek-see-oh-**nare**
soap	du savon	dew sah-**vohn**
city map	un plan de ville	uhn plahn de **veel**
road map	une carte routière	ewn cart roo-tee-**air**
magazine	une revue	ewn reh-**vu**
envelopes	des enveloppes	dayz ahn-veh-**lope**
writing paper	du papier à lettres	dew pa-pee-**ay** a **let**-ruh
postcard	une carte postale	ewn cart pos-**tal**
How much is it?	C'est combien?	say comb-bee-**ehn**
It's expensive/	C'est cher/pas cher share	say share/pa cheap
A little/a lot	Un peu/beaucoup	uhn peuh/bo-**koo**
More/less	Plus/moins	plu/mwehn
Enough/too (much)	Assez/trop	a-say/tro
I am ill/sick	Je suis malade	zhuh swee ma-**lahd**

Call a . . . doctor	Appelez un . . . docteur	a-play uhn dohk-**tehr**
Help!	Au secours!	o suh-**koor**
Stop!	Arrêtez!	a-reh-**tay**
Fire!	Au feu!	o fuh
Caution!/Look out!	Attention!	a-tahn-see-**ohn**

Dining Out

A bottle of . . .	une bouteille de . . .	ewn boo-**tay** duh
A cup of . . .	une tasse de . . .	ewn tass duh
A glass of . . .	un verre de . . .	uhn vair duh
Ashtray	un cendrier	uhn sahn-dree-**ay**
Bill/check	l'addition	la-dee-see-**ohn**
Bread	du pain	dew pan
Breakfast	le petit-déjeuner	luh puh-**tee** day-zhuh-**nay**
Butter	du beurre	dew burr
Cheers!	A votre santé!	ah vo-truh sahn-**tay**
Cocktail/aperitif	un apéritif	uhn ah-pay-ree-**teef**
Dinner	le dîner	luh dee-**nay**
Dish of the day	le plat du jour	luh plah dew **zhoor**
Enjoy!	Bon appétit!	bohn a-pay-**tee**
Fixed-price menu	le menu	luh may-**new**
Fork	une fourchette	ewn four-**shet**
I am diabetic	Je suis diabétique	zhuh swee dee-ah-bay-**teek**
I am on a diet	Je suis au régime	zhuh sweez oray-**jeem**
I am vegetarian	Je suis végé-tarien(ne)	zhuh swee vay-zhay-ta-ree-**en**
I cannot eat . . .	Je ne peux pas manger de . . .	zhuh nuh **puh** pah mahn-**jay** deh
I'd like to order	Je voudrais commander	zhuh voo-**dray** ko-mahn-**day**
I'm hungry/thirsty	J'ai faim/soif	zhay fahm/swahf
Is service/the tip included?	Est-ce que le service est compris?	ess kuh luh sair-**veess** ay comb-**pree**

It's good/bad	C'est bon/mauvais	say bohn/ mo-**vay**
It's hot/cold	C'est chaud/froid	say sho/frwah
Knife	un couteau	uhn koo-**toe**
Lunch	le déjeuner	luh day- zhuh-**nay**
Menu	la carte	la cart
Napkin	une serviette	ewn sair- vee-**et**
Pepper	du poivre	dew **pwah**- vruh
Plate	une assiette	ewn a-see-**et**
Please give me . . .	Donnez-moi . . .	doe-nay- **mwah**
Salt	du sel	dew sell
Spoon	une cuillère	ewn kwee-**air**
Sugar	du sucre	dew **sook**-ruh
Waiter!/Waitress!	Monsieur!/ Mademoiselle!	muh-**syuh**/ mad-mwa-**zel**
Wine list	la carte des vins	la cart day an

MENU GUIDE

French	English
General Dining	
Entrée	Appetizer/Starter
Garniture au choix	Choice of vegetable side
Plat du jour	Dish of the day
Selon arrivage	When available
Supplément/En sus	Extra charge
Sur commande	Made to order
Petit Déjeuner (Breakfast)	
Confiture	Jam
Miel	Honey
Oeuf à la coque	Boiled egg
Oeufs sur le plat	Fried eggs
Oeufs brouillés	Scrambled eggs
Tartine	Bread with butter
Poissons/Fruits de Mer (Fish/Seafood)	
Anchois	Anchovies
Bar	Bass
Brandade de morue	Creamed salt cod
Brochet	Pike
Cabillaud/Morue	Fresh cod
Calmar	Squid
Coquilles St-Jacques	Scallops
Crevettes	Shrimp
Cuisses de grenouilles	Frogs' legs
Daurade	Sea bream
Ecrevisses	Prawns/Crayfish
Harengs	Herring
Homard	Lobster
Huîtres	Oysters
Langoustine	Prawn/Lobster
Lotte	Monkfish
Maquereau	Mackerel
Moules	Mussels
Palourdes	Clams
Saumon	Salmon
Thon	Tuna
Truite	Trout
Viande (Meat)	
Agneau	Lamb
Boeuf	Beef
Boudin	Sausage
Boulettes de viande	Meatballs
Brochettes	Kabobs
Cassoulet	Casserole of white beans, meat
Cervelle	Brains

Chateaubriand	Double fillet steak
Choucroute garnie	Sausages with sauerkraut
Côtelettes	Chops
Côte/Côte de boeuf	Rib/T-bone steak
Cuisses de grenouilles	Frogs' legs
Entrecôte	Rib or rib-eye steak
Épaule	Shoulder
Escalope	Cutlet
Foie	Liver
Gigot	Leg
Porc	Pork
Ris de veau	Veal sweetbreads
Rognons	Kidneys
Saucisses	Sausages
Selle	Saddle
Tournedos	Tenderloin of T-bone steak
Veau	Veal

Methods of Preparation

A point	Medium
A l'étouffée	Stewed
Au four	Baked
Ballotine	Boned, stuffed, and rolled
Bien cuit	Well-done
Bleu	Very rare
Frit	Fried
Grillé	Grilled
Rôti	Roast
Saignant	Rare
Sauté/Poêlée	Sautéed

Volailles/Gibier (Poultry/Game)

Blanc de volaille	Chicken breast
Canard/Caneton	Duck/Duckling
Cerf/Chevreuil	Venison (red/roe)
Coq au vin	Chicken stewed in red wine
Dinde/Dindonneau	Turkey/Young turkey
Faisan	Pheasant
Lapin/Lièvre	Rabbit/Wild hare
Oie	Goose
Pintade/Pintadeau	Guinea fowl/Young guinea fowl
Poulet/Poussin	Chicken/Spring chicken

Légumes (Vegetables)

Artichaut	Artichoke
Asperge	Asparagus
Aubergine	Eggplant
Carottes	Carrots
Champignons	Mushrooms
Chou-fleur	Cauliflower
Chou (rouge)	Cabbage (red)
Laitue	Lettuce
Oignons	Onions
Petits pois	Peas

Pomme de terre	Potato
Tomates	Tomatoes

Fruits/Noix (Fruits/Nuts)

Abricot	Apricot
Amandes	Almonds
Ananas	Pineapple
Cassis	Blackcurrants
Cerises	Cherries
Citron/Citron vert	Lemon/Lime
Fraises	Strawberries
Framboises	Raspberries
Pamplemousse	Grapefruit
Pêche	Peach
Poire	Pear
Pomme	Apple
Prunes/Pruneaux	Plums/Prunes
Raisins/Raisins secs	Grapes/Raisins

Desserts

Coupe (glacée)	Sundae
Crème Chantilly	Whipped cream
Gâteau au chocolat	Chocolate cake
Glace	Ice cream
Tarte tatin	Caramelized apple tart
Tourte	Layer cake

Drinks

A l'eau	With water
Avec des glaçons	On the rocks
Bière	Beer
Blonde/brune	Light/dark
Café noir/crème	Black coffee/with steamed milk
Chocolat chaud	Hot chocolate
Eau-de-vie	Brandy
Eau minérale	Mineral water
gazeuse/non gazeuse	*carbonated/still*
Jus de . . .	. . . juice
Lait	Milk
Sec	Straight or dry
Thé	Tea
au lait/au citron	*with milk/lemon*
Vin	Wine
blanc	*white*
doux	*sweet*
léger	*light*
brut	*very dry*
rouge	*red*

INDEX

A

B

C

I

J

K

L

M